TABLE OF CONTENTS

INTRODUCTION XXIX

LESSON 1 Introducing Java 1

LESSON 2 Eclipse IDE 9

LESSON 3 Object-Oriented Programming with Java 21

LESSON 4 Class Methods and Constructors 37

LESSON 5 Java Syntax: Bits and Pieces 47

LESSON 6 Packages, Interfaces, and Encapsulation 61

LESSON 7 Programming with Abstract Classes and Interfaces 73

LESSON 8 Introducing the GUI with Swing 83

LESSON 9 Event Handling in Swing GUI 99

LESSON 10 Error Handling 115

LESSON 11 Introduction to Collections 127

LESSON 12 Introduction to Generics 141

LESSON 13 Lambda Expressions and Functional Style Programming 151

LESSON 14 Working with I/O Streams 171

LESSON 15 Java Serialization 185

LESSON 16 Network Programming Basics 195

LESSON 17 Concurrency and Multithreading 209

LESSON 18 Introduction to GUI with JavaFX 233

LESSON 19 Developing JavaFX Calculator and Tic-Tac-Toe 251

LESSON 20 Stream API 281

LESSON 21 Working with Relational DBMS Using JDBC 297

LESSON 22 Rendering Tabular Data in the GUI 311

LESSON 23 Annotations and Reflection 321

LESSON 24 Remote Method Invocation 335

LESSON 25 Java EE 7 Overview. 345
LESSON 26 Programming with Servlets. 355
LESSON 27 JavaServer Pages. 379
LESSON 28 Developing Web Applications with WebSockets. 395
LESSON 29 Introducing JNDI. 415
LESSON 30 Introducing JMS and MOM. 425
LESSON 31 Introduction to Enterprise JavaBeans. 447
LESSON 32 Overview of the Java Persistence API. 465
LESSON 33 Working with RESTful Web Services. 483
LESSON 34 Java Logging API. 501
LESSON 35 Introduction to Unit Testing with JUnit Framework. 515
LESSON 36 Build Automation with Gradle. 531
LESSON 37 Java Technical Interviews. 555

INDEX. 569

Java® Programming

24-Hour Trainer
Second Edition

Yakov Fain

Java® Programming 24-Hour Trainer, Second Edition

Published by
Wiley Publishing, Inc.
10475 Crosspoint Boulevard
Indianapolis, IN 46256
www.wiley.com

Published simultaneously in Canada

ISBN: 978-1-118-95145-3
ISBN: 978-1-118-95146-0 (ebk)
ISBN: 978-1-118-95157-6 (ebk)

Manufactured in the United States of America

10 9 8 7 6 5 4 3 2 1

For general information on our other products and services please contact our Customer Care Department within the United States at (877) 762-2974, outside the United States at (317) 572-3993 or fax (317) 572-4002.

Wiley publishes in a variety of print and electronic formats and by print-on-demand. Some material included with standard print versions of this book may not be included in e-books or in print-on-demand. If this book refers to media such as a CD or DVD that is not included in the version you purchased, you may download this material at http://booksupport.wiley.com. For more information about Wiley products, visit www.wiley.com.

Library of Congress Control Number: 2015930542

In memory of my friend, Felix Rubinchik.

CREDITS

EXECUTIVE EDITOR
Robert Elliott

PROJECT EDITOR
Adaobi Obi Tulton

TECHNICAL EDITORS
Chád Darby
Rajesuwer P. Singaravelu
Martijn Verburg

PRODUCTION MANAGER
Kathleen Wisor

COPY EDITOR
Charlotte Khugen

MANAGER OF CONTENT DEVELOPMENT & ASSEMBLY
Mary Beth Wakefield

MARKETING DIRECTOR
David Mayhew

MARKETING MANAGER
Carrie Sherrill

PROFESSIONAL TECHNOLOGY & STRATEGY DIRECTOR
Barry Pruett

BUSINESS MANAGER
Amy Knies

ASSOCIATE PUBLISHER
Jim Minatel

PROJECT COORDINATOR, COVER
Brent Savage

PROOFREADER
Jennifer Bennett, Word One

INDEXER
Johnna VanHoose Dinse

COVER DESIGNER
Wiley

COVER IMAGE
©iStock.com/gpointstudio

ABOUT THE AUTHOR

Yakov Fain works as a software architect for Farata Systems, a company that provides consulting services in the field of development of enterprise applications. He has authored several technical books and lots of articles on software development. Sun Microsystems has awarded Mr. Fain with the title of Java Champion, which has been given to only 150 people in the world. He leads the Princeton Java Users Group. Yakov blogs at yakovfain.com, and his Twitter ID is @yfain.

ABOUT THE TECHNICAL EDITORS

Chád (shod) Darby is an author, instructor and speaker in the Java development world. As a recognized authority on Java applications and architectures, he has presented technical sessions at software development conferences worldwide (U.S., U.K., India, Italy, Russia and Australia). In his fifteen years as a professional software architect, he's had the opportunity to work for Blue Cross/Blue Shield, Merck, Boeing, Red Hat and a handful of startup companies.

Chád is a contributing author to several Java books, including Professional Java E-Commerce (Wrox Press), Beginning Java Networking (Wrox Press), and XML and Web Services Unleashed (Sams Publishing). Chád has Java certifications from Sun Microsystems and IBM. He holds a B.S. in Computer Science from Carnegie Mellon University.

Stay connected with Chád by visiting his blog: www.luv2code.com and his YouTube channel: www.luv2code.com/youtube.

Rajesuwer P. Singaravelu has been working with Java and web technologies since the late '90s, creating distributed enterprise systems for financial services industry in New York City. When he isn't hacking, he enjoys spending time with his wife Rohini and two kids- Hassini and Arvind. His interests are in cross platform mobile development using Appcelerator Titanium and he is a Titanium Certified Expert (TCE). He is @rajesuwerps at the usual hangouts.

Martijn Verberg is the CEO of jClarity, a performance analysis and machine learning start-up in London. He is involved in various Java and open source communities, and co-leads the London's Java User Group (LJC, a JCP EC member). Martijn was recognized as a Java Champion in 2012 for his services to the community. You can find him speaking regularly at conferences (Devoxx, JavaOne, OSCON, etc.) on Java, open source, and software development as the "Diabolical Developer."

ACKNOWLEDGMENTS

First of all I want to thank my family for understanding that stealing (once again) time from family to write a computer book is OK.

I'd also like to thank the technical editors, Rajesuwer P. Singaravelu and Martijn Verberg, for their valuable input.

My special thanks to Chad Darby for producing the awesome videos for this book.

I give particular thanks to my business partners and colleagues at Farata Systems. They didn't contribute to this book directly, but working in the same team with these top notch professionals makes me a better programmer day in and day out.

Big thanks to the Wiley editors for doing a great job of editing and for not cursing me for not meeting deadlines.

CONTENTS

INTRODUCTION *XXIX*

LESSON 1: INTRODUCING JAVA 1

Why Learn Java? **1**
Setting the Goals **2**
The Life Cycle of a Java Program **2**
JDK and JRE **3**
Downloading and Installing Java SE **3**
Installing JDK 8 for MAC OS 3
Installing JDK 8 in Windows 4
Your First Java Program: Hello World **5**
Compiling and Running Hello World 7
Try It **7**
Lesson Requirements 8
Step-by-Step 8

LESSON 2: ECLIPSE IDE 9

Introducing Eclipse IDE **9**
Downloading and Installing Eclipse **10**
Creating Hello Project in Eclipse **11**
Creating the HelloWorld Class in Eclipse **14**
Java Packages **15**
Completing Code Generation **16**
Additional Materials **18**
Try It **18**
Lesson Requirements 19
Step-by-Step 19

LESSON 3: OBJECT-ORIENTED PROGRAMMING WITH JAVA 21

Classes and Objects **21**

Variables and Data Types 23
Declaring Variables 23
Final Variables 23
Primitive Data Types 24
Variable Scope 25
Wrappers, Autoboxing, and Unboxing 26
Program Comments 26
First Useful Program 27
Conditional Statement if 30
switch Statement 31
Inheritance 32
Method Overriding 33
Additional Materials 33
Try It 33
Lesson Requirements 33
Hints 34
Step-by-Step 34

LESSON 4: CLASS METHODS AND CONSTRUCTORS 37

Method Arguments 37
Method Overloading 38
Constructors 39
The Keyword super 40
The Keyword this 40
Passing by Value or by Reference 42
Variable Scopes 43
The Keyword static 44
Try It 45
Lesson Requirements 45
Step-by-Step 45

LESSON 5: JAVA SYNTAX: BITS AND PIECES 47

Arrays 47
More About Strings 49
Loops 50
Debugging Java Programs 54
More About if and switch Statements 57
The Flavors of if Statements 57
Command-Line Arguments 58

Try It **59**
Lesson Requirements 59
Step-by-Step 60

LESSON 6: PACKAGES, INTERFACES, AND ENCAPSULATION 61

Java Packages **61**
Encapsulation **62**
Access Levels 63
The Keyword final **63**
final Variables 64
final Methods 64
final Classes 64
Interfaces **65**
Marker Interfaces 66
Default Methods in Interfaces 67
Static Methods in Interfaces 68
Casting **68**
Try It **70**
Lesson Requirements 70
Step-by-Step 70

LESSON 7: PROGRAMMING WITH ABSTRACT CLASSES AND INTERFACES 73

Abstract Classes **73**
Assignment 73
Solution with an Abstract Class 74
Polymorphism **76**
Making the Interface Solution Polymorphic 77
Interfaces Versus Abstract Classes **78**
Try It **79**
Lesson Requirements 79
Step-by-Step 79

LESSON 8: INTRODUCING THE GUI WITH SWING 83

Swing Basics **83**
Layout Managers **86**
A Simple Calculator with FlowLayout 86
A Brief Introduction to Layout Managers 87

FlowLayout 88
GridLayout 88
BorderLayout 90
Combining Layout Managers 90
BoxLayout 93
GridBagLayout 94
CardLayout 95
Containers with Absolute Layout 96
More About Swing Widgets 96
Swing GUI Builders 97
Try It 97
Lesson Requirements 97
Step-by-Step 97

LESSON 9: EVENT HANDLING IN SWING GUI 99

Introduction to Event Listeners 99
Teaching the Calculator to Calculate 100
Registering Components with `ActionListener` 101
Finding the Source of an Event 102
How to Pass Data Between Objects 104
Design Pattern Model-View-Controller 107
More Swing Listeners 108
How to use Adapters 109
Inner Classes 110
Anonymous Inner Classes 111
Try It 112
Lesson Requirements 112
Step-by-Step 112

LESSON 10: ERROR HANDLING 115

Stack Trace 115
Java Exceptions 116
Exception Hierarchy 117
Try/Catch Blocks 118
Using the throws Clause 119
Using the finally Clause 120
Try-With-Resources 121
The throw Keyword 122
Creating Your Own Exceptions 123

Try It **125**
Lesson Requirements 125
Step-by-Step 125

LESSON 11: INTRODUCTION TO COLLECTIONS 127

Arrays Revisited **128**
Collection Interfaces From *java.util* **128**
Dynamic Arrays with ArrayList **129**
Classes Hashtable and Hashmap **132**
Class Properties 133
Classes Enumeration and Iterator **135**
Class LinkedList **135**
Class BitSet **137**
Choosing the Right Collection **138**
Try It **139**
Lesson Requirements 139
Step-by-Step 139

LESSON 12: INTRODUCTION TO GENERICS 141

Generics with Classes **141**
Declaring Generics **144**
Wildcards **144**
Creating Custom Parameterized Classes **146**
Bounded Type Parameters **147**
Generic Methods **149**
Try It **150**
Lesson Requirements 150
Step-by-Step 150

LESSON 13: LAMBDA EXPRESSIONS AND FUNCTIONAL STYLE PROGRAMMING 151

Imperative vs Functional Style **152**
What's Lambda Expression **153**
Functional Interfaces **155**
Methods Versus Functions **157**
Passing Functions to Methods 158
Iterating Collections with forEach() **160**
Lambdas Versus Inheritance and Polymorphism **162**

Eliminating Inheritance 165
Interfaces Function and BiFunction 167
Try It 170
Lesson Requirements 170
Step-by-Step 170

LESSON 14: WORKING WITH I/O STREAMS 171

Byte Streams 172
Buffered Streams 173
Character Streams 174
Bringing Together GUI and I/O Streams 175
Data Streams 178
Utility Classes for Working with Files 179
The Class File 179
NIO.2: Using Files, Path, and Paths 180
What NIO Is About 182
Try It 184
Lesson Requirements 184
Step-by-Step 184

LESSON 15: JAVA SERIALIZATION 185

The Class ObjectOutputStream 187
The Class ObjectInputStream 188
The Interface Externalizable 189
Class Versioning 191
Serializing into Byte Arrays 192
Try It 193
Lesson Requirements 193
Step-by-Step 194

LESSON 16: NETWORK PROGRAMMING BASICS 195

Reading Data from the Internet 196
Connecting Through HTTP Proxy Servers 198
How to Download Files from the Internet 199
Specifying Command-Line Parameters for FileDownload 200
The Stock Quote Program 200
Socket Programming 203
Why Use Sockets? 204

The Stock Quote Server with Sockets 204
Try It 207
Lesson Requirements 207
Hints 207
Step-by-Step 207

LESSON 17: CONCURRENCY AND MULTITHREADING 209

The Class Thread 210
The Interface Runnable 211
Eliminating Inheritance 213
Sleeping Threads 213
How to Kill a Thread 215
Thread Priorities 217
Thread Synchronization and Race Conditions 217
Thread States 219
Wait and Notify 219
Closures in Java 221
Joining Threads 222
Goodies From java.util.concurrent 224
ReentrantLock Versus Synchronized 224
Executor Framework 225
A Brief Review of Concurrent Collections 228
Swingworker Thread 229
Try It 232
Lesson Requirements 232
Step-by-Step 232

LESSON 18: INTRODUCTION TO GUI WITH JAVAFX 233

JavaFX Application Basics 233
Using the E(fx)clipse Plug-in 234
Layouts 236
A Sample Application with the HBox Layout 238
A Sample Application with the GridPane Layout 239
Skinning with CSS 241
Event Handling 244
Properties and Binding 246
Try It 250
Lesson Requirements 250
Step-by-Step 250

LESSON 19: DEVELOPING JAVAFX CALCULATOR AND TIC-TAC-TOE 251

Designing a Calculator with Scene Builder **251**
Designing the Calculator GUI with Scene Builder 254
Handling Events in the Controller Class **260**
Recognizing the Source of the Event 261
Passing Data from View to Controller and Back 263
Programming Tic-Tac-Toe **265**
The Game Strategy 265
Designing Tic-Tac-Toe GUI with FXML and CSS 266
Implementing Game Strategy in Tic-Tac-Toe Controller 273
Handling the Tic-Tac-Toe Menu Play 277
Tic-Tac-Toe: What to Try Next 277
JavaFX on the Web and Mobile Devices **278**
Try It **278**
Lesson Requirements 278
Step-by-Step 279

LESSON 20: STREAM API 281

Stream Basics **281**
Intermediate and Terminal Operations 282
Parallel Versus Sequential Processing 285
Sorting Collections and Streams **285**
Sorting Java Collections 286
Sorting Streams 289
Other Stream Sources **290**
Creating Finite Size Streams 290
Creating Infinite-Size Streams 291
Short-Circuit Operations **293**
Try It **294**
Lesson Requirements 294
Step-by-Step 294

LESSON 21: WORKING WITH RELATIONAL DBMS USING JDBC 297

JDBC Driver Types **298**
Installing Derby DB and Creating a Database **298**
Sample JDBC Program **300**
Processing Result Sets **302**
The PreparedStatement Class **304**

The CallableStatement Class **304**
The ResultSetMetaData Class **305**
Scrollable Result Sets and Rowset **307**
Transactional Updates **308**
Connection Pools and DataSource **308**
Try It **309**
Lesson Requirements 309
Hint 309
Step-by-Step 309

LESSON 22: RENDERING TABULAR DATA IN THE GUI 311

JTable and the MVC Paradigm **311**
The Model **312**
Mandatory Callbacks of Table Models 313
Optional Callbacks of Table Models 316
Introduction to Renderers **318**
Summary **320**
Try It **320**
Lesson Requirements 320
Step-by-Step 320

LESSON 23: ANNOTATIONS AND REFLECTION 321

Javadoc Annotations **321**
Java Annotations Basics **322**
@Override 323
@Deprecated 324
@Inherited 324
@FunctionalInterface 324
@Documented 325
Custom Annotations **325**
Reflection **328**
Run-Time Annotation Processing **330**
Summary **332**
Try It **332**
Lesson Requirements 332
Step-by-Step 333

LESSON 24: REMOTE METHOD INVOCATION 335

Developing Applications with RMI 336
Defining Remote Interfaces 336
Implementing Remote Interfaces 337
Registering Remote Objects 338
Writing RMI Clients 339
Security Considerations 340
Finding Remote Objects 341
Try It 341
Lesson Requirements 342
Hints 342
Step-by-Step 342

LESSON 25: JAVA EE 7 OVERVIEW 345

The Big Picture 345
JCP, JSR, and Other Acronyms 346
Tiers of Java EE Applications 346
Containers Versus Application Servers 348
Profiles and Pruning 350
Why Java EE? 350
Try It 352
Lesson Requirements 352
Step-by-Step 352

LESSON 26: PROGRAMMING WITH SERVLETS 355

The Big Picture 355
The Thin Client 357
How to Write a Servlet 357
How to Deploy a Servlet 358
Configuring Glassfish in Eclipse IDE 359
How to Create a Servlet in Eclipse 362
Deploying a Web Application as WAR 366
Browser-Servlet Data Flow 366
HTTP Get and Post Requests 367
Session Tracking 368
Cookies 368
URL Rewriting 369
Server-Side HttpSession 370
Filters 373

Asynchronous Servlets **375**
Try It **376**
Lesson Requirements 376
Step-by-Step 377

LESSON 27: JAVASERVER PAGES 379

Embedding Java Code into HTML **380**
Implicit JSP Objects **383**
Overview of the JSP Tags **383**
Directives 384
Declarations 384
Expressions 384
Scriptlets **385**
Comments 385
Standard Actions 385
Error Pages **386**
Java Beans **387**
Using JavaBeans in JSP 388
How Long Does a Bean Live? 388
Loading JSP from Servlets **389**
Tag Libraries **390**
JSTL **392**
Try It **393**
Lesson Requirements 393
Step-by-Step 393

LESSON 28: DEVELOPING WEB APPLICATIONS WITH WEBSOCKETS 395

HTTP Drawbacks **396**
HTTP Hacks for Server-Side Data Push 397
Client-Server Communication with Websockets **397**
Web Browser as a WebSocket Client 398
Communication with the Server Using WebSockets 399
Sending Messages 403
Receiving Messages Using @OnMessage 404
Encoders and Decoders **406**
Publishing to All Clients **409**
Try It **412**
Lesson Requirements 412
Step-by-Step 412

LESSON 29: INTRODUCING JNDI 415

Naming and Directory Services **415**
Using the Class InitialContext **416**
Getting a Reference to InitialContext 416
Injecting JNDI Resources 417
Administering JNDI Objects in Glassfish **418**
Datasource and JNDI **419**
Lightweight Directory Access Protocol **421**
Try It **423**
Lesson Requirements 423
Step-by-Step 423

LESSON 30: INTRODUCING JMS AND MOM 425

Messaging Concepts and Terminology **425**
Two Modes of Message Delivery **427**
Introducing OpenMQ MOM **428**
JMS API Overview **431**
Types of Messages 431
How to Send a Message Directly to MOM 432
How to Receive a Message Directly from MOM 433
How to Publish a Message 436
How to Subscribe for a Topic 436
Message Acknowledgments and Transactions Support 437
Message Selectors 439
Sending Messages from Java EE Containers **439**
Administering JMS Objects in GlassFish 441
Try It **443**
Lesson Requirements 444
Hints 444
Step-by-Step 444

LESSON 31: INTRODUCTION TO ENTERPRISE JAVABEANS 447

Who Needs EJB Containers? **447**
Types of EJBs **448**
Stateless Session Beans **449**
The Bean 449
The Client's View 450
Asynchronous Methods and Concurrency 455

Stateful Session Beans **456**
Singleton Beans **457**
Deploying EJB **458**
Message-Driven Beans **460**
EJB and Transactions **461**
Timer Service **462**
Summary **463**
Try It **463**
Lesson Requirements 463
Hint 463
Step-by-Step 463

LESSON 32: OVERVIEW OF THE JAVA PERSISTENCE API 465

The Big Picture **465**
Mapping Objects to Database Tables **466**
Querying Entities **468**
JPQL 469
Criteria API 469
Entity Manager **471**
Bean Validation **473**
Try It **475**
Lesson Requirements 475
Step-by-Step 475

LESSON 33: WORKING WITH RESTFUL WEB SERVICES 483

The Soap Web Services **483**
The RESTful Web Services **484**
Working with JSON-Formatted Data **485**
Reading JSON with the Streaming API 487
Writing JSON with the Streaming API 487
Writing JSON with the Object Model API 488
The RESTful Stock Server **489**
Creating the Application 490
Creating the Java Bean Stock 490
Creating the Endpoint StockService 491
Creating RESTFful Clients 495
Contexts and Dependency Injection **495**
Try It **498**
Lesson Requirements 498

Hints 498
Step-by-Step 498

LESSON 34: JAVA LOGGING API 501

Java Logging API **502**
Hello World with the Java Logging API 503
Using Handlers and Setting Log Levels 505
Formatters and Filters 508
Logging Frameworks **511**
Try It **512**
Lesson Requirements 512
Step-by-Step 512

LESSON 35: INTRODUCTION TO UNIT TESTING WITH JUNIT FRAMEWORK 515

Introduction to JUnit **516**
Installing JUnit 517
Changing the Default Directory Structure in Eclipse 517
Your First JUnit Test Case 518
JUnit Annotations 521
Applying Annotations for Testing Tax 522
Test Suites 524
JUnit Test Runners 527
Try It **528**
Lesson Requirements 528
Step-by-Step 528

LESSON 36: BUILD AUTOMATION WITH GRADLE 531

Hello World in Ant **532**
Hello World in Maven **533**
Gradle Basics **536**
Hello World in Gradle 537
Changing Gradle Conventions **540**
Managing Dependencies with Gradle **542**
Repositories 544
Dependencies and Configurations 545
Using Gradle in Eclipse IDE **551**
Gradle Eclipse Plug-ins 551

Eclipse IDE and Gradle 552
Try It 553
Lesson Requirements 554
Step-by-Step 554

LESSON 37: JAVA TECHNICAL INTERVIEWS 555

Getting the Interview 555
Doing Well at the Interview 556
Considering the Offer 557
Interviewing Enterprise Developers 558
To Get or Not to Get Certified? 559
Technical Questions and Answers 559
Epilogue 567

INDEX 569

INTRODUCTION

Thank you for considering learning Java with the second edition of my book. This book may look thick, but it's rather thin given the number of topics covered, and it comes with well-produced and helpful videos.

I like this *24-Hour Trainer* series from Wiley Publishing. This is not to say that you can learn the software covered in these books within 24 hours.

It's about having a trainer that's with you 24 hours a day. Each book in this series, which is accompanied by a set of videos, contains a minimum of theory to get you started on a subject that is new to you.

This book comes with more than six hours of Java programming screencasts that demonstrate modern concepts, techniques, and technologies in a way that facilitates learning and promotes a better understanding of the development process.

Software developers are often categorized into junior, mid-level, and senior developers. If you master all the materials of this book, rest assured that you will have achieved the technical skills of a mid-level Java developer. I often run technical interviews for the company I work for, and I would be happy if a candidate for a mid-level position could demonstrate an understanding of all the topics covered in this book.

Who This Book Is For

This book is for anyone who wants to learn how to program with the Java language. No previous programming experience is expected.

- This tutorial can be used by Java developers looking for simple working examples that use certain features of the language.
- Accomplished Java developers can also use this book as a refresher while preparing for a technical job interview.
- This tutorial can be used by university students who are interested in learning from a practitioner who has spent 25-plus years developing enterprise software for a living.
- University professors should appreciate the fact that each lesson ends with a Try It section—a prepared assignment for each lesson. Solutions to these assignments are provided as well.

This book is a tutorial, but not in an academic sense. It's written by a practitioner and is for practitioners.

What This Book Covers

To be called a Java developer, a person has to know not only the core syntax of this programming language, but also the set of server-side technologies called Java EE (Enterprise Edition). This book covers both. At the time of this writing, the latest version of core Java is 8 and the latest release of Java EE is 7. These are the versions covered in this book.

Java is a general-purpose language—you can program applications that run independently on the user's computer, and applications that connect to remote servers. You can program applications that run exclusively on the server. You can use Java for writing applications for mobile phones and programming games. We live in the Internet of Things (IoT) era, and Java can be embedded into sensors inside cars or in household appliances.

The bulk of this book covers Java programming syntax and techniques that can be used on both users' computers and the servers. Nine lessons are dedicated to Java EE technologies used for Java programs that run on servers. The final lesson is dedicated to the process of getting prepared for Java technical job interviews for those who are interested in applying for a job as a Java software developer.

How This Book Is Structured

This book is a tutorial. Each lesson walks you through how to use certain elements and techniques of the Java language or gives an introduction to the server-side Java EE technologies. The Try It sections serve as continuations of materials explained in the lessons. The screencasts that come with the book usually illustrate how to complete the assignments from Try It sections.

You can choose to read the lesson and then try to run the examples and work on the lesson assignment, or you can read the lesson, watch the video, and then try to do the assignment on your own.

The lessons are short and to the point. The goal is to explain the material quickly so you can start applying it hands-on as soon as possible. Some readers may feel that more explanation of certain subjects are required; you are encouraged to do some extra research. There are lots and lots of online materials available on any Java-related subject, but the coverage of the material given in this book definitely helps in understanding what to focus on and what to look for.

What You Need to Use This Book

To run the examples and complete the assignments from this book, you do not need to purchase any software—freely available software is used here. Installing Java Development Kit and Eclipse Integrated Development Environment (IDE) is explained in the first two lessons, and this is all you need to get started. In Lesson 21 you download an open source database management system called Derby DB. In Lesson 25 you install Java Application Server GlassFish, which is used for explanation of the Java EE (server-side) technologies covered in Lesson 25 through Lesson 33. Finally, in Lesson 36 you install Gradle—the modern build-automation tool used by professional Java developers. Whenever you need to download certain software, detailed instructions are given in the book and/or in the screencasts.

From the hardware perspective, you can use either a PC running Windows or one of the Apple computers running Mac OS X. Linux fans are also able to run all book samples. You should have at least 2GB of RAM on your computer to run all code examples from this book, but adding more memory can make your Java compiler and Eclipse IDE work faster.

How To Read This Book

This book is a tutorial, and I assume in each lesson that you are already familiar with the materials from the lessons that came before it. If you are new to Java, I highly recommend that you read this book sequentially.

Typically, I give you just a little theory, followed by the working code that you can either read or use for trying the concept in a hands-on mode.

Each lesson except the last one has a corresponding video screencast that shows you how to work on the assignment from the Try It section of the lesson, run code samples, or simply install and configure some software. Ideally, you should try to do all the assignments from the Try It sections on your own and use the videos only if you get stuck or don't understand the instructions. But if you prefer to learn by following the instructor, just watch the video first and then try to repeat the same actions on your own. Whatever works is fine.

Java is a multiplatform language, and programs written for Microsoft Windows, say, should work the same way in Mac OS X or on Linux computers. I'm using a Mac, but I also have special software that enables me to run Microsoft Windows. In this book I use the open-source Eclipse Integrated Development Environment, which exists on all major platforms and looks pretty much the same on each. So regardless of your preferred operating system, you'll be able to run all the code samples from this book.

Conventions

To help you get the most from the text and keep track of what's happening, I've used a number of conventions throughout the book.

> **NOTE** *Notes, tips, hints, tricks, and asides to the current discussion are offset and placed in italic like this.*

> **TIP** *References like this one point you to the URL to watch the instructional video that accompanies a given lesson.*

As for styles in the text:

- We *highlight* new terms and important words when we introduce them.
- We show filenames, URLs, and code within the text like so: `persistence.properties`.
- We present code like the following:

```
We use a monofont type with no highlighting for most code examples.
```

Source Code

As you work through the examples in this book, you may choose either to type in all the code manually or to use the source code files that accompany the book. All of the source code used in this book is available for download on the book's page at `www.wrox.com`.

When you're at the site, simply click the Download Code link on the book's detail page to obtain all the source code for the book.

After you download the code, just decompress it with your favorite compression tool. Alternatively, you can go to the main Wrox code download page at `www.wrox.com/dynamic/books/download.aspx` to see the code available for this book and all other Wrox books.

Errata

Wiley Publishing and Wrox make every effort to ensure that there are no errors in the text or in the code. However, no one is perfect, and mistakes do occur. If you find an error in one of our books, like a spelling mistake or faulty piece of code, we would be very grateful for your feedback. By sending in errata you may save another reader hours of frustration, and at the same time you will be helping us provide even higher quality information.

To find the errata page for this book, go to `www.wrox.com` and locate the title using the Search box or one of the title lists. Then, on the book details page, click the Book Errata link. On this page you can view all errata that has been submitted for this book and posted by Wrox editors. A complete book list including links to each book's errata is also available at `www.wrox.com/misc-pages/booklist.shtml`.

If you don't spot "your" error on the Book Errata page, go to `www.wrox.com/contact/techsupport.shtml` and complete the form there to send us the error you have found. We'll check the information and, if appropriate, post a message to the book's errata page and fix the problem in subsequent editions of the book.

P2P.Wrox.Com

For author and peer discussion, join the P2P forums at `p2p.wrox.com`. The forums are a web-based system for you to post messages relating to Wrox books and related technologies and interact with other readers and technology users. The forums offer a subscription feature to e-mail you topics of interest of your choosing when new posts are made to the forums. Wrox authors, editors, other industry experts, and your fellow readers are present on these forums.

At `p2p.wrox.com` you will find a number of different forums that will help you not only as you read this book, but also as you develop your own applications. To join the forums, just follow these steps:

1. Go to `p2p.wrox.com` and click the Register link.
2. Read the terms of use and click Agree.
3. Complete the required information to join as well as any optional information you wish to provide and click Submit.
4. You will receive an e-mail with information describing how to verify your account and complete the joining process.

> **TIP** *You can read messages in the forums without joining P2P but in order to post your own messages, you must join.*

After you join, you can post new messages and respond to messages other users post. You can read messages at any time on the web. If you would like to have new messages from a particular forum e-mailed to you, click the Subscribe to this Forum icon by the forum name in the forum listing.

For more information about how to use the Wrox P2P, be sure to read the P2P FAQs for answers to questions about how the forum software works as well as many common questions specific to P2P and Wrox books. To read the FAQs, click the FAQ link on any P2P page.

1

Introducing Java

During the last two decades Java has maintained its status as one of the most popular programming languages for everything from programming games to creating mission-critical applications, such as those for trading on Wall Street or controlling Mars rovers. For the current popularity chart see the Tiobe Index at `http://www.tiobe.com/index.php/content/paperinfo/tpci/index.html`. In this lesson you are introduced to some of the very basic Java terms. You also download and install the Java Development Kit (JDK) and compile your first program.

WHY LEARN JAVA?

The Java programming language was originally created in 1995 by James Gosling from Sun Microsystems (acquired by Oracle Corporation in 2010). The goal was to provide a simpler and platform-independent alternative to C++. Java programs run inside the Java Virtual Machine (JVM), which is the same on every platform from the application programmer's perspective. You find out what *platform independence* means a little later, in the section "The Life Cycle of a Java Program". For now, let's look at some of the reasons why Java can be your language of choice.

Java is a general-purpose programming language that's used in all industries for almost any type of application. If you master it, your chances of getting employed as a software developer will be higher than if you specialize in some domain-specific programming languages.

There are more than nine million professional Java developers in the world, and the majority of them are ready to share their knowledge by posting blogs and articles or simply answering technical questions online. If you get stuck solving some problem in Java, the chances are very high that you'll find the solution on the Internet.

Because the pool of Java developers is huge, project managers of large and small corporations like to use Java for the development of new projects—if you decide to leave the project for whatever reason, it's not too difficult to find another Java programmer to replace you. This would not be the case if the project were being developed in a powerful, but less popular language, such as Scala. At this point you may ask, "Does that also mean that my

Java skills will be easily replaceable?" It depends on you. To improve your value and employability, you need to *master* not only the syntax of the language but also the right set of Java-related technologies that are in demand (you learn them in this book in the Java EE section).

Not only is Java open-source, but there are thousands and thousands of open-source projects being developed in Java. Joining one of these projects is the best way to get familiar with the process of project development and secure your very first job without having any prior real-world experience as a programmer.

The Java language is *object-oriented* (OO), which enables you to easily relate program constructs to objects from the real world (more on this in Chapter 3-Chapter 7). On the other hand, recently added lambda expressions (see Chapter 14) allow you to program in Java in a functional style.

The IT world is changing and people often use more than one language in the same project. Java is not the only language that runs in JVM. Such languages as Scala, Groovy, Clojure, JavaScript and others also run on JVM. So being familiar with the JVM opens the doors to being a polyglot programmer within the same operating environment.

The server-side applications that are deployed in the JVM scale well. The processing of thousands of users requests can be arranged in parallel by splitting the job between rather inexpensive servers in a cluster.

Java as a development platform has many advantages over other environments, which makes it the right choice for many projects, and you'll have a chance to see this for yourself while reading this book, watching the screencasts from the accompanying DVD, and deploying all code samples from the book on your computer.

SETTING THE GOALS

The goal of this rather slim tutorial is to give you just enough information about most of the Java language elements, techniques, and technologies that are currently being used in the real world. The first 25 lessons of the book are about the Java Standard Edition, whereas the remaining part is about Java Enterprise Edition—it covers server-side Java technologies, and this is where Java shines in the enterprise world.

The brevity of some of the lessons may make you wonder if it's even possible to explain a subject in just 10 pages when there are whole books devoted for the same topic. My approach is to cover just enough for you to understand the concept, important terms, and best practices. Prerecorded screencasts on the DVD help you to repeat the techniques explained in the lesson on your own.

There are plenty of additional materials online that help you to study any specific topic more deeply. But you'll get a working and practical knowledge about Java just by using the materials included with this book.

The goal of this book is not just to get you familiar with the syntax of the Java language, but to give you practical Java skills that will enable you to develop business applications either on your own or by working as a team member in a larger-scale project.

THE LIFE CYCLE OF A JAVA PROGRAM

There are different types of programming languages. In some of them you write the text of the program (aka the source code) and can execute this program right away. These are interpreted languages (for example, JavaScript).

But Java requires the source code of your program to be compiled first. It gets converted to a bytecode that is run by Java Virtual Machine, which may turn some of it into a platform-specific machine code using the so-called Just-In-Time (JIT) compiler.

Not only will the program be checked for syntax errors by a Java compiler, but other libraries of Java code can be added (*linked*) to your program after the compilation is complete (deployment stage). There are plenty of readily available libraries of reusable components, and a vast majority of them are free of charge.

In this lesson you start with writing a very basic Java program that outputs the words "Hello World" on your computer's monitor.

Technically you can write the source code of your Java program in any plain text editor that you prefer (Notepad, TextEdit, Sublime Text, vi, and so on), but to compile your program you need additional tools and code libraries that are included in the Java Development Kit (JDK).

JDK AND JRE

If you are planning to use a specific computer to develop Java programs, you need to download and install JDK. If you are planning to use this computer only to run Java programs that were compiled somewhere else, you just need the Java Runtime Environment (JRE).

If you have JDK installed on your machine, it includes JRE.

Java's platform independence comes from the fact that your Java program doesn't know under which operating system (OS) or on which hardware it's being executed. It operates inside the pre-installed JRE.

You need to get familiar with two more terms: Java SE (Standard Edition) and Java EE (Enterprise Edition). The latter includes the server-side tools and libraries that you get familiar with starting in Chapter 25.

DOWNLOADING AND INSTALLING JAVA SE

Start with downloading the latest version of the JDK SE Development Kit, which at the time of this writing is Java SE 8. Download and install JDK for your platform from Oracle's Java SE Downloads site: `http://goo.gl/X68FzJ`. In some literature you see references like JDK 1.8, which is the same as JDK 8. The number 8 is followed by the letter *u* and a number. For example, JDK 8u5 means that Oracle has released an update number 5 for JDK 8.

Installing JDK 8 for MAC OS

Download the *dmg* file marked as MAC OS X x64. Running this program on a Mac OS X computer installs Java in `/Library/Java/JavaVirtualMachines/jdk1.8.0.jdk`. MAC OS X is my platform of choice, but Java works practically the same on all platforms, and all the book examples work under Windows and Linux as well.

Open the Terminal window and enter `java -version`. You should see an output similar to this one:

```
Last login: Sun Apr 27 08:41:47 on ttys000
Yakov:~ yfain11$ java -version
java version "1.8.0"
Java(TM) SE Runtime Environment (build 1.8.0-b132)
Java HotSpot(TM) 64-Bit Server VM (build 25.0-b70, mixed mode)
Yakov:~ yfain11$
```

FIGURE 1-1: Checking the Java version in MAC OS

Installing JDK 8 in Windows

Select and download the Windows x86 executable file, which is a Java version for 32-bit computers. This version is perfectly fine to start working with Java. Run this file, click the Next button two or three times, and then click Close. In about a minute the installation is complete. By default JDK is installed in the directory named something like `c:\Program Files\Java\jdk1.8.0_05`. This is the place where both JDK and JRE are installed.

Now you need to add the `bin` folder from your java installation directory to the environment variable PATH of your Windows OS. Click Start, Control Panel and search for the environment variables. Click the Edit the System Environment Variables link and press the Environment Variables button. Edit the system variable PATH (if you don't have one, create it) to include the path to `c:\Program Files\Java\jdk1.8.0_05\bin` unless you have it in a different location. Don't forget to add a semicolon as a separator as in Figure 1-2.

FIGURE 1-2: Java location is added to the Path variable in Windows

If you have previous versions of the JDK installed on your computer, each of them is located in its own directory, and they don't conflict with each other.

To ensure that you'll be working with the freshly installed Java, open a command window (in Windows 7 just click the Start button and in the search box enter command `cmd`) and enter `java -version` in the command window. Figure 1-3 shows the confirmation that I have Java 1.8.0_05.

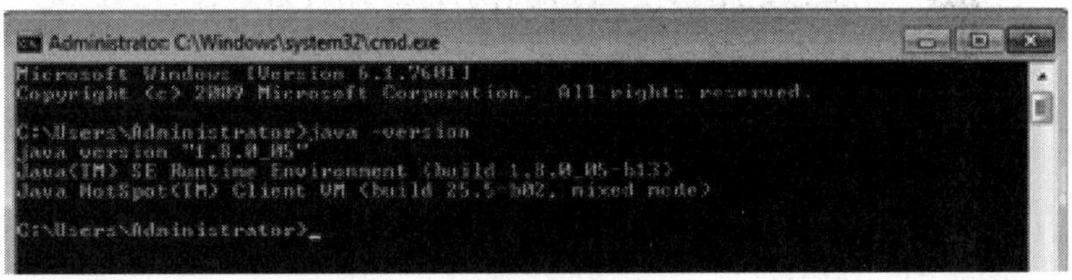

FIGURE 1-3: Checking the Java version in Windows

If you still don't see the proper version, reopen the command window. Congratulations! Your JDK and JRE are installed.

YOUR FIRST JAVA PROGRAM: HELLO WORLD

Historically, the first program you write while learning a new programming language is the program Hello World. If you can write a program that outputs Hello World on your monitor, it proves that you have properly installed the compiler and the run time environment, and your program doesn't have syntax errors.

To start writing a Java program you could use any plain text editor, such as Notepad, TextEdit, or Sublime Text. The file that contains the Java code must be saved in a file with its name ending in `.java`.

Enter the following code in the text editor.

LISTING 1-1 HelloWorld.java

```
public class HelloWorld {

   public static void main(String[] args){
            System.out.println("Hello World!!!!!");
   }
}
```

Create a directory, `c:\PracticalJava\Lesson1`, and save the program you just created in the file `HelloWorld.java` (if you use Notepad, select All Files in the Save as Type drop-down to avoid auto-attachment of the `.txt` suffix).

Keep in mind that Java is a case-sensitive language, which means that if you named the program HelloWorld with a capital H and a capital W, don't try to start the program helloworld. Your first dozen syntax errors will probably be caused by improper capitalization.

What follows is a really short explanation of some of the terms and language elements used in the HelloWorld program. You'll get more comfortable with them after mastering the first several lessons in this book.

The first program contains a *class*, `HelloWorld`. Give the Java class and its file the same name. (There could be exceptions to this rule, but not in this simple program.) While writing Java programs, you create *classes*, which often represent objects from real life. You learn more about classes in Chapter 3.

The class `HelloWorld` contains a *method*, `main()`. Methods in Java classes represent functions (actions) that a class could perform. A Java class may have several methods, but if one of them is called `main()` and has the same *method signature* (the declaration line) as in our class, this makes this Java class executable. If a class doesn't have a method `main()`, it can be used from other classes, but you can't run it as a program. Here is the *method signature* (similar to a title) of the method `main()`:

```
public static void main(String[] args)
```

This method signature includes the access level (`public`), instructions on usage (`static`), return value type (`void`), name of the method (`main`), and argument list (`String[] args`).

- The keyword `public` means that the method `main()` can be accessed by any other Java class.
- The keyword `static` means that you don't have to create an instance of this class to use this method.
- The keyword `void` means that the method `main()` doesn't return any value to the calling program.
- The keyword `String[] args` tells you that this method will receive an array of strings as the argument (you can pass external data to this method from a command line).

The `main()` method is the starting point of your program. You can write a program in Java SE that consists of more than one class, but at least one of them has the method `main`. A Java class can have more than one method. For example, a class `Employee` can have the methods `updateAddress()`, `raiseSalary()`, `changeName()`, and so on.

The *body* of the method `main()` contains the following line:

```
System.out.println("Hello World!!!!!");
```

The preceding `println()` method is used to print data on the system console (command window). Java's method names are always followed by parentheses.

`System` here represents another Java class.

The dot notation, as in `System.out`, means that the variable `out` is defined inside the class `System`.

`out.println()` tells you that there is an object represented by a variable called `out` and it has a method called `println()`.

You will be using this dot notation to refer to class methods or variables.

All these explanations may sound too short and inadequate, and they really are. Bear with me; I go into greater detail in subsequent chapters.

Compiling and Running Hello World

The program HelloWorld is written, and now you need to *compile* this program. Java compiler is a program that will convert your source code into so-called bytecode that JRE understands. The `javac` compiler is a part of the JDK, so open a command window on your PC or Terminal on MAC, change the current directory to `c:\PracticalJava\Lesson1`, and try to compile the following program:

```
cd PracticalJava\Lesson1
 javac HelloWorld.java
```

Even though there is no program javac in the Chapter 1 directory, your OS found it in the *bin* directory of your Java install. MAC OS knows where the bin directory is located. In Windows OS you've added it to the PATH environment variable.

You won't see any confirmation of a successful compilation; just type *dir* on Windows (or *ls* on MAC OS) to confirm that a new file named `HelloWorld.class` has been created. This proves that your program has been successfully compiled.

If the program has syntax errors, the compiler prints error messages. In this case, fix the errors, and recompile the program again. You may need to do it more than once until the file `HelloWorld.class` is successfully created.

Now run the program by typing the following command:

```
java HelloWorld
```

Note that this time you didn't use the *javac* program, but java, which starts the Java run time and loads the HelloWorld program into the Java Virtual Machine (JVM). The words "Hello World" are displayed in the command window. Figure 1-4 is a screenshot that shows how in MAC OS looks the compilation command (`javac HelloWorld.java`), the content of the Chapter 1 folder (`ls`) after the compilation—the `dir` in Windows is an equivalent to `ls`, how to run the program (`java HelloWorld`), and the output of the HelloWorld program (`Hello World!!!!!`).

```
Yakov:Lesson1 yfain11$ pwd
/Users/yfain11/practicalJava/Lesson1
Yakov:Lesson1 yfain11$ javac HelloWorld.java
Yakov:Lesson1 yfain11$ ls
HelloWorld.class        HelloWorld.java
Yakov:Lesson1 yfain11$ java HelloWorld
Hello World!!!!!
Yakov:Lesson1 yfain11$
```

FIGURE 1-4: Compiling and running HelloWorld

TRY IT

In this lesson your goal is to write your first Java program that outputs the words "Hello World." After this goal is achieved, add more lines to this program to print your address.

Lesson Requirements

For this lesson download and install the current version of JDK as explained in the section Downloading and Installing Java SE.

Step-by-Step

1. Open a plain text editor of your choice and enter the text of the Hello World program. Keep in mind that Java is case sensitive.
2. Save the program in the file `HelloWorld.java`.
3. Compile the program in the command window using the command `javac HelloWorld.java`.
4. Run the program by using the command `java HelloWorld`.

> **TIP** *Please select the videos for Lesson 1 online at* `www.wrox.com/go/javaprog24hr2e`. *You will also be able to download the code and resources for this lesson from the website.*

Eclipse IDE

Your first Java program was written in a plain text editor and compiled from a command window, but this is not a productive way of developing software. Professional programmers use an Integrated Development Environment (IDE), which includes an editor, a compiler, context-sensitive help, a debugger, and a lot more (you become familiar with these features later in this lesson). There are several popular Java IDEs, such as Eclipse, IntelliJ IDEA, and NetBeans.

Eclipse is by far the most widely used IDE, and I use it for compiling and running most of the examples in this book. But switching from one IDE to another is a pretty simple process, and if you see that in some areas one IDE makes you more productive than the other, just use the best one for the job. As a matter of fact, I prefer IntelliJ IDEA IDE, but this doesn't stop me from enjoying Java development in Eclipse, too.

INTRODUCING ECLIPSE IDE

Eclipse IDE is an open-source product that was originally created with a substantial code donation by IBM to the Java community, and from that moment Eclipse was a community-driven product. It started as an IDE for developing Java programs, but today it's a development platform used for building thousands of tools and plug-ins. Some people are using its Rich Client Platform (RCP) API to develop user interfaces (UIs) for applications. With Eclipse you can easily generate and deploy web applications, start and stop servers, use it as a Database admin tool, and a lot more. Some use its plug-ins for developing reports. Visit the Downloads page at `www.eclipse.org/downloads` to see some of the Eclipse-based products available.

Besides being an IDE, Eclipse supports plug-in development, and each developer can add only those plug-ins that he or she is interested in. For example, there is a plug-in to display UML diagrams, another offers a reporting system, and there are plug-ins for developing applications in C, JavaScript, Apache Flex, and other languages.

DOWNLOADING AND INSTALLING ECLIPSE

There are different versions of Eclipse IDE, and this book uses *Eclipse IDE for Java EE Developers*. Each version of Eclipse IDE has a name. At the time of this writing, the current version is called Luna, and you should download it from `http://www.eclipse.org/downloads`.

The installation of Eclipse IDE comes down to a simple unzipping of the downloaded file into a disk drive of your choice. Depending on your OS, you find either the file Eclipse.exe or Eclipse.app in the Eclipse folder — just run this program. You immediately see a pop-up window asking you to select a *workspace*, which is a directory on your hard disk where one or more of your *projects* is going to be stored.

Eclipse for Java EE IDE starts with showing the Welcome panel; just close it by clicking the little x on the Welcome tab. Figure 2-1 is a snapshot of the *workbench* of the freshly installed Eclipse IDE.

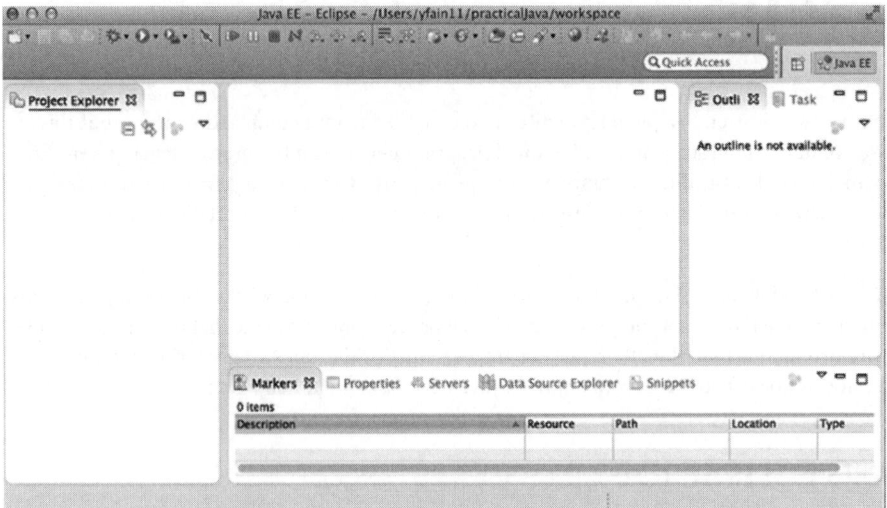

FIGURE 2-1: The Java EE perspective in Eclipse IDE workbench

In Eclipse you start with creating a project. In the real world, the source code of a decent-sized application can consist of several Eclipse projects.

For code samples of this book, I selected the following workspace directory: `practicalJava/workspace`.

To be precise, in Figure 2-1 you are looking at Java EE *perspective* (note the Java EE tab at the top), which is a collection of default *views* that are opened for Java EE developers. On the left you see a Project Explorer view; creating a Hello project is your next task. The area in the middle is reserved for the code editor view. You start entering Java code in there after creating your first Java class. The Outline view is on the right; you'll see the names of your classes, methods, and variables (see Chapter 3) there.

There are many other views that you can open and close by yourself by selecting Window → Show View. These include Console, Search, Problems, Servers, and others. If you don't see some of these menu items, find them in Windows → Show View → Other.

Because you are just starting to learn the language, there is no need to work in the Java EE perspective; you can get by in the Java perspective. Click the little icon with the plus sign on the toolbar by the Java EE tab and select Java perspective. You'll see a slightly different set of views with the Package Explorer and Hierarchy views on the left, Task List on the right, and the Problems, Javadoc, and Declaration tabs at the bottom, as shown in Figure 2-2.

FIGURE 2-2: The Java perspective in Eclipse IDE workbench

CREATING HELLO PROJECT IN ECLIPSE

In Chapter 1 you simply created the class `HelloWorld`, but in Eclipse you have to create the project first. Select File → New → Java Project and enter `Hello` as the name of the project in the pop-up window, as shown in Figure 2-3.

You can select the version of the JRE you want to work with. In Chapter 1 I've installed the JDK and JRE of version 1.8, but you may have more than one version of JRE, and Eclipse can compile the code that will run in another version of JRE. This might be useful if some of your projects have to run with the older versions of JRE. Typically enterprises don't rush to install the newest version of Java because it requires substantial investments of time and resources to ensure that their production applications are not broken in the new version of JRE. Eclipse allows you to select for your projects any of the installed versions of JRE.

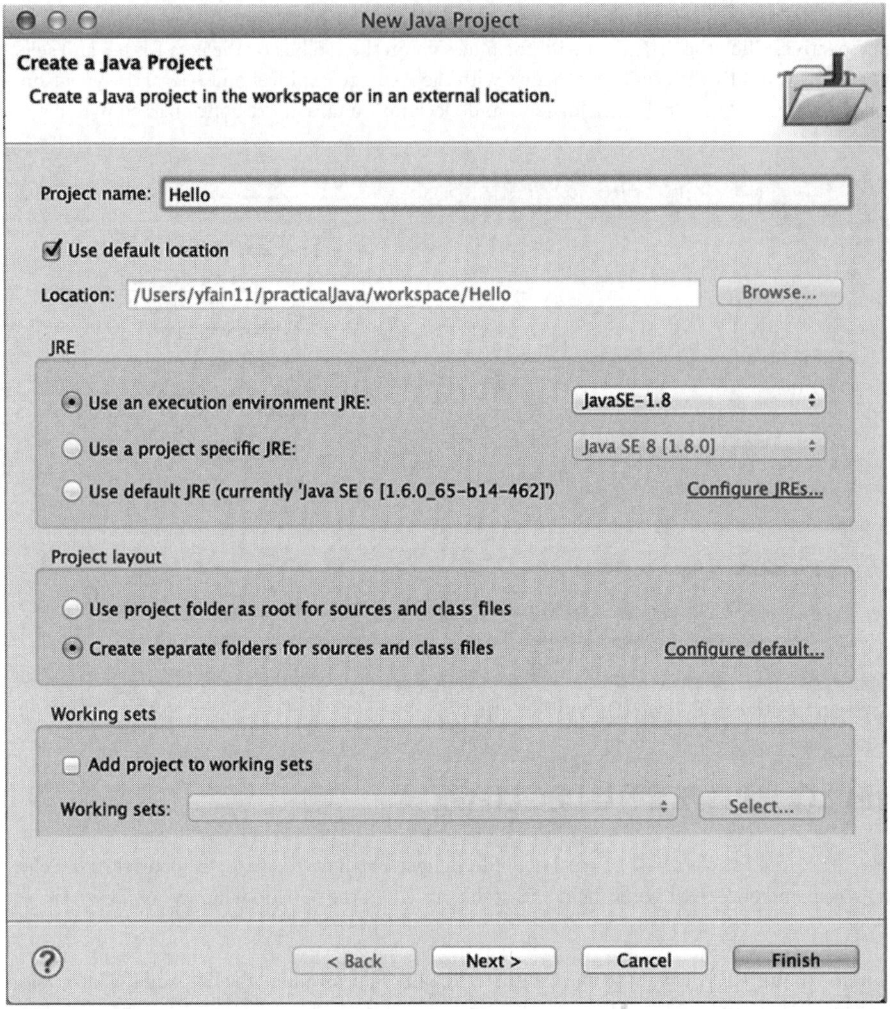

FIGURE 2-3: Creating a Java project in Eclipse (step 1)

After you click Next, you're asked to specify the folders where the source code and compiled Java classes of the Hello project should be created (see Figure 2-4). By default, Eclipse creates a Hello folder for this project with a *bin* subfolder for compiled classes and an *src* subfolder for the source code. In Chapter 1 both `HelloWorld.java` and `HelloWorld.class` were sitting in the same folder, which is OK for a one-class project, but the good practice is to keep `.java` and `.class` files in separate folders.

Don't change the name of the output directory; just click Finish on that window. In Figure 2-5 you see a new project, Hello, in the Package Explorer view of Eclipse. This project has an empty folder named *src*—you will save the source code of `HelloWorld.java` there.

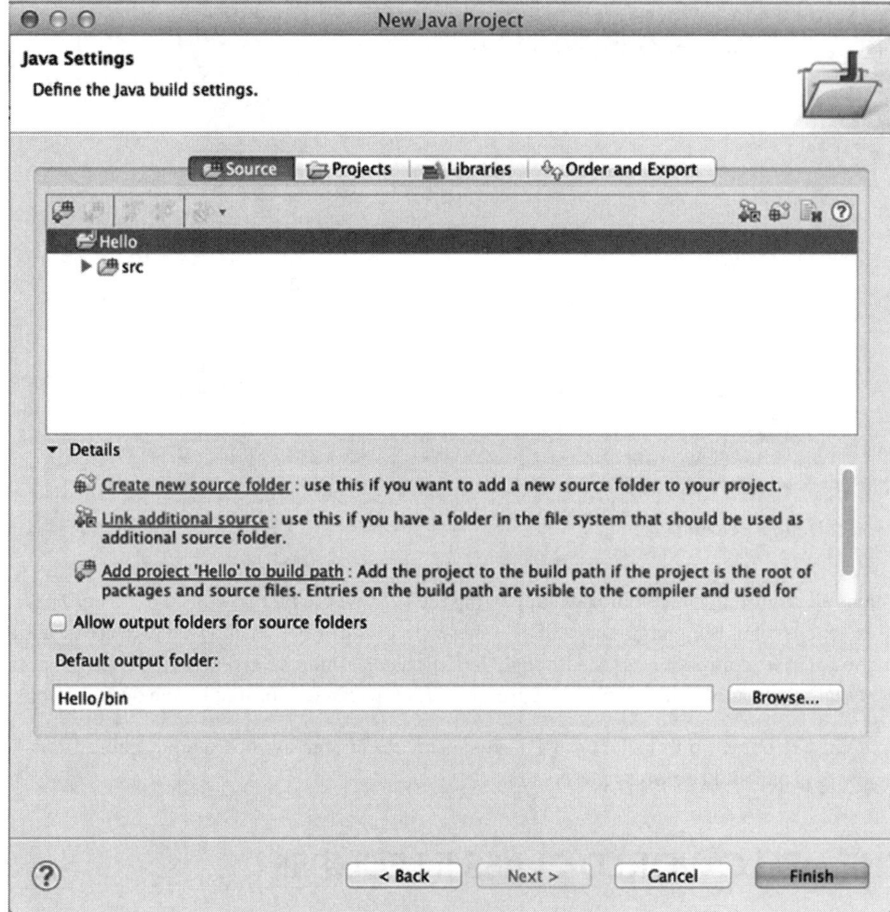

FIGURE 2-4: Creating a Java project in Eclipse (step 2)

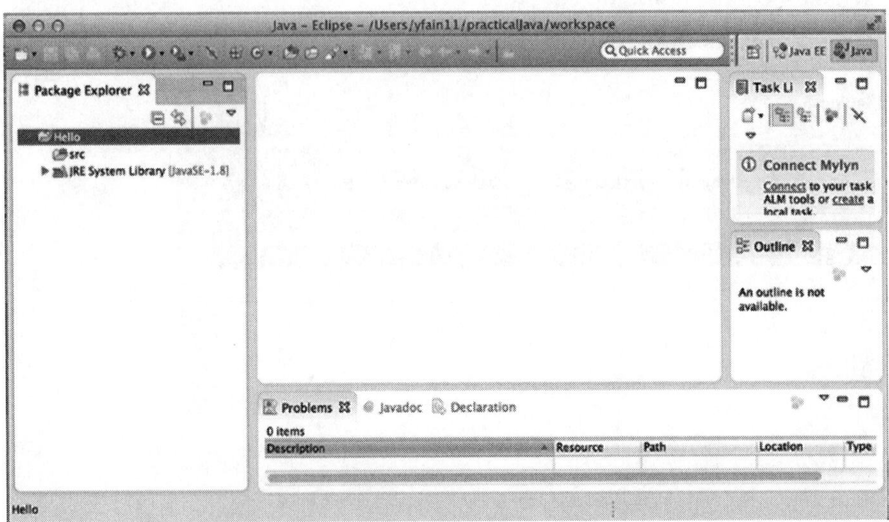

FIGURE 2-5: The project Hello is created

The JRE folder contains all required Java 1.8 libraries supporting the JVM where `HelloWorld` will run. These library files have `.jar` extension in their names. Java SDK comes with a jar utility that allows you to create a file archive that contains one or more compiled classes. Although the JRE folder contains classes created by developers of the JRE itself, most real-world applications consist of groups of files (packages) located in one or more jars.

It doesn't make much sense to put the only `HelloWorld` class inside the jar, but as your sample applications grow, you find out how to group and compress files in jars.

CREATING THE HELLOWORLD CLASS IN ECLIPSE

Your Hello project will contain one Java class: `HelloWorld` from Chapter 1. Select File → New → Class and enter `HelloWorld` in the Name field in the pop-up window shown in Figure 2-6.

Then enter `com.practicaljava.lesson2` in the Package field. The *package name* is a new addition to the previous version of `HelloWorld` from Chapter 1.

FIGURE 2-6: Creating a HelloWorld class in Eclipse

JAVA PACKAGES

Packages in Java are used to better organize multi-file projects and for data protection. It's not unusual for a project to have several hundreds of Java classes. Keeping them all in one directory is never a good idea. Consequently, the files will be located in various directories and subdirectories (also known as packages).

What are the naming conventions for packages? Java developers use *reverse-domain name* conventions. Let's say you work on a project called Sales for a company called Acme, which has an Internet site at `acme.com`. Every package name will start with the reverse URL of the company, followed by the project name: `com.acme.sales`.

Accordingly, all Java classes that belong to this package are stored in the following directory structure: `com/acme/sales`.

If some of the Java classes are specific to domestic sales, whereas others are used in international sales at Acme, you can create two more subdirectories: `com/acme/sales/domestic` and `com/acme/sales/international`.

Whereas directory names are separated by a forward slash or backslash, the corresponding Java package names are separated with periods. Java has a special keyword `package`, and its declaration has to be the first line of the class (program comments don't count). For example:

```
package com.acme.sales.domestic;
```

Let's assume that you work for a company called Practical Java on the project named Chapter 2; the name of the package will be `com.practicaljava.lesson2`, which is exactly what I've entered in the Package field shown in Figure 2-6.

Besides being used for better organization of Java classes, packages help in controlling data access. You learn about this feature in the section access_levels in programming_with_abstract_classes_and_in.

COMPLETING CODE GENERATION

From Figure 2-6 you may have noticed that I also checked off the box asking Eclipse to generate the main method for me.

Click Finish, and in no time Eclipse generates the initial code for the class `HelloWorld`, as shown in Figure 2-7.

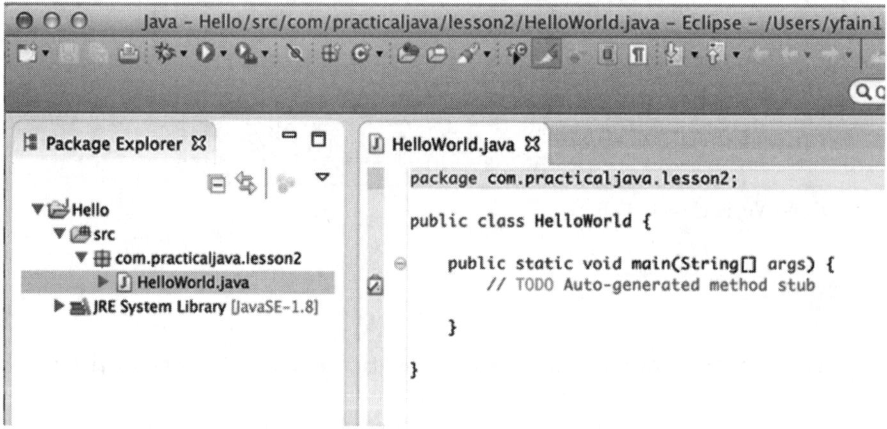

FIGURE 2-7: The auto-generated code of the HelloWorld class

The generated code is shown in Eclipse's editor view. It starts with the `package` statement, and the class declaration with the method name goes next. The line that starts with two slashes is a single-line comment. Programmers use comments to describe code fragments in a free form to explain to author's intentions to whoever will read the code. Comments are ignored by the compiler.

Place the cursor under the TODO comment, type **sysout**, and then press Ctrl+Space; Eclipse turns this abbreviation into `System.out.println();`. From the first seconds of coding Eclipse makes you more productive! Eclipse IDE has lots of useful hot key combinations that will allow you to do less manual typing.

Just add "Hello World!!!!!" between parentheses and save the code by pressing the little diskette image on the toolbar or using the Ctrl+S key combination.

By default, saving the code results in an invocation of the Java compiler. If you didn't make any syntax errors, Eclipse creates `HelloWorld.class` in the `bin` directory of the Hello project. In case of compilation errors, Eclipse puts a little red round bullet in front of problematic lines.

Now you can run the program by pressing the round green Play button on the toolbar. The output of the program is shown in the Console view panel in the lower part of the Eclipse workbench, as in Figure 2-8.

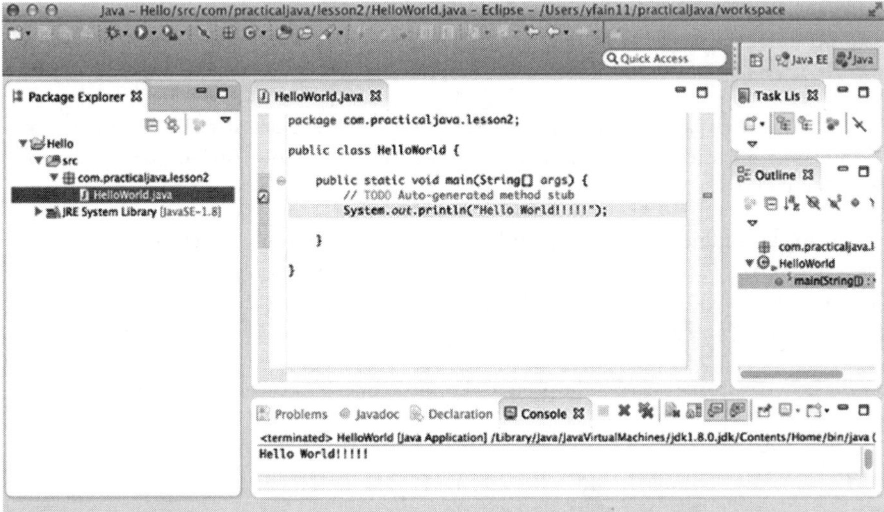

FIGURE 2-8: The output of the program is shown in the Console view

As you type, Eclipse displays context-sensitive help suggesting a selection of possible values, which minimizes guesswork and typing errors. You can try to bring up the context-sensitive help by pressing Ctrl+Space. In some cases, Eclipse won't have any suggestions, but sometimes it becomes pretty helpful. For example, place the cursor after the dot behind the `System` and press Ctrl+Space. You see a list of method names available inside the class `System`. Selecting `out` from this list displays the content of online Help for this object.

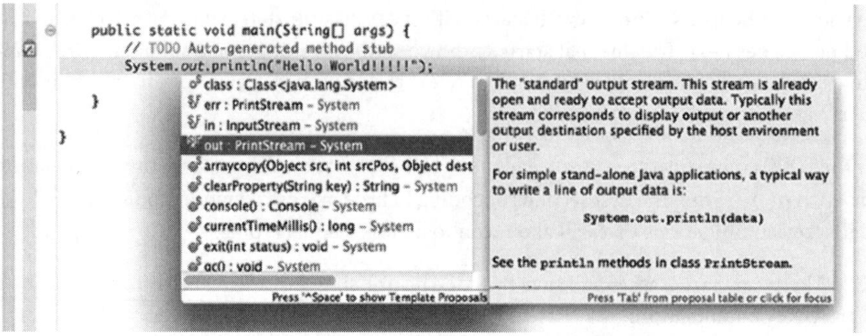

FIGURE 2-9: Ctrl-Space shows context-sensitive proposals and help

In Chapter 31 I explain how to use the debugger of Eclipse IDE. In Chapter 25 I show you how to start Java servers from Eclipse. In Chapter 26 you use Eclipse IDE for creating web projects. The format of this book doesn't have space for more detailed coverage of all the features of Eclipse. The next section contains additional online resources that can help you in getting more comfortable with Eclipse.

ADDITIONAL MATERIALS

The Eclipse IDE Documentation web page at `http://www.eclipse.org/documentation/` contains comprehensive Eclipse documentation. Select the latest version of Eclipse there and follow the Getting Started section under the Workbench User Guide.

I can also recommend to you the online Eclipse IDE Tutorial by Lars Vogel. It's available at `http://www.vogella.com/tutorials/Eclipse/article.html`. Lars Vogel has also published a list of useful Eclipse shortcuts that will increase your productivity. It's available at `http://www.vogella.com/tutorials/EclipseShortcuts/article.html`.

You can also watch Eclipse IDE Tutorial on Youtube produced by luv2code. It's available at `http://bit.ly/1uTYOR2`.

TRY IT

In this lesson your first task is to write, compile, and run `HelloWorld` in Eclipse IDE.

The second task is to create the new Eclipse project named Sale containing one Java class `FriendsAndFamily`. This class should also have the method `main()`. Include inside the method `main()` several `System.out.println()` lines that announce that your favorite store runs a 30% off sale on selected products. Output the names of the products that go on sale.

Now your Eclipse project contains two classes with the `main()` method. Which program will run when you press the green button? Click the class you want to run, and then press the green button. If no class is selected, the class that was run the last time you pressed the green button will run again.

Lesson Requirements

For this lesson, download and install the current version of Eclipse IDE for Java EE Developers from `www.eclipse.org/downloads`.

Step-by-Step

1. Create the Hello project in Eclipse IDE.
2. Create a new Java class, `HelloWorld`, with the method `main()`, as described earlier.
3. Compile the program by clicking Save.
4. Run the program by clicking the green button in the Eclipse toolbar.

Repeat the steps for the second task, but this time your program will have several lines of code invoking `println()`.

> **TIP** *Please select the videos for Lesson 2 online at* `www.wrox.com/go/javaprog24hr2e`. *You will also be able to download the code and resources for this lesson from the website.*

Object-Oriented Programming with Java

Starting with this lesson, you study various elements of the Java language with brief descriptions to get you started with programming in the shortest possible time. But you are certainly encouraged to refer to the extensive Java SE documentation that's available online at `http://docs.oracle.com/javase/8/`.

CLASSES AND OBJECTS

Java is an object-oriented language, which means that it has constructs to represent objects from the real world. Each Java program has at least one class that knows how to do certain things or how to represent some type of object. For example, the simplest class, `HelloWorld`, knows how to greet the world.

Classes in Java may have methods and fields (also known as attributes). Methods represent actions or functions that a class can perform. Up until Java 8, every function had to be represented as a method of some class. Lambda expressions (see working_with_streams) give more freedom to functions, but for now the focus is on the Java foundation — classes, methods, and fields.

Let's create and discuss a class named `Car`. This class will have *methods*, describing what this type of vehicle can do, such as start the engine, shut it down, accelerate, brake, lock the doors, and so on.

This class will also have some *fields*: body color, number of doors, sticker price, and so on.

LISTING 3-1 Class Car

```
class Car{
    String color;
    int numberOfDoors;
```

```
        void startEngine() {
           // Some code goes here
        }
        void stopEngine() {
             int tempCounter=0;
          // Some code goes here
        }
    }
```

In some code samples you'll see the comments, "Some code goes here." I do this to avoid distracting you from something that is not relevant to the subject of discussion. At this point, you couldn't care less about the algorithm of starting the engine. You're getting familiar with the structure of a Java class.

`Car` represents common features for many different cars: All cars have such attributes as color and number of doors, and all of them perform similar actions. You can be more specific and create another Java class called `JamesBondCar`. It's still a car, but with some attributes specific to the model created for James Bond (see Listing 3-2). You can say that the class `JamesBondCar` is a *subclass* of `Car`, or, using Java syntax, `JamesBondCar extends Car`.

LISTING 3-2 Class JamesBondCar

```
class JamesBondCar extends Car{
    int currentSubmergeDepth;
    boolean isGunOnBoard=true;
    final String MANUFACTURER;

    void submerge() {
        currentSubmergeDepth = 50;
      // Some code goes here
    }
    void surface() {
      // Some code goes here
    }
}
```

As you can guess from the method names, the James Bond's car not only drives, but it can go under water and then resurface. But even after defining all the attributes and methods for the class `JamesBondCar`, you can't "drive it," even on the computer screen. A Java class is like a blueprint in construction or engineering; until you build real objects based on this blueprint, you can't use them.

Creating objects, also known as *instances*, based on classes is the equivalent of building real cars based on blueprints. To create an instance of a class means to create the object in the computer's memory based on the class definition.

To instantiate a class (to put a car on the road), you declare a *variable* of this class's type, and use the `new` operator for each new instance of the car:

```
JamesBondCar car1 = new JamesBondCar();
JamesBondCar car2 = new JamesBondCar();
```

Now the variables `car1` and `car2` can be used to refer to the first and second instance of the `JamesBondCar`, respectively. To be precise, declaring the variables pointing at the instances is needed if you are planning to refer to these instances in the program. The variables `car1` and `car2` become your access points to the corresponding instance of a `Car`, as Figure 3-1 depicts.

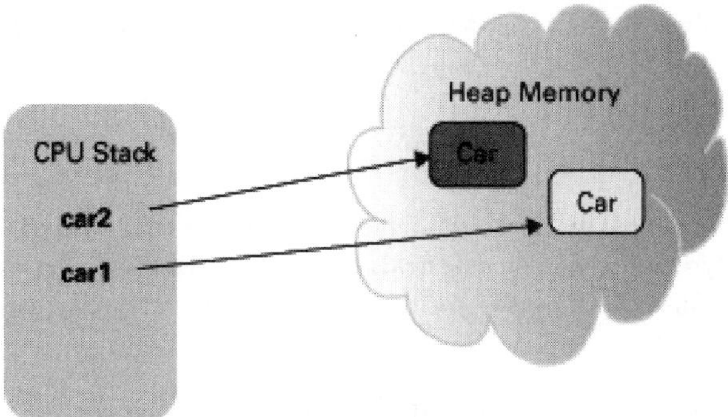

FIGURE 3-1: Instantiating two Car objects

The statement `new JamesBondCar()` creates the instance of this class in *heap memory*. In the real world, you can create many cars based on the same specification. Even though they all represent the same class, they may have different values in their attributes — some of them are red and some yellow, some of them have two doors whereas others have four, and so on.

VARIABLES AND DATA TYPES

Some values representing an object can change over the program's lifetime (variables) and some remain the same (constants). This section sheds more light on the use of both types.

Declaring Variables

Java is a statically typed language: A program *variable* must be declared (given a name and a data type) first, and then you can assign them values either at the time of declaration or later on in one of the class methods. For example, the variable `isGunOnBoard` has been initialized during its declaration in Listing 3-2, and `currentSubmergeDepth` got its value in the method `submerge()`.

The class `Car` from Listing 3-1 defines a *variable* `color` of type `String`, which is used to represent text values; for example, "Red," "Blue," and so on.

Final Variables

To store the value that never changes, you need to declare a *final variable* (or *constant*); just add the keyword `final` to the declaration line, as in Listing 3-2:

```
final String MANUFACTURER = "J.B. Limited";
```

Java developers usually name final variables in upper case. If you are wondering how Java developers agree on naming conventions, check out one of the coding standards guides. For example, Google publishes coding standards at `https://code.google.com/p/google-styleguide/` for various languages.

The value of a constant can be assigned only once, and because you are creating an instance of a specific car, its manufacturer is known and can't change during the life span of this object. Declare a `final` variable and initialize it right away, as shown earlier.

Primitive Data Types

When you're declaring a class, you create a new data type and can declare variables of this type as you saw above with the class `Car`. But these are not a simple data type as they can include fields and methods describing the object of this type. On the other hand, Java has predefined data types for storing simple values, such as an integer number or a character.

There are eight *primitive* data types in Java: four are for integer values; two are for values with a decimal point; one is for storing single characters; and one is for boolean data that allows only either `true` or `false` as a value. Following are some examples of variable declarations and initializations:

```
int chairs = 12;
char grade = 'A';
boolean cancelJob = false;
double nationalIncome = 23863494965745.78;
float hourlyRate = 12.50f;   // add an f at the end of
                             //float literals
long totalCars = 46372836483921; // add an l at the end
                                 // of long literals
```

The last two literals in the preceding list end with the letters `f` and `l` to indicate that you want to store these data as `float` and `long` data types correspondingly. The `double` data type fits most of the needs in non-integer calculations.

Each primitive data type occupies a certain amount of memory and has a range of values that it can store. The following table summarizes some characteristics of the Java data types.

PRIMITIVE TYPE	SIZE	MIN VALUE	MAX VALUE	WRAPPER CLASS
`byte`	8 bits	`-128`	`127`	`Byte`
`short`	16 bits	`-32,768`	`32,767`	`Short`
`int`	32 bits	`-2,147,483,648`	`2,147,483,647`	`Integer`
`long`	64 bits	`-9,223,372,036,854,775,808`	`9,223,372,036,854,775,807`	`Long`

float	32 bits	Single-precision floating point; see Java language specification at http://bit.ly/9nlwjh	Single-precision floating point; see Java language specification at http://bit.ly/9nlwjh	Float
double	64 bits	Double-precision floattingpoint; see Java language specification at http://bit.ly/9nlwjh	Double-precision floating point; see Java language specification at http://bit.ly/9nlwjh	Double
char	16 bits	Unicode 0	Unicode 2 in a power of 16 value	Character
boolean	-	false (not a min)	true (not a max)	Boolean

Have you noticed that the char data type uses two bytes of memory to store the data? This enables you to store character sets that have a lot more symbols than traditional alphabets because a single byte can only represent up to 256 different characters, whereas two bytes can represent 65,536 characters.

If you need to store very large numbers, Java has a class BigDecimal, but it's not a primitive data type.

VARIABLE SCOPE

If you declare a variable inside any method or a code block surrounded with curly braces, the variable has a local scope (for example, tempCounter in Listing 3-1 is local). This means that it's only visible for the code within the method stopEngine(). A local variable is accessible within the method only after the variable is declared, and only within the block in which it is declared. For instance, a variable declared inside a for loop is not accessible outside the for loop even within the same method.

When the method completes its execution, all local primitive variables are automatically removed from stack memory. If a variable was pointing to an instance of an object (for example, car1 on Figure 3-1), the corresponding object instance is removed from heap memory by Java's *Garbage Collector (GC)*, but it won't happen immediately. Periodically GC walks around the heap memory and removes all objects that have no reference variables.

If a variable has to be accessible from more than one class method, declare it on a class level. Listing 3-1 shows the class Car, where color and numberOfDoors are *class* or *member variables*. These variables remain "alive" while the instance of the Car object exists in memory. They can be shared and reused by all methods within the class, and they can even be visible from external classes (read about access levels in Chapter 7). There are some differences in passing primitive variables and those that point at object instances. Read the section Passing by Value or by Reference in the next chapter.

> **NOTE** *If a variable is declared with a* `static` *qualifier (see Chapter 4) it will be shared by all instances of the class. Instance variables (without* `static`*) store different values in each object instance.*

WRAPPERS, AUTOBOXING, AND UNBOXING

All primitive data types have corresponding *wrapper classes* that contain useful methods dealing with respective data types. The wrapper classes serve two purposes:

1. They contain a number of useful functions for manipulation with their primitive counterparts. For example, the class `Integer` offers such useful methods as conversion of a `String` into an `int`, or turning an `int` into a `float`, and more. The `Integer` class also enables you to set the minimum and maximum values for the number in question.

2. Some Java collections can't store primitives (such as `ArrayList`), so primitives have to be wrapped into objects. For example:

```
ArrayList myLotteryNumbers = new ArrayList();
myLotteryNumbers.add(new Integer(6));
myLotteryNumbers.add(new Integer(15));
```

Java has a feature called autoboxing, which spares you from explicitly creating a new instance for every primitive as in the preceding code snippet. You can simply write `myLotteryNumbers.add(6);` and the primitive value `6` is automatically wrapped into an instance of the `Integer` class.

On the same note, the next line is also valid:

```
int luckyNumber= myLotteryNumber.get(23);
```

Even though `get(23)` returns the value of the 24th element (the numbering in the Java collections starts with zero) as an `Integer` object, that object is automatically converted into a primitive. This is called *unboxing*.

PROGRAM COMMENTS

While writing code in Java, you should add comments, which is the text that explains what the program does. Programs are being read a lot more often than they are being written. At some point, other software developers will read and try to understand your code. Be nice and make their jobs easier. A typical software developer doesn't like writing comments (regardless of what programming language he or she uses).

I suggest you use a simple technique: Write comments first and then write the code. By the time your program is written it already has a comment. You can write comments pretty much everywhere — before or inside the class, or inside the methods.

In Java you can use three types of comments:

- Block comments contain more than one line of text located between the symbols `/*` and `*/`. For example:

```
/* This method will calculate the cost of shipping, handling,
     and all applicable taxes
*/
```

  The compiler ignores the text in comments and you can write whatever you want.

- If you want to write a short comment that fits on a single line, start this line with two forward slashes (`//`). You can also place comments with two forward slashes at the end of the line.

  For example:

```
// Calculate the cost of shipping
   int cost = calcShippingCost();   // results depends on country
```

- Some comments start with `/**` and end with `*/`. These are used by a special utility, javadoc, that can automatically extract the text from these comments and create program documentation. Javadoc also allows the use of special annotations (for example, `@param`, `@return`, `@see`) that allow producing professional-looking program documentation. To get a feeling for what javadoc can generate, read Oracle's whitepaper on writing javadoc comments at `http://goo.gl/imDMU`.

First Useful Program

It's time to write a program that does something more useful than print "Hello World." This program emulates the calculation of state tax. The goal is to show you how Java classes communicate, how methods are called, and how variables can be used.

First you need to decide what Java class(es) you need to write for the task at hand. Then think about the attributes (class variables) and methods (behavior) these classes should have.

Declaring a Tax Class

Because you are planning to calculate tax, it doesn't take a rocket scientist to figure out that you need to define a class called `Tax`. Start with the class name and curly braces — this is the simplest class you can create:

```
class Tax{
}
```

What data does this class need to perform tax calculations? You definitely need to know the gross income of a person for the tax year. Gross income is a good candidate for an attribute of this class. Attributes in Java are represented by *variables*. Pick one of the numeric data types. Gross income is not always an integer number, so use the `double` data type, as it's a number with a decimal point. You could use `float` instead, but using `double` enables you to be ready to process larger incomes, too:

```
class Tax{
      double grossIncome;
}
```

You also need to know what state the person lives in; taxation rules vary by state. These are a few of the abbreviations for the states in the USA: NY, NJ, CT. Use the data type `String` for storing text data:

```
class Tax{
        double grossIncome;
        String state;
 }
```

Add one more attribute for dependents of the taxable person. `Integer` works just fine here — a person can't have two-and-a-half dependents:

```
class Tax{
        double grossIncome;
        String state;
        int  dependents;
 }
```

Adding a Method to the Tax Class

Variables store data, and methods perform actions. It's time for actions. The first method, `calcTax()`, calculates the state tax based on the values of gross income, number of dependents, and state:

LISTING 3-3 Class Tax

```
class Tax{
           double grossIncome;
           String state;
           int dependents;

           public double calcTax() {

              return 234.55;
           }
}
```

The `calcTax()` method signature tells the following:

- Any external class can access this method (`public`).
- This method returns a value of type `double`.
- The name of the method is `calcTax`.

The empty parentheses after the method name mean that it does not have any arguments, or, in other words, it does not need any values from outside `Tax` to perform calculations. As a matter of fact, this version of `calcTax()` doesn't even use the values from class variables for tax calculation. It just always returns a hard-coded tax value of 234.55.

How do you decide if a method should return a value? If your method performs some calculations and has to give a value back to a calling program, it has to return a value. If a method directly modifies the class variables or simply outputs data somewhere (monitor, disk, server) it may not need to return any values. You still need to declare a "no return" in a method signature by using a special keyword, `void`:

```
public void printAnnualTaxReturn() {
    //Code goes here
}
```

With the Java `return` statement, a method can return data contained in a variable to a calling program, for example:

```
return calculatedTax;
```

Keep in mind that if you declare a return type in the method signature but forget to include the `return` statement in the body of the method, the Java compiler will give you an error.

Declaring Another Class: TestTax

`Tax` will know how to calculate tax, but in a real-world application you'll have many classes that represent the various workflows of this process. For example, you may need to create a class called `Customer`. Depending on the type of employment or income, accountants use many different forms to file taxes, and each form can be represented by a separate class: `Form1040`, `Form1099`, and so on.

Each of these classes represents some entity, but none of them is an executable program; that is, none of them will have the method `main()`. You need to create one more class to start the application and instantiate other classes as needed. I'm calling this class `TestTax`. The class `TestTax` should be able to perform the following actions:

- Create an instance of the class `Tax`.
- Assign the customer's data (gross income, state, dependents) to the class variables of the class `Tax`.
- Call the method `calcTax()`.
- Print the result on the screen.

The class `TestTax` is stored in a separate file named `TestTax.java`.

LISTING 3-4 Class TestTax

```
class TestTax{
     public static void main(String[] args){
            Tax   t = new Tax(); // creating an instance

            // assigning the values to class members
            t.grossIncome= 50000;
```

```
            t.dependents= 2;
            t.state= "NJ";

            double yourTax = t.calcTax(); //calculating tax

           // Printing the result
           System.out.println("Your tax is " + yourTax);
        }
    }
```

In the preceding code you've declared a variable, `t`, of type `Tax`. The method `main()` is an entry point to the tax-calculation program. This method creates an instance of the class `Tax`, and the variable `t` points to a place in your computer's memory where the `Tax` object was created. From now on, if you want to refer to this object use the variable `t`. Take another look at Figure 3-1, which shows a similar situation to what you have here.

The following three lines assign values to the fields of the object `Tax`:

```
t.grossIncome= 50000;
t.dependents= 2;
t.state= "NJ";
```

After that you can calculate tax on your object represented by `t` by calling the method `calcTax()`, and the result returned by this method will be assigned to the variable `yourTax`. The method `calcTax()` still returns the hard-coded value, but you fix this in the "Try It" section of this lesson. The last line just displays the result on the system console.

At this point you already have two classes communicating with each other (`TestTax` and `Tax`). The class `TextTax` creates an instance of `Tax`, initializes its variables, and calls its method `calcTax()`, which returns the value back to the class `TextTax`.

Conditional Statement if

In the real life we make decisions all the time: "If she says this I'll answer with that, otherwise I'll do something else." Java has an `if` statement that determines whether some condition is `true` or `false`. Based on the answer to this question the execution of your program will be routed.

In the following code snippet, if the condition expression (`totalOrderPrice > 100`) evaluates to `true` then the code between the first curly braces is executed; otherwise the code after the `else` statement takes place:

```
if (totalOrderPrice > 100){
         System.out.println("You'll get a 20% discount");
}
else{
         System.out.println("Order books for more than a" +
                            " $100 to get a 20% discount");
}
```

Because this code sample has only one statement to execute in the `if` and `else` clauses, using curly braces is not a must, but they make the code more readable and prevent you from introducing hard-to-find bugs if, later on, you need to add more code in an `if` statement.

switch Statement

The `switch` statement is an alternative to `if`. The case label in the switch condition (`taxCode`) is evaluated and the program goes to one of the following `case` clauses:

```
int taxCode=someObject.getTaxCode(grossIncome);
switch (taxCode){
   case 0:
     System.out.println("Tax Exempt");
     break;
   case 1:
     System.out.println("Low Tax Bracket");
     break;
   case 2:
     System.out.println("High Tax Bracket");
     break;
   default:
     System.out.println("Wrong Tax Bracket");
}
// Some other code goes here
```

The preceding code invokes only one of the `println()` methods and continues with the execution with the other code below the closing curly brace, if any. Do not forget to put the `break` at the end of each `case` statement so the program jumps out of the `switch` statement after processing a case; otherwise the code "falls-through" and prints more than one line even though a `taxCode` can have only one value. For example, the following code prints both "Tax Exempt" and "Low Tax Bracket" even if the value of the `taxCode` is zero:

```
switch (taxCode){
   case 0:
     System.out.println("Tax Exempt");
   case 1:
     System.out.println("Low Tax Bracket");
     break;
   case 2:
     System.out.println("High Tax Bracket");
     break;
   default:
     System.out.println("Wrong Tax Bracket");
}
```

Starting from Java 7 you can use `String` values in the `case` expression:

```
switch (yourState){
   case "NY":
     System.out.println("Taxing by NY law");
     break;
   case "CA":
     System.out.println("Taxing by CA law");
     break;
   case "FL":
     System.out.println("Taxing by FL law");
     break;
```

```
        default:
          System.out.println("Wrong state");
    }
```

Inheritance

In object-oriented languages, the term *inheritance* means an ability to define a new class based on an existing one (not from scratch).

Imagine that the class Tax calculates tax properly in all states except New Jersey, which has introduced new educational tax deductions. If you have a kid in college, this makes you eligible for an additional $500 deduction from your taxes. In this case you have to either change the method calcTax() in the class Tax to introduce a special case for New Jersey, or create another class based on Tax, and add this new functionality there.

Every person inherits some features from his or her parents. A similar mechanism exists in Java. The special keyword extends is used to indicate that one class has been inherited from another:

```
class NJTax extends Tax{
}
```

The class NJTax has all the features of the class Tax, plus you can add new attributes and methods to it. In such a setup, the class Tax is called a *superclass*, and NJTax is called a *subclass*. You can also use the terms *ancestor and descendent*, respectively. This new class has access to all variables and methods of its superclass, unless those have a private or package access level, which is discussed in Chapter 5.

Let's extend the behavior of the class Tax in NJTax. The latter has a method called adjustForStudents():

LISTING 3-5 Class NJTax

```
class NJTax extends Tax{

    double adjustForStudents (double stateTax){
       double adjustedTax = stateTax - 500;
       return adjustedTax;
    }
}
```

To use this new method, the TestTax class should instantiate NJTax rather than Tax as it did in Listing 3-4:

```
NJTax t= new NJTax();
```

Now you can call methods defined in the class Tax as well as those from NJTax using the reference variable t; for example:

```
NJTax t= new NJTax();
double yourTax = t.calcTax();
double totalTax = t.adjustForStudents(yourTax);
```

I've added a new functionality to the tax-calculation program without changing the code of the class `Tax`. The preceding code fragment also shows how you can pass a result of processing from one method to another. The value of the variable `yourTax` was calculated by `calcTax()` and then passed to the method `adjustForStudents()` as an *argument*.

Method Overriding

Yet another important term in object-oriented programming is *method overriding*. Imagine class `Tax` with 20 methods. Most of them work fine for all states, but there is one method that is not valid for New Jersey. Instead of modifying this method in the superclass, you could create another method in the subclass *with the same name and argument list* (also known as *signature*). If a subclass has that method with the same signature, it overrides (suppresses) the corresponding method of its ancestor.

Method overriding comes in handy in the following situations:

- The source code of the superclass is not available, but you still need to change its functionality.
- The original version of the method is still valid in some cases and you want to keep it intact.
- You use method overriding to enable polymorphism, which will be explained in Chapter 7.

You have a chance to try method overriding in the "Try It" section. In Chapter 4 you read about method overloading, which is a completely different animal.

ADDITIONAL MATERIALS

Java Garbage Collector Basics `http://www.oracle.com/webfolder/technetwork/tutorials/obe/java/gc01/index.html`

TRY IT

In this section, you create in Eclipse the tax-calculation application described in this lesson, and then modify it to replace the hard-coded value returned by the method `calcTax()` with some calculations. After this is done, you subclass the class Tax and override `calcTax()`.

Lesson Requirements

For this lesson you must have Eclipse IDE installed.

> **NOTE** *You can download the code and resources for this "Try It" from the book's web page at* `www.wrox.com/go/javaprog24hr2e`. *You can find them in* `Lesson3.zip`.

Hints

This lesson has only brief introductions to basic Java language constructs. The online Java tutorial may be handy while completing this and future assignments. It's available at `http://download.oracle.com/javase/tutorial/java/index.html`.

Step-by-Step

1. In Eclipse, create a new project named Lesson3.
2. Create a new `Tax` class (File→New→Class). Enter the code shown in Listing 3-3.
3. Create another class, `TestTax`, and input the code from Listing 3-4.
4. Save both classes and run `TestTax` (right-click and select Run As→Java Application). The console view should display "Your tax is $234.55."
5. Replace the return of a hard-coded value with some tax calculations. Let's say that if the gross income was less than $30,000 you deduct 5% for state tax. If it's greater than $30,000 you deduct 6%. Modify the code of the method `calcTax` as follows. Run the program several times, modifying the values of the class variables of the class `Tax`. Make sure that the tax value on the console is properly calculated:

```
public double calcTax() {
       double stateTax=0;
       if (grossIncome < 30000) {
         stateTax=grossIncome*0.05;
       }
       else{
         stateTax= grossIncome*0.06;
       }
         return stateTax;
}
```

6. Create the `NJTax` class shown in Listing 3-5.
7. Change the functionality of `calcTax()` by overriding it in `NJTax`. The new version of `calcTax()` should lower the tax by $500 before returning the value.
8. Modify the code of the `TestTax` class to instantiate `NJTax` instead of `Tax`. Observe that the $500 deduction is properly calculated.

To get the sample database files, you can download Chapter 3 from the book's website at `www.wrox.com/go/javaprog24hr2e`.

TIP *Please select the videos for Lesson 3 online at* www.wrox.com/go/javaprog24hr2e. *You will also be able to download the code and resources for this lesson from the website.*

Class Methods and Constructors

Methods contain code for actions or functions a class can perform. Although you started working with methods in previous lessons, in this lesson you find out how to work with them in detail. You also get familiar with a special type of method called a constructor.

METHOD ARGUMENTS

Each class method performs some functionality, such as calculating tax, placing an order, or starting the car. If a method requires some external data to perform its function, such data can be provided in the form of arguments or parameters, as in the method `adjustForStudents()` shown in Listing 3-5, which has one argument: `stateTax`.

In the method signature, you need to declare the data type and the name of each argument. For example, the following method has three arguments: two of them are the `int` data type and one is `String`:

```
int calcLoanPayment(int amount, int numberOfMonths, String state){
   // Your code goes here
}
```

When you call (or invoke) a method, the Java run time tries to find the method that has been declared with the specified signature. For example, if you try to call the preceding method like this:

```
calcLoanPayment(20000, 60);
```

the Java compiler will give you an error complaining that no `calcLoanPayment()` function has been found that expects just two arguments.

METHOD OVERLOADING

If you want to allow the calling of a method with different numbers of arguments, you need to create multiple versions of this method. For example, you can create a method that will use the state of New York as default to spare developers from providing the state as an argument. If most of the loan calculation is done for New Yorkers, such a method may be a good idea. So in addition to the method `calcLoanPayment()` with three arguments, you create another one with just two arguments. To avoid code duplication, only the method with three arguments implements the logic calculating payments. The method with two arguments simply calls it, adding "NY" as the third argument.

```
int calcLoanPayment(int amount, int numberOfMonths){
   calcLoanPayment(amount, 12, "NY");

}
```

Method overloading means having a class with more than one method that has the same name but different argument lists. A method can be overloaded not only in the same class but also in a descendant. For example, the class `LoanCalulator` can have the method `calcLoanPayment()` defined with three arguments, while its descendant `MyLoanCalculator` may have a two-argument version of `calcLoanPayment()`.

Why overload methods in your classes? To provide programmers who use these classes with a more flexible application program interface (API). Coming back to the loan-calculation example, programmers now have a choice of calling either a three- or two-argument version of this method.

In Chapter 1 you used the method `println()` declared in the class `PrintStream` (see Figure 4-1 or its description at `http://docs.oracle.com/javase/8/docs/api/java/io/PrintStream.html`). The function `println()` has been overloaded there to give Java developers the freedom to call "the same" method with different types of arguments. In reality they are calling different methods with the same name.

void	**println(char[] x)** Prints an array of characters and then terminate the line.
void	**println(double x)** Prints a double and then terminate the line.
void	**println(float x)** Prints a float and then terminate the line.
void	**println(int x)** Prints an integer and then terminate the line.
void	**println(long x)** Prints a long and then terminate the line.
void	**println(Object x)** Prints an Object and then terminate the line.
void	**println(String x)** Prints a String and then terminate the line.

FIGURE 4-1: JavaDoc for the PrintStream class

CONSTRUCTORS

When a program creates an instance of a class, Java invokes the class's *constructor* — a special method that is called only once when the instance is being built with the operator `new`:

```
Tax t = new Tax();
```

Empty parentheses in the preceding code snippet mean that this code calls a no-argument constructor on the class `Tax`. If you didn't declare a constructor on a class, Java creates a no-argument constructor for you.

Constructors have the following characteristics:

- They are called when the class is being instantiated.
- They must have the same name as the class they're in.
- They can't return a value and you don't specify the keyword `void` as a return type.

Typically constructors have very little code. There you just assign initial values to class variables. In the next code snippet, a three-argument constructor is defined:

LISTING 4-1 Class Tax with constructor

```
class Tax {
    double grossIncome; // class variables
    String state;
    int dependents;

    // Constructor
    Tax (double gi, String st, int depen){

      // Initializing class variables
       grossIncome = gi;
       state = st;
       dependents=depen;
    }
}
```

Creating an instance of this class can look like this:

```
Tax t = new Tax(65000,"NJ",3);
```

Note the difference in the initialization of the class variables: Here you pass the values during the class instantiation via the constructor's arguments, whereas in Listing 3-4 it took four lines of code to create an instance of `Tax` and then initialize the variables. But in the preceding code snippet you killed two birds with one stone: instantiated `Tax` and initialized its variables via class `constructor`.

Note that after defining a constructor with arguments, the rule of automatic creation of a default no-argument constructor does not apply anymore. If you need a class to have more than one constructor, and one of the constructors with no arguments, you have to explicitly write a no-argument constructor.

The preceding code snippet declares the variable `t` that points at an instance of the object `Tax` in memory. To refer to any specific field or call a method on this instance, you need to use dot-notation — the name of the reference variable followed by a dot and the name of the field or a method. For example:

```
public static void main(){
...
Tax t = new Tax(65000,"NJ",3);
t.dependents = 4; // changing the number of dependents from 3 to 4
...
```

THE KEYWORD SUPER

If a method is overridden in a subclass, there are two versions of the method with the same signature. If you just call a method by name; for example, `calcTax()` in the class `NJTax` from Chapter 3, the JVM calls the overridden version of the method. Once in a while you may need to call the ancestor's version of a method. The keyword `super` enables you to explicitly call the method or a constructor from the ancestor's class. For example, to call the ancestor's method `calcTax()`, you just write `super.calcTax();` in the descendant:

If one class is inherited from another, each of them may have its own constructor explicitly defined. As opposed to regular class methods, a constructor of a subclass cannot override the constructor of a superclass; they even have different names. But sometimes you may need to add into the subclass's constructor some functionality that has to be called after the ancestor's constructor code. To avoid code duplication, just add the explicit call to the constructor of a superclass followed by additional code you want to run during instantiation of the descendant (see Listing 4-2). Invocation of the constructor of the superclass must be the first line in the constructor.

LISTING 4-2 Calling the constructor of the ancestor

```
class SmallerTax extends Tax{
    // Constructor
    SmallerTax (double gi, String st, int depen){
       super(gi,st,depen);

       // Adding code specific to descendant's constructor
       System.out.println("Applying special tax rates for my friends.");
    }
}
```

THE KEYWORD THIS

The keyword `this` is useful when you need to refer to the instance of the class from its method. Review the code of the constructor from Listing 4-1. The names of the constructor's arguments were different from the names of the class variables. But the code in Listing 4-3 shows how you can use the same variable names, both in the arguments and in the class variables. Besides pointing at the current object, the keyword `this` helps to resolve name conflicts. To instruct JVM to use the instance variable `grossIncome`, use the following syntax:

```
this.grossIncome = 50000;
```

If there were only one `grossIncome` variable in the class `Tax`, you could simply omit the `this` prefix. But in Listing 4-3 the absence of the `this` keyword would lead to ambiguity, and the instance variable would never be initialized.

LISTING 4-3 Resolving name conflicts with the this keyword

```
class Tax {
    double grossIncome; // class member variables
    String state;
    int dependents;

    // Constructor
    Tax (double grossIncome, String state, int dependents){
       this.grossIncome = grossIncome;
       this.state = state;
       this.dependents=dependents;
    }
}
```

Consider a class called `SomeOtherClass` with a method defined as `verifyTax(Tax t)`. As you can see, it expects an instance of the `Tax` object as an argument. Listing 4-4 shows how you can call it from the class `Tax` using the keyword `this` to pass a reference to the current instance of the object `Tax`.

LISTING 4-4 Calling a method using the keyword this as an argument

```
class Tax {
     void verifyTax(){

        SomeOtherClass s = new SomeOtherClass();
        s.verifyTax(this);
     }
}
```

Here's another use case: A class has several overloaded constructors with different numbers of arguments. As with method overloading, the overloaded constructors give more choices in instantiation objects and helps avoid code duplication. You can use the `this()` notation to call a specific version of the constructor. In Listing 4-5 the second constructor invokes the first one.

LISTING 4-5 Calling an overloaded constructor with the keyword this

```
class Tax {
    double grossIncome; // class member variables
    String state;
    int dependents;

    // First Constructor
    Tax (double grossIncome, String state, int dependents){
       this.grossIncome = grossIncome; // instance variable initialization
       this.state = state;
       this.dependents=dependents;
    }
   // Second Constructor
    Tax (double grossIncome, int dependents){
       this(grossIncome, "NY", dependents);     }

}
```

PASSING BY VALUE OR BY REFERENCE

Calling a method with arguments enables you to pass some required data to the method. The question is how JVM passes these values to the method. Does it create a copy of a variable in a calling program and give it to the method?

The primitive values are passed *by value* (meaning that an extra copy is created in memory for each variable). If you create an instance of Tax, as in Listing 4-6, there will be two copies of `grossIncome` and two copies of the variable `dependents` — one in `TestTax` and the other one in `Tax`. But objects are passed *by reference*. The following code creates only one copy of "NJ" in memory. In Java, String objects have special rules of treatment, which are discussed in Chapter 5, but the rule still holds: Non-primitives are passed by reference.

LISTING 4-6 The TestTax class

```
class TestTax{
     public static void main(String[] args){
            double grossIncome; // local variables
            String state;
            int dependents;

            grossIncome= 50000;
            dependents= 2;
            state= "NJ";

            Tax   t = new Tax(grossIncome, state, dependents);

            double yourTax = t.calcTax(); //calculating tax
```

```
            // Printing the result
            System.out.println("Your tax is " + yourTax);
        }
    }
```

In the preceding example, if you'll be changing the value of `grossIncome` or `dependents` in the constructor of the class `Tax`, it won't affect the values in the corresponding variables of the class `TestTax` because there will be two copies of these primitives.

Now consider another example. I'm declaring another variable of type `Tax` and assigning the value of `t` to it:

```
Tax   t2 = t;
```

The variable `t` is pointing to an instance of the object `Tax` in memory. In other words, the variable `t` holds the reference (the address in memory) to an object. The code line above does not create another copy of the `Tax` object in memory, but copies its address to the variable `t2`. You still have a single instance of the `Tax` object, but now you have two reference variables — `t` and `t2` — pointing at it. Until both of these variables go out of scope (something that's explained in the next section), the object `Tax` is not removed from memory.

As I mentioned before, the process of removal of unused objects from memory is called garbage collection. JVM runs GC automatically.

Here's another example of passing by reference: The code in ch04.html#calling_an_overloaded_constructor_with_t does not create a copy of the object `Tax` just to pass it to the method `verifyTax()`. A copy of just the reference variable pointing at the `Tax` instance can be created inside the method `SomeOtherClass.verifyTax()`, pointing at the one and only instance of the class `Tax`.

This means that if the code in `SomeOtherClass` is changing some properties of the `Tax` instance, the changes are applied to the only copy of the `Tax` instance and are visible from both `Tax` and `SomeOtherClass`.

VARIABLE SCOPES

Variable scope defines how long the variable lives and remains usable. If you declared the variable inside a method, it's a local variable that goes out of scope (becomes unavailable) as soon as the method finishes its execution. For example, variables `t`, `grossIncome`, `dependents`, and `state` from Listing 4-6 are local.

If a variable is defined inside any block of code between curly braces located inside the method, the scope of the variable is limited to the code within this block. In the following code fragment the variable `taxCredit` has a block scope and is visible only inside the code for the case when `grossIncome < 30000`.

```
public double calcTax() {
      double stateTax=0;
      if (grossIncome < 30000) {
        int taxCredit = 300;
        stateTax=grossIncome*0.05 - taxCredit;
      }
      else{
        stateTax= grossIncome*0.06;
```

```
        }
          return stateTax;
    }
```

If variables have been declared outside the method (such as grossIncome, dependents, and state in Listing 4-1) they are *class variables* and can be used by any method of this class. On the other hand, the variables grossIncome, dependents, and state in Listing 4-1 are also *instance variables* and store instance-specific data.

You can create more than one instance of the class Tax, and each instance can have different values in its instance variables. For example, the following lines of code create two instances of Tax, with different values for grossIncome, dependents, and state (these instance variables are initialized in the constructor):

```
Tax   t1 = new Tax(50000, "NY", 3 );
Tax   t2 = new Tax(65000, "TX", 4 );
```

THE KEYWORD STATIC

Java has a special keyword, static, that indicates that the class variable is shared by all instances of the same class. If the class Tax has the declaration static double grossIncome; then this variable's value is shared by all instances of the class Tax, which doesn't make sense in the tax calculation scenarios.

Besides, after the creation of two instances (t1 and t2), as in the preceding code, the first value of the variable (50000) is overwritten with the second one (65000).

But, if you introduce in Tax a class variable to count the number of its instances (think the number of customers whose taxes have been calculated), such a variable has to be declared as static, so its only version can be incremented by each instance on creation, as in Listing 4-7.

LISTING 4-7 The Tax class with the keyword static

```
class Tax {
    double grossIncome; // class member variables
    String state;
    int dependents;
    static int customerCounter;

    // Constructor
    Tax (double gi, String st, int depen){
       grossIncome = gi; // member variable initialization
       state = st;
       dependents=depen;
       customerCounter++;    // increment the counter by one
    }
}
```

You can also declare methods with the `static` qualifier. Such methods can be called without the need to instantiate the class first. This is usually done for utility methods that don't use any instance variables, but do get input via the argument and return the result.

The following function converts Fahrenheit to Celsius and returns the result:

```
class WeatherReport{
      static double convertToCelsius(double far){
           return ((far - 32) * 5 / 9);
    }
}
```

You can call this function from another class without the need to instantiate `WeatherReport` first:

```
double centigrees=WeatherReport.convertToCelsius(98.7);
```

Note that because you never instantiated the class `WeatherReport`, there is no reference variable to any object. You just use the name of the class followed by dot and the method name.

Java 8 introduced static methods in interfaces, which is covered in Lesson 6.

TRY IT

In this section you create yet another version of the `Tax` class with a three-argument constructor and add a utility function to convert the tax value from dollars to euros, assuming the dollar-to-euro conversion rate is 1.25.

Lesson Requirements

For this lesson you should have Eclipse IDE installed.

> **NOTE** *You can download the code and resources for this "Try It" from the book's web page at* `www.wrox.com/go/javaprog24hr2e`. *You can find them in* `Lesson4.zip`.

Step-by-Step

1. In Eclipse IDE, create a new project named Lesson4.
2. Create a new class called `Tax` (File → New → Class). Enter the code shown in Listing 4-7.
3. Add the following statement as the last line of the constructor of the class `Tax`:

```
System.out.println("Preparing the tax data for customer #" +
customerCounter);
```

4. Add the method `calcTax()` to the class `Tax` and calculate tax by multiplying the gross income by 0.33 and deducting the number of dependents multiplied by one hundred:

```
return (grossIncome*0.33 - dependents*100);
```

5. Add the `static` function to `Tax` to convert the calculated tax to euros, applying the currency-conversion rate of 1.25.

```
public static void convertToEuros(double taxInDollars){
    System.out.println("Tax in Euros: " + taxInDollars/1.25);
}
```

6. Create a `TestTax` class and input the code from Listing 4-6. Add to this class's `main()` method a line to create another instance of the class `Tax`:

```
Tax   t2 = new Tax(65000, "TX”, 4 );
```

Calculate the tax using the second instance of the class `Tax`:

```
double hisTax = t2.calcTax();
```

7. Call the method `convertToEuros()` twice to convert the currency, passing the calculated tax from `t` and `t2` as an argument.

8. Run the class `TestTax` (right-click and select Run As → Java Application). The Console view should display the two “Preparing the tax...” messages followed by the two messages with the calculated tax in Euros as follows:

Preparing the tax data for customer #1

Preparing the tax data for customer #2

Tax in Euros: 13040.0

Tax in Euros: 16840.0

To get the sample files, download the content of the Chapter 4 folder from the book's website at `www.wrox.com/go/javaprog24hr2e`.

> **TIP** *Please select the videos for Lesson 4 online at* `www.wrox.com/go/javaprog24hr2e`. *You will also be able to download the code and resources for this lesson from the website.*

Java Syntax: Bits and Pieces

This tutorial didn't start with detailed coverage of basic constructs of the Java language such as the syntax of `if` statements, loops, and the like. You started learning Java programming with getting used to object-oriented terms and constructs of the language. This lesson is a grab bag of basic language elements, terms, and data structures. You also find out how to debug Java programs in Eclipse IDE and how to pass parameters to a program started from a command line.

ARRAYS

An *array* is data storage that's used to store multiple values of the same type. Let's say your program has to store names of 20 different girls, such as Masha, Matilda, Rosa, and so on. Instead of declaring 20 different `String` variables, you can declare one `String` array with the capacity to store 20 elements:

```
String []  friends = new String [20]; // Declare and instantiate array
friends[0] = "Masha";                //Initialize the first element
friends[1] = "Matilda";              //Initialize the second element
friends[2] = "Rosa";

// Keep initializing other elements of the array here

friends[19] = "Natasha";              //Initialize the last element
```

The first element of an array in Java always has an index of `0`. Arrays in Java are *zero-based*. While declaring an array you can place brackets either after the data type or after the variable name. Both of the following declarations are correct:

```
String friends[];
String[] friends;
```

You must know the size of the array before assigning values to its elements. If you want to be able to dynamically change the size of an array during run time, consider other Java collection classes from the package `java.util`, such as `Vector` and `ArrayList`. Besides arrays, Java has lots of collection classes that can store multiple related values; for example, `HashMap`, `List`, and `LinkedList`. You have a chance to see their use in the code samples accompanying this book. Listing 5-1 contains sample code that partially populates an array.

LISTING 5-1 Populating a simple array

```
public class Girlfriends1 {

 public static void main(String[] args) {
    String [] friends = new String [20]; // Declare and instantiate array
    friends[0] = "Masha";              //Initialize the first element
    friends[1] = "Matilda";            //Initialize the second element
    friends[2] = "Rosa";
    // ...
    friends[18] = "Hillary";
    friends[19] = "Natasha";

    System.out.println("The third girl's name is " + friends[2]);
    System.out.println("The twentieth girl's name is " + friends[19]);
 }
}
```

An array has a property `length` that "knows" the number of elements in the array. The next line shows how you can get this number:

```
int totalElements = friends.length;
```

If you know all the values that will be stored in the array at the time of its declaration, you can declare and initialize an array at the same time. The following line declares, instantiates, and populates an array of four elements:

```
String []  friends = {"Masha", "Matilda", "Rosa", "Sharon"};
```

Our array `friends` is not as practical as a contacts list in your phone, though — it does not store girls' phone numbers. Luckily, Java supports multidimensional arrays. For example, to create a two-dimensional array (names and phone numbers), declare it with two sets of square brackets:

```
String friends [][] = new String [20][2];
friends[0][0] = "Masha";
friends[0][1] = "732 111-2222";
friends[1][0] = "Matilda";
friends[1][1] = "718 111-2222";
...
friends[19][0] = "Sharon";
friends[19][1] = "212 111-2222"
```

More About Strings

Strings are special objects in Java. They are stored in a pool of strings for reusability. They are immutable; you can't change the value of a `String` that has been initialized. However, this doesn't mean that you can't create new `Strings` based on the existing one. Consider the following code sample:

```
String bestFriend = "Mary";
bestFriend = bestFriend + " Smith";
String greeting = "Hello " + bestFriend;
```

The first line creates an entry in the pool of strings with the value of "Mary." The second line doesn't modify the first one but creates a new entry with the value "Mary Smith." The third line creates yet another entry in the pool with the value "Hello Mary Smith."

A program can consist of hundreds classes, and if any other class will need a `String` with any of these three values, they'll be taken from the pool.

If your program needs to do lots of manipulations with strings, consider using a class `StringBuffer`, which is mutable. For example:

```
StringBuffer sbf = new StringBuffer();
sbf.append("Mary");
sbf.append(" Smith");

String fullName = sbf.toString();  // Converting back to String
```

Another way to create a mutable object for storing textual data is the class `StringBuilder`. It's based on arrays and has capacity. For example, you can allocate memory for 50 characters and fill 10 of them as follows:

```
StringBuilder sbld = new StringBuilder(50);
sbld.append("Mary");
sbld.append(" Smith");

String fullName = sbld.toString(); // Converting back to String
```

`StringBuilder` has lots of convenient methods, such as methods that insert characters into a certain position in a character sequence or remove one or more characters. Refer to Oracle's tutorial at `http://docs.oracle.com/javase/tutorial/java/data/buffers.html` for more examples.

Have you noticed that although `String` is an object (not a primitive), I have not used the `new` operator to instantiate these objects? You can instantiate strings as regular objects, too. For example:

```
String friend1=new String("Mary");
String friend2=new String("Joe");
String friend3=new String("Mary");
```

Now, I'd like to bring your attention to `String` comparison. Revisit the beginning of Lesson 3, and take another look at the diagram illustrating two instances of the car. The variables `car1` and `car2` point at different memory addresses. On the same note, the variables `friend1`, `friend2`, and `friend3` point at three different memory locations, and the values stored in these variables are the addresses of two different objects. Hence, even though the name of the first and third friend are the same, comparing `friend1` and `friend3` returns false. You can test it by trying the following line of code:

```
System.out.println("Is friend1==friend3? " + (friend1==friend3));
```

THE == OPERATOR

Note the double equal sign in the code above. You are comparing the variables for equality and not assigning one value to another.

But if you'd like to compare values of the strings (not the memory addresses), use the `equals()` method. The following code prints the sentence that ends with true:

```
System.out.println("Is friend1.equals(friend3)? " +
                                     (friend1.equals(friend3)));
```

LOOPS

Loops are used to repeat the same action multiple times. When you know in advance how many times you want to repeat an action, use the `for` loop. Try printing the names from the one-dimensional array `friends`.

```
int  totalElements = friends.length;

for (int i=0; i < totalElements;i++){
   System.out.println("I love " + friends[i]);
}
```

The preceding code reads "Print the value of the element `i` from the array `friends` starting from `i=0` and incrementing `i` by one (`i++`) until `i` reaches the value equal to the value of `totalElements`." Listing 5-2 adds a `for` loop to the program shown in Listing 5-1.

LISTING 5-2 Looping through the array

```
public class Girlfriends2 {

        public static void main(String[] args) {
              String [] friends = new String [20];
              friends[0] = "Masha";
              friends[1] = "Matilda";
              friends[2] = "Rosa";
              friends[18] = "Hillary";
              friends[19] = "Natasha";

              int  totalElements = friends.length;
              int i;
```

```
                for (i=0; i<totalElements;i++){
                   System.out.println("I love " + friends[i]);
                }
            }
        }
```

Because the `friends` array has been declared with a size of `20`, the Java run time has allocated memory for 20 elements. But the code in Listing 5-2 has populated only five of the 20 elements of the array, which explains why the output of this program looks as follows:

```
I love Masha
I love Matilda
I love Rosa
I love null
I love null
I love null
I love null
I love null
I love null
I love null
I love null
I love null
I love null
I love null
I love null
I love null
I love null
I love null
I love Hillary
I love Natasha
```

The keyword `null` represents an absence of any value in an object. Even though the size of this array is `20`, only five elements were initialized.

There's another syntax of the `for` loop, known as the `for-each` loop. You simply declare a variable of the same type as the objects stored in an array and specify the array to iterate. The following code snippet declares the variable `girl`, and the colon means "in." Read this loop's condition expression as "for each element in `friends`." This syntax allows you to not worry about checking the size of the array, and there is no need to increment any loop variable either. This is an elegant and short loop notation:

```
for (String girl: friends){
    System.out.println("I love " + girl);
}
```

LOOPING THROUGH COLLECTIONS WITH FOREACH()

Java 8 introduced a new way of looping through data collection with the method `forEach()`. You see it in action in Lesson 13. Just keep in mind that for-each loops and the `forEach()` method are different animals.

You can rewrite the program in Listing 5-2 using the `while` loop, which is used when you do not know the exact size of the array but do know the condition of exit from the loop. Use the keyword `while`:

```
int  totalElements = friends.length;
int i=0;
while (i<totalElements){
  System.out.println("I love " + friends[i]);
     i++;    // the same as i=i+1;
}
```

Just think of a program that reads and processes the records from a database (see Chapter 21). When you write a Java program, you don't know how many elements the database has, and even if you do know, this number can change in the future, so it's better to use loops with the exit condition than to use a hard-coded number of repetitions.

Use the keyword `break` to prematurely jump out of the loop on the line below the ending curly brace. For example, if you want to find the first `null` element in the `friends` array, write the following:

```
while (i<totalElements){
       if (friends[i]==null){
          System.out.println("The element " + (i+1) + " is null");
          break;
       }

      System.out.println("I love " + friends[i]);
      i++;
}  // closing curly brace for the loop
```

The `if` statement in the preceding code checks the value of each element of the array, and as soon as it finds `null`, the loop prints the message about it, stops the iteration process, and goes to the line below the closing curly brace of the loop, if any.

The keyword `continue` enables you to force the loop to return to its first line and retest the loop exit condition. The following code snippet prints only those values from the array that are not `null`:

```
while (i<totalElements){
    if (friends[i]==null){
        i++;
        continue;
    }

    System.out.println("I love " + friends[i]);
    i++;
                     }
    System.out.println("The iteration is over");
```

The preceding code uses an `if` statement, which allows you to check a certain condition and redirect the program to execute or skip a portion of the code. In this case, if the loop runs into a `null` value, it increments by one the value of the variable `i` and goes to the beginning of the `while` loop, skipping the rest of the code within the loop body. (Later in this lesson there's a section explaining the syntax of the various `if` statements in greater detail.) The complete code of the program, illustrating a `while` loop with a `continue` statement, is shown in Listing 5-3.

LISTING 5-3 While loop with continue statement

```
public class WhileLoopDemo {

       public static void main(String[] args) {
              String [] friends = new String [20];
              friends[0] = "Masha";
              friends[1] = "Matilda";
              friends[2] = "Rosa";
              friends[18] = "Hillary";
              friends[19] = "Natasha";

              int  totalElements = friends.length;
              int i=0;

              while (i<totalElements){
                       if (friends[i]==null){
                                 i++;
                                 continue;
                        }

                        System.out.println("I love " + friends[i]);
                        i++;
                        }
                        System.out.println("The iteration is over");
       }
}
```

The output of the WhileLoopDemo program is shown here:

```
I love Masha
I love Matilda
I love Rosa
I love Hillary
I love Natasha
The iteration is over
```

There is a rarely used do-while version of the while loop. It starts with the do keyword followed by the body of the loop in curly braces, and the while condition comes last. Such loop syntax guarantees that the code written in the body of the loop will be executed at least once, because the loop condition will be tested only after the first pass into the loop. In the following loop, at the very minimum the statements about reading the element zero of array friends will be printed for each element of the array even if every one of them is null:

```
do {
   System.out.println("Reading the element" + i +" of array friends");
    if (friends[i]==null){
       i++;
       continue;
    }

    System.out.println("I love " + friends[i]);
```

```
        i++;

    } while (i<totalElements);
```

The worst thing that can happen in any loop is a programmer's mistake in the loop exit condition that always evaluates the loop condition as `true`. In programming this is known as an *infinite loop*. To get a better feeling for what this term means, comment out the line that increments the value of the variable `i` inside the `if` statement in the `do-while` sample, and your program will never end unless you forcefully stop it or your computer runs out of power. The reason is clear: If the program enters the code block that just has the statement `continue`, the value of the variable `i` will never increase and the loop execution condition `i<totalElements` will hold true forever.

DEBUGGING JAVA PROGRAMS

In programmer's lingo, a *bug* is an error in a program that causes the program to work in an unexpected way. Don't confuse a bug with a syntax error in the code. The latter will be caught by the Java compiler before you even start the program, while bugs are your run-time enemies. To *debug* a program is to identify and fix the run-time errors in code.

The simplest way to debug a program is to print the value of the "suspicious variables" with `System.out.println()` or the like. You may think that a certain variable will get a particular value during the execution, but you might be wrong, and printing its value from the running program may reveal why your code produces unexpected results.

LOGGING API

Java also comes with a logging application program interface (API) — see`http://docs.oracle.com/javase/8/docs/technotes/guides/logging/index.html` — that allows you to *log* the run-time values in a file or other destination. Logging is out of the scope of this book, but you can find `Logger` and other supporting classes in the Java package `java.util.logging`.

You'll find daily use for the debugger that comes with your IDE.

Even though Chapter 2 was dedicated to Eclipse IDE, explaining debugging back then would have been a bit premature because it didn't have much Java code to debug. Now you're ready to learn how the Eclipse debugger can help you.

Let's see how the `while` loop from Listing 5-3 works by running the `WhileLoopDemo` program with the Eclipse debugger. First, download `Lesson5.zip` from this book's website and import it into Eclipse. Open the source code of the class `WhileLoopDemo` and set a breakpoint on the line of code where you want the program to pause execution so you can start watching the program internals.

I'd like to pause this program right before it enters the `while` loop, so set the breakpoint on the following line:

```
while (i<totalElements){...}
```

Double-click the blue vertical bar located at the left side of the Editor view — you should see an image of a little bullet there. This line becomes a breakpoint, and if the program runs into the code with the set breakpoint, Eclipse IDE switches to Debug perspective and pauses the program, highlighting the line that's about to execute.

To run `WhileLoopDemo` in the debugger, right-click the name of this program in Package Explorer and select the Debug As Java Application menu option.

On the first run you will see a warning that Eclipse wants to switch to the Debug perspective; agree with this. Figure 5-1 shows how the Debug perspective looks when the program reaches the breakpoint.

Note the little arrow in the Editor view next to the bullet; it shows you the line of code that will be executed next. The Variables view shows you the values of the program variables at this moment. The variable `i` is equal to `0`; the value of `totalElements` is `20`. If you click the little plus sign by the variable `friends`, you see the contents of this array.

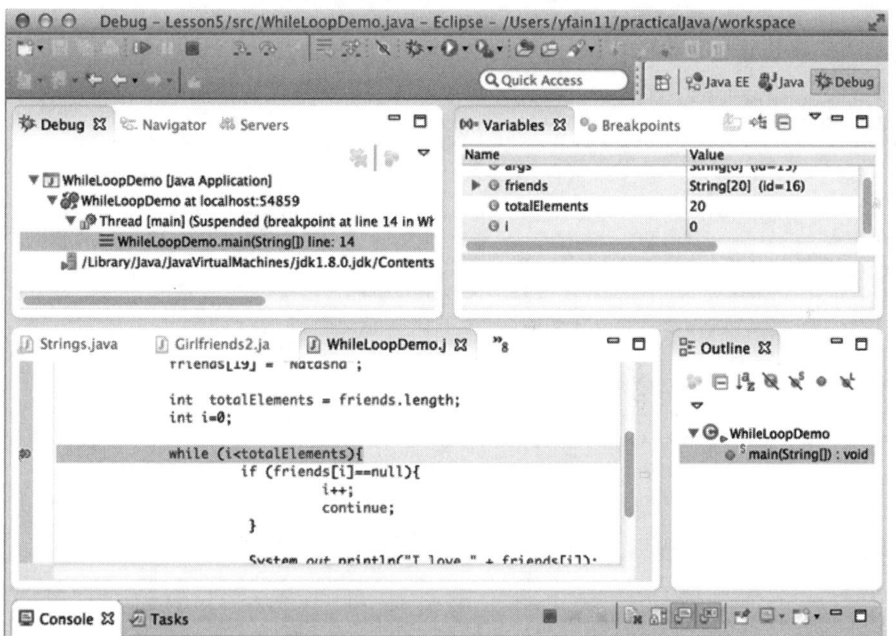

FIGURE 5-1: Debugger paused at the breakpoint

Now try to execute this program step by step, watching how the value of the variable `i` changes. You control program execution by clicking the buttons in the toolbar for the Debug view (see Figure 5-2).

FIGURE 5-2: The Debug View tab

The green play button means "Continue executing the program until it ends or hits another breakpoint." The red square button stops the debugging process. The first curvy yellow arrow (Step Into) is used if the code has been paused on a line that calls a method, and you'd like to debug the code of the method being called. The second curvy arrow (Step Over) allows you to execute the current line without stepping into any methods that may be called in this line of code.

There are other and less frequently used buttons on this toolbar, which you can study on your own; for now, enter the loop by clicking the Step Over button. Keep clicking this button and observe that the program doesn't enter the `if` statement, which is correct — the first element of the friends `array` is not `null`. Then `if` prints "I love Masha" in the console view, increments the value of the variable `i` to `1` (see the Variables view in Figure 5-3), and returns to the loop condition to check whether the value of `i` is still less than the value of `totalElements`.

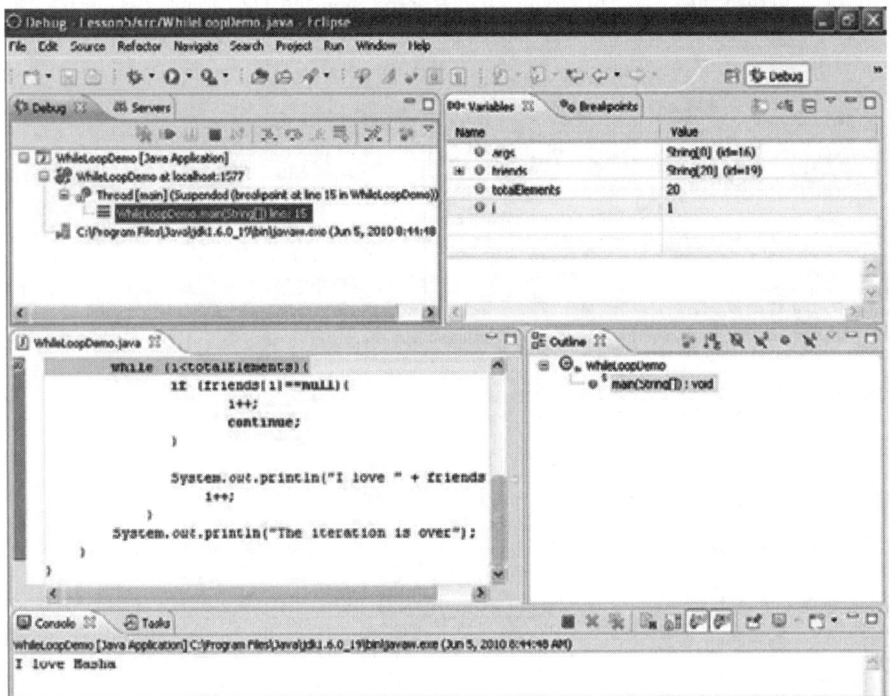

FIGURE 5-3: A snapshot of a Debug perspective

Keep clicking the Step Over button, and expand the variable `friends` in the Variables view to see its elements in order to better understand why the program skips or enters the `if` statement in the loop. Note the moment when the program exits the loop and prints the message "The iteration is over." After spending some time debugging the program, you should appreciate the value of the Eclipse Debugger. In my opinion, the best way to learn a new programming language is to run someone else's code through a good debugger. The program may be bug-free, but running the program through the debugger helps you to better understand the program's flow.

MORE ABOUT IF AND SWITCH STATEMENTS

If you need to change the execution of the program based on a certain condition then you can use either `if` or `switch` statements, which were introduced in Chapter 3. In this section you see more flavors of the conditional statements.

The Flavors of if Statements

In Listing 5-3 you saw one version of the `if` statement:

```
if (friends[i]==null){
    i++;
    continue;
}
```

The curly braces must be used in the `if` statement to specify a block of code that has to be executed if the condition is true. Even though the curly braces are not required if there's only one statement in the code block, using the braces is considered a good practice. They make the program more understandable for other people who may need to read your code (or for yourself six months from now):

```
if (friends[i]==null){
    System.out.println("I found an array element with null value");
}
// Some other code goes here
```

The code below the closing curly brace is always executed, which may not be desirable. In this case use the `if-else` syntax:

```
if (friends[i]==null){
    System.out.println("I found an array element with null value");
} else{
    // Some other code goes here
}
```

In the preceding code snippet, the "some other code" is executed only if the current element of the array is not `null` (or, as it's put it in Java, `friends[i]!=null`). You can write an `if` statement with multiple `else` clauses. For example, the following code prints only one love confession:

```
if (friends[i]==null){
    System.out.println("I found an array element with null value");
} else if (friends[i] == "Natasha"){
    System.out.println("I love my wife so much!");
} else if (friends[i] == "Masha"){
    System.out.println("I fell in love with Masha when I was in the 8th grade.");
} else{
    System.out.println("I used to love " + friends[i] + " at some point.");
}
```

Using conditional statements can be a lot more complex than comparing two values. You can build expressions using `boolean` AND, OR, and NOT operators. The AND operation is represented as &&, like this:

```
if (age<20 && gender=="male") {
      // do something only for males under 20 years old
}
```

For the OR condition use ||; for example:

```
if (age < 30 || yearsInArmy > 0) {
    // do something with people younger than 30 or those who served
    // in the army regardless of their age
}
```

For the NOT condition (aka negation) use the ! sign:

```
boolean hasBachelorDegree;
// Read the person record and assign the value true or false
// to the variable hasBachelorDegree
if (!hasBachelorDegree) {
      // do something with people without bachelor degree
}
```

The negation symbol can be placed either in front of a `boolean` variable, as in the preceding code snippet, or in front of the expression that returns `boolean`. The next code example shows how to use negation. Note that the comparison expression was placed inside the parentheses; otherwise the Java compiler would assume that you're trying to negate a `String` value called `friends[i]`, which is not allowed.

```
if (!(friends[i]=="Hillary")){
       System.out.println("Still looking for Hillary.");
}
```

Imagine a situation in which you need to assign a value to a variable, but the value depends on the result of a certain condition. To assign the variable in a verbose way you can use a regular `if` statement and test some condition, writing one assignment operator for a result of `true`, and another in the `else` section for a result of `false`. But if you use a special construct called a *conditional operator* (?), the same task can be done more simply.

The conditional operator consists of the following parts: an expression that returns `boolean`, a question mark, an expression that returns some value if the first expression evaluates to `true`, a colon, and an expression that returns a value to be used if the first expression returns `false`. It sounds complicated, but it's not. The following code sample shows how to assign a $3,000 bonus if a person's salary is greater than $90,000, and only $2,000 otherwise:

```
float salary;
// Retrieve the salary of the person from some data source here
int bonus = salary > 90000 ? 3000 : 2000;
```

COMMAND-LINE ARGUMENTS

In Chapter 1 you learned how to start a Java program from a command line. After development in Eclipse or another IDE is done, Java programs are *deployed in production* and will be started from a command line — usually you get an icon to click that runs a command to start a program, but under the hood the operating system executes a command that starts your program. You can't expect an accountant to have Eclipse installed to run a tax calculation program, right? For example, to run the `TestTax` program (see Lesson 4) from the command window you need to open a command (or Terminal) window, change the directory to `Lesson4` in your Eclipse workspace, and enter the following:

```
java TestTax
```

You can run as standalone programs only those Java classes that have the method `main`, which takes a `String` array as an argument. This array is the means of passing some data from the command line to your program during start-up. For example, you can pass gross income, state, and number of dependents to `TestTax` by starting it from the command line as follows:

```
java TestTax 50000 NJ 2
```

The method `main(String[] args)` of the class `TestTax` receives this data as a `String` array that I decided to call `args`. This array is automatically created by JVM, and it's large enough to accommodate all the arguments entered from the command line. This array will be populated as follows:

```
args[0] = "50000";
args[1] = "NJ";
args[2] = "2";
```

Command-line arguments are always being passed to a program as `String` arrays. It's the responsibility of the programmer to convert the data to the appropriate data type. The wrapper Java classes that were introduced in Chapter 3 can come in handy. For example, the wrapper class `Double` has the function `parseDouble` to convert `String` to `double`:

```
double grossIncome = Double.parseDouble(args[0]);
```

Review the code of the `TestTax` program from Listing 4-6, which has hard-coded values of gross income, state, and number of dependents. By using command-line arguments you can make the program more generic and use for more people — not only those from New Jersey who have two dependents and an annual income of $50,000.

You'll work on this assignment in the Try It section.

TRY IT

Your assignment is to introduce command-line arguments into the program from Listing 4-6.

Lesson Requirements

For this lesson you should have Java installed.

> **NOTE** *You can download the code and resources for this "Try It" from the book's web page at* www.wrox.com/go/javaprog24hr2e. *You can find them in* `Lesson5.zip`.

Step-by-Step

1. In Eclipse IDE, copy the `TestTax` class from the Lesson4 project to the *src* folder of the project Lesson5. Also, copy the `Tax` class from the project Chapter 3 that has an `if` statement in the `calcTax()` method.
2. Remove the three lines that initialize `grossIncome`, `state`, and `dependents` with hard-coded values.
3. Add the following code fragment to ensure that the program has been started with three arguments. If it has not, print the error message and exit the program.

```
if (args.length != 3){
      System.out.println("Sample usage of the program:" +
                              "  java TestTax 50000 NJ 2");
      System.exit(0);
}
```

4. Add the following statements to the method `main()` to get the values passed from the command line, convert them to appropriate data types, and initialize the variables `grossIncome`, `state`, and `dependents`:

```
double grossIncome = Double.parseDouble(args[0]);
String state = args[1];
int dependents = Integer.parseInt(args[2]);
```

5. Even though there is a way to specify command-line arguments in Eclipse, I want you to leave the IDE and do the rest in the command-line window. Right-click the Lesson5 project in Eclipse IDE and select the Properties menu item (note the location of the compiled classes of your project — in my case it was `c:\practicalJava\workspace\Lesson5\bin`).
6. Open the command window and change the directory to the one that contains the file `TestTax.class`.
7. Run your program several times, specifying different values for the command-line arguments. The program should print different values for the calculated tax.

> **TIP** *Please select the videos for Lesson 5 online at* `www.wrox.com/go/javaprog24hr2e`. *You will also be able to download the code and resources for this lesson from the website.*

Packages, Interfaces, and Encapsulation

A programming language is considered *object-oriented* if it supports *inheritance*, *encapsulation*, and *polymorphism*. You know by now that Java supports inheritance, which lets you design a class by deriving it from an existing one. This feature allows you to reuse existing code without copy-pasting code fragments from other classes. The class `NJTax` from Listing 3-5 was designed this way.

In Chapter 6 and Chapter 7 you learn what encapsulation means, and continue studying coding techniques and best practices. Although this lesson shows you several short code examples illustrating certain programming topics, the next one brings all the pieces you've learned so far together in one larger application.

JAVA PACKAGES

A decent size project can have hundreds of Java classes, and you need to organize them in *packages* (think file directories). This will allow you to categorize files, control access to your classes (see the section "Access Levels" later in this chapter), and avoid potential naming conflicts: If both you and your colleague coincidentally decide to name a class `Util`, this won't be a problem as long as these classes are located in different packages.

Sometimes you'll be using third-party libraries of Java classes written in a different department or even outside your firm. To minimize the chances that package names will be the same, it's common to use so-called *reverse domain name* notation. For example, if you work for a company called Acme, which has the website `acme.com`, you can prefix all package names with `com.acme`. To place a Java class in a certain package, add the package statement at the beginning of the class (it must be the first non-comment statement in the class). For example, if the class `Tax` has been developed for the accounting department, you can declare it as follows:

```
package com.acme.accounting;
class Tax {
  // the code goes here
}
```

If you declare the class Tax as shown in the preceding code, the file Tax.java must be stored in the corresponding directory tree:

```
com
   acme
      accounting
```

Java classes are also organized into packages, and the fully qualified name of a class consists of the package name followed by the class name. For example, the full name of the Java class Double is java.lang.Double, where java.lang is the package name. As a matter of fact, java.lang is the only package name that you don't have to explicitly mention in your code in order for its classes to be found, unless all classes are located in the same package.

The program documentation on all Java 8 packages is available at http://download.oracle.com/javase/8/docs/api/.

Let's say your Tax class needs to connect to some URL with the help of the class URL located in the java.net package. You can write code containing the fully qualified name of this second class:

```
java.net.URL myURL = new java.net.URL ("http://www.acme.com");
```

But instead of using this rather long notation, include the import statement right above the class declaration, and then use just the name of the class:

```
import java.net.URL;
class Tax{
   URL myURL = new URL("http://www.acme.com");
   ...
}
```

If you need to import several classes from the same package, use the wild card (*) in the import statement rather then listing each of the classes on a separate line:

```
import java.net.*;
```

But using the wild card makes your program less readable. The preceding code sample makes it not clear which specific classes from the java.net package are used in the program. Don't be lazy and list import statements for each class separately. It doesn't affect the size of the compiled code, but it will make your program easier to understand to whomever reads it in the future (even you, by the way).

ENCAPSULATION

Encapsulation is the ability to hide and protect data stored in Java objects. You may ask, "Who are the bad guys who want to illegally access my data?" It's not about bad guys. When a developer creates a Java class, he or she plans for a certain use pattern of this code by other classes. For example, the variable grossIncome should not be modified directly; instead, it should be modified via a method that performs some validation procedures to ensure that the value to be assigned meets application-specific rules.

A Java developer may decide to "hide" 15 out of 20 variables, say, so other classes can't access them. Imagine how many parts exist in a car and how many functions those parts can perform. Does the driver need to know about all of them? Of course not. The driver needs to know how to start and stop the car, signal turns, open the windows, turn on the wipers, and do a few dozen other simple operations, which in programming jargon can be called the car's *public interface*. Java has special keywords to control which elements of your programs should be made public, and which should not.

Access Levels

Java classes, methods, and member variables can have `public`, `private`, `protected`, and `package` access levels; for example:

```
public class Tax {
   private double grossIncome;
   private String state;
   private int dependents;
   protected double calcTax(){
      // the method code goes here
   }
}
```

The keyword `public` means that this element (a class, a method, or a variable) can be accessed from any other Java class. The keyword `protected` makes the element "visible" not only in the current class but also to its subclasses, even if they are located in different packages.

The keyword `private` is the most restrictive one, as it makes a member variable or a method accessible only inside this class. For example, our class `Tax` may need some additional methods that could be internally called from the method `calcTax()`. The users of the class `Tax` do not need to know about these methods, and they should be declared as `private`.

If you do not specify any access level, the default is *package* (it's not a keyword), which means that only classes located in the same package will have access to this method or variable. Java classes should expose only the methods that outsiders have to know, such as `calcTax()`.

If you are not sure which access level to give to methods or variables, just make them all `private`; as you're doing later development, if some other class needs to access them, you can always change the access level to be less restrictive. This will protect all the internals of your application from misuse. Think of it this way: "I want to sell my class `Tax` to various accounting firms across the country. If their software developers integrate my class with their existing systems, what are the methods that they must know about to be able to calculate tax?" If car designers did not ask themselves similar questions, drivers would need to press dozens of buttons just to start the engine.

THE KEYWORD FINAL

The keyword `final` can have different meanings depending on the context. It's explained in the next sections.

final Variables

You can use the keyword `final` while declaring variables, methods, and classes. A `final` variable becomes a constant (see Chapter 3) that can be initialized only once and can't change its value during the run time. Some people may argue that a constant and a variable that can get initialized only once are not the same thing, but the fact that you can't change their values makes them very similar.

Even though you can declare constants inside a method, it's more common to declare them on the class level so they can be reused by several methods of the same class:

```
final int BOILING_TEMP = 212; // in Fahrenheit
```

final Methods

If you declare a class method with a `final` keyword, this method can't be overridden if someone decides to extend the class. At the moment it may seem obvious to you that a particular method will never ever need to be overridden. What are the chances that the formula to convert Fahrenheit to Celsius will be changed any time soon?

```
static final double convertToCelsius(double far){
          return ((far - 32) * 5 / 9);
}
```

But in many cases developers create reusable libraries of Java classes, finalizing functionality that's not written in stone. Although it may seem to you that a particular method will never need to be overridden, you might not have predicted all use patterns of this class. If this happens, some other developer will have to jump through hoops to create another version of your method in a subclass.

Many years ago the Java compiler optimized (inlined) final methods. It doesn't do that anymore — all methods are optimized by the Hotspot JVM. Just think twice before making a method `final`

final Classes

If you declare a class as `final`, no one will be able to subclass it. For example, the class `String` has been created as immutable and therefore was declared as `final` (see `http://docs.oracle.com/javase/8/docs/api/java/lang/String.html`). If a class is declared as `final`, all its methods become implicitly `final`.

FINAL IN EXCEPTION HANDLING

There is one more use of the final keyword. You can use it in the error-handling blocks (`try-catch`). You see an example of using `finally` in Lesson 10 covering error handling

INTERFACES

There are different approaches to how to start designing a class. Most people start with thinking over the behavior it should support. For example, an employee should get paid; hence the class `Employee` should implement `Payable` interface. The name *Payable* is an arbitrary one. What represents payable behavior? Let's say that you want to implement it in a method with a signature `boolean increasePay(int percent)`.

Of course, you can just add such a method straight to the class `Employee` and implement business logic right there. The other choice is to just declare this method in a separate entity called an *interface*, and then have your class implement this interface:

```
class Employee implements Payable{
   // the implementation goes here
}
```

Listing 6-1 shows an interface with one method declaration.

You should have a reason for declaring some methods separately from the class that will implement them, and you see these reasons in the next lesson when you learn about polymorphism. For now, just get familiar with the syntax of defining and using interfaces. Interfaces before Java 8 didn't allow for any method implementations — just declarations. Let's start with the case when an interface has only declared behavior.

When a class declares that it implements a certain interface, *it guarantees* to provide implementation for all methods declared in this interface. And a class can implement more than one interface: just separate their names with commas.

Let's say there are two types of workers in your organization — employees and contractors — and that you create the classes `Employee` and `Contractor` to implement functionalities that reflect specifics of these different groups. Each person is entitled to a pay raise, though for employees this means a salary increase and for contractors it's an increase of an hourly or daily rate.

Instead of creating two different methods in these classes (for example, `increateSalary()` and `increaseRate()`), it's better to define an interface called, say, `Payable` that contains the declaration of the method `increasePay()`, and to have both classes implement it, as in Listing 6-1, Listing 6-2, and Listing 6-3. Every method declared in the interface automatically becomes `public`.

LISTING 6-1 Payable interface

```
public interface Payable {
       boolean increasePay(int percent);
}
```

LISTING 6-2 Class Employee

```
public class Employee implements Payable {
```

```
        public boolean increasePay(int percent) {
                // implement salary raise here
        }
}
```

LISTING 6-3 Class Contractor

```
public class Contractor implements Payable {
        public boolean increasePay(int percent) {
                // implement hourly rate increase here
        }
}
```

Because both Employee and Contractor contain the clause `implements Payable`, you must implement the `increasePay()` method in each of the classes, or your code won't compile. Creating classes with common interfaces leads to a cleaner design of your application and makes the code more readable. But what's more important is that, with the help of interfaces, you can introduce polymorphic behavior to your program, which is illustrated in Chapter 7.

Besides method signatures, Java interfaces can contain declarations of `final` variables. For example, you can create a `final` variable in the `Payable` interface for the maximum percentage of a pay increase (all variables declared in the interface automatically become `public static final`):

```
int INCREASE_CAP = 20;
```

Because both the `Employee` and `Contractor` classes implement `Payable`, they can both (or just the `Contractor`) include `if` statements in the implementation of `increasePay()` to ensure that the provided percentage increase is less than `INCREASE_CAP`. If the cap changes in the future, you need to change it in only one place — the `Payable` interface. Moreover, if a new type of worker is introduced later (for example, `ForeignContractor`), the implementation of `increasePay()` may be completely different.

Some software developers create Java interfaces that contain only `final` variables storing important application constants. Implementing such interfaces will make these constants available in the class that implements the interface(s). Not everyone approves of such usage of interfaces because it can create a messy situation when a class that implements interfaces with static constants exposes a new set of public APIs (those `final` variables) rather than just using these values internally. The code readability suffers, too; it's not immediately clear where a certain variable was declared, especially if there are several layers of inheritance, where classes implement multiple interfaces. You can read more about this Constant Interface Antipattern at `http://goo.gl/WBQm9d`.

Marker Interfaces

Marker interfaces are those that don't have any methods declared. One example of such an interface is `Serializable`, which is covered in Chapter 15. You don't need to write any implementation of these interfaces; the Java compiler takes care of this for you. Objects of a class that implement a marker interface support a certain functionality. For example, if a class implements `Serializable`, JVM is able to *serialize* it — turn it into a string of bytes (in the server's JVM) in such a way that the string can be sent to another JVM (on the client's machine), which will be able to re-create the instance of the object, or *de-serialize* it. Marker interfaces are used internally by the Java compiler to generate the byte code that will implement the functionality required by such interfaces.

Also, Java has an operator `instanceof` (see the next section) that can check during the run time whether an object is of a certain type. You can use the operator `instanceof`, as shown in the following code, to check whether the object implements a marker interface, or any other type of interface for that matter:

```
if (receivedFromServerObj instanceof Serializable) {
    // do something
}
```

This may look strange — is it an instance of an interface? The proper way to read it is if the variable `receivedFromServerObj` points to the object that prompts `Serializable` to do something.

Default Methods in Interfaces

A new keyword, `default`, was introduced in Java SE 8. Now you can provide a default method implementation in interfaces, too. For example, you can create an interface `Payable` with default implementation of the method `increasePay()`:

```
public interface Payable {
    default boolean increasePay(int percent){
        System.out.println(
          "The default code implementing pay increase goes here");
        return true;
    };
}
```

Now, if a class that implements `Payable` doesn't have its own implementation of the `increasePay()` then the default method implementation is used. The compiler will not complain. Default methods are also known as *defender methods*.

COMPILER COMPLIANCE LEVEL IN ECLIPSE IDE

If the preceding code doesn't compile in your Eclipse IDE, most likely your project is set to support syntax that's older than Java 8. To fix it, right-click the project name, select the Project Properties menu, and then select Java Compiler. Make sure that the JDK Compliance is set to support Java 1.8.

You need to handle default methods with care as sometimes you might run into the name conflicts. Consider the following situation:

```
package defendermethods;
class Employee extends Person implements Payable, Promotionable{
   public static void main(String[] args){
       Employee emp = new Employee();
```

```
            emp.increasePay(10);
        }
    }
```

What if there is the method increasePay() in the class Person and in the interfaces Payable and Promotionable? How is such a conflict resolved? If a program creates an instance of the class Employee and invokes the method increasePay() on it, which version of this method is invoked?

If a method with the same signature exists in the ancestor class and the interface, the one in the class is invoked. If the defender methods with the same signature exists only in the interfaces Payable and Promotionable, the compiler complains with the following error:

Duplicate default methods named increasePay with the parameters (int) and (int) are inherited from the types Promotionable and Payable Employee.java

Static Methods in Interfaces

As of Java 8, you are allowed to include static methods in interfaces. For example:

```
public interface Payable {
    default boolean increasePay(int percent){
        System.out.println(
          "The default code implementing pay increase goes here");
        return true;
    };

    static double checkThePayIncreaseLimit(){
        // do something
        return 12345.00;
    }
}
```

If a static method is declared in a class, it's invoked by using a class name followed by the dot and the method name, as shown in Lesson 4: WeatherReport.convertToCelsius(98.7).

Accordingly, if a static method was declared in the interface, a class can invoke it using the interface name. For example, this is how you could do it from our class Employee:

```
double limit = Payable.checkThePayIncreaseLimit();
```

CASTING

All Java classes form an inheritance tree with the class Object on top of the hierarchy — all Java classes are direct or indirect descendants of Object. When you eclare a non-primitive variable, you are allowed to use either the exact data type of this variable or one of its ancestor data types. For example, if the class NJTax extends Tax, each of the following lines is correct:

```
NJTax myTax1   = new NJTax();
Tax myTax2     = new NJTax();  // upcasting
Object myTax3  = new NJTax();  // upcasting
```

Java is smart enough to automatically *cast* an instance of the class to its ancestor. When the variable has a more generic type than an instance of the object, it's called *upcasting*. Let's say the class `Object` has 10 methods and class variables defined, the class `Tax` (an implicit subclass of `Object`) adds five more methods and variables (making 15), and `NJTax` adds another two (totaling 17). The variable `myTax1` has access to all 17 methods and variables, `myTax2` sees only 15, and `myTax3` just 10. Why not always use exact types in variable declarations?

Say you need to write a program that will process data about workers of a certain company. Some of them are full-time employees and some are contractors, but you'd like to read their data from some data source and store them in the same array. Arrays can store only objects of the same type, remember? Because Java can automatically upcast the objects, you can create a class called `Person` with two subclasses, `Employee` and `Contractor`, and then read the records from a database. Based on the employment type you can then create an appropriate object instance and put it into an array of type `Person`:

```
Person workers[] = new Person [20];
workers[0] = new Employee("Yakov", "Fain");
workers[1] = new Employee("Mary", "Lou");
workers[2] = new Contractor("Bill", "Shaw");
...
```

Of course, you could've created two separate arrays, one for employees and one for contractors, but I'm laying the foundation here for explaining polymorphism — a powerful concept in object-oriented languages. You see a concrete example of polymorphism in Chapter 7.

At some point you need to process the data from the array `workers`. In a loop you can test the data type of the current element of the array with the operator `instanceof`, downcast the object (it can't be done automatically) to `Employee` or `Contractor`, and process it accordingly:

```
for (int i; i<20; i++){
     Employee currentEmployee;
     Contractor currentContractor;

     if (workers[i] instanceof Employee){
          currentEmployee = (Employee) workers[i];
          // do some employee processing here
     } else if (workers[i] instanceof Contractor){
          currentContractor = (Contractor) workers[i];
          // do some contractor processing here
     }
}
```

Placing a data type in parentheses in front of another object means that you want to *downcast* this object to the specified type. You can downcast an object only to one of its descendant data types. Even though the preceding code has correct syntax, it doesn't represent the best practice for processing similar objects. In the next lesson you see how to use polymorphism in a more generic way.

If a class implements an interface, you can cast its instance to this interface. Say that a class called `Employee` implements `Payable`, `Insurable`, and `Pensionable` interfaces:

```
class Employee extends Person implements
                                   Payable, Insurable, Pensionable {
// implementation of all interfaces goes here
}
```

Assume you have an array of workers of type `Person`. If you are interested only in the `Insurable` behavior of employees, there is no need to cast each element of this array to the type `Employee`. Just cast them to the `Insurable` type, as shown in the following code fragment. However, keep in mind that if you do so, the variable `currentEmployee` exposes access only to those methods that were declared in the `Insurable` interface:

```
Insurable currentEmployee;

if (workers[i] instanceof Insurable){
  currentEmployee = (Insurable) workers[i];
  // do some insurance-specific processing here
}
```

TRY IT

The goal of this assignment is to start using packages, protect data using private variables, and define first interfaces. You create a simple program that will increase pay, which is implemented differently for employees and contractors. After completing this assignment you'll have working but not perfect code. What can be improved is explained in Chapter 7.

Lesson Requirements

For this lesson you should have Java installed.

> **NOTE** *You can download the code and resources for this "Try It" from the book's web page at* `www.wrox.com/go/javaprog24hr2e`. *You can find them in* `Lesson6.zip`.

Step-by-Step

1. In the Eclipse IDE, create a new project called Lesson6.
2. Create the `Payable` interface as per Listing 6-1 in the package `com.practicaljava.lesson6` — you can enter the name of the package in the Eclipse New Java Class window. Declare a `final` variable there:

   ```
   int INCREASE_CAP = 20;
   ```

3. Create a class called `Person`:

   ```
   package com.practicaljava.lesson6;

   public class Person {
   ```

```
        private String name;

        public Person(String name){
              this.name=name;
        }

        public String getName(){
              return "Person's name is " + name;
        }
  }
```

4. Create the classes `Employee` and `Contractor` in the package `com.practicaljava.lesson6`. Each class should extend `Person` and implement `Payable`. While creating a new class, click the Add button in Eclipse to automatically include the `Payable` interface in declarations of the classes `Employee` and `Contractor`.
5. Check your filesystem to ensure that the files were created in your workspace in the directory `com/practicaljava/lesson6`.
6. Create a class called `TestPayIncrease` with a method called `main()`. Don't specify any package; this class will be created in a different directory.
7. Try to create an instance of the class `Employee` in the method `main()` of `TestPayIncrease`:

```
Employee myEmployee = new Employee();
```

You'll get an error: `Employee` can't be resolved to a type. No wonder — it's located in a different package. Move the mouse over `Employee` and Eclipse will offer you a fix. Add an `import` statement:

```
import com.practicaljava.lesson6.Employee;
```

Select this fix and later add the `import` statement for all required classes.

8. In the `main()` method of the class `TestPayIncrease`, create an array of employees and contractors and call the function `increasePay()` for each element of the array:

```
public static void main(String[] args) {

        Person workers[] = new Person[3];
             workers[0] = new Employee("John");
             workers[1] = new Contractor("Mary");
             workers[2] = new Employee("Steve");

                   Employee currentEmployee;
                   Contractor currentContractor;

              for (Person p: workers){
                  if (p instanceof Employee){
                       currentEmployee = (Employee) p;
                       currentEmployee.increasePay(30);

                  }else if (p instanceof Contractor){
                      currentContractor = (Contractor) p;
```

```
                currentContractor.increasePay(30);
            }
        }
}
```

9. Implement the `increasePay()` method in `Employee` — don't put any restrictions on pay increases. Here's the body of `increasePay()`:

```
System.out.println("Increasing salary by " + percent + "%. "+
                                                   getName());
return true;
```

10. Implement the `increasePay()` method in the class `Contractor`. If the percentage of the increase is less than `INCREASE_CAP`, print a message similar to the one in the preceding code. Otherwise, print a message explaining that you can't increase a contractor's rate by more than 20 percent.

11. Run the `TestPayIncrease` program. It should produce output similar to the following:

```
Increasing salary by 30%. Person's name is John
Sorry, can't increase hourly rate by more than 20%. Person's name is Mary
Increasing salary by 30%. Person's name is Steve
```

> **TIP** *Please select the videos for Lesson 6 online at* `www.wrox.com/go/javaprog24hr2e`. *You will also be able to download the code and resources for this lesson from the website.*

Programming with Abstract Classes and Interfaces

In this lesson you learn about *abstract classes*, and then you build a complete application that illustrates how to design and implement programs with abstract classes and interfaces. You also learn about the notion of *polymorphism*.

ABSTRACT CLASSES

If a class is declared *abstract* it can't be instantiated. The keyword `abstract` has to be placed in the declaration of a class. The abstract class may have abstract method(s). The question is, "Who needs a class that can't be instantiated?"

It's easiest to answer this question by showing you how to use abstract classes while designing an application. Previous lessons ended with assignments, but this lesson starts with one.

Assignment

A company has employees and contractors. Design the classes without using interfaces to represent the people who work for this company. The classes should have the following methods:

```
changeAddress()
promote()
giveDayOff()
increasePay()
```

A one-time promotion means giving one day off and raising the salary by a specified percentage. The method `increasePay()` should raise the yearly salary for employees and increase the hourly rate for contractors.

Solution with an Abstract Class

Classes Employee and Contractor should have some common functionality, but because increasePay() has to be implemented differently for Employee and Contractor, let's declare a superclass Person for them with an abstract (not implemented) method increasePay(). The class Person also has three concrete (implemented) methods. The fact that the abstract class Person cannot be instantiated forces you, the developer, to implement abstract methods in its subclasses.

Start by redesigning the class Person from the "Try It" section of Chapter 6. That version of the class didn't have the method increasePay(), which was a part of the Payable interface back then. As per the previous lesson's assignment, add the following concrete methods to the class Person: changeAddress(), giveDayOff(), and promote() (see Listing 7-1).

This is a different approach from the one in Chapter 6, which used interfaces. In this case some methods are implemented in the superclass and some are not. As per the assignment, this solution won't be using any interfaces.

LISTING 7-1 Abstract class Person

```
package com.practicaljava.lesson7;

public abstract class Person {

       private String name;
       private String address;

       int INCREASE_CAP = 20; // cap on pay increase

       public Person(String name){
              this.name=name;
       }

       public String getName(){
              return "Person's name is " + name;
       }

       public void changeAddress(String address){
           this.address = address;
           System.out.println("New address is" + address);
       }

       private void giveDayOff(){
              System.out.println("Giving a day off to " + name);
       }

       public void promote(int percent){
                 System.out.println(" Promoting a worker...");
                 giveDayOff();

                 //calling an abstract method
```

```
            increasePay(percent);
        }

        // an abstract method to be implemented in subclasses
        public abstract boolean increasePay(int percent);
}
```

The method `increasePay()` is abstract, and the author of the class `Person` doesn't have to know the specifics of implementing raising pay. The subclasses may even be programmed by other developers. But the author of `Person` can write code that even invokes `increasePay()`, as in the method `promote()`. This is allowed because by the time the concrete class is instantiated, the method `increasePay()` will definitely have been implemented. For simplicity, I didn't write any code that looks like an actual increase of pay — this is irrelevant for understanding the concept of abstract classes.

The next step is to create the subclasses `Employee` and `Contractor`, implementing the method `increasePay()` in two different ways, as shown in Listing 7-2 and Listing 7-3.

LISTING 7-2 Class Employee

```
package com.practicaljava.lesson7;

public class Employee extends Person{

        public Employee(String name){
                super(name);
        }
        public boolean increasePay(int percent) {
                System.out.println("Increasing salary by " +
                        percent + "%. "+ getName());
                return true;
        }
}
```

LISTING 7-3 Class Contractor

```
package com.practicaljava.lesson7;

public class Contractor extends Person {

        public Contractor(String name){
                super(name);
        }
        public boolean increasePay(int percent) {
                if(percent < INCREASE_CAP){
                   System.out.println("Increasing hourly rate by " +
                                          percent + "%. "+ getName());
                  return true;
               } else {
```

```
                System.out.println("Sorry, can't increase hourly rate by more
                      than " + INCREASE_CAP + "%. "+ getName());
                return false;
            }
        }
}
```

Programmers writing subclasses are forced to write an implementation of `increasePay()` according to its signature, declared in the abstract class. If they declare a method increasing pay that has a different name or argument list, their classes remain abstract. So they don't have a choice and have to play by the rules dictated in the abstract class.

The class `TestPayIncrease` in Listing 7-4 shows how to use the classes `Employee` and `Contractor` for promoting workers.

LISTING 7-4 Class TestPayincrease

```
import com.practicaljava.lesson7.Person;
import com.practicaljava.lesson7.Contractor;
import com.practicaljava.lesson7.Employee;

public class TestPayIncrease {

      public static void main(String[] args) {

        Person workers[] = new Person[3];
              workers[0] = new Employee("John");
              workers[1] = new Contractor("Mary");
              workers[2] = new Employee("Steve");

              for (Person p: workers){
                        p.promote(30);
              }
        }
}
```

Compare the code of the preceding class `TestPayIncrease` with the one from the "Try It" section of Chapter 6. Which one do you like better? I like this version better; it exhibits polymorphic behavior, explained next.

POLYMORPHISM

Polymorphism is easier to understand through an example. Let's look at the classes `Person`, `Employee`, and `Contractor` from a different angle. The code in Listing 7-4 populates an array, mixing up the instances of the classes `Employee` and `Contractor` with hard-coded names. In real life, the data about workers usually comes from an external data source. For example, a program could get a person's work status from the database and instantiate an appropriate concrete class. The earlier class `TestPayIncrease` gives an additional vacation day and attempts to increase the salary or hourly rate of every worker by 30 percent.

Note that even though the loop variable p is of its ancestor's type Person in Listing 7-4, at every iteration it actually points at either an Employee or a Contractor instance. The actual object type will be evaluated only during the run time. This feature of object-oriented languages is called *run-time binding* or *late binding*.

The output of the class TestPayIncrease looks like the following:

```
Promoting a worker...
Giving a day off to John
Increasing salary by 30%. Person's name is John
 Promoting a worker...
Giving a day off to Mary
Sorry, can't increase hourly rate by more than 20%. Person's name
is Mary
 Promoting a worker...
Giving a day off to Steve
Increasing salary by 30%. Person's name is Steve
```

Both classes, Employee and Contractor, were inherited from the same base class, Person. Instead of having different methods for increasing the worker's compensation based on the worker's type, you give a polymorphic behavior to the method increasePay(), which applies different business logic depending on the type of the object.

You're calling the same method, promote(), on every object from the array workers, but because the actual object type is evaluated during run time, the pay is raised properly according to this particular object's implementation of the method increasePay(). This is polymorphism in action.

The for loop in the class TestPayIncrease remains the same even if you add some other types of workers inherited from the class Person. For example, to add a new category of worker — a foreign contractor — you have to create a class called ForeignContractor derived from the class Person and implement yet another version of the method increasePay() there. The class TestPayIncrease keeps evaluating the actual type of Person's descendants during run time and calls the proper implementation of the method increasePay().

Polymorphism enables you to avoid using switch or if statements with the rather slow operator instanceof, which you used in Chapter 6. Would you agree that even though TestPayIncrease from Lesson 6 is producing the same results, its code looks pretty ugly compared to this version of this class? The code in the Lesson 6 version of TestPayIncrease works more slowly than the polymorphic version, and its if statement will have to be modified every time a new type of worker is added.

Making the Interface Solution Polymorphic

After discussing the abstract class version of the assignment's solution, it's time to modify its interface version from Chapter 6 with the polymorphic solution. Note that the array workers has been declared of type Payable . It is populated by objects of types Employee and Contractor, which implement the Payable interface.

You've eliminated not only the need of using instanceof, but even the casting to Payable is not required. The array is of type Payable, and you use only the behavior defined in Payable (that is, the increasePay() method) without worrying too much about whether the current worker is an employee or a contractor (see Listing 7-5).

LISTING 7-5 Class TestPayincreasePoly

```
// For reusing the interface version of Employee and Contractor
// let's keep this sample in the code for Lesson 6
import com.practicaljava.lesson6.*;

public class TestPayInceasePoly {

    public static void main(String[] args) {

        Payable workers[] = new Payable[3];
        workers[0] = new Employee("John");
        workers[1] = new Contractor("Mary");
        workers[2] = new Employee("Steve");

            for (Payable p: workers){
                      p.increasePay(30);
             }
        }
}
```

Note that the variable p can "see" only the methods declared in `Payable`. The variable p could not be used to invoke any methods from `Person` regardless of the fact that both `Employee` and `Contractor` are inherited from this class.

What can go wrong during the execution of the code from Listing 7-5? What if a developer creates a class called `ForeignContractor` without implementing the `Payable` interface, and by mistake tries to add its instance to the array `workers`? You get a compile-time error "Cannot convert from `ForeignContractor` to `Payable`." Compiler errors are easy to fix. In the "Try It" section you purposely create a situation that causes a run-time casting error.

INTERFACES VERSUS ABSTRACT CLASSES

The next question is, "When should you use interfaces and when should you use abstract classes?" If two or more classes have lots of common functionality, but some methods should be implemented differently, you can create a common abstract ancestor and as many subclasses inheriting this common behavior as needed. Declare those methods abstract so subclasses implement them differently, and implement these methods in subclasses.

If several classes don't have common functionality but need to exhibit some common behavior, do not create a common ancestor; have them implement an interface that declares the required behavior. This scenario was not presented in the "Interfaces" section of Chapter 6, but it's going to be a part of the hands-on exercise in the "Try It" section of this lesson.

Interfaces and abstract classes are similar in that they ensure that required methods are implemented according to required method signatures. But they differ in how the program is designed. Whereas abstract classes require you to provide a common ancestor for the classes, interfaces don't.

Interfaces could be your only option if a class already has an ancestor that cannot be changed. Java doesn't support multiple inheritance; a class can have only one ancestor. For example, to write Java applets you must inherit your class from the class `Applet`, or, in the case of Swing applets, from `JApplet`. Using your own abstract ancestor here is not an option.

Although using abstract classes, interfaces, and polymorphism is not a must, it certainly improves the design of Java code by making it more readable and understandable to others who may need to work on programs written by you. In general, it's a good habit to think over the behavior of the classes you're about to write and list it in separate interfaces.

In Lesson 11 I give you another reason for using interfaces in the note titled "Programming to Interfaces".

TRY IT

In the first part of the assignment your goal is to break the code from Listing 7-5 to produce the run-time error `ClassCastException`. You create a situation when the array workers will be of type `Person`, which can store any `Person` or its descendants. Then, you purposely add its subclass that doesn't implement `Payable`, but will try to cast it to `Payable` anyway to generate a run-time exception. In the second part of the assignment you need to rewrite the assignment from Chapter 6 to keep the `Payable` interface but remove the common ancestor `Person`.

Lesson Requirements

For this lesson you should have Java installed.

> **NOTE** *You can download the code and resources for this "Try It" from the book's web page at* `www.wrox.com/go/javaprog24hr2e`. *You can find them in* `Lesson6.zip` *and in* `Lesson7.zip`.

Step-by-Step

Part 1

1. In Eclipse, open the project Lesson6 — yes, the one you've imported in the previous lesson.
2. Create a new class called `ForeignContractor`, as shown in the following code. Note that this class doesn't implement the `Payable` interface:

```
package com.practicaljava.lesson6;

public class ForeignContractor extends Person {

        public ForeignContractor(String name){
               super(name);
        }
        public boolean increasePay(int percent) {
```

```
                System.out.println("I'm just a foreign worker");
                return true;
            }
    }
```

3. Create the class `TestPayIncreasePolyError`, adding an instance of the `ForeignContractor` class. Note that you're casting every element of the array to `Payable`:

```
import com.practicaljava.lesson6.*;

public class TestPayIncreasePolyError {

    public static void main(String[] args) {

        Person workers[] = new Person[3];
        workers[0] = new Employee("John");
        workers[1] = new Contractor("Mary");
        workers[2] = new ForeignContractor("Boris");

                for (Person p: workers){
                        ((Payable)p).increasePay(30);
                }
        }
}
```

4. Run the program `TestPayIncreasePolyError`. Observe the output in the console view. You get the run-time error `java.lang.ClassCastException` on the third element of the array. Note the number `14` — this is the line number of `TestPayIncreasePolyError` program, which casts each object to the `Payable` interface:

```
Increasing salary by 30%. Person's name is John
Sorry, can't increase hourly rate by more than 20%. Person's name is Mary
Exception in thread "main" java.lang.ClassCastException:
com.practicaljava.lesson6.ForeignContractor cannot be cast to
com.practicaljava.lesson6.Payable
         at TestPayInceasePolyError.main(TestPayInceasePolyError.java:14)
```

5. Modify the code of `TestPayIncreasePolyError`, changing the type of the array from `Person` to `Payable` and changing the type of the loop variable accordingly:

```
Payable workers[] = new Payable [3];
workers[0] = new Employee("John");
workers[1] = new Contractor("Mary");
workers[2] = new ForeignContractor("Boris");

        for (Payable p: workers){
                p.increasePay(30);
        }
```

6. Observe that now you are getting a Java compiler error preventing you from even adding to the array the instance of `ForeignContractor` because it doesn't implement `Payable`. Predicting and preventing run-time errors is a very important task for every software developer, and this subject is covered in detail in Chapter 10.

Part 2

1. Open the the project Lesson7 in Eclipse, select the menu File → New → Package, and create the new package `com.practicaljava.lesson7.tryit`.
2. Using Ctrl+C/Ctrl+V copy the `Payable` interface from Eclipse project Lesson6 to the package `com.practicaljava.lesson7.tryit`. Change the package name to be `com.practicaljava.lesson7.tryit`.
3. In the same package create the class `Employee` as follows:

```
package com.practicaljava.lesson7.tryit;

public class Employee implements Payable{
       private String name;

       public Employee(String name){
              this.name=name;
       }

       public boolean increasePay(int percent) {
         System.out.println("Increasing salary by " + percent
             + "%: " + name);
         return true;
       }
}
```

4. In the same package create the class `Contractor` as follows:

```
package com.practicaljava.lesson7.tryit;

public class Contractor implements Payable {

       private String name;

       public Contractor(String name){
              this.name=name;
       }
       public boolean increasePay(int percent) {
         if(percent < Payable.INCREASE_CAP){
           System.out.println("Increasing hourly rate by " +
                          percent + "%. ");
           return true;
         } else {
            System.out.println(
            "Sorry,can't increase hourly rate by more than "
                + Payable.INCREASE_CAP + "%: " + name);
```

```
                return false;
            }
        }
}
```

5. Create a class called `TestPayIncreaseInterface`:

```
public class TestPayIncreaseInterface {

    public static void main(String[] args) {

      Payable workers[] = new Payable [3];
            workers[0] = new Employee("John");
            workers[1] = new Contractor("Mary");
            workers[2] = new Employee("Steve");

                for (Payable p: workers){
                        ((Payable)p).increasePay(30);
                }
            }
}
```

6. Run this program. It should produce the following output:

```
Increasing salary by 30%: John
Sorry, can't increase hourly rate by more than 20%: Mary
Increasing salary by 30%: Steve
```

Note that neither `Employee` nor `Contractor` extends `Person` any longer. Both classes are free to extend any other classes now, but on the other hand, each of them has to declare the variable name and the method `getName()`, which was done once in the class `Person` before.

> **TIP** *Please select the videos for Lesson 7 online at* `www.wrox.com/go/javaprog24hr2e`. *You will also be able to download the code and resources for this lesson from the website.*

Introducing the GUI with Swing

These days people are accustomed to working with applications that have rich user interfaces. JavaFX is Oracle's newest platform for development of such applications. Lessons 11 and 12 introduce you to JavaFX. JavaFX is a layer on top of Java Swing — a library of components, which for many years was used for building graphic user interfaces (GUIs) for desktop applications, as well as a web program called *applets* (GUI programs running inside the web browser's Java run-time plug-in).

Today Java applets are rarely used, which is the reason why I decided not to include chapters about applets in this edition of the book. Instead, I've added coverage of the more modern JavaFX framework. In this and the following lesson you learn the principles of building GUIs while developing a simple desktop calculator using the Java Swing library.

> **NOTE** *Eclipse Foundation offers another library of UI components called the Standard Widget Toolkit (SWT), available at* `https://wiki.eclipse.org/SWT`*, which is outside of the scope of this book.*

SWING BASICS

Originally Java offered a pretty basic library of UI-related classes called the Abstract Windowing Toolkit (AWT). A couple of years later a new widget toolkit called Swing was introduced. Swing offers a lighter set of UI components while keeping the main idea intact — to keep UI development independent of the end user's operating system. Run the same program on Windows and on Mac OS, and GUI components look native to the corresponding operating system (OS) (see Figure 8-1). You can also create a Swing GUI application with a cross-platform look and feel (see Nimbus at `http://docs.oracle.com/javase/tutorial/uiswing/lookandfeel/nimbus.html`).

Today developers are trying to create UIs that appear to be native to the OS, whether that is Windows, Mac OS, iOS, or Android. Eventually the market share of Swing-based UIs may diminish, but at the time of this writing it's still widely used by enterprises, and skilled Swing developers remain in demand.

Swing offers you everything you need to build UIs in Java: There are controls to represent buttons, drop-down menus, grids, scrollbars, trees, tab folders, and so on. Typically you create UIs by combining controls into containers (for example, JPanel or JFrame) that support various layouts that enable controls to be arranged as you or a graphic designer envision. In this lesson you use some of the Swing components while creating a UI for a simple desktop calculator.

A complete discussion of the Swing library is out of the scope of this book, but there are plenty of books and technical articles covering this subject. The official online Swing tutorial is located at http://bit.ly/1o7JeuE.

Swing classes are located in the javax.swing package, and the process of creating a UI comes down to extending some of these classes to display the UI and respond to various user- and system-generated events. You create a top-level window with a title and border by instantiating the class JFrame, as in Listing 8-1.

LISTING 8-1 An empty descendant of JFrame

```
import javax.swing.JFrame;
import javax.swing.JButton;

public class HelloWorld extends JFrame {
  public static void main(String[] args) {
    JFrame myWindow = new HelloWorld();

    // Creating and adding a button to the container
    JButton myButton = new JButton ("Click me");
    myWindow.add(myButton);
    myWindow.setSize(200,300);
    myWindow.setTitle("Hello World");
    myWindow.setVisible(true);
  }
}
```

The class HelloWorld creates and adds a button to the container, sets the size and title of the window, and makes it visible. JFrame is an example of a container that can hold UI controls, which must be instantiated first and then added to the container. Run this program, and it shows a small window that looks like Figure 8-1 (the left image shows the Windows OS version, and the right one was taken from Mac OS).

The code in Figure 8-1 doesn't specify the size of the button, where to put it, or whether there should be space between the components and the borders. Without layout instructions, the entire empty space in Figure 8-1 will be occupied by one huge button.

FIGURE 8-1: HelloWorld on Windows (left) and Mac OS (right)

DEFAULT CLOSE OPERATION

Run the earlier `HelloWorld`program and try to click the window's Close button. It doesn't work. The JRE sent an event to close the window, but the program didn't have event-handling code for this.You find out how to add it in the next lesson, but meanwhile you can make the window close by adding the following line to `HelloWorld.java`:

```
myWindow.setDefaultCloseOperation(JFrame.EXIT_ON_CLOSE);
```

Usually `JFrame` includes some nested containers where you place controls such as `JButton`, `JTable`, and `JList`.Java Swing comes with *layout managers* that help you arrange all these controls appropriately. For example, a sample coding process for creating a `JFrame` containing `JPanel` can go like this:

1. Create a `JPanel`.
2. Assign a layout manager to it.
3. Instantiate some Swing controls and add them to the panel.
4. Add the panel to the top-level container—`JFrame`—by calling the `setContentPane()` method.
5. Set the frame's size and make it visible.

You can assign different layout managers to your containers to create very sophisticated windows. But displaying a window with properly laid-out components is only half of the job because these controls should know how to respond to various *events*, such as a click on a button. This lesson covers the basics of displaying UI components; Lesson 9 is about writing code for responding to events.

LAYOUT MANAGERS

The simplest layout manager is `FlowLayout`, which allocates all components being added to the container horizontally. When there's no room for the next component, `FlowLayout` uses the next row, and the process repeats.

A Simple Calculator with FlowLayout

The best way to learn layout management is by trying to use it in practice. You're going to create a UI for a simple calculator that can accept two numbers and display the result. Create a new Eclipse project called Lesson8 and a new class called `SimpleCalculator` with the following code:

LISTING 8-2 Calculator with FlowLayout

```
public class SimpleCalculator {
 public static void main(String[] args) {
  // Create a panel
       JPanel windowContent= new JPanel();

  // Set a layout manager for this panel
       FlowLayout fl = new FlowLayout();
       windowContent.setLayout(fl);

  // Create controls in memory
       JLabel label1 = new JLabel("Number 1:");
       JTextField field1 = new JTextField(10);
       JLabel label2 = new JLabel("Number 2:");
       JTextField field2 = new JTextField(10);
       JLabel label3 = new JLabel("Sum:");
       JTextField result = new JTextField(10);
       JButton go = new JButton("Add");

  // Add controls to the panel
       windowContent.add(label1);
       windowContent.add(field1);
       windowContent.add(label2);
       windowContent.add(field2);
       windowContent.add(label3);
       windowContent.add(result);
       windowContent.add(go);

  // Create the frame and add the panel to it
  JFrame frame = new JFrame("My First Calculator");
```

```
        // Add the panel to the top-level container
        frame.setContentPane(windowContent);

        frame.setDefaultCloseOperation(JFrame.EXIT_ON_CLOSE);

        // set the size and make the window visible
        frame.setSize(400,100);
        frame.setVisible(true);
    }
}
```

Compile and run this program, and it displays the window shown in Figure 8-2.

This may not be the best-looking calculator, but it demonstrates the use of `FlowLayout`. In the next section you make it look better with the help of more suitable layout managers.

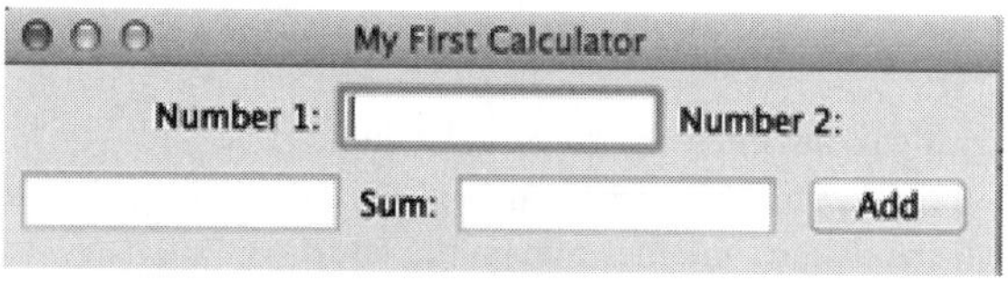

FIGURE 8-2: Running the SimpleCalculator class

Grab the corner of the window and make it wider. You see how `FlowLayout` starts reallocating controls, trying to fill the new area. If you make the window wide enough, all the components fit in one row, as in Figure 8-3.

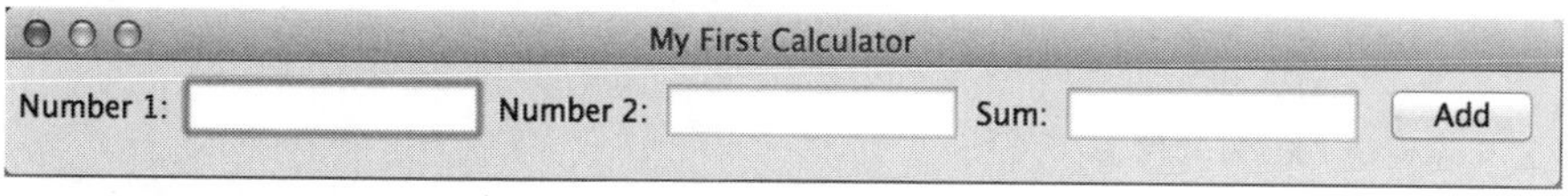

FIGURE 8-3: Resizing the window of SimpleCalculator

Even though you can enforce exact coordinates and sizes for each window component, Swing has layout managers that can maintain relative positions for all controls without assigning strict positions to them. Layout managers ensure that the content of a container looks nice regardless of the current window size. The `FlowLayout` is not about looking nice, though. It's about showing all visual components based on the current container's width.

A Brief Introduction to Layout Managers

Swing offers the following layout managers:

- `FlowLayout`
- `GridLayout`
- `BoxLayout`
- `BorderLayout`
- `CardLayout`
- `GridBagLayout`

To use any layout manager, instantiate it first and then assign this instance to a container via `setLayout()`, as you did with the class `SimpleCalculator` in Listing 8-2.

FlowLayout

This layout arranges components in a container row by row. For example, labels, text fields, and buttons are added to the first imaginary row until there is no room left in this row.

When the current row is filled, the rest of the components go to the next row, and so on. Components can be added to the container from left to right or from right to left according to the container's `componentOrientation` property. If a user changes the size of the window, this layout manager reflows the components, which changes the GUI as illustrated in Figure 8-2. Indeed, `FlowLayout` is not the best choice for the calculator. Let's try something different.

GridLayout

The class `java.awt.GridLayout` enables you to arrange components as rows and columns in a grid. You'll be adding components to imaginary cells of this grid. If the container gets resized, grid cells may become larger or smaller, but the relative positions of the components inside the container remain the same.

So far your calculator has seven components: three labels, three text fields, and a button. You may arrange them as a grid of four rows and two columns (one cell stays empty) by creating an instance of `GridLayout` like this:

```
GridLayout gr = new GridLayout(4,2);
```

You can also assign some horizontal and vertical spaces of, for example, five pixels, between the cells:

```
GridLayout gr = new GridLayout(4,2,5,5);
```

Replace `FlowLayout` with `GridLayout` in Listing 8-2 and the calculator looks a little prettier. Create and compile a new class called `SimpleCalculatorGrid` (see Listing 8-3).

LISTING 8-3 Calculator with GridLayout

```
import javax.swing.*;
import java.awt.GridLayout;
public class SimpleCalculatorGrid {
public static void main(String[] args) {

      JPanel windowContent= new JPanel();

      // Set the layout manager for the panel
      GridLayout gl = new GridLayout(4,2);
      windowContent.setLayout(gl);

      JLabel label1 = new JLabel("Number 1:");
      JTextField field1 = new JTextField(10);
```

```
            JLabel label2 = new JLabel("Number 2:");
            JTextField field2 = new JTextField(10);
            JLabel label3 = new JLabel("Sum:");
            JTextField result = new JTextField(10);
            JButton go = new JButton("Add");

        // Add controls to the panel
            windowContent.add(label1);
            windowContent.add(field1);
            windowContent.add(label2);
            windowContent.add(field2);
            windowContent.add(label3);
            windowContent.add(result);
            windowContent.add(go);

         // Create the frame and add the panel to it
            JFrame frame = new JFrame("My First Grid Calculator");

            frame.setContentPane(windowContent);

            frame.setDefaultCloseOperation(JFrame.EXIT_ON_CLOSE);

        // set the size and display the window
            frame.setSize(400,100);
            frame.setVisible(true);
        }
    }
```

Run the program `SimpleCalculatorGrid` to see a calculator that looks a little better than before (see Figure 8-4).

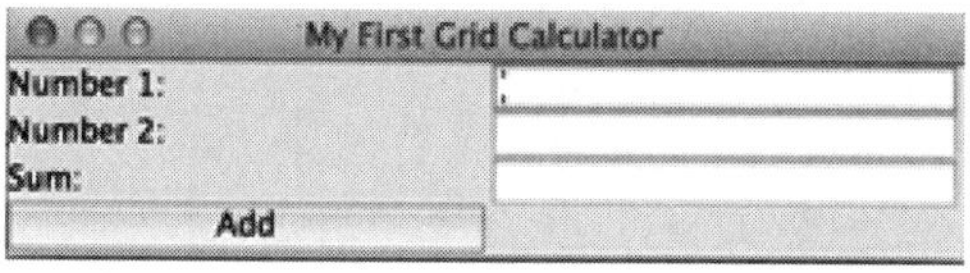

FIGURE 8-4: Running the SimpleCalculatorGrid

Try to resize this window; controls grow with the window, as shown in Figure 8-5, but their relative positions won't change. Note that with `GridLayout` all cells of the grid have the same width and height.

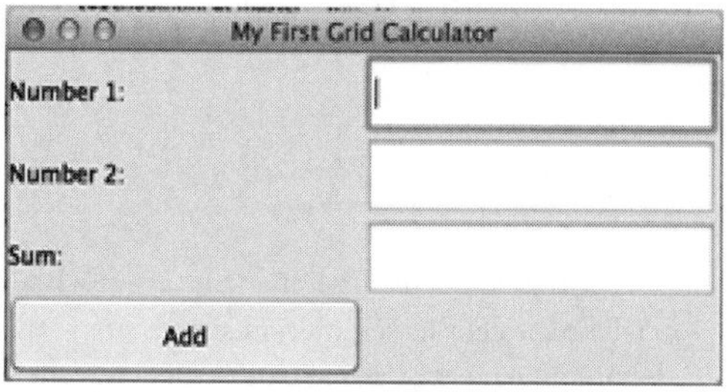

FIGURE 8-5: Resizing SimpleCalculatorGrid

BorderLayout

The layout manager `java.awt.BorderLayout` divides a container into `South`, `West`, `North`, `East`, and `Center` areas. The `North` area stays on top of the window, `South` at the bottom, `West` on the left, and `East` on the right. For example, in the calculator shown in Figure 8-6, a text field that displays numbers is located in the `North` area, and the panel `p2` is in the `West`.

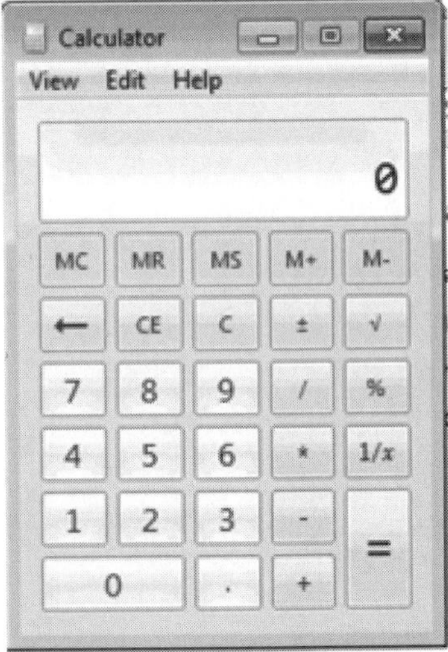

FIGURE 8-6: The Windows 7 Calculator

You can use the following code to create a `BorderLayout` and place a text field there:

```
BorderLayout bl = new BorderLayout();
this.setLayoutManager(bl);

JTextField  txtDisplay = new JTextField(20);
this.add(BorderLayout.NORTH, txtDisplay);
```

You are not required to have window controls in all five areas. If you need only `North`, `Center`, and `South` areas, the `Center` area becomes wider because you are not going to use the `East` and `West` areas. I use a `BorderLayout` later in this lesson in the next version of the calculator: `Calculator.java`.

`BorderLayout` is a default layout manager for content panes.

Combining Layout Managers

Do you think that `GridLayout` will enable you to design a calculator that looks like the one that comes with Microsoft Windows, shown in Figure 8-6? Unfortunately, it won't, because cells have different sizes there — the text field is wider than the buttons. You can, however, combine layout managers by using panels that have their own layout managers.

You can create such a calculator by using `GridBagLayout`, which is explained later. In the meantime, you can create a simpler version of it by combining layout managers you know. The end result looks like Figure 8-7.

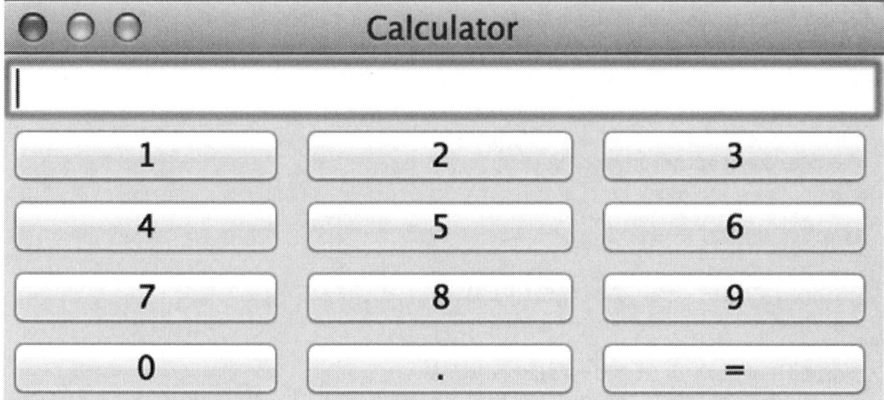

FIGURE 8-7: Calculator with combined layouts

Create a new class, `Calculator`, as per Listing 8-4, and run the program. Read the program comments; you should be able to understand how the code works by reading the comments, shouldn't you? Running this program shows the calculator, as shown in Figure 8-7.

LISTING 8-4 Calculator with combined layouts

```
import javax.swing.*;
import java.awt.GridLayout;
import java.awt.BorderLayout;

public class Calculator {

  // Declare all calculator's components.
     JPanel windowContent;
     JTextField displayField;
     JButton button0;
     JButton button1;
     JButton button2;
     JButton button3;
     JButton button4;
     JButton button5;
     JButton button6;
     JButton button7;
     JButton button8;
     JButton button9;
     JButton buttonPoint;
     JButton buttonEqual;
     JPanel p1;

     // Constructor creates the components
```

```
    // and adds them to the frame using combination of
    // Borderlayout and Gridlayout

Calculator(){

        windowContent= new JPanel();

       // Set the layout manager for this panel
         BorderLayout bl = new BorderLayout();
         windowContent.setLayout(bl);

       // Create the display field and place it in the
       // North area of the window

         displayField = new JTextField(30);
         windowContent.add("North",displayField);

    // Create buttons using constructor of the
    // class JButton that takes the label of the
    // button as a parameter

         button0=new JButton("0");
         button1=new JButton("1");
         button2=new JButton("2");
         button3=new JButton("3");
         button4=new JButton("4");
         button5=new JButton("5");
         button6=new JButton("6");
         button7=new JButton("7");
         button8=new JButton("8");
         button9=new JButton("9");
         buttonPoint = new JButton(".");
         buttonEqual=new JButton("=");

        // Create the panel with the GridLayout with 12 buttons -
        //10 numeric ones, period, and the equal sign

                p1 = new JPanel();
                GridLayout gl =new GridLayout(4,3);
                p1.setLayout(gl);

        //  Add window controls to the panel p1
                p1.add(button1);
                p1.add(button2);
                p1.add(button3);
                p1.add(button4);
                p1.add(button5);
                p1.add(button6);
                p1.add(button7);
                p1.add(button8);
                p1.add(button9);
                p1.add(button0);
                p1.add(buttonPoint);
                p1.add(buttonEqual);
```

```
            // Add the panel p1 to the center of the window
                    windowContent.add("Center",p1);

            //Create the frame and set its content pane
                  JFrame frame = new JFrame("Calculator");
                  frame.setContentPane(windowContent);

            // Set the size of the window big enough
            // to accommodate all controls
                    frame.pack();

                // Display the window
                frame.setVisible(true);
                frame.setDefaultCloseOperation(JFrame.EXIT_ON_CLOSE);
        }

        public static void main(String[] args) {

            Calculator calc = new Calculator();
        }
}
```

BoxLayout

The class `javax.swing.BoxLayout` allows multiple window components to be laid out either horizontally (along the x axis) or vertically (along the y axis). Unlike with the `FlowLayout` manager, when the window with the `BoxLayout` is resized, its controls do not wrap. And unlike with `GridLayout`, with `BoxLayout`, window controls can have different sizes.

The next two lines of code assign `BoxLayout` with vertical alignment to `JPanel`. To make this code shorter, I have not declared a variable to store a reference to the object `BoxLayout`, but rather create an instance of this object and immediately pass it to the method `setLayout()` as an argument.

```
JPanel p1= new JPanel();
setLayout(new BoxLayout(p1, BoxLayout.Y_AXIS));
```

If you just add several buttons to the panel `p1`, they all display one under another.

You can use combinations of various containers implementing horizontal or vertical `BoxLayout` to build a fairly sophisticated UI. Think of a front page of a game that has to have several items next to each other on the top of the window, some controls located vertically on the left sidebar, and the rest of the window's real estate allocated for the main battlefield. You can use `BorderLayout` having a panel with a horizontal `BoxLayout` on the `North`, and a panel with vertical `BoxLayout` on the `West`.

The next section shows you a sophisticated yet more verbose `GridBagLayout`, but you should always try to see if the `BoxLayout` can do the job and use it, if possible.

GridBagLayout

In this section you are familiarized with yet another way of designing the calculator by using the `java.awt.GridBagLayout` layout manager instead of combining panels with different layouts. `GridBagLayout` is an advanced grid that allows the creation of cells of different sizes. `GridBagLayout` works in combination with another class called `GridBagConstraints`.

Constraints are just attributes of a cell, and you have to set them for each cell separately. All constraints for a cell have to be set before you place a component in the cell. For example, one of the constraint's attributes is called `gridwidth` (see Figure 8-8). It enables you to make a cell as wide as several other cells. The display field in the example is as wide as five other cells. The top-left cell has the coordinates 0,0.

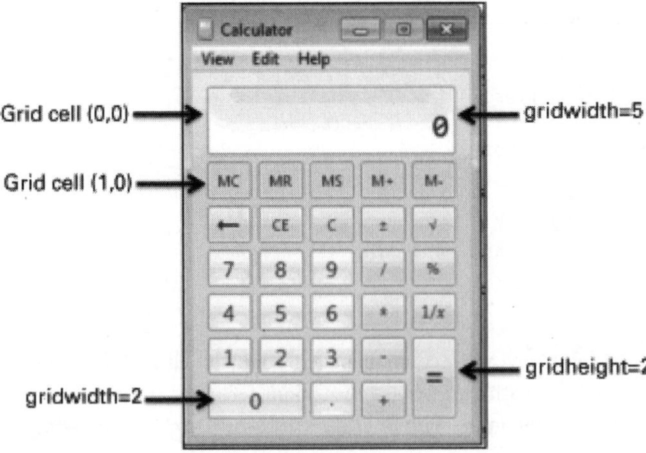

FIGURE 8-8: GridBagConstraints in Calculator

When working with the grid layout you should create an instance of the constraint object first, and set the values to its properties. Then you can add a UI component to the cell with specified coordinates in your container. After that you repeat the procedure: populate the same instance of `GridBagConstraints` with properties of another cell and add it to the container and so on.

The code sample in Listing 8-5 is heavily sprinkled with comments to help you understand how to use `GridBagLayout`. While working on this lesson's assignment you'll be using this code.

LISTING 8-5 Creating constraints for GridBagLayout

```
// Set the GridBagLayout for the window's content pane
 GridBagLayout gb = new GridBagLayout();
 this.setLayout(gb);

// Create an instance of the GridBagConstraints
// You'll have to repeat these lines for each component
// that you'd like to add to the grid cell
```

```
 GridBagConstraints constr = new GridBagConstraints();

//setting constraints for the Calculator's displayField:

// x coordinate in the grid
 constr.gridx=0;
// y coordinate in the grid
 constr.gridy=0;

// this cell has the same height as other cells
 constr.gridheight =1;

// this cell is as wide as 5 other ones
 constr.gridwidth= 5;

// fill all space in the cell
 constr.fill= constr.BOTH;
// proportion of horizontal space taken by this
// component
 constr.weightx = 1.0;

// proportion of vertical space taken by this component
 constr.weighty = 1.0;
// position of the component within the cell
 constr.anchor=constr.CENTER;

 displayField = new JTextField();
// set constraints for this field
 gb.setConstraints(displayField,constr);

// add the text field to the window
 windowContent.add(displayField);
```

CardLayout

Think of a deck of cards lying on top of each other — only the top card is visible. You can use the `java.awt.CardLayout` manager to create a component that shows one panel at a time, such as the tabbed folder in Figure 8-9.

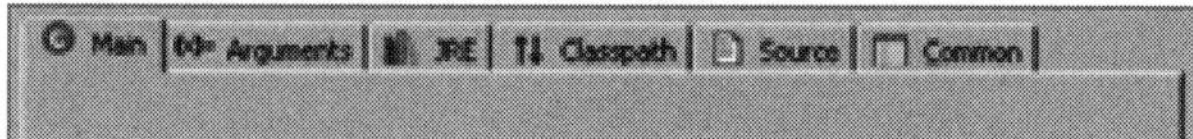

FIGURE 8-9: Tab folder as a card layout example

When the user clicks a tab, the content of the window changes. In fact, all the panels needed for this screen are already preloaded and lie on top of each other. When the user clicks a tab, the program just brings this "card" to the top and makes the other "cards" invisible. The tabbed folder here was used for illustration; the Swing library includes a ready-to-go component for windows with tabs, called `JTabbedPane`.

Containers with Absolute Layout

If you want a container's content to look the same regardless of the user's window size, set the x and y coordinates, width, and height (the bounds) of each component while adding them to the window. Your class has to explicitly state that it won't use any layout manager by passing `null` to `setLayout()`:

```
windowContent.setLayout(null);
```

The next code snippet shows how you can set a button's width to 40 pixels and its height to 20, and place the button so its top-left corner is 100 pixels to the right of and 200 pixels down from the top-left corner of the window:

```
JButton myButton = new Button("New Game");
myButton.setBounds(100,200,40,20);
```

More About Swing Widgets

It's not possible to describe all the Swing components in a short lesson. Use the Swing online tutorial mentioned in the beginning of this lesson to get more information. Here's a list of all the Swing widgets:

JButton	JScrollBar
JLabel	JSlider
JCheckBox	JProgressBar
JRadioButton	JComboBox
JToggleButton	JList
JScrollPane	JTabbedPane
JSpinner	JTable
JTextField	JToolTip
JTextArea	JTree
JPasswordField	JViewPort
JFormattedTextField	ImageIcon
JEditorPane	

You can also create menus (JMenu and JPopupMenu), pop-up windows, and frames inside other frames (JInternalFrame), and you can use the standard-looking windows (JFileChooser, JColorChooser, and JOptionPane).

Java used to come with an excellent demo application, SwingSet3, that showed all the available Swing components in action. Now it's available online at https://swingset3.java.net. Check it out.

SWING GUI BUILDERS

Java developers use various tools to speed the process of designing UIs. See what's available for the IDE that you use. For example, there is design tool for Eclipse called WindowBuilder that simplifies creation of GUI without writing too much code. You can find it at the following URL: http://www.eclipse.org/windowbuilder.

Matisse was originally developed for the NetBeans IDE, and you can find it here: http://netbeans.org/kb/trails/matisse.html.

Finally, consider yet another Eclipse plug-in, called Jigloo GUI Builder (http://marketplace.eclipse.org/content/jigloo-swtswing-gui-builder). You can definitely find a tool that will substantially speed up your design of UIs with the Java Swing library.

TRY IT

Your task for today is to create another version of the calculator in Figure 8-8, using only one layout: GridBagLayout.

Lesson Requirements

For this lesson you should have Java installed.

> **NOTE** *You can download the code and resources for this "Try It" from the book's web page at* www.wrox.com/go/javaprog24hr2e. *You can find them in the* Lesson8.zip.

Step-by-Step

This assignment comes down to creating appropriate constraints for each UI component shown in Figure 8-8, so there is just one long step in this assignment: Follow the example given in Listing 8-5 for each UI component needed for the calculator.

> **TIP** *Please select the videos for Lesson 8 online at* www.wrox.com/go/javaprog24hr2e. *You will also be able to download the code and resources for this lesson from the website.*

Event Handling in Swing GUI

Java Swing, like any other UI library, is *event-driven*. When a user interacts with a GUI program (such as by clicking a button or pressing a key) a Java Swing program receives an *event* that can initiate an appropriate reaction.

If you wrote the code to react to a particular event, this code will be invoked. If you haven't written such code, the event will be fired anyway, but the program won't respond to it. In this lesson you learn how to handle events in Java GUI programs.

INTRODUCTION TO EVENT LISTENERS

I'm sure you've tried to click the buttons of the calculator from Chapter 8, but they were not ready to respond to your actions yet. Swing widgets can process various events, or in the programmers' jargon can *listen to events*. To listen to events, a program has to register window components with Java classes called *listeners*.

You should have components listen only to the events they are interested in. For example, when a person clicks a button, it's not important where exactly the mouse pointer is as long as it is on the button's surface. That's why you do not need to register the button with `MouseMotionListener`. On the other hand, this listener comes in handy for all kinds of drawing programs.

To process button clicks, Swing provides `ActionListener`. All listeners are declared Java interfaces and their methods have to be implemented in an object that listens to events.

This is how Java documentation describes the `ActionListener` interface:

> *This is the listener interference for receiving action events. The class that is interested in processing an action event implements this interface, and the object created with that class is registered with a component, using the component's* `addActionListener()` method. When the action event occurs, that object's `actionPerformed()` method is invoked.

This interface `ActionListener` is defined in the `java.awt.event` package, as presented in Listing 9-1. It declares only one method.

LISTING 9-1 ActionListener Interface

```
public interface ActionListener extends EventListener
  void actionPerformed(ActionEvent e);
}
```

> **NOTE** *Starting from Java 8, interfaces that declare a single method are called functional interfaces. You learn more about them in Lesson 15.*

The `actionPerformed()` method is invoked by the JVM if the action happened. Let's use this listener in the calculator you created in Chapter 8.

TEACHING THE CALCULATOR TO CALCULATE

The calculator's buttons should register themselves with a class that implements `ActionListener`, which means that its method `actionPerform()` contains the calculation logic. Even though you can implement `ActionListener` in the `Calculator` class itself, for better readability and code maintainability it's best to separate the code defining the UI from the code containing processing logic. Let's start writing a separate class, `CalculatorEngine`:

```
import java.awt.event.ActionListener;
public class CalculatorEngine implements ActionListener {

}
```

The preceding class won't compile; Java gives an error message stating that the class must implement the method `actionPerformed(ActionEvent e)`. You remember the rules for interfaces, right? The interface `ActionListener` declares a single method `actionPerformed()`, which makes it a *functional interface*, as discussed in Lesson 15. The code in Listing 9-2 fixes this error.

LISTING 9-2 First implementation of ActionListener interface

```
import java.awt.event.ActionListener;
import java.awt.event.ActionEvent;
public class CalculatorEngine implements ActionListener {

   public void actionPerformed(ActionEvent e){
       // An empty method body
```

```
    }
}
```

Even though the actionPerformed() method doesn't contain any code yet, it's considered implemented in Listing 9-2 (the curly braces make the compiler happy). JVM calls this method on the class that's registered as an event listener and implements the ActionListener interface whenever the user clicks the button.

The next version of CalulatorEngine (see Listing 9-3) will display a message box from the method actionPerformed(). You can display any messages using the Swing class JOptionPane and its method showConfirmDialog().

LISTING 9-3 This class displays a message box

```
import java.awt.event.ActionListener;
import java.awt.event.ActionEvent;
import javax.swing.JOptionPane;
public class CalculatorEngineMsg implements ActionListener {

   public void actionPerformed(ActionEvent e){
       JOptionPane.showConfirmDialog(null,
               "Something happened...",
               "Just a test",
               JOptionPane.PLAIN_MESSAGE);
   }
}
```

If you register the class CalculatorEngineMsg from Listing 9-3 as a listener for the class Calculator from Listing 8-4, it displays the message box shown in Figure 9-1 when the user clicks inside the calculator window.

The class JOptionPane declares several overloaded methods named showConfirmDialog() — I used the version with four arguments in Listing 9-3. The first argument is null, which means that this message box does not have a parent window. The second argument contains the title of the message box. The third contains the message itself, and the fourth argument allows you to select a button(s) to be included in the box; PLAIN_MESSAGE means that it only needs the OK button.

FIGURE 9-1: A message box with JOptionPane

Registering Components with ActionListener

Which program invokes the code in the method actionPerformed() shown in Listing 9-3 and when? Register the calculator's buttons with the class CalculatorEngine, and Java run time obediently invokes this class's method actionPerformed() every time any button is clicked.

CALLBACK METHODS

The methods that are not called by the Java run time on your application code are often referred to as *callback methods*.

Add the following two lines at the end of the constructor of the class `Calculator` (Listing 8-4), and one button (zero) starts responding to clicks with the box from Figure 9-1:

```
CalculatorEngine calcEngine = new CalculatorEngine();
button0.addActionListener(calcEngine);
```

The other calculator buttons remain silent because they have not been registered with the action listener yet. Keep adding similar lines to bring all the buttons to life:

```
button1.addActionListener(calcEngine);
button2.addActionListener(calcEngine);
button3.addActionListener(calcEngine);
button4.addActionListener(calcEngine);
```

Finding the Source of an Event

The next step is to make the listener a little smarter: It has to display message boxes with different text, depending on which button was pressed. When an action event happens, Java run time calls the method `actionPerformed(ActionEvent)` on your listener class, and this method provides valuable information about the event in the argument `ActionEvent`. In particular, the method `getSource()` in the object `ActionEvent` supplied to `actionPerformed()` in Listing 9-3 tells you what object caused this method invocation.

But according to Java documentation for the class `ActionEvent`, the method `getSource()` returns an instance of type `Object`, which is a superclass of all Java classes, including window components. Since buttons in your calculator can be the only reason for an action event, cast the returned `Object` to the type `JButton`:

```
JButton clickedButton = (JButton) evt.getSource();
```

Only after performing casting from `Object` to `JButton` can you call methods that `JButton` supports; for example, `getText()`, which returns the button's label, as shown in Listing 9-4. If you press the button labeled 5, you see a message box that reads, "You pressed 5."

LISTING 9-4 Getting the label of the clicked button

```
import java.awt.event.ActionListener;
import java.awt.event.ActionEvent;
import javax.swing.JOptionPane;
import javax.swing.JButton;
public class CalculatorEngine implements ActionListener {
```

```
        public void actionPerformed(ActionEvent e){
            // Get the source object of this action
            JButton clickedButton=(JButton) e.getSource();
            // Get the button's label
            String clickedButtonLabel = clickedButton.getText();

            // Concatenate the button's label
            // to the text of the message box
            JOptionPane.showConfirmDialog(null,
                    "You pressed " + clickedButtonLabel,
                    "Just a test",
                    JOptionPane.PLAIN_MESSAGE);
        }
    }
```

What if the window events are produced not only by buttons, but by some other components as well? Then don't cast every object that has arrived with `ActionEvent` to `JButton`. Use the operator called `instanceof` to perform the proper casting. The next example first determines what type of object caused the event, and then performs casting to either `JButton` or `JTextField`:

```
public void actionPerformed(ActionEvent evt){

   JTextField myDisplayField=null;
   JButton clickedButton=null;

   Object eventSource = evt.getSource();

   if (eventSource instanceof JButton){
       clickedButton = (JButton) eventSource;
   } else if (eventSource instanceof JTextField){
       myDisplayField = (JTextField)eventSource;
   }
}
```

Consider the buttons that perform arithmetic operations. Our calculator has to execute different code for each button:

```
public void actionPerformed(ActionEvent e){

     Object src = e.getSource();

     if (src == buttonPlus){
        // Call the method that adds numbers here
     } else if (src == buttonMinus){
       // Call the method that subtracts numbers here
     }else if (src == buttonDivide){
      // Call the method that divides numbers here
     } else if (src == buttonMultiply){
     // Call the method that multiplies numbers here

     }
}
```

How to Pass Data Between Objects

When you click a numeric button on the real calculator, it does not show a message box, but rather displays the number in the text field on top. Here's a new challenge: You need to be able to reach the attribute displayField from the object Calculator from the method actionPerformed() defined in another class —CalculatorEngine. In other words, two objects need to communicate. There are different ways of arranging this; for instance, in the class CalculatorEngine you can declare a private variable to store a reference to the instance of the object Calculator.

The next version of the class CalculatorEngine declares a one-argument constructor, which takes an argument of type Calculator.

JVM executes the constructor of the CalculatorEngine class during instantiation of this class in memory. The Calculator object instantiates CalculatorEngine and passes to the engine's constructor a reference to itself (note this):

```
CalculatorEngine calcEngine = new CalculatorEngine (this);
```

The reference this contains the location of the calculator's instance in memory. The engine's constructor can store the value from the variable this in its own variable, say parent, and eventually use it from the method actionPerformed() to access the calculator's display field.

Attention, Bad Practice!

The variable parent in the following code listing serves as a bridge from the object CalculatorEngine to Calculator. And the easy way to access Calculator's displayField from CalculatorEngine is this:

```
parent.displayField.getText();
...
parent.displayField.setText(dispFieldText + clickedButtonLabel);
```

These two lines were taken from the code sample in Listing 9-5. This code works, but it violates one of the principles of object-oriented programming: encapsulation. The problem is that code from CalculatorEngine has direct knowledge of the internals of another object: Calculator. The engine "knows" that there is a field called displayField in Calculator, and the preceding code gets and sets its value directly.

LISTING 9-5 Bad execution of object communication

```
import java.awt.event.ActionListener;
import java.awt.event.ActionEvent;
import javax.swing.JButton;

public class CalculatorEngine implements ActionListener {

 Calculator parent; // a reference to the Calculator

 // Constructor stores the reference to the
```

```
  // Calculator window in the member variable parent
  CalculatorEngine(Calculator parent){
    this.parent = parent;
  }

  public void actionPerformed(ActionEvent e){
    // Get the source of this action
    JButton clickedButton = (JButton) e.getSource();

    // Get the existing text from the Calculator's
    // display field. Reaching inside another object is bad.
    String dispFieldText = parent.displayField.getText();

    // Get the button's label
    String clickedButtonLabel = clickedButton.getText();

    parent.displayField.setText(dispFieldText +
                                clickedButtonLabel);
  }
}
```

Imagine that for whatever reason you decide to use in `Calculator` something other than the `JTextField` widget to display the results of calculations. That other widget may not even have such application programming interfaces (APIs) as `setText()` and `getText()`. Now you need to modify not only the `Calculator` class but also the code of the `CalculatorEngine` to replace the part that displays or reads the `displayField`. This is not the right way to design interactions between objects.

A Better Solution with a Public API

If `Calculator` needs to communicate with other objects, it should expose a public API to get or set data but hide details about its internals. The class `Calculator` from Listing 8-4 declares widgets without using any access-level qualifiers, so default package access level is applied. Hide these user interface (UI) components, as shown in the following code by using the keyword `private`:

```
private JPanel windowContent;
private JTextField displayField;
private JButton button0;
private JButton button1;
...
```

Now `CalculatorEngine` isn't able to access `displayField` directly as it did in Listing 9-5. Defining public *getter* and *setter* methods in `Calculator` allows outsiders to access `displayField` without knowing it exists. Listing 9-6 demonstrates how a small change can protect data and enforce encapsulation.

LISTING 9-6 Adding a public API to Calculator

```
public class Calculator{
    private JTextField displayField;
```

```
    public void setDisplayValue(String val){
        displayField.setText(val);
    }

    public String getDisplayValue() {
        return displayField.getText();
    }

    // The rest of the code goes here
}
```

Now if you decide to replace the `JTextField` widget with another one, only the methods `setDisplayValue()` and `getDisplayValue()` need a change; the code of `CalculatorEngine` don't need to be touched. Listing 9-7 shows the proper way to access `Calculator` from the `CalculatorEngine`.

LISTING 9-7 Using a public API of Calculator

```
import java.awt.event.ActionListener;
import java.awt.event.ActionEvent;
import javax.swing.JButton;

public class CalculatorEngine implements ActionListener {

 Calculator parent; // a reference to the Calculator

  // Constructor stores the reference to the
  // Calculator window in the member variable parent
 CalculatorEngine(Calculator parent){
   this.parent = parent;
 }

 public void actionPerformed(ActionEvent e){
   // Get the source of this action
   JButton clickedButton =  (JButton) e.getSource();

   // Get the existing text from the Calculator's
   // display field. Reaching inside another object is bad.
   String dispFieldText = parent.getDisplayValue();

   // Get the button's label
   String clickedButtonLabel = clickedButton.getText();

   parent.setDisplayValue(dispFieldText +
                               clickedButtonLabel);
 }
}
```

DESIGN PATTERN MODEL-VIEW-CONTROLLER

Software engineers often have to implement similar architectural solutions in their projects. Over the years a number of design patterns were published online and in books. One of such architectural patterns is model-view-controller (MVC). The main idea of MVC is that you should separate code that deals with UI (view), stores the application data (model), and triggers the changes of the views and data (controller). The implementation of MVC may vary depending on the application, but the principle remains the same.

Even in such a simple application as your calculator, you can start separating the code. For example, the `Calculator` class represents *view*, is responsible only for the UI, and has no application logic.

The event listener `CalculatorEngine` plays the role of the controller. It serves as a trigger to engage the application logic when the user clicks on the button or updates the view when the result has been calculated.

You don't have the model layer here as you don't store any data. But if you need to implement a calculator that remembers the history of calculations, you could create a class `CalculationsHistory` that would serve as a model in MVC, as shown in Figure 9-2.

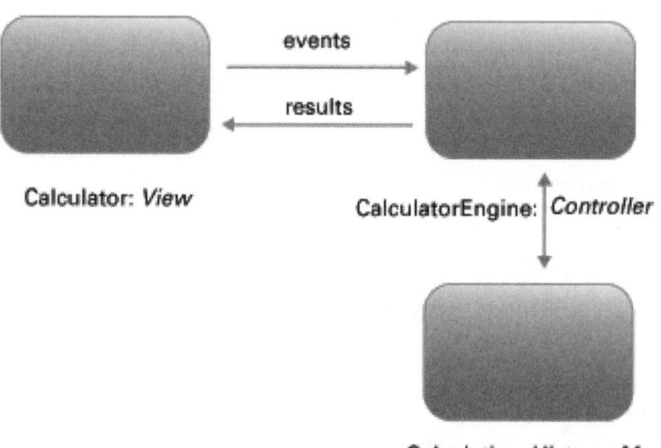

FIGURE 9-2: MVC in Calculator

Design patterns became a part of the software developer's jargon. If one programmer says, "We need to implement MVC here," both know what this is all about.

I keep bringing your attention to various design patterns in the future chapters of this book. Meanwhile you can refer to the online resource Computer Science Design Patterns (`http://en.wikibooks.org/wiki/Computer_Science_Design_Patterns`).

MORE SWING LISTENERS

JDK comes with a number of event listeners (`http://docs.oracle.com/javase/tutorial/uiswing/events/api.html`)

located in the package `java.awt.event`. Here are some of them:

- `FocusListener` is notified when a widget gains or loses focus (for example, we say that a text field has focus if it has a blinking cursor).
- `ItemListener` reacts to the selection of items from a list or a drop-down box.
- `KeyListener` responds to user keypresses.
- `MouseListener` responds to mouse clicks or the cursor hovering over a widget.
- `MouseMotionListener` tells you if the mouse is being moved or dragged. To *drag* means to move the mouse while holding its left button down.
- `WindowListener` gives you a chance to catch the moments when the user opens, closes, minimizes, or activates the window.

Table 9-1 shows the names of selected listener interfaces and the methods declared in these interfaces. For example, `FocusListener` declares two methods: `focusGained()` and `focusLost()`. This means that even if your class is interested only in knowing when a particular field gains focus, you also must include the empty method `focusLost()`. Java provides special *adapter classes* for most of the event listeners to spare you from having to manually code empty methods enforced by listener interfaces.

TABLE 9-1 Selected Swing Listeners

INTERFACE	METHODS TO IMPLEMENT
`FocusListener`	`focusGained(FocusEvent)` `focusLost(FocusEvent)`
`ItemListener`	`itemStateChanged(ItemEvent)`

`KeyListener`	`keyPressed(KeyEvent)`
	`keyReleased(KeyEvent)`
	`keyTyped(KeyEvent)`

`MouseListener`	`mouseClicked(MouseEvent)`
	`mouseEntered(MouseEvent)`
	`mouseExited(MouseEvent)`
	`mousePressed(MouseEvent)`
	`mouseReleased(MouseEvent)`

`MouseMotionListener`	`mouseDragged(MouseEvent)` `mouseMoved(MouseEvent)`

`WindowListener`	`windowActivated(WindowEvent)`
	`windowClosed(WindowEvent)`
	`windowClosing(WindowEvent)`
	`windowDeactivated(WindowEvent)`

	windowDeiconified(WindowEvent) windowIconified(WindowEvent) windowOpened(WindowEvent)

Java run time has to take care of multiple things: update the content of the screen, apply processing logic and data, and react to events.

Multiple events can be happening at the same time, and Java run time constantly runs a GUI event loop, placing these events in the event queue, as shown in Figure 9-3.

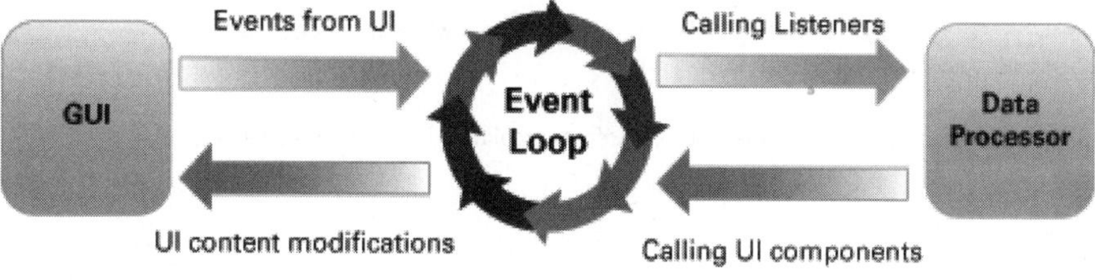

FIGURE 9-3: GUI event loop

The code that updates the GUI should be processed by a special worker thread (`SwingWorker`), which we'll discuss in Lesson 17.

HOW TO USE ADAPTERS

Swing adapters are classes with implemented empty functions required by listener interfaces. Let's say you need to display a warning message and save some data on the disk when the user closes the window. According to table_9-1, a class that implements the `WindowListener` interface has to include seven methods. This means that you'll have to write the code that saves the data in the method `windowClosing()` and also include six empty methods.

The package `java.awt.event` includes a number of adapter classes that implement corresponding listener interfaces, such as `KeyAdapter` and `WindowAdapter`. Instead of implementing `WindowListener` in a class that handles the window's events, just extend a class from `WindowAdapter` and override only the methods you are interested in; for example, the method `windowClosing()`:

```
class MyWindowEventProcessor extends java.awt.event.WindowsAdapter {

  public void windowClosing(WindowEvent e) {
    // your code that saves the data goes here.
  }
}
```

The rest is easy: Register the class `MyWindowEventProcessor` as an event listener in your GUI class (for example, `Calculator`), as shown in Listing 9-8.

You can register multiple listeners by using adapters in `Calculator`. For example, to allow the user to enter a number by pressing numeric keys, create a class based on `KeyAdapter`, instantiate it, and register it with `Calculator`, too.

LISTING 9-8 Registering an adapter-based listener

```
MyWindowEventProcessor myWindowListener = new MyWindowEventProcessor();
addWindowListener(myWindowListener);
```

You can achieve the same result using anonymous *inner classes*, as explained in the next section.

INNER CLASSES

A class declared inside another one is called an inner class. Listing 9-9 shows an example of the class `TaxOptimizer` declared inside the class `Tax`. The class `TaxOptimizer` is a member inner class and has access to all variables of the class `Tax`. Placing one class inside another is just a way of saying that the classes belong together. After compilation, the class `Tax` file produces two output files: `Tax.class` and `Tax$TaxOptimizer.class`.

LISTING 9-9 Tax class including an inner Taxoptimizer class

```
class Tax{
    double grossIncome;
    int dependents;

  double calcStateTax(){
        TaxOptimizer tOpt = new TaxOptimizer();
        return tOpt.optimize(grossIncome, dependents);
  }

      TaxOptimizer getTaxOptimizer(){
          return new TaxOptimizer();
      }

      class TaxOptimizer{

       int taxCode;

        void setTaxCode(int tCode){
              taxCode=tCode;
       }

       int optimize(double grossIncome, int dep){
```

```
            // Some optimization code goes here
               return 0;
            }
     }
    }
```

An inner class defined as static can access only static variables of the outer class. The inner class can even be defined inside a method of an outer class. In this case this local inner class is available only when the outer method is called, and it can access only static variables of the top-level class.

The method getTaxOptimizer() in Listing 9-9 returns an instance of the inner class if external classes need it. For example, if the class TestTax needs to access the method setTaxCode() from the inner class, it could do so as follows:

```
Tax t = new Tax(2, "NY", 50000);
Tax.TaxOptimizer tOptimizer = t.getTaxOptimizer();
tOptimizer.setTaxCode(12345);
```

Here's another syntax producing the same result:

```
Tax t = new Tax(2, "NY", 50000);
Tax.TaxOptimizer tOptimizer = t.new TaxOptimizer();
tOptimizer.setTaxCode(12345);
```

Anonymous Inner Classes

If an inner class does not have a name, it's called *anonymous*. The use of anonymous inner classes is pretty easy to understand in examples of implementing Swing adapters. You've learned by now that using adapters is a three-step process: Extend the adapter class, instantiate it, and register it as an event listener (see Listing 9-8). With anonymous inner classes you can perform all three steps in one shot, as in Listing 9-10.

LISTING 9-10 Using an anonymous class as adapter

```
this.addWindowListener(new WindowAdapter() {
            public void windowClosing(WindowEvent e) {
                   System.exit(0);
            }
       }
);
```

Imagine that this code is placed in the Calculator class. The method addWindowListener() requires a subclass of WindowAdapter, and the section in bold in Listing 9-10 demonstrates the syntax of declaring an anonymous class that extends WindowAdapter and overrides the method windowClosing().

The new operator instantiates the adapter, and because this is done inside the parentheses of the method addWindowListener() the newly created object is used as its argument. This adapter's implementation doesn't have a name, and we don't need to know its name in this context, do we? The instance of the adapter was created and registered as an event listener, and this is all that matters.

LAMBDA EXPRESSIONS AS AN ALTERNATIVE TO INNER CLASSES

For many years anonymous inner classes were used as method (function) wrappers because Java did not allow a function to pass as an argument to a method. Java 8 introduced lambda expressions that in many cases eliminate the need to use anonymous inner classes. You read about lambda expressions in Lesson 13.

Try It

The goal of this lesson is to complete the code of the calculator. It has to look as in Figure 9-2 and implement the functionality of all the buttons.

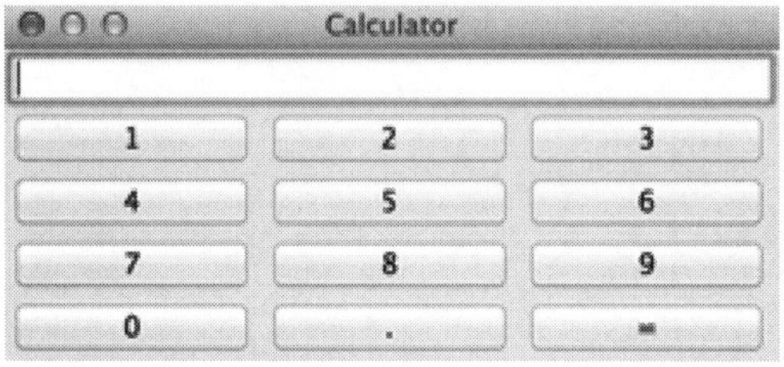

FIGURE 9-4: The Calculator GUI

Lesson Requirements

For this lesson you should have Java installed.

NOTE *You can download the code and resources for this "Try It" from the book's web page at* `www.wrox.com/go/javaprog24hr2e`. *You can find them in* `Lesson9.zip`.

Step-by-Step

1. Create a new Eclipse project called Lesson9 and copy the `Calculator` from Chapter 8 into it (see Listing 8-4).
2. Create all missing UI components — use Figure 9-4 as a prototype.
3. Create the event listener `CalculatorEngine` — all event processing and calculations should be performed there.
4. From `Calculator`, pass to the `CalculatorEngine` engine a reference to itself.
5. Register with `CalculatorEngine` all GUI components that can generate events.
6. Implement the code for the following scenario:

a. The user enters all the digits of the first number.

b. If the user hits one of the action buttons (+, -, /, or *), this indicates that the first number has been entered. Store this number and selected action in class variables (declare them first) and erase the number from the display text field. You need to convert the `String` value to `double` with the help of class `Double`.

c. The user enters the second number and clicks the = button.

d. Convert the `String` value from the text field into a numeric type `double` so it is able to store numbers with a decimal point. Perform the selected action using this value and the number stored in the numeric variable from Step b.

e. Display the result in the display field and store this value in the variable that was used in Step b, for future calculations.

f. Run the calculator. If it works, show it to your friends.

> **TIP** *Please select the videos for Lesson 9 online at* `www.wrox.com/go/javaprog24hr2e`*. You will also be able to download the code and resources for this lesson from the website.*

10

Error Handling

Fixing the compiler's errors becomes trivial as you become more comfortable with the Java syntax. But you also should ensure that your programs handle runtime errors that may happen regardless of your proficiency with the language itself.

Let's say you have a Java program that reads customers' data from a file deployed in production. What's going to happen if this file gets corrupted? Will the program crash with a scary geeky error message, or will it stay alive, displaying a user-friendly message such as, "There seems to be a problem with the file *Customers*. Please make sure that the file is not corrupted"? Error processing in the Java world is called *exception handling*, which is the subject of this lesson. An exception is a runtime error that may stop the execution of your program.

STACK TRACE

When a Java application is running, the JVM performs a number of internal and application-specific method calls. If a runtime error occurs that's not handled by the program, the program prints a *stack trace*, which reflects in the call stack the sequence of unfortunate events that caused this error. A stack trace helps software developers follow the workflow of the program that led to the error.

To illustrate what a stack trace may look like, consider the program shown in Listing 10-1, which deliberately divides by zero.

LISTING 10-1 Generating stack trace by dividing by zero

```
public class TestStackTrace{
   TestStackTrace()
   {
       divideByZero();
   }
```

```
6
7    int divideByZero()
8    {
9       return 25/0;
10   }
11
12    public static void main(String[] args)
13    {
14            new TestStackTrace();
15    }
16 }
```

Listing 10-2 depicts the output of this program, which has traced what happened in the program stack before the error occurred. Read the output from the last line upward. It shows that the program was executing the methods `main()`, `init()` for the constructor, and `divideByZero()`. The line numbers 14, 4, and 9, respectively, indicate where in the program these methods were called. After that the `ArithmeticException` was thrown—the code in line 9 tried to divide by zero. Turning the line numbers on in the Eclipse IDE helps you locate problematic code.

LISTING 10-2 Sample stack trace

```
c:\temp>java TestStackTrace

      Exception in thread "main"
      java.lang.ArithmeticException: / by zero
         at TestStackTrace.divideByZero(TestStackTrace.java:9)
         at TestStackTrace.<init>(TestStackTrace.java:4)
         at TestStackTrace.main(TestStackTrace.java:14)
```

Executing any Java program means running multiple threads, as explained in introduction_to_multi-threading, and the stack trace output reflects what was happening in the main thread of the simple `TestStackTrace` program.

JAVA EXCEPTIONS

In many programming languages, error processing depends on the programmer's good will and experience. Java forces a programmer to include the error-handling code for certain errors; otherwise the programs won't even compile.

Say you need to write a piece of code that reads a file containing data about customers. It's easy to foresee that unless the code includes error handling there is a chance that one day you'll see a stack trace instead of a customer list.

The creators of Java didn't want to allow this code to fail just because some programmers are too lazy to include error-handling code. Java forces you to place such code inside a `try/catch` block, as in Listing 10-3. Whenever you read or write files you have to process input/output (I/O) errors.

LISTING 10-3 Catching I/O errors

```
try {
    fileCustomer.read(); // the file may be corrupted or missing
}
catch (IOException ioe) {
    System.out.println(
           "There seems to be a problem with the file customers.");
}
```

Read the code from Listing 10-3 as follows: "Try to execute `fileCustomer.read()`, and if an error occurs, jump into the `catch` section and execute the code from there." `IOException` is a class that contains information about input/output errors.

In the case of an I/O error, the method `read()` *throws an exception* (for more details on reading files refer to Chapter 14). The `catch` block catches this error and processes it. The program doesn't terminate, and this exception is considered handled. If the method `read()` finishes successfully, the code in the *section* `catch` isn't executed.

EXCEPTION HIERARCHY

Errors in Java are represented as classes that can be divided into two major types: those that were caused by bad programming and those that were thrown because of some other external condition. For example, if a program declares a variable of type `Tax`, but this object was never instantiated, any attempts to call the (non-static) method `calcTax()` result in `NullPointerException`:

```
Tax tax;
tax.calcTax();
```

This situation could have been predicted and properly handled by the programmer.

If a runtime error can be handled programmatically, the exception is called *checked*. The method `reads()` from Listing 10-3 throws an exception and the JVM tries to find the code that handles this error. Such an exception can be anticipated and recovered from without the need to change the code. While the program remains operational, the user can find the missing file containing the list of customers and try again to populate the GUI with this list.

All exceptions are subclasses of `Throwable`, which has two immediate descendants: `Error` and `Exception`.

Subclasses of the class `Error` are fatal errors and are called *unchecked exceptions*, and are not required to be caught. You don't have to put them in `try/catch` blocks as there is not much you can do if, say, the JVM runs out of memory and crashes.

Subclasses of `Exception` (excluding `RuntimeException`) are called checked exceptions and have to be handled in your code.

You can declare and throw your own application-specific exception; for example, `LoveFailedException` or `ShipmentCreationException`.

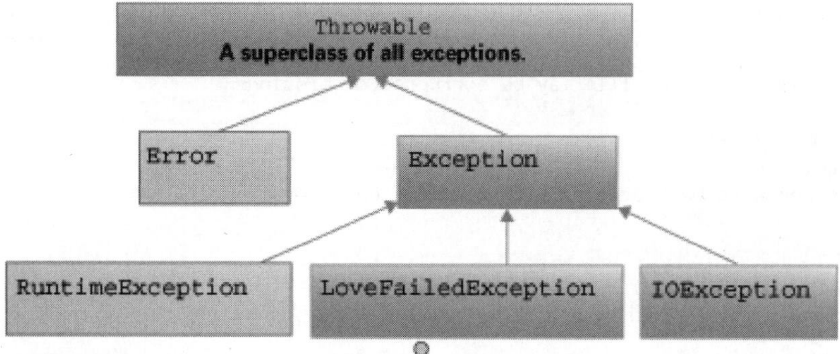

FIGURE 10-1: Figure 10.1. Sample Exceptions hierarchy with custom exception

How is a programmer supposed to know in advance if some Java method may throw a particular exception and that the `try/catch` block should therefore be used? No need to memorize anything. If a method throws an exception, the Java compiler prints an error message similar to this one:

```
"Tax.java":  unreported exception: java.io.IOException; must be
caught or declared to be thrown at line 57
```

If you see a message like this, find the description of the class method being invoked or search for the documentation for the exception itself. For example, here's the description of the java.io.IOException (`http://docs.oracle.com/javase/8/docs/api/java/io/IOException.html`). Add the appropriate try/catch block to handle this exception, as explained in the following section.

TRY/CATCH BLOCKS

There are five Java keywords that can be used for exception handling: `try`, `catch`, `finally`, `throw`, and `throws`. One `try` block can have multiple `catch` blocks, to provide handling for more than one type of error. For example, when a program tries to read a file, the file may not be there—you must catch the `FileNotFoundException`. If the file is there, but the code tries to read past the end of file, the `catch` clause for `EOFException` is necessary. Listing 10-4 illustrates a multi-`catch` block.

LISTING 10-4 One try with multiple catch statements

```
public void getCustomers() {
   try {
       fileCustomers.read();
   } catch(FileNotFoundException fileEx) {
       System.out.println("Cannot find file Customers");
```

```
        } catch(EOFException eof) {
            System.out.println("Done with file read");
        } catch(IOException ioe) {
            System.out.println("Problem reading file: " +
                                           ioe.getMessage());
        }
    }
```

The order of the `catch` statements may be important if the exceptions being caught belong to the same inheritance branch. For example, the class `EOFException` is a subclass of the more generic `IOException`, and you have to put the `catch` block for the subclass first. If you place the `catch` block for `IOException` before the one for `EOFException`, the latter block will never be reached—the end-of-file errors will be intercepted by the `IOException catch` block.

Starting from Java 7 you can catch multiple exceptions in one `catch` block. For example, the preceding code may be rewritten as follows:

```
public void getCustomers() {
   try {
       fileCustomers.read();  // may throw an error
   } catch(FileNotFoundException | EOFException | IOException ioe) {
     System.out.println("Problem reading file" + ioe.getMessage());
   } catch (Exception ex) {
     System.out.println("Exception in getCustomers:" +
                          ex.getMessage());
   }
}
```

A `catch` block receives an instance of the `Exception` object that contains a short explanation of a problem, and the method `getMessage()` of the `Exception` object returns this info. If the description of an error returned by `getMessage()` is not clear enough, try the method `Exception.toString()` instead.

If you need more detailed information about the exception, use the method `printStackTrace()` on the received `Exception` object (see Listing 10-6). It prints all internal method calls that led to this exception, as described in the section “Stack Trace” earlier in this lesson.

USING THE THROWS CLAUSE

In some cases it makes more sense to handle an exception not in the method where it happened, but in the calling one. Let’s use the same example of code that reads a file. Because the method `read()` may throw an `IOException`, you should either handle it or declare that the calling method may throw it. The latter is done in Listing 10-5.

LISTING 10-5 Using the throws clause

```
public class CustomerList {
```

```
    public void getAllCustomers() throws IOException {

        // Some other code goes here

        // Don't use try/catch if you are not handling
        // exceptions here
        file.read();
    }

    public static void main(String[] args) {
        System.out.println("Customer List");

        // Some other code goes here

        try {
            // Since getAllCustomers() declared an exception,
            // either handle it over here, or rethrow it
            // (see the throw keyword explanation below)
            getAllCustomers();
        } catch(IOException ioe) {
            System.out.println("Customer List is not available");
        }
    }
}
```

In Listing 10-5 `IOException` has been propagated from the method `getAllCustomers()` to the `main()` method, and it has been handled there.

USING THE FINALLY CLAUSE

The code can exit the `try/catch` block in several ways:

- The code inside the `try` block successfully ends and the program continues.
- The code inside the `try` block runs into a `return` statement and the program control returns to the calling method.
- The code inside the `try` block throws an exception and control goes to the `catch` block.

As you can see, in some cases only the code from the `try` block works; in some cases part of the code from the `try` block and all the code in `catch` is invoked. If there is a piece of code that must be executed regardless of the success or failure of the code in the `try` block, put it under the `finally` clause.

LISTING 10-6 Using the finally clause

```
try {
    file.read();
    // file.close();   don't close files inside try block
}
catch(Exception e) {
```

```
        e.printStackTrace();
    }
    finally {
        try {
            file.close();
        } catch(IOException ioe) {
            ioe.printStackTrace();
        }
    }
```

The code in Listing 10-6 will try to close the file regardless of the success of the `read` operation because the `close()` function is called in the `finally` block. If you had placed the `close()` function *inside* the `try` block, then when an exception was thrown, the next code to execute would be in the `catch` block, skipping the `close()` operation, which would result in resource leak, the object referred by the `file` variable would get stuck in memory for some time. As a summary, you should always use the `finally` clause for the release of system resources. To minimize the programmer's errors with unclosed resources Java introduced try-with-resources.

USING PRINTSTACKTRACE

In some of the code snippets I invoke the method `printStackTrace()` just to make the code samples short. But the `printStackTrace()` is a slow operation and it's better to extract the error message from the exception object rather than printing the entire stack trace that led to the error.

Try-With-Resources

Starting from Java 7 you can simplify the code in try/catch blocks by using *try-with-resources* syntax, which directs Java run time to automatically close resources without using the `finally` clause. You just need to open the resources in the parentheses right after the `try` keyword, and they're automatically closed. The next code fragment illustrates try-with-resources. The object `InputStream` (explained in Lesson 17) is closed automatically without the need to use `finally`.

```
InputStream myFileInputStream = null;

try (myFileInputStream = new FileInputStream("customers.txt");) {
    // the code that reads data from customers.txt goes here
} catch (Exception e) {
    e.printStackTrace();
}
```

THE AUTOCLOSABLE INTERFACE

The automatic closing works only if the resource implements `java.lang.AutoCloseable` or `java.io.Closeable` interface, which is the case with `FileInputStream (http://`

docs.oracle.com/javase/8/docs/api/java/io/FileInputStream.html). If you want to create your classes that automatically close some resources, have them implement one of these interfaces.

If you are not planning to handle exceptions in the current method, they will be propagated to the calling method. In this case you can use the `finally` clause without the `catch` clause where it would be mandatory otherwise:

```
public void myMethod() throws IOException {
    try {
        // If an exception occurs the method calling this one
        // will deal with it
        file.read();
    } finally {
        file.close();
    }
}
```

THE THROW KEYWORD

If an exception has occurred in a method, you may want to do one of the following:

1. Catch the exception.
2. Do some partial error processing (such as error logging).
3. Throw the exception to the calling method for further processing.
4. Just make the user aware of the problem.

In some cases you may want to catch an exception and handle it by throwing another exception (with modified error information) to the calling method.

The `throw` statement is used to throw Java exception objects. The object that a program throws must be `Throwable`. This means that you can throw only subclasses of the `Throwable` class and that all Java exceptions are its subclasses:

```
public class CustomerList {

    public void getAllCustomers() throws Exception {

    // some other code can go here

    try {
        file.read(); // this line may throw an exception
    } catch (IOException ioe) {

        // Log this error here, and rethrow another exception
        // with a custom error description
        throw new Exception ("Customer List is not available"+
                                         ioe.getMessage());
```

```
        }
    }

    public static void main(String[] args){
        System.out.println("Customer List");
        // some other code can go here
        try {
            // Since the getAllCustomers() declares an exception,
            // you should either handle. Rethrowing is also an
            // option unless you are in the main() method already.
            getAllCustomers();
        }
        catch(Exception e) {
            System.out.println(e.getMessage());
        }
    }
}
```

CREATING YOUR OWN EXCEPTIONS

You can also create exceptions customized to fit their business applications. Just create a class that's a subclass of one of the classes from the `Throwable` hierarchy.

Let's say you are in business of selling bikes and need to validate a customer's order. You can create a new class, `TooManyBikesException`, and throw it if someone tries to order more bikes than can fit into the store's truck. The class `BikeOrder` shown in Listing 10-7 highlights this idea.

LISTING 10-7 Creating and throwing your own exceptions

```
public class TooManyBikesException extends Exception {

    TooManyBikesException (String msgText){
        super(msgText);
    }
}

public class BikeOrder {
    ...
    public static void validateOrder(String bikeModel,
                      int quantity) throws TooManyBikesException {

        // perform some data validation, and if the entered
        // the quantity or model is invalid, do the following:

        throw new TooManyBikesException("Cannot ship" +
          quantity + "bikes of the model" + bikeModel +);
    }
}

public class OrderWindow extends JFrame {
```

```
    ...
    public void actionPerformed(ActionEvent e) {

    // the user clicked on the "Validate Order" button

    try {
        bikeOrder.validateOrder("Model-123", 50);

        // the next line will be skipped in case of exception
        txtResult.setText("Order is valid");

        } catch(TooManyBikesException e) {
            txtResult.setText(e.getMessage());
        }
    }
}
```

TooManyBikesException shown in Listing 10-8 has a unique name, and the text includes some information specific to the shipping business. But another way to provide application-specific information is to declare one or more additional variables in the custom exception. These variables can store multiple pieces of data that describe the erroneous situation.

LISTING 10-8 A custom exception with an extra property

```
public class TooManyBikesException extends Exception{

    // Declare an application-specific property
    ShippingErrorInfo shippingErrorInfo;

    TooManyBikesException(String msgText,
                          ShippingErrorInfo shippingErrorInfo) {
        super(msgText);
        this.shippingErrorInfo = shippingErrorInfo;
    }
}
```

Listing 10-8 illustrates the code that adds an application-specific object, ShippingErrorInfo, to the custom exception class TooManyBikesException. An application can prepare the object describing a shipping error and pass it as an argument to the constructor of the exception. The latter stores it in the class variable shippingInfo, and whatever method catches this exception can extract the ShippingErrorInfo object and act accordingly.

In distributed Java EE applications, an exception can travel through several tiers (such as JMS, EJB, Servlet, Swing client), and not only does having a custom property inside the exception object ensure that the valuable information isn't lost, but each tier can add more specifics to this custom property, which helps in tracing the error.

There is also a class called RemoteException, with a field called detail, that's used for reporting communication errors. You can extend this class to make remote exceptions more descriptive. This subject may be more appropriate for lessons 25 through 35 about the server-side technologies, but because this is the lesson dedicated to exceptions, I mentioned it here.

Handling programming errors is a must. Unfortunately I've seen how some of the Java developers were quietly ignoring errors. Literally, they would write an empty `catch` clause. This is the worst thing that could be done. It's like a time bomb that will definitely blow the program up one day, and finding such bombs is usually a time-consuming process. Don't cut corners; exception handling should be taken very seriously. For more details on Java exceptions refer to Oracle's tutorial at `http://bit.ly/1n03wIO`.

TRY IT

Create a Swing application for placing bike orders. It has to have a drop-down list (`JComboBox`) containing several bike models, `JTextField` for entering quantity, and `JButton` for validating the order.

Make up several combinations of bike models and quantities that throw an exception. Use the code snippets from Listing 10-7 as examples. The validation should start when the user clicks the button to validate the order.

Lesson Requirements

You should have Java installed.

> **NOTE** *You can download the code and resources for this "Try It" from the book's web page at* `www.wrox.com/go/javaprog24hr2e`. *You can find them in* `Lesson10.zip`.

Step-by-Step

1. Create a new Eclipse project called Lesson10.
2. Learn how to work with `JComboBox` at the following tutorial: `http://bit.ly/1qfPjbs`.
3. Process events and revalidate the order whenever the user selects a new bike model or changes the quantity of the order.
4. Throw and handle `TooManyBikesException` if the order can't be shipped.

> **TIP** *Please select the videos for Lesson 10 online at* `www.wrox.com/go/javaprog24hr2e`. *You will also be able to download the code and resources for this lesson from the website.*

11

Introduction to Collections

So far you've been introduced to only one way of storing a collection of objects—with Java arrays, which are good for storage but fall short when you need to dynamically add, remove, or traverse the data. There are a number of classes and interfaces in the package `java.util` that are quite handy when multiple instances of some objects (collections) have to be co-located in memory. This lesson introduces you to several of them.

You can find more collections in the `java.util.concurrent` package, but you review those in digging_deeper_into_concurrent_execution after you become familiar with the concept of multithreading. Together, the collection classes and interfaces located in `java.util` and `java.util.concurrent` are often called Java Collection Framework.

Collection classes implement different interfaces, and several are covered in this lesson. The image in Figure 11-1 is taken from Oracle Java documentation (`http://bit.ly/1kV9EAh`). It depicts the top-level core collection interfaces.

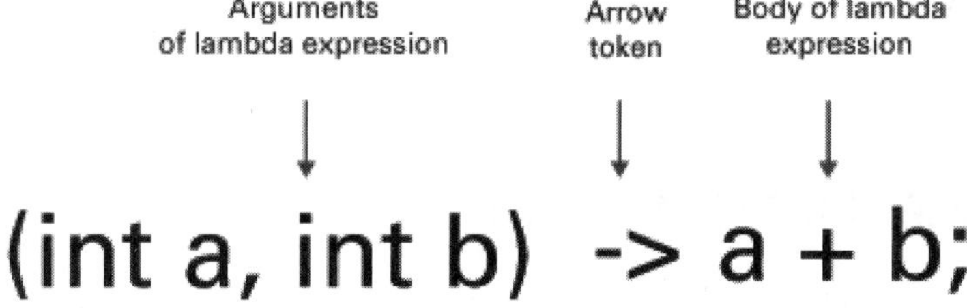

FIGURE 11-1: Figure 11-1. Core Collection Interfaces

Java 8 introduced substantial improvements in collection data manipulation, and I highlight these changes in this lesson as well as in Lesson 20.

ARRAYS REVISITED

Java collection classes enable the storing of primitives or object references in one place in memory. You were introduced to arrays in Chapter 5: Arrays let you store and access a group of variables of the same type. Let's go over the steps you follow to declare and populate an array.

First, declare a variable of the type that matches the types of the objects (or primitives) that will be stored in the array, and reserve enough memory to accommodate all objects. For example, to reserve memory enough for storing 10 instances of class `Customer` you can declare a variable `customers`, as follows:

```
Customer customers[] = new Customers[10];
```

At this point you've allocated enough space for the storage of 10 memory references, not for the actual objects. Next, create instances of the objects and store their references in the array.

```
Customer[] customers = new Customer[10];

customers[0] = new Customer("David","Lee");
customers[1] = new Customer("Ringo","Starr");
    ...
customers[9] = new Customer("Lucy","Mann");
```

Now give a 15 percent discount to all customers who spent more than $500 in the online store:

```
for (Customer c: customers){
  if (c.getTotalCharges() > 500){
      c.setDiscount(15);
  }
}
```

Note the use of the `for-each` loop here. It safely iterates through this array without trying to access elements beyond its boundaries. If a programmer forgot to check the size of the array (remember, if an array has `n` elements then the last element's index is `n - 1`) and tried to access, say, the eleventh element like `customers[10].setDiscount(15)`, Java would throw a runtime `ArrayIndexOutOfBoundsException`.

COLLECTION INTERFACES FROM *JAVA.UTIL*

A typical collection class implements several interfaces, which represent a well-designed hierarchy. For example, `ArrayList` implements the `List` interface, which extends `Collection`. For allowing a program to iterate over the collection without worrying about specific implementation of a particular collection. The interface `Collection` extends `Iterable`, so the application code can request a reference to the `Iterator` object and simply ask for the next element in the collection. You'll see an example of using `Iterator` later in this chapter.

You can use a for-each loop with classes that implement `Iterable`, and this would be external (a.k.a. imperative) iteration of a collection. But Java 8 has introduced a new and preferable way of iterating collections with

Iterable.forEach() method, which would be an internal iteration. I'll explain why internal iteration is better in Lesson 13.

The List interface is used by the ordered collections like ArrayList and LinkedList. It allows duplicate elements. For example, the following code snippet will create two elements in ArrayList:

```
myArrayList.add("Mary");
myArrayList.add("Mary");
```

The Set interface is implemented by collections that don't allow duplicate elements—for example, HashSet and SortedSet. For example, the following code snippet creates one element in HashSet. The second line finds out that Mary already exists, doesn't change it, and returns false:

```
myHashSet.add("Mary");
myHashSet.add("Mary"); // Returns false
```

The Map interface is for storing key/value pairs. A map can't contain duplicate keys, and each key can be mapped to only one value (object). You see some relevant code examples later in this lesson.

The Queue interface is mainly for collections that require first-in-first-out (FIFO) operation (so-called *priority queues* are the exception). Every new element is added to the tail of the queue and the elements are retrieved from the head of the queue. You can restrict the size of the queue if need be. LinkedList is one of the classes that implement the Queue interface.

Now let's look at some of the classes that implement these interfaces.

DYNAMIC ARRAYS WITH ARRAYLIST

Arrays offer the fastest access to the collection of data, but you have to know in advance the number of elements to be stored there. Luckily Java has classes that don't have this restriction, and you can add more elements to a collection during the run time if needed. This lesson shows you several collection classes starting from ArrayList.

Internally this collection uses an array for storage, but when you keep adding elements to ArrayList, it increases (by small increments) the size of the underlying array. Correspondingly, as elements are deleted, this collection shrinks in size. You can store duplicate objects in ArrayList.

ArrayList implements the List interface and can store only objects; primitives are not allowed. Having said this, keep in mind that Java supports autoboxing (see Chapter 3), and if you try to add a primitive to a collection, it is automatically converted into the corresponding wrapper object. You have to pay a price for this convenience; ArrayList is a little slower than the array as it needs to do internal copying from one array to another to change the collection's size.

To create and populate an ArrayList object you should first instantiate it, and then you add instances of other objects to the ArrayList by calling the method add(), as in Listing 11-1.

LISTING 11-1 Populating ArrayList

```
ArrayList customers = new ArrayList();
Customer customer1 = new Customer("David","Lee");
customers.add(customer1);
Customer customer2 = new Customer("Ringo","Starr");
customers.add(customer2);
```

The method `add()` doesn't copy the instance of the object into the `customers` collection, it just stores the memory address of the object being added. The element numbering in `ArrayList` starts with `0`. If you know that an `ArrayList` will store, say, 20 objects, instantiate it with the constructor that allocates the right amount of memory on creation:

```
ArrayList customers = new ArrayList(20);
```

You can still add more than 20 elements, but JVM allocates additional memory as needed. The method `get()` is used to extract a particular element from `ArrayList`. Because `ArrayList` is generic storage for any type of object, the method `get()` returns elements as `Object` data types. It's the responsibility of the programmer to provide proper casting, such as the following:

```
Customer theBestCustomer =  (Customer) customers.get(1);
```

To illustrate a possible runtime error that will occur if the casting was not properly done, add an object of another type to your `customers` collection from Listing 11-1:

```
Order order = new Order(123, 500, "IBM");
customers.add(order);
```

The Java compiler does not complain because `ArrayList` can store any objects. At this point you have the elements in `customers`—two customers and one order. The following code throws the `IllegalCastException` on the third iteration of the loop:

```
int totalElem = customers.size(); // number of elements
for (int i = 0; i < totalElem; i++){
  Customer currentCustomer = (Customer) customers.get(i);
  currentCustomer.doSomething();
}
```

Listing 11-2 shows how the operator `instanceof` helps you avoid this exception. But before using `instanceof`, see if you can come up with a more elegant solution, as you learned to do in the section "Polymorphism" in Chapter 7. In Lesson 12 you'll learn how to use generics, which allow to remove the need of using `instanceof` and in particular control during the compilation time which objects can be added to a collection.

LISTING 11-2 ArrayList and instanceof

```
ArrayList customers = new ArrayList(3);

// The code to populate customers with instances of
// Customer and Order objects is omitted for brevity

int totalElem = customers.size();

// Iterate through the list customers and do something with each
// element of this collection

for (int i=0; i<totalElem;i++){
  Object currentElement = customers.get(i);
  if (currentElement instanceof Customer){
    Customer currentCustomer= (Customer)customers.get(i);
    currentCustomer.doSomething();
  }
  else if (currentElement instanceof Order){
    Order currentOrder = (Order) customers.get(i);
    currentOrder.doSomething();
  }
}
```

In the section Programming to Interfaces I'll show you what has to be changed in the declaration of the variable `customers`.

ARRAYLIST AND CONCURRENT ACCESS

In Lesson 17 you learn about concurrent access to the data from multiple threads. If the data is stored in an `ArrayList`, you may run into concurrency issues (*race condition*). To prevent this from happening, you can turn on synchronization by invoking the method `Collections.synchronizedList()` on an `ArrayList` object.

PROGRAMMING TO INTERFACES

In this section code samples start with declaring a variable of type `ArrayList`; for example:

```
ArrayList customers = new ArrayList(3);
```

While this code is correct, there a better way of declaring the variable `customers`:

```
List customers = new ArrayList(3);
```

You can read the first example as follows: "I want to declare a variable `customers` that will have all access to all API offered by the class `ArrayList`." The second version means the following: "I want to declare a variable `customers` that has a behavior declared in the `List` interface".

The first example declares a variable of a specific implementation— `ArrayList`—of the `List` interface.

`ArrayList` implements several interfaces besides `List`, which means that it has more methods that the `List` defines. But if you read the documentation (`http://docs.oracle.com/javase/8/docs/api/java/util/List.html`) on the `List` interface, you'll see that among others it includes the methods as `add()`, `get()`, and `size()`, which are the only ones used with our collection `customers`. If this is all we need, declaring a variable `customers` of type `List` gives us more flexibility. If later we decide to switch to a different implementation of the List (e.g., `LinkedList` instead of `ArrayList`) we won't need to change the type of the variable `customers`.

You may say that changing a variable declaration from `ArrayList` to `LinkedList` it's not a big deal—it's still the same line of code. But it may be a bigger deal if, say, your program needs to pass the object referred by `customers` to another object's method that also was declared with the argument of type `ArrayList`. Now we need to make changes in two places. In large projects such a refactoring may become a time-consuming process.

If you just need a behavior defined in a particular interface, declare the variable of this interface type rather than of a concrete implementation of this interface.

CLASSES HASHTABLE AND HASHMAP

The classes `Hashtable` and `HashMap` implement the `Map` interface and stores key/value pairs. These classes offer a convenient way of storing and accessing the elements of a collection by key. You can assign a key to an instance of some Java object and use it as a reference. Let's say you need to store instances of the classes `Customer`, `Order`, and `Portfolio` in the same collection. The code snippet from Listing 11-3 creates these instances first, and then puts them in the collection under some identifiers (keys).

LISTING 11-3 Hashtable for key/value pairs

```
Customer customer = new Customer("David", "Lee");
Order order = new Order(123, 500, "IBM");
Portfolio portfolio = new Portfolio(123);

Map data = new Hashtable();  // programming to interfaces
data.put("Customer", customer);
data.put("Order",order);
data.put("Portfolio", portfolio);
```

The values in double quotes represent keys by which the objects could be retrieved. In this example the keys are represented by the Java class `String`, but you can use any objects as keys. The keys are selected based on the application needs; for example, the code in Listing 11-3 could be written in some order management application.

If you have an idea of how many elements you are planning to store in a `Hashtable`, use the constructor with the capacity argument:

```
Hashtable data = new Hashtable(10); // 10-element capacity
```

The method `get()` provides access to these objects via the key. You need to either perform the proper casting as shown in the following code or use *generics* (explained in Chapter 12):

```
Order myOrder = (Order) data.get("Order");
```

The method `size()` returns the number of elements in the `Hashtable`:

```
int totalElem = data.size();
```

Methods `containsKey()` and `containsValue()` help you to find out if the collection contains a specific key or value.

The class `HashMap` is similar to `Hashtable`, but it allows `null` as a key or value and is not *synchronized* (explained in Lesson 19). If you are writing code that doesn't need to access the same element concurrently without using multithreading, use `HashMap` because it performs faster than `Hashtable`. If you do need concurrent access, the other alternative to `Hashtable` is `ConcurrentHashMap`.

To speed up the table lookup, both `HashMap` and `Hashtable` index the data by applying a *hash function* that (based on the contents of the object) generates a *hash code*, one number that represents a large object. There's a slight chance that two different objects will generate the same hash code, but the same object always produces the same hash code. You can read more about hash functions in Wikipedia at `http://en.wikipedia.org/wiki/Hash_function`.

THE JAVA.UTIL.COLLECTIONS CLASS

The class `java.util.Collections` consists of useful static methods that work with collection classes; for example, `sort()`, `reverse()`, `swap()`, and more.

Class Properties

Pretty often a desktop application offers you a way to specify and store user preferences such as fonts and colors. This is a use case in which storage of key/value pairs is exactly what's needed. You can store such preferences locally or on remote servers. In Chapter 14 you find out how to work with files and other I/O streams, but from a data structure perspective you'll be dealing with a collection of key/value pairs, such as *color=red, font=verdana*.

Windows-based applications often store some configurable parameters in the `.ini` files. In general, Java applications store their properties in plain text files, XML files, database tables, and others.

In this section you see some code fragments illustrating how the Java class `Properties`, which extends `Hashtable`, can be used to manipulate with properties using key/value pairs. The class `Properties` has one restriction that `Hashtable` does not. For example, if you'd need to write a program that sends e-mails, you can store the URL of the mail server and from/to addresses from the `mailman.properties` file, which has the following contents:

```
SmtpServer=mail.xyz.com
to=abc@xyz.com
cc=mary@xyz.com
from=yakov@xyz.com
```

To load this file into the `Properties` object, just define an input I/O stream on this file (see Chapter 14) and call the method `load()`, as shown in Listing 11-4. After the file has been loaded into the `Properties` object, each individual property can be obtained with the method `getProperty()`.

LISTING 11-4 Reading file mailman.properties into the Properties object

```
Properties properties=new Properties();
FileInputStream in =null;
try{
  in = new FileInputStream ("mailman.properties");
  properties.load(in);
}catch(Exception e){...}
finally{... in.close();...}

String from = properties.getPropery("from");
String mailServer=properties.getProperty("SmtpServer");
...
```

Java does not have global variables, but as a workaround you can make these properties available to any object in your application by turning them into system properties available from any class in your application:

```
System.setProperties(properties);
```

Keep in mind that the preceding line also replaces the existing system properties, which you may or may not want to do. Now you can get these values from any other class in your application; for example:

```
String mailServer = System.getProperty("SmtpServer");
```

If you decide to store properties in XML files, the class `Properties` offers you the method `loadFromXML()` to read properties and the method `storeToXML()` to store them in a simple XML format.

You see a practical example of using the `Properties` class in Lesson 29 while learning about Java Naming and Directory Interface (JNDI).

CLASSES ENUMERATION AND ITERATOR

In general, enumerations are sets of items that are related to each other. For example, shipment options or ice cream flavors—such enumerations are supported by the Java keyword `enum` (see Chapter 17). But because we are talking about collections, the meaning of the term *enumeration* is somewhat different. If a collection object implements the interface `Enumeration`, you can traverse its elements sequentially, without even knowing the total number. You just need to obtain the enumeration of all elements and use the methods `hasMoreElements()` and `nextElement()`. For example, to process all elements of `ArrayList` `customers` you can do the following:

```
Enumeration enumCustomers = Collections.enumeration(customers);
while(enumCustomer.hasMoreElements()){
  Customer currentCustomer = (Customer)enumCustomer.nextElement());
  currentCustomer.doSomething();
}
```

You can also obtain the enumeration of a `Hashtable`'s keys or elements. For example:

```
Hashtable customerData = new Hashtable();

// Get the keys
Enumeration enumKeys = customerData.keys();
while(enumKeys.hasMoreElements()){
  // do some keys processing
}
// Get the elements
Enumeration enumElements = customerData.elements();
// do some customer objects processing
```

The `Iterator` interface is `Enumeration` on steroids. It also offers a standard way to process elements of a collection sequentially. The main difference between the two is that `Enumeration` is a read-only means of traversing a collection, whereas `Iterator` has a method called `remove()` that enables you to delete unwanted elements of the collection. `Enumeration` is considered a legacy interface, and you should use `Iterator`. For example, you can iterate through the `ArrayList` `customers` as follows:

```
Iterator iCust = customers.iterator();
while (iCust.hasNext()){
   System.out.println(iCust.next())
}
```

CLASS LINKEDLIST

Java collection classes differ in how you can retrieve and insert objects. If you need to work with a sequential list of objects and often insert (remove) the object into (from) the list, the data structure called *linked list* can fit the bill.

Linked lists store elements so that each contains a reference to the next one. *Doubly linked lists* also contain a reference to both the next and the previous elements. Java includes the the doubly linked class

`LinkedList`, which enable you to create the data structures known as *queues* (first-in-first-out or FIFO) and *stacks* (last-in-first-out or LIFO).

Insertion of a new object inside the list comes down to a simple update of two references: The previous element of the list has to be pointed to the newly inserted object, which has to include a reference to the next element, if any. Compare this to the complexity of lots of memory allocations and objects moving in memory to increase the size of an `ArrayList`, and you'll appreciate the value that linked lists bring to the table. On the other hand, collections that use arrays for the underlying data storage offer random access to the data elements, whereas linked lists can be processed only sequentially.

You can navigate through the list using the class `ListIterator`, which supports going through the list in both directions via its methods `next()` and `previous()`. Listing 11-5 shows you an example, in which a standby passenger list is created at the boarding gate of some airline company.

LISTING 11-5 LinkedList example

```
import java.util.LinkedList;
import java.util.ListIterator;
public class TestLinkedList {

 public static void main(String[] args) {
   LinkedList passengerList = new LinkedList();
   passengerList.add("Alex Smith");
   passengerList.add("Mary Lou");
   passengerList.add("Sim Monk");

   ListIterator iterator = passengerList.listIterator();
   System.out.println(iterator.next());
   System.out.println(iterator.next());
   System.out.println(iterator.next());
  }
}
```

The code in Listing 11-5 iterates and prints all the objects from the list using `ListIterator` interface, which allows a program to traverse the list in both directions.

You might be wondering how the `println()` method knows how to print an object returned by the iterator. It tries to find the method `toString()` defined on the object and call it. In our example the object is a string itself, but in a real-world situation you might need to print objects, and defining the `toString()` method is the right way to do so.

If you use `add()` or `remove()` while iterating through the list, the new element is either inserted or removed at the iterator's current position.

CLASS BITSET

The class `BitSet` stores a sequence of bits. It's a pretty efficient class when you need to pass to a program a number of flags that indicate certain conditions. Think of a financial trading application that must be extremely fast. One way to improve the performance is to represent the maximum amount of information in a minimal number of bytes.

Another use case for `BitSet` are programs that send signals with information about the state of a certain device or as sensor. For example, some vending machines have smart chips that can automatically dial their owner's phone number and send a signal containing status information. Sending a set of flags (bits that are set to `1` or `0`) instead of text or numbers is the most economical way to do this.

The `BitSet` class does not have a size limit and can grow as needed. Depending on which bit is set (for example, has the value of `1`) the class could indicate the following:

- **Bit 0**: The coin box is empty.
- **Bit 1**: The coin box is half full.
- **Bit 2**: The coin box is full.
- **Bit 3**: The coin box has been removed.
- **Bit 4**: The Coca-Cola row is empty.

One instance of a `BitSet` object carries multiple parameters describing its status. The program that receives this signal could print a nice report, and the owner of this remote machine could decide if he or she needs to send a technician to look at the machine.

The Java class `BitSet` is nothing more than a collection of bits. The following code prepares a signal indicating that the coin box is full and there are no Coca-Cola bottles left:

```
import java.util.BitSet;
class VendingMachineSender {
   public static void main(String args[]){
       BitSet report = new BitSet();
       report.set(2);   // box is full
       report.set(4);   // no Coca-Cola
   }
}
```

When the phone call comes in, the callback method `phoneRinging()` is invoked and the signal can be decoded like this:

```
import java.util.BitSet;
class VendingMachineListener {
   public void phoneRinging(BitSet signal)
      int size = signal.size();

      for (int i=0;i<size;i++){
          if (signal.get(i)){
            switch (i){
               case 0:
```

```
                System.out.println("Box is empty");
                break;
              case 1:
                System.out.println("Box is half full");
                break;
              case 2:
                System.out.println("Box is full");
                break;
              // more cases come here
            }
          }
        }
      }
    }
```

INTERNET OF THINGS

The Internet Of Things (IoT) is a buzzword that's used to describe Internet applications that deal with small, sensor-like devices, which have a limited amount of memory and processing power. Consider using the class `BitSet` if you need to program sensors.

CHOOSING THE RIGHT COLLECTION

Java has dozens of collection classes and interfaces. In this lesson I've shown just a few of them. But which collection is the right one for your needs? Below are some of the considerations that may help you to choose one.

- If you need to access data by index, consider using `ArrayList`.
- If you need to often insert or remove data in/from a collection, a `LinkedList` should be a good choice
- If you need a collection that doesn't allow duplicate elements, use one of the collections that implements `Set` interface. For fast access use `HashSet`. For sorted set use `TreeSet`.
- For storing key/value pairs use a collection that implements the `Map` interface; e.g. `HashMap` or `HashTable`.
- If you need a collection for a fast search that remains fast regardless of the size of the data set use `HashSet`.

These recommendations are applicable for cases when there is no need to access data concurrently by multiple threads (see Lesson 17). Java has many concurrent collections (`http://docs.oracle.com/javase/tutorial/essential/concurrency/collections.html`) located in the package `java.util.concurrent`, and these collections have to be used for concurrent data access. Oracle's Collections tutorial (`http://docs.oracle.com/javase/tutorial/collections/`) and Java API on collection classes is a good resource for finding the right collection for your application.

> **THE BIG O NOTATION**
>
> In computing there is something called *Big O notation* (`http://en.wikipedia.org/wiki/Big_O_notation`), which describes how the time to do a certain thing grows when the size of the input data grows. The Big O notation is represented as O(n). The higher value of n represents greater dependency of the task from the data size. Hence O(1) means that the speed of a task doesn't depend on the collection size. The article on Performance of Java Collections (`http://infotech-gems.blogspot.com/2011/11/java-collections-performance-time.html`) includes Big O notations for various Java collections and operations.

TRY IT

Modify the `LinkedList` example from Listing 11-5 to add an arbitrary object, say, the VIP customer after the very first element of the list. You must do this while iterating through the list. When the program is ready it should print the following:

```
Alex Smith
VIP Customer
Mary Lou
Sim Monk
```

Lesson Requirements

You should have Java installed.

> **NOTE** *You can download the code and resources for this "Try It" from the book's web page at* `www.wrox.com/go/javaprog24hr2e`. *You can find them in the* `Lesson11.zip`.

Step-by-Step

1. Create a new Eclipse project called Lesson11.
2. After the first call to `iterator.next()` add the following line: `iterator.add("VIP Customer");`
3. Run the program and observe that it doesn't print "VIP Customer." This happens because the iterator is already positioned after the newly inserted object.
4. Add the line `iterator.previous()` right after the "VIP Customer" to move the iterator one element back.
5. Add one more print statement (otherwise the program won't reach Sim Monk). Compile and run the program. It prints all four elements as requested.

6. Now break the code by changing the line that you added in Step 2 to `passengerList.add("VIP Customer");`.
7. Run the program. It prints the first element of the linked list and then produces a runtime exception:

```
Alex Smith
Exception in thread "main"
     java.util.ConcurrentModificationException
     at java.util.LinkedList$ListItr.checkForComodification(
               LinkedList.java:761)
     at java.util.LinkedList$ListItr.next(LinkedList.java:696)
     at TestLinkedList.main(TestLinkedList.java:20)
```

The reason for this concurrent modification exception is that one *thread of execution* was iterating through a collection, and at the same time another thread was trying to modify the underlying collection in an unsafe way. The concept of threads is introduced in Chapter 17.

> **TIP** *Please select the videos for Lesson 11 online at* `www.wrox.com/go/javaprog24hr2e`. *You will also be able to download the code and resources for this lesson from the website.*

12

Introduction to Generics

In the previous lesson you saw an example of a collection that stores objects of different types (see Listing 11-2). During the run time, that program would test the actual type of each object and cast it to an appropriate type—`Customer` or `Order`. If some code adds an element of another (unexpected) data type, this will result in a casting error, `ClassCastException`. Instead of leaving it until run time, it would be nice if during the compilation the compiler would prevent using unexpected types with collection, objects, or even method arguments and return types.

Java supports *generics*, which enable you to use parameterized data types—you can declare an object, collection, or method without specifying a concrete data type, shifting the definition of concrete types to the code that will use these objects, collections, or methods. In other words, a generic type is one that can work with parameterized data types.

PARAMETERIZED CLASSES

Not only Java methods can accept parameters (also known as arguments), but classes can have them as well. I'll show you how to do it in the section on custom parameterized classes.

By using generic notation, you get help from Java compiler, which does not allow you to use objects of the "wrong" types that don't match the declaration. In other words, you can catch improper data types earlier, during the compilation phase. This concept is easier to explain by examples, and so we'll get right into it.

GENERICS WITH CLASSES

Consider the `ArrayList` from Listing 11-2, which is a kitchen sink–like storage that can hold pretty much any object. But if you add the parameterized type `Customer` in angle brackets (`ArrayList<Customer>`) to the declaration of the `customers` collection (see Listing 12-1), any attempt to place an `Order` object there generates the following compiler error:

```
The method add(Customer) in the type ArrayList<Customer> is not
applicable for the arguments (Order).
```

Think of it this way: `ArrayList` can be used to store any objects, and using generics enables you to put a constraint on the types of objects allowed in a specific instance of `ArrayList`. This is an example of a parameterized class, which is just one use for generics.

LISTING 12-1 Using generics in the collection

```
import java.util.List;
import java.util.ArrayList;

public class TestGenericCollection {

        public static void main(String[] args) {

            List<Customer> customers = new ArrayList<>();

            Customer customer1 = new Customer("David","Lee");
            customers.add(customer1);
            Customer customer2 = new Customer("Ringo","Starr");
            customers.add(customer2);

            Order order = new Order();

            customers.add(order); // Compiler error
        }
}
```

Getting an error during compilation is better than getting runtime cast exceptions. Note the empty angle brackets in the preceding example. Those are called the *diamond operator*—you don't need to repeat `<Customer>` on the right because this type has been specified already on the left. As a refresher, I've been using the List interface to declare the variable customers as explained in the previous lesson in the section "Programming to Interfaces."

What makes the `ArrayList` class capable of rejecting the unwanted data types? Open the source code of the `ArrayList` itself (pressing F3 in Eclipse shows the source code of any class or interface, if available). It starts as follows:

```
public class ArrayList<E> extends AbstractList<E>
    implements List<E>, RandomAccess, Cloneable, Serializable
```

This magic `<E>` after the class name tells the Java compiler that this class can use some types of elements, but which ones remains unknown until a concrete instance of `ArrayList` is created. In Listing 12-1, the *type parameter* `<Customer>` replaces `<E>` during compilation, and the compiler ensures that the code stores only instances of `Customer` objects in the collection `customers`.

TYPE ERASURE

I'd like to stress that this <E> notation is used only during the declaration of the type. The code in Listing 12-1 does not include <E>. The compiler replaces <E> with `Customer` and erases the parameterized data type in the byte code. This process is known as *type erasure;* it's primarily done for compatibility with code written in older versions of Java that didn't have generics. The generated byte code is the same with parameterized and with *raw* data types.

Now you can simplify the code from Listing 11-2 by removing casting (see Listing 12-2). Why? Because with generics, when the compiler sees a specific type, it automatically generates the bytecode, which performs casting internally! That's why you don't even need to cast the data returned by the method `get(i)` from `Object` to `Customer` any longer. Besides, you're guaranteed that the collection `customers` will have only `Customer` instances. Java compiler has the ability to look at the method invocation and properly guess the type of the argument. It's called *type inference* (*http://docs.oracle.com/javase/tutorial/java/generics/genTypeInference.html*). It's used not only with generics, but with lambda expressions as well, which will be covered in Lesson 13.

LISTING 12-2 Iterating through customers without casting

```
List<Customer> customers = new ArrayList<>();

// The code to populate customers is omitted for brevity

// Iterate through the list customers and do something with each
// element of this collection. No casting required.

for (Customer customer: customers){
    customer.doSomething();
}
```

RAW TYPES

Using the parameterized `ArrayList` in this example is not a must. You can still write the following:

```
List customers = new ArrayList();
```

The compiler gives you a warning that `ArrayList` is a raw type and should be parameterized. This basically means that compiler won't help you if you add to this collection an object of a type that might blow up in some other place in the program. While using raw types is not an error, it should be avoided.

DECLARING GENERICS

If you'll be creating your own class for storing objects, you can use any letter(s) in angle brackets to declare that your class will use parameterized types. You can use any letters to represent parameterized types, but traditionally developers use `<E>` for *element,* `<T>` for *type,* `<K>` for *keys,* `<V>` for *value,* and so on. The letter is replaced by a concrete type during concrete variable declaration. Open the source code of the Java class `Hashtable`, and you see `<K,V>`, which stands for *key* and *value*:

```
public class Hashtable<K,V> extends Dictionary<K,V>
    implements Map<K,V>, Cloneable, Serializable
```

Again, what types are used for storing keys and values is decided when the `Hashtable` is being declared. You can use a parameterized type for declaring variables wherever you can use regular data types. Listing 12-3 shows a fragment from the source code of the interface `java.util.List`. This interface declaration uses `<E>` as a data type.

LISTING 12-3 Fragment from java.util.List interface

```
package java.util;

public interface List<E> extends Collection<E> {

    Iterator<E> iterator();
    <T> T[] toArray(T[] a);
    boolean add(E e);
    boolean containsAll(Collection<?> c);
    boolean addAll(Collection<? extends E> c);
    boolean addAll(int index, Collection<? extends E> c);
    boolean removeAll(Collection<?> c);
    E set(int index, E element);
    void add(int index, E element);
    ListIterator<E> listIterator();
    ListIterator<E> listIterator(int index);
    List<E> subList(int fromIndex, int toIndex);
}
```

WILDCARDS

Listing 12-3 contains question marks that represent unknown types. It's easier to explain them with an example. Let's turn the `for` loop from Listing 12-2 into a method. In Eclipse, highlight the code of the `for` loop, right-click, and select Refactor → Extract Method. In the pop-up window enter the method name `processCustomers` and click OK.

LISTING 12-4 Refactored class TestGenericCollection

```
import java.util.ArrayList;
import java.util.Hashtable;
import java.util.List;

public class TestGenericCollection {

       public static void main(String[] args) {

         List<Customer> customers = new ArrayList<Customer>();
         Customer customer1 = new Customer("David","Lee");
         customers.add(customer1);
         Customer customer2 = new Customer("Ringo","Starr");
         customers.add(customer2);
         Order order = new Order();
         //customers.add(order); // Compiler error

         // Iterate through the list customers and do something
         // with each element of this collection.
         // No casting required.

         processData(customers);
       }

       private static void processData(List<Customer> customers){
              for (Customer customer: customers){
                    customer.doSomething();
              }
       }
}
```

What if you want to make the method `processData()` more generic and useful not only for a collection of `Customer` objects but for others, too? Without generics you'd be using `instanceof` and writing something similar to Listing 12-5.

LISTING 12-5 Back to casting

```
private static void processData(ArrayList data) {

    for (Object object: data){
       if(object instanceof Customer){
          ((Customer) object).doSomething();
       }
    }
}
```

But now, armed with the new knowledge, you can try to change the signature of the method `processData()` to the following:

```
private static void processData(List<Object> data){
  // do something with data
}
```

Unfortunately, this solution won't work, because there is no such thing as inheritance of parameterized types. In other words, even though the class `Customer` is a subclass of `Object`, such inheritance does not apply to parameters `<Customer>` and `<Object>`. This is when the question mark that represents an unknown type becomes handy. The next step in making `processData()` more generic is to change the method signature like so:

```
private static void processData(List<?> data){
   // do something with data
}
```

Using such a method signature is different from simply declaring the method argument data of type `List`, which would require casting, as in Listing 12-5. With the wildcard notation you state, "At this point the type of data is not known, but whenever some code uses the method `processData()` it'll be known and properly compiled so casting won't be needed."

The next challenge you face is to compile the code calling the method `doSomething()` on the objects of unknown types.

CREATING CUSTOM PARAMETERIZED CLASSES

Let's consider an example with the bike store from the "Try It" section for Lesson 10. That online store has a truck that's used to deliver bikes and, say, spare wheels for customers. We want to allow only bikes and wheels to be loaded into the truck; people are not allowed there. Consider the class hierarchy in Figure 12-1:

An object of type `Truck` can contain instances of `Product`. The object `Ferry` can contain `Truck` instances. The classes `Product`, `Bike`, `Wheel`, and `Person` don't implement any business logic in this small application as it's irrelevant for understanding generic types. But the fact that `Product` is a superclass of `Bike` and `Model` is important. The parameterized class `Truck` can look as follows:

```
public class Truck<T> {

    private List<T> products = new ArrayList<>();

    // load the product on the truck
    public void add (T t){
        products.add(t);
    }

    // Return products loaded on the truck
    public List<T> getProducts(){
        return products;
    }
```

```
}
```

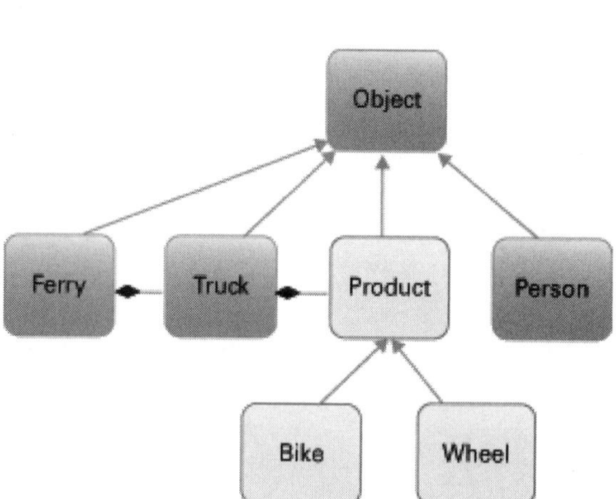

FIGURE 12-1: Figure 12-1. The bike store class hierarchy

This declaration uses a parameter of type T that's unknown at this point yet. You specify a concrete type when you create a program that instantiates `Truck`; for example:

```
public class TestGenericType {

    public static void main(String[] args) {

        Truck<Product> shipment = new Truck<>();

        Bike bike = new Bike();
        Wheel wheel = new Wheel();
        Person person = new Person();

        shipment.add(bike);
        shipment.add(wheel);
     // shipment.add(person); // Compiler error
    }
}
```

The variable `shipment` points at the instance of the `Truck` that allows adding only the objects of type `Product` or its subclasses. Because `Person` is not a `Product`, the compiler won't let you add it to the `Truck` load.

BOUNDED TYPE PARAMETERS

Bounded type parameters enable you to specify generic types with restrictions related to class inheritance hierarchies. Let's continue using the same example of a bike store. Although `Product` is a superclass of a `Bike`, `ArrayList<Product>` is not a superclass of `ArrayList<Bike>`. Hence, if there is a method that expects `ArrayList<Product>` as an argument, you can't provide `ArrayList<Bike>` instead. With generics, you should use the keyword `extends` to specify the upper bound of allowed types in the inheritance hierarchy. In this case it would be `ArrayList<? extends Product>`. This means that only `ArrayList` containing object of `Product` type and its subclasses are allowed. The question mark is a wildcard here.

To illustrate this, let's change the rules in our bike store: You can't mix bikes and wheels in the same truck. Also, you want to be able to load trucks on a ferry. The class `Ferry` looks like the following:

```
public class Ferry {

  public void loadTruck(Truck<? extends Product> truck){ }

  public void unloadToDock(List<? extends Product> ferryTrucks,
                           List<? super Product> dockTrucks){

      for (Product product: ferryTrucks){
          dockTrucks.add(product);
      }
  }
}
```

The method `loadTruck()` declares the argument with the *upper bounded wildcard*—only the trucks with `Product` and its subclasses can be loaded to the ferry. The class `TestGenericBounded` creates one truck loaded with two bikes, and another one loaded with three wheels. Then it loads both trucks on the ferry.

```
public class TestGenericBounded {

    public static void main(String[] args) {

        Ferry ferry = new Ferry();

        // Load a truck with two bikes
        Truck<Bike> bikes = new Truck<>();
        bikes.add(new Bike());
        bikes.add(new Bike());

        // Load a truck with three wheels
        Truck<Wheel> wheels = new Truck<>();
        wheels.add(new Wheel());
        wheels.add(new Wheel());
        wheels.add(new Wheel());

        // Load two trucks on the ferry
        ferry.loadTruck(bikes);
        ferry.loadTruck(wheels);
    }
}
```

If the ferry's `loadTruck()` method would be declared as `loadTruck(Truck<Product> truck)`, you wouldn't be able to load either the truck with bikes or the one with wheels.

The class `Ferry` also has the method `unloadToDock()` that illustrates lower bounded wildcards by using the keyword `super`.

```
public void unloadToDock(List<? extends Product> ferryTrucks,
                         List<? super Product> dockTrucks){
    for (Product product : ferryTrucks){
        dockTrucks.add(product);
    }
}
```

Note the `super` keyword here. You are copying the data from a collection that can contain any subclasses of `Product` into another one. Revisit the class hierarchy diagram and think of a standard Java upcasting. The destination collection can be of a type of any class that the `Product` extends from (for example, of type `Object`). Moreover, you may introduce yet another class located between `Object` and `Product` in the inheritance hierarchy—this won't break the code. The keyword `super` means exactly this; the destination collection can hold any types as long as they are superclasses of `Product`.

There is a simple *in-out* rule that may help you to figure out if you need to use `extends` or `super` keywords. If you're creating a parameterized class to read data from it, use `extends`. If you are planning to put or copy data into a parameterized class, use `super`.

GENERIC METHODS

While declaring a method you can either predefine data types for its arguments and return values or use generics. For example, the method `toArray()` from Listing 12-3 starts with a declaration of a new parameterized type (<T> in that case), which has to be placed in angle brackets right before the return type in the method signature. The very fact that a method declares a new type makes it generic. The following declaration of the `toArray()` method takes an array of objects of type T and returns an array of T objects:

```
<T> T[] toArray(T[] a);
```

Figure 12-2 explains the above line in greater details.

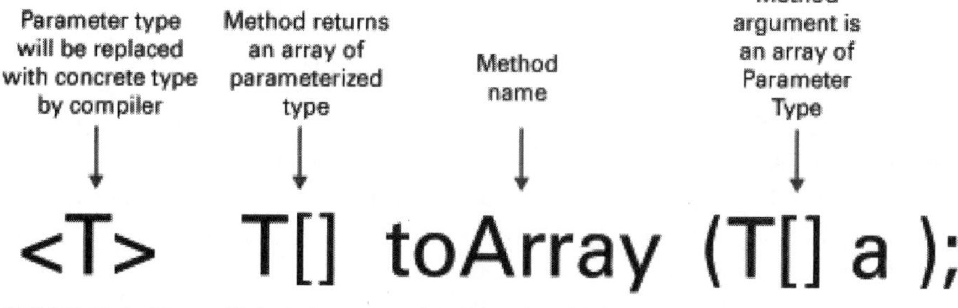

FIGURE 12-2: Figure 12-2. A signature of a generic method

If you have an `ArrayList` of integers, you can declare and convert it to an array as follows:

```
List<Integer> myNumericList = new ArrayList<>();
...
Integer myNumericArray[] = new Integer[myNumericList.size()];
myNumericArray = myNumericList.toArray();
```

If you need to use the same method `toArray()` with a list of customers, the data type `<T>` magically transforms (by compiler) into the `Customer` type:

```
List<Customer> myCustomerList = new ArrayList<Customer>();
...
Customer myCustomerArray[] = new Customer[myCustomerList.size()];
myCustomerArray = myCustomerList.toArray();
```

As in examples from the "Bounded Type Parameters" section, you are allowed to put constraints on the type. For example, you can restrict the `toArray()` method to work only with types that implement the `Comparable` interface:

```
<T extends Comparable> T[] toArray(T[] a);
```

TRY IT

Create a simple program that uses generics with the class `RetiredEmployee` (which extends the class `Employee`) from Listing 7-2. Write a generic method that accepts a collection of `RetiredEmployee` objects and copies it into a collection of `Employee` objects. Use the method `unloadToDock()` from class `Ferry` as an example.

Lesson Requirements

You should have Java installed.

> **NOTE** *You can download the code and resources for this "Try It" from the book's web page at* `www.wrox.com/go/javaprog24hr2e`. *You can find them in* `Lesson12.zip`.

Step-by-Step

1. Create a new Eclipse project called Lesson12.
2. Create classes `Employee` and then `RetiredEmployee` that extends `Employee`.
3. Create an executable Java class, `TestGenericMethod`, that accepts a `List` of `RetiredEmployee` objects and copies it into a `List` of `Employee` objects. This method should print on the system console the name of each `Employee` from the resulting collection.
4. Run the `TestGenericMethod` program and observe the printed names.

> **TIP** *Please select the videos for Lesson 12 online at* `www.wrox.com/go/javaprog24hr2e`. *You will also be able to download the code and resources for this lesson from the website.*

13

Lambda Expressions and Functional Style Programming

Presenting materials of this chapter is somewhat challenging. From the beginning of this book you've gotten to know that Java is an object-oriented language (as opposed to a functional language). You've learned that to start any program you'll need to define classes with attributes and methods, instantiate them as objects, and invoke methods (think functions) on these instances. If a method is declared as `static`, you can invoke it without the need to instantiate a class, but still you were defining the class first and then a static method inside of it. For example, to process a click on a Swing `JButton`, you would need to implement and instantiate a listener class containing just one method `actionPerformed()`.

Now I need to tell you that the object-oriented approach may have some drawbacks, and there is a large group of functional programming languages (`http://en.wikipedia.org/wiki/List_of_programming_languages_by_type#Functional_languages`) in which you don't need to wrap functionality inside classes. Proponents of functional languages say (and rightly so) that creating objects with fields that can be changed (*mutated*) by the methods' code may be error prone and more difficult to debug. They prefer thinking in terms of functions that don't depend on the external context.

A function takes the values from the outside world in the form of arguments, apply some application logic and returns the result. A function doesn't change any external values (including those that were provided as arguments). A function can take a single value (or a data collection) and produce another value, but doesn't modify the input. So no matter how many times you'll be invoking any given function with the same input, the returned value will be the same.

In languages such as Haskell, JavaScript, Scala, Closure, and Ruby, functions are treated as first-class citizens, and they don't require you to write and instantiate classes. In functional languages, you can do the following:

- Assign a function to a variable.
- Pass a function as an argument to another function.
- Define a function inside another function.

- Return a function from another function.

For example, this is how you can create a function that returns another function, in JavaScript:

```
function () {
    var taxDeduction = 500;

    return function (income) {
       // Implement calculating tax using taxDeduction here
       // ...
       return calculatedTax;
    }
}
```

Java 8 introduced *lambda expressions* (from Lambda Calculus (http://en.wikipedia.org/wiki/Lambda_calculus)), which are anonymous functions. Since the lambda expression has no name, it can be assigned as a value to a named variable.

With lambda expressions, object-oriented Java (as well as C#) allows programing in a mixed style. When you need an object with state, declare a class and instantiate it. If you just need to implement some algorithm define a lambda expression.

In this lesson you find out how to make your Java code more concise with lambda expressions. Java 8 blends functional into object-oriented style by representing a `Function` as a an object in the Java type system. Also, the interfaces that declare just one abstract method (functional interfaces) now can be implemented without the need to create an object just to contain this method.

IMPERATIVE VS FUNCTIONAL STYLE

Java is not a functional programming language, but even without lambda expressions it allows writing programs with elements of functional style. I'll show you a quick example illustrating the concept of *imperative* vs *functional* styles of programming. The following class `ImperativeVsFunctional` creates a collection `winners` and populates it with names. Then it tries to find if this collection contains the winner named "Ringo" using two different styles - imperative and then functional.

```
public class ImperativeVsFunctional {

 public static void main(String[] args) {

   List<String> winners = new ArrayList<>();

   winners.add("Mary");
   winners.add("Ringo");
   winners.add("Joe");
   winners.add("Paul");

   // Imperative style
   boolean gotRingo = false;
   for (String winner: winners){
```

```
            if ("Ringo".equals(winner)){
              gotRingo = true;
              System.out.println("Imperative style. Ringo won?"
                                                    + gotRingo);
               break;
            }
          }

          // Functional style
          System.out.println("Functional style. Ringo won?"
                                            + winners.contains("Ringo"));
       }
    }
```

Running this program will produce the following output:

```
    Imperative style. Ringo won? true
    Functional style. Ringo won? true
```

In imperative style the program dictates what has to be done: create a flag, then in a for-loop check the value of each element and if Ringo is found, change the value of the flag to true and break out of the loop. In this case we assume that `ArrayList` is just a storage of the winner's names.

In functional style, we don't dictate *how* to search for Ringo, and just call the method `contains()`. No external loops, no mutable flags, a no breaks. It's short, concise, and easy to understand. How the method `contains()` is implemented in the current version of Java? It's an internal business of the `ArrayList`. It very well can be that either in this or in the future version of Java the method `contains()` will split the collection (especially the large one) into smaller chunks and will do a parallel search for Ringo if the computer has multiple processors, while the imperative version will always process this collection sequentially.

This example uses a function that already exists in the collection. But with lambda expressions you can define your own functions and give it for the execution to a class or a collection. And again, depending on what your lambda does, the Java run time may decide to execute it in parallel.

You'll see some examples comparing imperative and functional styles of programming in the section "Iterating Collections with foreach" later in this chapter. With imperative style we tell Java *how* to do things, but with functional we tell Java *what* we want to do. In Lesson 20 on Stream API you'll see more examples of writing code in declarative and functional style. Let's learn the syntax of the lambda expressions now.

WHAT'S LAMBDA EXPRESSION

A lambda expression is an anonymous function that you can

- Assign to a variable.
- Pass as an argument to another function.
- Return from a method.

If in earlier versions of Java only objects and primitives could represent values, as of Java 8, functions can be values as well. In Lesson 9 you learned about anonymous inner classes served as wrapper for methods. Lambda expressions can eliminate the need for such wrappers. For example, consider the following lambda expression (let's call them *lambdas* for brevity):

```
(int a, int b) -> a + b;
```

Assume that there is an interface that declares a single abstract method that takes two `int` arguments and returns an `int` value. The lambda in the preceding code is an anonymous function that takes two `int` arguments `a` and `b`. The arguments are placed inside the parentheses similarly to Java methods. Actually, if lambda expression has only one argument then even those parentheses are not needed. On the right side of the -> sign (a.k.a. arrow token) you see the body of the lambda expression. In this case it's just a one-liner that calculates and returns the sum of arguments. If the body of lambda is a single-line expression as in the preceding example, there is no need to write a `return` statement. The result of the lambda expression is returned implicitly.

While the syntax of a lambda expression may look unusual, it's pretty easy to understand. Just take a regular Java method declaration, remove everything to the left of the opening paren, and add the -> sign after the closing paren. So if you wanted to rewrite the above lambda expression as a Java method, it could look like this:

```
public int addNumbers(int a, int b){
 return a + b;
}
```

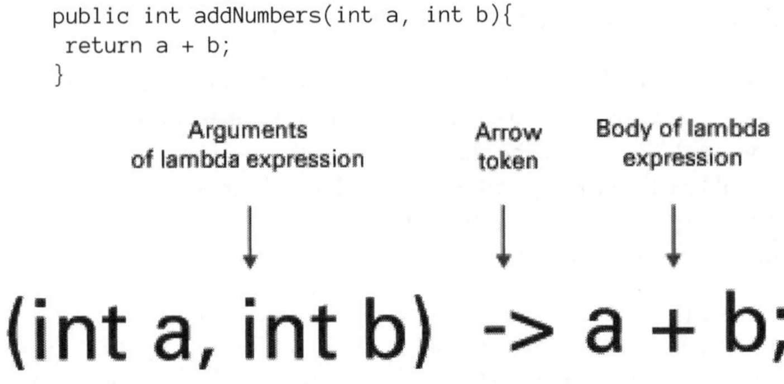

FIGURE 13-1: Parts of a lambda expression

In lambda expressions, specifying argument types is optional. Lambdas support inferred data types; the Java compiler properly "guesses" the types based on the context of your code. So our lambda expression can be rewritten as follows:

```
(a, b) -> a + b;
```

If the lambda expression consists of several lines of code, you need to put the code inside the curly braces and add an explicit `return` statement. You can pass lambda expressions to a method *to be applied* there. You'll see the example of using `apply()` in the section titled "Interfaces Function and BiFunction." The Java 8 lambdas can represent single-method interfaces in a concise way, which is discussed next.

Functional Interfaces

A Java interface can declare any number of methods, but to be implemented as lambdas, the interface has to declare a single *non-implemented method*. Such interfaces are called *functional interfaces*. Technically, functional interfaces can have more than one method; some of them can be static, some of them can be implemented as default methods—these don't count. The important part is that there is only one abstract method that has to be implemented.

Consider the `ActionListener` interface that you used in Lesson 9 to process button clicks:

```
public interface ActionListener extends EventListener {

    public void actionPerformed(ActionEvent actionEvent);

}
```

The old way of implementing such an interface with an anonymous inner class could look like this:

```
myButton.addActionListener(new ActionListener() {
    public void actionPerformed(ActionEvent actionEvent) {
        someTextField.setText("Someone clicked on the button");
    }
});
```

Because `ActionListener` defines a single method `actionPerformed()` it can be called *functional interface*. Hence it can be represented in a concise form with a lambda expression:

```
myButton.addActionListener(actionEvent -> {
    someTextField.setText("Someone clicked on the button);
});
```

It is a lot simpler to write and read, isn't it? No need to declare and instantiate anonymous classes. This lambda expression has one argument represented by the variable `actionEvent` (you could name it anything and no data type is needed). The method `actionPerformed()` is a callback, and Java run time would pass the instance of `ActionEvent` to it. But because it is a single method interface, the compiler is smart enough to figure out the type of the argument so you don't even need to declare it. Because any functional interface has a single method, it is easy for the compiler to figure out its name, so you just can write a lambda expression as its implementation.

Method References

In some cases your lambda expression just calls a predefined method. Java 8 introduces method references that can be used instead of lambda expressions. The new syntax introduces a double colon operator `::`, and you can write something like this:

```
myObject::myMethod
```

There is no parentheses after the method name and you can't specify the arguments in method references. So this syntax applies to the cases when either the method has no arguments or the compiler can "figure out" what such method expects as an argument. For example, the following method has no arguments and can be invoked using method reference syntax:

```
public void myMethod(){
    System.out.println("Hello from myMethod");
}
```

The case with inferred arguments, which the compiler figures out, can be illustrated by the event listener callback methods. The following class `MethodReferenceSample` uses method reference syntax in `addActionListener()`. The compiler figures out that the `processButtonClick()` method expects the argument of the type `ActionEvent`.

```
public class MethodReferenceSample extends JFrame {

   public void processButtonClick(ActionEvent actionEvent){
      System.out.println("Someone clicked on the button");
   }

   public static void main(String args[]){
       MethodReferenceSample mrs = new MethodReferenceSample();
       JButton myButton = new JButton("Click me");
       mrs.add(myButton);

       myButton.addActionListener(mrs::processButtonClick);

       mrs.pack();
       mrs.setVisible(true);
       mrs.setDefaultCloseOperation(JFrame.EXIT_ON_CLOSE);
   }
}
```

ECLIPSE LUNA AND LAMBDAS

Eclipse Luna (as well as NetBeans and IntelliJ IDEA) offers help in converting anonymous inner classes that implement functional interfaces into lambda expressions. Highlight the anonymous class creation (starting with `new`), and select the Quick Fix option by pressing Ctrl+1 (or Cmd+1 on Mac). Eclipse opens a menu. Select the Convert to Lamba Expression option to turn the anonymous inner class into a lambda expression.

ANNOTATION @FUNCTIONALINTERFACE

In Lesson 23 you'll be learning about Java annotations, which are metadata about Java code. Some annotation affect the process of compilation while other instruct Java run time to do certain things with the code. Java 8 introduces a new annotation that you can use for explicitly marking your interfaces as functional like this:

```
@FunctionalInterface
public interface Payable {
   boolean increasePay(int percent);
}
```

Using the annotation `@FunctionalInterface` is optional. It just shows your intention to implement this interface as a lambda expression. People who read your code may appreciate this hint. In the section "Passing Functions to Methods" I'll show you an example of using this annotation.

METHODS VERSUS FUNCTIONS

The difference between methods and functions is that functions are not attached to any class instance. You can say that static methods are also not attached to the instances, but static methods have to be declared inside a class or an interface, whereas functions don't.

You can try using lambdas just to simplify your code in places where you need to implement functional interfaces while maintaining an object-oriented style of programming. The code sample of replacing anonymous an inner class implementing `ActionListener` is an illustration of such simplification.

On the other hand, you may start experimenting with a functional style of programming, where a function just gets some input, applies its business logic, and returns the results. A function doesn't know anything about the context it operates in unless it was given to it as an argument. A function doesn't belong to any object hence it cannot rely on the fact that certain external values can be used in performing its action. A function does not change the state of any object.

The following example of the class `Tax` is written in object-oriented style. After the object of type `Tax` is instantiated, its fields `grossIncome` and the method `calcTax()` are not functions, as it expects to get some values from class variable `grossIncome` that modifies `federalTax`. It's a situation with mutable state.

```
class Tax{
    double grossIncome;
    double federalTax;

    public void calcTax() {

        if (grossIncome < 30000) {
          federalTax=grossIncome*0.05;
        }
        else{
          federalTax= grossIncome*0.06;
        }
  }
}
```

In the object-oriented world it's perfectly fine, because an object is the center of the universe there. To eliminate mutable attributes (`grossIncome` and `federalTtate`), change the definition of this class to:

```
class TaxNoState{

 public static double calcTax(double grossIncome) {
        double federalTax=0;
        if (grossIncome < 30000) {
          federalTax=grossIncome*0.05;
        }
        else{
          federalTax= grossIncome*0.06;
        }
          return federalTax;
  }
}
```

in TaxNoState the method calculateStateTax() gets the required values via its arguments. It's still a method since it lives inside the class, but is closer to being a function. After applying business logic calculateStateTax() returns the calculated federalTax. Returns to whom? It's none of the function's business. Note that I've used the keyword static in the method declaration to remove any attachments to specific instances of the class TaxNoState. After all, the tax calculation should be done the same way for Mary and Joe if they have the same income.

In the class TaxNoState we removed class variables and used the method arguments instead. The question is why the tax calculation logic that doesn't use any class fields have to live inside class method? Can you provide the code to calculate the tax from outside? Prior to Java 8, primitives or objects were the only values that you could pass to a method. But now you can also pass lambda expressions as method arguments, and I'll give you an example of this in the next section.

Passing Functions to Methods

In functional programming, you can pass a function as an argument to another function (or a function can return a function). Such outer functions are called *higher-order functions*.

This section shows you how to pass a function to a Java method. We'll create a class with three fields: name, grossIncome, and state to represent a customer of some accounting office. This class will have a method applyTaxCalculationFunction(), but the code of this function will be provided to this method as an argument. Here's the code of the class Customer:

```
public class Customer{
   public String name;
   public double grossIncome;

   public void applyTaxCalcFunction(TaxFunction taxFunc) {

      double calculatedTax = taxFunc.calcTax(grossIncome);
      System.out.println( "The calculated tax for " + name +
                                           " is "+ calculatedTax );

   }
}
```

The argument of the method `applyTaxCalcFunction()` is an implementation of the functional interface `TaxFunction`, which is shown here:

```
@FunctionalInterface
public interface TaxFunction {
    double calcTax(double grossIncome);
}
```

The implementation of this interface is provided by lambda expressions defined in the class `TestTaxLambda`. This class creates two customer instances and invokes the method `applyTaxCalculationFunction()` providing the lambda to execute. The customer's method `applyTaxCalculationFunction()` receives the implementation of this interface and invokes its method `calcTax()`. Here's the code of the class `TestTaxLambda`:

```
public class TestTaxLambda {

    public static void main(String[] args) {

        // Define one function as a lambda expression
        // and store it in a variable
        TaxFunction taxFunction = (double grossIncome) -> {

            double federalTax=0;
            if (grossIncome < 30000) {
              federalTax=grossIncome*0.05;
            }
            else{
              federalTax= grossIncome*0.06;
            }
            return federalTax;
        };

        // Define another function as a lambda expression
        // for calculating tax for mafia members
        TaxFunction taxFunctionMafia = (double grossIncome) -> {

            double stateTax=0;
            if (grossIncome < 30000) {
              stateTax=grossIncome*0.01;
            }
            else{
              stateTax= grossIncome*0.02;
            }
            return stateTax;
        };

        Customer customer1 = new Customer();
        customer1.name = "Mary Lou";
        customer1.grossIncome=50000;
        customer1.applyTaxCalcFunction(taxFunction);

        Customer customer2 = new Customer();
        customer2.name = "Al Capone";
```

```
            customer2.grossIncome=25000;
            customer2.applyTaxCalcFunction(taxFunctionMafia);
        }
    }
```

The implementation of two different algorithms of tax calculation is stored in lambda expressions is stored in the variable `taxFunction` and `taxFunctionMafia`. If you run `TestTaxLambda`, you see the following output on the console:

```
The calculated tax for Mary Lou is 3000.0
The calculated tax for Al Capone is 250.0
```

Lambda expressions spare you from needing to wrap a function inside a class. The big question is what's better: providing the tax calculation function inside the class `Customer` or passing it from outside. There is no general answer for this. Just know that if the business rules of your application require you to apply a the same or different pieces of a functionality to different objects, lambda expressions allow you to do this.

Java 8 lambdas still have some restrictions, and you can pass it to a method that expects a lambda that implements an interface of a specified type (`TaxFunction` in this case). In functional languages like JavaScript, you can attach an arbitrary function to any object and execute in the context of that object with functions `call()` or `apply()`. You see the Java version of `apply()` in the last section of this lesson.

ITERATING COLLECTIONS WITH FOREACH()

In the previous lesson you iterated a collection of objects by writing a loop. To perform some actions on each object of a collection you can implement these actions in the method `doSomething()` that's called in the loop body:

```
List<Customer> customers = new ArrayList<>();
// The code to populate customers is omitted for brevity
// Iterate through the list customers and do something with each
// element of this collection.

for (Customer customer : customers){
     customer.doSomething();
}
```

This is an *imperative* way of programming, you say, "I want get every element of the collection sequentially and do something with it." But there is a *functional* approach to this task, "Hey, collection, I'll give you a function to perform on each of your elements. Please figure out the best way to do it."

You may say, "What do you mean by the best way? Does collection know better than me how to process its elements?" Yes, it does. Starting with Java 8, collection became smarter and can parallelize execution, especially on multiprocessor computers. For example, it may internally split the collection in half and apply `doSomething()` in parallel for each half, and then it merges the results back. So you'd better give your function to a collection; there is a chance the processing will finish faster.

I'll show you the implementation of both imperative and functional styles in the class `TestCollectionsForEach` below. It'll iterate through the collection of workers represented by the instances of the class `Person`, which has a `boolean` variable `workerStatus` to store the employment: `E` means employee, and C means contractor.

```
public class Person {
    private String name;
    private char workerStatus;  // 'E' or 'C'

    public Person (String name, char workerStatus){
        this.name = name;
        this.workerStatus = workerStatus;
    }

    public String getName() {
        return name;
    }

    public char getWorkerStatus() {
        return workerStatus;
    }
}
```

The program `TestCollectionsForEach` creates an array of `Person` instances and then turns it into a `List` with `Arrays.asList()`. After that it iterates through the list using two different techniques: imperative and functional.

```
public class TestCollectionsForEach {

  public static void main(String[] args) {

        Person workers[] = new Person[3];
        workers[0] = new Person("John", 'E');
        workers[1] = new Person("Mary", 'C');
        workers[2] = new Person("Steve", 'E');

        List<Person> workersList = Arrays.asList(workers);

        // Imperative loop
        System.out.println("1. Running imperative loop");
        for (Person person : workersList){
          if ('E' == person.getWorkerStatus()){
            System.out.println(person.getName() + " is employee");
          } else if ('C' == person.getWorkerStatus()){
            System.out.println(person.getName() + " is contractor");
          }
        }

        // Functional loop
        System.out.println("2. Running functional loop");
        workersList.forEach(person -> {
          if ('E' == person.getWorkerStatus()) {
            System.out.println(person.getName() + " is employee");
          } else if ('C'==pers.getWorkerStatus()){
```

```
                System.out.println(person.getName() + " is contractor");
            }
        });
    }
}
```

The output of this program is shown here:

```
1. Running imperative loop
John is employee
Mary is contractor
Steve is employee
2. Running functional loop
John is employee
Mary is contractor
Steve is employee
```

The output is the same from both loops. In the functional loop you're passing a lambda expression to the `forEach()` method of the collection.

In Lesson 20 you learn about the new Stream API, and you see there how to specifically request parallel processing.

I'd like to bring your attention to the variable `person` in the argument to the `forEach()` method. I've never declared this variable, so what its type? It's yet another example of the *type inference*. Java is smart enough to see that the lambda expression is being applied to the collection of the class `Person` (see, generics are helpful!). Hence the variable `person` will be typed as `Person`. You can name this variable anything you want; the Java compiler will figure out its inferred type.

LAMBDAS VERSUS INHERITANCE AND POLYMORPHISM

Lambda expressions promote a functional style of programming. In previous lessons you've learned about the object-oriented style and its major concepts: inheritance, which can be implemented as polymorphism or composition. This section shows you how to take the example from the section "Making the Interface Solution Polymorphic" from Lesson 7 where you processed a collection of employees and contractors in polymorphic ways and rewrite it using composition with lambdas.

INHERITANCE VS COMPOSITION

To create a class that can reuse features of another class you can use either inheritance or composition as a design technique. In case of inheritance you can simply create a `ClassB` that extends `ClassA` and use the ancestor's elements from a descendent class. The following example demonstrates inheritance, where the `ClassB` invokes in constructor a method `doSomething()` declared in its ancestor:

```
ClassA {
 public void doSomething(){
 }
}
```

```
ClassB extends ClassA{
   ClassB(){
      doSomething();
   }
}
```

In case of composition, you don't need to inherit from ClassA, but just instantiate (and hold a reference) ClassA in ClassB:

```
ClassA {
 public void doSomething(){
 }
}

ClassB{
   ClassB(){
      ClassA classA = new classA();
      classA.doSomething();
   }
}
```

For pros and cons of inheritance vs composition, read the JavaWorld article "Inheritance versus Composition: Which one Should You Choose? (http://www.javaworld.com/article/2076814/core-java/inheritance-versus-composition--which-one-should-you-choose-.html)"

In that Lesson 7 example you used the Payable interface to increase pay for employees and contractors. First, refresh your memory about that application. Figure 13-2 shows the class diagram (http://en.wikipedia.org/wiki/Class_diagram) of that application (in UML notation arrows mean *extends,* and dashed arrows means *implements*):

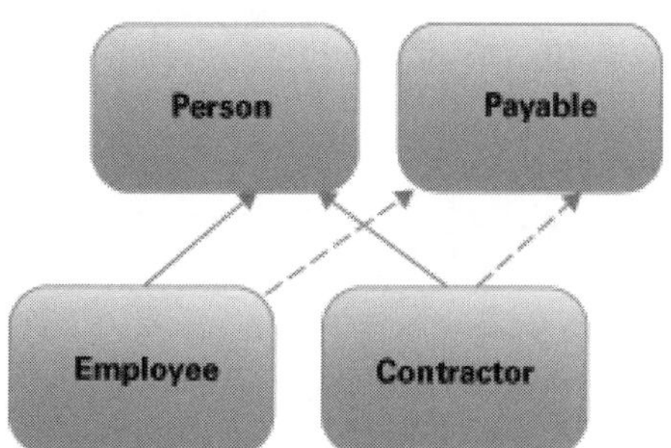

FIGURE 13-2: Figure 13-2. Extending Person and implementing Payable

The code of the superclass Person is shown next:

```
public class Person {
    private String name;
```

```
    public Person(String name){
        this.name = name;
    }

    public String getName(){
        return "Person's name is " + name;
    }
}
```

This is the Payable interface:

```
public interface Payable {
    int INCREASE_CAP = 20;
    boolean increasePay(int percent);
}
```

Classes Employee and Contractor had different implementations of the Payable interface. This is what Employee looked like:

```
public class Employee extends Person implements Payable {

    public Employee(String name){
        super(name);
    }

    public boolean increasePay(int percent) {
      System.out.println("Increasing salary by " + percent + "%. "+
                                                      getName());
      return true;
    }
}
```

The class Contractor looked as follows:

```
public class Contractor extends Person implements Payable {

    public Contractor(String name){
        super(name);
    }

    public boolean increasePay(int percent) {
        if(percent < Payable.INCREASE_CAP){
            System.out.println("Increasing hourly rate by " +
                                        percent + "%. "+ getName());
            return true;
        } else {
            System.out.println(
             "Sorry, can't increase hourly rate by more than " +
              Payable.INCREASE_CAP + "%. "+ getName());
            return false;
        }
    }
}
```

The program TestPayIncreasePoly demonstrated the polymorphic behavior of Employee and Contractor objects.

```
public class TestPayInceasePoly {

    public static void main(String[] args) {

        Payable workers[] = new Payable[3];
        workers[0] = new Employee("John");
        workers[1] = new Contractor("Mary");
        workers[2] = new Employee("Steve");
            for (Payable p: workers){
                p.increasePay(30);
            }
        }
}
```

Eliminating Inheritance

The only difference between Contractor and Employee was the implementation of the increasePay() method, extracting the implementation of this method into a lambda expression. This enables you to get rid of the classes Employee and Contractor and simply pass the proper function to the class Person. To be able to distinguish contractors and employees you use the version of the class Person from the section "Iterating collection with forEach() Method." But this time add a method validatePayIncrease() that takes the lambda expression as one parameter and the amount of pay increase as another. This is the new version of the class Person:

```
public class Person {

    private String name;
    private char workerStatus;  // 'E' or 'C'

    public Person (String name, char workerStatus){
        this.name = name;
        this.workerStatus = workerStatus;
    }

    public String getName(){
        return name;
    }

    public char getWorkerStatus(){
        return workerStatus;
    }

    public boolean validatePayIncrease(Payable increaseFunction,
                                                    int percent) {

         boolean isIncreaseValid =
                increaseFunction.increasePay(percent);

         System.out.println( " Increasing pay for " + name +
```

```
            " is " + (isIncreaseValid? "valid.": "not valid."));
          return isIncreaseValid;
    }
}
```

The Payable interface remains the same, and its implementation will be represented by two lambda expressions —one for employees and another one for contractors, as shown in the program TestPayIncreaseLambda:

```
public class TestPayIncreaseLambda {

  public static void main(String[] args) {

        Person workers[] = new Person[3];
        workers[0] = new Person("John", 'E');
        workers[1] = new Person("Mary", 'C');
        workers[2] = new Person("Steve", 'E');

       // Lambda expression for increasing Employee's pay
       Payable increaseRulesEmployee = (int percent) -> {
               return true;
       };

        // Lambda expression for increasing Contractor's pay
        Payable increaseRulesContractor = (int percent) -> {
            if(percent > Payable.INCREASE_CAP){
              System.out.print(
               " Sorry, can't increase hourly rate by more than " +
                         Payable.INCREASE_CAP + "%. ");
              return false;
            } else {
              return true;
            }
       };

       for (Person p: workers){
           if ('E'==p.getWorkerStatus()){
               // Validate 30% increase for every worker
               p.validatePayIncrease(increaseRulesEmployee, 30);
           } else if ('C'==p.getWorkerStatus()){
               p.validatePayIncrease(increaseRulesContractor, 30);
           }
       }
  }
}
```

Running this program produces the same output as the version with class inheritance and polymorphism:

```
Increasing pay for John is valid.
Sorry, can't increase hourly rate by more than 20%.
Increasing pay for Mary is not valid.
Increasing pay for Steve is valid.
```

The result is the same, so what have you achieved? Using lambdas made it possible to remove two classes: `Contractor` and `Employee`. This is good. But it seems that by removing these classes you've lost the strict contract enforcement to implement the `Payable` interface. Actually, though, you didn't! Using the `Payable` type is still enforced but in a different way; now it's a type of the argument in the method `validatePayIncrease()`. If a new type of a worker will be introduced (for example, foreign workers), you just need to add another lambda expression to the class `TestPayIncreaseLambda` that implements business rules for foreign workers.

CLOSURES WITH LAMBDAS

The "Closures in Java" section in Lesson 17 demonstrates an important concept of functional programming: *closures*.

Interfaces Function and BiFunction

On the other hand, even the interface `Payable` can be eliminated from the increase pay example. Revisit the class `Person` from the section "Eliminating Inheritance." It has a method `validatePayIncrease` where the first argument is strictly typed as `Payable`. But Java 8 allows passing any arbitrary function to a method as an argument. There is a new package java.util.function (`http://docs.oracle.com/javase/8/docs/api/java/util/function/package-summary.html`) that has a number of useful interfaces for those who like functional programming. For example, the interface `Function` has the following declaration:

```
@FunctionalInterface
public interface Function<T, R>
```

As you see, it uses generics. This interface has two parameters: T for type and R for the type of the return value of the method `apply()` declared in the interface `Function`. Using T for type and R for the type of the return value became idiomatic in Java, so you should also use these letters in your code. You can pass the code of such a function to a class method and apply this function to a provided argument.

The interface `BiFunction` declares two arguments (T and U) and a return value (R):

```
@FunctionalInterface
public interface BiFunction<T, U, R>
```

Accordingly, the `BiFunction` interface declares a method `R apply(T, U)`. Let's see if you can use it in the increase pay example, which is built using the techniques you've learned in this lesson.

First, take a look at the new version of the class `Person`. Note the change in the arguments of the method `validateIncreasePay()`:

```
public class Person {

    private String name;
    private char workerStatus;  // 'E' or 'C'
```

```
    public Person (String name, char workerStatus){
        this.name = name;
        this.workerStatus=workerStatus;
    }

    public String getName(){
        return name;
    }

    public char getWorkerStatus(){
        return workerStatus;
    }

    public boolean validateIncreasePay(
        BiFunction<Person, Integer, Boolean> func
, int percent) {

        boolean isIncreaseValid = func.apply(this, percent);
        System.out.println( " Increasing pay is " +
                  (isIncreaseValid? "valid.": "not valid."));
        return isIncreaseValid;
    }
}
```

The method `validateIncreasePay()` has two arguments: a `BiFunction` for the function to apply and a proposed increase pay percent to validate. In turn, `BiFunction` declares two arguments—one of type `Person` and the other of type `Integer`—and a `Boolean` return type. When actual implementation of `BiFunction` is passed to the method `validateIncreasePay()`, it invokes it using the method `apply()`. The keyword `this` represents the current instance of a `Person`, and percent is the proposed increased amount.

Once again, the term *higher order function* is a function (or method) that either takes a function as an argument or returns a function. In other words, higher order functions work on other functions.

The program `TestPayIncreaseFunctionInterface`, which declares the lambdas for contractors and employees and validates a list of workers, is shown here:

```
public class TestPayIncreaseFunctionInterface{

 public static void main(String[] args) {

      final int INCREASE_CAP = 20;  // cap for pay increase in %

      int proposedIncrease = 30;  // percent

        Person workers[] = new Person[3];
        workers[0] = new Person("John", 'E');
        workers[1] = new Person("Mary", 'C');
        workers[2] = new Person("Steve", 'E');

        List<Person> workersList = Arrays.asList(workers);

       // Define functions with 2 args Person and percent
       // that returns Boolean
```

```
        // Lambda expression for increasing Employee's pay
      BiFunction <Person, Integer, Boolean> increaseRulesEmployee =
           (pers,percent) -> {
              System.out.print(" Increasing pay for " +
                                      pers.getName() + " is valid");
             return true; // allow any increases for employees
           };

        // Lambda expression for increasing Contractor's pay
      BiFunction <Person, Integer, Boolean> increaseRulesContractor =
        (pers,percent) -> {
            if(percent > INCREASE_CAP){
               System.out.print(
                 " Sorry, can't increase hourly rate by more than " +
                          INCREASE_CAP + "%. for " + pers.getName());
                return false;
            } else {
                return true;
            }
        };

        // Validate pay increase
         workersList.forEach(pers -> {
               if ('E'==pers.getWorkerStatus()){
                 pers.validateIncreasePay(increaseRulesEmployee,
                                                  proposedIncrease);
               } else if ('C'==pers.getWorkerStatus()){
                   pers.validateIncreasePay(increaseRulesContractor,
                                                  proposedIncrease);
               }
        });
   }
 }
```

In the previous section you stored lambdas in the variables of type `Payable`, but in this version it's stored as a `BiFunction`; for example:

```
BiFunction <Person, Integer, Boolean> increaseRulesEmployee
```

The `Payable` interface is gone. I just moved the final variable `INCREASE_CAP`in the class `TestPayIncreaseFunctionInterface`. In the beginning of this lesson we designed the increase pay application using four classes and one interface. Now we have just two classes and the code became shorter.

The goal of this lesson was to explain the concept of lambdas and show some practical use cases where they can simplify your code. I didn't want to repeat all syntax details of lambdas. Please visit Oracle's tutorial on lambda expressions (`http://goo.gl/xS3ejB`) for further studying of this subject.

TRY IT

The goal of this lesson is to add another lambda expression to the class `TestPayIncreaseLambda` to process pay increases for foreign workers.

Lesson Requirements

You should have Java installed.

> **NOTE** *You can download the code and resources for this "Try It" from the book's web page at* `www.wrox.com/go/javaprog24hr2e`. *You can find them in* `Lesson13.zip`.

Step-by-Step

1. Import into Eclipse the project Lesson13 from the file `Lesson13.zip`. Review the code of all examples from this lesson.
2. Introduce the new type of workers: a foreign worker.
3. Come up with some business logic for increasing rate for foreigners.
4. Create a new lambda expression implementing these rules and assign it to the variable `Payable increaseRulesForeigner`.
5. Add an instance of the foreign worker (worker status `'F'`) to the array `workers`.
6. Modify the `for` loop in the class `TestPayIncreaseLambda` to process pay increase for foreigners.
7. Extra challenge: Modify the class `Person` to remove the `workerStatus` attribute. Add a second parameter to its constructor—a lambda expression—so you can pass the rules of increasing pay during instantiation of a worker.

> **TIP** *Please select the videos for Lesson 13 online at* `www.wrox.com/go/javaprog24hr2e`. *You will also be able to download the code and resources for this lesson from the website.*

14

Working with I/O Streams

Most programs work with some kind of data, which could be stored in a local database, on a remote computer, or in a file located on your disk. Java has a concept of working with *streams of data*. You can say that a Java program reads sequences of bytes from an input stream (or writes into an output stream) byte after byte, character after character, primitive after primitive. Accordingly, Java defines various types of classes supporting streams; for example, `InputStream` or `OutputStream`. There are classes specifically meant for reading character streams such as `Reader` and `Writer`. `DataInputStream` and `DataOutputStream` can read and write Java primitives, and to work with files you may consider such classes as `FileInputStream` and `FileReader`.

Classes that work with streams are located in two packages: `java.io` and `java.nio`. Classes from the former implement blocking input/output (I/O): When bytes are being read/written by a process, they become unavailable for other threads of execution. The latter package offers non-blocking I/O with improved performance. Most of this chapter covers the fundamentals of I/O, but at the end I'll show you how to work with files using classes from the package `java.nio`.

Before deciding which Java class to use for I/O in each particular case, you need to understand what kind of data is coming from (or going to) the stream in question. No matter what you select, your code needs to perform three operations:

1. Open a stream that points at a specific data source: a file, a socket, a URL, and so on.
2. Read or write data from/to this stream.
3. Close the stream.

If a Java program uses third-party programs, such as database management systems (DBMS), you won't need to program streams directly—the database drivers or object-relational mapping framework is all you need. But in this lesson you see examples of performing I/O operations with different streams.

BYTE STREAMS

A program can read or write any file one byte at a time with the help of one of the subclasses of InputStream or OutputStream, respectively. The following example in Listing 14-1 shows how to use the class FileInputStream to read a file named abc.dat. This code snippet reads and prints each byte's value:

LISTING 14-1 Using FileInputStream

```
try (FileInputStream myFile = new FileInputStream("abc.dat")){

     boolean eof = false;

     while (!eof) {
          int byteValue = myFile.read();
          System.out.print(byteValue + " ");
          if (byteValue  == -1)
              eof = true;
     }
   } catch (IOException ioe) {
            System.out.println("Could not read file: " +
                                                ioe.toString());
   }
}
```

Because the code in Listing 14-1 doesn't specify the directory where abc.dat is located, the program tries to find this file in the current directory, which is the root directory of the Eclipse project (if you use Eclipse). At any given time you can easily find out the current directory programmatically by calling the method System.getProperty("user.dir").

The output of this program will be a sequence of numbers, which represents the codes of the characters located in the file. For example, if abc.dat contains the text *"This is a test file,"* the output on the system console will look like this:

```
84 104 105 115 32 105 115 32 97 32 116 101 115 116 32 102 105 108 101 -1
```

When you are reading with FileInputStream, the end of the file is represented by a negative one, and this is how you know when to stop. The code in Listing 14-1 checks for -1 and sets the boolean variable eof to false to finish the loop.

Note that the above example automatically closes streams by using try-with-resources, as explained in Lesson 10. This code will work starting from Java 7.

The code fragment in Listing 14-2 writes into a file called xyz.dat using the class FileOutputStream.

LISTING 14-2 Using FileOutputStream

```
// byte values are represented by integers from 0 to 255
  int somedata[]= {56,230,123,43,11,37};

  try (FileOutputStream myFile= new FileOutputStream("xyz.dat");){
     for (int i = 0; i <somedata.length; i++){
        file.write(somedata[i]);
     }
  } catch (IOException ioe) {
     System.out.println("Could not write to a file: " +
                                                 ioe.toString());
  }
```

BUFFERED STREAMS

The code in the previous section was reading and writing one byte at a time. In general, disk access is much slower than the processing performed in memory; that's why it's not a good idea to access the disk a thousand times to read a file of 1,000 bytes. To minimize the number of times the disk is accessed, Java provides *buffers*, which serve as reservoirs of data.

The class `BufferedInputStream` works as a middleman between `FileInputStream` and the file itself. It reads a big chunk of bytes from a file into memory in one shot, and the `FileInputStream` object then reads single bytes from there, which is memory-to-memory operations. `BufferedOutputStream` works similarly with the class `FileOutputStream`. The main idea here is to minimize disk access.

Buffered streams are not changing the type of the original streams—they just make reading more efficient. Think of it this way: A program performs stream chaining (or stream piping) to connect streams, just as pipes are connected in plumbing. Listing 14-3 shows an example in which a file is read so the data from `FileInputStream` fills `BufferedInputStream` before processing.

LISTING 14-3 Chaining FileInputStream with BufferedInputStream

```
try (FileInputStream myFile = new  FileInputStream("abc.dat");
     BufferedInputStream buff = new BufferedInputStream(myFile);){

            boolean eof = false;
            while (!eof) {
                int byteValue = buff.read();
                System.out.print(byteValue + " ");
                if (byteValue  == -1)
                    eof = true;
            }
        } catch (IOException ioe) {
            ioe.printStackTrace();
```

```
            }
    }
```

While reading a stream with the help of `BufferedInputStream`, watch for the end-of-file character to know that all the bytes have been read from the buffer. The class `BufferedOutputStream` is for writing, and you'd need to call its method `write()`.

The default buffer size is 8Kb, but you can control it using a two-argument constructor of the `BufferedInputStream` or `BufferedOutputStream`. For example, to set the buffer size to 5,000 bytes, instantiate the buffered stream as follows:

```
BufferedInputStream buff = new BufferedInputStream(myFile, 5000);
```

CHARACTER STREAMS

The text in Java is represented as a set of `char` values (two-byte characters), which are based on the Unicode Standard. The Java classes `FileReader` and `FileWriter` were specifically created to work with text files, but they work only with default character encoding and don't handle localization properly.

The recommended way is to pipe the class `InputStreamReader` with specified encoding and the `FileInputStream`. The class `InputStreamReader` reads bytes and decodes them into characters using a specified `CharSet`. Each JVM has a default *charset,* which can be specified during the JVM start-up and depends on the locale. Some of the standard charsets are US-ASCII, UTF-8, and UTF-16.

Listing 14-4 reads bytes from a text file and converts them from UTF-8 encoding into Unicode to return results as a `String`. For efficiency, the reading is piped with the `BufferReader`, which reads text from the stream buffering characters. Note that this code uses mutable `StringBuffer` that usually works faster than `String` when it comes to performing text manipulations. Using a mutable `StringBuffer` was a recommended way to concatenate strings. That's why I decided to illustrate its use.

If you'll be concatenating regular `String` values, Java compiler will optimize this code anyway and will replace `String` concatenation with yet another helper class `StringBuilder`. You can also manually use `StringBuilder` instead of `StringBuffer`, as shown in Lesson 16.

LISTING 14-4 Reading text files

```
StringBuffer buffer = new StringBuffer();
    try (
       FileInputStream myFile = new FileInputStream("abc.txt");
       InputStreamReader inputStreamReader =
                 new InputStreamReader(myFile, "UTF8"
);
      Reader reader = new BufferedReader(inputStreamReader);){

      int ch; // the code of one character

      while ((ch = reader.read()) > -1) {
```

```
                buffer.append((char)ch);
        }

        buffer.toString();

    } catch (IOException e) {
            e.printStackTrace();
    }
```

For writing characters to a file, pipe `FileOutputStream` and `OutputStreamWriter`. For efficiency, use `BufferedWriter`; for example:

```
try (FileOutputStream myFile = new FileOutputStream("abc.txt");
     Writer out = new BufferedWriter(
                        new OutputStreamWriter(myFile, "UTF8"));) {

  String myAddress = "123 Broadway, New York, NY 10011";
  out.write(myAddress);
} catch(IOException e){
      e.printStackTrace();
}
```

Bringing Together GUI and I/O Streams

Listing 14-5 shows yet another version of the tax calculation program. This time I've added a text file, `states.txt`, that includes states that will be used to populate a drop-down box, `chStates`. My file is located in the root directory of the Eclipse project Lesson14, and it looks like this:

```
New York
New Jersey
Florida
California
```

The program in Listing 14-5 requires a class, `Tax`, that you can borrow from Lesson 4 class_methods_and_constructors. Make sure that it has the method `calcTax()`.

LISTING 14-5 Bringing together Swing and streams

```
public class TaxGuiFile extends JFrame {
    JLabel lblGrIncome;
    JTextField txtGrossIncome = new JTextField(15);
    JLabel lblDependents=new JLabel("Number of Dependents:");
    JTextField txtDependents = new JTextField(2);
    JLabel lblState = new JLabel("State: ");

    //Define a data model for the ComboBox chState
    Vector<String> states = new Vector<>(50);

    //Create a combobox to get data from the model
    JComboBox chState = new JComboBox(states);
```

```
JLabel lblTax = new JLabel("State Tax: ");
JTextField txtStateTax = new JTextField(10);
JButton bGo = new JButton("Go");
JButton bReset = new JButton("Reset");

TaxGuiFile() {
    lblGrIncome = new JLabel("Gross Income: ");
    GridLayout gr = new GridLayout(5,2,1,1);
    setLayout(gr);

    add(lblGrIncome);
    add(txtGrossIncome);
    add(lblDependents);
    add(txtDependents);
    add(lblState);
    add(chState);
    add(lblTax);
    add(txtStateTax);
    add(bGo);
    add(bReset);

    // Populate states from a file
    populateStates();

    chState.setSelectedIndex(0);
    txtStateTax.setEditable(false);

   // The Button Go processing using lambda expression
   bGo.addActionListener(evt -> {
    try{
     int grossInc=Integer.parseInt(txtGrossIncome.getText());
     int dependents=Integer.parseInt(txtDependents.getText());
     String state = (String)chState.getSelectedItem();

     Tax tax=new Tax(grossInc, state,dependents);
     String sTax =Double.toString(tax.calcTax());
     txtStateTax.setText(sTax);
    }catch(NumberFormatException e){
       txtStateTax.setText("Non-Numeric Data");
    }catch (Exception e){
       txtStateTax.setText(e.getMessage());
    }
   });

   // The Button Reset processing using lambda expression
   bReset.addActionListener(evt ->{
        txtGrossIncome.setText("");
        txtDependents.setText("");
        chState.setSelectedIndex(0);
        txtStateTax.setText("");
   });

 // Define, instantiate and register a WindowAdapter
```

```
        // to process windowClosing Event of this frame
        this.addWindowListener(new WindowAdapter() {
            public void windowClosing(WindowEvent e) {
                System.exit(0);
            }});
        }

    // The code below will read the file states.txt and
    // populate the drop-down chStates

     private void populateStates(){

         states.add("Select State");

         try (FileInputStream myFile =
                             new FileInputStream("states.txt");
                 InputStreamReader inputStreamReader=
                             new InputStreamReader(myFile, "UTF8");
                 BufferedReader reader =
                         new BufferedReader(inputStreamReader);){

             String stateName;
             while ( (stateName = reader.readLine()) != null ){
                 states.add(stateName);
             }

            }catch (IOException ioe){
                txtStateTax.setText("Can't read states.txt: " +
                                                ioe.getMessage());
            }
     }

     public static void main(String args[]){
        TaxGuiFile taxFrame = new TaxGuiFile();
        taxFrame.setSize(400,150);
        taxFrame.setVisible(true);
     }
}
```

The code in Listing 14-5 reads the content of the file `states.txt` and populates a collection—a `Vector` with states. The `Vector` collection (it's like `ArrayList` but synchronized) plays the role of a data model for the combo box states. I used a constructor of JComboBox that takes a data model as an argument. This Swing component knows how to display the content of its data model.

This is an example of the implementation of the *MVC (model-view-controller)* design pattern, which promotes the separation of data and user interface (UI). JComboBox plays the role of a view, the `Vector` is a model, and the user works as a controller when she selects a particular state and the view has to be updated.

Note that the `TaxGuiFile` class doesn't implement the `ActionListener` interface. The click event handling for the Go and Reset buttons is implemented using lambda expressions.

The output of the program from Listing 14-5 is shown in Figure 14-1.

> **SPLITTING GUI AND PROCESSING**
>
> In a larger application it would make sense to separate the class `TaxGuiFile` into two: one would be only creating GUI components, and the other would read the data from files or other data sources. I illustrated this in Lesson 9 for the calculator program that had two classes: `Calculator` and `CalculatorEngine`.

FIGURE 14-1: Running the TaxGuiFile program

DATA STREAMS

If you are expecting to work with a stream of known data primitives (for example, two integers, three floats, and a double) use either `DataInputStream` for reading or `DataOutputStream` for writing. A method, `readInt()`, of `DataInputStream` reads the whole integer number (four bytes) at once, and `readLong()` gets you a long number (eight bytes).

The class `DataInputStream` is yet another "pipe" that can be connected to another stream. Listing 14-6 has an example of how you can "build a pipe" from the following pieces:

```
FileInputStream □ BufferedInputStream □ DataInputStream
```

LISTING 14-6 Using DataInputStream

```
try (FileInputStream myFile = new FileInputStream("myData.dat");
     BufferedInputStream buff = new BufferedInputStream(myFile);
     DataInputStream data = new DataInputStream(buff);) {

     int num1 = data.readInt();
     int num2 = data.readInt();
     float num2 = data.readFloat();
     float num3 = data.readFloat();
     float num4 = data.readFloat();
     double num5 = data.readDouble();
} catch (IOException ioe) {
    ioe.printStackTrace();
}
```

In this example, FileInputStream opens the file myData.dat for reading, BufferedInputStream makes the read more efficient, and DataInputStream extracts from the buffer two integers, three floats, and a double. The assumption here is that the file myData.dat contains exactly these data types, and they're in the specified order. Such a file could have been created with the help of DataOutputStream, which allows you to write primitive Java data types to a stream in a portable way. It has a variety of methods to choose from: writeInt(), writeByte(), writeFloat(), and so on.

UTILITY CLASSES FOR WORKING WITH FILES

Often you need to do some operations with files that do not always include reading or writing into files. For example, you may need to check for the existence of a file or rename it programmatically. Java includes utility classes File, Files, and Path that can become handy.

The Class File

The class java.io.File enables you to rename or delete a file, perform an existence check, create a directory, check the file size, and more. If you need this functionality, start by creating an instance of this class:

```
File myFile = new File("abc.txt");
```

This line does not create a file; it just creates in memory an instance of the class File that's ready to perform its action on the file named abc.txt. If you want to create a physical file, use the method createNewFile() defined in the class File. Here's the list of some methods of the class File:

- createNewFile(): Creates a new, empty file named according to the file name used during the file instantiation. Creates a new file only if a file with this name does not exist.
- delete(): Deletes a file or directory.
- renameTo(): Renames a file.
- length(): Returns the length of the file in bytes.
- exists(): Tests whether the file with the specified name exists.
- list(): Returns an array of strings containing a file and directory.
- lastModified(): Returns the time that the file was last modified.
- mkDir(): Creates a directory.

The next code fragment checks for the existence of the file customers.txt.bak, deletes it if it is found, and then renames the file customers.txt to customers.txt.bak:

```
File file = new File("customers.txt");
File backup = new File("customers.txt.bak");
if (backup.exists()){
       backup.delete();
}
file.renameTo(backup);
```

NIO.2: Using Files, Path, and Paths

Java 7 introduced a number of new classes and interfaces for more efficient work with files and directories often referred as NIO.2 (`http://docs.oracle.com/javase/tutorial/essential/io/fileio.html`).

The interface `Path` is a programmatic representation of the full path to the file, a directory, or a URI (`http://en.wikipedia.org/wiki/Uniform_resource_identifier`). While the full path to the file is represented differently in Windows and Unix OS, each of the file systems is a hierarchical tree of directories, subdirectories, and files that start from some root node (e.g., `c:\` in Windows or / in Unix).

The path can be absolute that starts from the root directory on the drive like `/Users/yfain11/practicalJava/workspace/Lesson14/states.bak` and relative that starts with the directory where the application was launched from; e.g., `Lesson14/states.bak`. A file can also be represented by a so-called *symbolic link*, that looks like a file but is actually a reference to a different file in a different branch of the files hierarchy. If you want to write a program that can be launched from any directory and work with a certain file, consider using absolute path. If your application is deployed in a way that a file will always be located in the same place relative to the location of the main application, use relative path.

The interface `Path` allows you to programmatically represent a full path according to the underlying OS being used. First your program should create a `Path` object, and then work with files or directories located there.

The class `java.nio.file.Files` is similar to `java.io.File` in that it contains static methods that operate on files and directories. Most of these methods delegate the processing to the underlying operating system (OS) file system. In addition to functionality of the class `File`, the class `Files` can walk directory trees, check a file's attributes (e.g., read/write access), understand if a file is a symbolic link, and work with streams. Using the class `Files` you can copy, move, and delete files, too.

You can get a file path by using the method `Paths.get()`. The following class `TestFilesPaths` checks if the file `states.txt` exists, then checks its size, outputs its absolute path, and creates a backup copy of this file named `states.bak`.

```
public class TestFilesPaths {

  public static void main(String[] args) {

    // Get the path to the file states.txt located in dir
    // this program was launched from
    Path sourceFilePath = Paths.get("states.txt");

    // Will copy the source file to this destination
    Path destFilePath = Paths.get("states.bak");

    if (Files.exists(sourceFilePath)){
      System.out.println("The file  " + sourceFilePath + " exists");
      System.out.println("The absolute path is " +
                              sourceFilePath.toAbsolutePath());
       try{
          // Check the file size (in bytes)
          System.out.println("It's size is " +
                                   Files.size(sourceFilePath));
```

```
            // Copy the file from states.txt to states.bak
            Files.copy(sourceFilePath, destFilePath,
                               StandardCopyOption.REPLACE_EXISTING);
            System.out.println(
                   "Copy completed. The backup file is at " +
                                 destFilePath.toAbsolutePath());

        } catch(IOException ioe){
            ioe.printStackTrace();
        }
    }
  }
}
```

The output of the program `TestFilesPaths` looks as follows:

```
The file states.txt exists
The absolute path is
/Users/yfain11/practicalJava/workspace/Lesson14/states.txt
It's size is 41
Copy completed. The backup file is at
/Users/yfain11/practicalJava/workspace/Lesson14/states.bak
```

COPY OPTIONS

In the class `TestFilesPaths` I was using the option `StandardCopyOption.REPLACE_EXISTING` to replace the destination file if it exists. Now let's make a little experiment. The class `Files` has an overloaded version of the method copy that takes only two parameters: the source and the destination. If you'll remove the parameter `StandardCopyOption.REPLACE_EXISTING`, the program will work fine as long as the output file doesn't exist in the specified destination. So if you'll run `TestFilesPaths` more than once, the method `copy()` will generate an exception, which on my computer looks as follows:

```
java.nio.file.FileAlreadyExistsException: states.bak
    at sun.nio.fs.UnixCopyFile.copy(UnixCopyFile.java:551)
    at sun.nio.fs.UnixFileSystemProvider.copy(UnixFileSystemProvider.java:
253)
    at java.nio.file.Files.copy(Files.java:1274)
    at TestFilesPaths.main(TestFilesPaths.java:29)
```

I'm using a computer with MAC OS, which is Unix based. Read the exception message: The Java runtime properly figured out the type of my OS and, under the hood, engaged Unix-specific classes that implement file copying. If you'll do the same experiment in Window, the exception stack trace will look different.

As a matter of fact, you can specify more than one copy option while invoking `copy()` or `move()`. The option `COPY_ATTRIBUTES` will set the same security attributes on the destination files. The option ATOMIC_MOVE will ensure that the copy or move operation will roll back in case of failure.

The class Files can also open input and output streams and read/write into them. You can find the complete list of all methods of the class Files in the Java documentation at http://goo.gl/LBhZYF.

WHAT NIO IS ABOUT

In this lesson you've learned how to work with I/O streams using small files. The real-world applications, sometimes, need to process files that are hundreds of megabytes in size. While the file is being read, the main program may need to perform other application-specific functions. I'll give you an example from the GUI-related programming. Imagine that the TaxGuiFile program has to read not a small but a large file, which takes 20 seconds. The GUI will become non-responsive for 20 seconds if you'll be using blocking I/O in a wrong way. In Lesson 17 you'll be learning about concurrent processing and multi-threading. You should run a long-running code in a separate *thread of execution*, so the main thread that's responsible for the communication with GUI will remain operational. In particular, I'll explain what SwingWorker thread is for in Lesson 17 and how to avoid "frozen screens" in JavaFX applications in Lesson 19.

Blocking I/O may become a bottleneck in your application, if you need to come up with a scalable solution that reads/writes large amounts of data. Yes, you can use blocking I/O in a separate thread of execution. But a better alternative is to use non-blocking I/O that was first introduced in Java 1.4, and improved in Java 7. The non-blocking mode of Java NIO allows to create channels so a thread can read (or write) only the data that's currently available. The thread doesn't wait till all the data is available and can continue processing some other tasks. Working with NIO channels is not covered in this book. Please refer to Oracle documentation (http://docs.oracle.com/javase/tutorial/essential/io/file.html).

I'll show you just a couple of examples of using the class java.nio.Files for working with text files. This helper class consists of multiple static methods that can help you with various file operations. For the complete list of available operations refer to the javadoc (https://docs.oracle.com/javase/8/docs/api/java/nio/file/Files.html) on Files.

Reading a file with the class Files is even easier than with the classes from the java.io package. For example, to read the file states.txt that I used in the TestGuiFile class can be done as follows:

```
public class TestBufferedReaderNio {
    public static void main(String[] args){
        Path statesFile = Paths.get("states.txt");

        try (BufferedReader reader =
                Files.newBufferedReader(statesFile,
                                         StandardCharsets.UTF_8)){

            String stateName;
            while ( (stateName = reader.readLine()) != null ){
                System.out.println("Got the state " + stateName);
            }
```

```
        } catch (IOException ioe){
            System.out.println("Error while reading states.txt: " +
                                                    ioe.getMessage());
        }
    }
}
```

The class TestBufferedReaderNio uses the method newBufferedReader() that spares you from manually creating an input stream.

If you want to read all lines from a file into a Java collection it can be easily done with the method readAllLines() from the class Files.

```
public class TestReadAllNio {
    public static void main(String[] args){
        Path statesFile = Paths.get("states.txt");

        try {
            // Populate the collection
            List<String> states = Files.readAllLines(statesFile,
                                           StandardCharsets.UTF_8);

            // Print state names
            states.forEach(System.out::println);

        } catch (IOException ioe){
            System.out.println("Error while reading states.txt: "
                                                  + ioe.getMessage());
        }
    }
}
```

Writing into a text file is simple, too:

```
Path myOutputFile = Paths.get("someOutputFile.txt");
try (BufferedWriter writer = Files.newBufferedWrite(myOutputFile,
             StandardCharsets.UTF_8, StandardOpenOption.CREATE)) {
    writer.write("Whatever you want to write");
}
```

The enumeration StandardOpenOption allows you to specify how you want to open the file; e.g., append to an existing file, create a new file if none exists, et al. See the javadoc (https://docs.oracle.com/javase/8/docs/api/java/nio/file/StandardOpenOption.html) for details.

Another interesting feature of NIO is the ability to perform input/output operations asynchronously, which may substantially increase the scalability of your application. If you'll need to work with large amounts of data, research asynchronous classes and interfaces located in the package java.nio.channels (https://docs.oracle.com/javase/8/docs/api/java/nio/channels/package-summary.html). For more detailed coverage of NIO get the book titled "The Well-Grounded Java Developer" published by Manning in 2012.

TRY IT

Write a program that will read a `.zip` archive file and print on the system console the list of files included in the zip archive. Do a little research about the class `java.util.zip.ZipInputStream` and use it together with `FileInputStream`. Read about the class `ZipEntry`, too.

Lesson Requirements

You should have Java installed.

> **NOTE** *You can download the code and resources for this "Try It" from the book's web page at* `www.wrox.com/go/javaprog24hr2e`. *You can find them in the* `Lesson14.zip` *folder in the download.*

Step-by-Step

1. Create a new Eclipse project called Lesson14.
2. Copy any `.zip` file into its root directory.
3. Open `FileInputStream` and connect it with `ZipInputStream`.
4. Write a loop that uses the method `getNextEntry()` from `ZipInputStream`. This method reads the `ZipEntry`, if any, and positions the stream at the beginning of the entry data.
5. Call the function `getName()` on each `ZipEntry` instance found.
6. Print the entry name on the system console.
7. Close the entry inside the loop.
8. Run the program and observe that it properly prints the filenames from the selected `.zip` file.
9. If you want to learn how to create `.zip` files from Java, read about the class `ZipOutputStream`.

> **TIP** *Please select the videos for Lesson 14 online at* `www.wrox.com/go/javaprog24hr2e`. *You will also be able to download the code and resources for this lesson from the website.*

15

Java Serialization

Imagine a building that, with a push of a button, can be turned into a pile of construction materials and the possessions of its residents. Push another button and the building is re-created in its original form in a different location. This is what Java serialization is about. By "pushing the serialize button" you turn an instance of an object into a pile of bytes, and "pushing the deserialize button" magically re-creates the object.

Wikipedia defines the term *serialization* as

> *the process of translating data structures or object state into a format that can be stored (for example, in a file or memory buffer, or transmitted across a network connection link) and reconstructed later in the same or another computer environment. When the resulting series of bits is reread according to the serialization format, it can be used to create a semantically identical clone of the original object ... This process of serializing an object is also called deflating or marshalling an object. The opposite operation, extracting a data structure from a series of bytes, is deserialization (which is also called inflating or unmarshalling).*

In Chapter 14 you became familiar with streams that deal with single bytes, characters, Java primitives, and text. Now you see why and how to write objects into streams, or how to serialize Java objects.

Consider the following scenario: `ClassA` creates an instance of the object `Employee`, which has the fields `firstName`, `lastName`, `address`, `hireDate`, `salary`, and so on. The values of these fields (that is, the object's state) have to be saved in a stream. Later, `ClassB`, which needs these data, somehow has to re-create the instance of the object `Employee` in memory. The instances of `ClassA` and `ClassB` may live in two different Java Virtual Machines (JVMs) running on different computers.

Sure enough, your program can memorize the order of the fields and their data types of `firstName`, `lastName`, `address`, `hireDate`, and `salary`, and loop through the fields performing the output with `DataOutputStream`. The program that reads this stream needs to know the fields' order and their types.

Here's another use case: Your application has a Preferences menu where the user can select fonts, colors, and user interface (UI) controls that should be displayed on the opening view. To support such functionality, the Preferences panel creates an instance of a class, `UserPreferences`, with 50 configurable properties (some of which are of custom data types) that have to be saved in a local file. On the next start of the application, the previously saved data should be read from this file with the re-creation of the `UserPreferences` object.

Writing a manual procedure that uses, say, `DataOutputStream` on each primitive property and then recursively performs the same operation for each non-primitive type is tedious. Besides, this code would need to be changed each time the properties of class `UserPreferences` change.

You can achieve the same result in a more elegant way, not one property at a time, but one object at a time, with the help of such streams as `ObjectOutputStream` and `ObjectInputStream`. This process is known as *Java serialization*, which enables you to save objects in a stream in one shot.

> **NOTE** *This lesson discusses only core Java serialization. But the process of converting an instance of Java into XML, JSON, or another text format is also referred to as serialization. You see an example of serialization into JSON and XML formats in Lesson 33 on RESTFul Web Services.*

`ClassA` serializes the object `Employee`, and `ClassB` *deserializes* (reconstructs) this object. To support this mode, the class `Employee` has *to be serializable*—that is, it has to implement the `Serializable` interface, as shown in Listing 15-1.

LISTING 15-1 Serializable class Employee

```
class Employee implements java.io.Serializable{
     String lName;
     String fName;
     double salary;
}
```

The interface `Serializable` does not define any methods, so the class `Employee` has nothing to implement. If an interface doesn't declare any methods it's called a *marker interface*. The marker interfaces are just affecting the way compiler generates the bytecode.

Two use cases described in this section represent the main uses for Java serialization: distribution of the Java objects between different JVMs and object persistence for future reuse. Often serialization is implemented internally by various Java frameworks to pass objects between tiers of a distributed application that runs on multiple servers and client computers.

Some Java frameworks use serialization to load or unload objects to free the JVM's memory (these are known as *passivation* and *activation* of objects, respectively). Later in the book you learn about RMI and EJB, which use serialization a lot. But even in regular business application development you may need to serialize and deserialize application-specific objects. This process comes down to reading from and writing into streams, namely `java.io.ObjectInputStream` and `java.io.ObjectOutputStream`, respectively.

THE CLASS OBJECTOUTPUTSTREAM

To serialize an object perform the following actions:

1. Open an output stream.
2. Chain it with `ObjectOutputStream`.
3. Call the method `writeObject()`, providing the instance of a `Serializable` object as an argument.
4. Close the stream.

Listing 15-2 shows a code sample that serializes an instance of the `Employee` object into the file `c:\practicalJava\BestEmployee.ser`. This code first opens `FileOutputStream` and then chains it with `ObjectOutputStream`. The method `writeObject()` performs the serialization of the `Employee` instance in one shot.

LISTING 15-2 Serializing an Employee object into a file

```
class ClassA {

  public static void main(String args[]){

    Employee emp = new Employee();
    emp.lName = "John";
    emp.fName = "Smith";
    emp.salary = 50000;

    try (FileOutputStream fOut =
                       new FileOutputStream("BestEmployee.ser");
         ObjectOutputStream oOut =
                                 new ObjectOutputStream(fOut);){

     oOut.writeObject(emp);  //serializing employee
   } catch (IOException ioe){
      ioe.printStackTrace();
   }
   System.out.println(
     "Employee object has been serialized into BestEmployee.ser");
  }
}
```

All Java primitive data types are serializable. All member variables of the serializable class must be either Java primitives or reference variables pointing to objects that are also serializable. The class `Employee` from Listing 15-1 contains only serializable data types. But if a class has fields of custom data types, each of them has to be serializable. The `Employee` class from Listing 15-3 can be serialized only if the class `PromotionHistory` (and all data types it uses) was declared with `implements Serializable`.

LISTING 15-3 Class Employee with custom data types

```
class Employee implements java.io.Serializable{
     String lName;
     String fName;
     double salary;

     PromotionHistory promos; // A custom data type
}
```

If you do not want to serialize some sensitive information, such as salary, declare this variable using the keyword `transient`. If you declare the field salary of the class `Employee` with the `transient` qualifier, its value won't be serialized. The serialized set of bytes will still contain the `transient` field, but it's not going to be the actual value; such a field will have a default value for its type.

```
transient double salary;
```

Typically, you declare a variable as `transient` if it contains some sensitive information or if its value is useless in the destination stream. Suppose a Java class that runs on the server has database connectivity variables. If such a class gets serialized to the client's machine, sending database credentials may be not only useless, but unsafe. Therefore, such variables have to be declared as `transient`. One more reason to use the `transient` keyword is to serialize an object that includes fields of non-serializable types.

THE CLASS OBJECTINPUTSTREAM

To deserialize an object perform the following steps:

1. Open an input stream.
2. Chain it with the `ObjectInputStream`.
3. Call the method `readObject()` and cast the returned object to the class that is being deserialized.
4. Close the stream.

Listing 15-4 shows a code sample that reads the previously serialized file `BestEmployee.ser`. This code opens a `FileInputStream` that points at `BestEmployee.ser` and then chains the `FileInputStream` with `ObjectInputStream`. The method `readObject()` resurrects the instance of the `Employee` object in memory.

LISTING 15-4 Deserializing Employee from file

```
import java.io.*;
class ClassB {

  public static void main(String args[]){
```

```
        try ( FileInputStream fIn =
                      new  FileInputStream("BestEmployee.ser");
              ObjectInputStream oIn = new ObjectInputStream(fIn);){

              Employee bestEmp=(Employee)oIn.readObject();

        }catch (ClassNotFoundException cnf){
            cnf.printStackTrace();
        } catch (IOException ioe){
          ioe.printStackTrace();
        }

        System.out.println(
                       "The Employee  object has been deserialized.");
    }
}
```

Note that the class that deserializes an object has to have access to its declaration or the `ClassNotFoundException` is thrown. During the process of deserialization all `transient` variables are initialized with the default values for their type. For example, `int` variables have a value of `0`.

Keep in mind that class variables with longer names produce larger footprints when the object is serialized. In time-critical applications this may be important. Imagine a Wall Street trading system in which each order is presented as an object, `TradeOrder`, with 50 fields, and you need to send 1,000 of these objects over the network using serialization. Simply shortening each field name by one character can reduce the network traffic by almost 50 KB! You find out how to open the network streams in Chapter 16.

THE INTERFACE EXTERNALIZABLE

Continuing with the example of the trade order, the knowledge of the values of all 50 fields from the class `TradeOrder` may be required to support certain functionality of the application, but when the program has to send a buy or sell request to the stock exchange, only ten fields may be needed.

This raises a question—can the process of serialization be customized so only some of the object fields are serialized?

The method `writeObject()` of `ObjectOutputStream` sends all the object's fields into a stream. But if you want to have more control over what is being serialized and decrease the footprint of your object, implement the `Externalizable` interface, which is a subclass of `Serializable`.

This interface defines two methods: `readExternal()` and `writeExternal()`. These methods have to be written by you to implement serialization of only the selected fields. Listing 15-5 shows a fragment of a class, `Employee2`, that implements `Externalizable`. It has several fields, but in a certain scenario only `id` and `salary` have to be serialized.

LISTING 15-5 Externalizable version of Employee

```
class Employee2 implements java.io.Externalizable {
       String lName;
       String fName;
       String address;
       Date hireDate;
       int id;
       double salary;

   public void writeExternal(ObjectOutput stream)
                               throws java.io.IOException {
    // Serializing only the salary and id
    stream.writeDouble(salary);
    stream.writeInt(id);
   }

   public void readExternal(ObjectInput stream)
                               throws java.io.IOException {
     salary = stream.readDouble(); // Order of reads must be the
                                   // same as the order of writes
     id = stream.readInt();
   }
}
```

Note that each property of the class is individually serialized and the methods `writeExternal()` and `readExternal()` must write and read properties, respectively, in the same order. The class `EmpProcessor` from Listing 15-6 shows how to *externalize* the object `Employee2`.

LISTING 15-6 Externalizing an Employee object

```
import java.io.*;
import java.util.Date;

public class ClassAExt {
  public static void main(String[] args) {
      Employee2 emp = new Employee2();
      emp.fName = "John";
      emp.lName = "Smith";
      emp.salary = 50000;
      emp.address = "12 main street";
      emp.hireDate = new Date();
      emp.id=123;

      try ( FileOutputStream fOut=
                  new FileOutputStream("NewEmployee2.ser");
            ObjectOutputStream oOut =
                  new ObjectOutputStream(fOut);){
```

```
            emp.writeExternal(oOut); //externalizing employee
            System.out.println(
              "An employee is externalized into NewEmployee2.ser");
        }catch(IOException ioe){
            ioe.printStackTrace();
        }
    }
}
```

You had to write a little more code to implement the `Externalizable` interface than to implement the `Serializable` interface, but the size of the file `NewEmployee2.ser` will be substantially smaller. First of all, you serialized the values of only two properties, and files created with the `Externalizable` interface contain only data, whereas files created with `Serializable` also contain class metadata that includes properties' names. The `ClassBExt` in Listing 15-7 shows you how to re-create in memory the externalized object `Employee2`.

LISTING 15-7 Re-creating the externalized object

```
public class ClassBExt {

  public static void main(String[] args) {

      try (FileInputStream fIn=
                      new FileInputStream("NewEmployee2.ser");
           ObjectInputStream oIn = new ObjectInputStream(fIn);){

          Employee2 emp = new Employee2();
          emp.readExternal(oIn);

          System.out.println("Deserialized employee with id "
                                                  + emp.id);
          // format the output as dollars
          System.out.printf("salary = $%7.2f", emp.salary);
      }catch (IOException ioe){
          ioe.printStackTrace();
      }

  }
}
```

CLASS VERSIONING

Imagine that a program, `ClassA`, serializes the `Employee` object from Listing 15-1 into a file on Mary's computer. Two days later Mary starts another program, `ClassB`, that offers a download of its new version with long-awaited features. After upgrade, `ClassB` starts generating errors, which are caused by the fact that the new upgrade includes a modified version of the class `Employee` that now has one property with a different data type than what exists in memory. The upgrade also includes one new property that wasn't in the previous version of the `Employee` object.

Now the deserialization process tries to ignore the new property but fails because of the mismatched property types between the serialized and in-memory versions of `Employee`. Serialization may also fail because of a change in the inheritance tree of `Employee`.

During serialization, JVM automatically calculates a special value: the *serial version unique ID*, which is based on the properties of the serializable object, the class name, the implemented interfaces, and the signatures of non-private methods. If you are curious to see how this number looks for your class, run the program serialver (it's located in the `bin` directory of your Java install), providing the name of your class as a command-line argument.

But if your class explicitly defines and initializes a `static final` variable called `serialVersionUID`, Java uses your value instead of trying to generate one. For example:

```
public static final serialVersionUID = 123;
```

Now, if you keep the value of this variable in the new version of `Employee` the same as in the old one, you have some freedom to add more methods to this class, and JVM assumes that both classes have the same version. If a new version has added a public field, the deserialization process ignores it. If a new version has removed a field, the deserialized version still has it initialized with a default value. But if you change the data type for the public field, the deserialization process fails anyway.

SERIALIZING INTO BYTE ARRAYS

You can also serialize objects into an in-memory array of bytes—`byte[]`. This can be the easiest way of creating a sort of memory blob that can be exchanged among different virtual machines (VMs).

The syntax of such serialization is pretty straightforward. Let's assume that you have a class called XYZ that implements `Serializable` and contains all the elements of your report in the proper format. To prepare a byte array from it, write the code in Listing 15-8.

LISTING 15-8 Turning an object into an array of bytes

```
XYZ myXyz = new XYZ();

// Code to assign values to the fields of myXyz goes here

//...

ByteArrayOutputStream baOut = new ByteArrayOutputStream(5000);
ObjectOutputStream oOut = new ObjectOutputStream(
                              new BufferedOutputStream(baOut));

//Here comes the serialization part

oOut.writeObject(myXyz);
oOut.flush();

// create a byte array from the stream
```

```
byte[] xyzAsByteArray = baOut.toByteArray();
oOut.close();
```

Another convenient use for serializing into a byte array is *object cloning*, which is the creation of an exact copy of an object instance. Even though the class `Object`, the root of all classes, includes the method `clone()`, it works only with objects that implement another marker interface `Cloneable`; otherwise the cloning fails. Things may get more complicated when an object contains instances of other objects: You need to program a *deep copy* of the object.

Serialization into a byte array with immediate deserialization creates a deep copy of the object in no time. After executing the code from Listing 15-9 you get two identical objects in memory. The variable `bestEmployee` points at one of them, and the variable `cloneOfBestEmployee` points at another.

LISTING 15-9 Object cloning with serialization

```
Employee bestEmployee = new Employee();

//Serialize into byte array
ByteArrayOutputStream baOut = new ByteArrayOutputStream();
ObjectOutputStream oOut = new ObjectOutputStream(baOut);
oos.writeObject(bestEmployee);

//Deserialize from byte array to clone the object
ByteArrayInputStream baIn =
                    new ByteArrayInputStream(baOut.toByteArray());
ObjectInputStream oIn = new ObjectInputStream(baIn);
Employee cloneOfBestEmployee = (Employee) oin.readObject();
```

TRY IT

Create a Java Swing program called `MyCustomizableGUI` that enables the user to specify her preferences, such as background color, font family, and size. Pick any GUI components that have these attributes. Selected values should be assigned to fields of the serializable class `UserPreferences` and be serialized into the file `preferences.ser`. Each time `MyCustomizableGUI` is started it should determine if the file `preferences.ser` exists. If the file does exist, `MyCustomizableGUI` should deserialize it and apply previously saved preferences to the GUI.

Lesson Requirements

You should have Java installed.

> **NOTE** *You can download the code and resources for this "Try It" from the book's web page at* `www.wrox.com/go/javaprog24hr2e`*. You can find them in the Lesson15.zip.*

Step-by-Step

1. Create a new Eclipse project and name it Lesson15.
2. Create an executable Swing class called `MyCustomizableGUI` with a text field and a User Preferences button.
3. Program the button to open a new window Preferences (based on `JDialog`) that has three drop-down menus (`JComboBox`), a Save button, and a Cancel button. The first drop-down menu enables the user to select a color, the second a font, and the third a font size.
4. Create a serializable class, `UserPreferences`, that remembers the user's selections. When the user has made her choices, the Save button has to serialize the instance of `UserPreferences` into a file named `preferences.ser`.
5. Each time `MyCustomizableGUI` starts it has to determine if the file `preferences.ser` exists, deserialize it if so, and apply the appropriate color as the background color of the window `MyCustomizableGUI`. The font preferences should be applied to the text field.
6. Run the program to ensure that you can change and save the preferences and that they are properly applied to the GUI.

> **TIP** *Please select the videos for Lesson 15 online at* `www.wrox.com/go/javaprog24hr2e`*. You will also be able to download the code and resources for this lesson from the website.*

16

Network Programming Basics

Computers connected to a network can communicate with each other only if they agree on the rules of communication, called *protocols,* that define how to request the data, if the data should be sent in pieces, how to acknowledge received data, if the connection between two computers should remain open, and so on. TCP/IP, UDP/IP, FTP, HTTP, and WebSocket are some examples of network protocols.

Local area network (LAN) refers to a computer network connecting devices in a small area—for example, the same office or house, or a rack. Interconnected computers located farther apart or that belong to different companies are part of a *wide area network (WAN).* The Internet consists of millions of networks and individual devices. Connected networks that belong to the same organization are referred to as an *intranet.* For security reasons intranets are shielded from the rest of the world by special software called *firewalls.* This lesson introduces networking using HTTP protocol and sockets.

The World Wide Web (WWW) uses *uniform resource locators (URLs)* to identify online resources. For example, the following URL says that there is (or will be generated on the fly) a document called `training.html` located at the remote host known as `mycompany.com`, and that the program should use the HTTP protocol to request this document. It also states that this request has to be sent via port 80.

```
http://www.mycompany.com:80/training.html
```

The hostname must be unique, and it is automatically converted to the Internet Protocol (IP) address of the physical server by your *Internet service provider (ISP),* which is also known as your hosting company. The IP address is a group of four numbers (IPv4)—for example 122.65.98.11—or up to eight hexadecimal numbers (IPv6) —such as 2001:cdba:0000:0000:0000:0000:3257:9652 . Most of the individuals connected to the Internet are getting *dynamic* (not *permanent*) IP addresses assigned to their computers, but for an extra fee you can request a static IP address that can be assigned to any server located in your basement, office, or garage. In enterprises, network computers usually get static (permanent) IP addresses. For individual use, it's sufficient to have a dynamically assigned IP address as long as your ISP can find your server by resolving a domain name to the current IP address.

Finding a resource online is somewhat similar to finding a person by his or her address. The role of an IP address is similar to the role of a street number of a building, and a port plays the role of an apartment number in that building. Many people can live in the same building, just as many programs can run on the same server. A port is simply a unique number assigned to a server program running on the computer.

Multiple Java technologies exist for providing data exchange among computers in a network. Java provides classes for network programming in the package `java.net`. This lesson shows you how to read data from the Internet using the class `URL` as well as direct socket-to-socket programming. Starting with Lesson 25 you become familiar with other technologies that you can use over the network: Java Servlets, RMI, EJB, Web Services, and JMS.

READING DATA FROM THE INTERNET

You learned in Chapter 14 that to read local file streams, a program has to know the file's location—for example, `c:\practice\training.html`. The same holds true for reading remote files—the only difference is that you open the stream over the network. Consider reading remote data using HTTP protocol. Java has a class, `java.net.URL`, that helps you connect to a remote computer on the Internet and get access to a resource there, provided that it's not protected from the public. First, create an instance of the `URL` of your resource:

```
try{
  URL xyz = new URL("http://www.xyz.com:80/training.html");
    ...
}
catch(MalformedURLException murle){
      murle.printStackTrace();
}
```

The `MalformedURLException` is thrown if an invalid URL has been specified—for example, if you typed `htp` instead of `http` or included extra spaces. If the `MalformedURLException` is thrown, it does not indicate that the remote machine has problems; just check "the spelling" of your URL.

Creation of the `URL` object does not establish a connection with the remote computer; you still need to open a stream and read it. Perform the following steps to read a file from the Internet via HTTP connection:

1. Create an instance of the class `URL`.
2. Create an instance of the `URLConnection` class and open a connection using the `URL` from Step 1.
3. Get a reference to the input stream of this object by calling the method `URLConnection.getInputStream()`.
4. Read the data from the stream. Use a buffered reader to speed up the reading process.

While using streams over the networks you'll have to handle possible I/O exceptions the way you did while reading the local files. The server you are trying to connect to has to be up and running, and, if you're using HTTP-based protocols, a special software—a web server—has to be "listening to" the specified port on the server. By default, web servers are listening to all HTTP requests on port 80 and to secure HTTPS requests directed to port 443.

The program in Listing 16-1 reads the content of the existing or generated file `index.html` from `google.com` and prints its content on the system console. To test this program your computer has to be connected to the Internet.

LISTING 16-1 Reading the content of the home page at google.com

```
public class WebSiteReader {
  public static void main(String args[]){
       String nextLine;
       URL url = null;
       URLConnection urlConn = null;

       try
       {
         // Assume index.html is a default home page name
          url  = new URL("http://www.google.com" );
          urlConn = url.openConnection();
       } catch( IOException e){
           System.out.println("Can't connect to the provided URL:" +
                                                e.toString() );
       }

       try( InputStreamReader inStream = new InputStreamReader(
             urlConn.getInputStream(), "UTF8");
            BufferedReader buff  = new BufferedReader(inStream);){

      // Read and print the content of the Google's home page
        while (true){
             nextLine =buff.readLine();
             if (nextLine !=null){
                System.out.println(nextLine);
             }
             else{
               break;
             }
        }
      } catch(IOException  ioe){
      System.out.println("Can't read from the Internet: "+
                                           ioe.toString());
     }
 }
}
```

The code in Listing 16-1 creates an instance of the class URL, then gets a reference to an instance of `URLConnection` to open a connection with the stream, and, finally, opens `InputStreamReader`, which is chained with `BufferedReader`. Run this program and you see the output shown in Listing 16-2.

LISTING 16-2 The fragment of console output shown after google.com is read

```
<!doctype html><html itemscope="" itemtype="http://schema.org/WebPage"
lang="en">
<head><meta content="Search the world's information,
including webpages, images, videos and more. Google has many special
```

```
features to help you find exactly what you're looking for."
name="description"><meta content="noodp" name="robots">
<meta content="/images/google_favicon_128.png" itemprop="image">
<title>Google</title><script>(function(){
window.google={kEI:"kJLGU6f4DJSqyAT614K4DA",getEI:function(a){
for(var c;a&&(!a.getAttribute||!(c=a.getAttribute("eid")));)
a=a.parentNode;return c||google.kEI},https:function()
{return"https:"==window.location.protocol},
kEXPI:"4791,25657,4000116,4007661,4008142,4009033,4009641,
...
</script></div></body></html>
```

The class `WebSiteReader` explicitly creates the object `URLConnection`. Strictly speaking, you could achieve the same result by using only the class `URL`:

```
URL url = new URL("http://www.google.com");
InputStream in = url.openStream();
BufferedReader buff= new BufferedReader(new InputStreamReader(in));
```

The reason you may consider using the `URLConnection` class is that it could give you some additional control over the I/O process. For example, by calling its method `setDoOutput(true)` you specify that this Java program is intended to write to the remote URL, too. In the case of HTTP connections, this will also implicitly set the type of request to `POST` (see Chapter 26). The method `useCaches()` of `URLConnection` also allows you to specify whether the protocol can use a cached object or should always request a fresh copy of the document at a specified URL. In general, if you are planning to write Java programs that will only use the HTTP protocol, use the class `HttpURLConnection`, which supports HTTP-specific features, such as processing header fields, getting HTTP response codes, setting request properties, and so on.

CONNECTING THROUGH HTTP PROXY SERVERS

For security reasons, most enterprises use *firewalls* (see `http://en.wikipedia.org/wiki/Firewall_%28computing%29`) to block unauthorized access to their internal networks. As a result their employees can't directly reach the outside Internet world (or even some internal servers), but go through *HTTP proxy servers*. Check the settings of your Internet browser to see if you are also sitting behind a firewall, and find out the hostname and port number of the proxy server if you are. Usually, web browsers store proxy parameters under the Advanced tabs of their Settings or Preferences menus.

If your browser has downloaded a page containing a Java applet, the latter knows the parameters of the proxy servers and can make requests to the remote servers through the firewall. But a regular Java application should specify networking properties (`http://docs.oracle.com/javase/8/docs/api/java/net/doc-files/net-properties.html`) `http.proxyHost` and `http.proxyPort` to "drill a hole" in the firewall. For example, if the name of your proxy server is `proxy.mycompany.com` and it runs on port 8080, the following two lines should be added to the Java application that needs to connect to the Internet:

```
System.setProperty("http.proxyHost","http://proxy.mycompany.com");
System.setProperty("http.proxyPort", 8080);
```

If you do not want to hardcode these values, pass them to your program from the command line:

```
java -Dhttp.proxyHost=http://proxy.mycompany.com
Dhttp.proxyPort=8080 WebSiteReader
```

The other option for programmatically specifying proxy parameters is to do it via the class `java.net.Proxy`. The code for the same proxy server parameter would look like this (you can replace the name of the server with an IP address):

```
Proxy myProxy = new Proxy(Proxy.Type.HTTP,
        new InetSocketAddress ("http://proxy.mycompany.com", 8080));
url  = new URL("http://www.google.com/index.html");
urlConn = url.openConnection(myProxy);
```

HOW TO DOWNLOAD FILES FROM THE INTERNET

Combine the class `URL` with the writing files techniques and you should be able to download practically any unprotected file (such as images, music, and binary files) from the Internet. The trick is in opening the file stream properly. Listing 16-3 shows the code of a Java class, `FileDownload`, which gets the URL and the destination (local) filename as command-line arguments, connects to this resource, and downloads it into a local file.

LISTING 16-3 Downloading an arbitrary file from the Internet

```
class FileDownload{

  public static void main(String args[]){
   if (args.length!=2){
     System.out.println(
    "Proper Usage:java FileDownload SourceFileURL OutputFileName");
     System.out.println(
     "For example: " +
        "java FileDownload http://myflex.org/yf/nyc.jpg nyc.jpg");
     System.exit(-1);
   }

    URLConnection fileStream=null;
    try{
        URL remoteFile=new URL(args[0]);
        fileStream=remoteFile.openConnection();
    } catch (IOException ioe){
      ioe.printStackTrace();
    }

   try(  FileOutputStream fOut=new FileOutputStream(args[1]);
        InputStream in = fileStream.getInputStream();){

    // Read a remote file and save it in the local one
    int data;
    System.out.println("Starting the download from " + args[0]);
    while((data=in.read())!=-1){
         fOut.write(data);
```

```
            }
            System.out.println("Finished downloading the file "+args[1]);
        } catch (Exception e){
            e.printStackTrace();
        }
    }
}
```

Specifying Command-Line Parameters for FileDownload

Note how this `FileDownload` program starts by checking the number of provided command parameters: If the number is anything but two, the program prints an error message and quits. Here's an example of how you can run this program from the command line to download a photo of New York City that I made in July of 2014.

```
java FileDownload http://myflex.org/yf/nyc.jpg nyc.jpg
```

If you prefer to run this program from Eclipse, select the Run Configurations menu (use the drop-down menu with the green button on the toolbar), select `FileDownload` as the main class, and enter `http://myflex.org/yf/nyc.jpg nyc.jpg` in the Program Arguments box (it's under the Arguments tab). The file will be downloaded in your project directory, and you can see it in Eclipse by selecting Refresh on the project.

THE STOCK QUOTE PROGRAM

This section shows you how to write a program that can read stock market price quotes from the Internet. There are many Internet sites providing such quotes; the Internet portal Yahoo! is one of them.

Visit `http://finance.yahoo.com`, enter the symbol of any stock (AAPL for example), and press the Search Finance button. You see the pricing information about Apple, Inc.—a fragment of this web page is shown in Figure 16-1.

The URL that can be used to get to this page directly is `http://finance.yahoo.com/q?s=AAPL (http://http://finance.yahoo.com/q?s=AAPL)`.

Right-click this web page and select View Page Source (or similar) from the pop-up menu to see the HTML contents of this page; you see lots of HTML tags, and the information about AAPL is buried somewhere deep inside. The class `WebSiteReader` that you used earlier in this lesson reads the content of the Google home page. Modify the line in the class `WebSiteReader` from Listing 16-1 to have it print the content of the Apple's price quote page on the system console:

```
url = new URL("http://finance.yahoo.com/q?s=AAPL");
```

You can also store the whole page in a Java `String` variable instead of printing the lines on the console. In the following code snippet I use the class `StringBuilder` that's a more efficient way of concatenating strings than the immutable class `String` itself. Just modify the `while` loop in Listing 16-1:

```
// Create an instance of StringBuilder with initial capacity ~10Kb
StringBuilder sb = new StringBuilder(10000);
```

```
String theWholePage;
String txt;
while (txt =buff.readLine() != null ){
     sb.add(txt);
 }

theWholePage=sb.toString()
```

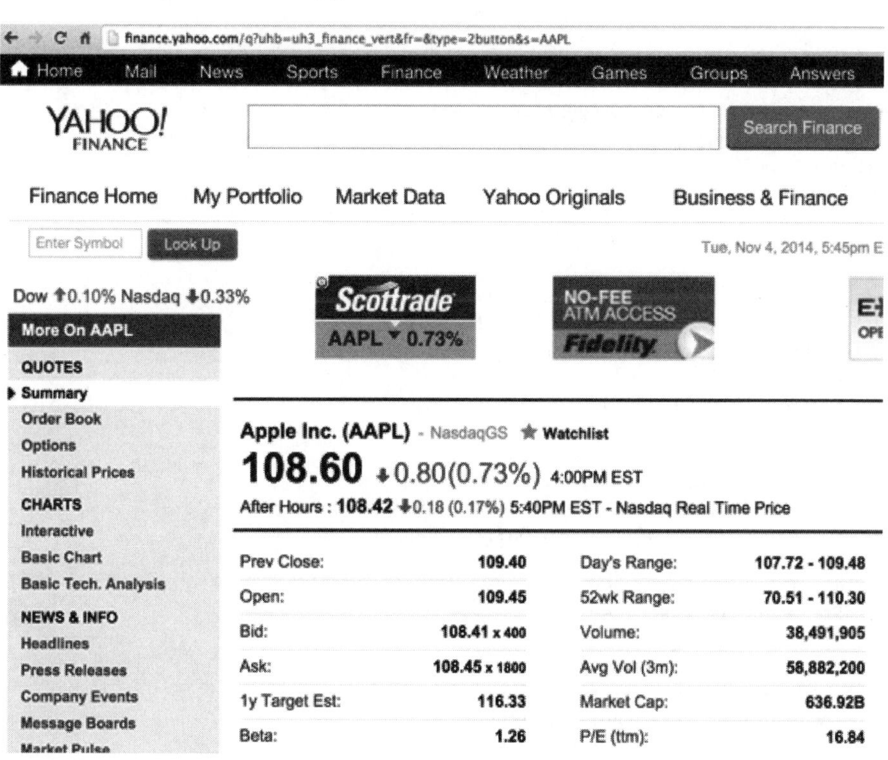

FIGURE 16-1: Figure 16-1. The Apple's stock in November of 2014

If you add some smart tokenizing (splitting into parts based on the specified tokens as in Listing 16-4) of `theWholePage` to get rid of all HTML tags and everything but a fragment around (AAPL), you can create your own little Stock Quote program. Although this approach is useful to sharpen your parsing skills, it may not be the best solution, especially if Yahoo! changes the presentation of the stock symbol on this page (e.g., removes parentheses). That's why the example uses another URL that provides stock quotes in a cleaner *comma-separated values (CSV)* format. Here's the URL that should be used for the symbol AAPL:

```
http://quote.yahoo.com/d/quotes.csv?s=AAPL&f=sl1d1t1c1ohgv&e=.csv
```

This URL produces a string that includes the stock symbol, last trade, date and time of the price quote, earning per share (EPS), opening price, day's range, and volume.

```
"AAPL",108.60,"11/4/2014","4:00pm",-0.80,109.45,109.49,107.72,414989
```

Now the task of tokenizing the entire web page comes down to parsing this short CSV line. The `StockQuote` class from Listing 16-4 does exactly this: It accepts the stock symbol from the command line, gets the data from Yahoo!, tokenizes the received CSV line, and prints the price quote on the console.

LISTING 16-4 Retrieving and printing stock quotes

```
public class StockQuote {

       static void printStockQuote(String symbol){
       String csvString;
       URL url = null;
       URLConnection urlConn = null;

       try{
           url  = new
               URL("http://quote.yahoo.com/d/quotes.csv?s="
                   + symbol + "&f=sl1d1t1c1ohgv&e=.csv" );
           urlConn = url.openConnection();
       } catch(IOException ioe){
           ioe.printStackTrace();
       }

       try(InputStreamReader inStream =
               new InputStreamReader(urlConn.getInputStream());
           BufferedReader buff  = new BufferedReader(inStream);){

        // get the quote as a csv string
        csvString =buff.readLine();

        // parse the csv string
        StringTokenizer tokenizer=new StringTokenizer(csvString, ",");
        String ticker = tokenizer.nextToken();
        String price  = tokenizer.nextToken();
        String tradeDate = tokenizer.nextToken();
        String tradeTime = tokenizer.nextToken();

        System.out.println("Symbol: " + ticker +
            " Price: " + price + " Date: "  + tradeDate
            + " Time: " + tradeTime);
     } catch(MalformedURLException e){
         System.out.println("Please check the spelling of "
                               + "the URL: " + e.toString() );
     } catch(IOException  e1){
      System.out.println("Can't read from the Internet: " +
                                          e1.toString() );
     }
   }

  public static void main(String args[]){
      if (args.length==0){
         System.out.println("Sample Usage: java StockQuote IBM");
```

```
                System.exit(0);
            }

            printStockQuote(args[0]);
        }
    }
```

If you've gone through all the previous lessons in this book, reading and understanding the code in Listing 16-4 should be a piece of cake for you. Test the `StockQuote` program. Enter AAPL or another stock symbol as an argument in the Run Configurations window of Eclipse, or run it from a command window as follows:

```
java StockQuote AAPL
```

Running `StockQuote` can produce something similar to this:

```
Symbol: "AAPL" Price: 108.60 Date: "11/4/2014" Time: "4:00pm"
```

SOCKET PROGRAMMING

Java-based technologies offer many options for network communications, and one of the technologies to consider is *sockets* (*http://docs.oracle.com/javase/tutorial/networking/sockets/definition.html*). A socket is *one endpoint* in the communication link. In this section you learn how to use the Java classes `Socket` and `ServerSocket` from the package `java.net`. Many communication protocols in IP networking are based on sockets. For example, *Transmission Control Protocol/Internet Protocol (TCP/IP)* maintains a socket connection for the whole period of communication, whereas *User Datagram Protocol (UDP)* is a connectionless protocol, which sends data in small chunks called *datagrams.*

The socket address is a pair: IP address and port. When a Java program creates an instance of the `ServerSocket` class, this instance becomes a server that just runs in memory and listens on the specified port for other program requests. The following lines create a server that is listening to port 3000:

```
ServerSocket  serverSocket = new ServerSocket(3000);
client = serverSocket.accept();
```

The client program should create a client socket—an instance of the class `Socket`—pointing at the computer/port on which the `ServerSocket` is running. The client program can connect to the server using hostnames or IP addresses, too; for example:

```
clientSocket = new Socket("124.67.98,101", 3000);
clientSocket = new Socket("localhost", 3000);
clientSocket = new Socket("127.0.0.1", 3000);
```

While deciding which port number to use for the `ServerSocket`, avoid using port numbers below 1024 to avoid conflicts with other system programs. For example, port 80 is typically used by HTTP servers; port 443 is reserved for HTTPS; port 21 is typically used for FTP communications; port 389 is for LDAP servers, and so on. After creating a socket-based connection, both client and server should obtain references to its input/output streams and use them for data exchange.

Why Use Sockets?

Why even use manual socket programming if you can easily establish inter-computer communication with, say, HTTP (it uses sockets internally), start one of many open-source or commercial web servers, and have clients connect to the server as shown in the preceding sample programs in this lesson? Because a socket connection has a lot less overhead than any standard protocol.

You can create your own very compact protocol that will allow you to send only the data you need, with no or minimal headers. Socket communication provides a duplex byte stream, whereon the data travels simultaneously in both directions, unlike protocols based on the request-response model. Think of financial trading systems: Speed is the king there, and the ability to send data up and down at the same time saves milliseconds, which makes a difference.

Compare with Hypertext Transfer Protocol (HTTP), which is used for request-response based communications and adds a couple of hundreds milliseconds of overhead to your data in the form of the HTTP request and response headers. To lower this overhead, a WebSocket protocol (`http://en.wikipedia.org/wiki/WebSocket`)has been created and standardized. WebSocket protocol is not covered in this book.

If you design your application to use sockets, the live connection is maintained for each user connected to `ServerSocket`. If your program has to maintain several thousand concurrent connections it requires more powerful servers than programs using the request-response system, with which a connection is maintained only during the time of the client's request.

The Stock Quote Server with Sockets

Let's build a socket-based client/server application that emulates both a server providing fake price quotes for requested stocks and a client consuming this data. The `StockQuoteServer` class is our socket server that listens to requests on port 3000 (see Listing 16-5).

LISTING 16-5 The server generating stock quotes

```
public class StockQuoteServer {
 public static void main(java.lang.String[] args) {
   ServerSocket serverSocket = null;
   Socket client = null;

   BufferedReader inbound = null;
   OutputStream outbound = null;

   try
     {
     // Create a server socket
     serverSocket = new ServerSocket(3000);

      System.out.println("Waiting for a quote request...");
     while (true)
     {
```

```
        // Wait for a  request
          client = serverSocket.accept();

          // Get the streams
        inbound=new BufferedReader(new
              InputStreamReader(client.getInputStream()));
           outbound = client.getOutputStream();

             String symbol = inbound.readLine();

          //Generate a random stock price
          String price= (new
                     Double(Math.random()*100)).toString();
           outbound.write(("\n The price of "+symbol+
                                " is " + price + "\n").getBytes());

         System.out.println("Request for " + symbol +
                   " has been processed - the price of " + symbol+
                          " is " + price + "\n" );
         outbound.write("End\n".getBytes());
     }
    }
    catch (IOException ioe) {
     System.out.println("Error in Server: " + ioe);
   }  finally{
       try{
           inbound.close();
           outbound.close();
         }catch(Exception e){
           System.out.println(
           "StockQuoteServer: can't close streams" + e.getMessage());
         }
     }
   }
  }
```

The method `accept()` of the `SocketServer` class is the one that puts this program into a wait mode. As soon as it starts you see the message *"Waiting for a quote request..."* on the system console, and nothing else happens until the request comes in from the client. Creating a `SocketServer` instance binds it to the specified port, but if this port is already in use by another process you get a `BindException`.

The client programs run in separate Java Virtual Machines (JVMs). When a client connects to the server's socket, our class `StockQuoteServer` gets references to its I/O streams and sends randomly generated quotes for the requested stock. In the real world this server would have to be connected to another server providing real-time market data, but for the purposes of this example, generating random numbers as "price quotes" will suffice.

The client program shown in Listing 16-6 has to be started with a command-line parameter such as AAPL, IBM, MSFT, and so on to produce a price quote. Because you might not have access to two connected computers, you can start the `Client` program on the same one, but it'll be running in a separate JVM.

LISTING 16-6 The client sending requests for stock quotes

```
public class Client {
public static void main(java.lang.String[] args) {

 if (args.length==0){
   System.out.println("Usage: java Client Symbol");
          System.exit(-1);
 }

  Socket clientSocket = null;
  try{
       // Open a client socket connection
        clientSocket = new Socket("localhost", 3000);
        System.out.println("Client: " + clientSocket);
    }catch (UnknownHostException uhe){
        System.out.println("UnknownHostException: " + uhe);
    } catch (IOException ioe){
       System.err.println("IOException: " + ioe);
    }

   try (OutputStream outbound = clientSocket.getOutputStream();
        BufferedReader inbound = new  BufferedReader(new
        InputStreamReader(clientSocket.getInputStream()));  ){

       // Send stock symbol to the server
     outbound.write((args[0]+"\n").getBytes());

     String quote;
     while (true){
            quote = inbound.readLine();
            if (quote.length() == 0) continue;

            if (quote.equals("End")){
                break;
             }
            System.out.println("Got the quote for " + args[0]+":" +
                                                          ➥ quote);
      }
   }catch (IOException ioe){
       ioe.printStackTrace();
     }
 }
}
```

Have you noticed that StockQuoteServer appends the word "End" to indicate that the price quote has ended? This is an example of a very simple custom-made networking protocol. I just came up with this rule—the word "End" indicates the end of data. While working with sockets it's your responsibility to decide on the data format being sent from client to server and back.

> **NON-BLOCKING SOCKETS**
>
> I used simple blocking sockets in the Stock Server example. The stock server calls the method `accept()`, which blocks on the socket, which may create a bottleneck in a multi-client application. The package java.nio.channels (`https://docs.oracle.com/javase/8/docs/api/java/nio/channels/package-summary.html`) includes a number of classes and interfaces that support asynchronous work with data in general and non-blocking sockets in particular.
>
> In real-world applications with multiple clients, consider learning and using nonblocking sockets, which are implemented in classes `SocketChannel` and `ServerSocketChannel`. Instead of invoking `SocketServer.accept()`, you'll need to open the socket channel, bind it to a particular port, and call `accept()`, which can be listening to the client's connection either in blocking or in non-blocking mode. To place the channel in a non-blocking mode invoke `configureBlocking(false)` on the channel.

TRY IT

The goal of this exercise is to test the socket communication in action, even if you have only one computer.

Lesson Requirements

You should have Java installed.

> **NOTE** *You can download the code and resources for this "Try It" from the book's web page at* `www.wrox.com/go/javaprog24hr2e`. *You can find them in* `Lesson16.zip`.

Hints

In this exercise you use two separate command windows to run the socket client and the server. Eclipse IDE enables you to have more than one Console view. Find a little icon that looks like a monitor in the Console view toolbar and click the little triangle next to it to switch between console views while running more than one application.

Step-by-Step

```
java sockets.StockQuoteServer
java sockets.Client IBM
```

1. Import Eclipse project from `Lesson16.zip` accompanying the book.

2. Even though you can run both programs from Eclipse, it's easier to observe the entire process if you run them from separate command windows. Open two command windows and imagine that they belong to different computers.
3. In each command window, go to the bin directory located in the Lesson16 directory under Eclipse workspace. In one of the command windows start the `StockQuoteServer` and in the other start the `Client`. Note that these classes are located in the package named `socket`.
4. In each command window, go to the bin directory located in the Lesson16 directory under Eclipse workspace. In one of the command windows start the `StockQuoteServer` and in the other start the `Client`. Note that these classes are located in the package named `socket`.
5. Observe that the server generates prices, and that both client and server print the same price on the respective console. By starting client and server in different command windows you are starting two separate JVMs, emulating network communication between computers.
6. Open a couple more command windows and start the `Client` program in them, providing different stock symbols as arguments. Observe that the same server can handle multiple clients' requests. If you have access to a real network in which each computer has Java runtime installed, run the client and server programs on different computers—just replace the `localhost` in the class `Client` with the network name or IP address of the server's computer.

> **TIP** *Please select the videos for Lesson 16 online at* `www.wrox.com/go/javaprog24hr2e`. *You will also be able to download the code and resources for this lesson from the website.*

17

Concurrency and Multithreading

Developing Java applications that implement concurrent processing gives you an amazing power and flexibility when it comes to building highly available, scalable, and responsive applications capable of processing thousands of concurrent requests of various types.

Up until now you've been creating Java programs that were executing code sequentially. But the main power of Java lies in its ability to do things in parallel, or, as they say, to run *multiple threads of execution*. As always, going through a practical use case is the best way to understand this feature.

Let's discuss a program that should display market news and information about the user's stock portfolio in the same window. While the market news feed is coming from a remote computer, stock portfolio data are retrieved from the database and may be located on the local server of your organization.

Suppose it takes three seconds to get the market news and only one second to get the portfolio data. If you run these two tasks sequentially (one after another), you need four seconds to complete the job.

But market news doesn't depend on your portfolio data, and these two tasks can run in parallel. They run on different computers and use different processors. If you can implement parallel processing, the total time should be less than four seconds (close to three seconds in the use case—the time it takes for the longer task to complete).

A Java program can start multiple threads of execution that will run in parallel. Even if you have only one processor in your computer, it still could be a good idea to run some tasks in parallel. Think of a web browser that allows you to download a file and perform page browsing at the same time. Web browsers maintain several connections to any website, and can download multiple resources (text, images, videos, music) at the same time. Any web browser works in a multithreaded mode.

If these jobs ran sequentially, the browser's window would be frozen until the download was complete. On a multiprocessor computer, parallel threads can run on different CPUs. On a single-processor computer, threads take turns getting "slices" of the processor's time. Because switching CPU cycles between threads happens fast, a user won't notice the tiny delays in each thread's execution, and browsing feels smooth.

In many cases, especially on the disappearing single-CPU computers, the benefit of many threads comes about because there's a lot of idle time in most operations. In particular, if an operation is I/O bound instead of CPU bound then using *multiple threads* helps take advantage of those otherwise unused blocks of time.

People also can work in a multithreaded mode. For example, they can drink coffee while talking on a cell phone and driving a car.

THE CLASS THREAD

If class A needs to initiate some parallel executions in classes B and C, the latter two must declare multithreading support from the get-go. Each of the classes B and C must either be inherited from the Java class `Thread` or implement one of the following interfaces: `Runnable` or `Callable` (the latter is covered in Callable). If a class is inherited from the class `Thread` then it has to override the method `run()`.

The first version of the market-portfolio example has three classes (see Listing 17-1, Listing 17-2, and Listing 17-3). Two of them are subclasses of the class `Thread` (`MarketNews` and `Portfolio`), and the third (`TestThreads`) is just a testing program that instantiates them and starts the execution of some code in each of them. You must initiate the code that has to work as a thread in the method `run()`.

LISTING 17-1 Class MarketNews

```
public class MarketNews extends Thread {
 public MarketNews (String threadName) {
        super(threadName); // name your thread
    }

 public void run() {
     System.out.println("The stock market is improving!");
    }
}
```

LISTING 17-2 Class Portfolio

```
public class Portfolio extends Thread {
    public Portfolio (String threadName) {
        super(threadName);
    }

    public void run() {
       System.out.println("You have 500 shares of IBM");
     }
}
```

LISTING 17-3 Class TestThreads starts MarketNews and Portfolio

```
public class TestThreads {
   public static void main(String args[]){
      MarketNews mn = new MarketNews("Market News");
      mn.start();

      Portfolio p = new Portfolio("Portfolio data");
      p.start();

      System.out.println("TestThreads is finished");
   }
}
```

The method `main()` in Listing 17-3 instantiates each thread, passing the name for the thread as a constructor argument and then calls its `start()` method declared in its ancestor. Each thread itself invokes internally the code written by you in the method `run()`. After calling `mn.start()`, the program `TestThread` does not wait for its completion but immediately executes the lines that follow, creating and starting the thread `Portfolio`. Even if the code in the `MarketNews.run()` is lengthy and takes several seconds to execute, the `Portfolio` thread starts immediately.

If you run the `TestThread` program it prints the output from threads `MarketNews` and `Portfolio` almost simultaneously—there is no lengthy and time-consuming code in their `run()` methods. A bit later, in the section "Sleeping Threads", you see how to emulate a lengthy execution. The output of the `TestThread` program can vary—it all depends on which thread finishes first.

THE INTERFACE RUNNABLE

The second way to create threads is to implement a `Runnable` interface, which is a functional interface with a single method `run()`. In this case, your class also has to have business logic in the method `run()`. First, you see an old-fashioned version of creating a thread with Runnable, and then more concise version with lambda expressions.

The second version of our market-portfolio example (Listing 17-4, Listing 17-5, and Listing 17-6) also has three classes (you eliminate two of them shortly), but `MarketNews2` and `Portfolio2` are not inherited from the class `Thread`—they implement the `Runnable` interface.

In environments before Java 8, creation of a thread iis a two-step process: create an instance of a class that implements `Runnable` and then give it as an argument to the constructor of the class `Thread` during instantiation.

LISTING 17-4 Class MarketNews2

```
public class MarketNews2 implements Runnable {
     public void run() {
```

```
            System.out.println("The stock market is improving!");
        }
    }
```

LISTING 17-5 Class Portfolio2

```
public class Portfolio2 implements Runnable {
    public void run() {
       System.out.println("You have 500 shares of IBM ");
    }
}
```

LISTING 17-6 Class TestThreads2

```
public class TestThreads2 {
    public static void main(String args[]){

     MarketNews2 mn2 = new MarketNews2();
     // passing Runnable object to a constructor
     Thread mn = new Thread(mn2,"Market News");
     mn.start();

     Runnable port2 = new Portfolio2();
     // passing Runnable object to a constructor
     Thread p = new Thread(port2, "Portfolio Data");
     p.start();

     System.out.println("TestThreads2 is finished");
    }
}
```

Run this program, and you see an output similar to this one:

```
The stock market is improving!
TestThreads2 is finished
You have 500 shares of IBM
```

The main thread finished earlier than the portfolio one!

Note that I've declared the variable `port2` in Listing 17-6 to not be of type `Portfolio2`; instead it is type `Runnable`. I did it for illustration purposes and to reiterate the fact that an interface is also a data type that can be used in variable declarations. It takes three lines of code in Listing 17-6 to instantiate and start a thread. The `Runnable` interface provides a more flexible way to use threads because it allows a class to be inherited from any other class, while having all the features of a thread.

Eliminating Inheritance

In Lesson 13 in the Eliminating Inheritance section I demonstrated how an inheritance hierarchy can be simplified by introducing lambda expressions. Let's do it again. The classes `Portfolio2` and `MarketNews2` differ only in the implementation of the method `run()` of the functional interface. You can easily get rid of both of these classes by providing implementation of the functional interface `Runnable` (the method `run()`)with lambda expressions directly to the constructors of the `Thread` objects.

```
public class TestThreads2Lambda {
    public static void main(String args[]){

     Thread mn = new Thread(()-> System.out.println(
                      "The stock market is improving!"),"Market News");
     mn.start();

     Thread p = new Thread(() -> System.out.println(
                      "You have 500 shares of IBM"),"Portfolio Data");
     p.start();

     System.out.println("TestThreads2Lambda is finished");
    }
}
```

The classes `MarketNews2` and `Portfolio2` are not needed any longer! This example is very simplistic because both implementations of `run()` just print a simple message. You can also pass a multiline lambda expression; just don't forget to declare the expression in curly braces. The next section includes an example.

SLEEPING THREADS

One of the ways to make the processor available to other threads is by using `Thread`'s method `sleep()`, which enables you to specify in milliseconds (and nanoseconds) how long the thread has to sleep. The next program demonstrates sleeping threads. The class `TestThreads3Lambdas` declares two lambda expressions to process market data and portfolio threads. The function for market news puts itself to sleep for a thousand milliseconds (one second) after each output of the message about market improvements.

When the market news thread goes to sleep, the portfolio gets the CPU and prints its message and then goes to sleep for 700 milliseconds on each loop iteration. Every second the market news thread wakes up and does its job. The portfolio thread has shorter sleep periods.

The program `TestThreads3Lambda` generates mixed console output about the market and portfolio from both threads—the threads are taking turns even on the single-processor machine.

LISTING 17-7 Class TestThreads3Lambda

```
public class TestThreads3Lambda {
```

```
    public static void main(String args[]){

      // Lambda expression for Market News
        Runnable mn = () -> {
           try{
            for (int i=0; i<10;i++){
             Thread.sleep (1000);  // sleep for 1 second
             System.out.println("The market is improving " + i);
            }
          }catch(InterruptedException e ){
             System.out.println(Thread.currentThread().getName()
                                                  + e.toString());
          }
      };

      Thread marketNews = new Thread(mn, "Market News");
      marketNews.start();

      // Lambda expression for Portfolio
      Runnable port = () ->{
          try{
               for (int i=0; i<10;i++){
                Thread.sleep (700);    // Sleep for 700 milliseconds
                System.out.println("You have " + (500 + i) +
                                                  " shares of IBM");
               }
             }catch(InterruptedException e ){
               System.out.println(Thread.currentThread().getName()
                                                      + e.toString());
             }
      };

     Thread portfolio = new Thread(port,"Portfolio data");
     portfolio.start();

     System.out.println(
           "The main method of TestThreads3Lambda is finished");
    }
  }
```

If you need to "wake up" a sleeping thread before its sleeping time is up, use the method `interrupt()`. Just add `mn.interrupt()` to the class `TestThreads3Lambda` right after starting the market news thread. This triggers `InterruptedException`, and the market news thread will wake up and continue its execution from the operator located below the `sleep()` method call. The class `Thread` has a method `interrupted()` that returns `true` if the current thread has been interrupted. The output of the program `TestThreads3Lambda` can look as follows:

```
The main method of TestThreads3Lambda is finished
You have 500 shares of IBM
The market is improving 0
You have 501 shares of IBM
The market is improving 1
You have 502 shares of IBM
```

```
You have 503 shares of IBM
The market is improving 2
You have 504 shares of IBM
The market is improving 3
You have 505 shares of IBM
You have 506 shares of IBM
The market is improving 4
You have 507 shares of IBM
The market is improving 5
You have 508 shares of IBM
The market is improving 6
You have 509 shares of IBM
The market is improving 7
The market is improving 8
The market is improving 9
```

These days it's hard to find a single-CPU server machine. Most of the readers of this book have personal computers with dual-core CPUs, which have two processors in the same chip. Modern JVMs use multiple cores for multi-threaded applications, but you shouldn't assume that your program will run twice as fast on such hardware. JVM optimization is a complex subject and is out of the scope of this tutorial. You may boost the performance of your system by increasing the number of threads running in parallel, but you should define the right ratio between the number of threads and the number of processors (see Amdahl's Law at `http://en.wikipedia.org/wiki/Amdahl's_law`) during the performance-tuning phase of application development.

HOW TO KILL A THREAD

The class `Thread` has a method, `stop()`, that was supposed to know how to kill the current thread. But it was deprecated many years ago because it could bring some of the objects in your program into an inconsistent state (`https://docs.oracle.com/javase/8/docs/api/java/lang/Thread.html#stop--`) caused by improper unlocking of the object instances.

There are different approaches to killing threads. One of them involves creating your own method on the thread, say `stopMe()`, in which you set your own `boolean` variable, say `stopMe`, to `false` and test its value periodically inside the thread's method `run()`. If application code changes the value of `stopMe` to `true`, just exit the code execution in the method `run()`. In Listing 17-8, the loop in the method `run` initializes the value of the variable `stopMe` with the reference to the current thread and then runs the infinite loop testing if the value of `stopMe` is still the same. As soon as it is changed (set to `null` in this case), the processing in the `PortfolioVolatile` stops.

LISTING 17-8 Killing a thread

```
class KillTheThread{
  public static void main(String args[]){

     PortfolioVolatile p =new PortfolioVolatile("Portfolio data");
     p.start();
```

```
            // Some code implementation business logic goes here
            int i=0;
            do {
               System.out.println(" i= " + i++);
            }while (i<100);

            // and now it's time to kill the thread
            p.stopMe();
        }
    }

    class PortfolioVolatile extends Thread{

    private volatile Thread stopMe;

        public PortfolioVolatile (String threadName) {
             super(threadName);
        }

        public void stopMe() {
            stopMe = null;
        }

        public void run() {
            stopMe = Thread.currentThread();

            while (stopMe == Thread.currentThread()) {
             //Do some portfolio processing here
             System.out.println("The Portfolio thread is running");
            }
           System.out.println("The Portfolio thread was killed");
        }
    }
```

Running the program `KillTheThread` produces the console output that can end as follows:

```
The Portfolio thread is running
 i= 97
 i= 98
 i= 99
The Portfolio thread is running
The Portfolio thread was killed
```

The variable `stopMe` has been declared with a `volatile` keyword, which warns the Java compiler that another thread can modify it, and that this variable shouldn't be cached in the CPU's registers, so all threads must always see its fresh value. The class `PortfolioVolatile` could be written differently—the variable `stopMe` could be declared as `boolean`.

Not every thread can be killed using the code shown in Listing 17-8. What if a thread is not doing any processing at the moment, but is waiting for the user's input? Call the method `interrupt()` on such a thread. Killing a thread by interrupting it may be the only technique you need to use in such cases.

If you need to kill a thread that's busy doing some blocking I/O operations and the preceding methods of killing such a thread don't work, try closing I/O streams. This causes `IOException` during the current read/write operation and the thread will be over.

If you'd like to read more comprehensive coverage of this subject, see Dr. Heinz Kabutz the Java Specialist's newsletter Issue #56, available at `www.javaspecialists.co.za/archive/Issue056.html`.

THREAD PRIORITIES

Single-processor computers use a special scheduling algorithm that allocates processor time slices to the running threads based on their priorities. If `Thread1` is using the processor and the higher-priority `Thread2` wakes up, `Thread1` is pushed aside and `Thread2` gets the CPU. It is said that `Thread2` *preempts* `Thread1`.

The class `Thread` has a method, `setPriority()`, that allows you to control its priority. There are 10 different priorities, which are `final integer` variables defined in the class `Thread`. Some of them are named constants `MIN_PRIORITY`, `NORM_PRIORITY`, and `MAX_PRIORITY`. Here's an example of their usage:

```
Thread myThread = new Thread("Portfolio");
myThread.setPriority(Thread.NORM_PRIORITY + 1);
```

If two threads with the same priority need the processor, it'll be given to one of them using an algorithm specific to the computer's operating system.

THREAD SYNCHRONIZATION AND RACE CONDITIONS

During the design stage of a multithreaded application's development, you should consider the possibility of a so-called *race condition*, which happens when multiple threads need to modify the same program resource at the same time (*concurrently*). The classic example is when a husband and wife are trying to withdraw cash from different ATMs *at the same time*.

Suppose the balance on their joint account is $120. If a `Thread` class is responsible for the validation as well as update of the balance of their bank account, there is a slight chance that if the validation starts at the same time it'll approve withdrawal of $100 for the husband and $50 for the wife because the each of the validated amounts is less than the total. A moment later the husband's thread withdraws $100, and a split second later the wife's thread attempts to withdraw $50—it was validated, right? Unless these two processes were synchronized the couple would be able to withdraw a total of $150, leaving a negative balance in their account. This is an example of a *race condition*.

A special keyword, `synchronized`, prevents race conditions from happening. This keyword places a *lock* on an object instance (*the monitor*) to make sure that only one thread at a time has access to the synchronized code. The code in Listing 17-9 locks the entire method `withdrawCash()` so no other thread gets access to the specified portion of code until the current (locking) thread has finished its execution of `withdrawCash()`. In this example, both validation and balance update can be performed by only one thread at a time.

LISTING 17-9 Declaring a synchronized method

```
class ATMProcessor extends Thread{

 synchronized withdrawCash(int accountID, int amount){
    // Some thread-safe code goes here, i.e., reading from
    // a file or a database
    //   ...
   boolean allowTransaction = validateWithdrawal(accountID,
                                                 amount);
   if (allowTransaction){
     updateBalance(accountID, amount, "Withdraw");
   }
   else {
    System.out.println("Not enough money on the account");
   }
  }
}
```

The locks should be placed for the shortest possible time to avoid slowing down the program: That's why synchronizing short blocks of code is preferable to synchronizing whole methods. Listing 17-10 shows how to synchronize only the portion of the code that may actually cause the race condition, rather then locking the entire method `withdrawCash()`.

LISTING 17-10 Declaring a synchronized block

```
class ATMProcessor extends Thread{
  ...
 withdrawCash(int accountID, int amount){
    // Some thread-safe code goes here, i.e., reading from
    // a file or a database
  ...
 synchronized(this) {
   boolean allowTransaction=validateWithdrawal(accountID, amount);
   if (allowTransaction){
      updateBalance(accountID, amount, "Withdraw");
   }
   else {
      System.out.println("Not enough money on the account");
   }
  }
 }
}
```

When a `synchronized` block is executed, the section of the code in parentheses is locked and can't be used by any other thread until the lock is released. Listing 17-10 locks the current instance of the class `ATMProcessor` (represented by the `this` key-word) only for the duration of the `validateWithdrawal()`

and updateBalance() methods, which is a shorter period of time than locking withdrawCash() would take.

Although synchronized is a Java keyword, there is a more efficient API for locking the code. It's called reentrantLock(), and you see it later in this lesson.

THREAD STATES

A thread goes through various states during its life span. The class Thread has a method, getState(), that returns one of the values defined in the enumeration Thread.State.

- BLOCKED: Thread state for a thread that is blocked and waiting to enter or reenter a synchronized method or block of code
- NEW: Thread state for a thread that has been instantiated but not started yet
- RUNNABLE: Thread state for a runnable thread
- TERMINATED: Thread state for a terminated thread
- TIMED_WAITING: Thread state for a waiting thread with a specified waiting time
- WAITING: Thread state for a waiting thread

The class Thread has a method, isAlive(), that can help you to find out the status of the thread. If it returns true, the thread has been started and hasn't died yet. If it returns false, the thread is either new or already dead.

WAIT AND NOTIFY

The class Object also has some methods relevant to threads: wait(), notify(), and notifyAll(). The method notify() allows one waiting thread to notify another about some important event. Accordingly, notifyAll() sends notification to all waiting threads. Because every Java class is inherited from the class Object, these methods can be called on any object. There is one more important rule: Both the wait and notification must be done in a synchronized block holding the lock *on the same object*.

Let's revisit our class TestThreads3Lambda, which spawns the threads for market news and portfolio. It has the following line at the end of the main() method:

```
System.out.println("The main method TestThreads3 is finished");
```

Run the program TestThreads3Lambda, and it prints something like this:

```
The main method of TestThreads3Lambda is finished
You have 500 shares of IBM
The market is improving 0
You have 501 shares of IBM
The market is improving 1
...
```

Note that the method `main()` did not wait for the portfolio and market news threads' completion! The next code sample shows you how one thread can wait for a notification from another using `wait()`. To simplify the understanding of the example I'm using just two threads: the main thread and the market news one. The new class is called `TestLambdaWaitNotify`. I want to kill two birds with one stone and explain an interesting use case for lambdas, too. To make the `main()` method wait for notifications, it can include the following code fragment:

```
TestLambdaWaitNotify thisInstance = new TestLambdaWaitNotify();

synchronized (thisInstance) {
  try{
             thisInstance.wait(20000);  // wait for up to 20 sec
  } catch (InterruptedException e){
             e.printStackTrace();
  }
}

System.out.println(
            "The main method of TestLambdaWaitNotify is finished");
```

The method call `wait(20000)` means "wait for up to 20 seconds." The last `println` statement is executed either after 20 seconds or when the main thread receives notification of some important event, whichever comes first. Calling `wait()` without the argument would make the program wait for the notification until it arrives. Examples of important events are a price drop on the auction for items you're interested in, the reopening of the airport after freezing rain, and the execution of your order to purchase 100 shares of IBM stock.

The difference between `sleep()` and `wait()` is that calling `sleep(20000)` puts a thread into a not-runnable state for exactly 20 seconds, although `wait(20000)` might mean that it will come back to a runnable state earlier.

Note that in the preceding example the main thread placed a lock on the instance of its own object—`thisInstance`. The other thread has to receive a reference to the same object to send the notification. If you were writing code in traditional object-oriented style, you could create a separate class implementing `Runnable` with a constructor that gets a reference to the parent thread for further notifications as shown here:

LISTING 17-11 Notification example

```
class MarketNews implements Runnable {
 Object parent;

  MarketNews(Object whoToNotify){
      parent=whoToNotify;
  }

  public void run(){
    // Do some lengthy processing here

    synchronized(parent){
     parent.notify(); // send notification to the waiting thread
```

```
            }
        }
    }
```

But I'd like to implement `Runnable` using a lambda expression and illustrate an interesting concept called *closures*.

Closures in Java

In functional languages like JavaScript, a *closure* is a nested function that knows the context where it was declared. In other words, during the invocation the nested function has access to variables from the outer one even though they were never declared inside the nested function. It's easier to explain this concept by example, and I will implement the market news thread not as a separate class, but as a lambda expression:

```
 Runnable mNews =() -> {
     // Do something
     // But who to notify????
};
```

This lambda gets the object of the inferred type `Runnable`, but how to pass it to yet another object, which is the reference to the parent thread to send notification to? You create an "outer function"—a method that takes a reference to the parent thread as an argument:

```
private Runnable getMktNewsRunnable(
   Object whoToNotify){
     return () -> {
        // Do something
        whoToNotify.notify();
     };
}
```

This is an example of a method returning a lambda expression so the following statement is valid:

```
Runnable mktNewsRunnable = getMktNewsRunnable(this);
```

The value of the variable is just the code returned by the method `getMktNewsRunnable()`. It's important to notice that this code just uses the variable `whoToNotify` from the outer method even though it was not declared inside the lambda expression! So the inner function "remembers" that when it was created, there was someone in the neighborhood named `whoToNotify`. This is the essence of the concept of closures, which remember the context they were declared in.

The variables from outer scope are inferred to be `final` and are immutable; you can't modify them. Even though I never declared the variable `whoToNotify` as `final`, it is `final`.

Following is the complete version of the class `TestLambdaWaitNotify` that creates a thread using lambda and gets notification when that thread is done with the processing.

```
public class TestLambdaWaitNotify {

  private static Runnable getMktNewsRunnable(Object whoToNotify){
    // returning a closure
```

```
        return  () -> {
             try{
               for (int i=0; i<10;i++){
                Thread.sleep (1000);  // sleep for 1 second
                System.out.println("The market is improving " + i);
               }

               synchronized(whoToNotify){
                  whoToNotify.notify(); // send notification to parent
               }
            }catch(InterruptedException e ){
               System.out.println(Thread.currentThread().getName()
                                                + e.toString());
            }
        };
      }

      public static void main(String args[]){

         TestLambdaWaitNotify thisInstance = new TestLambdaWaitNotify();

         Runnable mktNewsRunnable = getMktNewsRunnable(thisInstance);
         Thread marketNews = new Thread(mktNewsRunnable,"");
         marketNews.start();


         synchronized (thisInstance) {
               try{
                   thisInstance.wait(20000);  // wait for up to 20 sec
               } catch (InterruptedException e){
                   e.printStackTrace();
               }
             }

            System.out.println(
                "The main method of TestLambdaWaitNotify is finished");
      }
    }
```

Now the message that the main method is finished is printed after the loop inside the market news ends. Hopefully it takes less than 20 seconds. You can remove this time interval and just call `wait()` to ensure that even on the slow computers the main thread waits for as long as needed.

JOINING THREADS

Now let's consider a scenario in which you need to start multiple threads and continue program execution only when all threads are complete. You may have several threads that need to wait for each other's completion. The `Thread` class has a method, `join()`, that you can use in this case.

Revisit the `TestThreads3Lambda` program shown in Listing 17-7. If you want to make sure that the `main` method (the main thread) is waiting until the other two threads are finished, you can use the method `join()`.

The following code snippet shows the class `TestThreads3LambdaJoin` that links together three threads: main, portfolio, and market news.

LISTING 17-12 Joining threads

```
public class TestThreads3LambdaJoin {

  public static void main(String args[]){

    // Lambda expression for Market News
      Runnable mn = () -> {
         try{
          for (int i=0; i<10;i++){
           Thread.sleep (1000);  // sleep for 1 second
           System.out.println("The market is improving " + i);
          }
        }catch(InterruptedException e ){
           System.out.println(Thread.currentThread().getName()
                                                   + e.toString());
        }
     };


     // Lambda expression for Portfolio
     Runnable port = () ->{
         try{
              for (int i=0; i<10;i++){
               Thread.sleep (700);   // Sleep for 700 milliseconds
               System.out.println("You have " +  (500 + i) +
                                                 " shares of IBM");
              }
           }catch(InterruptedException e ){
              System.out.println(Thread.currentThread().getName()
                                                   + e.toString());
           }
     };

     Thread marketNews = new Thread(mn, "Market News");
     Thread portfolio = new Thread(port,"Portfolio data");

     marketNews.start();
     portfolio.start();

     try{
        marketNews.join();
        portfolio.join();

     }catch (InterruptedException e){
        e.printStackTrace();
     }

     System.out.println(
```

```
                "The main method of TestThreads3LambdaJoin is finished");
    }
}
```

Running the class TestThreads3LambdaJoin prints the outputs of market news and portfolio first, and only after the message that the main method is finished. The main thread waits for the other two by joining them.

GOODIES FROM JAVA.UTIL.CONCURRENT

The package java.util.concurrent has lots of goodies that make thread programming a lot more robust and flexible, and most importantly that increase the performance of multithreaded applications. This section highlights some of the must-know techniques, classes, and interfaces from this package. For detailed coverage of this subject get the book *Java Concurrency in Practice* by Brian Goetz et al. (Addison-Wesley, 2006).

ReentrantLock Versus Synchronized

The package java.util.concurrent.locks includes the class ReentrantLock, which can be used as a replacement for the synchronized keyword. Using it gives you more flexibility, and it can be used across methods. The idea is to place a lock (invoke lock()) before the section of your program that may cause a race condition, and to remove the lock afterward. The next code snippet is a revision of the code shown earlier in Listing 17-10:

```
private Lock accountLock = new ReentrantLock();

witdrawCash(int accountID, int amount){
    // Some thread-safe code goes here, e.g. reading from
    // a file or a database

   accountLock.lock(); // place a lock here

   try{
    if (allowTransaction){
      updateBalance(accountID, amount, "Withdraw");
    } else {
      System.out.println("Not enough money on the account");
    }
   }finally {
     accountLock.unlock(); //allow other threads to update balance
  }
}
```

Note that the lock has to be removed in the finally section to ensure that unlocking always gets executed, even if there is an exception thrown from the try block. When the code is unlocked it can be given to one of the waiting threads. The class ReentrantLock has an overloaded constructor with a boolean argument—if you specify true while creating the lock, the control is given to the longest-waiting thread.

There is another useful class, Condition, that can be associated with the lock. This object enables a locked block of code to suspend its execution until other threads notify the current one that some condition has become true —for example, the bank account has enough funds now for you to make a withdrawal.

If you don't need the flexibility offered by the ReentrantLock/Condition combo, just use the synchronized keyword with notify()/notifyAll() methods to control thread locking. Or, even better, see if using one of the concurrent collections (reviewed in the section "A Brief Review of Concurrent Collections") can take care of all your locking needs so you don't need to create explicit locks in your code.

Executor Framework

Creating threads by subclassing Thread or implementing Runnable works, but there are certain shortcomings to these approaches. First, the method run() cannot return a value. Second, an application may spawn so many threads that it can take up all the system resources, and if this happens the application will stop functioning. In other words, you need to be able to control the number of threads allowed for each application.

You can overcome the first shortcoming by using the Callable interface, and the second one by using classes from the *Executor framework*. The Executors class spawns the threads from Runnable objects, ExecutorService knows how to create Callable threads, and ScheduledExecutorService allows you to schedule threads for future execution.

The utility class Executors has static methods that enable you to create an appropriate executor. In particular, its method newFixedThreadPool() creates a pool of threads of a specified size. For example, Executors.newFixedThreadPool(5) gives you an instance of ExecutorService that automatically supports a pool of not more than five threads. If all five threads are busy when a request to create a new thread comes in, that request waits until one of the running threads completes. Using thread pools ensures that you can control system resources better.

If you need a thread to return some data on completion, create a class that implements the Callable interface and defines a method call() that plays the same role as run() in Runnable. In this case you need to create threads differently; the class Thread doesn't take a Callable object as an argument. The class Executors comes to the rescue: it offers a number of static methods that create a thread from your Callable class and return the result of its execution packaged inside the special object implementing the interface Future.

The method call() is defined with a parameterized value (remember generics?):

```
public interface Callable <V>{
   V call() throws Exception;
}
```

Accordingly, if some method needs to create a thread using Callable, the code should instantiate the Callable thread with a specific data type in place of <V>. For example, the thread Portfolio may return an Integer as a result of some processing in its call() method:

```
public class Portfolio implements Callable<Integer>{

   public Integer call() {
      // Perform some actions
      return someInteger;
```

```
    }
}

public class MarketData implements Callable<Integer>{

    public Integer call() {
        // Perform some actions
        return someInteger;
    }
}
```

One way to create a Future object is by submitting an instance of the Callable thread to the Executor. Call the function get() on the Future instance, and it blocks on the thread until its call() method returns the result:

```
//Threads' results can be stored in the collection of Futures
List<Future<Integer>> threadResults=
                              new ArrayList<Future<Integer>>();

// Submit Callables for execution
threadResults.add(myExecutorService.submit(new Portfolio()));
threadResults.add(myExecutorService.submit(new MarketData()));

for (Future<Integer> future : threadResults) {
       future.get();
}
```

Calling methods get() on several instances of the Future objects is equivalent to joining threads.

The process of spawning threads using Executors, Callable, and Future may go like this:

1. Declare and instantiate a class that implements the Callable interface, and program the business logic in its method call(). Alternatively, you can use a lambda expression because Callable is a functional interface.
2. Create an instance of the Future object.
3. Create an instance of an ExecutorService using Executors.newFixedThreadPool().
4. Call the function submit() on the ExecutorService, providing an instance of the Callable object (or lambda expression) as an argument.
5. Call the function get() on the Future object from Step 2. This function waits until the thread returns the result (or throws an exception).
6. Accept the result of the thread execution into a variable of the data type used in Step 1.
7. Call the function shutdown() on the ExecutorService from Step 3.

The following class TestCallableThreads creates a collection of Future objects—one per thread. Executors creates a pool of two threads, and each thread is submitted for execution. The method get() waits for the completion of each thread, and the result of each call() method is stored in the collection results. Lambda expressions implement Callable.

LISTING 17-13 Spawning threads with the Executor framework

```
public class TestCallableThreads {

 public static void main(String[] args)
               throws InterruptedException, ExecutionException {

   // Lambda expression for Market News
  Callable<Integer> mn = () -> {
     for (int i=0; i<10;i++){
      Thread.sleep (1000);  // sleep for 1 second
      System.out.println("The market is improving " + i);
     }
      // Just return some number to illustrate return
      return 12345;
  };

    // Lambda expression for Portfolio
  Callable<Integer> port = () ->{
         for (int i=0; i<10;i++){
          Thread.sleep (700);    // Sleep for 700 milliseconds
          System.out.println("You have " +  (500 + i) +
                                        " shares of IBM");
         }

      // Just return some number
      return 10;
  };

  //A placeholder for Future objects
   List<Future<Integer>> futures =
    new ArrayList<Future<Integer>>();

   // A placeholder for results returned by threads
   List<Integer> results = new ArrayList<Integer>();

  final ExecutorService service =
    Executors.newFixedThreadPool(2);

  try {
    futures.add(service.submit(port));
    futures.add(service.submit(mn));

    for (Future<Integer> future : futures) {
     results.add(future.get());
    }
  } finally {
     service.shutdown();
  }

  for (Integer res: results){
     System.out.println("\nGot the result: " + res);
```

```
            }
        }
    }
```

The output of this program is shown next. But if you change the number of threads in the pool from two to one, the program first prints all messages from the portfolio thread and only after that prints all messages from the market news.

```
You have 500 shares of IBM
The market is improving 0
You have 501 shares of IBM
The market is improving 1
You have 502 shares of IBM
You have 503 shares of IBM
The market is improving 2
You have 504 shares of IBM
The market is improving 3
The market is improving 4

Got the result: 10
Got the result: 12345
```

A Brief Review of Concurrent Collections

The package `java.util.concurrent` offers a number of data structures that simplify programming with threads. This section briefly names some of them.

Queues

The concept of a *queue* (First In First Out or FIFO) fits well in any process that involves asynchronous intra-object communications. Instead of object A trying to place a direct lock on object B, the former (also known as the *producer*) can place some data objects in a queue, and the latter (also known as the *consumer*) retrieves (*dequeues*) them from the queue asynchronously. Most importantly, the queues from the `java.util.concurrent` package are *thread-safe*, which means that you can add an object to a queue without worrying about race conditions.

If the queue is blocking, the thread also blocks while trying to add an object to a full queue or remove an object from an empty one. The following classes implement the `BlockingQueue` interface: `LinkedBlockingQueue`, `ArrayBlockingQueue`, `SynchronousQueue`, `PriorityBlockingQueue`, and `DelayQueue`. To add an object to a queue you can use such methods as `add()`, `put()`, and `offer()`. To retrieve an object from a queue use `poll()`, `remove()`, `take()`, or `peek()`.

Unbound queues don't place limitations on the number of elements. `ConcurrentLinkedQueue` is an example of such a queue.

Java has introduced a `Deque` interface for inserting and removing elements from both ends of the queue. The class `LinkedBlockingDeque` is a concurrent implementation of this interface.

Collections

Using concurrent collections is a recommended way of creating thread-safe data structures. Such collections include `ConcurrentHashMap`, `ConcurrentSkipListMap`, `ConcurrentSkipListSet`, `CopyOnWriteArrayList`, and `CopyOnWriteArraySet`. Java documentation describes when to use each of these collections. For example, a `CopyOnWriteArrayList` is preferable to a `synchronized ArrayList` when the expected number of reads and traversals is much greater than the number of updates to a list. These collections were written to minimize the time during which data is locked.

The utility class `java.util.Collections` has a number of static methods that create thread-safe collections. Their method names start with the word *synchronized*. For example, `synchronizedList()` takes a regular `List` (such as `ArrayList`) as an argument and makes it thread-safe. You can read more about Java Collections Framework in Oracle documentation at `http://goo.gl/yknUje`.

Finding a ready-to-use synchronized collection is better than writing `synchronized` blocks on your own. The chances are slim that you'll write more efficient synchronization code than already exists in Java.

SWINGWORKER THREAD

Any Java Swing application spawns a number of threads. At the very minimum it runs the main application thread, the second thread captures system events, and the third one communicates with the graphical user interface (GUI). The application itself may spawn additional threads. But if more than one thread needs to update the user interface (UI) components, the changes may not be rendered properly, because Swing components were not made thread-safe to minimize the number of locks that hurt performance.

To avoid this problem, UI updates shouldn't be made directly, but rather submitted to an *event dispatch thread*. Swing uses a single-threaded model, which means that all UI updates are rendered via a single thread.

Suppose your GUI application is written with Java Swing, and a click on `JButton` initiates some server-side data request that takes about 10 seconds to complete. You should never execute long requests in the event dispatch thread. If you do, then the UI will become frozen, as no updates can be made until the long running process releases the lock on the thread. Therefore, you need to start a separate thread for such a long process, and when it finishes, the program has to modify the GUI via the event dispatch thread.

For example, if the result of a button click has to update a `JTextField`, you may create a new thread in the button's `actionPerformed()` method and, from within the `run()` method of this thread, update the text field. This will work most of the time, if there are no conflicts with other threads running in your application.

All UI-related Swing events (such as button clicks and window repaints) are placed in a special queue, and the object `java.awt.EventQueue` retrieves them from this queue. You should direct modification of the UI (the `JTextField` in our example) to this queue.

In the older version of Java, to ensure that all application-specific data would modify the GUI via this queue, developers used the method `invokeLater()` to ensure that UI changes were placed in the `EventQueue`:

```
SwingUtilities.invokeLater(
   new Runnable(){
    public void run(){
```

```
            // Do some processing here
            //... and then update the UI
            myTextField.setText(someData);
        }
      }
    );
```

You may use lambda to make the preceding code shorter. The class `javax.swing.SwingWorker` gives you a cleaner (though not necessarily simpler) means of dealing with the event dispatch thread. This thread class implements `Runnable` and `Future`, and so can be submitted to the `Executor` for execution and return a result.

Let's say a Swing application needs to make a request to the server to get the market news information, which may take a couple of seconds. So that the UI isn't frozen for these seconds, this request has to be performed in a background thread, and when the result is ready the UI has to be updated. To arrange this, create a subclass of `SwingWorker` and override its `doInBackground()` method, then instantiate it and call its `execute()` method, as in Listing 17-14.

LISTING 17-14 Basic use of SwingWorker

```
class MarketNewsWorker extends SwingWorker <List<String>, String>{

   @Override public List<String> doInBackground(){
       // Make a request to the server and return a result,
       // i.e., a list of Strings
      return myListOfTextData;
  }
     // method method overrides go here

 }

class TestMarketNews{
     ...
     public static void main(String[] args){
          new MarketNewsWorker().execute();
     }
}
```

This code gives you a high-level picture, but there is more to executing the thread with `SwingWorker`. First, you probably noticed the unknown syntax element `@Override`, which is Java *annotation* stating that the method `doInBackground()` is being overridden. Adding the `@Override` annotation is not required here; it's just an example of an annotation. You learn about annotations in Chapter 23.

Second, the class `MarketNewsWorker` uses generics and has two parameters, `<List<String>` and `String>`. The reason for this is that the overridden method `doInBackground()` *might* call the `SwingWorker`'s `process()` method, and *will* call its `done()` method on completion; this is where the UI is being updated. Two parameters indicate what types of data will be returned by `doInBackground()` and given to `process()` respectively.

Why might you consider calling the method `process()` during your thread execution? You might do it to support some kind of progress meter or other means of reporting the progress of long-running processes. If, for example, a long-running thread is reading a large file or performing some lengthy calculations, you might want to calculate the percentage of completion and report it to the calling Swing application.

You are not allowed to call the `process()` method directly, but have to call a method called `publish()`, which internally calls `process()`. Override `process()` to add some messages to the log file or update the progress meter. The code to display the result of the calculations on the UI should be written in the method `done()`.

Listing 17-15 shows you a typical way to program with `SwingWorker`. I left out the details on purpose so you'd have something to do for this lesson's homework.

LISTING 17-15 A typical way to use SwingWorker

```
class MarketNewsWorker extends SwingWorker <List<String>, String>{

   @Override public List<String> doInBackground(){
      // Make a request to the server and return a result,
      // i.e., a list of Strings
      for (String news: someNewsCollection){
            //process each news and report the progress
            // ...
         publish("Processed the news " + news); //this calls process()
      }
      return myListOfTextData;
  }

   @Override protected void process(String progressMessage){
       // display the progress information here
   }

   @Override protected void done(){
       // modify UI components here by calling get()
       // Future's get() gives you the result of
       // the thread execution
   }
}

class TestMarketNews{

     public static void main(String[] args){
          new MarketNewsWorker().execute();
     }
}
```

You just completed a rather long and advanced lesson of this book. The subject definitely requires more research and practice. Some good content to read next is the lesson on concurrency in Oracle's Java tutorial, which is at `http://docs.oracle.com/javase/tutorial/essential/concurrency`. As always, trying it hands-on will deepen your understanding.

TRY IT

Create a Swing application with the GUI that consists of two `JTextArea` controls and one `JButton` with the label "Get the News." Prepare two text files with some text information (the news), and write the code that reads them to the left and right text areas respectively. File reading has to be implemented concurrently using two `SwingWorker` threads.

Lesson Requirements

You should have Java installed.

> **NOTE** *You can download the code and resources for this "Try It" from the book's web page at* `www.wrox.com/go/javaprog24hr2e`. *You can find them in the Lesson17.zip.*

Step-by-Step

1. Create a new Eclipse project.
2. Create a class called `NewsReader` as a subclass of `SwingWorker`. This class should have a constructor that takes one argument of type `File`, and another of type `JTextArea` (the content of the file should be displayed there).
3. Prepare two text files with some news in each.
4. Create a Swing application with two text areas and a button.
5. On the click of the button instantiate two `NewsReader` threads. Each thread should get an instance of the `File` object pointing to the corresponding news file and the corresponding text area.
6. Override the `NewsReader`'s methods `doInBackground()` and `done()` to read the files and populate the Swing view.
7. Test this program.
8. This step is optional. Override the method `process()` and make sure that it updates the view with progress information about the reading process. The progress should be displayed as a percentage: The percentage formula is `progressToDisplay=readBytes/FileSize*100`. Use the Swing class `JProgressBar` for displaying the progress bar.

> **TIP** *Please select the videos for Lesson 17 online at* `www.wrox.com/go/javaprog24hr2e`. *You will also be able to download the code and resources for this lesson from the website.*

18

Introduction to GUI with JavaFX

JavaFX was created to compete with formerly popular Rich Internet Application (RIA) frameworks, such as Adobe Flex and Microsoft Silverlight. In reality JavaFX never became competitive in the RIA space, but it presents a better and more modern alternative for Swing when it comes to developing a graphical user interface (GUI) in Java. Whereas Swing was built on top of the old AWT library, JavaFX is not. Also, while JavaFX is bundled with Java SE 8, it's not a part of it.

With JavaFX you can develop the GUI either in Java or use a mix of FXML and Java. The FXML is an XML-based markup language that enables you to define GUI components in a declarative way. The sources of such GUI definitions would be stored in a text files with the extension `.fxml`, which represent a view in the Model View Controller (MVC) architecture. The business code and access to data would be still written in Java using a rich library of JavaFX components. Using FXML for GUI promotes the clean separation of the code between the MVC layers. JavaFX offers a design tool called Scene Builder (`http://www.oracle.com/technetwork/java/javase/downloads/sb2download-2177776.html`)that allows designing the GUI by dragging the GUI components from a toolbar onto the window's real estate.

In this lesson you'll learn how to program JavaFX application in Java. In Lesson 19 you'll see how to use Scene Builder to make a GUI design process a lot more enjoyable and simple by using FXML.

You can find JavaFX documentation at the following Oracle website: `http://docs.oracle.com/javase/8/javase-clienttechnologies.htm`.

In this lesson you discover the basics of creating GUI with JavaFX 8. In the next lesson you create a tic-tac-toe game with JavaFX .

JAVAFX APPLICATION BASICS

JavaFX uses theater terminology. To create an application, you instantiate a *stage* object first. Pretend that you're a play director and need to set up one or more *scenes* (think views). The backbone of each scene is a *scene graph* (*`http://docs.oracle.com/javafx/2/architecture/jfxpub-architecture.htm#A1106328`*)—a hierarchical tree of GUI *nodes* (think GUI containers and components). Each node can be styled using the Cascading Style Sheet (CSS) file. You can also apply effects and transitions to nodes. You can assign event handlers to nodes if need be. On the top of the scene graph you create a *root node.*

JavaFX classes are located in the packages `javafx.stage` and `javafx.scene`. The main class of a JavaFX application extends `Application` and has the following structure:

```
public class Main extends Application {
    public void start(Stage primaryStage) {
        // Create your stage and scenes here
    }

    public static void main(String[] args) {
        launch(args);
    }
}
```

The JavaFX framework calls the `Application` 's methods `launch()`, `init()` , and then `start()`. The method `init()` is called on the launcher thread, and is the right place to create all required GUI components. The `start()` method is the main entry point to the JavaFX application. The `start()` method is called on the application thread and is the right place for creating objects to be placed on the first scene of the stage, which plays a similar role as `JFrame` or `JDialog` in Swing.

EMBEDDING SWING IN JAVAFX

Swing and the Java FX application run on different threads. To reuse existing Swing components inside JavaFX applications, use the class `SwingNode`.

Using the E(fx)clipse Plug-in

Modern IDE speed up JavaFX programming by providing code generators, embedded Scene Builder and good support of FXML. The best IDE for developing JavaFX application is NetBeans (`https://netbeans.org/features/java-on-client/javafx.html`). IntelliJ IDEA (`http://blog.jetbrains.com/idea/2014/11/intellij-idea-14-is-released/`) goes next. Since we use Eclipse IDE in this book, we'll need to install an Eclipse plug-in called E(fx)clipse (`https://www.eclipse.org/efxclipse/index.html`).

Open the Eclipse menu Help → Install New Software. Click the Add button and include the following URL in the location field to get the latest version: `http://download.eclipse.org/efxclipse/updates-nightly/site` as shown in Figure 18-1.

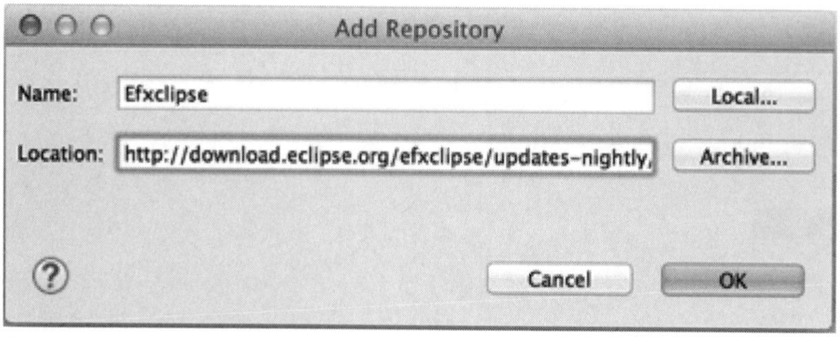

FIGURE 18-1: Adding the location of the E(fx)clipse plug-in

Click OK, and check all components as shown in Figure 18-2.

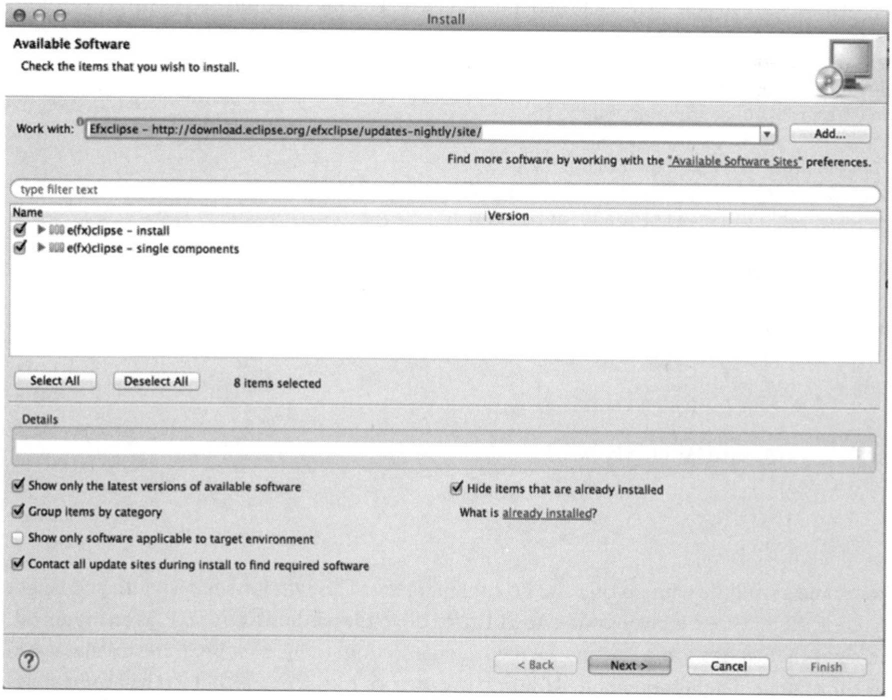

FIGURE 18-2:
Selecting the plug-in's components for installation

Complete the install by clicking Next and then clicking Finish. Eclipse restarts and you're ready to create JavaFX projects.

Create a new HelloFX project. Select File→New→Other→JavaFX→JavaFX Project and give your project a name HelloFX. You see a new project with content like that shown in Figure 18-3.

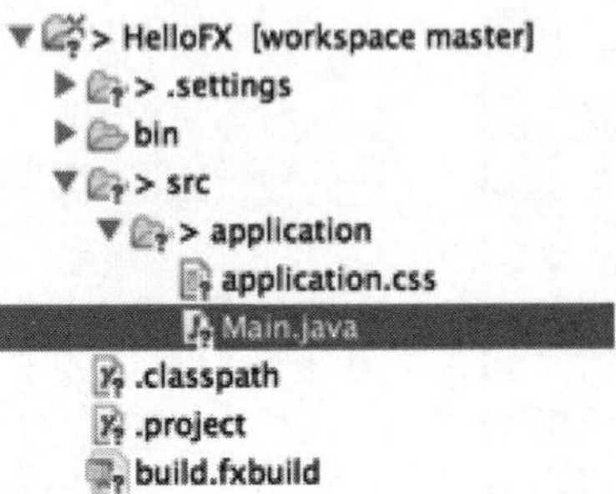

FIGURE 18-3: The newly generated JavaFX project

This project has auto-generated a `Main` class that launches the application; it also auto-generated the empty file `application.css`, where you can add styles. The generated class `Main` looks like this:

```
public class Main extends Application {
    @Override
    public void start(Stage primaryStage) {
        try {
            BorderPane root = new BorderPane();
            Scene scene = new Scene(root,400,400);
            scene.getStylesheets().add(getClass()
                 .getResource("application.css").toExternalForm());
            primaryStage.setScene(scene);
            primaryStage.show();
        } catch(Exception e) {
            e.printStackTrace();
        }
    }

    public static void main(String[] args) {
        launch(args);
    }
}
```

Run the `Main` program, and a window with no title and no content opens. This windows has a width and height of 400 pixels. The reference to the stage is given by the `Application` to the method `start()` as an argument. After that the code assigns the `BorderPane` layout (see the Layouts section) to the root node and creates a 400 x 400 scene with this empty node. The auto-generated file `application.css` is empty, but if it had some styles defined, the scene would be styled accordingly.

In the next section you modify this code to use JavaFX layouts.

LAYOUTS

Similarly to Java Swing layout managers (see Lesson 9), JavaFX has layouts that help with arranging GUI controls on the scene and keeping the arrangement for different stage sizes. In addition to using the built-in layouts, you can customize the positioning of the nodes on the scene using CSS.

This section includes only two code samples of using layouts, and it assumes that you've mastered Lessons 8 and 9 and understand the concept. Refer to the product documentation (`http://docs.oracle.com/javafx/2/layout/jfxpub-layout.htm`) to see how other layouts work.

JavaFX has the following layout container classes (*layout panes*):

- `HBox`
- `VBox`
- `FlowPane`
- `GridPane`
- `BorderPane`
- `StackPane`
- `TilePane`
- `AnchorPane`

The `HBox` class (the horizontal box) places controls in a row next to each other. The vertical box `VBox` places controls vertically. The `FlowPane` places the nodes in a row and then wraps to the next row if there is no room in the current one.

The `GridPane` is similar to Swing's `GridBagLayout` described in Lesson 8. It enables you to arrange user interface (UI) controls in rows and columns and assign constraints to each cell.

The `BorderPane` can split the scene into as many as five regions, similar to Swing's `BorderLayout`, but in JavaFX these areas are called `left`, `top`, `right`, `bottom`, and `center`.

The `TilePane` layout is similar to the `FlowPane`, but it places each node in a cell of the same size (like tiles on the wall). Say, you need to display several images in a tile layout. Adding the `ImageView` nodes to the `TilePane` shows them as tiles next to each other.

The `StackPane` layout is similar to the Swing's `CardLayout`. Only one child node is shown at a time covering the other nodes.

The `AnchorPane` enables you to anchor nodes at the left, top, right, and bottom of the scene. Imagine a music player application with the Rewind button on the left and the Fast Forward button on the right. Say you want to ensure that the Rewind button always remains 20 pixels away from the left border of the window and 10 pixels from the bottom. You want to maintain this positioning even if the user resizes the window. For that you can use the `leftAnchor` and `bottomAnchor` properties. For example,

```
AnchorPane.setLeftAnchor(rewindBtn, 20);
AnchorPane.setBottomAnchor(rewindBtn, 10);
```

Each of these layouts can be configured in terms of alignments, padding, margins and other properties.

Typically you'll be going through the following steps with any layout:

1. Create instances of child nodes to be used within the layout container.

2. Create an instance of the selected layout class (for example, `HBox`). This instance serves as a container and a layout manager for all child nodes that you add to it.

3. Add the child nodes to the container using either the `add()` or `addAll()` method.

4. If this layout instance needs to be used inside another layout (for example, an HBox can be placed inside the `BorderPane`), add the instance created in Step 1 to the parent container by using the method `add()`.

Let's see how it works using the HBox example.

A Sample Application with the HBox Layout

Say you need to ask the user to enter his or her e-mail and send it to some Java code that knows how to process it. This example use sthe following JavaFX components: `Label`, `Button`, and `TextField`, which are located in the `javafx.scene.control` package.

With the help of the E(fx)clipse plug-in, create a new JavaFX Main class `HBoxSample` (use File→New→Other→JavaFX→Classes). It creates the following class:

```
public class HBoxSample extends Application {

    public void start(Stage primaryStage) {
    }

    public static void main(String[] args) {
        launch(args);
    }
}
```

Now you need to create instances of `Label`, `TextField`, and `Button` set their properties, and add them to the instance of HBox. Add the following code to the `start()` method:

```
Label emailLbl = new Label("Email:");

TextField emailTxt = new TextField();
emailTxt.setPrefColumnCount(20);
emailTxt.setPromptText("Your email");

Button submitBtn = new Button("Submit");

HBox emailBox = new HBox(5);  // spacing between children 5 px
emailBox.setPadding(new Insets(3));  // space around HBox
emailBox.getChildren().addAll(emailLbl, emailTxt, submitBtn);

Scene scene = new Scene(emailBox,750,100);
primaryStage.setScene(scene);
primaryStage.show();
```

Run the `HBoxSample` program, and you see a window similar to the one shown in Figure 18-4.

FIGURE 18-4: Running the HBoxSample

The prompt "Your email" is not shown in the text field because it has focus, but as soon as this control loses focus you see it.

Make a small change to this program by replacing instantiation of the `HBox` with `VBox`, and these components will be laid out vertically one under another (you need to increase the height of the scene to see all three components).

A SAMPLE APPLICATION WITH THE GRIDPANE LAYOUT

`GridPane` divides the selected scene area into rows and columns and places nodes into the grid cells. Cells don't have to be of the same size—nodes can span. If the screen size changes, the content doesn't wrap and maintains the grid.

Before placing the node into a cell, you have to specify grid constraints, such as `rowIndex` and `columnIndex` (the coordinate of the cell, which starts with 0,0). The `rowSpan` and `columnSpan` allow to make the cell as wide (or as tall) as several other cells. The `GridPane` documentation (`http://docs.oracle.com/javase/8/javafx/api/javafx/scene/layout/GridPane.html`)describes lots of various constraints that can define the behavior of each cell's content if the windows are resized. This section shows you a basic example that uses some of the constraints.

This example creates a login window where the user can enter the ID and password, and then press the Sign In button. The scene uses the `GridPane` layout. The first row contains a `Label` and `TextField` for the user ID; the second row has a setup for the password; and the third row of the grid has one button (Sign In) that should span two columns. Figure 18-5 below shows how the window should look.

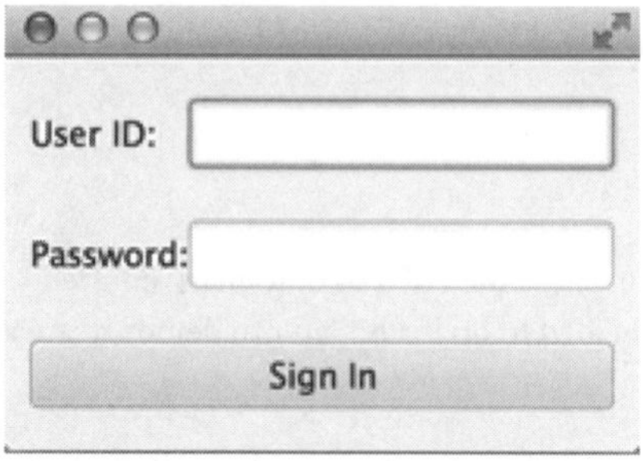

FIGURE 18-5: The Sign In window

Following is the code of the class `GridPaneSample` that rendered this window:

```
public class GridPaneSample extends Application {

    public void start(Stage primaryStage) {

        final int TWO_COLUMN_SPAN = 2;

        Label userIdLbl = new Label("User ID:");
        TextField userIdTxt = new TextField();
        Label userPwdLbl = new Label("Password:");
```

```
        PasswordField userPwdTxt = new PasswordField();

        GridPane root = new GridPane();
        root.setVgap(20);
        root.setPadding(new Insets(10));
        root.setAlignment(Pos.CENTER);

        // Using static methods for setting node constraints
        GridPane.setConstraints(userIdLbl, 0, 0);
        GridPane.setConstraints(userIdTxt, 1, 0);
        GridPane.setConstraints(userPwdLbl, 0, 1);
        GridPane.setConstraints(userPwdTxt, 1, 1);

        root.getChildren().addAll(userIdLbl, userIdTxt,
                                  userPwdLbl, userPwdTxt);

        Button signInBtn = new Button ("Sign In");

        // Allow the button to be wider overriding preferred width
        signInBtn.setPrefWidth(Double.MAX_VALUE);

        // using instance method for directly adding the node
        root.add(signInBtn,0,2,TWO_COLUMN_SPAN,1);

        Scene scene = new Scene(root,250,150);
        primaryStage.setScene(scene);
        primaryStage.show();

    }

    public static void main(String[] args) {
        launch(args);
    }
}
```

The code creates two instances of the `Label` , one `TextField` and one `PasswordField`, to mark entered characters. I could have created the instance of the `Button` too, but decided to do it a bit later to demonstrate a different way of setting constraints.

Then the code calls a static method `setConstraints()` on the class `GridPane` to allocate the GUI controls to the appropriate cells. The coordinates of the top-left cell are (0,0). The label User ID goes there. The next cell to the right has the coordinates (1,0). Note that the column's number goes first. The label Password goes to the cell (0,1), and the text field for the password is placed in the cell (1,1).

Note that the width of the second column is noticeably wider than the first one. The width of the column is automatically determined to accommodate the widest node. The same applies to the height of the rows.

After that the code creates an instance of a `Button` and sets its preferred width to large. Without setting the width, I was not able to specify that this button should span two columns. To demonstrate a different syntax of setting constraints, I've placed the button to the cell (0,2) using the `GridPane` instance method `add()`. The third and fourth arguments are for specifying the row and column spans. My button's cell is twice as wide as regular cells of this grid.

The examples in the next sections further modify the class `GridPaneSample` to demonstrate event handling and skinning.

SKINNING WITH CSS

Using CSS became a de facto standard way of styling UI in web applications. This process is known as *skinning*. You can apply different skins on the same GUI components to change the look of the UI. Applying the skin comes down to loading the CSS file into your JavaFX application. Even though you can style JavaFX GUI components programmatically (for example, using `setFont()` or `setFill()`) separating styling from programming allows professional web designers to take care of the look and feel while software developers implement application logic. Besides, changing the style doesn't require recompilation and redeployment of your application.

Covering CSS is out of scope of this book, but you can get familiar with the CSS syntax by going through the CSS specification (`http://www.w3.org/TR/CSS21/`)(JavaFX supports CSS 2.1) or by reading a CSS books. This section shows you a simple example of how the look of the GUI can be changed without the need to modify the Java code. Keep in mind, though, that JavaFX style names are similar, but they're not the same as those defined in the CSS specification. JavaFX styles start with the prefix `fx-`.

You can create *CSS selectors* to style a specific GUI component, a type of components (for example, all labels), or create a reusable style that can be applied programmatically to selected components.

To style a specific component, the component has to have a unique ID, which can be set in your Java code using the method `setId()`. For example, if a button has an ID of `submitBtn`, you can add the following section to the CSS file to make its background color red (you can find the names of the main CSS colors online (`http://www.w3schools.com/cssref/css_colornames.asp`)):

```
#submitBtn{
    -fx-background-color: red;
}
```

In CSS, the ID type selectors start with the # sign. To make the style in the preceding code work, your Java code should have something like this:

```
Button signInBtn = new Button ("Sign In");
signInBtn.setId("submitBtn");
```

If you want to apply a style to several components of the same type, you need to define a *type selector*. For example, to make the text of all `Label` components red, you can define the following CSS type selector:

```
.label{
  -fx-text-fill: red;
}
```

Note that CSS type selectors start with the dot. To create a CSS *class selector* that can be applied to any component, define under the selector under an arbitrary name and apply it programmatically to the components of your choice. For example, you can specify the following class selector:

```
.bluelabel{
   -fx-text-fill: blue;
   -fx-font-weight: bold;
   -fx-font-family:verdana;
   -fx-font-style:italic;
}
```

This class selector defines rules that displays the text of the label in blue **bold** verdana font in *italic style.* To apply this class selector to a specific label, your Java code should have something like this:

```
Label userPwdLbl = new Label("Password:");
userPwdLbl.getStyleClass().add("bluelabel");
```

For this particular label, the style `bluelabel` overrides the type selector that may have been applied to all other labels on stage.

You may ask, "How am I supposed to know which style properties are available for a given JavaFX component?" For styles that are supported by JavaFX, refer to the online document titled "JavaFX CSS Reference Guide (`http://docs.oracle.com/javase/8/javafx/api/javafx/scene/doc-files/cssref.html`)."

It's time to find out how to apply all these styling techniques to the `GridPaneSample` from the previous section. I named the new version of this class `GridPaneSampleCSS`, and its code is shown next. I've added only three lines to the `GridPaneSample` code, which are shown in bold.

```
public class GridPaneSampleCSS extends Application {

    public void start(Stage primaryStage) {

        final int TWO_COLUMN_SPAN = 2;

        Label userIdLbl = new Label("User ID:");
        TextField userIdTxt = new TextField();
        Label userPwdLbl = new Label("Password:");
        userPwdLbl.getStyleClass().add("bluelabel");
        PasswordField userPwdTxt = new PasswordField();

        GridPane root = new GridPane();
        root.setVgap(20);
        root.setPadding(new Insets(10));
        root.setAlignment(Pos.CENTER);

        // Using static methods for setting node constraints
        GridPane.setConstraints(userIdLbl, 0, 0);
        GridPane.setConstraints(userIdTxt, 1, 0);
        GridPane.setConstraints(userPwdLbl, 0, 1);
        GridPane.setConstraints(userPwdTxt, 1, 1);

        root.getChildren().addAll(userIdLbl, userIdTxt,
                                  userPwdLbl, userPwdTxt);

        Button signInBtn = new Button ("Sign In");
        signInBtn.setId("submitBtn");  // used in CSS
```

```
            // Allow the button to be wider overriding preferred width
            signInBtn.setPrefWidth(Double.MAX_VALUE);

            // using instance method for directly adding the node
            root.add(signInBtn,0,2,TWO_COLUMN_SPAN,1);

            Scene scene = new Scene(root,250,180);
            scene.getStylesheets().add(getClass()
                      .getResource("application.css").toExternalForm());
            primaryStage.setScene(scene);
            primaryStage.show();
        }

        public static void main(String[] args) {
            launch(args);
        }
    }
```

This application loads the `application.css` file with the following content:

```
#submitBtn{
    -fx-background-color: lightskyblue;
    -fx-font-family:verdana;
    -fx-font-size:20;
    -fx-font-weight: bold;
    -fx-stroke:navy;
    -fx-font-style:italic;
    -fx-border-radius: 20;
    -fx-background-radius: 20;
    -fx-padding: 5;
}

.label{
    -fx-text-fill: red;
}

.bluelabel{
   -fx-text-fill: blue;
   -fx-font-weight: bold;
   -fx-font-family:verdana;
   -fx-font-style:italic;
}
```

First, it defines the style for the JavaFX component with the ID `submitBtn`. Then it defines a rule that all labels should be red. There is no need to write any JavaFX code to apply these styles. There is also a class selector named `bluelabel`, which can be applied selectively. Note that you need to add a `-fx-` prefix to the standard CSS properties for them to be recognizable by JavaFX applications. Running the program `GridPanelSampleCSS` produces the output shown in Figure 18-6.

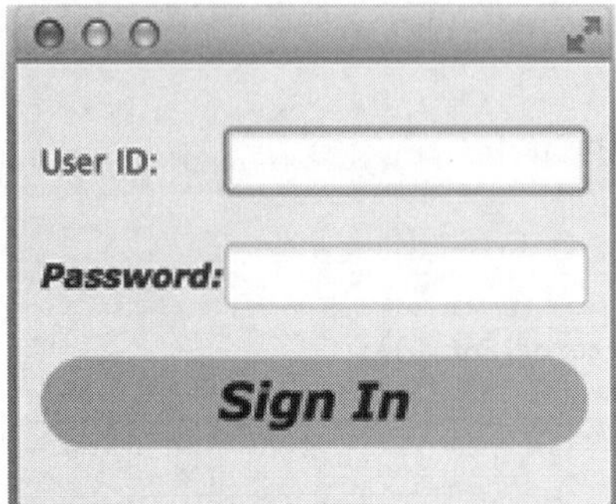

FIGURE 18-6: The styled Sign In window

For further details of skinning the JavaFX GUI, read Oracle's online tutorial "Skinning JavaFX Applications with CSS (`http://docs.oracle.com/javafx/2/css_tutorial/jfxpub-css_tutorial.htm`)."

EVENT HANDLING

Similarly to the Swing framework events covered in Lesson 9, JavaFX applications are also event-driven. In JavaFX, an event object is represented by the instance of the class `javafx.event.Event`. There are different ways of handling events. Depending on how you structured your application, you can assign event handlers either in Java or in FXML. Lesson 19 shows you how to hook up event handlers to GUI components declared in FXML. But if your program is written in purely in Java, you'll be assigning event handlers in Java as well. But in any case, the code that handles events will be always written in Java.

Before writing event handlers for your application you need to decide which events are important and have to be handled in your application. For example, there is no need to write and event handler for the label from the Sign In application. But we do need to handle the Sign In and Cancel button click events. If the user ID would be represented by an email, we would need to intercept and handle the moment when the text field loses focus. In this lesson I'll only show you how to handle the button clicks. For detailed coverage of handling JavaFX events read the Oracle tutorial (`http://docs.oracle.com/javafx/2/events/jfxpub-events.htm`).

You can handle events using one of the following techniques:

- Create an instance of an anonymous class overriding its `handle()` callback method. Pass it to the the event handler for a specific event.
- Use lambda expressions.
- Use Java *method references*.

This example creates yet another version of the Sign In window, but this time the window has the Sign In and Cancel buttons as well as the Forgot Password hyperlink. Each of these controls use a different way of handling the click event. The new Sign In window will look like the one in Figure 18-7.

FIGURE 18-7:
The Sign In window with event handlers

The event handler for the Sign In button is implemented using an anonymous inner class. The event handler for the Cancel button is implemented using a lambda expression. Finally, I implement the click handler for the Forgot Password hyperlink using a method reference. The code of the class `GridPaneSampleEvents` is shown next.

```
public class GridPaneSampleEvents extends Application {

    public void start(Stage primaryStage) {

        Label userIdLbl = new Label("User ID:");
        TextField userIdTxt = new TextField();
        Label userPwdLbl = new Label("Password:");
        PasswordField userPwdTxt = new PasswordField();
        Button signInBtn = new Button ("Sign In");
        Button cancelBtn = new Button ("Cancel");
        Hyperlink forgotPwdLink = new Hyperlink("Forgot password");

        GridPane root = new GridPane();
        root.setVgap(20);
        root.setPadding(new Insets(10));
        root.setAlignment(Pos.CENTER);

        // Using static methods for setting node constraints
        GridPane.setConstraints(userIdLbl, 0, 0);
        GridPane.setConstraints(userIdTxt, 1, 0);
        GridPane.setConstraints(userPwdLbl, 0, 1);
        GridPane.setConstraints(userPwdTxt, 1, 1);
        GridPane.setConstraints(signInBtn, 0, 2);
        //Cancel button: span 1, right aligned
        GridPane.setConstraints(cancelBtn, 1,2, 1, 1, HPos.RIGHT,
                                                     VPos.CENTER);
        GridPane.setConstraints(forgotPwdLink, 0, 3,2,1);

        root.getChildren().addAll(userIdLbl, userIdTxt, userPwdLbl,
                    userPwdTxt,signInBtn, cancelBtn, forgotPwdLink);

        // Event handlers
```

```
        //1. Anonymous class
        signInBtn.setOnAction(new EventHandler<ActionEvent>(){
            public void handle(ActionEvent evt){
              System.out.println(
                      "Anonymous class handler. Sign in clicked.");
            }
        });

        // lambda expression
        cancelBtn.setOnAction(evt ->
            System.out.println("Lambda handler. Cancel clicked.")
        );

        // method reference
        forgotPwdLink.setOnAction(this::forgotPwdHandler);

        // Show the window
        Scene scene = new Scene(root,250,200);
        primaryStage.setScene(scene);
        primaryStage.show();
    }

    private void forgotPwdHandler(ActionEvent evt){
        System.out.println(
              "Method reference handler. Forgot password clicked");
    }

    public static void main(String[] args) {
        launch(args);
    }
}
```

If you run this program, and click Sign In, Cancel, or Forgot Password, the console output shows the following:

```
Anonymous class handler. Sign in clicked.
Lambda handler. Cancel clicked.
Method reference handler. Forgot password clicked.
```

Although each of the event handlers works the same, I prefer the lambda expression version because it's concise and is easy to read. Each of the JavaFX GUI controls has a set of `setOnXXX()` methods (for example, `setOnAction()` and `setOnMouseMoved()`) that should be called for the events you're interested in handling.

PROPERTIES AND BINDING

Although Java developers casually use the words properties referring to class attributes, JavaFX properties are more than just class attributes. JavaFX defines an interface `javafx.beans.property.Property`, which has a very useful functionality enabling you *to bind* (`http://docs.oracle.com/javafx/2/binding/jfxpub-binding.htm`) the GUI components (the view) with properties of the Java classes (the model) and automate notifications of the GUI components when the value in the model changes or vice versa.

Imagine that you're developing a financial application that receives notification from the server about the stock price changes. When a Java object receives a new price, you need to modify the content of the corresponding GUI component. With JavaFX you can simply bind a property `price` of a Java class to the property of, say, a `Label` component. No more coding is required. As soon as the `price` value changes, the `Label` is automatically updated. JavaFX properties greatly simplify the process of synchronization of the data and the GUI.

Existing implementations of the `Property` interface serve as wrappers to Java attributes adding the change notification functionality. The interface `Property` declares the following methods: `bind()`, `unbind()`, `bindBidirectional()`, `unbindBidirctional()`, and `isBound()`. Can you bind any value to a JavaFX property? No—the value has to be of an `ObservableValue` type.

OBSERVER DESIGN PATTERN

In software development there is a design pattern called *Observer*. It's used to implement scenarios when one object (*the observer*) wants to watch changes in other object(s) (*the observables*). For example, if a Twitter user (the observable) posts a tweet, all of his followers (observers) are notified. You can read more about this and other design patterns at `http://www.javacamp.org/designPattern`.

JavaFX property classes are located in the package `javafx.beans.property`. For each property type there are two classes: read-only and read-write. For example, if you need to work with a `String` property, use either `SimpleStringProperty` or `ReadOnlyStringWrapper`. Both of these implement the `StringProperty` interface. Similarly named classes exist for other data types and some collections too.

As you always do in this book, you can learn by coding. This time you're going to modify the `GridPaneSampleEvents` class from the previous section by placing an additional `Label` component at the bottom of the Sign In window. It'll display the messages about the events as the user clicks the buttons and the hyperlink. Initially this label does not have any text:

```
Label messageLbl = new Label();
```

JavaFX properties are observables. Hence you can add a listener (observer) to the property to be notified when the property value changes. But it's much easier to simply use a property in a binding expressions. You *bind* this label to the string property, and as soon as the value of this property changes, the label component `messageLbl` displays this value.

```
private StringProperty message = new SimpleStringProperty();
messageLbl.textProperty().bind(message);
```

In the previous section, the class `GridePaneSampleEvents` was just printing messages on the system console when the user clicked the buttons or the hyperlink. The new class `GridPaneSampleBinding` modifies the property `message` instead, for example:

```
cancelBtn.setOnAction(evt ->
   message.set("Cancel clicked.")
);
```

The click on the cancelBtn changes the value of the the message property, which was bound to the text property of messageLbl; the GUI changes automatically! Figure 18-8 below shows how the Sign In window will look like after the user has pressed the Cancel button.

FIGURE 18-8: Binding in action

The complete code of the GridPaneSampleBinding class is shown here:

```
public class GridPaneSampleBinding extends Application {

    //Declaring a JavaFX property
    private StringProperty message = new SimpleStringProperty();

    public void start(Stage primaryStage) {

        Label userIdLbl = new Label("User ID:");
        TextField userIdTxt = new TextField();
        Label userPwdLbl = new Label("Password:");
        PasswordField userPwdTxt = new PasswordField();
        Button signInBtn = new Button ("Sign In");
        Button cancelBtn = new Button ("Cancel");
        Hyperlink forgotPwdLink = new Hyperlink("Forgot password");

        // A label to display messages using binding
        Label messageLbl = new Label();
        // binding the StringProperty to a GUI component
        messageLbl.textProperty().bind(message);

        GridPane root = new GridPane();
        root.setVgap(20);
        root.setPadding(new Insets(10));
        root.setAlignment(Pos.CENTER);

        // Using static methods for setting node constraints
        GridPane.setConstraints(userIdLbl, 0, 0);
        GridPane.setConstraints(userIdTxt, 1, 0);
        GridPane.setConstraints(userPwdLbl, 0, 1);
        GridPane.setConstraints(userPwdTxt, 1, 1);
```

```
        GridPane.setConstraints(signInBtn, 0, 2);

        //Cancel button: span 1, right aligned
        GridPane.setConstraints(cancelBtn, 1,2, 1, 1,
                                      HPos.RIGHT, VPos.CENTER);
        GridPane.setConstraints(forgotPwdLink, 0, 3,2,1);

        // Message label: span 2
        GridPane.setConstraints(messageLbl, 0,4,2,1);

        root.getChildren().addAll(userIdLbl, userIdTxt, userPwdLbl,
        userPwdTxt,signInBtn, cancelBtn, forgotPwdLink, messageLbl);

        // event handlers
        //1. Anonymous class
        signInBtn.setOnAction(new EventHandler<ActionEvent>(){
            public void handle(ActionEvent evt){
                  message.set("Sign in clicked.");
            }
        });

        // lambda expression
        cancelBtn.setOnAction(evt ->
           message.set("Cancel clicked.")
        );

        // method reference
        forgotPwdLink.setOnAction(this::forgotPwdHandler);

        // Show the window
        Scene scene = new Scene(root,250,220);
        primaryStage.setScene(scene);
        primaryStage.show();
    }

    private void forgotPwdHandler(ActionEvent evt){
        message.set("Forgot password clicked");
    }

    public static void main(String[] args) {
        launch(args);
    }
}
```

The binding can be bidirectional. If the value of the GUI component changes, it can change the value of the underlying model (remember MVC?), and if the value of the model changes then the GUI is updated, too. If you want to stop binding at any time, use the method `unbind()`—for example:

```
messageLbl.textProperty().unbind();
```

I tried to fit as much information as possible in this introductory lesson so you can start working on the assignment. In Lesson 19 you apply all these techniques while developing a game.

TRY IT

Re-create the the calculator from Chapter 8 as a JavaFX application.

Lesson Requirements

You should have Java installed.

> **NOTE** *You can download the code samples from this lesson from the book's web page at* `www.wrox.com/go/javaprog24hr2e`*. You can find them in the* `Lesson18.zip`*.*

Step-by-Step

1. Create a new JavaFX project in Eclipse.
2. Create a class `Calculator` that extends `Application` (you can rename the `Main` class).
3. Using JavaFX layouts, re-create the `Calculator` GUI.
4. Create the class `CalculatorController` that implements `EventHandler` to process clicks on the buttons with digits.
5. Use JavaFX binding between the display field of the `Calculator` and a `String` property of the `CalculatorController` to display the entered number
6. Implement at least one operation (e.g., addition) and display the result using binding. See Try It section of Lesson 19 for a sample implementation of calculator's functionality.

> **TIP** *Please select the videos for Lesson 18 online at* `www.wrox.com/go/javaprog24hr2e`*. You will also be able to download the code and resources for this lesson from the website.*

19

Developing JavaFX Calculator and Tic-Tac-Toe

Now that you're familiar with the basics of JavaFX, it's time to write some practical applications. In this lesson you program the calculator and the game of Tic-Tac-Toe. In Lesson 18 you wrote the application in Java, but this time you create the graphical user interface (GUI) part with a declarative language—FXML. The application logic and event handling remain in Java.

In this lesson you get familiar with Scene Builder—a design tool that enables you to create a GUI by dragging and dropping components (buttons, text fields, labels, and so on) right onto the content panel (the center area of Scene Builder as shown in Figure 19-4). While you design the view with Scene Builder it generates a file with the name extension `.fxml`, which contains XML-like tags with attributes that reflect your design.

You also see how to dynamically change the styling of components using cascading style sheets (CSS).

DESIGNING A CALCULATOR WITH SCENE BUILDER

I assume that you already have the Efxclipse plug-in installed as described in Lesson 18. Now you need to download and install Scene Builder from Oracle at `http://bit.ly/1rnw1S5`.

AN ALTERNATIVE SITE FOR SCENE BUILDER DOWNLOADS

Starting from Java 8 update 40 Oracle stopped offering installer for Scene Builder. You can download a build of Scene Builder 8, based off of the latest sources from OpenJFX from Gluon (`http://gluonhq.com/products/downloads/`).

If you've completed the assignment from the Try It section of Lesson 18 you should have a program that shows the GUI of a calculator that might look similar to the one shown in Figure 19-1.

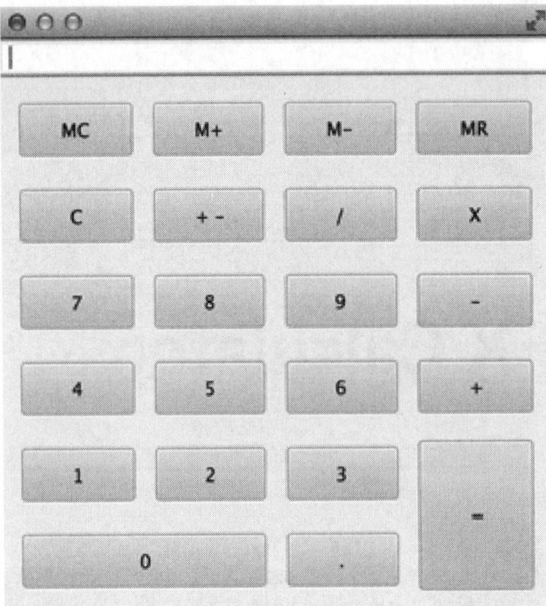

FIGURE 19-1: The calculator

Now you find out how this calculator can be created using Scene Builder. You still start with creating a JavaFX project in Eclipse by selecting menus File → New → Other → JavaFX.

I'm naming this project Lesson19. During creation of this project I specify the package name `mycalculator`, the language FXML, and the file name `Calculator`, and the controller name `CalculatorController` as shown in Figure 19-2.

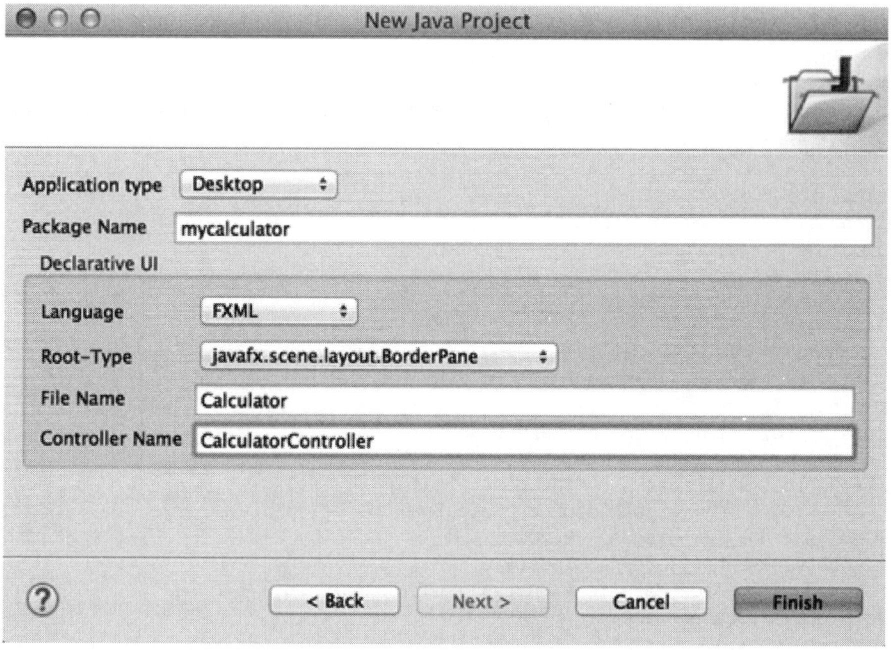

FIGURE 19-2: Configuring a new JavaFX project in Eclipse

Clicking the Finish button creates a new Eclipse project that includes two Java classes—`Main` and `CalculatorController`—the FXML file `Calculator.fxml` shown on Figure 19-3, and the CSS file called `application.css`.

FIGURE 19-3: The generated project Lesson19

Note that the `<BorderPane>` contains the attribute `fx:controller` with the name of the class that plays the role of the controller in your MVC-based application.

The file `Calculator.fxml` (shown in Figure 19-3) contains the calculator's GUI represented by XML-like tags. In particular, the tag `<BorderPane>` corresponds to the JavaFX `BorderLayout` container.

The `Main` class launches the application. In Lesson 18 you had to write the Java application manually, but now it is generated by the E(fx)clipse plug-in as shown here:

```
package mycalculator;
import javafx.application.Application;
import javafx.stage.Stage;
import javafx.scene.Scene;
import javafx.scene.layout.BorderPane;
import javafx.fxml.FXMLLoader;

public class Main extends Application {

  @Override public void start(Stage primaryStage) {
     try {
       BorderPane root = (BorderPane)FXMLLoader.load(getClass()
                              .getResource("Calculator.fxml"));
       Scene scene = new Scene(root,400,400);
       scene.getStylesheets().add(getClass()
               .getResource("application.css").toExternalForm());
       primaryStage.setScene(scene);
       primaryStage.show();
    } catch(Exception e) {
         e.printStackTrace();
    }
  }

  public static void main(String[] args) {
      launch(args); }
}
```

There is a new for you element in this code—the annotation `@Override`, which indicates that the method `start()` overrides its superclass's version. I explain annotations in Lesson 23. In the next section you see how to design the GUI in Scene Builder, which saves it in the `.fxml` file. Your `Main` class loads it using the class `FXMLLoader` and creates a Java object in memory according to FXML content.

The generated project includes an empty file `application.css`, which is the right place for customizing the look of the GUI with CSS.

According to the MVC design pattern, the class `CalculatorController` is the place where you program event handler methods in Java. It's empty at this point. You separate the creation of the GUI in a declarative language (FXML) from the application logic written in Java.

Designing the Calculator GUI with Scene Builder

The content of the file `Calculator.fxml` is generated by Scene Builder. Right-click its name and use the menu Open → Other → Scene Builder. It looks like Figure 19-4.

The middle section is called Content Panel. From the left panel, you drag and drop the GUI controls and containers onto the Content Panel. At the bottom left you see the hierarchy of GUI components, which, at this point, includes nothing but the `BorderPane`. Now place a `TextField` in the TOP area of the `BorderPane` and the `GridPane` with `Button` controls in the CENTER.

Open the Controls panel on the left, select a `TextField`, and drop it on the *insert TOP* line in the Hierarchy panel. Scene Builder looks like Figure 19-5.

After Saving (Ctrl+S) the current design, open the `Calculator.fxml` file in Eclipse. You see that Scene Builder has generated the `<top>` tag inside `<BorderPane>`:

```
<BorderPane xmlns:fx="http://javafx.com/fxml/1"
            xmlns="http://javafx.com/javafx/8"
            fx:controller="mycalculator.CalculatorController">
   <top>
      <TextField BorderPane.alignment="CENTER" />
   </top>
</BorderPane>
```

Now select `GridPane` in the Containers panel on the left and drag and drop it on the *insert CENTER* line in the Hierarchy panel. The Scene Builder looks like Figure 19-6.

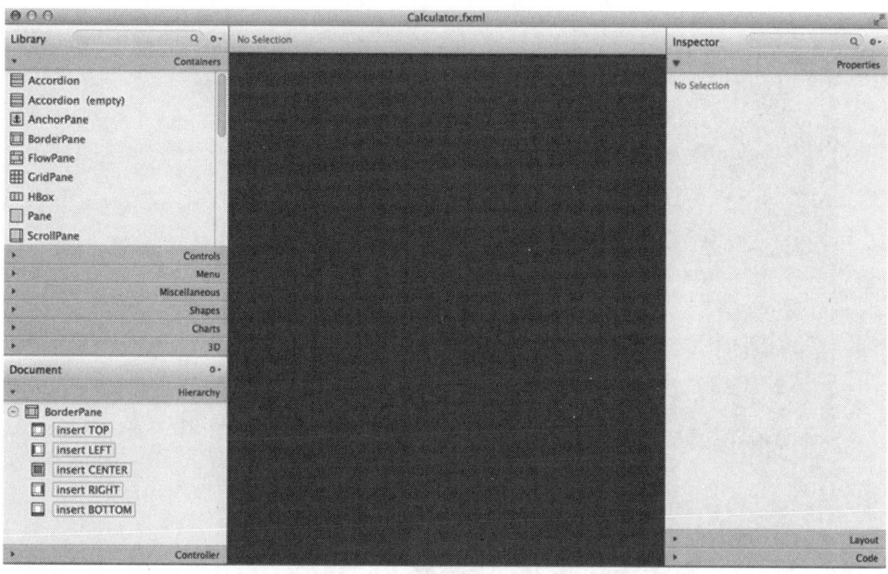

FIGURE 19-4: Calculator.fxml in Scene Builder

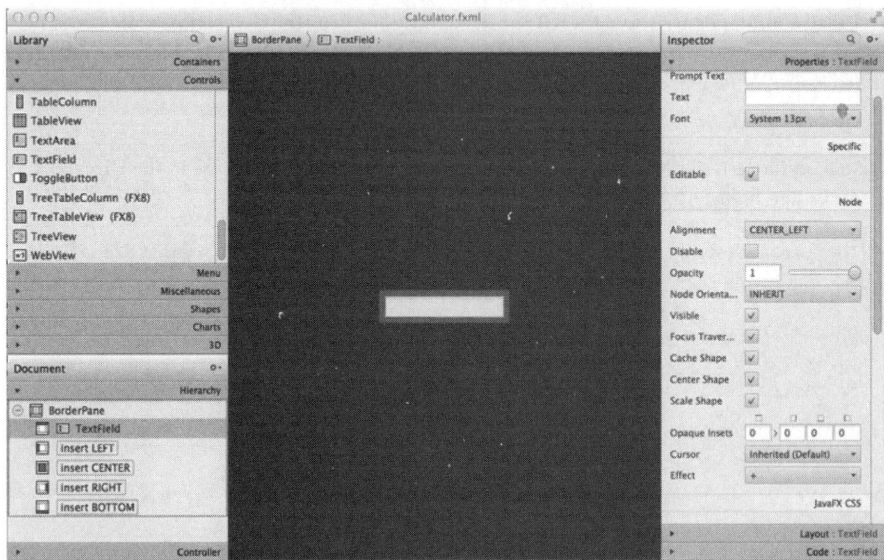

FIGURE 19-5: The TextField control is placed in the TOP area

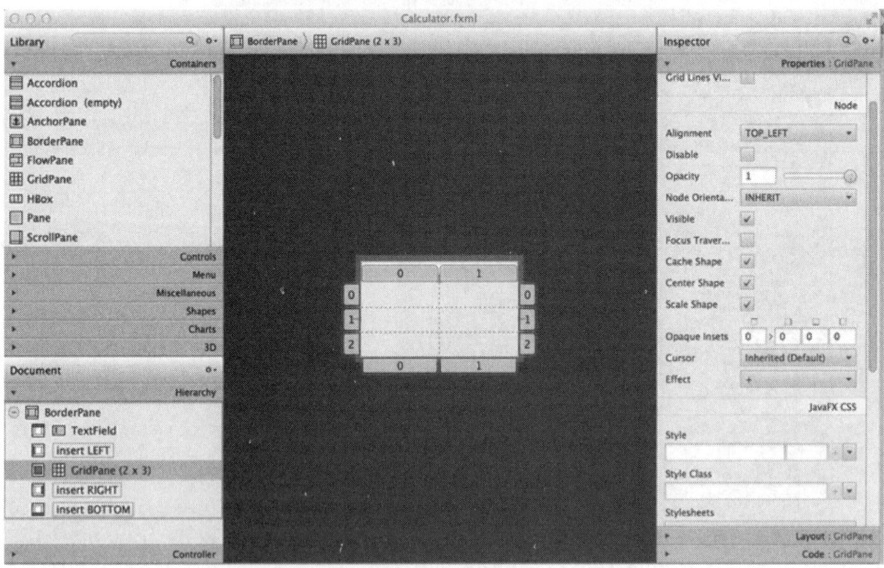

FIGURE 19-6: Adding the GridPane to the CENTER.

After saving the design, the `Calculator.fxml` file includes new content:

```
<BorderPane xmlns:fx="http://javafx.com/fxml/1"
      xmlns="http://javafx.com/javafx/8"
      fx:controller="mycalculator.CalculatorController">
   <top>
```

```
        <TextField BorderPane.alignment="CENTER" />
    </top>
    <center>
        <GridPane BorderPane.alignment="CENTER">
          <columnConstraints>
            <ColumnConstraints hgrow="SOMETIMES" minWidth="10.0"
                                                  prefWidth="100.0" />
            <ColumnConstraints hgrow="SOMETIMES" minWidth="10.0"
                                                  prefWidth="100.0" />
          </columnConstraints>
          <rowConstraints>
            <RowConstraints minHeight="10.0" prefHeight="30.0"
                                                  vgrow="SOMETIMES" />
            <RowConstraints minHeight="10.0" prefHeight="30.0"
                                                  vgrow="SOMETIMES" />
            <RowConstraints minHeight="10.0" prefHeight="30.0"
                                                  vgrow="SOMETIMES" />
          </rowConstraints>
        </GridPane>
    </center>
</BorderPane>
```

In the `GridPaneSample` class in Lesson 18 you specify all the attributes of the `GridPane` by invoking methods in the Java classes, but now they are represented by the FXML tag attributes. By default, a `GridPane` container is initially created with two columns and three rows, hence you see two tags `<ColumnConstraints>` and three tags `<RowConstraints>`.

The little tabs labeled with numbers in Figure 19-6 correspond to the row and column numbers of the grid. But the calculator shown in Figure 19-1 has four columns and six columns filled with buttons. To add more rows and columns you need to right-click the grid and keep selecting the GridPane | Add Rows Below or Add Column After until you see a 4x6 grid as shown in Figure 19-7.

After saving the design, the `Calculator.fxml` file includes the FXML tags for a 4x6 grid. Next, in Scene Builder you add the padding of 10 pixels to have some space between the grid and the border of the window and the horizontal and vertical gap to have space between the cells of the grid. This is done by filling the values of Padding, Hgap, and Vgap in the GridPane Properties panel on the right as shown on Figure 19-8.

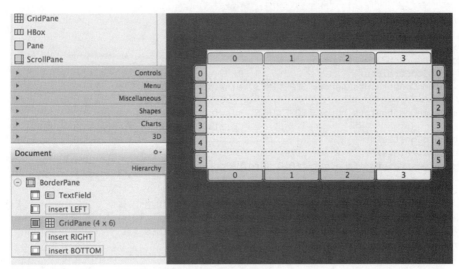

FIGURE 19-7: The 4x6 GridPane under the TextField

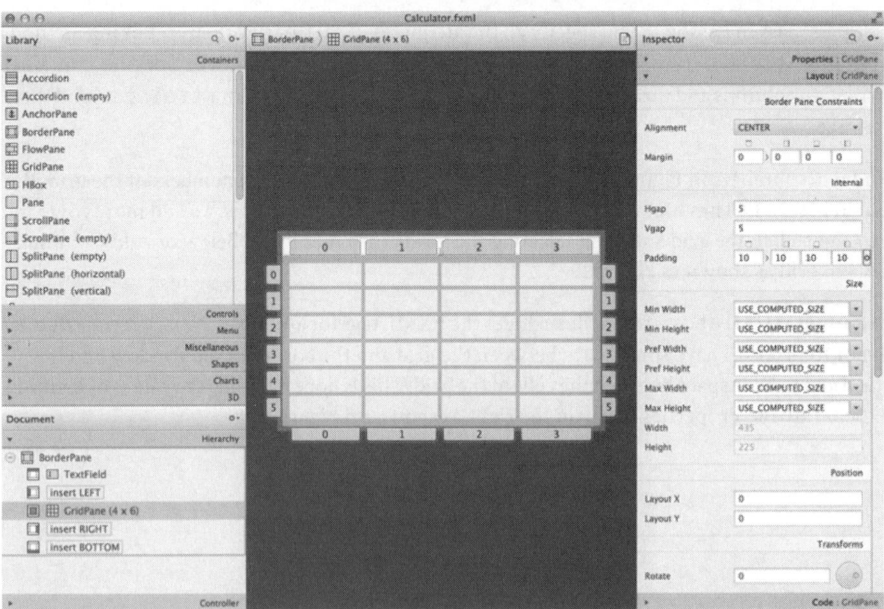

FIGURE 19-8: Setting Hgap, Vgap, and Padding properties of the GridPane

The next step is to add buttons into the grid cells. Drag and drop a `Button` from the Controls panels on the left into the top left cell of the grid as shown in Figure 19-9. Drag the button's right border to make it larger. Set the `Margin` property to 5 for each side of the button; this is the distance between the button and cell borders. Finally, change the text on the button to read MC to match the top left button from Figure 19-1. Figure 19-9 shows how the Scene Builder's window should look now.

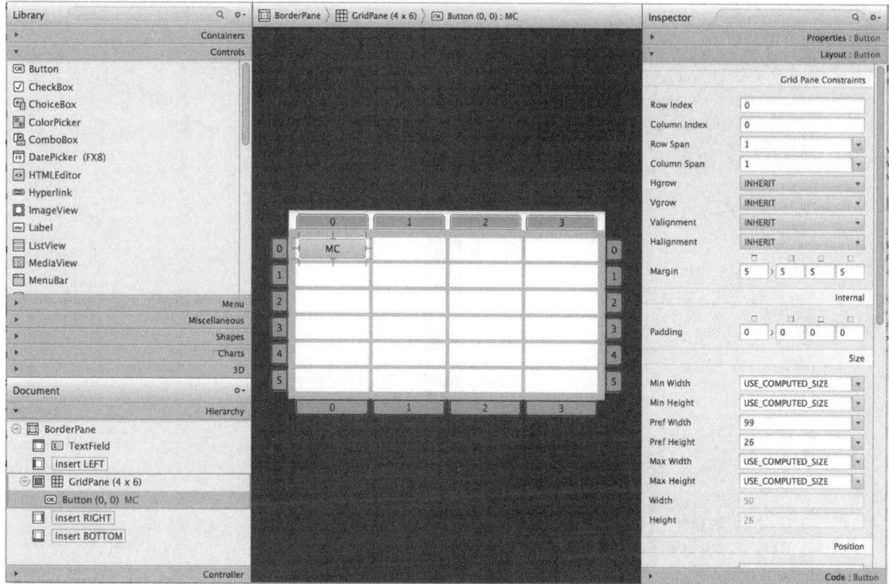

FIGURE 19-9: The button MC added to the top left grid cell

After saving this design in `Calculator.fxml`, a new section `<children>` is inside the `<GridPane>`. It has just one button for now:

```
<children>
  <Button mnemonicParsing="false" prefHeight="26.0"
                                   prefWidth="99.0" text="MC">
     <GridPane.margin>
        <Insets bottom="5.0" left="5.0" right="5.0" top="5.0" />
     </GridPane.margin>
  </Button>
</children>
```

There is no indication of the cell (0,0) because zeros are the default values for `GridPane.columnIndex` and`GridPane.rowIndex` properties. Now you need to replicate this button in other cells. You can use multiple Ctrl+C/Ctrl+V keystrokes and then drag/drop the buttons into other cells. Set the proper text for each button. While doing this, watch how the content of the`Calculator.fxml` changes as you add more buttons. I find it faster to copy and paste the code directly in the FXML file than use Scene Builder for mass duplication.

Note that in Figure 19-1 the button located in the cell (0,5) spans two columns, and the button with coordinates (3,4) spans two rows. For these buttons you need to enter 2 as the row (or column) span, and select `MAX_VALUE` as maximum width (or height) using the Properties panel on the right. After all this done, the Scene Builder's window should look like Figure 19-10.

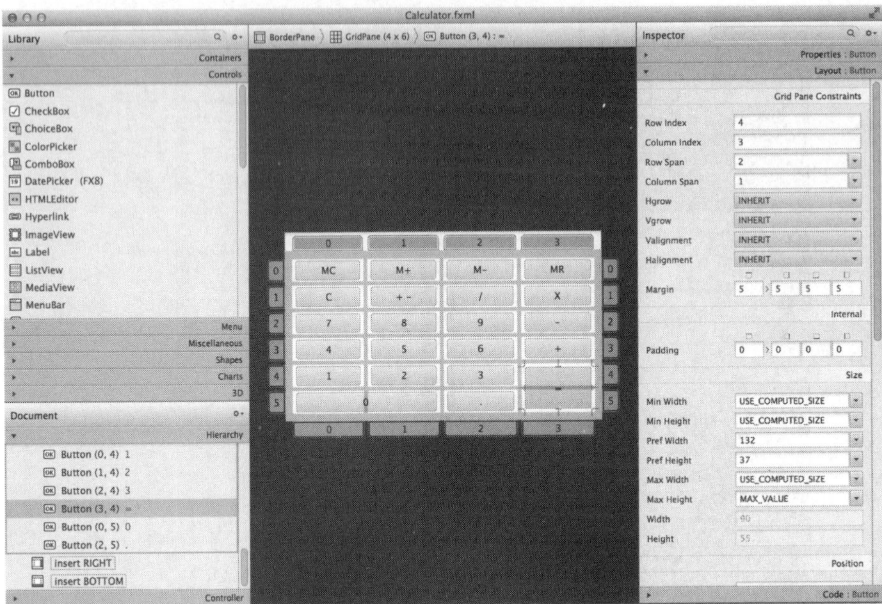

FIGURE 19-10: All buttons in the grid

Run the `Main` class and you see the calculator that looks like Figure 19-1.

This concludes a very brief introduction to Scene Builder. If you invest more time into mastering this tool, your productivity in developing GUI applications will increase. Refer to Scene Builder User Guide (`https://docs.oracle.com/javase/8/scene-builder-2/user-guide/`) for more details.

Handling Events in the Controller Class

As per MVC design pattern, you've created the view `Calculator.fxml`. Now you can write a controller and hook it up to the view. When the file `Calculator.fxml` was initially generated, it included the name of the controller that will be handling events of all components located in the root container:

```
<BorderPane xmlns="http://javafx.com/javafx/8"
      xmlns:fx="http://javafx.com/fxml/1"
      fx:controller="mycalculator.CalculatorController">
```

You add the event handler method to the class `CalculatorController` and link the GUI components to the corresponding event handlers. Initially the generated class `CalculatorController` is empty. Add a simple event handler method `buttonClickHandler()`:

```
package mycalculator;

import javafx.event.ActionEvent;

public class CalculatorController {
```

```
    public void buttonClickHandler(ActionEvent evt){

      System.out.println("Hello from controller!");
    }
}
```

If you remember, the class `GridPaneSampleEvents` from Lesson 18 invoked the method `setOnAction()` on the `Button` objects to assign the event handlers to button clicks. But if you develop the GUI in FXML, there are no Java objects there. Instead, you use the `<Button>` property `onAction` to assign the controller's `buttonClickHandler()` as the event handler for the calculator's buttons. The following snippet is for the button with the label `1`.

```
<Button prefHeight="37.0" prefWidth="132.0"
      text="1" onAction="#buttonClickHandler" GridPane.rowIndex="4">
    <GridPane.margin>
       <Insets bottom="5.0" left="5.0" right="5.0" top="5.0" />
    </GridPane.margin>
</Button>
```

The root container knows its controller, and the children of the container know the name of controller's method that handles events. In the calculator's example I have just one event handler for all buttons, and I copy and paste `onAction="#buttonClickHandler"` to each of button. Alternatively, I could assign one event handler for the digit buttons and another for the buttons that perform operations.

Now running the `Main` class and clicking on any button prints the message "Hello from controller" on the console, which is not exactly what the calculator should do. But at least this proves that controller receives events from the view. The next step is to enable the controller to send data back to the view.

Basically, there are two use cases for clicking the calculator's buttons:

1. The user clicked the digit button, and the event handler should get the current value from the `TextField` control, concatenate the label of the clicked button, and set the `TextField` to the new value.

2. The user clicked the operation button, and the event handler has to recognize the selected operation and apply the appropriate business logic.

You fully implement all calculator's logic as an assignment in the Try It section of this lesson, but I explain you how to recognize which button has been clicked and how to send the data from controller to view.

Recognizing the Source of the Event

Each JavaFX event is inherited from javafx.event.Event (`https://docs.oracle.com/javase/8/javafx/api/javafx/event/Event.html`), which has such fields as `source` and `target`. The `source` stores a reference to the object where the event initially occurred. The `target` defines the object where the event is handled. If the user clicks the component and the program is inside the event handler for this component, both source and target point at the same object.

But each event travels through the container(s), where the component is located. This is a *capturing phase*. Then the event reaches the target, the event handler processes it, and then event *bubbles up* back to the root container.

But the container(s) may also have event handlers, so while the event travels to the target, it may be processed by the container's handler, in which case the `target` doesn't have the same value as the `source`.

For example, JavaFX has `KeyEvent`, which the run time provides to the keyboard event handlers. If your calculator has a keyboard event handler on the `BorderPane` and on the nested `TextField`, and the user clicked the key while the focus was in the `TextField`, the container's event handler receives the `KeyEvent` object where the `target` points at the `TextField`, while the `source` points at the `BorderPane`. By the time the event object reaches the event handler of the `TextField`, the `KeyEvent` has both `source` and `target` pointing at the `TextField`.

In your calculator you don't process container's events, hence both the `source` and the `target` point at the clicked button. So checking the value of the `ActionEvent.source` gives you the reference to the specific button, and by calling the `getText()` method on the button you can find out its label and act accordingly. The following version of the calculator recognizes and prints the label of the clicked button on the console.

```
package mycalculator;

import javafx.event.ActionEvent;
import javafx.scene.control.Button;

public class CalculatorController {

  public void buttonClickHandler(ActionEvent evt){

    Button clickedButton = (Button) evt.getTarget();
    System.out.println("You clicked on " + clickedButton.getText());
  }
}
```

Now let's separate the processing of the operation and digit buttons using the `switch` statement. All digits and the period button should simply change the content of the calculator's `TextField`. The private method `processDigit()` should do it. All operation buttons should apply the application logic based on the selected operation. The private method `processOperation()` should take care of that.

```
public class CalculatorController {

  public void buttonClickHandler(ActionEvent evt){

    Button clickedButton = (Button) evt.getTarget();
    String buttonLabel = clickedButton.getText();

    // Tell apart digits from operations
    switch(buttonLabel){
      case "0": case "1": case "2": case "3": case "4": case "5":
      case "6": case "7": case "8": case "9": case "10": case ".":
         processDigit(buttonLabel);
         break;
     default:
         processOperation(buttonLabel);
    }
  }
```

```
    private void processDigit(String buttonLabel){
        System.out.println("You clicked on " + buttonLabel);
    }

    private void processOperation(String buttonLabel){
        System.out.println("You selected operation " + buttonLabel);
    }
}
```

Run the `Main` class now, and you see that system console properly recognizes the clicked button and invokes either the method `processDigit()` or `processOperation()`.

Passing Data from View to Controller and Back

How can the controller class access GUI components that were declared in FXML? If you create both GUI and controller as Java classes, you write the code passing a GUI object to the controller as you did with `Calculator` and `CalclulatorEngine` in Lesson 9 in the section "How to Pass Data Between Objects." But when the GUI is declared in FXML, you don't instantiate the GUI—`FXMLLoader` does.

For such cases, JavaFX offers a simple solution: assign an ID to a component in the FXML file and the variable with the same name *annotated* with `@FXML` in the controller class. This ensures that the Java variable is linked with the GUI component. You read about Java annotations in Lesson 23. For now, just trust me that the `@FXML` annotation magically *injects* the GUI component's reference into the controller's variable. As a matter of fact, why just trust me if you can easily see it in action?

First, add the `fx:id` attribute to the `<TextField>` tag of your calculator in `Calculator.fxml`. I decided to name this ID `displayField`.

```
<top>
   <TextField fx:id="displayField" BorderPane.alignment="CENTER" />
</top>
```

Accordingly, declare a variable `displayField` in the `CalculatorController` class as follows:

```
@FXML
private TextField displayField;
```

Now you can use the variable `displayField` knowing that it always has the same value as the GUI component having the same ID. The next version of `CalculatorController` uses this variable in the method `processDigit()`. First it gets the current value of the `displayField` via `getText()`, then attaches the selected digit to it, and puts it back into the variable `displayField` using the `setText()` method.

```
package mycalculator;

import javafx.event.ActionEvent;
import javafx.fxml.FXML;
import javafx.scene.control.Button;
import javafx.scene.control.TextField;
```

```
public class CalculatorController {

  @FXML
  private TextField displayField;

  public void buttonClickHandler(ActionEvent evt){

    Button clickedButton = (Button) evt.getTarget();
    String buttonLabel = clickedButton.getText();

    // Tell apart digits from operations
    switch(buttonLabel){
      case "0": case "1": case "2": case "3": case "4": case "5":
      case "6": case "7": case "8": case "9": case "10": case ".":
         processDigit(buttonLabel);
         break;
     default:
         processOperation(buttonLabel);
    }
  }

  private void processDigit(String buttonLabel){

      displayField.setText(displayField.getText() + buttonLabel);
  }

  private void processOperation(String buttonLabel){
      System.out.println("You selected operation " + buttonLabel);
  }
}
```

In Lesson 3 I mention that if you forget to write the `break` statement in a `case` clause, the code falls through. In the method `processDigit()` I do this on purpose to avoid writing `processDigit()` and `break` for each clause. Figure 19-11 shows a screenshot of the running calculator after I clicked the buttons 1,5,9,.,2, and 3.

The `processDigit()` method illustrated the process of passing data from GUI to controller and back. In the Try It section you need to implement the `processOperation()` method to complete the calculator.

THE @FXML ANNOTATION

You can annotate fields and methods that return void with the `@FXML` annotation. If you add to the controller class the method `initialize()` annotated with `@FXML`, `FXMLLoader` . Java runtime invokes this method *after* all GUI components are constructed. In particular, this can be useful if you want to use binding and want to make sure that all GUI components are already constructed.

```
@FXML public void initialize() {
  myComponent1.textProperty().bind(myComponent2);
}
```

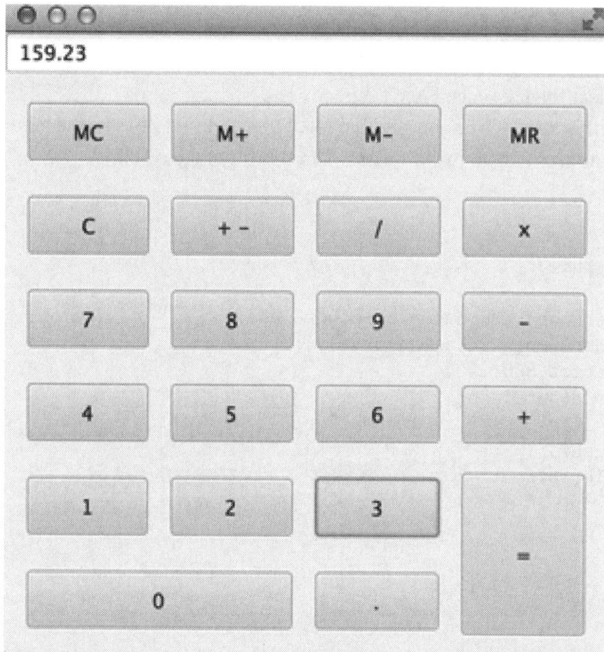

FIGURE 19-11: The Calculator view after entering the number 159.23

PROGRAMMING TIC-TAC-TOE

Now that you are familiar with the basics of creating a GUI with FXML and Scene Builder, this section shows you how easy it is to program a tic-tac-toe game.

The Game Strategy

Every game implements some algorithm—a set of rules or a strategy that has to be applied depending on the player's actions. You need to come up with a simple algorithm for the tic-tac-toe game.

If you aren't familiar with tic-tac-toe, or if it has a different name in your part of the world, read the Wikipedia article (`http://en.wikipedia.org/wiki/Tic-tac-toe`) about this game. For the version of the popular game that you're building, implement the following strategy:

- The game is played by two players on a two-dimensional 3x3 board.
- Two players can play this game. One plays with the symbol X, and the other uses the symbol O.
- The winner must have a full row, column, or diagonal of Xs or Os.
- After each move, the program has to check whether there is a winner.
- The winning combination has to be highlighted.
- After the winner is found or there is no empty square left the players may select Actions → Play to play again.
- In a new game the first player plays with Xs.

Designing Tic-Tac-Toe GUI with FXML and CSS

Create new JavaFX project titled TicTacToe. Select the language FXML, specify the package name `tictactoe`, the class name `TicTacToe` and the controller's name as `TicTacToeController`. In the generated `Main` class make two changes: set the scene size to 300 by 320 pixels and disable stage resizing.

```
public class Main extends Application {
    @Override
    public void start(Stage primaryStage) {
        try {
            BorderPane root = (BorderPane)FXMLLoader.load(getClass()
                              .getResource("TicTacToe.fxml"));
            Scene scene = new Scene(root,300,320);
            scene.getStylesheets().add(getClass()
                .getResource("application.css").toExternalForm());
            primaryStage.setScene(scene);
            primaryStage.setResizable(false);
            primaryStage.show();
        } catch(Exception e) {
            e.printStackTrace();
        }
    }

    public static void main(String[] args) {
        launch(args);
    }
}
```

Your tic-tac-toe game is going to have a menu bar in the `Top` area of the `BorderPane`, and in the `Center` you add a `GridPane` having three rows and three columns.

JavaFX menus are created as a hierarchy. A `Menu` component can contain one or more `MenuItem`'s and other `Menu` components. You can also create a `MenuBar` or a `ContextMenu` that includes one or more `Menu` components. I'm just explaining how to create a menu for the tic-tac-toe application, but you can read more about JavaFX menus by visiting the Oracle tutorial (`https://docs.oracle.com/javafx/2/ui_controls/menu_controls.htm`) on this subject.

In Scene Builder, drop the `MenuBar` component from the Controls panel onto the line that reads "Insert TOP" in the `BorderPane` at the bottom left panel.

Expand the `MenuBar` in the Hierarchy panel. It has the default menus named File, Edit, and Help. There is nothing to edit in tic-tac-toe, so right-click Edit and select Delete. Rename the File menu as Actions using the Properties panel of Scene Builder. The `Menu` File was created with the `MenuItem` Close, which you should rename as Quit.

Drop a `MenuItem` onto the menu Actions. Scene Builder automatically creates the menu item Unspecified Action. Rename it as Play.

The `Menu` Help was originally created with the `MenuItem` About. Drop another `MenuItem` component onto the menu Help. Scene Builder by default creates the menu item Unspecified Action. Rename it as How to Play.

Now drop a `GridPane` from the Containers panel onto the center of the `BorderPane` and add a column to change the grid dimensions to be 3x3.

Change the preferred height of each row to 100 by selecting each row and entering 100 in the Pref Height field on the right panel named Layout: RowConstraints. Your Scene Builder's window should look like Figure 19-12.

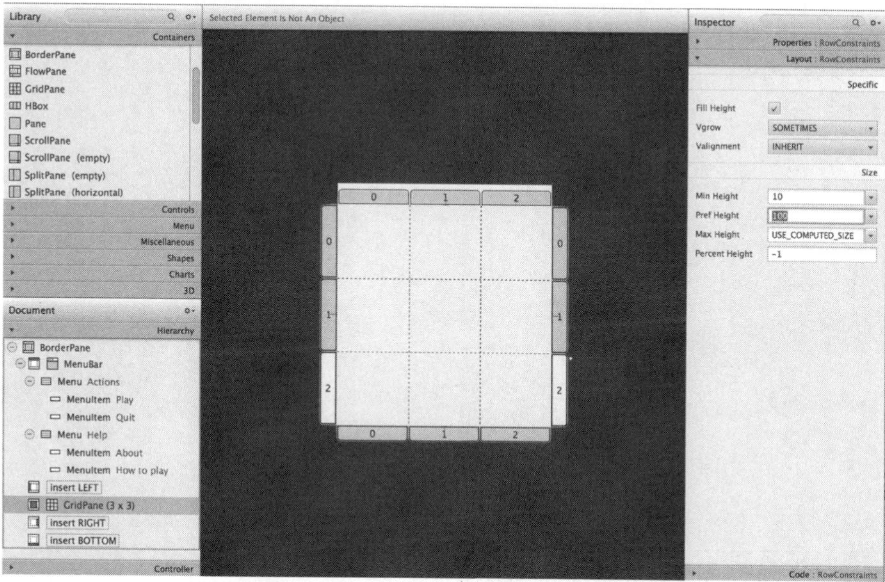

FIGURE 19-12: The BorderPane layout with the menu bar and the 3x3 grid

If you run the `Main` class, it opens the window with the menu bar on top as shown in Figure 19-13.

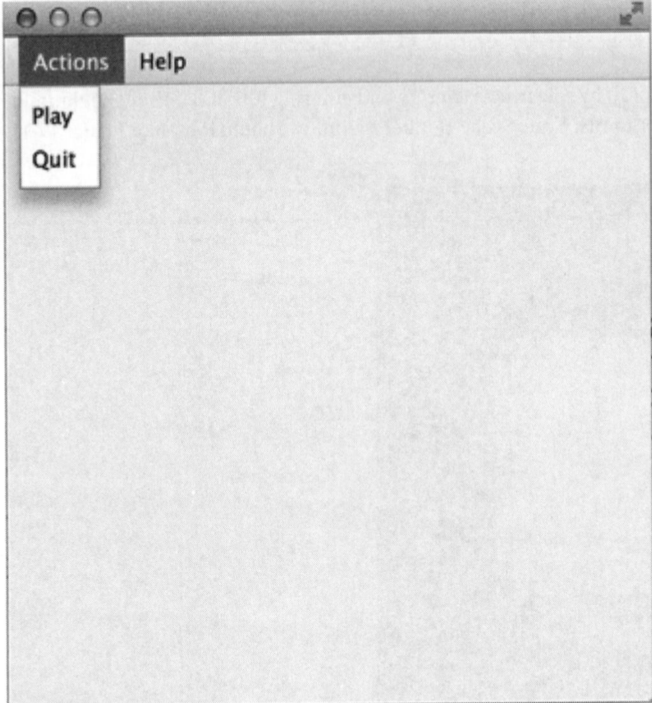

FIGURE 19-13: TicTacToe with the menu bar and the empty grid

Now you need to add nine buttons to the grid as youdid for the calculator earlier in this lesson. Each button should occupy the entire cell. Buttons should have no labels; you set them programmatically to X or O during the game play.

Open the generated file `TicTacToe.fxml` in Eclipse and simplify it. Remove rows and columns constraints and add nine buttons with preferred width and height of 100 to the `GridPane` so it looks like the following snippet:

```
<?xml version="1.0" encoding="UTF-8"?>

<?import java.lang.*?>
<?import javafx.scene.control.*?>
<?import javafx.scene.layout.*?>
<?import javafx.scene.layout.BorderPane?>

<BorderPane xmlns="http://javafx.com/javafx/8"
            xmlns:fx="http://javafx.com/fxml/1"
            fx:controller="tictactoe.TicTacToeController">
    <top>
       <MenuBar BorderPane.alignment="CENTER">
         <menus>
           <Menu text="Actions">
             <items>
               <MenuItem text="Play" />
```

```
                <MenuItem text="Quit" />
              </items>
            </Menu>
            <Menu text="Help">
              <items>
                <MenuItem text="About" />
                <MenuItem text="How to play" />
              </items>
            </Menu>
          </menus>
        </MenuBar>
    </top>
    <center>
       <GridPane fx:id ="gameBoard" BorderPane.alignment="CENTER">
          <children>
           <Button fx:id="b1" prefHeight="100.0" prefWidth="100.0" />
           <Button fx:id="b2" prefHeight="100.0" prefWidth="100.0"
                                  GridPane.columnIndex="1" />
           <Button fx:id="b3" prefHeight="100.0" prefWidth="100.0"
                                  GridPane.columnIndex="2" />
           <Button fx:id="b4" prefHeight="100.0" prefWidth="100.0"
                                  GridPane.rowIndex="1" />
           <Button fx:id="b5" prefHeight="100.0" prefWidth="100.0"
                      GridPane.columnIndex="1" GridPane.rowIndex="1" />
           <Button fx:id="b6" prefHeight="100.0" prefWidth="100.0"
                      GridPane.columnIndex="2" GridPane.rowIndex="1" />
           <Button fx:id="b7" prefHeight="100.0" prefWidth="100.0"
                                  GridPane.rowIndex="2" />
           <Button fx:id="b8" prefHeight="100.0" prefWidth="100.0"
                      GridPane.columnIndex="1" GridPane.rowIndex="2" />
           <Button fx:id="b9" prefHeight="100.0" prefWidth="100.0"
                      GridPane.columnIndex="2" GridPane.rowIndex="2" />
          </children>
       </GridPane>
    </center>
</BorderPane>
```

Run the `Main` class, and you see the tic-tac-toe board with the menu on top as shown in Figure 19-14. Note that the first button has a focus rendered as a blue border.

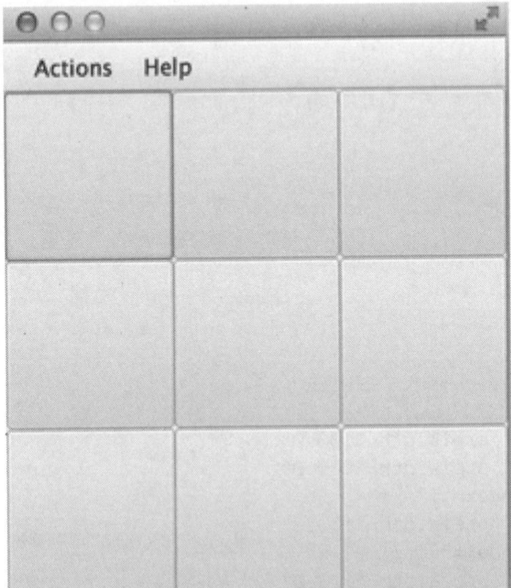

FIGURE 19-14: TicTacToe with the focus border on the first button

To remove the focus border you need to change the attributes of the buttons in the generated empty `application.css` file. Theoretically, the style attribute `-fx-focus-color: transparent;` should do the trick, but in programming not everything works by the book. Here's the style that removes the focus border:

```
.button{
    -fx-focus-color: transparent;
    -fx-background-insets: -1, 0, 1, 1;
}
```

The class `Main` loads the file `application.css` and applies its styles to the matching components on stage. (See Figure 19-15.)

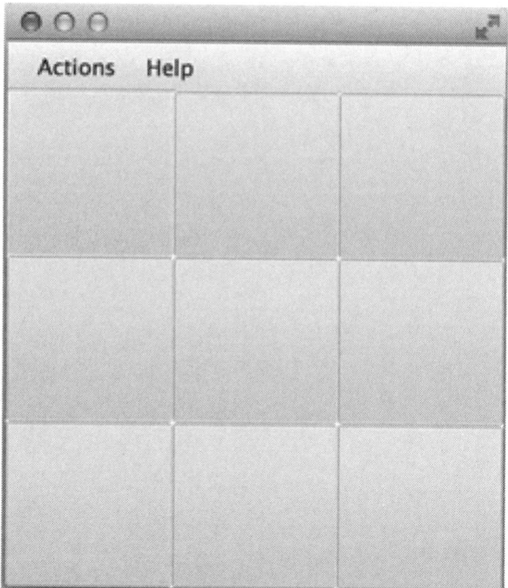

FIGURE 19-15: TicTacToe without the focus border on the first button

The GUI is ready. Now program the application logic in the controller class. There are two players in this game. The first one places Xs on the blank buttons and the other one uses Os. Hence, you need to keep track of the player's number. When the player clicks the button, the event handler should place the appropriate label on the button. The code of the `TicTacToeController` takes care of this functionality:

```
public class TicTacToeController {
   private boolean isFirstPlayer = true;

   public void buttonClickHandler(ActionEvent evt){

        Button clickedButton = (Button) evt.getTarget();
        String buttonLabel = clickedButton.getText();

        if ("".equals(buttonLabel) && isFirstPlayer){
            clickedButton.setText("X");
            isFirstPlayer = false;
        } else if("".equals(buttonLabel) && !isFirstPlayer){
            clickedButton.setText("O");
            isFirstPlayer = true;
        }
   }
}
```

Add `onAction="#buttonClickHandler"` to each `Button` tag in the `TicTacToe.fxml` and run the `Main` program. Start clicking empty squares, and the program takes turns in placing the Xs and Os on them as shown in Figure 19-16.

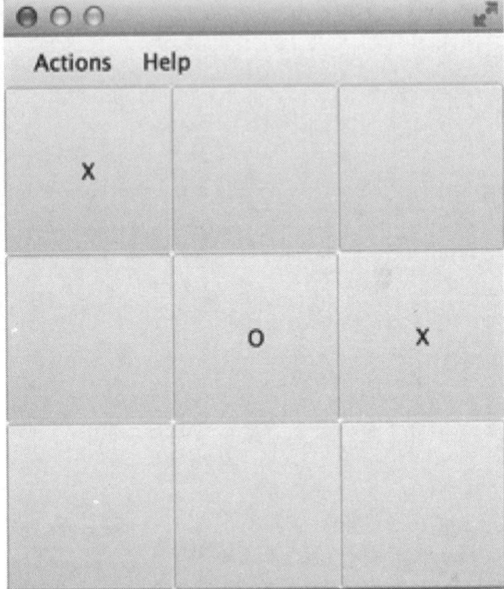

FIGURE 19-16: The game after the three clicks on the buttons

Increase the size of the letters X and O by adding font style attributes to the `application.css` file to make it looks like this:

```
.button{
    -fx-focus-color: transparent;
    -fx-background-insets: -1, 0, 1, 1;
    -fx-font-weight: bold;
    -fx-font-size: 36;
    -fx-text-fill: blue;
}
```

Now the tic-tac-toe window shows large and bold Xs and Os in blue, as shown in Figure 19-17.

FIGURE 19-17: TicTacToe with the styled button labels

> **STYLING WITH SCENE BUILDER**
>
> All JavaFX components are pre-styled, and the combination of the styles is called *a theme*.
>
> The default theme of all JavaFX components is called caspian. By defining your own CSS rules you can override the defaults. Scene Builder includes the View → Show CSS Analyzer menu to enable you to see the default styles of your GUI components. If you're interested in learning more about styling with Scene Builder, watch the video titled "In-Depth Layout and Styling with the JavaFX Scene Builder (`https://www.youtube.com/watch?v=7Nu3_5doZK4`)".

Both the FXML and CSS files of the tic-tac-toe game are ready and the class `TicTacToeController` knows how to properly set the buttons' labels for the first and second players.

Now's the time to write some Java code in the controller to implement the game rules.

Implementing Game Strategy in Tic-Tac-Toe Controller

It's time to implement the game rules in the `TicTacToeController` class. On each button click you need to check whether there is a winner. If there is, the program should highlight the winning combination.

You're going to write a method `find3InARow()`, which checks each row, column, and diagonal on the board to see if they have the same labels. The method `find3InARow()` is invoked from the method `buttonClickHandler()`. If the winning combination is found, the program invokes the method `highlightWinningCombo()` to show the winning combination in a different style.

To compare the labels of the buttons you need to have references to their `Button` objects, which you get using the injection mechanism offered by the `@FXML` annotation. You also need to have a reference to the `GridPane`, which is a container for all buttons. You see its use in the section "Handling the Tic-Tac-Toe Menu Play."

```
@FXML Button b1;
@FXML Button b2;
@FXML Button b3;
@FXML Button b4;
@FXML Button b5;
@FXML Button b6;
@FXML Button b7;
@FXML Button b8;
@FXML Button b9;

@FXML GridPane gameBoard;
```

The code of the method `find3InARow()` is shown next and is self-explanatory:

```
private boolean find3InARow(){
        //Row 1
        if (""!=b1.getText() && b1.getText() == b2.getText()
            && b2.getText() == b3.getText()){
            highlightWinningCombo(b1,b2,b3);
            return true;
        }
        //Row 2
        if (""!=b4.getText() && b4.getText() == b5.getText()
            && b5.getText() == b6.getText()){
            highlightWinningCombo(b4,b5,b6);
            return true;
        }
        //Row 3
        if (""!=b7.getText() && b7.getText() == b8.getText()
            && b8.getText() == b9.getText()){
            highlightWinningCombo(b7,b8,b9);
            return true;
        }
        //Column 1
        if (""!=b1.getText() && b1.getText() == b4.getText()
            && b4.getText() == b7.getText()){
            highlightWinningCombo(b1,b4,b7);
            return true;
        }
        //Column 2
        if (""!=b2.getText() && b2.getText() == b5.getText()
            && b5.getText() == b8.getText()){
            highlightWinningCombo(b2,b5,b8);
            return true;
        }
        //Column 3
        if (""!=b3.getText() && b3.getText() == b6.getText()
            && b6.getText() == b9.getText()){
            highlightWinningCombo(b3,b6,b9);
```

```
            return true;
        }
        //Diagonal 1
        if (""!=b1.getText() && b1.getText() == b5.getText()
            && b5.getText() == b9.getText()){
            highlightWinningCombo(b1,b5,b9);
            return true;
        }
        //Diagonal 2
        if (""!=b3.getText() && b3.getText() == b5.getText()
            && b5.getText() == b7.getText()){
            highlightWinningCombo(b3,b5,b7);
            return true;
        }
        return false;
    }
```

To highlight the winning combination you need to dynamically change the styles of the winning buttons by invoking the method `setStyle()` on them. I want to change the background to a gradient color and the color of the button labels to red. You can read about gradients in the JavaFX CSS Reference (`https://docs.oracle.com/javase/8/javafx/api/javafx/scene/doc-files/cssref.html`) and find the popular CSS color names (`https://docs.oracle.com/javafx/2/api/javafx/scene/doc-files/cssref.html#typecolor`) there, too. The first version of the method `highlightWinningCombo()` may look as follows:

```
private void highlightWinningCombo(Button first, Button second,
                                                   Button third){
  first.setStyle("-fx-background-color:
       radial-gradient(radius 100%, white, lightyellow, lawngreen);
                 -fx-text-fill: red;");
  second.setStyle("-fx-background-color:
       radial-gradient( radius 100%, white, lightyellow, lawngreen);
                 -fx-text-fill: red;");
  third.setStyle("-fx-background-color:
       radial-gradient( radius 100%, white, lightyellow, lawngreen);
                 -fx-text-fill: red;");

}
```

Figure 19-18 shows how the winning combination may look.

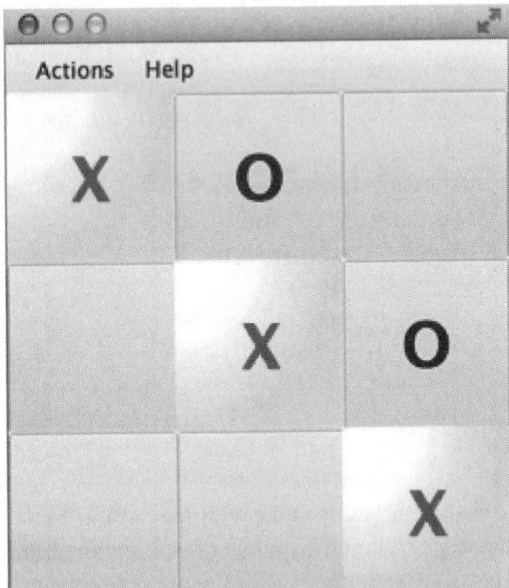

FIGURE 19-18: Highlighting the winning combination with gradient colors

Changing the styles of the buttons works, but I don't like the fact that the CSS styles are hardcoded in the Java code. The better way is to define a class selector in the CSS file and apply it when needed. Add the following CSS class selector to the file `application.css`:

```
.winning-button {
  -fx-background-color:
       radial-gradient( radius 100%, white, lightyellow, lawngreen);
  -fx-text-fill: red;
}
```

Now the method `highlightWinningCombo()` can apply this style to the button by adding the style `winning-button` as needed. The better version of `highlightWinningCombo()` looks like this:

```
private void highlightWinningCombo(Button first, Button second,
                                                    Button third){

  first.getStyleClass().add("winning-button");
  second.getStyleClass().add("winning-button");
  third.getStyleClass().add("winning-button");
}
```

Now if you (or the graphic designer) decide to change the style of the winning button, there is no need to modify Java code and recompile the program. Modifying the content of the file `application.css` in any plain text editor is all that's needed.

Handling the Tic-Tac-Toe Menu Play

The good news is that clicks on menu items are processed the same way as clicks on buttons. You just implement the menu Play so the users can start a new game when either a winning combination is found or there is no winner at all.

In the file `TicTacToe.fxml`, assign an event handler for the menu Play, like so:

```
<MenuItem text="Play" onAction="#menuClickHandler"/>
```

When the user clicks the Play menu item, the controller needs to reset the labels of all the buttons and remove styling from the winning buttons. The most concise way to do it is to get a hold of all children of `GridPane` and call `forEach()` passing a short lambda expression to it. This is what the method `menuClickHandler()` looks like:

```
public void menuClickHandler(ActionEvent evt){
     MenuItem clickedMenu = (MenuItem) evt.getTarget();
     String menuLabel = clickedMenu.getText();

     if ("Play".equals(menuLabel)){
         ObservableList<Node> buttons =
                  gameBoard.getChildren();

         buttons.forEach(btn -> {
             ((Button) btn).setText("");

             btn.getStyleClass().remove("winning-button");
         });

         isFirstPlayer = true;  // new game starts with X
     }
}
```

The package `javafx.collections` contains classes and interfaces or JavaFX Collection API (`https://docs.oracle.com/javase/8/javafx/collections-tutorial/collections.htm`), which is an extension of Java Collections Framework, and you can find the description of all of them in Oracle documentation (`https://docs.oracle.com/javase/8/javafx/api/javafx/collections/package-summary.html`). Your method `menuClickHandler()` uses one of these interfaces: `ObservableList`. This collection was created to listen to the events that may happen to its elements, but I use it to store references to children of the `GridPane`.

The method `getChildren()` returns a collection of `Node` instances (each `Button` is a descendant of `Node`). Then you"erase" the label of each button and remove that fancy style of winning buttons. Finally youreset the value of `isFirstPlayer` so the first move places X on the clicked button. That's all there is to it. Play the game!

Tic-Tac-Toe: What to Try Next

Your tic-tac-toe game is ready. Of course, there are things that can be improved to make this game more of a commercial grade. For example, you can remove all event handlers by calling `removeEventHandler()` on all buttons when the winner is found. You may consider offering the user to set the dimensions of the playing board rather than using a 3x3 board. In this case, I recommend you create the GUI in Java and dynamically create arrays of buttons based on the user's selection. You may add the Save History feature, too.

You can add an option to play against the computer instead of having a second player. In that case, you may need to get familiar with the Minimax, a decision rule algorithm from Game Theory. This YouTube video (`https://www.youtube.com/watch?v=3sbGRBjsf0o`) will help you to see how it can be applied to the tic-tac-toe game.

JAVAFX ON THE WEB AND MOBILE DEVICES

JavaFX applications can run inside web browsers provided the user's computer has JavaFX run time installed. There is a Deployment Kit (`http://docs.oracle.com/javafx/2/deployment/deployment_toolkit.htm`) to auto-detect whether the user has such a run time and install it if necessary. Unfortunately the detection and installation process is not a simple one, so using JavaFX application inside web browsers is not a good idea for consumer-oriented applications. It's possible in controlled environments, such as inside an organization where the required Java run time can be installed on the user's desktops.

If you're wondering whether it's possible to use JavaFX for writing applications for smartphones, Oracle doesn't offer the JavaFX libraries for mobile platforms, but it's possible.

To develop JavaFX applications for iOS, you need to install and learn some additional software, namely RoboVM (`http://www.robovm.com/`), which is a software development kit (SDK) for converting Java bytecode into the native device code as if it was written in the C programming language.

There is also a community site called JavaFXPorts (`http://javafxports.org/page/home`), where people offer solutions for deployment of JavaFX applications on iOS and Android devices.

TRY IT

The goal of the next assignment is to implement the application logic for the operation buttons in the Calculator project created earlier in this lesson. By the time the user clicks one of the operation buttons, the `displayField` variable in `CalculatorController` already has some value. I've written the step-by-step instructions for implementing only the plus operation, and you need to implement other operations similarly.

Lesson Requirements

You should have Eclipse with the E(fx)clipse plug-in installed.

> **NOTE** *You can download the code and resources for this Try It from the book's web page at* `www.wrox.com/go/javaprog24hr2e`. *You can find them in the Lesson19.zip.*

Step-by-Step

As you see, I use the wrapper class Double to convert String into a numeric value before using it in the addition.

1. Import the Eclipse project Lesson19.
2. Run the Main class from the mycalculator package to see that clicks on digit buttons are properly shown in the display field.
3. To perform an operation on two numbers you need to know their values and the selected operation. The calculator's display field shows only one number at a time, so you need to store the first entered value in a program variable. You may also store the result of the performed operation in a separate variable. Keep in mind that the value in the display field is represented by a string of characters. Declare the following fields in the CalculatorContoller class:

```
private String previousValue="";
private String currentValue="";
private double result;
```

4. Write a method to add two numbers. Initially, if the user enters the first number and clicks on the plus button, you just need to store the entered value in previousValue and clean the display field so the user can enter the second one. If the user clicks the plus button and the previousValue is not empty, sum the current and previous values and display the result. The first version of the method may look as follows:

```
private void addNumbers(){
    if ("".equals(previousValue)){
        previousValue = displayField.getText();
        displayField.setText("");
    } else{
        currentValue = displayField.getText();
        result = Double.parseDouble(previousValue) +
                 Double.parseDouble(currentValue);
        displayField.setText("" + result);
    }
}
```

5. The controller should call the method addNumbers() if the user clicked one of the buttons: plus or equal. You may also need to remember the last operation being performed. Hence, add the following variable declaration:

```
private String lastOperation;
```

Modify the method processOperation() in CalculatorController to look like this:

```
private void processOperation(String buttonLabel){
    switch (buttonLabel) {
      case "+":
            lastOperation = "+";
            addNumbers();
            break;
```

```
            case "=":
                  processOperation(lastOperation);   // recursion
          }
      }
```

The term *recursion* (`http://en.wikipedia.org/wiki/Recursion_(computer_science)`) describes a situation when a function or a method calls itself. Recursion helps avoiding code duplication. Because you want to repeat the same actions if the user clicks the plus or equal button, using recursion makes sense.

6. Run the `Main` class, and you should be able to enter and add two numbers. But to support a scenario when the user wants to perform several consecutive additions, you need to add a little more code to catch the moment if the user continues clicking a digit right after the operation has been performed. In this case you need to store the `result` value in the variable `previousValue`, and clean the display field so the user can enter the next number to add.

7. Implement other operations similarly to addition. Add input validation: Don't allow the user to enter more than one period in the number. Don't allow division by zero.
8. Compare the FXML implementation of the calculator's GUI with the Java version from Try It section from Lesson 18 .

> **TIP** *Please select the videos for Lesson 19 online at* `www.wrox.com/go/javaprog24hr2e`*. You will also be able to download the code and resources for this lesson from the website.*

Stream API

In this lesson you'll learn how to work with the new Stream application programming interface (API) introduced in Java 8 (not to be confused with I/O Streams). Stream API enables you to write data processing in a simpler and more understandable way. Most of the examples in this chapter illustrate iterating and manipulating data from Java collections, but you should know from the very start that the Stream API is not just another type of a data collection. It's an abstraction over a bunch of data that your program needs to process.

The data can come from a collection, from some function that generates data, or from an I/O stream. Using the Stream API and lambda expressions, you can write simple-to-read and efficient iterators that will result in a subset of the incoming data or some kind of a data aggregation.

All new classes and interfaces supporting the Stream API are located in the package java.util.stream (`http://docs.oracle.com/javase/8/docs/api/java/util/stream/package-summary.html`), and the `Stream` interface is the main player there. Some old classes (for example, `BufferedReader`) located in other packages now include new methods returning the reference to its data as a `Stream`.

STREAM BASICS

A stream is an abstraction that represents zero or more values. Think of it as a fancy iterator that enables you to declare one or more operations on the data and then perform these operations *in one pass*. But whereas a regular Java `Iterator` works sequentially, streams can also be processed in parallel.

Let's start with a simple example. This chapter uses a collection of beers to make working with stream API more fun. The class `Beer` is shown here:

```
public class Beer {
  public String name;
  public String country;
  public float price;

  Beer(String name, String country,float price){
```

```
        this.name=name;
        this.country=country;
        this.price=price; }

    public String toString(){
            return "Name: " + name + ", price: " + price;
    }
}
```

Say you have a collection named `beers` that can be populated by the method `loadCellar()`. Now you want to create another collection that includes only American beers. This is how you can do it using the Stream API:

```
List<Beer> beers = loadCellar(); // populating beer collection

List<Beer> americanBeers = new ArrayList<>();

americanBeers = beers.stream()
                    .filter(brr -> "USA".equals(brr.country))
                    .collect(Collectors.toList());
```

Calling the method `stream()` sets the `beers` collection as a source of the stream. Then your code filters out only the beer objects where country is not the United States. Finally, the code invokes the method `collect()` to place filtered beers into another list: `americanBeers`. In this example I've chained only two operations—filter and collect. But you can specify a lot more, including map, reduce, find, sort, and match.

Note that I've used a lambda expression to specify the filter criteria. Another interesting thing to note in the preceding code is type inference; the variable `brr` was never declared. Because I've used generics in declaring the `beers` collection, the Java compiler knows that it stores objects of the `Beer` type, and if we're using lambdas to process these objects, `Beer` is assumed as the argument type.

Intermediate and Terminal Operations

There are two types of operations that you can apply to a stream: *intermediate* and *terminal*. You can specify multiple intermediate operations and only one terminal at the end. In the example, `filter()` is an intermediate and `collect()` is a terminal operation.

Each intermediate operation declares *what* you want to do with the stream data before applying the terminal operation, which produces a concrete result, for example sum or average, print some output, or a new collection (as in the case of this example).

How can you say that a particular operation is intermediate or terminal? Intermediate operations always return a `Stream`, whereas terminal ones return anything but a `Stream` (including `void`). As a matter of fact, stream operations can be chained into a pipeline because each intermediate operation returns a `Stream`.

Lazy Operations

Intermediate operations don't even try to read data until the terminal operation is invoked. The whole idea of using intermediate operations is to express your intentions in a declarative form. Consider the following code snippet:

```
OptionalDouble averagePrice = beers.stream()
                .filter(brr -> "USA".equals(brr.country))
                .mapToDouble(brrr -> brrr.price)
                .average();
```

I explain you this code a bit later, but it reveals the intentions: "We want to filter out non-American beers and then apply the map operation to extract the beer price. Finally we calculate an average beer price." Neither `filter()` nor `mapToDouble()` is invoked until the `average()` method is called (I prove it to you in the next code sample). But knowing upfront what are you planning to do with the data allows Java to create the most efficient plan for executing this code. By lazy execution I mean that `mapToDouble()` isn't performed on the beers that are not produced in the United States.

Before giving you the proof that intermediate operations are not being called until the terminal operation is invoked, you should have an understanding of what the terms *filter, map,* and *reduce* mean. Assuming that you know the basics of working with relational databases, the explanations use the analogy of SQL statements.

- **Filter:** Select the object that meet certain criteria. It's like using `select *` with a `where` clause in the SQL statement. The size of the resulting collection can be smaller than the original, but the resulting objects include all attributes (think columns).
- **Map:** Select only a subset of properties of the objects without filtering. It's like selecting specific columns in the SQL query without the `where` clause, for example `select price from beers`. Map creates a new stream as a result of applying the specified function to each stream element. The size of the resulting stream is the same as the original.
- **Reduce:** Aggregate the data. The relevant SQL examples would be `select count(*)` or `select sum(price)`.

Now let's look at the proof that intermediate operations don't access the data. In the class `LazyStreamsDemo` I'm not going to chain the operations on the stream:

```
public class LazyStreamsDemo {

    // Populate beer collection
    static List<Beer> loadCellar(){
      List<Beer> beerStock = new ArrayList<>();

      beerStock.add(new Beer("Stella", "Belgium", 7.75f));
      beerStock.add(new Beer("Sam Adams", "USA", 7.00f));
      beerStock.add(new Beer("Obolon", "Ukraine", 4.00f));
      beerStock.add(new Beer("Bud Light", "USA", 5.00f));
      beerStock.add(new Beer("Yuengling", "USA", 5.50f));
      beerStock.add(new Beer("Leffe Blonde", "Belgium", 8.75f));
      beerStock.add(new Beer("Chimay Blue", "Belgium", 10.00f));
      beerStock.add(new Beer("Brooklyn Lager", "USA", 8.25f));

      return beerStock;
    }

    public static void main(String[] args) {

    List<Beer> beers = loadCellar();
```

```
        // First intermediate operation
        Stream<Beer> americanBeers = beers.stream()
                     .filter(brrsssss -> {
                         System.out.println("Inside filter: " +
                                                brrsssss.country);
                         return "USA".equals(brrsssss.country);
                     });
        // Second intermediate operation
        DoubleStream americanBeerPrices = americanBeers
                       .mapToDouble(brrr -> {
                          System.out.println("Inside mapToDouble: "
                                 + brrr.name + ": " + brrr.price);
                         return brrr.price ;
                     });

        // Commented out terminal operation
        //System.out.println("The average American beer price is $"+
        //        americanBeerPrices.average().getAsDouble());
        }
    }
```

The preceding program creates a stream from the beers collection and then applies two intermediate operations: `filter()` and `mapToDouble()`. The first one filters out non-American beers, and the second performs the map operation to keep only the beer price, ignoring beer's other fields. The `LazyStreamsDemo` class has a terminal operation that's supposed to calculate an average price of American beers, but I commented it out on purpose.

Note that each intermediate operation has a `println()` statement. If you run the program `LazyStreamsDemo` as is, you don't see any outputs on the system console. The intermediate operations are not invoked on a stream until the terminal operation is specified! The intermediate operations just declare your intentions. Now uncomment the last two lines in `LazyStreamsDemo` and rerun it. This time you see plenty of output:

```
Inside filter: Belgium
Inside filter: USA
Inside mapToDouble: Sam Adams: 7.0
Inside filter: UkraineInside filter: USA
Inside mapToDouble: Bud Light: 5.0
Inside filter: USA
Inside mapToDouble: Yuengling: 5.5
Inside filter: Belgium
Inside filter: BelgiumInside filter: USA
Inside mapToDouble: Brooklyn Lager: 8.25
The average American beer price is $6.4375
```

The `mapToDouble()` operation worked only for the American beers. Note that `mapToDouble()` returns a stream of type `DoubleStream`. It's a special type of a stream that works on primitive `double` values. We use it to calculate the average value of `double` beer prices. There are also `IntegerStream` and `LongStream` to work with `int` and `long` data types, respectively.

To summarize, treat intermediate operations as a laundry list of required actions that are performed along with a terminal operation in one pass. Neither intermediate nor terminal operations can't modify the source data. Streams are immutable.

Parallel Versus Sequential Processing

A party of ten walk into an Octoberfest tent. They are seated at a table, and the waiter stops by. One of the guys say, "Please bring us ten mugs of Leffe Blonde, and do it as follows: go to the bar, fill the first mug and bring it here; then return and do the same with the second one. Repeat ten times." The waiter politely replies, "Please don't tell me how to bring your beer." He went to the bar that had ten beer dispensers, filled all ten in parallel, and brought them all at the same time. The waiter optimized the process. He just needed the customers to tell him *what* to do but not *how* to do it.

Parallel processing rules! I've already mentioned this while describing iterating collections with the `forEach()` method in Lesson 13. The same applies to streams. When you invoke the method `stream()` on a data source, there is a chance that the data processing will be optimized and performed in parallel; the Java runtime may internally split the data into chunks, perform the operations in parallel, and reconstruct the result.

If you want to make sure that the processing is performed in parallel, use the method `parallelStream()` on your data, which may internally create multiple threads for processing the stream's data. Java 7 introduced the Fork/Join framework for implementing parallelism, but it was not simple to code. In Java 8 the Fork/Join routine is hidden from application developers inside the stream implementation.

However, there is no guarantee that your application code will perform faster with `parallelStream()`. You need to benchmark your code by comparing the speed of `parallelStream()` versus the speed of `stream()`. The results depends on your application code as well as on the Java internals for your data source. Even the Java documentation states that `parallelStream()` returns a possibly parallel stream (`http://docs.oracle.com/javase/8/docs/api/java/util/Collection.html#stream--`).

WHEN TO USE PARALLEL STREAMS

If you're interested in deeper understanding of when to use parallel streams, read the online article "When to use Parallel Streams (`http://gee.cs.oswego.edu/dl/html/StreamParallel-Guidance.html`)" written by a group of Java experts led by Dr. Doug Lea.

SORTING COLLECTIONS AND STREAMS

Sometimes you need to sort data values in ascending or descending order. Hence the Java runtime needs to be able to compare values. It's a simple task for primitive data types: 3 is greater than 2, and 27 is less than 28. But how do you compare complex data types such as objects? What does it mean to sort the collection of `Beer` objects? Which of the `Beer` 's properties should be compared to place beers in a sorted order: prices, names, countries, or a combinations of these attributes?

A programmer needs to specify the rules for object comparison—for example, sort beers by price in an ascending order. Let's see how to specify sorting rules for general Java collections first and then how to sort streams.

Sorting Java Collections

A collection can consist of multiple objects, but you just need to know how to compare two objects to place them in a certain order. Then the method `sort()` on your collection compares each pair of objects. On rare occasions, people need to apply different sorting algorithms, and most likely invoking the method `sort()` is all you need. Java interfaces `Comparable` and `Comparator` enable you to specify the comparison rules.

Using the Comparable Interface

If a class implements the `Comparable` interface, a program can compare the current instance of an object with another object of the same type. You need to add `implements Comparable` to the class declaration and implement the method `compareTo()` there. See how the `Beer` class may look if we want to be able to compare beers by price.

```
public class Beer implements Comparable<Beer>{
    public String name;
    public String country;
    public float price;

    Beer(String name, String country,float price){
        this.name=name;
        this.country=country;
        this.price=price;
    }

    public int compareTo(Beer otherBeer) {

        if (this.price > otherBeer.price){
            return 1;   // This beer is "larger" than the other
        } else if (this.price < otherBeer.price) {
            return -1;  // This beer is "smaller" than the other
        } else {
            return 0;   // The beers are "equal"
        }
    }

    public String toString(){
        return "Name: " + name + ", price: " + price;
    }
}
```

The method `compareTo()` takes one argument—the object to be compared with. If according to our rule this beer value is "larger" than the other, the method `compareTo()` must return 1. If this beer value is "smaller", then it returns a -1. If values are "equal," `compareTo()` returns zero. The current example compares prices.

We're going to reuse the same beer collection used earlier in this lesson. The following code snippet uses the class `java.util.Collections` and shows you how you can sort it by prices:

```
List<Beer> beers = loadCellar();  // populate beer collection

Collections.sort(beers);
beers.forEach(System.out::println);
```

Here's the expected output:

```
Name: Obolon, price: 4.0
Name: Bud Light, price: 5.0
Name: Yuengling, price: 5.5
Name: Sam Adams, price: 7.0
Name: Stella, price: 7.75
Name: Brooklyn Lager, price: 8.25
Name: Leffe Blonde, price: 8.75
Name: Chimay Blue, price: 10.0
```

`Comparable` interface can sort objects by a single attribute only, which limits its use. If you'd want to sort beers by names and prices, you need to consider another solution using the `Comparator` interface.

Using the Comparator Interface

You can use the class that implements the `Comparator` interface to specify the rules for comparison of any two objects of a certain type. For example, you can have the class `Beer` that doesn't implement any interfaces and separately the class `PriceComparator` that implements the `Comparator` interface and has the rules for comparing prices. As of Java 8, you don't even need to create a separate class with comparison rules; you can use lambdas instead. And yes, `Comparator` is a functional interface with only one abstract method: `compare()`.

Let's see a couple of examples of sorting beers by one or more attributes using the `Comparator` interface and lambda expressions. These examples use the original class `Beer` that doesn't implement any interfaces:

```
public class Beer {
    public String name;
    public String country;
    public float price;

    Beer(String name, String country,float price){
        this.name=name;
        this.country=country;
        this.price=price;
    }

    public String toString(){
        return "Name: " + name + ", price: " + price;
    }
}
```

The class `Comparator` has a method `comparing()`, which takes a lambda expression that extracts the attribute that needs to be used for comparison—for example, `price`:

```
List<Beer> beers = loadCellar();  // load the beer collection
```

```
System.out.println("=== Sorting by ascending price");

beers.sort(Comparator.comparing(beer -> beer.price));
beers.forEach(System.out::println);
```

Running this code against your beer collection properly sorts the beers by ascending price. It prints the following:

```
=== Sorting by ascending price
Name: Obolon, price: 4.0
Name: Bud Light, price: 5.0
Name: Yuengling, price: 5.5
Name: Sam Adams, price: 7.0
Name: Stella, price: 7.75
Name: Brooklyn Lager, price: 8.25
Name: Leffe Blonde, price: 8.75
Name: Chimay Blue, price: 10.0
```

The method `reversed()` allows sorting in descending order, for example:

```
Comparator<Beer> priceComparator =
                        Comparator.comparing(beer -> beer.price);

System.out.println("=== Sorting by descending price");
beers.sort(priceComparator.reversed());
beers.forEach(System.out::println);
```

The following is the output of the preceding code snippet:

```
=== Sorting by descending price
Name: Chimay Blue, price: 10.0
Name: Leffe Blonde, price: 8.75
Name: Brooklyn Lager, price: 8.25
Name: Stella, price: 7.75
Name: Sam Adams, price: 7.0
Name: Yuengling, price: 5.5
Name: Bud Light, price: 5.0
Name: Obolon, price: 4.0
```

If you want to sort by multiple fields you should use method chaining with one or more invocations of `thenComparing()`. The following code shows how you can sort beers by name and price:

```
System.out.println("=== Sorting by name and price");
beers.sort(Comparator.comparing((Beer beer) -> beer.name)
                .thenComparing(beer -> beer.price));
beers.forEach(System.out::println);
```

The method `comparing()` expects to get *a method extractor* as an argument. The method extractor (a getter) returns a field that should be used for comparison. The preceding code snippet uses lambda expressions instead of method extractors, which requires you to specify the type in case of method chaining. That's why this example uses explicit casting `(Beer beer)`.

If I had getters in the `Beer` class, I could have used method references and casting wouldn't be required:

```
beers.sort(Comparator.comparing(Beer::getName)
                .thenComparing(Beer::getPrice));
```

MUTABLE COLLECTIONS

Using `Collections.sort()` with both `Comparable` and `Comparator` interfaces modifies (re-orders) the original data collection. Hence a collection is *mutable*. This is not the case when sorting streams, which is explained next.

Sorting Streams

Now that you are familiar with the basics of general sorting of data collections, it's time to see how you can use Stream API for sorting any data sources. As a reminder, when you work with streams, the original data source stays *immutable*—no changes are made to the data source. To store the sorted data in another collection or an array you need to use the terminal operation `collect()`.

The method sorted works together with `Comparator`, and to sort your beer collection by price just write something like this:

```
beers.stream()
        .sorted(Comparator.comparing(b -> b.price))
        .forEach(System.out::println);
```

Sorting by multiple fields is done similarly to the code sample from the section on `Comparator`. The next example shows you how to sort beers by country and price. Slightly modify the method `toString()` from `Beer` to print the country too:

```
public String toString(){
   return "Country: " + country +
            " Name: " + name + ", price: " + price;
}
```

This is how sorting by beer country and price can look like:

```
 beers.stream()
       .sorted(Comparator.comparing((Beer b) -> b.country)
                         .thenComparing(b -> b.price))
       .forEach(System.out::println);
```

Running this code snippet produces the following output:

```
Country: Belgium Name: Stella, price: 7.75
Country: Belgium Name: Leffe Blonde, price: 8.75
Country: Belgium Name: Chimay Blue, price: 10.0
Country: USA Name: Bud Light, price: 5.0
Country: USA Name: Yuengling, price: 5.5
Country: USA Name: Sam Adams, price: 7.0
```

```
Country: USA Name: Brooklyn Lager, price: 8.25
Country: Ukraine Name: Obolon, price: 4.0
```

To store the result of the stream sorting in a new `List` collection, you need to add a terminal operation:

```
List<Beer> sortedBeers = beers.stream()
        .sorted(Comparator.comparing(b -> b.price))
        .collect(Collectors.toList());
```

Now you have two collections. The original (`beers`) collection is unsorted and the new one (`sortedBeers`) is sorted.

PARALLEL STREAMS AND SORTING

If you decide to use `parallelStream()`, the method `forEach()` can't be used with the sorted data. Per Oracle documentation (`http://docs.oracle.com/javase/8/docs/api/java/util/stream/IntStream.html#forEach-java.util.function.IntConsumer-`), "For parallel stream pipelines, this operation does not guarantee to respect the encounter order of the stream, as doing so would sacrifice the benefit of parallelism." You need to use the `forEachOrdered()` method instead.

OTHER STREAM SOURCES

So far, all the code samples in this chapter use a collection of objects as a stream's data source. But this doesn't have to be the case. You can process both finite and infinite data sources with the Stream API.

Creating Finite Size Streams

You can take a bunch of arbitrary values and turn them into a stream using the `Stream.of()` method. For example, the following code snippet creates and prints a stream of strings of a *finite size*:

```
Stream<String> beerNames = Stream.of("Leffe Blonde",
                                     "Chimay Blue","Sam Adams");
beerNames.forEach(System.out::println);
```

The method `builder()` is yet another way of creating finite size streams. The following code snippet creates a stream of three long primitives and finds the maximum value. Because `max()` returns the `OptionalLong` type (it may or may not have a value), I call the `getAsLong()` to get the primitive `long`. After running this code, `maxValue` is equal to 21.

```
long maxValue = LongStream.builder()
                .add(10)
                .add(21)
                .add(15)
                .build()
                .max().getAsLong();
```

Creating Infinite-Size Streams

Although data collections have finite size, you can use the Stream API for working with infinite streams of data.

Generating Stream Data

The method `Stream.generate()` can take a lambda expression that generates values by some arbitrary algorithm. This lambda has to be an implementation of the functional interface `java.util.function.Supplier`. Implementing a `Supplier` comes down to writing a function that returns some result.

The following class `StreamOfDates` uses the class `LocalDateTime`, which is a part of the new Java 8 Date and Time API (`http://docs.oracle.com/javase/tutorial/datetime/`) located in the package java.time (`http://docs.oracle.com/javase/8/docs/api/java/time/package-summary.html`). The supplier repeatedly sleeps for a second (1000 millisec) and then queries the system time using the method `now()`. The method `Stream.generate()` generates an *infinite stream* that is feeding the stream with the current time about every second.

```
import java.time.LocalDateTime;
import java.util.function.Supplier;
import java.util.stream.Stream;

public class StreamOfDates {

  public static void main(String[] args){

     // Implementing a Supplier interface
    Supplier<LocalDateTime> myStopWatch = () -> {
           try{
               Thread.sleep(1000);
           } catch (InterruptedException e){
               e.printStackTrace();
           }
           return LocalDateTime.now(); // get the current time
           };

     // Generating a stream using lambda expression

     Stream<LocalDateTime> timeStream =
                                  Stream.generate(myStopWatch);

     timeStream.forEach(System.out::println);
   }
}
```

Running this program starts producing an output that never stops and looks like this (without ellipses):

```
2014-09-18T17:41:36.017
2014-09-18T17:41:37.026
2014-09-18T17:41:38.027
2014-09-18T17:41:39.028
2014-09-18T17:41:40.028
2014-09-18T17:41:41.029
2014-09-18T17:41:42.029
2014-09-18T17:41:43.030
2014-09-18T17:41:44.031
2014-09-18T17:41:45.033
...
```

You see how to stop an infinite stream in the section Short-Circuit Operations.

Yet another way of generating the infinite stream is the method `iterate()`, which requires a rule for generating the next data value.

```
LongStream evenNumbers = LongStream.iterate(0, num -> num+2);
evenNumbers.forEach(System.out::println);
```

The preceding code prints even numbers, but because they are being generated extremely fast, you might need to limit the number of generated values (see the section Short-Circuit Operations) to see the expected results.

Using Stream API with I/O Streams

As of Java 8, some of the classes used for processing I/O streams include new methods that allow data processing with the Stream API. For example, the class `java.io.BufferedReader` has a new method lines() (`http://docs.oracle.com/javase/8/docs/api/java/io/BufferedReader.html#method.summary`)that returns a `Stream`, the elements of which are lines read from this `BufferedReader` object. As with other data sources, the `Stream` (`http://docs.oracle.com/javase/8/docs/api/java/util/stream/Stream.html`) is lazily populated—that is, read only occurs during the terminal operation.

You can see it in action by rewriting the class `WebSiteReader` from Lesson 16. That class was reading and printing the content of the web page www.google.com. The new version of this class is called `WebSiteReaderStream`.

```
public class WebSiteReaderStream {
  public static void main(String args[]){
       String nextLine;
       URL url = null;
       URLConnection urlConn = null;

       try
       {
         // Assume index.html is a default home page name
          url  = new URL("http://www.google.com" );
          urlConn = url.openConnection();
       } catch( IOException e){
           System.out.println(
                    "Can't connect to the provided URL:" +
                                              e.toString() );
```

```
        }

        try( InputStreamReader inStream = new InputStreamReader(
                 urlConn.getInputStream(), "UTF8");
                 BufferedReader buff  =
                                 new BufferedReader(inStream);){

       // Read and print the content of the Google home page
       // using Stream API

          buff.lines()
                 .forEach(System.out::println);

        } catch(IOException  e1){
       System.out.println("Can't read from the Internet: "+
                                              e1.toString() );
       }
    }
  }
```

Not only does the reading part of the stream becomes simpler—just call the `lines()`—but you can now add some intermediate operations to perform some filtering as the data is coming in. For example, you can create a matching pattern using regular expressions (`http://docs.oracle.com/javase/tutorial/essential/regex/`)(not covered in this book) and read only those data that match this pattern. You can research this further by finding examples that use the Java class Matcher (`http://docs.oracle.com/javase/8/docs/api/java/util/regex/Matcher.html`).

SHORT-CIRCUIT OPERATIONS

In some cases you want to stop stream processing prematurely. Say you want to show only the first five elements from the stream. Short-circuit operations serve this purpose. Revisit the example that prints even numbers. With it you generated an infinite stream of even numbers. To print only the first five numbers you use the short-circuit operation `limit()`:

```
LongStream evenNumbers = LongStream
                    .iterate(0, num -> num+2)
                    .limit(5);

evenNumbers.forEach(System.out::println);
```

This code prints the following five numbers:

```
0
2
4
6
8
```

Another short-circuit method is the `findFirst()` element of the stream. This method returns an object of type `Optional`, which was introduced in Java 8. It allows avoiding `NullPointerException` if the requested object is not found. If the requested value is not found, the method `findFirst()` returns an empty `Optional` object. The next code sample prints the first element from the beers collection:

```
Optional<Beer> firstBeer = beers.stream()
                 .findFirst();

System.out.println("The first beer in collection: " +
              firstBeer.orElse(new Beer("No name","No country",0 )));
```

Running this code against your collection of beers prints the following:

```
The first beer in collection: Name: Stella, price: 7.75
```

If your collection is empty, the `println()` method uses the code from the `orElse()` method. An attempt to simply print `firstBeer` from an empty collection would output `Optional.empty`.

Some other short-circuit methods on the class `Stream` are `skip()`, `findAny()`, `allMatch()`, `noneMatch()`, and `anyMatch()`.

TRY IT

In the following assignments you need to use method references while working with streams. You also try using short-circuit operations.

Lesson Requirements

You should have Java installed.

> **NOTE** *You can download the code and resources for this "Try It" from the book's web page at* `www.wrox.com/go/javaprog24hr2e`. *You can find them in the Lesson20.zip.*

Step-by-Step

In this exercise you need to use static method references with streams.

1. Import the project Lesson20 into the Eclipse IDE.
2. In the class `StreamOfDates`, add a static method titled `myStopWatchFunction()` and move the code from the lambda expression `myStopWatch` there. This is how the lambda expression `myStopWatch` was originally implemented:

```
Supplier<LocalDateTime> myStopWatch = () -> {
       try{
           Thread.sleep(1000);
       } catch (InterruptedException e){
           e.printStackTrace();
```

```
}
return LocalDateTime.now(); // get the current time
};
```

3. Remove the declaration of the lambda expression `Supplier myStopWatch` from the class.
4. The existing invocation of the method generate() looks like this:

```
Stream.generate(myStopWatch)
```

   Replace the argument of the method `generate()` with the method reference `StreamOfDates::myStopWatchFunction`.
5. Run the program. It should start printing the infinite messages with the current time.
6. Add the short-circuit operation `limit()` so the program stops after printing the current time five times.
7. Are `limit()` and `findFirst()` intermediate or terminal operations?
8. Modify the class `Beer` to include getters and change the `Comparator` code sample that use to use method references instead of lambda expressions.

> **TIP** *Please select the videos for Lesson 20 online at* `www.wrox.com/go/javaprog24hr2e`. *You will also be able to download the code and resources for this lesson from the website.*

21

Working with Relational DBMS Using JDBC

Business applications usually store data in the databases. In most of the enterprise applications, Relational Database Management Systems (RDBMSes) are used as data storage. They store the data records in *tables*. Each record (such as that of an employee) is represented by a table row, which consists of one or more columns or *record fields* (for example, name, address, hire date). RDBMSes understand the SQL language.

The most popular RDBMSes are Oracle, DB2, Sybase, Microsoft SQL Server, and MySQL Server. This lesson uses Apache Derby DB (`http://db.apache.org/derby/`) (also known as Java DB), which is included with Java SE for Windows, or you can separately install it on a Mac or Linux machine.

> **NOSQL DATABASE MANAGEMENT SYSTEMS**
>
> Some database management systems are not relational—they don't store data as rows and columns. Such database management systems are known as *NoSQL databases* (for example, MongoDB, Cassandra, Couchbase, and so on). This book doesn't cover NoSQL databases. Refer to `http://nosql-database.org` for further information.

Java includes two packages that contain classes required for work with DBMSes: `java.sql` and `javax.sql`. The former contains commonly used classes such as `Connection`, `Statement`, and `ResultSet`. The latter is used for supporting database connectivity on the server side, containing classes such as `DataSource` and `RowSet`.

The JDBC API is not DBMS-specific—if you write a program that uses JDBC classes to retrieve/update data in Oracle, you'll be using the same classes to work with MySQL Server or DB2. You just need the JDBC drivers from the corresponding DBMS vendor; the drivers hide their database specifics behind the same public JDBC API.

JDBC drivers either pass SQL statements from Java to a DBMS for execution or simply execute a program stored inside a DBMS (called a *stored procedure*). If some data has been retrieved as the result of these actions, your Java program will handle it by making appropriate calls to the JDBC API. Over the past 15 years the JDBC specification has been evolving and, at the time of this writing, most drivers comply with JDBC version 4.1 (`http://download.oracle.com/otndocs/jcp/jdbc-4_1-mrel-spec/index.html`).

In this lesson, all communications with the DBMS are made by supplying SQL statements to the JDBC API. There is an alternative way of working with data by using Java Persistence API (JPA), which is covered in Lesson 32. Some people prefer using object-relational mapping (ORM) frameworks, such as Hibernate, or those that reduce mundane JDBC programming like MyBatis (`http://mybatis.github.io/mybatis-3/`); these frameworks are not covered in this book.

JDBC DRIVER TYPES

A JDBC driver plays the role of the middleman between a Java program and a DBMS. Drivers are available from database vendors, from Oracle, and from third-party vendors of Java application servers.

There are four general types of JDBC drivers:

- A Type 1 driver is a JDBC-ODBC bridge that enables Java programs to work with the database using ODBC drivers from Microsoft. The drawbacks of ODBC drivers are that they are slower than the others, must be installed and configured on each user's machine, and work only on Windows machines. The Type 1 JDBC driver has rarely been used lately, and Oracle has removed it as of Java 8 run time.
- A Type 2 driver consists of Java classes that work in conjunction with the non-Java native drivers provided by the DBMS vendor. These drivers work much faster than Type 1, but they also require installation and configuration on the machine on which Java programs run.
- A Type 3 driver is called a *middleware driver* and can be provided by vendors of application servers. It consists of two parts: The *client* portion performs a DBMS-independent SQL call, which is then translated to a specific DBMS protocol by the *server* portion of the driver.
- A Type 4 driver is a pure Java driver, which usually comes as a `.jar` file and performs direct calls to the database server. It does not need any configuration on the client's machine, other than including the name of the main driver's class in your Java code. That's why it's also known as the *thin driver*. For example, Java applets can be packaged with this type of driver, which can be automatically downloaded to the user's machine along with the applets themselves.

For simplicity, this lesson uses JDBC drivers of Type 4, but many production systems can deploy Type 3 drivers to provide better performance.

INSTALLING DERBY DB AND CREATING A DATABASE

Derby DB (also known as JavaDB) is a small DBMS that you wouldn't use for serious production systems, but it's great for learning JDBC or to use for many small systems. If you're using Windows OS, it's already installed with Java SDK in the folder that looks similar to this one: `c:\Program Files\Java\jdk1.8.0_25\db`. The numbers reflect the major and minor versions of Java.

Modify your system variable `PATH` so it starts with the following: `c:\Program Files\Java\jdk1.8.0_25\db\bin;`

If you work in something other than Windows OS, download and install Derby DB from `http://db.apache.org/derby`. Derby DB is well-documented and if you haven't had a chance to work with relational DBMSes, download and read the "Getting Started with Derby" manual. The installation of Derby DB comes down to downloading and unzipping one file. At the time of this writing the filename is `db-derby-10.10.2.0-bin.zip`. Unzip it and rename the folder as *derby*.

The configuration process is also simple; read the steps required for your operating system at the Swinburne University web page at `http://goo.gl/` (`http://goo.gl/Q5a01N`)Q5a01N (`http://goo.gl/Q5a01N`). You need to set the `DERBY_HOME` environment variable to point to your Derby DB installation directory. For example, I've unzipped Derby into my root directory on my Mac OS computer and added the following two lines to the file `.bash_profile`:

```
export PATH=~/derby/bin:$PATH
export DERBY_HOME=~/derby
```

To insure that your Derby DB is properly installed, open a Command or Terminal window and enter the command `sysinfo`. You should see an output describing the Derby DB install.

Derby DB has an interactive command-line utility called *ij* that you can use to create databases and tables and populate them with data, among other actions. I show you how to create a sample database and a table to store data about employees.

First open a Command or Terminal window and issue the command `startNetworkServer.exe` (or `startNetworkServer` if you use Mac OS).

The Derby DB server starts by displaying the message similar to this one:

```
Apache Derby Network Server - 10.10.2.0 - (1582446) started and ready to
accept connections on port 1527
```

Open another command window and start ij—you'll see the *ij>* prompt. Now try connecting to the database Lesson21 by issuing the following command:

```
connect 'jdbc:derby://localhost:1527/Lesson21;create=true';
```

This command tries to connect to the database Lesson21 and creates it if no such database is found. The next *ij* command creates a database table—Employee—to store records that consist of three fields: `EMPNO`, `ENAME`, and `JOB_TITLE`. The first field is stored as an integer, and the other two as simple text (`varchar`) allowing 50 and 150 characters respectively.

```
CREATE TABLE Employee (
    EMPNO int NOT NULL,
    ENAME varchar (50) NOT NULL,
```

```
    JOB_TITLE varchar (150) NOT NULL
);
```

Finally, to populate the table with some data, issue the INSERT command in ij:

```
INSERT INTO Employee values (7369,'John Smith', 'Clerk'), (7499,
'Joe Allen','Salesman'), (7521,'Mary Lou','Director');
```

If you want to ensure that the records were successfully created in the database, in the ij utility issue the SELECT SQL statement to retrieve the data:

```
Select * from Employee;
```

You see the data about the three employees that were added by the INSERT SQL command. If you are not familiar with the syntax of SQL, refer to the tutorial at `http://www.sqlcourse.com`.

SAMPLE JDBC PROGRAM

In this section you see the steps that you can perform to retrieve the data in any Java program that works with a relational database using JDBC. A sample program implements all of these steps to display the list of employees from the database table Employee.

1. Load the JDBC driver using the method `forName()` of the Java class `Class`. You have to find out the name of the class to load from the JDBC driver's documentation. In the case of JavaDB, you can skip this step. If you work with Oracle DBMSes, you can load a Type 4 JDBC driver with the following Java statement:

   ```
   Class.forName("oracle.jdbc.driver.OracleDriver");
   ```

2. Get the database connection to the database Lesson21 by calling

   ```
   DriverManager.getConnection(url, user, password);
   ```

   In the case of Derby DB, you don't have to supply the user and the password; simply provide the URL of your database, for example:

   ```
   DriverManager.getConnection("jdbc:derby:Lesson21");
   ```

3. Create an instance of the Java class `Statement`:

   ```
   Connection.createStatement();
   ```

   As an alternative, you can create `PreparedStatement` or `CallableStatement`, which are explained later in this lesson in the "The PreparedStatement Class" and "The CallableStatement Class" sections.

4. To run SQL `Select` queries, your program can include a statement similar to this one:

```
Statement.executeQuery("Select * from Employee");
```

For SQL queries, which produce more than one result, you can use the method `execute()` of the class `Statement`.

For `Insert`, `Update`, and `Delete` SQL statement, use the method `updateQuery()`. For example:

```
String myInsertStmt = "INSERT INTO Employee values " +
                      "(1234,'John Bush', 'Clerk')";
Statement.updateQuery(myInsertStmt);
```

5. To process a received data loop through the `ResultSet` object, use the following:

```
while (ResultSet.next()) {
   // get the values from each column here
}
```

6. Free system resources by closing the `ResultSet`, `Statement`, and `Connection` objects.

All these steps are implemented in the class `EmployeeList`, shown in Listing 21-1, which prints the records from the table Employee. Even though you don't need to explicitly load the driver for Derby DB with `Class.forName()`, the location of the driver class has to be known to your program, otherwise you'll get a "No suitable driver" error. Either add `derbyclient.jar` located in the lib directory in your Derby installation to the CLASSPATH system variable, or just add it as an external `.jar` to your Eclipse project (see the project menu Properties → Java Build Panel → Add External JARs).

LISTING 21-1 The EmployeeList program

```
class EmployeeList {

  public static void main(String argv[]) {

   String sqlQuery = "SELECT * from Employee";

   // Open autocloseable Connection, Statement and get the result set
   try (Connection conn = DriverManager.getConnection(
                    "jdbc:derby://localhost:1527/Lesson21");
        Statement stmt = conn.createStatement();
        ResultSet rs = stmt.executeQuery(sqlQuery); ) {

      // Process each column in the result set and print the data
      while (rs.next()){
         int empNo = rs.getInt("EMPNO");
         String eName = rs.getString("ENAME");
         String job = rs.getString("JOB_TITLE");
         System.out.println(""+ empNo + ", " + eName + ", " + job );
      }
   } catch( SQLException se ) {
      System.out.println ("SQLError: " + se.getMessage ()
```

```
                + " code: " + se.getErrorCode ());

        } catch( Exception e ) {
           System.out.println(e.getMessage());
           e.printStackTrace();
        }
    }
    }
```

The output of the EmployeeList program looks like this:

```
7369, John Smith, CLERK
7499, Joe Allen, SALESMAN
7521, Mary Lou, Director
```

When you execute any SQL statements, always include error-handling code. Catching the SQLException is the right way to get the error message. Note that the code in Listing 21-1 calls the method getErrorCode() to extract the database-specific error code from the SQLException object.

PROCESSING RESULT SETS

Let's take a closer look at the code in Listing 21-1. After rs = stmt.executeQuery(sqlQuery), the cursor rs is positioned before the very first record (row) of the result set in memory, if any. Each row contains as many fields (columns) as were specified in the SQL Select statement. Each of the values is extracted by an appropriate method based on the data type of the field. The names of these methods are self-explanatory: rs.getString(), rs.getInt(), and so on. If you know the name of a column from the result, use it as a method argument:

```
int empNo = rs.getInt("EMPNO");
String eName = rs.getString("ENAME");
```

If you don't know the column names, specify the relative position of the column (they start with 1) from the result set:

```
int empNo = rs.getInt(1);
String eName = rs.getString(2);
```

You can also query the database table to figure our the column names and their types with the help of the class ResultSetMetaData explained later in this lesson. JDBC drivers automatically convert the data from the database types to the corresponding Java types: For example, Derby's varchar becomes Java'sString.

The class EmployeeList just prints the retrieved data in a loop. You can also place the result set data in a Java collection object for further processing. The ResultSet object holds the database connection and is not serializable. That's why common practice for programming server-side operations with DBMSes is to create a class representing a row from the result set and populate, say, an ArrayList or other Java collection with its instances.

Listing 21-2 shows an example of such a class, which can represent one employee record. Classes that hold only the value of some data are often called *value objects*. Because in distributed applications such objects may need to be transferred between different computers, they are also known as *Data Transfer Objects (DTOs)*.

LISTING 21-2 The EmployeeDTO

```
class EmployeeDTO{

  //private properties
  private int empNo;
  private String eName;
  private String jobTitle;

  //setters
  public void setEmpNo(int val){empNo=val;}
  public void setEName(String val){eName=val;}
  public void setJobTitle(String val){jobTitle=val;}

  // getters
  public int getEmpNo(){return empNo;}
  public String getEName(){return eName;}
  public String getJobTitle(){return jobTitle;}
}
```

EmployeeDTO declares private variables to store the data but access to this data is performed via public *setters* and *getters*, the methods that allow external code to set and get the appropriate values. This technique can be useful when some application-specific logic has to be applied at the moment when some code needs to get or modify the properties of the class EmployeeDTO.

For example, you can place some authorization code inside the setter to ensure that the external object has enough permissions to change the property jobTitle. If the business logic of obtaining such authorization changes in the future, you need to modify only the code inside the setter, but the external code remains unchanged.

The next code snippet shows how to prepare a collection of EmployeeDTO objects while processing the result set retrieved by the SQL Select statement.

```
// Create an object for collection of employees
ArrayList<EmployeeDTO> employees = new ArrayList<>();

// Process ResultSet and populate the collection

while (rs.next()){
 EmployeeDTO currentEmp = new EmployeeDTO();
 currentEmp.setEmpNo(rs.getInt("EMPNO"));
 currentEmp.setEName(rs.getString("ENAME"));
 currentEmp.setJobTitle(rs.getString("JOB_TITLE"));

 employees.add(currentEmp);
}
```

If this code is deployed on the server's JVM and you need to send the data to another computer that runs, say, a Swing client, you can consider applying Java serialization here for sending a collection of employees to the front. But make sure that the class EmployeeDTO implements the Serializable interface. In case of a web client, consider serializing the EmployeeDTO into JSON data format discussed in Lesson 33.

THE PREPAREDSTATEMENT CLASS

Listing 21-1 uses the class Statement to create an object capable of executing SQL. But this is not the only way to supply SQL to the JDBC API. The class PreparedStatement is a subclass of Statement, but it pre-compiles the SQL statement before executing it.

With PreparedStatement you can create SQL with parameters that are dynamically passed by the program. Suppose you need to execute the query "SELECT * from EMP WHERE empno=..." multiple times, providing the empno values from the array empNumbers[]. If you use the class Statement as in the following code snippet, the variable sqlQuery has to be modified and pre-compiled on each iteration of the loop:

```
for (int i=0;i<empNumbers.length; i++){
  sqlQuery="SELECT * from Employee WHERE empno=" + employees[i];
  stmt.executeQuery(sqlQuery);
}
```

The class PreparedStatement offers a more efficient solution:

```
PreparedStatement stmt=conn.prepareStatement(
                        " SELECT * from Employee WHERE empno=?");

for (int i=0;i<employees.length; i++){

  // pass the array's value that substitutes the question mark
  stmt.setInt(1,employees[i]);
  stmt.executeQuery();
}
```

In this case, the SQL statement is compiled only once and parameters are provided by the appropriate setXXX() method depending on the data type. The SQL statement may have several parameters (question marks), and the first argument of the setter enables you to specify each parameter's number. For example:

```
PreparedStatement stmt=conn.prepareStatement(
      "SELECT * from Employee WHERE empno=? and ename=?");

for (int i=0;i<empNumbers.length; i++){
  stmt.setInt(1,empNumbers[i];)
  stmt.setString(2,empNames[i];)
  stmt.executeQuery();
}
```

If you need to pass a NULL value as a parameter, use the method setNull().

THE CALLABLESTATEMENT CLASS

This class extends PreparedStatement and is used for executing database stored procedures from Java. Let's say there is a stored procedure entitled changeEmpTitle that takes two parameters: empno and title. Here's the code to execute this stored procedure:

```
CallableStatement stmt = conn.prepareCall("{call changeEmpTitle(?,?)}");

stmt.setInt(1,7566);
stmt.setString (2,"Salesman");
stmt.executeUpdate();
```

If a stored procedure returns some values using output parameters, each of the OUT data types has to be registered before the statement is executed. The next code snippet shows you an example of executing a stored procedure that has two parameters: The first is an input parameter, and the second is an output parameter by which the stored procedure can return the result of its execution to the Java program:

```
CallableStatement stmt = conn.prepareCall(
                  ("{call getEmpTitle(?,?) }");
stmt.setInt(1, 7566);
stmt.registerOutParameter(2,java.sql.Types.VARCHAR);
stmt.executeQuery();
String title=stmt.getString(2);
```

THE RESULTSETMETADATA CLASS

JDBC enables you to process result sets when the number of returned values is unknown. Imagine that you need to write a program that can accept any SQL `Select` statement, execute it, and display the retrieved data. With the class `ResultSetMetaData`, you can dynamically find out how many columns there are in the result set, as well as their names and data types. The following code fragment gets the number of the database table columns in the result set and for each of them identifies and prints the column name and type:

```
String sqlQuery = "select * from Employee";
ResultSet rs = stmt.executeQuery(query);

ResultSetMetaData rsMeta = rs.getMetaData();
int colCount = rsMeta.getColumnCount();

for (int i = 1; i <= colCount; i++) {
  System.out.println(
      " Column name: " + rsMeta.getColumnName(i) +
      " Column type: " + rsMeta.getColumnTypeName(i));
}
```

This simple but powerful technique is used internally by ORM frameworks that can "magically" generate database models and automatically generate Java classes representing database entities.

Listing 21-3 shows a Java program called `ShowAnyData` that prints a result set based on any SQL `Select` statement passed from the command line. For example, it can be started as follows:

```
java ShowAnyData "Select * from Employee"
```

LISTING 21-3 Using ResultSetMetaData

```
class ShowAnyData {

  public static void main(String args[]) {

   if (args.length==0){
     System.out.println(
      "Usage: java ShowAnyData SQLSelectStatement");
     System.out.println(
      "For example: java ShowAnyData \"Select * from Employee\"");
     System.exit(1);
   }

   try (Connection conn = DriverManager.getConnection(
                          "jdbc:derby://localhost:1527/Lesson21");
        Statement stmt = conn.createStatement();
        ResultSet rs = stmt.executeQuery(args[0]);) {

    // Find out the number of columns, their names
    // and display the data
    ResultSetMetaData rsMeta = rs.getMetaData();
    int colCount = rsMeta.getColumnCount();

     for (int i = 1; i <= colCount; i++)  {
      System.out.print(rsMeta.getColumnName(i) + " ");
    }
    System.out.println();

    while (rs.next()){
       for (int i = 1; i <= colCount; i++)  {
         System.out.print(rs.getString(i) + " ");
       }
       System.out.print("\n");    // new line character
    }
   } catch( SQLException se ) {
      System.out.println ("SQLError: " + se.getMessage ()
           + " code: " + se.getErrorCode ());

   } catch( Exception e ) {
      e.printStackTrace();
   }
  }
}
```

The output of the ShowAnyData program is the same as that of EmployeeList shown in Listing 21-1. But the ShowAnyData program can execute any SQL SELECT statement as long as you are specifying valid database and table(s) names. Note that the code in ShowAnyData first ensures that you have passed the command-line argument. If you run this program from a command line, don't forget to include the SQL statement in double quotes. In Eclipse you can specify a command-line argument by selecting the Arguments tab in the Run Configuration panel.

SCROLLABLE RESULT SETS AND ROWSET

In all the preceding examples, the code traversed the result set using the method `next()`, which moves the cursor only forward. Another option is to create a scrollable result set so the cursor can be moved back and forth if need be. There is a two-argument version of the method `createStatement()`. The first argument specifies the type of scrolling (`TYPE_FORWARD_ONLY`, `TYPE_SCROLL_INSENSITIVE`, or `TYPE_SCROLL_SENSITIVE`) and the second makes the result set updateable or read-only (`CONCUR_READ_ONLY` or `CONCUR_UPDATABLE`). For example,

```
Statement stmt = con.createStatement(
ResultSet.TYPE_SCROLL_INSENSITIVE, ResultSet.CONCUR_READ_ONLY);
ResultSet rs = stmt.executeQuery("SELECT * from Employee");
```

The `TYPE_FORWARD_ONLY` parameter allows only forward movement of the cursor. The difference between `TYPE_SCROLL_INSENSITIVE` and `TYPE_SCROLL_SENSITIVE` is in whether scrolling reflects changes that have been made to the result set. The next example sets the cursor at the end of the result set and moves the cursor backward:

```
rs.afterLast();
while (rs.previous()){
 int empNo = rs.getInt("EMPNO");
 String eName = rs.getString("ENAME");
 String job = rs.getString("JOB_TITLE");
 System.out.println(""+ empNo + ", " + eName + ", " + job);
}
```

You can also move the cursor to a specific row by using the following self-explanatory methods:

```
rs.absolute(25); // moves the cursor to the 25th row
rs.relative(-4); // moves the cursor to the 21st row
rs.first();
rs.last();
rs.beforeFirst();
```

If the result set is updatable (`CONCUR_UPDATABLE`) then you can modify the underlying database table while scrolling. For example, the following statements update the job title of the employee based on the current cursor's position:

```
rs.updateString("JOB_TITLE","Manager");
rs.updateRow();
```

Scrollable result sets enable you to traverse the result set in both directions, but they have a drawback: They hold the database connection, which may be required by another thread or program. The package `javax.sql` includes the interface `RowSet`, which is inherited from `ResultSet`. `RowSet` gets the data from the database, then disconnects, but still allows Java to work with the data. The package `javax.sql.rowset` has several concrete classes that implement `RowSet`, such as `CachedRowSet`, `FilteredRowSet`, and `WebRowSet`. The latter can turn `RowSet` into an XML stream to be sent to another tier in the distributed application.

TRANSACTIONAL UPDATES

Transaction is a logical unit of work. Sometimes several database modifications have to be processed as one transaction, and if one of the updates fails, the whole transaction has to be *rolled back*. These database operations have to be explicitly *committed* (finalized) in case of success. If you set the auto-commit parameter on the database connection to `false`, the database transaction is not committed until the code explicitly calls the method `commit()`, as in the following example:

```
try{
  conn.setAutoCommit(false);

  Statement stmt = con.createStatement();

  stmt.addBatch("insert into Orders " +
              "values(123, 'Buy','IBM',200)");
  stmt.addBatch("insert into OrderDetail " +
              "values('JSmith', 'Broker131', '05/20/02')");
  stmt.executeBatch();

  conn.commit(); // Transaction succeded

}catch(SQLException e){
  conn.rollback(); // Transaction failed
  e.printStackTrace();
}
```

In the preceding code snippet, two `Insert` statements have to be executed as one transaction, and if any of them fails, an exceptionis thrown and the method `rollback()` undoes all the changes, including those that succeeded.

CONNECTION POOLS AND DATASOURCE

Up until now you've been running all sample Java programs on your own computer. But imagine a distributed application in which multiple clients make requests to the same server, which has to process their SQL queries. Because obtaining a connection to the database is a slow process, it would be very inefficient to start every SQL request by obtaining a database connection and disconnecting after the request is complete. Such applications should reuse the same opened connection for multiple requests.

The package `javax.sql` includes the interface `DataSource`, which is an alternative to `DriverManager`. Vendors of JDBC drivers for servers implement this interface, and a `DataSource` is typically preconfigured for a certain number of connections (the *connection pool*). It is published in a directory using the JNDI interface. In such a setup, all clients' requests get their database connections from this `DataSource` object, eliminating the need to open and close a new connection for each request. The `DataSource` objects are typically used on the server side bound to JNDI. But you can create an instance of a `DataSource` in any Java application. Chapter 29 provides an example of working with `DataSource` objects.

TRY IT

In this assignment you modify the class `Portfolio` from Chapter 21, which was just printing some hard-coded statements. Now you create and populate the database table Portfolio and then read and display the data from there.

Lesson Requirements

You should have Java installed.

> **NOTE** *You can download the code and resources for this "Try It" from the book's web page at* `www.wrox.com/go/javaprog24hr2e`. *You can find them in the Lesson21.zip.*

Hint

Obtaining a database connection is a slow operation, and doing it from inside the method `run()` every time you start a new thread is not the best solution. Consider creating a database connection up front and passing it to the thread before starting it.

Step-by-Step

1. In the database Lesson21 create the table Portfolio using the following SQL statement:

```
create table Portfolio(
id INTEGER NOT NULL,
symbol VARCHAR(10) NOT NULL,
quantity INTEGER NOT NULL,
price NUMERIC NOT NULL, PRIMARY KEY (id)
);
```

2. Populate the table Portfolio with three records, for stocks traded under the symbols IBM, AMZN, and AAPL respectively:

```
insert into Portfolio values (1,'IBM',500,105.50),
 (2,'AMZN',1000,15.25),(3,'AAPL',2000,272.50);
```

3. Create a new Eclipse project.
4. Create a class called `Portfolio` that is similar to the one shown in Listing 17-5 from Lesson 17:

```
public class Portfolio implements Runnable {
    public void run() {
       System.out.println( "You have 500 shares of IBM ");
     }
}
```

5. Modify the code of `Portfolio`: instead of just printing "You have 500 shares of IBM," have it connect to the database, select all the data from the table `Portfolio`, and print the symbol, quantity, and total value. Calculate the total value by multiplying price by quantity.
6. Create a testing class called `ShowMyPortfolio` that instantiates and starts the thread `Portfolio`.
7. Test this program.

> **TIP** *Please select the videos for Lesson 21 online at* `www.wrox.com/go/javaprog24hr2e`. *You will also be able to download the code and resources for this lesson from the website.*

22

Rendering Tabular Data in the GUI

This lesson shows you how to display tabular data on the graphical user interface (GUI). Data grids and spreadheet-like data are very popular in the enterprise applications. Most of this lesson is dedicated to working with a powerful Swing component called `JTable`. This user interface (UI) component enables you to present data in a grid with rows and columns. After learning the basics of working with `JTable`, you see how to display tabular data using the JavaFX TableView control. In the "Try It" section you apply these new skills to display the portfolio data that, as of Chapter 21, is stored in the database.

In other words, you build a client-server application, where the Java GUI is a client and the RDBMS is a server. Such architecture was pretty popular in the mid-1990s. Rich clients were developed in Visual Basic, PowerBuilder, Delphi, Java, or C++, and they connected directly to database servers such as Oracle, DB2, Sybase, Microsoft SQL Server, and Informix.

In the late '90s, thin clients (plain-looking HTML-based web pages with almost no code implementing business logic) became the trend. These days applications with rich UIs are coming back, but typically you'll be using an application server as a middleman between the client and the data storage. I describe such middlemen starting in Chapter 25, but your UI skills need to include the ability to program data grids.

JTABLE AND THE MVC PARADIGM

The Swing class `JTable` is a powerful UI component created for displaying tabular data like a spreadsheet. The data is represented as rows and columns; that's why the `JTable` component is often used to display data from relational databases, which store data similarly. `JTable` was designed according to the *MVC* design pattern introduced in Lesson 9. The components responsible for presentation (or the view) are separated from components that store data (or the model) for that presentation.

`JTable` is responsible for the visible portion of the grid (the V part of MVC), but the data has to be stored in a different Java class that implements the `TableModel` interface (the M part). Any other UI component can play the role of the controller (the C part) and initiate some actions that will move the data from model to view or vice versa. For example, a click on the JButton can initiate the population of the table model from the database and display the data in JTable.

THE MODEL

Swing includes the classes DefaultTableModel and AbstractTableModel, which implement the TableModel interface and have methods to notify a JTable when the data is changing.

A programmer usually creates a model as a subclass of AbstractTableModel, and this class has to contain the data in some collection, for example ArrayList. When JTable needs to be populated, it requests the data from a class that implements TableModel, invoking such callback methods as getColumnCount() and getValueAt(). When a Swing program creates an instance of JTable, it has to assign to it a corresponding table model class. Listing 22-1 shows how the class MyTableModel (created by you) is given to the constructor of JTable.

Typically, the UI class that creates JTable defines one or more event listeners that are notified of any changes in the table's data. The incomplete class MyFrame in Listing 22-1 implements the TableModelListener interface that defines just one method—tableChanged(). This method should contain the code performing data modifications—for example, code to save the data in the database.

LISTING 22-1 A window with JTable

```
public class MyFrame extends JFrame implements TableModelListener{

  private MyTableModel myTableModel;
  private JTable myTable;

  MyFrame (String winTitle){
  super(winTitle);

  myTableModel = new MyTableModel();
  myTable = new JTable(myTableModel );

  //Add the JTable to frame and enable scrolling
  add(new JScrollPane( myTable));

  // Register an event listener
  myTableModel.addTableModelListener(this);
}

public void tableChanged(TableModelEvent e) {
  // Code to process data changes goes here
}

public static void main(String args[]){
  MyFrame myFrame = new MyFrame( "My Test Window" );

  myFrame.pack();
```

```
        myFrame.setVisible( true );
    }
        class MyTableModel extends AbstractTableModel {
          // The data for JTable should be here
        }
    }
```

In very simple cases you can create a JTable without declaring a table model class (JTable has a no-argument constructor), but Java internally uses its DefaultTableModel class anyway. My sample class MyFrame, though, uses the data model that's a subclass of the AbstractTableModel.

Note that the class MyTableModel is an inner class declared inside the class MyFrame. Having a model as an inner class is not a must, but if the data model is used with only one specific JTable, it can be created in the inner class.

The code in Listing 22-1 is not complete; it doesn't include any data yet, and the table model must include the mandatory callbacks described in the next section.

Mandatory Callbacks of Table Models

The class that implements the TableModel interface and feeds data to JTable must include at least three callback methods: getColumnCount(), getRowCount(), and getValueAt(). To populate the table, the Java run time needs to know the number of columns, number of rows, and the value for each cell (an intersection of the row and a column).

The method getColumnCount() must return an integer value—the number of columns in this JTable. This method is called once by the Java run time for a JTable instance. For example, if you are planning to display orders, each of which consists of four fields—order ID, stock symbol, quantity, and price—just put one line in the method getColumnCount():

```
return 4;
```

The callback method getRowCount() must return an integer; it will also be called only once. The data has to be placed into an array or a data collection (for example, an ArrayList) before it appears on the screen, and the code for this method could look like this assuming that myData is prepopulated with data:

```
return myData.size(); //myData is an ArrayList in this sample
```

The method getValueAt(int row, int col) returns an Object and is called once for each cell of JTable. You have to write the code that returns the value for the requested row and column.

Let's say you have a class called Order, as shown in Listing 22-2, and you want to store instances of this class in ArrayList myData.

LISTING 22-2 The Order class

```
public class Order {
 private int orderID;
 private String stockSymbol;
 private int quantity;
 private float price;

    public Order(int id, String stockSymbol, int quantity,
                 float price){
           orderID=id;
           this.stockSymbol=stockSymbol;
           this.quantity=quantity;
           this.price=price;
    }
}
```

Whenever the callback `getValueAt(int row, int col)` is called on the model, you have to return the cell value based on the given row and column. The inner class `MyTableModel` from Listing 22-3 includes the method `getValueAt()` working with `myData`, which is an `ArrayList` of `Order` objects.

LISTING 22-3 The JFrame window with implemented table model

```
public class MyFrame extends JFrame implements TableModelListener{

 MyTableModel myTableModel;
 JTable myTable;

  MyFrame (String winTitle){
    super(winTitle);

    myTableModel = new MyTableModel();
    myTable = new JTable(myTableModel );

    //Add the JTable to frame and enable scrolling
    add(new JScrollPane( myTable));

   // Register an event listener
   myTableModel.addTableModelListener(this);
  }

  public void tableChanged(TableModelEvent e) {
   // Code to process data changes goes here
 }

public static void main(String args[]){
 MyFrame myFrame = new MyFrame( "My Test Window" );

 myFrame.pack();
```

```
     myFrame.setVisible( true );
    }

    // Inner class for data model
    class MyTableModel extends AbstractTableModel {

      ArrayList<Order> myData = new ArrayList<>();

      MyTableModel(){
          myData.add(new Order(1,"IBM", 100, 135.5f));
          myData.add(new Order(2,"AAPL", 300, 290.12f));
          myData.add(new Order(3,"MOT", 2000, 8.32f));
          myData.add(new Order(4,"ORCL", 500, 27.8f));
      }

      public int getColumnCount() {
        return 4;
      }

      public int getRowCount() {
        return myData.size();
      }

      public Object getValueAt(int row, int col) {
          switch (col) {
            case 0:    // col 1
              return myData.get(row).orderID;
            case 1:    // col 2
                  return myData.get(row).stockSymbol;
            case 2:    // col 3
                  return myData.get(row).quantity;
            case 3:    // col 4
                  return myData.get(row).price;
            default:
              return "";
          }
      }
     }
    }
```

Note the use of generics in the declaration of the `myData` collection. Another Java feature not to be missed here is *autoboxing*; the primitive `Order` fields `int` and `float` are automatically converted into the corresponding wrapper objects `Integer` and `Float`.

Running the program from Listing 22-3 displays the window shown in Figure 22-1 (I ran it on Mac OS).

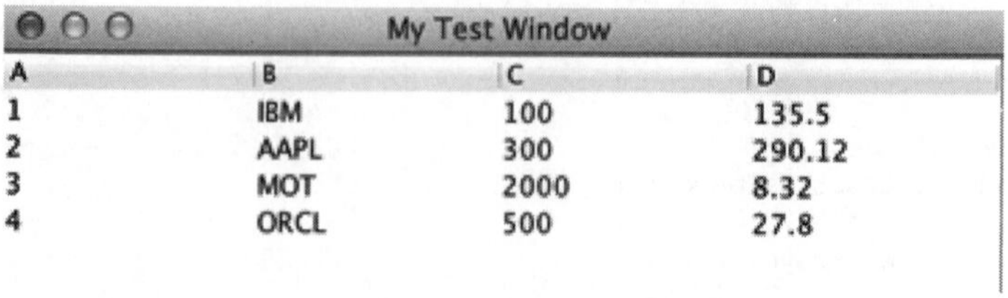

My Test Window

A	B	C	D
1	IBM	100	135.5
2	AAPL	300	290.12
3	MOT	2000	8.32
4	ORCL	500	27.8

FIGURE 22-1: Running MyFrame with no column titles

Optional Callbacks of Table Models

The `JTable` shown in Figure 22-1 doesn't show the proper titles of the columns; the auto-generated A, B, C, and D don't count. You can fix this easily by overriding the `getColumnName()` method in the table model class. This callback, if present, is called (once for each column) to render the column titles. Add the following code to the class `MyTableModel` and the window looks as it does in Figure 22-2.

```
String[] orderColNames =
                    { "Order ID", "Symbol", "Quantity", "Price"};

public String getColumnName(int col) {
     return orderColNames[col];
 }
```

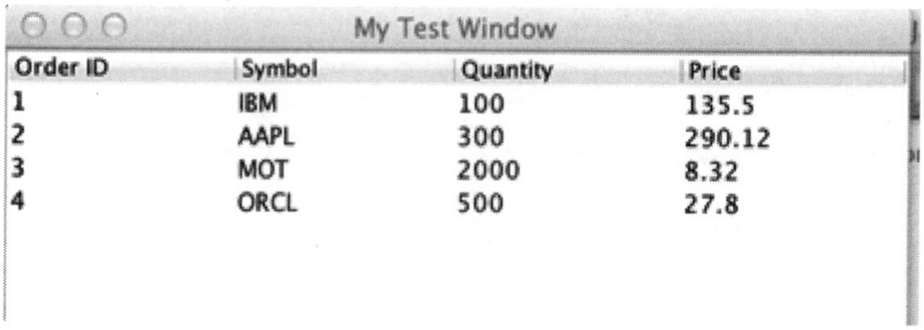

My Test Window

Order ID	Symbol	Quantity	Price
1	IBM	100	135.5
2	AAPL	300	290.12
3	MOT	2000	8.32
4	ORCL	500	27.8

FIGURE 22-2: Running MyFrame with column titles

If you want to make some of the columns or cells editable, just override the `isCellEditable()` method and return `true` from this callback for the editable columns. Here's how to make the third column (the column numbers are zero based) of your `JTable` editable:

```
public boolean isCellEditable(int row, int col) {

   if (col ==2){
       return true;
   } else {
     return false;
   }
 }
```

If your table has editable columns you need to override the method `setValueAt(Object value, int row, int col)` and include the code that copies the data from the UI component —`JTable`—to the appropriate field in its model objects. This method is called automatically when the user changes the value in a table cell and moves the cursor out of that cell by pressing the Enter or Tab key or by clicking a different cell.

The following method, `setValueAt()`, takes the modified order quantity and sets the new value for the `quantity` field in the appropriate `Order` in the model. By default, all the data shown in `JTable`'s cells have the `String` data type, and it's your responsibility to do proper casting.

```
public void setValueAt(Object value, int row, int col){

  if (col== 2){
   myData.get(row).quantity=(Integer.valueOf(value.toString()));
  }

  //Notify listeners about the data change
   TableModelEvent event = new TableModelEvent(this, row, row, col);
   fireTableChanged(event);
}
```

The `fireTableChanged()` method has been placed in the `setValueAt()` method to notify any listener(s) that want to know about the data changes. For example, if the quantity on any order has been changed and has gone over a certain threshold, the application may need to immediately perform some actions to report this to some authority.

Review the code in Listing 22-3. The class `MyFrame` implements `TableModelListener`, so the method `tableChanged()` is invoked as a result of the `fireTableChanged()` method call. Add the following line to the `tableChanged()` method:

```
System.out.println("Someone modified the data in JTable!");
```

Now run the program and modify the quantity in any row of `JTable`. The message is printed on the system console. But JVM fires an event with a payload—`TableModelEvent`—that carries useful information about what exactly has changed in the table model.

IMPLEMENTING TABLEMODELLISTENER WITH LAMBDA EXPRESSION

Instead of writing that the class implements `TableModelListener` and implementing the method `tableChanged()`, you can just use a lambda expression:

```
myTableModel.addTableModelListener(e ->
System.out.println("Someone changed the data in JTable!"))
```

`TableModelEvent` has several constructors; I've chosen the one that takes modified rows and columns as arguments. For example, if you change the quantity in the last row, as shown in Figure 22-2, the method `tableChanged()` receives an instance of `TableModelEvent` that encapsulates the reference to the entire model encapsulating the following values describing the change:

```
column=2     // the third column
firstRow=3   // starting from the row #4
lastRow=3    // ending with the row #4
```

Based on this information you can implement any further processing required by the functional specification of your application. If you need to apply the UI changes to the database, the method `tableChanged()` can be the right place to use the JDBC API or other communication with the server-side code to persist the changes.

There are several functions with names that start with the word `fire`. For example, to apply each cell's change to the database, call the method `fireTableCellUpdated()`. To apply all changes at once, call the method `fireTableDataChanged()`. Refer to the documentation of the class `AbstractTableModel` to decide which method fits your needs.

INTRODUCTION TO RENDERERS

The process of transferring data from the table model to the `JTable` view is performed by *cell renderers*. Accordingly, when the user is modifying the content of the cell, the *cell editor* is cengaged. By default, the content of each cell in a `JTable` is rendered using one of three default renderers, based on the type of data in the column. `Boolean` values are rendered as checkboxes, `javax.swing.Icon` is rendered as an image, and any other object is rendered as a string of characters.

To change the default rendering (for example, if you don't want to see checkboxes for `Boolean` values) you can either override the callback `getColumnClass()` or define a *custom cell renderer*. The latter option gives you a lot more flexibility. For example, you may need to display a photo of a person and his or her name in each cell. Or you may need to show cell values that meet certain criteria in a different color. To do something like one of these, you need to create a *custom renderer*.

The UI portion of each column is represented by the class `TableColumn`, which has a property, `cellRenderer`, of type `TableCellRenderer`, which defines the only method: `getTableCellRendererComponent()`. This method prepares the content for each column's cells of `JTable` and returns an instance of the `Component` class to be used for the cell rendering. This process uses `DefaultTableCellRenderer` unless you create a custom renderer. Custom renderers give you full control over how the cell is displayed.

The class `DefaultTableCellRenderer` extends `JLabel` and is Swing's implementation of the `TableCellRenderer` interface. Let's look at an example that formats the text in the `Price` column shown in Figure 22-2 to be right-justified and to display in red all prices greater than $100.

First the code fragment from Listing 22-4 gets a reference to the fourth column of `JTable` (remember, column numbering is zero-based). Then it needs to call the method `setCellRenderer()` on this column, provided that the custom renderer class was defined and instantiated. But you can define, instantiate, and set the custom renderer in one shot by using the mechanism of *anonymous inner classes*.

The anonymous inner class in Listing 22-4 extends the class `DefaultTableCellRenderer` and overrides the callback method `getTableCellRendererComponent()`. The latter sets the cell value to be right-justified and to be red if it is greater than 100. At the end, the method `getTableCellRendererComponent()` returns a `JLabel` object to be rendered in the current cell of `JTable`.

LISTING 22-4 Custom rendering of the Price value

```
//Assign custom cell renderer to the Price column
// Get the reference to the fourth column - Price

TableColumn column = myTable.getColumnModel().getColumn(3);

// Create a new cell renderer as an anonymous inner
// class and assign it to the column price

column.setCellRenderer(
      new DefaultTableCellRenderer(){
  public Component getTableCellRendererComponent(
           JTable table, Object value, boolean isSelected,
                    boolean hasFocus, int row, int col) {

       JLabel label = (JLabel) super.getTableCellRendererComponent(
             table, value, isSelected, hasFocus, row, col);

     // right-align the price value
     label.setHorizontalAlignment(JLabel.RIGHT);

     // display stocks that cost more than $100 in red
     if (((Float) value)>100){
        label.setForeground(Color.RED);
     } else{
           label.setForeground(Color.BLACK);
     }

     return label;
    } // end of getTableCellRendererComponent
   }  // end of new DefaultTableCellRenderer
);    // end of setCellRenderer
```

Add this code fragment at the end of the constructor in the class `MyFrame` from Listing 22-3 and run the application. The screen shows the text in the Price column right-justified and the first two prices printed in red (see Figure 22-3).

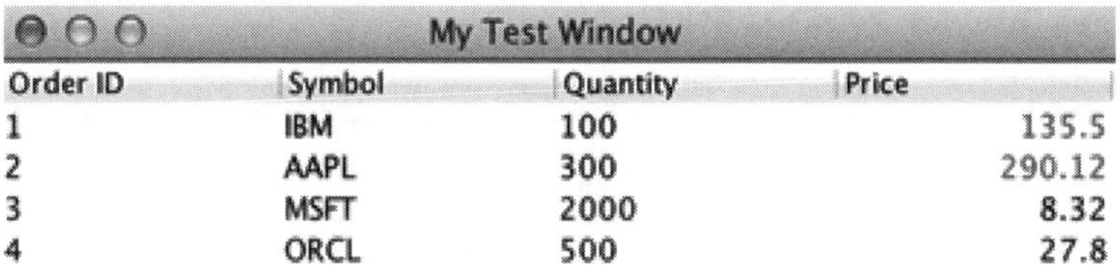

My Test Window

Order ID	Symbol	Quantity	Price
1	IBM	100	135.5
2	AAPL	300	290.12
3	MSFT	2000	8.32
4	ORCL	500	27.8

FIGURE 22-3: Running MyFrame with custom price renderer

SUMMARY

This lesson was a high-level overview of the `JTable` component, which is probably the most advanced UI component that deserves serious study if you are planning to develop Java Swing applications. You can continue studying all the features of `JTable` by following the section "How to Use Tables (`http://docs.oracle.com/javase/tutorial/uiswing/components/table.html`)" in the online Oracle tutorial.

TRY IT

Create a Portfolio application that displays your portfolio data that's stored in the database table. You need to use the database and the Portfolio table you created in the "Try It" section of Chapter 21.

Lesson Requirements

You should have Java installed.

> **NOTE** *You can download the code and resources for this "Try It" from the book's web page at* `www.wrox.com/go/javaprog24hr2e`. *You can find them in the Lesson22.zip.*

Step-by-Step

1. Create a new Eclipse project. Copy there the classes `MyFrame` and `Order` from the accompanying book code samples for Lesson 22. Compile and run the program to ensure that it displays hard-coded portfolio data, as shown in Figure 22-2.
2. Replace the hard-coded table model `ArrayCollection myData` with the JDBC code to connect to the database Lesson21 created in the Try It section of Lesson 21. Use the records from the database table Portfolio to populate orders.
   Don't forget to add the file `derbyclient.jar` to the Java Build Path of your project.
3. Run the appropriate SQL `Select` statement, and populate the `myData` collection with data received from the database.
4. Run the `MyFrame` program. The data should be displayed in the GUI.

> **TIP** *Please select the videos for Lesson 22 online at* `www.wrox.com/go/javaprog24hr2e`. *You will also be able to download the code and resources for this lesson from the website.*

23

Annotations and Reflection

In general, *metadata* is data about your data. In the context of DBMSes, metadata can be information describing the way you store data, such as the table and field names or primary keys. Program code metadata is data about your code. Any Java class has its metadata embedded, and you can write a program that "asks" another class, "What methods do you have?" or similar questions about class fields, constructors, and ancestors.

You can use annotations to include metadata about your code. There are a number of predefined annotations (for example, `@Override` and `@SuppressWarning`). The Java annotation model enables you to add custom metadata anywhere in your code. You can apply custom annotations to a class, a method, or a variable—just specify allowed *targets* when the annotation is being defined. Java annotations start with the @ sign and may optionally have one or more parameters. Some of the annotations are built into Java SE and are used by the javac compiler, but most of them are consumed by some kind of processing program or tool.

The subject of Java reflection doesn't require the use of annotations; reflection is used widely in various areas of Java development. But because this subject has to be covered before you can proceed with annotation processing, I decided to cover both topics in the same lesson.

JAVADOC ANNOTATIONS

If you've ever looked at the source code of any Java class, you can easily identify Javadoc-style comments for classes, interfaces, variables, and methods. These comments may include specially formatted words called tags. These tags are special annotations. They also start with the @ sign and help the Javadoc tool (`http://www.oracle.com/technetwork/java/javase/documentation/index-137868.html`) to generate the online documentation with the standardized look and feel.

In Eclipse you can select any Java class and press F3 to open the source code of this class. Because the previous lesson was about working with `JTable`, open the source code of this class. In the top part of the code you find a description similar to the one that follows (I removed a large portion of the text for brevity):

```
/**
 * The <code>JTable</code> is used to display and edit regular
```

```
* two-dimensional tables of cells.
* To enable sorting and filtering of rows, use a
* {@code RowSorter}.
*  * As for all <code>JComponent</code> classes, you can use
* {@link InputMap} and {@link ActionMap} to associate an
* {@link Action} object with a {@link KeyStroke} and execute the
* action under specified conditions.
* <p>
* <strong>Warning:</strong> Swing is not thread safe. For more
* information see <a
* href="package-summary.html#threading">Swing's Threading
* Policy</a>.
* <p>
*
* @version 1.292 05/30/08
* @author Philip Milne
* @author Shannon Hickey (printing support)
* @see javax.swing.table.DefaultTableModel
* @see javax.swing.table.TableRowSorter
*/
```

The special words marked with an @ sign are Javadoc metadata describing links, version, author, and related classes to see in Java documentation. If you run the source code of this class through the Javadoc utility, the utility generates HTML output that can be opened by any web browser. It's a good practice to include Javadoc comments in your classes.

Javadoc acts as a processing tool that extracts from the source code all comment blocks that start with `/**` and end with `*/`. It then formats this text using HTML tags and embedded annotations to generate program documentation. The preceding text is an example of the use of specific tags that are predefined and understood by Javadoc. This was an example of metadata that are understood by just one utility: Javadoc.

But Java allows you to declare your own custom annotations and define your own processing rules that route the execution of your program and produce configuration files, additional code, deployment descriptors, and more. No matter what your goals, when you create annotations you also need to create or use an *annotation processor* to get the expected output.

Starting from Lesson 26 you learn about annotations defined by the creators of Java EE technologies. In this lesson you become familiar with Java SE annotations, which you will eventually use in your projects.

JAVA ANNOTATIONS BASICS

There are about a dozen predefined annotations already included with Java SE. You can find them, along with their supporting classes, in the packages `java.lang`, `java.lang.annotation`, and `javax.annotation`. You can get familiar with the content of these packages in the latest online documentation on the Java SE API, which at the time of this writing is located at `http://goo.gl/sVZ8bI`.

Some of these annotations are used by the compiler (`@Override`, `@SuppressWarning`, `@Deprecated`, `@Target`, `@Retention`, `@Documented`, and `@Inherited`); some are used by the Java SE run time or third-party run times and indicate methods that have to be invoked in a certain order (`@PostConstruct`,

@PreDestroy), or mark code that was generated by third-party tools (@Generated). I'm not going to repeat a detailed description of how to use each of these annotations, but I am going to give you selected examples to help you get started with annotations.

@Override

In the "Try It" section of Chapter 3 you overrode the method public double calcTax() in the class NJTax. The method signature of calcTax() was the same in both NJTax and its superclass Tax. Now deliberately add an argument to calcTax() in NJTax, as if you had done so by accident. The code compiles with no errors. But you could have done this by mistake, and instead of overriding the method as planned, you've overloaded it. This doesn't happen if you use the annotation @Override whenever you are planning to override a method:

```
@Override public double calcTax(String something)
```

Now the compiler complains with the following error:

```
The method calcTax(String) of type NJTax must override or implement a supertype method
```

The annotation @Override signals the compiler that overriding is expected, and that it has to fail if an override does not occur. This annotation indicates your intentions and helps other people who may be reading your code in the future.

@SuppressWarning

The compiler can generate warning messages that don't stop your program from running but that do indicate potential problems. In some cases, though, you want to suppress some or all warnings so the output of the project build looks clean. For example,–Xlint:none disables all warnings, whereas –Xlint:fallthrough instructs the compiler to warn you if you forget to add the break statement to the switch statement (see Chapter 5). In Eclipse IDE, to set the compiler's options you right-click the project and select Properties → Java Compiler → Errors/Warnings → Potential Programming Problems.

But what if you want to omit the break keyword in the switch statement on purpose? You still want to be warned in all other cases about a missing break, but not in this particular method. This is where the @SupressWarnings annotation becomes quite handy, and Listing 23-1 illustrates it. To see this example at work, turn on the compiler's option that warns you about the switch case fall-throughs.

LISTING 23-1 Custom rendering of the Price value

```
package com.practicaljava.lesson24;

public class SuppressWarningDemo {

      @SuppressWarnings("fallthrough")
      public static void main(String[] args) {
        int salaryBand=3;
```

```
            int bonus;
           // Retrieve the salary band of the person from some
           // data source here
                switch(salaryBand){
                 case 1:
                      bonus=1000;
                      System.out.println("Giving bonus " + bonus);
                      break;
                 case 2:
                      bonus=2000;
                      System.out.println("Giving bonus " + bonus);
                      break;
                 case 3:
                      bonus=6000;
                      System.out.println("Giving bonus " + bonus);
                 case 4:
                      bonus=10000;
                      System.out.println("Giving bonus " + bonus);
                      break;
                 default:
                      // wrong salary band
                      System.out.println("Invalid salary band");
                }
           }

     }
```

Note that the `break` keyword is missing in the `case 3` section. In this code it's done on purpose: All employees in `salaryBand` 3 are entitled to two bonuses—$6,000 in addition to $10,000. The compiler's annotation `@SuppressWarnings("fallthrough")` suppresses compiler warnings only for this method. In all other classes or methods that may have `switch` statements, the warning is generated.

@Deprecated

If you are developing classes that are going to be used by someone else, mark as `@Deprecated` any classes or methods that may be removed in future versions of your code. Other developers will still be able to use this code, but they'll be warned that switching to newer versions is highly recommended.

@Inherited

This annotation simply means that the annotation has to be inherited by descendants of the class in which it is used. The next section includes an example of its use.

@FunctionalInterface

An informative annotation type used to indicate that an interface type declaration is intended to be a *functional interface.* If you'll ever be defining interfaces with a single abstract method, you may optionally mark such an interface with `@FunctionalInterface` just to hint that this interface can be implemented as a lambda expression.

@Documented

If you want an annotation to be included in the Javadoc utility, mark it as @Documented. The next section includes an example of this annotation.

CUSTOM ANNOTATIONS

Creating your own annotations is more interesting than using core Java or third-party annotations. First of all, you have to decide what you need an annotation for and what properties it should have. Then you need to specify the allowed *targets* for this annotation (for example, class, method, or variable). Finally, you have to define your *retention policy*: how long and where this annotation will live. Let's go through an example to illustrate all these steps.

Suppose you need to create an annotation that allows the user to mark class methods with a SQL statement to be executed during the run time. These classes are loaded dynamically. The goal is to declare your own annotation to be used by other Java classes and to write the annotation processor that reads these Java classes, identifies and parses annotations and the values of their parameters, if any, and does whatever is required accordingly. Usually creators of object-relational mapping (ORM) frameworks of code generators need to implement such tasks.

Declaring annotations is very similar to declaring interfaces, but don't forget to add the @ sign at the beginning. I'm naming my annotation MyJDBCExecutor:

```
public @interface MyJDBCExecutor{

}
```

If metadata is data about data, then *meta-annotations* are annotations about annotations. This is not as confusing as it sounds. To specify where you can use this newborn annotation, define the meta-annotation @Target. The enumeration ElementType defines possible target values: METHOD, TYPE, CONSTRUCTOR, FIELD, PARAMETER, PACKAGE, LOCAL_VARIABLE, TYPE_PARAMETER, TYPE_USE, and ANNOTATION_TYPE. If you don't use @Target, the annotation can be used anywhere. For example, this is how you can allow use of the annotation only with methods and constructors:

```
import java.lang.annotation.*;

@Inherited
@Documented
@Target({ ElementType.METHOD, ElementType.CONSTRUCTOR })
@Retention(RetentionPolicy.SOURCE)
public @interface MyJDBCExecutor {

}
```

Starting from Java 8 you can create custom annotations that can be used anywhere where you can declare a type, for example:

```
@MyAnnotation String employeePhone;
```

The retention policy in the preceding code snippet is set to SOURCE, which means that this annotation will be used for processing only during the compilation of your program. The other two allowed values for retention policy are RUNTIME and CLASS.

Annotations with the CLASS retention policy stay in the compiled class, but are not loaded during run time. The CLASS retention policy is used by default if a retention policy is not explicitly specified.

Annotations with the RUNTIME retention policy have to be processed by a custom processing tool (someone has to write it) when the compiled code is running.

Annotations may have parameters. Say you want to add a single parameter that will allow you to specify an SQL statement to be processed. Your annotation MyJDBCExecutor has to be declared as follows:

```
@Target({ ElementType.METHOD, ElementType.CONSTRUCTOR })
@Retention(RetentionPolicy.SOURCE)
public @interface MyJDBCExecutor {
   String value();
}
```

A sample Java class, HRBrowser, may use this annotation like this:

```
class HRBrowser{

  @MyJDBCExecutor (value="Select * from Employee")
  public List getEmployees(){
     // add calls to some JDBC executing engine here
  }
}
```

If the annotation has only one parameter named value, the "value=" part in the preceding code snippet is not required. But I'd like this annotation to have three parameters: SQL to execute, transactional support, and a notification flag to inform other users of the application about any database modifications. Add more parameters to your annotation:

```
@Target({ ElementType.METHOD})
@Retention(RetentionPolicy.SOURCE)
public @interface MyJDBCExecutor {
         String sqlStatement();
         boolean transactionRequired() default false;
         boolean notifyOnUpdates() default false;
}
```

You've replaced the parameter value with a more meaningful sqlStatement, and added two more: transactionRequired and notifyOnUpdates. The latter has two default values. If a Java class doesn't need to support transactions and notify other applications about updates, why force software developers to provide values for these parameters?

If you don't specify default values then the Java compiler generates compilation errors if the values for transactionRequired and notifyOnUpdates are missing in classes that use @MyJDBCExecutor. The following code is an example of a class, `HRBrowser`, with the method `getEmployees()` that's annotated with `@MyJDBCExecutor` having only a `sqlStatement` parameter; no other actions are needed here:

```
class HRBrowser{

  @MyJDBCExecutor (sqlStatement="Select * from Employee")
  public List<Employee> getEmployees(){
      // The code to get the the data from DBMS goes here,
      // result set goes in ArrayList myEmployeeList,
      // which is returned to the caller of getEmployees()
      // ...
      return myEmployeeList;
  }
}
```

The code sample in Listing 23-2 adds the method `updateData()` and uses all three annotation parameters.

LISTING 23-2 Using the annotation MyJDBCExecutor

```
class HRBrowser{

 @MyJDBCExecutor (sqlStatement="Select * from Employee")
 public List<Employee> getEmployees(){
        // Generate the code to get the the data from DBMS,
        // place them in ArrayList and return them to the
        // caller of my getEmployees
           ...
               return myEmployeeList;
 }

 @MyJDBCExecutor (sqlStatement="Update Employee set bonus=1000",
                  transactionRequired=true,
                  notifyOnUpdates=true)
 public void updateData(){
   // JDBC code to perform transactional updates and
   // notifications goes here
 }
}
```

ANNOTATIONS AND CODE GENERATION

I was involved in the development of an open-source code generator called Clear Data Builder (CDB). The CDB allows the user to write a simple Java class that has an abstract method annotated with an SQL statement and several other parameters, and within seconds to generate complete code for the functional application that has JavaScript on the client side talking to Java at the server, which is accessing data stored in any relational DBMS via JDBC. In this project we used only the annotations with the SOURCE retention policy, and, before compiling, classes would generate additional code according to specified annotations.

If CDB would be processing the annotation @MyJDBCExecutor, it would engage additional tools and generate and compile all JDBC code for the methods getEmployees() and updateData() automatically.

For the annotations with the RUNTIME retention policy you should know how to write an annotation processor, however, as it has to "extract" the values from the annotations during run time, and, based on those values, engage the appropriate code. But there is one Java feature, *reflection*, that you must understand before you can write your own annotation-processing class.

REFLECTION

Reflection enables you to find out about the internals of a Java class (its methods, constructors, and fields) during the run time, and to invoke the discovered methods or access public member variables. A special class called Class can load the class in memory, and then you can explore the content of the class by using classes from the package java.lang.reflect. Consider the classes Person and Employee in the following code.

LISTING 23-3 Class Employee extends Person

```
abstract public class Person {
  abstract public void raiseSalary();
}

public class Employee extends Person{
 public void raiseSalary() {
   System.out.println("Raising salary for Employee...");
  }
}
```

The ReflectionSample class in Listing 23-4 loads the class Employee, prints its method signatures, and finds its superclass and methods. The process of querying an object about its content during run time is called *introspection.*

LISTING 23-4 Introspecting Employee

```
import java.lang.reflect.*;
public class ReflectionSample {
  public static void main(String args[]) {
     try {
       Class c = Class.forName("Employee");
       Method methods[] = c.getDeclaredMethods();
       System.out.println("The Employee methods:");
```

```
            for (int i = 0; i < methods.length; i++){
                 System.out.println("*** Method Signature:" +
                                         methods[i].toString());
            }

            Class superClass = c.getSuperclass();
            System.out.println("The name of the superclass is "
                                        + superClass.getName());

            Method superMethods[] = superClass.getDeclaredMethods();
            System.out.println("The superclass has:");

            for (int i = 0; i < superMethods.length; i++){
                 System.out.println("*** Method Signature:" +
                                    superMethods[i].toString());
                 System.out.println("      Return type: " +
                     superMethods[i].getReturnType().getName());
            }

          } catch (Exception e) {
                e.printStackTrace();
          }
      }
    }
```

Here's the output of the program `ReflectionSample`:

```
The Employee methods:
*** Method Signature:public void Employee.raiseSalary()
The name of the superclass is Person
The superclass has:
*** Method Signature:public abstract void Person.raiseSalary()
      Return type: void
```

Some other useful methods of the class `Class` are `getInterfaces()`, `getConstructors()`, `getFields()`, and `isAnnotationPresent()`. The following code snippet shows how to get the names, types, and values of the public member variables of the loaded class:

```
Class c = Class.forName("Employee");

Field[] fields = c.getFields();
for (int i = 0; i < fields.length; i++) {
   String name = fields[i].getName();
   String type = fields[i].getType().getName();

   System.out.println("Creating an instance of Employee");
   Object obj = c.newInstance();
   Object value = fields[i].get(obj);
   System.out.println("Field Name: " + name + ", Type: "
              + type + " Value: " + value.toString());
}
```

The process of reflection uses introspection to find out during run time what the methods (or properties) are, but it also can call these methods (or modify these properties). The method `invoke()` lets you call methods that were discovered during run time:

```
Class c= Class.forName("Employee");
Method raiseSalary = c.getMethod( "raiseSalary", null);
raiseSalary.invoke(c.newInstance(),null);
```

Note that the method `forName()` loads the class and the `newInstance()` creates an instance of `Employee`. The first argument of the method `invoke()` represents an instance of the object `Employee`, and `null` means that this method doesn't have arguments. With reflection, the arguments are supplied as an array of objects. You can find out what the method arguments are by calling the method `Method.getParameterTypes()`, or create and populate them on your own. Add the following method to the class `Employee`:

```
public void changeAddress(String newAddress) {
    System.out.println("The new address is "+ newAddress);
}
```

Note the `public` qualifier: It's needed for proper introspection. Otherwise the `NoSuchMethodException` is thrown by the following code snippet. The `ReflectionSample` class can invoke `changeAddress()` as follows:

```
Class c= Class.forName("Employee");
Class parameterTypes[]= new Class[] {String.class};
Method myMethod = c.getMethod( "changeAddress", parameterTypes);

Object arguments[] = new Object[1];
arguments[0] = "250 Broadway";
myMethod.invoke(c.newInstance(),arguments);
```

Reflection helps in building dynamic component-based applications that can load different classes based on certain business logic and invoke this logic during run time. Many third-party Java frameworks read configuration files and then instantiate and use required objects.

RUN-TIME ANNOTATION PROCESSING

The author of a custom run-time annotation usually gives it to other developers along with the processing tool. Developers add the annotation to their classes and compile them, and the processing tool consumes these classes during run time. To illustrate the concept I reuse the code example from Listing 23-2, but this time imagine that `@MyJDBCExecutor` becomes the annotation with the `RUNTIME` retention policy and that there is no need to generate additional source code for the compilation time. Suppose this annotation is being used in `HRBrowser`, and another class has to analyze the annotation parameters and route the execution accordingly.

Now I'll write the annotation processor class called `MyJDBCAnnotationProcessor`, and the class `HRBrowser` in Listing 23-2 can serve as a command-line argument to that processor:

```
c:/>java MyJDBCAnnotationProcessor HRBrowser
```

The class MyJDBCAnnotationProcessor has to load the class HRBrowser, introspect its content, find the annotations and their values, and process them accordingly. I'll show you how to write such a processor, or rather its annotation-discovery part.

Listing 23-5 shows MyJDBCAnnotationProcessor, which starts by loading another class, whose name was supplied in the command line. After that it introspects the loaded class and places all references to its method definitions into an array called methods. Finally, it loops through this array, and for each method that has annotations it finds and prints the values of the parameters sqlStatement, notifyOnUpdates, and transactionRequired.

LISTING 23-5 MyJDBCAnnotationProcessor

```
import java.lang.reflect.*;
import com.practicaljava.lesson24.MyJDBCExecutor;

public class MyJDBCAnnotationProcessor {

 public static void main(String[] args) {
  // TODO add a check for the number of command line arguments
   // has to be the name of the class to load.

   String classWithAnnotation = args[0];

     try {
        //Load provided on the command line class
       Class loadedClass = Class.forName(classWithAnnotation);

       // Get references to class methods
       Method[] methods = loadedClass.getMethods();

       //Check every method of the class.If the annotation is present,
       //print the values of its parameters

        for (Method m: methods){
         if (m.isAnnotationPresent(MyJDBCExecutor.class)){
                   MyJDBCExecutor jdbcAnnotation =
                              m.getAnnotation(MyJDBCExecutor.class);

           System.out.println("Method: " + m.getName() +
             ". Parameters of MyJDBCExecutor are: " +
             "sqlStatement="+ jdbcAnnotation.sqlStatement() +
             ", notifyOnUpdates="+ jdbcAnnotation.notifyOnUpdates() +
             ", transactionRequired="+
             jdbcAnnotation.transactionRequired());
        }
     }

   }catch (ClassNotFoundException e) {
                e.printStackTrace();
   }
```

```
        }
    }
```

After running this processor with the class `HRBrowser`, the former correctly identifies the annotated methods and prints the values of their parameters:

```
Method: getEmployees. Parameters of MyJDBCExecutor are: sqlStatement=Select * from
Employee, notifyOnUpdates=false, transactionRequired=false

Method: updateData. Parameters of MyJDBCExecutor are: sqlStatement=Update Employee set
bonus=1000, notifyOnUpdates=true, transactionRequired=true
```

If a class may have several annotations, the annotation processor would need to start by getting all annotations of the loaded class using `loadedClass.getAnnotations()`. It would then process these annotations in a loop.

SUMMARY

In real-world applications you wouldn't simply be printing the values of the annotation parameters, but rather would be executing different branches of your code based on these values. This is the point of run-time annotation processing. You may ask, "OK, now I know the annotations and their values, so what do I do with them?" The big idea is that you've written a generic processor that can work with any classes that include your annotations. It's a pretty powerful mechanism for all software developers who are creating tools for other people to use.

You'll probably be using annotations and run-time processors written by other people rather than ones you write yourself. You'll see lots of examples of using annotations starting from Chapter 26, while learning about Java EE development. But now that you know what's going on under the hood in annotation processors, learning about Java EE annotation will be a lot easier.

The reflection mechanism allows you to find out the members of any class during the run time. This nice feature should be used sparingly because such discovery would require additional processing time.

TRY IT

Create a class-level run-time annotation called `@DBParams` that enables you to specify the name of the database, the user ID, and the password. Write a processor for this annotation.

Lesson Requirements

You should have Java installed.

> **NOTE** *You can download the code and resources for this "Try It" from the book's web page at* `www.wrox.com/go/javaprog24hr2e`. *You can find them in the Lesson23.zip.*

Step-by-Step

1. Create a new Eclipse project.
2. Declare there the annotation DBParams with the retention policy RUNTIME targeted to TYPE.
3. Define three parameters in this annotation: dbName, uid, and password.
4. Create the class MyDBWorker and annotate it with @DBParms populated with some initial values.
5. Write an annotation processor class called DBParamProcessor to find and print the annotation values in the class MyDBWorker.
6. Run and test DBParamProcessor.

> **TIP** *Please select the videos for Lesson 23 online at* www.wrox.com/go/javaprog24hr2e. *You will also be able to download the code and resources for this lesson from the website.*

24

Remote Method Invocation

So far most of the Java programs in this tutorial have been running in a single Java virtual machine (JVM). There were two exceptions: In Lesson 16 in the section on "Socket Programming" you used two JVMs, and your JDBC programs from Chapter 21 communicated with another JVM running a database server. The application running on the user's computer isn't always allowed to access remote data directly—that's one of the reasons *distributed Java applications* came into the picture. (The word distributed means having parts of the applications running on several computers.) The other reason was to provide a centralized server catering to multiple lightweight clients.

There are lots of ways to create Java distributed applications that run on more than one JVM, and Remote Method Invocation (RMI) is one of them even though it's seldom used these days. For example, a client Java application (JVM1) connects to a server Java application (JVM2), which connects to the DBMS that runs on a third computer. The client application knows nothing about the DBMS; it gets the data, an `ArrayList` (or other data collection) of `Employee` objects, from the server's application that runs in JVM2. RMI uses object serialization for the data exchange between JVM1 and JVM2.

But unlike with socket programming, where the client simply connects to a port on the server, with RMI one Java class can *invoke methods* on Java objects that live in another (remote) JVM. Although from a syntax perspective it looks as if the caller and the server's class are located in the same JVM, they may be thousands of miles away. The RMI client won't have a copy of the server-side method; it just has the method's local representative—a *proxy*, or, using the RMI terminology, a *stub*.

Any RMI application consists of an RMI server, a client, and the *registry* (a naming service). These three components could run on three different JVMs running on different networked computers. The RMI server creates Java objects that implement business logic, registers them with the naming service, and waits for remote clients to invoke the server's methods.

A client application gets a reference to a remote server object or objects from the registry and then invokes methods on this remote object. RMI uses the transport layer that hides the communications between the client's stub and the server-side Java objects, and even though the methods are called in the client's JVM, they are executed on the server's. All RMI supporting classes and the registry tool are included with the Java SE.

DEVELOPING APPLICATIONS WITH RMI

This lesson is written as an illustration of a sample RMI application with a minimum theory. For a more detailed description of RMI, refer to Oracle's online tutorial (`http://docs.oracle.com/javase/tutorial/rmi/`) on the subject.

Writing distributed RMI applications involves the following steps:

1. Declaring the remote interface.
2. Implementing the remote interface.
3. Writing a Java client that connects to the remote server and calls remote methods.
4. Starting the registry and registering the RMI server with it. The server associates (binds) its services with the registry names.
5. Starting the server and the client applications. The client looks up services by names and invokes them.

Let's perform each of these steps by developing the RMI version of the Stock Quotes Server (see its version with sockets in socket programming), which provides a client with price quotes for a specified stock. Some of the preceding steps could be combined—for example, creating a registry and binding a service to it. The package `java.rmi` contains all RMI supporting classes used in the following code samples.

Defining Remote Interfaces

The Java classes that you are planning to deploy on the server side have to implement *remote interfaces*, which declare business method(s) to be invoked remotely by RMI clients. The client's code looks as if it's calling local methods, but these calls are redirected to a remote server via the RMI protocol. Following are the rules for creating remote interfaces:

- The remote interface must declare public methods to allow clients to perform remote method invocation.
- The remote interface must extend `java.rmi.Remote`.
- Each method must declare `java.rmi.RemoteException`.
- If method arguments are not primitives, they should be serializable objects to be able to travel across the network.

In RMI, development of a the server-side layer starts with answering the question, "What business methods have to be exposed to the client applications and what should their signatures be?" When you know the answer, define remote interfaces that declare those methods and classes that implement them. Let's see how to apply this rule for the server that can serve stock prices.

Listing 24-1 shows the code of the `StockServer` remote interface that will be implemented on the server but *also must exist on the client side*. This interface declares two business methods: `getQuote()` and `getNasdaqSymbols()`. The first method generates a random price quote for the specified symbol, and the second returns the list of valid stock symbols.

LISTING 24-1 StockServer interface

```
public interface StockServer extends Remote {
  public String getQuote(String symbol) throws RemoteException;

  public List<String> getNasdaqSymbols()throws RemoteException;
}
```

In RMI, class definitions are dynamically loaded from one JVM to another. Implementation of the classes resided on the server side may change—for example, new methods may be introduced to the implementation of the class. But the client sees the stubs with only the methods defined in the interface that extends `Remote`. In our example, to make more server-side methods available to the RMI client, you'd need to add them to the `StockServer` interface and make this new version available on both the client and the server.

Implementing Remote Interfaces

Although the remote interface just declares the methods, you need to create a class that runs on the server side and provides implementation for those methods. There is a special requirement to *export* such a class to the Java RMI runtime to enable the class to receive remote calls. This is somewhat similar to binding to a port in the case of `ServerSocket` (see Listing 16-5), but in the case of Java RMI, the server also creates a stub—a dummy class (for the client side) that contains proxies of each implemented method from remote interfaces.

One RMI client communicates to one server. It's known as *unicast* as opposed to *multicast* (one to many) or *broadcast* (one to all). The easiest way to export an RMI server instance is by extending it from `java.rmi.server.UnicastRemoteObject`, as in Listing 24-2. If your server has to be extended from another class you can explicitly export the server object by calling `UnicastRemoteObject.export()`.

Listing 24-2 shows an implementation of the class `StockServerImpl`, which processes the client's requests. This class generates random price quotes for the stocks located in `ArrayList nasdaqSymbols`.

LISTING 24-2 StockServerimpl class

```
public class StockServerImpl extends UnicastRemoteObject
                             implements StockServer {
  private String price=null;
  private ArrayList<String> nasdaqSymbols = new ArrayList<>();

  public StockServerImpl() throws RemoteException {
    super();

     // Define some hard-coded NASDAQ symbols
     nasdaqSymbols.add("AAPL");
     nasdaqSymbols.add("MSFT");
     nasdaqSymbols.add("YHOO");
     nasdaqSymbols.add("AMZN");
  }
```

```
    public String getQuote(String symbol)
                          throws RemoteException {

      if(nasdaqSymbols.indexOf(symbol.toUpperCase()) != -1) {

          // Generate a random price for valid symbols
          price = (new Double(Math.random()*100)).toString();
      }
      return price;
    }

    public ArrayList<String> getNasdaqSymbols()
                                    throws RemoteException {
      return nasdaqSymbols;
    }
}
```

Registering Remote Objects

To make a remote object available to clients, you need to bind it to some name in a registry, a naming service that knows where exactly in the network your RMI server `StockServerImpl` is running. This allows Java clients to look up the object on the host machine by name.

Listing 24-3 depicts the code that binds the instance of `StockServerImpl` to port 1099 on the host machine, which is the local computer in my example. To the rest of the world this server is known as `QuoteService`.

LISTING 24-3 Creating registry, starting the server, and binding it to a registry

```
public class StartServer {

  public static void main (String args[]) {

   try {
    // Create the registry on port 1099
    LocateRegistry.createRegistry(1099);

    // Instantiate the StockServerInmpl and bind it
    // to the registry under the name QuoteService
      StockServerImpl ssi = new StockServerImpl();
      Naming.rebind("rmi://localhost:1099/QuoteService",ssi);

    }catch (MalformedURLException e1){
         System.out.println(e1.getMessage());
    }catch(RemoteException ex) {
          ex.printStackTrace();
    }
```

```
    }
  }
```

There are two methods in the class `java.rmi.Naming` that can bind an object in the registry. The method `bind()` binds an RMI server to a name. It throws `AlreadyBoundException` if the binding already exists. The method `rebind()` replaces any possibly existing binding with the new one. In addition to binding a server to a name, this also ensures that the clients requesting such services as `getQuotes()` or `getNasdaqSymbols()` receive their stubs—the local proxies of the remote methods.

The registry must be up and running by the time you start the program in Listing 24-3. One way to start the registry is by entering `start rmiregistry` in the Windows command window or `rmiregistry` in Mac OS. Instead of starting the registry manually, you can start it from within the `StartServer` program itself by calling the following method:

```
LocateRegistry.createRegistry(1099);
```

If you know that another process has already pre-created the registry, just get its reference and bind the server to it. The `getRegistry()` method can be called without arguments if the RMI registry runs on the default port 1099. If this is not the case, specify the port number (5048 in the following example). The variable `registry` in the following code fragment is a stub to the remote object `StockServerImpl`:

```
StockServerImpl ssi = new StockServerImpl();
Registry registry = LocateRegistry.getRegistry(5048);
registry.bind("QuoteService", ssi);
```

Writing RMI Clients

The client program, running anywhere on the Internet, performs a lookup in the registry on the host machine (using the host machine's domain name or IP address) and obtains a reference to the remote object. Listing 24-4 shows a sample client program. Notice the casting to the `StockServer` type of the data returned by the method `lookup()`.

Even though the class `StockServerImpl` has been bound to the name `QuoteService`, because this class implements the `StockServer` interface you can cast the returned object to it. The variable `myServer` sees only the methods defined in this interface, while the class `StockServerImpl` may have other public methods, too.

LISTING 24-4 RMI client

```
public class Client {

  public static void main (String args[]) {

   if (args.length == 0) {
     System.out.println(
                "\n Sample usage: java client.Client AAPL");
     System.exit(0);
   }
```

```
        try {
            StockServer myServer = (StockServer)
            Naming.lookup("rmi://localhost:1099/QuoteService");

           String price = myServer.getQuote(args[0]);
            if  (price != null){
              System.out.println("The price of " + args[0] +
                                   " is: $" + price);
            }
            else{
               System.out.println("Invalid Nasdaq symbol. " +
                  "Please use one of these:" +
                  myServer.getNasdaqSymbols().toString());
           }

        } catch (MalformedURLException exMF) {
            System.out.println(exMF.getMessage());
        } catch (NotBoundException exNB) {
            System.out.println(exNB.getMessage());
        } catch (RemoteException exRE) {
            System.out.println(exRE.getMessage());
          }
        }
      }
```

Multiple clients can connect to the same RMI server, but each client/server communication is done over the separate socket connection. This is done internally, so the application programmer doesn't need to explicitly program sockets. If you remember, in Lesson 16 we had to invent a simple communication protocol in the example on socket connection. RMI uses its own proprietary protocol called JRMP (`http://en.wikipedia.org/wiki/Java_Remote_Method_Protocol`), hence it can be used only in Java-to-Java communications.

Security Considerations

Can any RMI client restrict the actions that remotely loaded code can perform on the local computer? Can the server restrict access? You can specify a security policy file containing access restrictions. For example, in the code in Listing 24-3 and Listing 24-4 you can start the `main()` method with the following code:

```
if (System.getSecurityManager() == null) {
        System.setSecurityManager(new RMISecurityManager());
 }
```

The class `java.rmi.RMISecurityManager` extends the class `java.lang.SecurityManager` and provides a security context under which the RMI application executes. In RMI clients, the goal is to prevent remotely loaded stub code from downloading unsecured code via remote method invocation.

The RMI client uses a file in which security policies are defined. You can use the default security file, `java.policy`, located in your JDK or JRE installation directory under `lib/security`. The default policy file gives all permissions to the code, but you can create your own file and supply it either via the command-line parameter or in the code before the security manager is set:

```
System.setProperty("java.security.policy", "mypolicyfile");
```

For a more detailed description of security policy files, refer to the documentation at `http://docs.oracle.com/javase/8/docs/technotes/guides/security/PolicyFiles.html`.

Java applets can also serve as RMI clients, but they don't need RMI security managers. The only restriction on them is that they can connect only to the RMI server running on the same host on which they were deployed.

Finding Remote Objects

RMI clients find remote services by using a *naming* or *directory service*. A naming service runs on a known host and port number. The subject of naming and directory services is covered in more detail in Chapter 29.

By now you know that an RMI server can start its own registry that offers naming services for RMI clients. The behavior of the registry is defined by the interface `java.rmi.registry.Registry`, and you saw an example of binding to the registry in the section "Registering Remote Objects".

By default, the RMI registry runs on port 1099, unless another port number is specified. When the client wants to invoke methods on a remote object it obtains a reference to that object by looking up the name. The lookup returns to the client a remote reference, also known as a *stub*.

The method `lookup()` takes the object name's URL as an argument in the following format:

```
rmi://<host_name>[:<name_service_port>]/<service_name>
```

`host_name` stands for the name of a computer on the local area network (LAN), or the name of a domain name system (DNS) on the Internet. `name_service_port` has to be specified only if the naming service is running on a port other than the default. `service_name` stands for the name of the remote object that should be bound to the registry.

Figure 24-1 illustrates the architecture of an RMI application. In the "Try It," section you implement this architecture for the sample stock quote service.

TRY IT

In this exercise your goal is to start and test all the parts of the distributed Stock Server application, and you run all these parts on the same computer. The `StartServer` program creates a registry and binds the `StockServerImpl` under the name *QuoteService*. To emulate multiple computers you start the client from a command window. If everything is done properly you should be able to start the RMI client with one of the stock symbols known to the server, and get a price quote back.

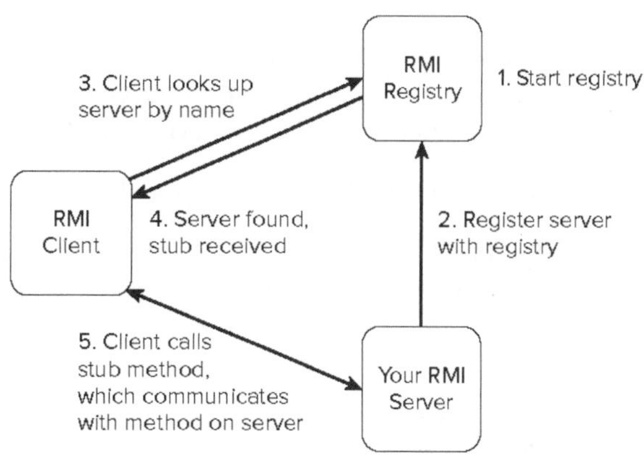

FIGURE 24-1

Lesson Requirements

You should have Java installed.

> **NOTE** *You can download the code and resources for this "Try It" from the book's web page at* `www.wrox.com/go/javaprog24hr2e`. *You can find them in the file Lesson24.zip.*

Hints

There is an RMI plug-in for the Eclipse RMI that may be handy for developing RMI-based distributed applications. It contains a useful utility called RMI Spy that shows all outgoing and incoming method calls, and measures execution times. Another useful utility in this plug-in is Registry Inspector, which displays information about objects in the registry. The RMI plug-in is available from `www.genady.net/rmi/index.html`.

Step-by-Step

1. Import the Eclipse project called Lesson24. It has two packages: `client` and `server`.
2. Rebuild the project (use the menu Project → Clean). Note the location of the Eclipse workspace; you need it because you run all code samples from command windows. Make sure that after importing the project it points at the JRE that's installed on your compute (right-click on the project name and use the menu Properties → Java Build Path).
3. Run the program `StartServer` to start and register `StockServer` with the registry (note the creation of registry with `LocateRegistry`). After you enter a command similar to the one shown below, the server starts and binds to the registry, printing the following message in the Eclipse console:

   ```
   <QuoteService> server is ready.
   ```

   The server stays up and running waiting for requests from the clients.
4. You can run the client from Eclipse, too, but to better illustrate the fact that you use different JVMs, run the client from a command window. Open a command (or Terminal) window and go to the `bin` directory of the project Lesson24 in your Eclipse workspace. On my computer I did it as follows:

   ```
   cd /Users/yfain11/practicalJava/workspace/Lesson24/bin
   ```

5. Run the `Client` program located in the `client` package, passing the stock symbol as a command-line argument, and the `Client` connects to your "remote" server and receives the price quote—for example:

   ```
   java client.Client AAPL
   ```

   On my computer the output looked as follows:
   `The price of AAPL is: $91.85776369781252`

6. Open several command windows and run the client program in each of them, emulating multiple clients sending requests to the same server.

7. Add the following statement to the method `getQuote()` of `StockServerImpl` class and note how the server reports each quote request in the Eclipse console:

```
System.out.println("Got the price quote request for " +
                                                    symbol);
```

TIP *Please select the videos for Lesson 24 online at* `www.wrox.com/go/javaprog24hr2e`*. You will also be able to download the code and resources for this lesson from the website.*

25

Java EE 7 Overview

Starting from this lesson you'll be learning about Java Enterprise Edition (Java EE, formerly J2EE), which is a powerful, mature, and widely used platform for development of distributed applications. The word *enterprise* doesn't imply that it is meant only for large-scale applications. Java EE components are used for the development of everything from an application for a local pizza parlor's website running on a five-hundred-dollar computer to a super-powerful Wall Street trading application that runs on a *cluster* of hundreds of interconnected servers.

This lesson is an overview of the Java EE architecture, concepts, components, and terms that will be covered in detail in the remaining lessons of this book. The goal of these lessons is to give you an understanding of how to approach the development of Java EE applications by showing you how to build small applications rather than making you read the 1,000-page manuscript that would otherwise be required for detailed coverage of this subject.

There are an abundance of online materials and books published on the subject of Java EE, and when you figure out which components are a good fit for your project, finding materials on the selected topic will not be difficult at all. My task is to help you in making that decision and getting you started in the quickest possible way. Oracle's white paper "Introduction to Java Platform Enterprise Edition 7 (`http://www.oracle.com/technetwork/java/javaee/javaee7-whitepaper-1956203.pdf`)" is a good complement for this lesson. If you start browsing the Internet trying to find more information on Java EE, you can easily get confused by trying to compare the features of different versions of Java EE components. I highly recommend that you stay focused on the features of Java EE 7, which is the most current platform and the easiest to use. It was released in 2013.

THE BIG PICTURE

Go to your favorite online job search engine and search for job listings with the keyword *Java*. You'll find thousands of job descriptions, but recruiters are looking for software developers that know more than just the Core Java that was covered in the first 24 lessons of this book. Here's an example of one of the job ads:

Title: Java Software Developer

Skills: Java, JMS, Spring, Websphere MQ, EJB, Servlets, JDK, JUnit, Oracle, SQL

The candidate should know:

- Core Java
- Have expertise in EJB and Servlets
- Have experience with RESTFulWeb Services and JAX-RS
- JDBC (Oracle) and JPA
- JUnit
- SQL
- Eclipse IDE
- Spring Framework
- WebSphere Application Server
- JMS and WebSphere MQ

How many items from this list of skills did you recognize? You know Core Java (also known as Java SE), JDBC, Eclipse, and hopefully SQL. After studying the remaining lessons you'll understand what most of the other skills are, why they are required, and how they all fit together. You'll also have technical knowledge of many of the buzzwords listed there.

JCP, JSR, and Other Acronyms

The Java community is accustomed to using lots of acronyms. Initially these acronyms might sound intimidating and confusing, but with a little effort they will make perfect sense and explain the way the Java ecosystem lives and functions.

Each version of Java EE includes a set of specifications for various technologies, such as Servlets, JavaServer Pages (JSP), Enterprise Java Beans (EJB), and Java Messaging Service (JMS). Each of these specifications has been defined by an organization called the Java Community Process (JCP). If a person or a group of people decides to propose a specification for some future technology, it creates a Java Specification Request (JSR) and forms a group of experts to work on this specification. JSRs are numbered. For example, the specification for Servlets 3.1 is described in JSR 340.

If you decide to get familiar with any specific JSR, visit the website `http://jcp.org`. Both Java EE and Java SE implement multiple JSRs. In other words, Java EE is based on standards. If you'd like to see which JSRs are included in Java EE 7, visit `http://en.wikipedia.org/wiki/Java_EE_version_history#Java_EE_7_.28June_12.2C_2013.29`. This book doesn't cover all of the JSRs, but it explains some of the main ones. Most importantly, this book tries to show you how to architect Java applications that use the Java EE 7 platform.

Tiers of Java EE Applications

A typical distributed Java application can be divided into three or four logical tiers. (If the application is getting data directly from a DBMS, as described in Chapter 21, it has a two-tier client-server architecture, and Java EE components are not needed.) Figure 25-1 shows selected technologies and some of the ways of building a distributed application that includes Java EE tiers or layers.

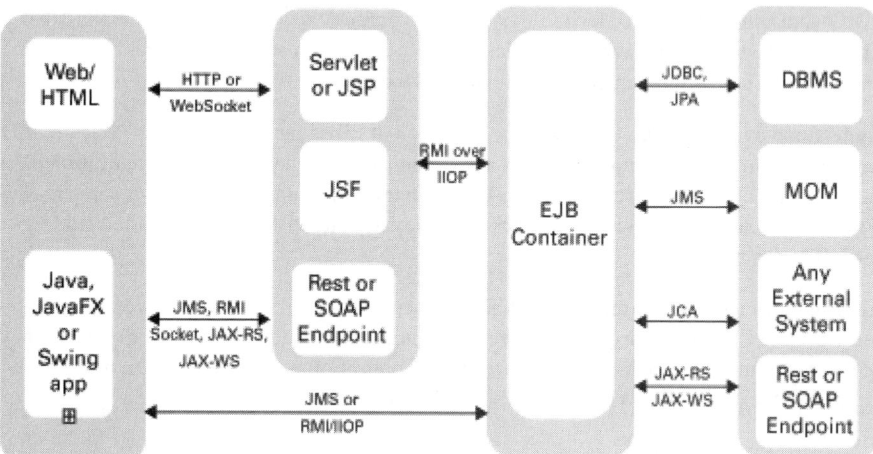

FIGURE 25-1: Architecting Java EE applications

FULL JAVA EE DIAGRAM

To see the full Java EE diagram, see the "Profiles" section in the document titled Java Platform, Enterprise Edition (Java EE) Specification, v7 (`http://download.oracle.com/otn-pub/jcp/java_ee-7-fr-eval-spec/JavaEE_Platform_Spec.pdf`).

The client tier can be implemented on a user's desktop, notebook, mobile phone, or any other device that has embedded JRE or can connect with Java on the web server. Applications that interconnect multiple devices are known as Internet of Things (`http://en.wikipedia.org/wiki/Internet_of_Things`) (IoT); they can utilize small sensors with embedded Java and servers that use Java EE technologies. You can create a client as an independent Java application, an applet, or a *thin client* (an HTML/JavaScript file running in a web browser). The word *thin* refers to the fact that no business processing (except the input validation) is being done on the client side, so the server has to work hard processing all application logic for all clients, and Java EE shines on the server side.

If you're building a web application, the web tier (also known as the *presentation tier*) comes into the picture. You have your choice of JSP, JavaServer Face (JSF), Servlets, or Web Services. These components are responsible for the look of your thin client. Java Swing and JavaFX are often used as *fat clients* working with the server-side applications. The word *fat* here refers to the fact that the client can contain some business logic, which lowers the load on the server. Any non-graphical user interface (GUI) Java application can be a client of the server-side application created with the help of one or more Java EE technologies.

The business logic of your application is deployed in the *business tier*, which is represented by EJBs in the Java EE world. In the past EJBs were pretty heavy components and third-party frameworks such as Spring became a popular alternative for implementing the business tier. But Java EE regains its market share in this department because it's a light POJO- and annotation-based technology that incorporates the best features of the third-party framework. POJO stands for *plain old Java object*—a Java class that can be written any way you want and doesn't have to extend any framework class or implement mandatory interfaces.

This term is easily understood by people who witnessed the evolution of EJBs that started with Java classes that had to be written and deployed in a certain convoluted way and accompanied by heavy XML configuration files. Things changed drastically, and now EJBs have turned into POJOs marked with annotations. If for some reason you skipped Chapter 23 on annotations, you should go back and study it; otherwise you won't understand most of the remaining material in this book.

While drawing the diagram for Figure 25-1, I moved the Web Services box a couple of times between the tiers. On one hand, Web Services (see Chapter 33) are based on web communication protocols; on the other hand they can serve as a façade that hides anything, including an entire legacy application written in COBOL or other languages on mainframes. In the real world, Web Services span all server-side tiers and could even be placed in a separate box in the data tier.

Using DBMSes remains the most popular way to store data in enterprise Java EE applications, but it's not the only way. The data can be served by an external web service or arrive as a real-time feed from some messaging infrastructure. MOM stands for *message-oriented middleware*, and you find out what it is in Chapter 30.

Without some practical example, all these new buzzwords may not make much sense to you. You see examples in the upcoming lessons, but for now, I'm just briefly discussing several (not all) ways or re-architecting of the Stock Market application that you've seen already implemented with sockets and RMI.

- Have a JavaFX client to connect to `StockQuoteServlet`, which creates what is known as a *session EJB* called `StockMarketQuote`, which connects to external stock exchange software and requests a price quote on the specified symbol(s). This session bean has a timer that updates and sends to the client the price quotes every second.
- Do as described in the previous bullet, but replace the JavaFX application with a thin HTML client.
- The same as before, but replace the Servlet with a JSP.
- The same as before, but replace the JSP with a JSF.
- The same as above, but replace JSF with RESTFul Web Service.
- The same as above, but replace HTTP with WebSocket protocol.
- The same as before, but replace the Web Service with a session EJB that interacts with a message-driven bean (MDB) that subscribes via MOM to the external stock exchange application that sends back new prices only when they change.
- The same as before, but add another session bean that will process every price quote received by MDB and apply a modeling algorithm, and on certain conditions send a message to buy or sell a specific number of shares of the suggested stock to a third-party trading system via a call to a Web Service.

I can keep going. As you can see, there are many ways to design a distributed Java EE application. This is what Java architects do for a living.

Containers Versus Application Servers

Java EE tiers are implemented in *containers*. Containers contain Java objects. In the Java EE world containers not only contain, but also control the birth, life, and death of Java components. For example, you don't need to use the `new` operator to create a new instance of an EJB; the container creates a pool of them based on configuration parameters. Basically, a container is an area inside JVM that can support a life cycle of certain types of Java objects, such as servlet, EJB, and so on. The word container applies to clients too; for example, Java SE run time serves as a container for Java client applications.

Containers perform useful functions, and one of them is thread safety. It's great that multiple clients can connect and make requests to the same server, but can you be sure that a thread initiated by Mary won't interfere with John's thread? An EJB container implements a single-threaded model ensuring that each client's request operates in a dedicated thread. Containers may offer transactional support with Java Transaction API (JTA) and persist data for you with Java Persistence API (JPA).

In the first few lessons I used a blueprint analogy to explain the relationship between Java classes and objects. I'm using this analogy again, but this time I'm explaining the relationship between the Java EE specification and application servers. The Java EE is a specification, and when its release is published, vendors who want to implement it in their software products create application servers that support this specification.

Multiple vendors offer their versions of a Java EE application server. The question is what version of the Java EE specification they support. Currently four application servers—GlassFish (Oracle), WildFly (Red Hat), WebLogic (Oracle), and Tmax JEUS (TMaxSoft)—support Java EE 7. To see the latest list of servers that support Java EE 7 visit the Java EE Compatibility (`http://www.oracle.com/technetwork/java/javaee/overview/compatibility-jsp-136984.html`) web page.

Java EE application servers have to support multiple containers; for example, a Servlet container and an EJB container. Some vendors prefer to create products supporting only certain technologies defined in the Java EE specification. For example, Tomcat (Apache Foundation), Jetty (Eclipse Foundation), and Resin (Caucho) offer support for selected technologies (such as Servlets and JSP), which makes them suitable for implementing web applications, but if you are planning to create web applications based on one of these products, you need to figure out what other tools or frameworks are needed to support transactions, the business tier, data persistence, and more. TomEE (Apache Foundation) supports Servlets, JSP, EJB, and other Java EE technologies.

This book uses GlassFish 4.1 from Oracle, which is fully compliant with Java EE 7. I have selected the most widely used technologies in Java EE development today. In particular you'll be learning about the following:

- Java Servlets (JSR 340)
- JavaServer Pages (JSR 245)
- Enterprise Java Beans (JSR 345)
- Java Persistence API (JSR 338)
- Context and Dependency Injection (JSR 346)
- Java Message Service (JSR 343)
- Java API for RESTFul Web Services (JSR 339)
- Java API for JSON Processing (JSR 353)
- Java API for WebSocket (JSR 356)

You may feel overwhelmed with all these terms, but I try to explain them in easy-to-understand language.

PROFILES AND PRUNING

Although Java EE offers a full stack of server technologies, most of the real-world applications don't need all of them. In the past, to get Java EE certified, a vendor of an application server had to implement all JSRs that were listed in the Java EE specification. But most of the applications don't use all technologies included in the full Java EE specification (`https://jcp.org/en/jsr/detail?id=342`). This is how that concept of a profile came about. A profile is a preconfigured subset of Java technologies geared toward solving a specific type of application. Currently, besides the full profile, there is the Web Profile (`https://java.net/downloads/javaee-spec/WebProfile.pdf`), which is designed specifically for the development of web applications. The Web Profile defines required components (for example, Servlets, JSF, JSP, CDI, EJB Lite, JPA, JTA), but vendors may include technologies from the full Java EE specification, too. In the future, new profiles may be created to address specific needs of developers.

JAVA SE PROFILES

Java SE 8 also has profiles. So-called compact profiles (`https://blogs.oracle.com/jtc/entry/a_first_look_at_compact`) were introduced to offer configurable lightweight runtimes for small devices with embedded Java.

Pruning is a way to reduce the size of the Java EE platform. The pruning process starts with marking in JavaDoc the technologies that are candidates for removal. Then, based on the reaction of the Java community, they will be either removed from the future specifications or not. It's up to the application server vendor to define the process of removal, but it's done carefully so the existing application won't break. Some of the technologies (such as JAXR 1.0) are optional for implementation in Java EE 7 servers.

WHY JAVA EE?

You may say, "I want my RMI-based stock server application back. Why make things so complex?" The reason is that a single instance of `UnicastRemoteObject` in your RMI `StockServer` may need to process tens of thousands of concurrent user requests. Because of this you'll need to write code ensuring that such concurrent processing is thread safe.

Servlet and EJB containers are scalable, and they take care of all multithreading issues, enabling you to write application code as if the application were the only user! This alone should be a good reason for using the Java EE stack as opposed to RMI. Without going into a detailed comparison between RMI and other Java EE technologies, I'll just add that if you need to deploy your `StockServer` application on the web, corporate firewalls may not allow clients to open certain ports and use the JRMP communication protocol required by RMI.

JAVA EE AND MULTITHREADING

One of the major changes in Java EE 7 compared to previous versions is that you are allowed to introduce multiple threads in your application code that run inside Java EE containers. It was not

> allowed before—only the container could create and manage threads. Now with the help of such classes as `ManagedExecutorService` and `ManagedThreadFactory` you can create threads from your code, too.

Java EE is a very robust, reliable, and scalable platform and you will appreciate what its container will do for your code. This section mentions a couple of concepts.

If you want Java EE containers to help you, help them by providing configuration parameters (annotations) that specify how many instances of the same session bean `StockMarketQuote` you want pre-created for you by the EJB container. Each of these session beans may be "rented" from a pool to the client's request, and then put back. How many beans do you need? I don't know. It depends on the load on your system—the number of concurrent (simultaneous) requests for price quotes that have to be supported by your system.

Java EE implements *dependency injection*. An object doesn't have to reach out to get the resources it needs because the container can inject its resources (and your code can inject application objects) into your object using annotations. You see examples of CDI later in the book.

WebSocket protocol allows you to switch from the request-response-based communications typical in web applications to a simultaneous two-way data exchange between the client and server. The server can initiate data push without waiting for the client requests. Consequently, creating real-time web applications becomes a lot easier.

JSON stands for JavaScript Object Notation. JSON became a de facto standard data format used in data communication between web browsers and servers. Java EE 7 defines a standard way of generating and parsing JSON data.

Interceptors offer a mechanism by which containers can intercept methods invoked on your session beans. When the call is intercepted, you can specify additional code to be called before or after the method is executed. For example, imagine that you need to add logging before certain methods are called. Adding interceptors is an easy way to do this.

Messaging allows you to introduce asynchronous processing into the business workflow of your application. Instead of making direct requests to business objects of your application, your code can place messages into queues maintained by special servers—Message-Oriented Middleware (MOM).

Starting in Lesson 26 you have a chance to apply these concepts and features. Oracle published a complete Java EE 7 Tutorial (`http://docs.oracle.com/javaee/7/tutorial/doc/`) that covers each and every technology in detail. The tutorial uses GlassFish server (`https://glassfish.java.net/`), and this book uses it, too.

> **JAVA EE CODE SAMPLES**
>
> More than 200 code samples illustrating various Java EE 7 technologies are available at `https://github.com/javaee-samples/javaee7-samples`.

TRY IT

This lesson was a high-level overview of the Java EE 7 platform. The hands-on exercises starting in the next lesson require that you have an application server installed, and installing the GlassFish server is your next assignment.

Lesson Requirements

You should have Java installed.

Step-by-Step

One instance of the GlassFish server may run several domains, and domain1 is the default. The command to stop a domain looks similar, but instead of using the command `start-domain` use `stop-domain`.

1. Download GlassFish Server Open Source Edition. At the time of this writing the latest version, GlassFish 4.1, is available at the following URL: `https://glassfish.java.net/download.html`.
2. Download and unzip the file titled Java EE Full Platform.
3. In the command (or Terminal) window switch to the directory `glassfish4/bin`. If you use Mac OS, start the server using the following command:

    ```
    ./asadmin start-domain domain1
    ```

    Windows users start the server using the following command:

    ```
    asadmin.bat start-domain domain1
    ```

    On my computer after starting GlassFish the Terminal window looked like Figure 25-2.

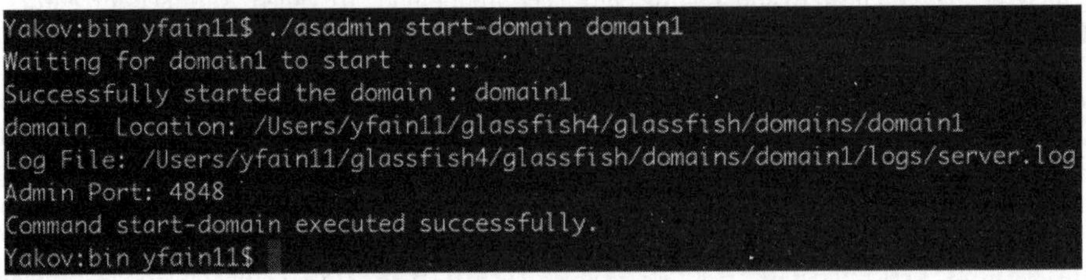

    ```
    Yakov:bin yfain11$ ./asadmin start-domain domain1
    Waiting for domain1 to start .....
    Successfully started the domain : domain1
    domain  Location: /Users/yfain11/glassfish4/glassfish/domains/domain1
    Log File: /Users/yfain11/glassfish4/glassfish/domains/domain1/logs/server.log
    Admin Port: 4848
    Command start-domain executed successfully.
    Yakov:bin yfain11$
    ```

    FIGURE 25-2: Starting GlassFish from the Terminal window in Mac OS

4. By default GlassFish Server runs on port 8080 and the port for server administration is 4848. Open your web browser and enter `http://localhost:8080`—you should see the GlassFish welcome page.
5. Open the GlassFish administration console by entering in your browser `http://localhost:4848`. The web browser should display the window shown in Figure 25-3.

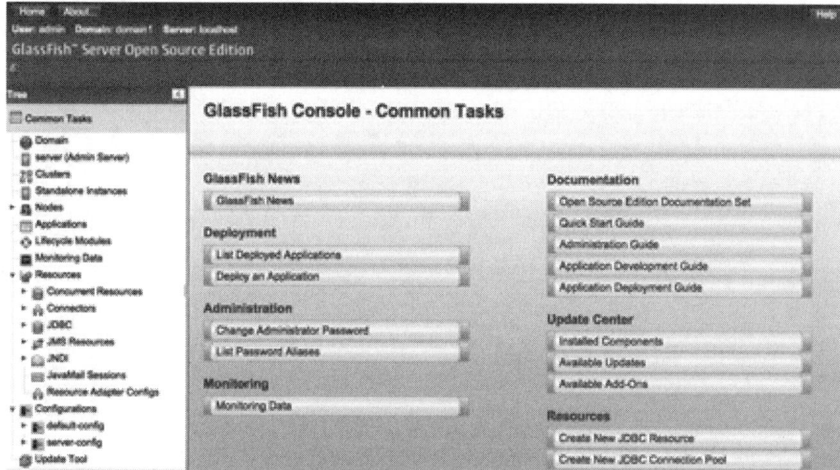

FIGURE 25-3: The GlassFish admin console

6. Download the Oracle GlassFish Server Quick Start Guide from `https://glassfish.java.net/docs/4.0/quick-start-guide.pdf` for a description of the administrative commands for working with the GlassFish server.

> **TIP** *Please select the videos for Lesson 25 online at* `www.wrox.com/go/javaprog24hr2e`*. You will also be able to download the code and resources for this lesson from the website.*

26

Programming with Servlets

Web applications can serve static or dynamic content. Some examples of static content are text files with HTML markup, images, and video. Dynamic content is formed on the fly. Think of a web application that enables you to browse the inventory of an online store. The content you see on your screen is being created based on your queries—in other words, dynamically.

In the Java EE world, web content can be served by a program running in a container with deployed servlets, Java Server Pages (JSP), JavaServer Faces (JSF), or a third-party framework. You can also create a web application by implementing a SOAP or RESTful Web Service. You can also create a web application based on a Plain Old Java Object (POJO) utilizing WebSocket protocol. Servlets, JSP, and JSF not only return the data, but also present it as formatted HTML pages, hence the term *presentation layer* (refer to Figure 25-1). Web Services or WebSocket-based applications, on the other hand, return just the data (see Chapter 33).

A servlet is a Java class written by certain rules and deployed in a Java EE–compliant servlet container of your choice. The client program can be a lightweight HTML/JavaScript, a heavyweight applet, or a Swing or JavaFX program. This lesson uses the most popular means of web communication: Web browsers talk to servlets using HTTP, which stands for *Hypertext Transfer Protocol*.

All examples in this lesson work in any servlet container supporting the Servlet 3.1 specification. The lesson uses a full application server GlassFish, which may be an overkill if your application only needs the servlet support. If you want to experiment with a lightweight servlet container, consider using Apache Tomcat (`http://tomcat.apache.org/`) or Jetty (`http://www.eclipse.org/jetty/`). But every Java EE application server comes with a servlet container, and because you are going to study several Java EE technologies, installing a full featured Java EE application server covers you for all upcoming lessons.

THE BIG PICTURE

Figure 26-1 depicts a web browser making HTTP requests to the servlet named `MyServlet` and receiving HTTP responses that `MyServlet` sends back.

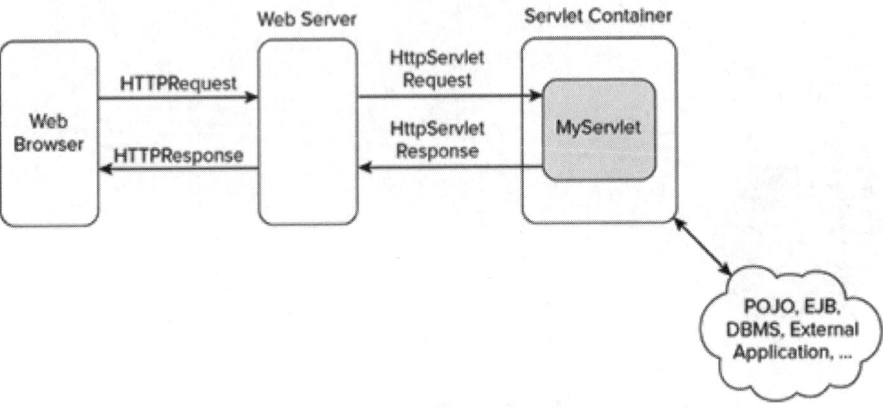

FIGURE 26-1: A sample client-servlet data flow

Before you even learn how to create and deploy servlets, take a look at the components and the workflow of an imaginary online store, `www.MyBooks.com`, which is developed and deployed with Java servlets.

- The client's machine just needs a web browser. The bookstore consists of a number of HTML web pages for interacting with users. The web browser sends the user requests to the server with the name `MyBooks.com` in the form of an `HttpRequest` object.
- The computer that hosts `MyBooks.com` has to run some web server software, usually on port 80. For secure communication with HTTPS (HyperText Transfer Protocol Secure) the default port is 443. These two ports are usually open on any web server, otherwise external clients wouldn't even be able to make any requests to the resources deployed under such a server.
- The web server "listens to" the users' requests. If a web server receives a simple request for static HTML content (such as a file or an image), the web server processes the request without needing to engage any additional software, and it sends back `HttpResponse` with the requested static content inside.
- The website `MyBooks.com` also runs a servlet container with deployed servlet(s). If the web server receives a user request to find books based on some search criteria, it creates and passes `HttpServletRequest` to the appropriate servlet (for example, `FindBooksServlet`), which should be deployed and running in the servlet container. The next section shows sample HTML containing a form that explicitly lists `FindBooksServlet` by name.
- The servlet invokes the Java code that performs the search and creates (on the fly) the HTML page listing the found books that meet the requested search criteria, and sends it to the web server wrapped in `HttpServletResponse`.
- The web server extracts the content from `HttpServletResponse`, wraps it inside the `HttpResponse` object, and sends it back to the user's web browser.
- The user's browser displays the received page without knowing if it was a static HTML page or a freshly baked one.

The user's web browsers don't need to know which server-side technology has been used to prepare dynamic content. It could be Java, .NET, Python, PHP, and so on. The browser just knows that to send data to the server using HTTP protocol, the data has to be placed inside `HttpRequest`. Web browsers also know how to display content arriving from the server in a form of `HttpResponse`. All other magic that's happening on the server is of no interest to the web browsers.

THE THIN CLIENT

Let's start with creating a simple HTTP page that can serve as a client for a Java servlet. Listing 26-1 shows a simple HTML file with a form containing a text input field and a Submit button, which users can use to find a book by its title.

LISTING 26-1 HTML that gives the 404 error

```
<html>
   <head>
    <title>Find a book</title>
   </head>

   <body>
     Enter a word from the book title:
     <form action=http://www.MyBooks.com/servlet/FindBooksServlet
                                                  method=Get>
       <input type=Text name=booktitle>
       <input type=Submit value="Search">
    </form>
   </body>
</html>
```

In any plain text editor, create a file called `BookSearch.html` containing the HTML from Listing 26-1. Open this file in a web browser (File → Open), enter any text in the input field, and press Search. You get an error message because there is neither a server behind the URL `www.MyBooks.com` nor a servlet called `FindBooksServlet` at this address. This was just an illustration of what the thinnest client could look like.

Clients communicate with servlets using HTTP protocol, and when no requested network resource is found, the `HttpResponse` object comes back with an error. If the server responds, but the requested resource (the `FindBooksServlet`) is not there, the error code 404 is returned. If the server doesn't respond, the web client shows an appropriate error code. If the client successfully receives the requested resource from the specified URL, the HTTP status code is anywhere in the range from 200 to 300. The HTTP may also return 304, which indicates that the browser found in its cache an unchanged local copy of the requested resource, so there was no need to send a request to the web server. The list of all possible HTTP status codes is available at `www.w3.org/Protocols/rfc2616/rfc2616-sec10.html`.

HOW TO WRITE A SERVLET

To create a servlet, write a class that extends from `HttpServlet` and annotate it with the `@WebServlet` annotation. The class `HttpServlet` extends `GenericServlet`, which defines the method `service()`. The method `service()` receives the client's response and directs it to one of the methods of your class that's a descendant of HttpServlet. Typically you have to override the methods doGet() and/or doPost(). Which one to override? This depends on the client's request method. If the client uses the HTTP request with the method Post, override doPost(), if the client uses the Get request (see Listing 26-1), override the callback doGet(), as shown in your_first_servlet.

LISTING 26-2 Your first servlet

```
@WebServlet(urlPatterns="/books", name="FindBooksServlet" )
public class FindBooksServlet extends HttpServlet {

  @Override
  public void doGet(HttpServletRequest request,
           HttpServletResponse response) throws ServletException {

         // The code processing the request goes here
         // The resulting Web page will be sent back via the
         // I/O stream that response variable contains

         PrintWriter out = response.getWriter();
         out.println("Hello from FindBooks");
    }
}
```

All the classes that support servlets are located in the package javax.servlet and are packaged in a JAR file, the location of which should be listed in the CLASSPATH environment variable. The javax.servlet package is not included with Java SE—you need to either have Java EE 7 SDK installed or read the documentation of the servlet container of your choice to know where they are located. GlassFish 4 comes with Java EE 7 files, so no separate download is needed.

If you properly deploy FindBooksServlet on www.MyBooks.com, the HTML client from Listing 26-1 gets as a response a web page containing the text "Hello from FindBooks."

HOW TO DEPLOY A SERVLET

The annotation @WebServlet is where you specify servlet deployment parameters. Prior to Java EE 6 you needed to specify deployment parameters in the web.xml file, but now that's optional. FindBooksServlet uses the deployment parameters urlPatterns and name. The former is used to match one of the servlets deployed on the server to the URL. The value /books means that whenever the client sends a request containing the pattern books in its URL, the request has to be redirected to the FindBooksServlet. For example, the servlet container forwards the request http://localhost:8080/books to the FindBooksServlet.

Each web server and servlet container has a directory known as a document root. It is used not only for servlet-based websites but also for the deployment of static HTML files. For example, if you put the HTML file TermsAndConditions.html in the subfolder legal of the document root of the server MyBooks.com, users would need to direct their web browsers to www.mybooks.com/legal/TermsAndConditions.html.

You can read the documentation for the server of your choice to find out the location of the document root directory. In the GlassFish application server, the default document root is the directory `/glassfish/domains/domain1/docroot`. In Apache Tomcat it's the directory `webapps`. If you are planning to create a servlet, its deployment directory is also located in the document root, but it's in the subdirectories `WEB-INF` and `META-INF`.

`WEB-INF` has the subdirectories `classes` and `lib` and might contain the optional file `web.xml`. It may be needed to configure filters; otherwise you can specify all deployment parameters using Java annotations. But if you use both annotations and `web.xml`, the values in this file override the corresponding values in the annotations. This allows changing deployment parameters without requiring recompilation of the servlets. The `WEB-INF` directory also may have some container-specific files.

The directory `META-INF` may have files containing metadata about this web application, like `manifest.mf` or other data specific to a third-party framework or application server content. For example, Apache Tomcat uses a file called `context.xml` where you may specify the information about JDBC drivers.

This is what the directory structure of the application deployed in the document root directory can look like:

```
document root dir
     WEB-INF
      classes
       com
         practicaljava
           lesson26
             FindBooksServlet.class
      lib
META-INF
    manifest.mf
```

The class `com.practicaljava.lesson26.FindBooksServlet` was compiled into the directory `classes`. If you have some third-party JAR files, add them to the `lib` directory.

When your web application is complete, most likely it'll consist of multiple files, and typically the entire directory structure is deployed as one compressed file with the extension `.war`, which stands for web archive. Such files can be created manually, by your Integrated Development Environment (IDE) plug-ins, or by one of the build tools such as Ant, Maven, or Gradle. Later in this lesson you see how to create a war file with Eclipse for Java EE Developers. Lesson 36 is about automating builds with Gradle, and you'll see how to automate creation of the `.war` files.

CONFIGURING GLASSFISH IN ECLIPSE IDE

In the "Try It" section in Lesson 25 you started and stopped GlassFish Server from a command window. However, it's a lot more convenient to develop and deploy web applications when you don't need to leave the IDE. Eclipse for Java EE is a good fit for the development of web projects. It supports a variety of Java EE application servers. In this section you configure GlassFish Server so you can do all the work inside Eclipse.

USING OTHER IDES

NetBeans IDE and IntelliJ IDEA also offer good support for Java EE developers.

If your GlassFish instance is still running, stop it from the command line. In Eclipse, switch to Java EE perspective by pressing the Java EE button on the top-right corner of the toolbar, as shown in Figure 26-2.

FIGURE 26-2: Switching to Java EE perspective in Eclipse

If you don't see this button, use the Eclipse menu Window → Open Perspective → Other → Java EE. Go to the Servers view and click the link to add a new server, as shown in Figure 26-3.

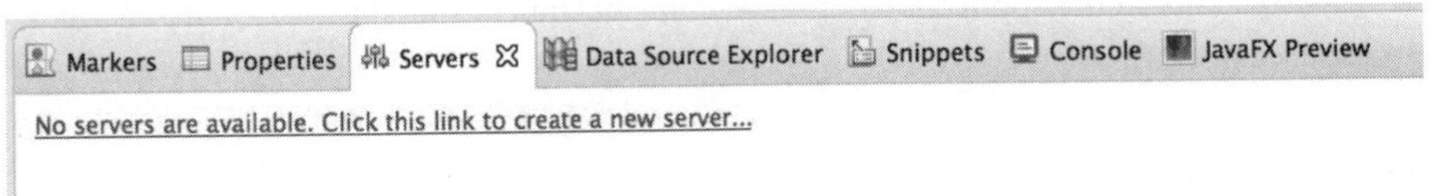

FIGURE 26-3: Configuring a new server in Eclipse

You see a new pop-up window with several server adapters, but to add GlassFish to the list click the Download Additional Server Adapters link (see Figure 26-4).

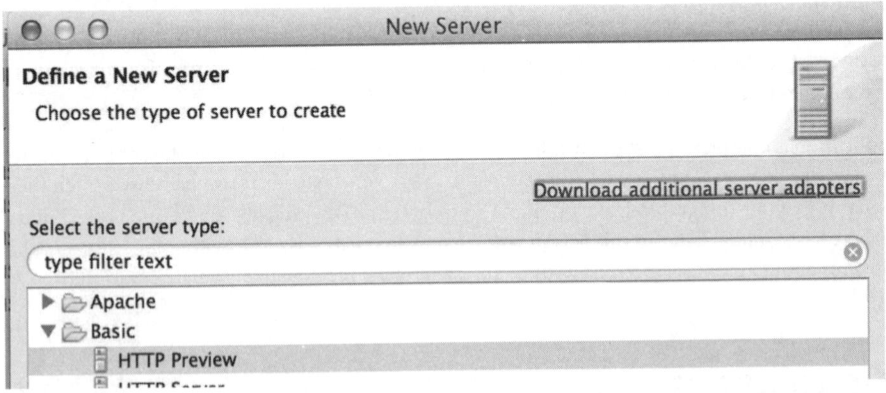

FIGURE 26-4: Download server adapters

Eclipse searches for available server adapters. If you see GlassFish Tools in the menu, install them. If not, you need to install the tools by selecting Help → Marketplace in Eclipse. In the marketplace window enter `GlassFish` in the Find field. Select GlassFish Tools for Luna and install them (make sure that during install Oracle Java EE tools are also selected). (See Figure 26-5.)

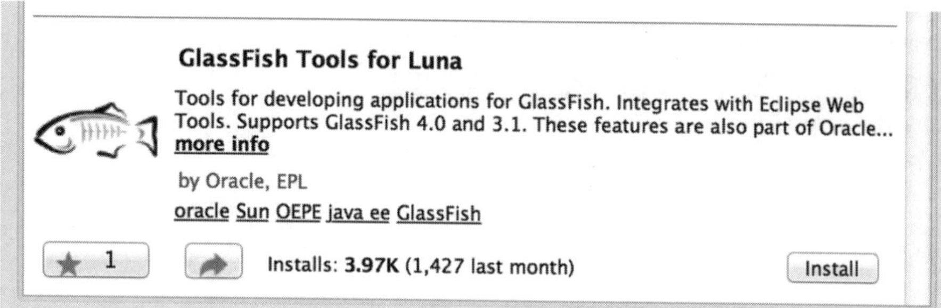

FIGURE 26-5: Installing GlassFish Tools for Luna from Eclipse Marketplace

Now go back to the Servers view and click the link to create new server. Select GlassFish 4 from the list (see Figure 26-6) and complete the configuration .

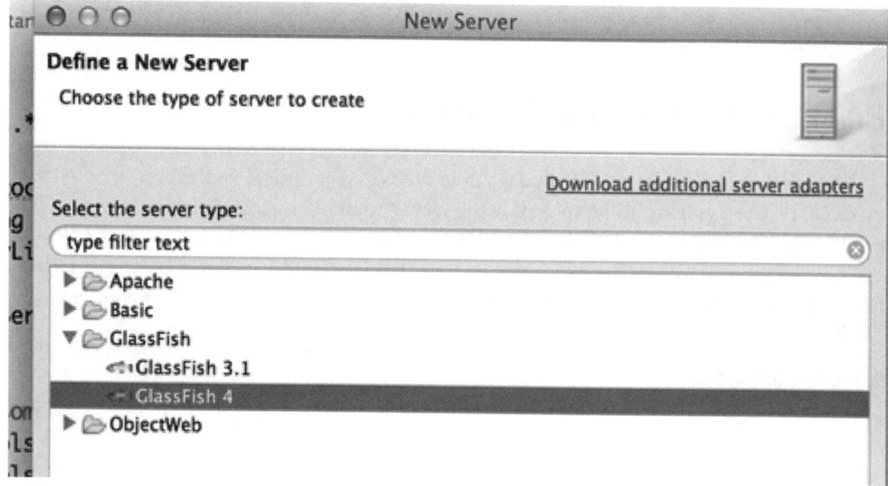

FIGURE 26-6: Configuring GlassFish in Eclipse

The next pop-up asks you about a default JRE (I use 1.8) and where GlassFish Server should be located. According to my installation I specified `/Users/yfain11/glassfish4/glassfish` and pressed Next. Accept the default parameters for `domain1`, don't enter any passwords for admin in the next window, and press Finish. Eclipse starts GlassFish, and the Eclipse console should look similar to a command window shown in the "Try It" section of Lesson 25.

You may configure several Java EE servers of the same or different vendors in Eclipse IDE. For example, I have Apache Tomcat 8, WildFly 8.1, and GlassFish 4.1 configured in my Eclipse, as shown in Figure 26-7.

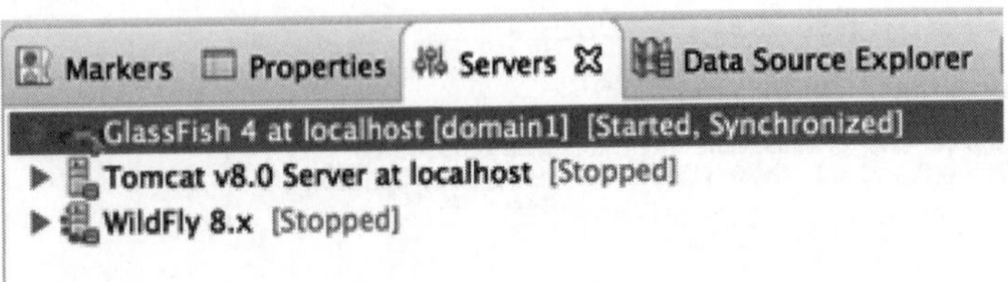

FIGURE 26-7: Three servers configured in Eclipse

> **STARTING AND STOPPING SERVERS IN ECLIPSE**
>
> To start or stop the configured server from Eclipse, visit the Servers view, right-click the server name, and select Start or Stop from the pop-up menu. If you want to debug the server-side code, select Debug instead of Start.

HOW TO CREATE A SERVLET IN ECLIPSE

Open File → New → Other → Web and select the Create Dynamic Web Project option. In the pop-up window, name the project Lesson26. Because you are going to deploy the servlet under GlassFish Server, make sure that GlassFish is selected in the Target Runtime combobox. Click Finish, and a new Eclipse project is created. It doesn't have the same structure as the projects you've been creating so far. It has a subfolder called *`WebContent`* that contains the *`WEB-INF`* and *`META-INF`* directories that will be used for deployment in the servlet container of your choice. (See Figure 26-8.)

FIGURE 26-8: Dynamic Web Project Structure

Right-click the project name, select New→Servlet, and then specify `com.practicaljava.lesson26` as the name of the package and `FindBooksServlet` as the class name. Click Next and edit the URL mapping field to be `/books` (see Figure 26-9; I'll explain it shortly).

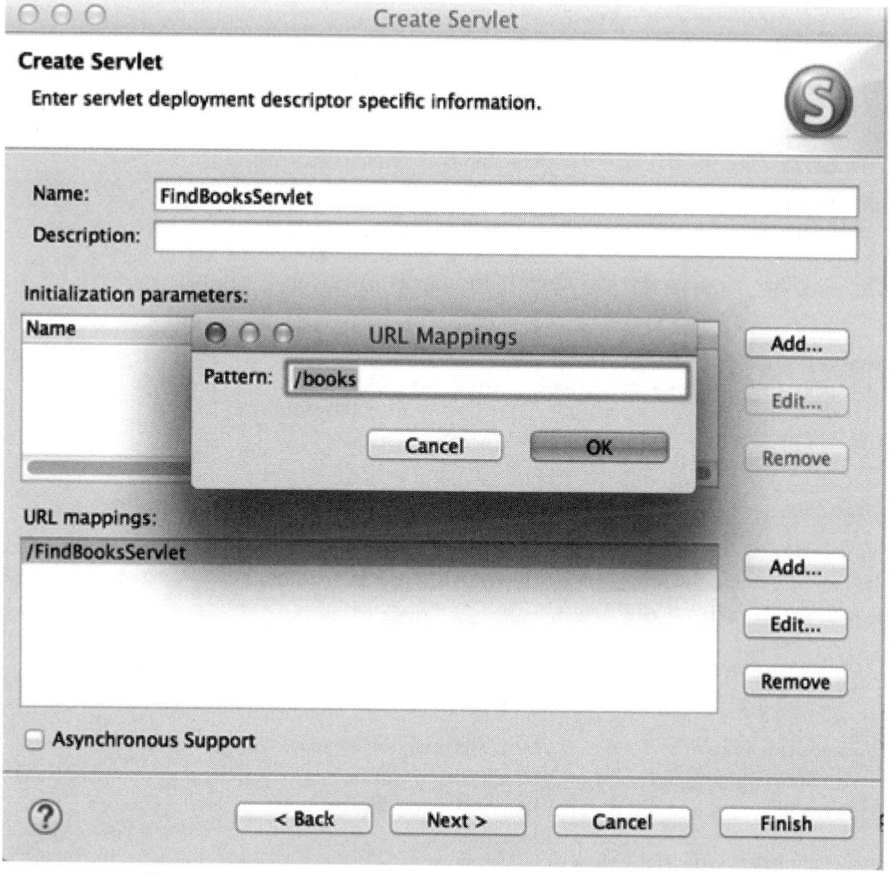

FIGURE 26-9: Changing the URL mapping for a servlet

Click Next again. The next window asks you which method stubs you'd like to have auto-generated; keep the default `doGet()` and `doPost()`. Finally, click Finish, and Eclipse generates the code shown in Listing 26-3 (I just removed some comments).

LISTING 26-3 Generated FindBooks servlet

```
package com.practicaljava.lesson26;

import java.io.IOException;
import javax.servlet.ServletException;
import javax.servlet.annotation.WebServlet;
import javax.servlet.http.;
import javax.servlet.http.HttpServletRequest;
import javax.servlet.http.HttpServletResponse;

@WebServlet(urlPatterns = {"/books"})
```

```
public class FindBooksServlet extends HttpServlet {
      private static final long serialVersionUID = 1L;

    public FindBooks() {
        super();
    }

      protected void doGet(HttpServletRequest request,
         HttpServletResponse response) throws ServletException,
                                                      IOException{

            // TODO Auto-generated method stub
      }

      protected void doPost(HttpServletRequest request,
         HttpServletResponse response) throws ServletException,
                                                      IOException{

            // TODO Auto-generated method stub
      }
}
```

I explain the servlet's data flow in the section "Browser-Servlet Data Flow." Meanwhile let's see the servlet `FindBooksServlet` in action. Add the following two lines in the `doGet()` method to get access to the output stream and send the message "Hello from FindBooks":

```
PrintWriter out = response.getWriter();
out.println("Hello from FindBooks");
```

Don't forget to add the import statement for `PrintWriter`. The final step is to deploy the servlet under GlassFish Server. Open the Servers view, right-click the server, and select Add and Remove from the pop-up menu. Select the project Lesson26 in the left panel and add it to the right one. Click Finish.

The servlet deployment is finished. Now right-click the class name `FindBooksServlet` in the Eclipse project, select Run on Server → GlassFish, and click Finish. If the server was not running, Eclipse first starts the server and then forms the URL to access the servlet `FindBooks`. Eclipse runs its internal web browser and displays the message shown in Figure 26-10.

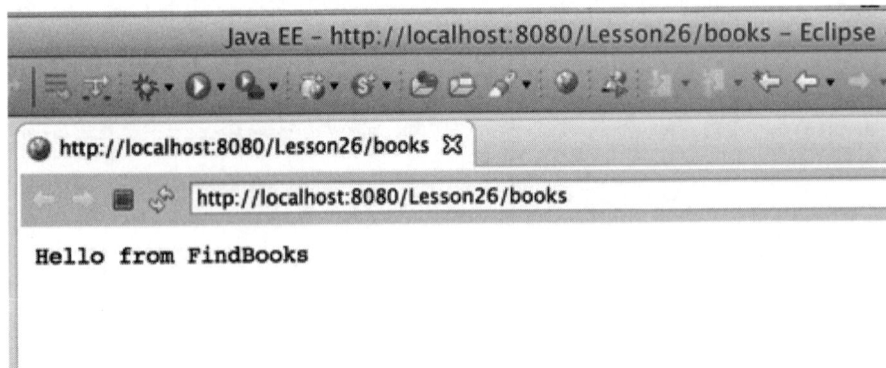

FIGURE 26-10: Running the servlet in Eclipse internal browser

You can copy this URL into any other web browser on your computer; the response will be the same. Starting the server from inside Eclipse doesn't change the fact that it listens to the port 8080, and any client can request and deploy servlets via this port.

Please note that the URL ends with `/books` and not `FindBooksServlet`. Take another look at Figure 26-8. You've changed the URL mapping instructing the servlet container to route all HTTP requests that include `/books` to the servlet `FindBooksServlet`. Eclipse has generated the proper annotation in the servlet's class that may look similar to this one:

```
@WebServlet(urlPatterns = {"/books"})
public class FindBooksServlet extends HttpServlet
```

Servlets belong to the presentation layer, so let's change the web page presentation a little bit. Replacing the code of the `doGet()` method with following three lines shows the output on yellow background and in the header `<H2>` style:

```
PrintWriter out = response.getWriter();
out.println("<html><body bgcolor=yellow>");
out.println("<h2>Hello from FindBooks</h2>");
```

The browser renders this HTML page, as shown in Figure 26-11.

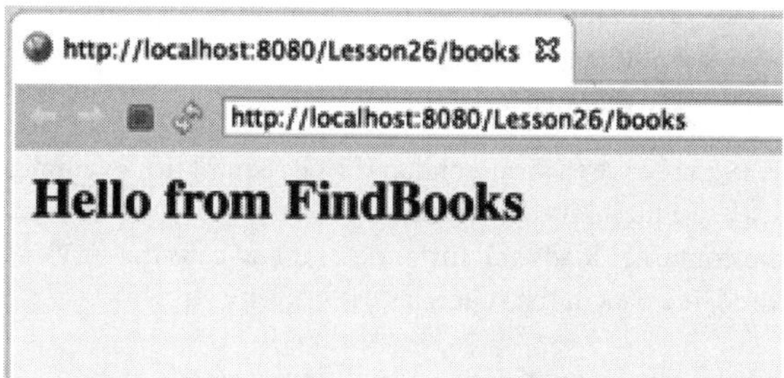

FIGURE 26-11: Changing the presentation of a web page from the servlet

Having HTML markup embedded inside servlets has some drawbacks though. You need to recompile the Java code every time the presentation changes. There are more drawbacks in having HTML embedded in Java, which are covered at the beginning of the next lesson.

HOT DEPLOYMENT

When you modify the code of a Java servlet or other application class, the server might need to be restarted or the servlet might need to be redeployed. This depends on the *hot deployment* (without the server restart) capabilities of a specific server you use. If you want to automate redeployments of your server-side Java code, consider using a third-party tool JRebel (`http://zeroturnaround.com/software/jrebel/`), which automatically reloads all your Java modifications in the server.

Deploying a Web Application as WAR

A real-world web application may consist of multiple files, and it would be easier if all of them are placed into a single archive file and deployed by placing such a file in the document root directory of your servlet container. Usually you create build scripts that that compile all required files, archive them in a WAR file, and copy this file into the deployment directory. You get familiar with a build tool called Gradle in Lesson 36.

But if you want to quickly create a WAR file by Eclipse means, just right-click the project name and select the menu Export → Web → WAR file.

In a couple of seconds you have `Lesson26.war`, a file that you can deploy in any Java EE–compliant container. Seasoned software developers wouldn't like this way of building WARs; they would argue that creating build scripts up front is the right thing to do. Because you're just making your first steps in the server-side development, though, using convenient features offered by IDE is justifiable.

BROWSER-SERVLET DATA FLOW

One servlet can serve multiple users, so let's review the entire process of client-servlet communication. Regular Java Servlets run in a container, which automatically spawns a new thread for every client's request without requiring you to do any thread programming. This sounds great and can work fine if the number of users is limited. Later in the section on asynchronous servlets you see a more scalable way of reusing threads, but for now you can concentrate on a traditional single-thread model—one thread per user.

A web page may include an HTML form, a link, or a JavaScript code that can sendan HTTP request (for example, `Get` or `Post`) to the web server. When the very first user's request hits the `FindBooksServlet` , the container check whether this servlet is up and running. If not, the container loads and instantiates it and calls the servlet's method `init()`. Even if you didn't override this method, it exists in the superclass `HttpServlet`.

SERVLET LIFE CYCLE EVENTS

If you'd like to perform some actions when the servlet is initialized or about to be destroyed, use `ServletContextListener` to intercept these events.

Then the container calls the method `service()` on your servlet's superclass, which redirects the request to `doGet()`, `doPost()`, or similar `doXXX()`, passing the arguments `HttpServletRequest` and `HttpServletResponse`. Your code can get the data that came from the web page by calling the method `getParameter()` on the `HttpServletRequest` object supplied by the servlet container to `doGet()`, `doPost()` and so on.

After you get the parameter(s), process it in the business layer, which can be implemented either as POJOs talking to some data store or as an EJB. Return the result to the client by getting the reference to the `PrintWriter` object; it knows how to send text data to the user. For non-textual results, use the class `OutputStream` instead of `PrintWriter`. Don't forget to set the content type (the MIME type (`http://en.wikipedia.org/wiki/MIME`)) by calling `setContentType()`. For example, if you are sending an object containing PDF content and want the browser to automatically open Acrobat Reader, call the function response.setContentType("application/pdf");.

The servlet container controls when the servlet is loaded, and when its init(), service(), and destroy() methods are called. The method destroy() is called when a server administrator decides to unload the servlet, the server is shutting down, or the server needs to free some memory.

If the HTTP client sent some data to the servlet, it can get them by calling getParameter() on the HttpServletRequest object. The following code gets the name of the book entered by the user in a field named booktitle and responds with the price of $65:

```
public void doGet(HttpServletRequest req, HttpServletResponse res)
                    throws ServletException, IOException {

  String title = req.getParameter("booktitle");
  PrintWriter out = res.getWriter();

  res.setContentType("text/html");

  out.println("<html><body>");
  out.println("<h2>the book "+title+" costs only $65");
  out.println("</body></html>");
}
```

HTTP GET AND POST REQUESTS

HTTP specification defines several methods for data exchange on the web, but with servlets the Get and Post methods were the most widely used ones. (In Lesson 33 you see the use of other HTTP methods.) If you don't specify the method, Get is used by default. Because I've used the method=Get in the tag <form> in Listing 26-1, the servlet container invokes the method doGet() on FindBooksServlet. With Get, the web browser appends the values entered in the form to the end of the URL after the question mark. For example, if the user enters the word Apollo as a book title, the URL may look like this:

```
http://www.mybooks.com?booktitle=Apollo
```

If a form (or a script) submits multiple values, the URL includes several key/value pairs separated by the & symbol after the question mark:

```
http://www.mybooks.com?booktitle=Apollo&author=Smith
```

With Get it's easy to copy and paste or bookmark the URL with parameters. On the other hand, with Get the data is not protected; you can see it in clear text.

The method Post is typically used to send data to the server. It also may be used for sending the binary data (for example, uploading an image) to the server. Of course, the log-in forms shouldn't use Get because you don't want the user's ID and password to be shown in the URL. To process Post requests, servlets have to override the method doPost(). It's common to use Get for data retrieval and Post for sending data to the server.

SESSION TRACKING

HTTP is a *stateless* protocol. If a user retrieves a web page with a list of books from the `FindBooksServlet` (or any other server-side program) and then goes to another web page, this second page does not know what was shown or selected on the first one. To preserve data to more than one web page, *session tracking* has to be implemented.

A session is a logical task, which the user is trying to complete by visiting a website. For example, the process of buying a book may involve several steps: book selection, input of billing and shipping information, and so on. These steps combined are an example of a session. When a purchase order is placed, the session is over.

The session information can be stored either on the client or on the server side. On the client side the user's session data can be stored using *cookies* (explained in the next section) or URL rewriting—this information is being sent back and forth from the client to the server as a part of the URL.

The server-side alternative for storing session data is a session tracking application programming interface (API) that offers a number of methods defined in the interface `HttpSession`. In this case the session data is stored only on the server, but the client gets only a session ID to identify a series of HTTP requests made by the same user. To create a session on the server, call the method on the `HttpServletRequest` object `getSession(true)`, which means "get a reference to an existing session, or create the new one." Calling this method without an argument gives you either a reference to the existing session or `null`. The next sections provide more details about session tracking.

Cookies

A cookie is a small piece of data that your servlet can send to the web client to be stored as a file on the user's computer. On every subsequent request from that client, the browser checks the local non-expired cookies (domain specific) and sends them to the server, uniquely associating the request with a given session. The cookies are persistent, but the user may disable them by selecting the appropriate setting in his web browser. Here's how the servlet can send a business-related `Cookie` to the client:

```
Cookie myCookie = new Cookie("bookName",
                             "Java Programming 24-hour trainer");
// Set the lifetime of the cookie for 24 hours
myCookie.setMaxAge(60*60*24);

response.addCookie(myCookie);
```

This is how a servlet can retrieve a client's cookies that arrive with `HttpServletRequest`:

```
Cookie[] cookies = request.getCookies();

if (cookies != null){

 // Get each cookie (a name/value pair)
 for (i=0; i < cookies.length; i++){
   Cookie currentCookie = cookie[i];
   String name = currentCookie.getName();
   String value = currentCookie.getValue();
```

```
    }
}
```

Even though you can store multiple cookies on the client, as in the preceding code, it's not a good idea to send the application data back and forth over the network. Typically the session data is stored in the `HttpSession` object described later in the section Server-Side HttpSession.

OTHER COOKIES

Besides the cookies that your servlet creates and sends to the web browser, search analytics engines may send their own cookies, too.

HTML 5 WEB STORAGE

HTML 5 supports web storage (local storage) that allows storage of key value pairs on the user's disk drive, but as opposed to cookies, these data always stay on the client side.

URL Rewriting

If a client disables cookies, the URL rewriting may be used for keeping track of the user's session. In this case the session ID and other required session data are attached to the URL string and are being sent back and forth with each client/server communication. If you've noticed something such as `jsessionid=12345` in the URL string of any website, it means that URL rewriting is being used.

SESSION ID AND SECURITY

OWASP stands for Open Source Web Application Security Project. It publishes a document titled "Top 10 Security Risks (`https://www.owasp.org/index.php/Category:OWASP_Top_Ten_Project`)." One of the top 10 risks is broken authentication and session management. Hackers can hijack a session ID presenting themselves as legitimate users.

Some applications configure the servers to switch from cookies to URL re-writing for delivering the session ID to allow the users who turned off the cookies to still use their application. Such configuration results in attaching the session ID to the URL, which makes hijacking the session easier. It's recommended to add a section `<session-config>` to the `web.xml` of your Java EE application server that includes the element `<tracking-mode>COOKIE</tracking-mode>` so that only cookies can be used for storing session IDs. This doesn't guarantee that the user's session ID won't be stolen, but will definitely lower the risk.

Server-Side HttpSession

You should keep the data that belong to a user's session (such as the shopping cart) inside the `HttpSession` object in the servlet container, which creates one such object per client. The servlet can store there any `Serializable` objects. The following line creates a session object (or finds a previously created one):

```
HttpSession mySession = request.getSession(true);
```

The `getSession(true)` call means "find this client's session object or create a new one if not found." For example, a shopping process usually consists of a number of subsequent servlet calls (list an inventory, add an item to the shopping cart, enter shipping information, and so on). The method call `getSession(true)` should be used in the very first servlet request that opens the business process qualified for a session opening. At this moment the application server generates a unique session ID (available by calling `session.getId()`) and sends it to the user's web browser using either a special cookie `JSESSIONID` or uses URL rewriting. When the browser sends an HTTP request to the server, the session ID is located in the request's header so the servlet container can find the matching session object.

The call `getSession(false)` means "find my session object," assuming that it has been created in the previous steps of the session. If this call returns `null`, the session object has been timed out or destroyed and you might want to display a message saying that the session has expired, and the user has to start the process from scratch.

I'll illustrate the concept of using `Httpsession` object by showing you an example, which includes an HTML page and a servlet. The HTML page has a form where you can enter a book title and a price to be added to your shopping cart on the server. Each time you add a book, the servlet returns a new HTML page that lists the content of the shopping cart and the form to add more books.

The initial file `ShoppingCart.html` is located in the document root directory of the project Lesson26. In the Eclipse Dynamic Web Project, the document root is represented by the directory `WebContent`. Here's the content of `ShoppingCart.html`:

```
<html>
   <head>
    <title>Add a book to shopping cart</title>
   </head>

   <body>
     Add the book title and price to the shopping cart:
     <form action=shoppingcart method=Get>
       <input type=Text name=booktitle>
       <input type=Text name=price>
       <input type=Submit value="Add to shopping cart">
    </form>
   </body>
</html>
```

Because this file is deployed in the same web application (that is, Lesson26) as the servlet, the form's action parameter doesn't include the complete URL of the servlet; the pattern—`shopingcart`—is all you need, assuming that the servlet is annotated with `@WerServlet("/shoppingcart")`. In Eclipse, you right-click the file `ShoppingCart.html` and select the Run on Server. The following URL is constructed (see Figure 26-12):

```
http://localhost:8080/Lesson26/ShoppingCart.html
```

localhost:8080/Lesson26/ShoppingCart.html

Add the book title and price to the shopping cart:

Add to shopping cart

FIGURE 26-12: Opening ShoppingCart.html deployed on the server

Don't enter the book title and the price just yet; the servlet is not ready. Before showing you the code of the servlet, let's agree that each shopping cart item will be represented as an instance of the following class `Book`:

```
class Book implements Serializable {
   String title;
   double price;
}
```

Note that the class `Book` implements `Serializable` because you're planning to keep it in the `HttpSession` object.

Next comes the `ShoppingCartServlet` class that has the URL mapping `/shoppingcart`; the web browser's request tries to find the server-side object that goes by the name `shoppingcart`. The `doGet()` method starts with printing the browser's cookies on the system console. I just want you to see that the value of the cookie `JSESSIONID` remains the same with each request made from the same browser. After that, the code works with the session object; the program comments give you some more explanations:

```
@WebServlet("/shoppingcart")
public class ShoppingCartServlet extends HttpServlet {

    protected void doGet(HttpServletRequest request,
                  HttpServletResponse response)
                   throws ServletException, IOException {

        Cookie[] cookies = request.getCookies();

        for (int i=0; i < cookies.length; i++){
              Cookie currentCookie = cookies[i];
              String name = currentCookie.getName();
              String value = currentCookie.getValue();

              System.out.println("Received the cookie "
                                             + name + "=" + value);
           }

        // Get or create a session object
        HttpSession session = request.getSession(true);

        // Try to get the shopping cart
        ArrayList<Book> myShoppingCart=(ArrayList<Book>)
                             session.getAttribute("shoppingCart");

        if (myShoppingCart == null){
```

```
            // This is the first call - instantiate the shopping cart
            myShoppingCart = new ArrayList<>();
        }

        // create an instance of a book object for received params
        Book selectedBook = new Book();
        selectedBook.title=request.getParameter("booktitle");
        selectedBook.price = Double.parseDouble(
                            request.getParameter("price"));

        // Add the book to our shopping cart
        myShoppingCart.add(selectedBook);

        // Put the shopping cart back into the session object
        session.setAttribute("shoppingCart", myShoppingCart);

        // Prepare the Web page and send it to the browser
        PrintWriter out = response.getWriter();

        // Add the content of the shopping cart to the Web page
        out.println("<body>Your shopping cart content:");
        myShoppingCart.forEach(book ->
              out.printf("<br>Title: %s, price: %.2f",
                          book.title, book.price)
           );

        //Add the HTML form to the Web page
        out.println("<p>Add another book to the shopping cart:");
        out.println("<form action=shoppingcart method=Get>");
        out.println("<input type=Text name=booktitle>");
        out.println("<input type=Text name=price>");
        out.println(
               "<input type=Submit value='Add to shopping cart'>");
        out.println("</form>");
        out.println("</body>");
    }
}
```

The very first time the servlet tries to get the shopping cart (represented by an `ArrayList`) from the session object, it won't be there, so the new instance of the `ArrayList<Book>` is created. Then the code gets the values of parameters `booktitle` and `price` (received from the web page), creates a new `Book` instance, adds it to `myShoppingCart` collection, and places it in the `HttpSession` instance for storage.

This code loops through the `myShoppingCart` collection using `forEach()` and a lambda expression just to send the content of the shopping cart with HTML to the web page. Finally, the servlet sends to the browser the same HTML form so the user can continue adding new books to the shopping cart. Figure 26-13 shows how my browser looks after adding several books to the shopping cart.

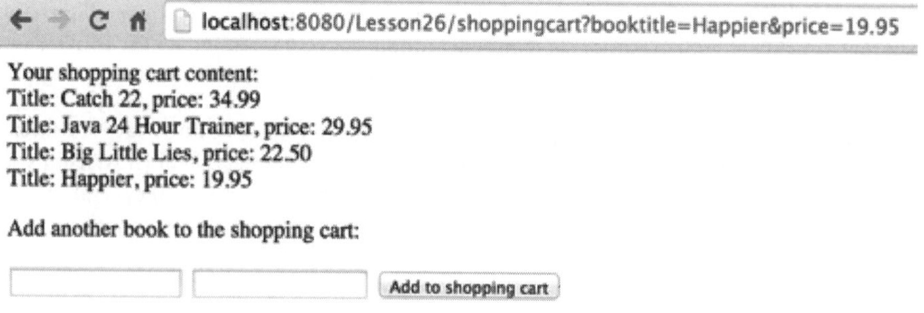

FIGURE 26-13: The web page after adding four books to the shopping cart

The `ShoppingCartServlet` doesn't have code to close the session. But you could add a Place Order to the Web Page button, and the corresponding method `placeOrder()` in the servlet, which could close the session by making the following call:

```
session.invalidate();
```

The simplest way of adding a Place Order button to ShoppingCart.html is to add yet another button of Submit type to the form:

```
<input type=Submit name=placeorder value="Place Order">
```

And in the `doGet()` method, check whether the user clicked on the button. If yes, invalidate the session.

```
if (request.getParameter("placeorder") != null) {
   session.invalidate();
}
```

If the session has not been invalidated explicitly, the application server does it automatically after a specific period (timeout). You can set the timeout programmatically by calling the method `setMaxInactiveInterval()` on the `HttpSession` object, or you can make it configurable in the external file `web.xml`. If the user closes the browser, the cookie associated with the session is destroyed and the session is closed.

SESSION LIFE CYCLE EVENTS

If you'd like to perform some actions when the HTTP session is created, invalidated, or timed out, use `HttpSessionListener`. To intercept adding or removing an attribute to a session, use `HttpSessionAttributeListener`.

Filters

Even after a servlet is deployed, you still can change the way it processes requests and responses without modifying the servlet's code. You can create *filters*, which are the Java classes that can be configured to process HTTP requests before they are passed to the servlet or when the servlet is about to return the response to the client. Filters are good for adding such functionality as authentication, logging, encryption, data compression, image conversion, and so on. Filters can even block request and response objects from passing any further.

None of these actions depend on the business logic implemented by servlets. Besides, you can create one filter (such as to authenticate the user) and apply it to multiple servlets deployed in the servlet container. What if you need to compress and encrypt the data before sending them to the client? Write two separate filters and chain them so both are applied to the same servlet. Filter classes are deployed in the `WEB-INF/classes` directory—in the same place where other compiled classes reside.

To create a filter, write a class that implements the interface `Filter` annotated with `@WebFilter`. There are three methods in this interface: `doFilter()`, `init()`, and `destroy()`. To allow filter chaining, you need to implement the `FilterChain` interface. The following code is a sample of a filter class to be used with two servlets: `FindBooksServlet` and `ShoppingCartServlet`:

```
@WebFilter(servletNames={"/FindBooksServlet","
                         /ShoppingCartServlet"})
public class MyAuthenticationFilter implements Filter {

      FilterConfig config;
      @Override
      public void doFilter(ServletRequest request,
                  ServletResponse response, FilterChain chain)
                           throws IOException, ServletException {

      // user authentication code goes here

      //Call the next filter, if need be
      chain.doFilter(request, response);

     }

     @Override
     public void init(FilterConfig filterConfig)
                           throws ServletException {

        this.config = filterConfig;
     }

     @Override
     public void destroy() {
       // Clean up system resources here
     }

}
```

The container gives the filter both request and response objects. You can check passed parameters by the client (such as by checking ID/password), perform authentication, and, if the user is not valid, call `response.getWriter()` and send the user the message "You don't belong here" without even passing control to the servlet.

The method `destroy()` is called once before the container removes the filter; if the filter has created some resources such as Database Management System (DBMS) connections, close them in the `destroy()` method.

The method `init()` is invoked on the filter object only once during its instantiation. The the servlet container gives to the `init()` method the instance of the `FilterConfig` object, which gives you access to the servlet context and initialization parameters if these are specified in the `@WebFilter` annotation (or in the file `web.xml`); for example:

```
@WebFilter(servletNames={"/FindBooksServlet",
                         "/ShoppingCartServlet"},
           initParams={@WebInitParam(name="community",
                                     value="adults")})
```

To assign several filters to the same servlet, configure them in the `web.xml` file in the the order you want them to be chained. So when you call `chain.doFilter()`, the container knows which filter to invoke next.

ASYNCHRONOUS SERVLETS

It's great that servlets automatically create and allocate a separate thread for each user's request, but each thread takes up system resources (both memory bytes and CPU cycles), and after a certain number of concurrent requests the server simply stops responding. Imagine if thousands of users simultaneously hit the `FindBooksServlet` that has to perform a three-second long DBMS search for each request. During these three seconds, the container is idling, but it holds the lock on each thread, doing nothing but waiting for the result of the DBMS query (running on another server!).

Is hard to say how many simultaneous blocking threads a specific servlet container can process in a timely manner; it all depends on the business application and the server hardware/software. Consider running load tests of your application with JMeter (`http://jmeter.apache.org/`)or similar software to get the real numbers for your hardware/software combination. I've seen a situation when a server started failing after just one of thousands of concurrent requests.

The idea of asynchronous servlets is to minimize the time of thread locking by reusing threads in the servlet container. If User A makes a request that takes three seconds on a DBMS server, his servlet container's thread is given to the request of User B, and when User A's result comes back from the DBMS, the container allocates this (or another) thread to return the result to User A. This architecture can substantially increase the number of concurrent requests that can be processed on the same server.

Java EE 7 includes Servlets 3.1, which supports asynchronous processing. In `doGet()` or `doPost()` you can instantiate the object `AsyncContext`, which creates an asynchronous worker thread and doesn't lock the client's thread while preserving the client's request and response objects. For example, the following servlet emulates a three-second blocking process, which runs in a separate thread:

```
@WebServlet(urlPatterns = {"/booksasync"}, asyncSupported=true)
public class FindBooksAsyncServlet extends HttpServlet {
    protected void doGet(HttpServletRequest request,
                         HttpServletResponse response)
              throws ServletException, IOException{
```

```
        // Don't send response when doGet ends
        AsyncContext aContext = request.startAsync();

          //Provide Runnable implementation to start method
          aContext.start(() ->{

            // a blocking operation goes here
            try{
                String title = aContext.getRequest()
                                       .getParameter("booktitle");

                PrintWriter out;
                try {
                    // Emulate a 3-second process
                    Thread.currentThread().sleep(3000);
                    HttpServletResponse resp =
                         (HttpServletResponse) aContext.getResponse();
                    out = resp.getWriter();
                    out.println("Hello from Async FindBooks");
                } catch (IOException e) {
                    e.printStackTrace();
                }
            }catch( InterruptedException e){
                e.printStackTrace();
            }finally{
                aContext.complete(); // close the response obj
            }
          });
        }
    }
```

For simplicity, I used `sleep()` on a `Thread` in this example just to emulate a long-running process. But keep in mind that in a real-world you should create threads in Java EE containers by using such classes as `ManagedExecutorService`, `ManagedThreadFactory`.

To catch some important events in the life cycle of asynchronous servlets, you can add `AsyncListener` on `AsyncContext` and provide callbacks `onComplete()`, `onError()`, and `onTimeout()`.

TRY IT

Write a simple HTML client with one text input field that has a Submit button. The user enters the stock symbol for which she wants to get a price quote. Generate a random quote and return a web page with the quote. Reuse the code from `StockServerImpl` from Listing 24-2 to generate the price quotes.

Lesson Requirements

You should have Java installed.

> **NOTE** *You can download the code and resources for this "Try It" from the book's web page at* `www.wrox.com/go/javaprog24hr2e`. *You can find them in Lesson26.zip.*

Step-by-Step

1. In the Eclipse project Lesson26 create an HTML client similar to the one from html_that_gives_404 to allow the user to enter the stock symbol. Name it `tryit.html`.
2. Create a servlet called `StockServerServlet` that takes one parameter, the stock symbol, and instantiates a class called `StockQuoteGenerator` that should have the code similar to Listing 24-2. You don't use RMI here, and there's no need to implement `Remote` interface.
3. Pass the stock symbol received from the client to `StockQuoteGenerator` and get the price.
4. Return the dynamically created HTML page to the client via the response object.
5. Test the servlet in the Eclipse IDE: right-click on the HTML file and select Run As → Run on Server. Enter the stock symbol and get the price quote.
6. Undeploy the Lesson26 project from GlassFish in Eclipse because you'll need to deploy this application directly in GlassFish. Stop GlassFish in Eclipse.
7. Export the project Lesson26 into a `Lesson26.war` file. Deploy this web application in GlassFish by copying it into the directory `glassfish/domains/domain1/autodeploy` of your GlassFish Server, installed in Chapter 25.
8. Start GlassFish Server from the command line, as described in the "Try It" section of Lesson 25.
9. Open the following URL in your web browser: `http://localhost:8080/Lesson26/tryit.html`. you should see the same Web page as in Step 5 above. Test this Web application by entering various stock symbols. You should be getting price quotes.

> **TIP** *Please select the videos for Lesson 26 online at* `www.wrox.com/go/javaprog24hr2e`. *You will also be able to download the code and resources for this lesson from the website.*

27

JavaServer Pages

The JavaServer Pages (JSP) technology was created as a next step in servlet evolution. JSP 2.3 is part of the Java EE 7 specification, and with JSP you can do everything that you can do with servlets, but more easily. In early Java EE specifications JSP was the only standardized web framework. But starting from Java EE 4 yet another web framework was introduced: JavaServlet Faces (JSF). While JSF has more features than JSP, I still see a lot more enterprise applications that use JSP, so this edition of the book covers JSP but not JSF. Now let's see why using servlets is not enough for developing of the presentation tier for all Java EE web applications.

Let's say you've created and deployed a servlet, which displays "Hello World." The servlet gets a hold of the output stream of the response object and executes the following line of code:

```
out.println("<html><body>Hello World </body></html>");
```

Now imagine that you run a software company that employs Alex, an expensive Java developer, and Matilda, a junior web designer who doesn't know Java but does know HTML. What if you need to change the layout of this HTML page, such as by adding several empty lines on top? It's not a big problem—Alex can modify the preceding line of code, recompile it, and redeploy the servlet. But for making small changes in the HTML-based user interface (UI) it's more cost-efficient to use Matilda. This is where JSP becomes very handy. Ask Matilda to create the following text file, `HelloWorld.jsp`:

```
<html>
 <body>
   Hello World
 </body>
</html>
```

Place this file into the document root directory (see Chapter 26) in your servlet container running at, say, `MyBooks.com`. Now the users can access this JSP by entering the following URL in their web browsers:

```
http://www.MyBooks.com/HelloWorld.jsp
```

Upon the first request to this page, the JSP container (all servlet containers support JSP, too) automatically generates, compiles, and deploys a servlet based on the content of the file `HelloWorld.jsp`. All subsequent calls to this JSP will be processed a lot faster because the servlet `HelloWorld` will already be deployed, loaded in memory, and running. As a matter of fact, JSP, as well as servlets, can be preloaded so that even the first user's request is responsive. You might think that you could make a simple web page by creating `HelloWorld.html` without all this extra code generation. This is true, as long as your page is static and does not use any external dynamically changed data. Remember that HTML is not a programming language but a markup language—it can't even add two and two, but JSP can (see `MyCalculator.jsp` in Listing 27-1).

EMBEDDING JAVA CODE INTO HTML

JSP defines tags that enable you to embed Java code into an HTML page. When the servlet is automatically generated behind the scenes, this Java code will also be included and executed as part of this servlet. JSP tags are included in angle brackets: for example, the `<%=...%>` tag displays the value of the variable or expression: `<%=2+2%>`. During the servlet generation process performed by the JSP engine, these tags are replaced with the regular Java code. For example, the tag `<%=2+2%>` is automatically replaced by a JSP container with the following Java statement:

```
out.println(2+2);
```

Listing 27-1 shows the content of the two-plus-two calculator called `MyCalculator.jsp`. `<br>` is an HTML tag for inserting line breaks. Note that Alex, the programmer, had to write only the expression inside the JSP tag; the rest was done by Matilda. Consider this task separation an example of the designer-developer workflow.

LISTING 27-1 MyCalculator.jsp

```
<html>
<body>
   HTML created by Matilda goes here...
   <br>
   You may not know that 2 + 2 is <%= 2 + 2%>
   <br>
   More HTML created by Matilda goes here...
 </body>
</html>
```

Deploying any JSP is a simple matter of copying the JSP file into the document root directory of your JSP container. Of course, if your JSPs are part of a multifile project, most likely you'll be deploying them in a war file, as described in Chapter 26.

As described in Lesson 26, create a Dynamic Web Project in Eclipse and name it Lesson27. Right-click the `WebContent` directory (the document root) and create a new JSP file named `index.jsp` by selecting the menu File → New → Other → Web → JSP file.

While creating the project make sure that GlassFish server is selected as the Target run time. Eclipse generates a file with the following content:

```
<%@ page language="java" contentType="text/html; charset=UTF-8"
    pageEncoding="UTF-8"%>
```

```
<!DOCTYPE html PUBLIC "-//W3C//DTD HTML 4.01 Transitional//EN"
                          "http://www.w3.org/TR/html4/loose.dtd">
<html>
<head>
<meta http-equiv="Content-Type" content="text/html; charset=UTF-8">
<title>Insert title here</title>
</head>
<body>

</body>
</html>
```

Add the following line in the <body> section of this file:

```
<h1>Hello World</h1>
```

The tag <hl> formats the text as a header, and Eclipse shows you how the future web page will be rendered (see the top portion on Figure 27-1).

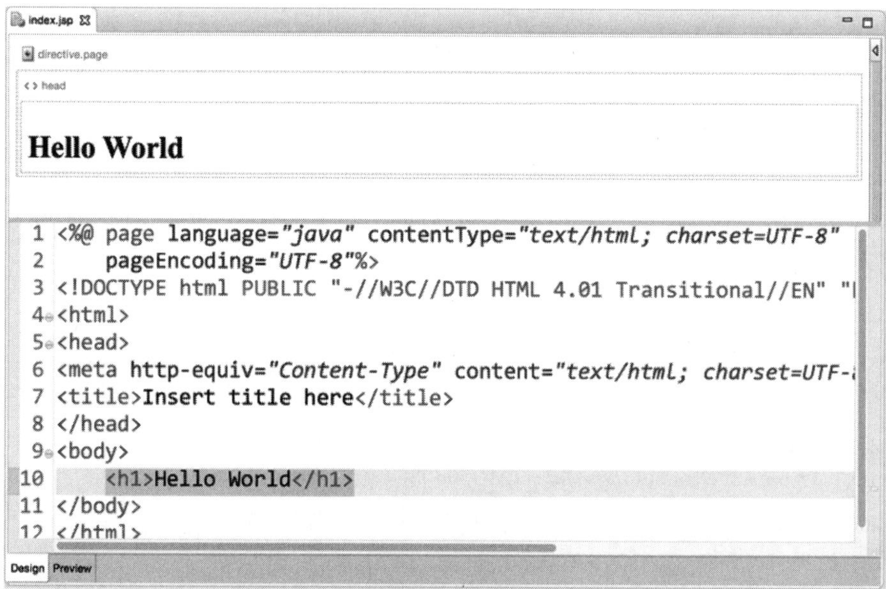

FIGURE 27-1: Viewing the page as you're adding tags

Right-click the name `index.jsp` and select Run on Server. If the GlassFish server is not running Eclipse launches it and deploys the Lesson27 project, and you see the Hello World web page in the internal Eclipse web browser, as shown in Figure 27-2.

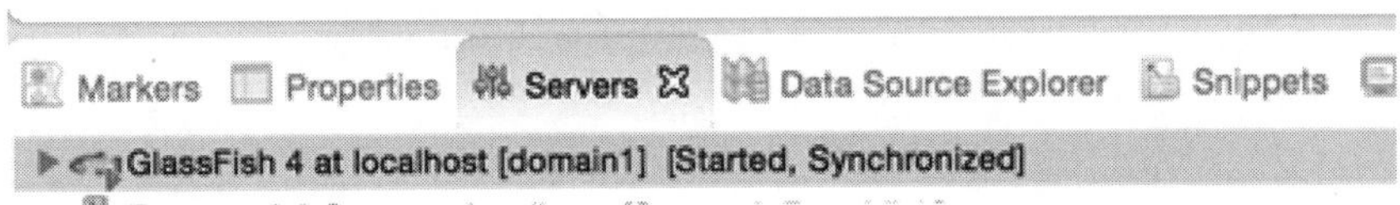

FIGURE 27-2: Runninng index.jsp in an Eclipse internal browser

Enter the same URL in your web browser, and you see the same result. The server is up and running on port 8080, and the application is deployed, so it's irrelevant which web browser you use as a client as long as it supports HTTP protocol.

Now test a JSP expression. Make a copy of `index.jsp` named `MyCalculator.jsp` in the project Lesson27 (Ctrl+C/Ctrl+V) and replace the content in the `<body>` part with the content from the `<body>` section from Listing 27-1. Run `MyCalculator.jsp` and you see the web page in Eclipse, as shown in Figure 27-3.

The expression `<%2+2%>` has been precompiled and replaced with `4`. A JSP is nothing more than a servlet that is automatically generated from a file containing valid HTML and JSP tags.

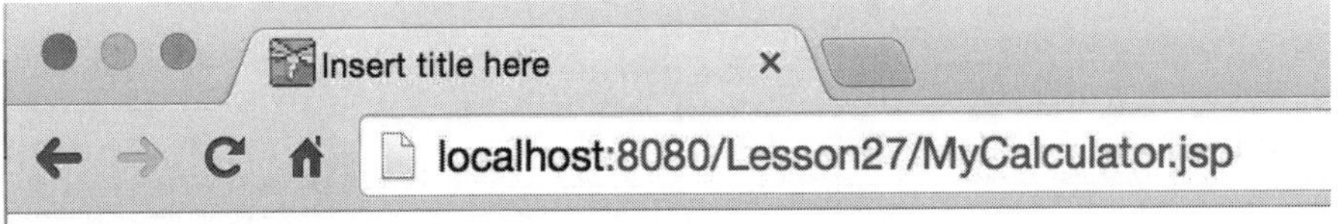

FIGURE 27-3: Running MyCalculator.jsp

If you need to change the appearance of the page (colors, fonts, data allocation) without changing the expression (2+2), Matilda can do it easily! After the changes are applied, the JSP is automatically regenerated into a new servlet and redeployed. Usually you do not even have to restart the server. The only exceptions are preloaded JSPs that are configured to be initialized on server startup. Any business logic changes inside the JSP tags will be programmed by Alex.

IMPLICIT JSP OBJECTS

Because JSPs are built on top of servlets, the main concepts remain the same. Following is the list of predefined variables that you can use in JSP pages. These variables are initialized by the JSP container, and you can use them without explicit declarations.

- `request` has the same use as `HttpServletRequest`.
- `response` has the same use as `HttpServletResponse`.
- `out` represents the output write stream `JspWriter`. This variable points at the same object as `HttpServletResponse.getWriter()` in servlets. For example, simplest JSP that returns a result from a Java class called `CurrencyConverter` might look like this:

```
<html>
  <body>
    <% out.println(CurrencyConverter.getDollarRate()); %>
  </body>
</html>
```

- `session` represents an instance of the user's `HTTPSession` object.
- `exception` represents an instance of the `Throwable` object and contains error information. This variable is available only from the JSP error page (described later in the section "Error Pages").
- `page` represents the instance of the JSP's servlet.
- `pageContext` represents the JSP context and is used with Tag Libraries (described later in this lesson in the section of that name).
- `application` provides access to web context. Its use is similar to that of `ServletContext`.
- `config` provides initialization information used by the JSP container. Its use is similar to that of the class `ServletConfig`.

OVERVIEW OF THE JSP TAGS

Each JSP tag starts and ends with an angle bracket and can be included in any HTML file, but you need to save your JSPs in `.jsp` files for proper identification and processing by JSP containers. This section is a brief overview of JSP tags. For more detailed coverage refer to the JSP documentation at `http://docs.oracle.com/javaee/5/tutorial/doc/bnagx.html`.

Directives

Directives do not generate screen output, but instruct the JSP container about the rules that have to be applied to the JSP. Some of the JSP directives are `page`, `include`, `attribute`, and `taglib`.

Page directives start with `<%@ page` and are only in effect within the current page. Directives are used with such attributes as `import`, `extends`, `session`, `errorPage`, `contentType`, and some others. For example, to import the `java.io` package use this directive:

```
<%@ page import="java.io.*" %>
```

Include directives to allow the inclusion of any text from a file or any code from another JSP, at the time when the page is compiled into a servlet, as in the following example:

```
<%@ jsp:include page="calcBankRates.jsp" %>
<%@ include file="bankRates.txt" %>
```

To use a third-party library of custom tags you need to specify where this library is located, as in the following example:

```
<%@ taglib uri="my_taglib.tld" prefix="test" %>
```

The `attribute` directive enables you to define attributes of custom tags, like this:

```
<%@ attribute name="corporate_logo_file_name" %>
```

Declarations

Declarations are used to declare variables before they are used. You can declare a variable `salary` like this:

```
<%! double salary; %>
```

The variable salary is visible only inside this page. You can declare Java methods in the JSP page the same way:

```
<%! private void myMethod(){
        ...
 }%>
```

The code contained in the declaration block turns into the Java code in the generated servlet.

Expressions

Expressions start with `<%=` and can contain any Java expression, which will be evaluated. The result will be displayed in the HTML page, replacing the tag itself, like this:

```
<%= salary*1.2 %>
```

SCRIPTLETS

Initially scriptlets were created to give JSP developers a place to put any valid Java code to be included in the generated servlet's `_jspService()` method, which is an equivalent of the servlet's method `service()`; for example, a scriptlet can look like this:

```
<% lastName = "Smith"; %>
```

With the creation of JSP Standard Tag Libraries (JSTL) and Expression Language (EL) there is now no need to use scriptlets, but this syntax still works.

Although directives, declarations, expressions, and scriplets may mix in your Java code inside the JSP, it's not a good idea. JSP was created to avoid embedding HTML into Java code, and you should also avoid embedding Java into HTML. You see how to avoid embedding Java into HTML in the section on tag_libraries. This thread (`http://stackoverflow.com/questions/9416049/removing-java-code-from-jsp-pages`) on Stack Overflow has several good recommendations on how to remove Java code from JSP.

Comments

Comments that start with `<%--` and end with `--%>` are visible in the JSP source code, but they are not be included in the resulting HTML page:

```
<%-- Some comments --%>
```

If you'd like to keep the comments in the resulting web page, use regular HTML comment notation:

```
<!-- Some comments -->
```

Standard Actions

Although the directive `include` adds the content of the included page during compile time, the element `jsp:include` does it during run time:

```
<jsp:include page "header.jsp" />
```

The element `forward` enables you to redirect the program flow from the current JSP to another one while preserving the `request` and `response` objects. The other way of redirecting the flow is to use `response.sendRedirect(someURL)` in the Java code, but in this case new `request` and `response` objects are created, which forces a web browser to make a new request to the server:

```
<jsp:forward page = "someOther.jsp" />
```

The `plugin` element ensures that your JSP includes an applet or a Java bean (described later in the "Java Beans" section). During run time the web browser replaces this tag with one of the HTML tags `<object>` or `<embed>` to embed the required Java class into the web page:

```
<jsp:plugin type=applet code="PriceQuotes.class" >
```

The nested tag `<jsp:param>` is used to pass parameters to an applet or a bean:

```
<jsp:plugin type=applet code="Login.class">
  <jsp:params>
    <jsp:param name="userID" value="SCOTT" />
    <jsp:param name="password" value="TIGER" />
  </jsp:params>
</jsp:plugin>
```

Even though it's possible to create web pages with embedded Java plug-ins, this is discouraged. These days people use a variety of web browsers and devices, and the chances that the user has the right version of the JRE installed on his or her device are slim. This was the main reason why Java Applets (`https://docs.oracle.com/javase/tutorial/deployment/applet/`) (they operate inside web browsers) are rarely being used with the exception of the back-office enterprise applications where the company system administrators can push the right version of the web browser and JRE to each user's desktop.

ERROR PAGES

Say you have a JSP called `calcTax.jsp` containing code that may throw Java exceptions. Instead of scaring users with stack trace output screens, prepare a friendly `taxErrors.jsp` explaining the problem in plain English.

`calcTax.jsp` may have an HTML `<form>` tag in which the user enters gross income and the number of dependents. The request for tax calculations is sent to the server's `CalcTax` Java class, which might throw an exception during its processing. Include in `calcTax.jsp` the name of the error page that has to be shown in case of exceptions:

```
<html>
   Some code to calculate tax and other HTML stuff goes here
       ...
      <%@ page errorPage=taxErrors.jsp %>

</html>
```

Next comes the error page `taxErrors.jsp`, which illustrates how to use the JSP variable `exception`, which displays the error message in a user-friendly way and also contains more technical error description for the technical support team:

```
<html>
 <body>
  Unfortunately there was a problem during your tax calculations.
  We are working on this issue - please try again in 10 minutes.
  If the problem persists, please contact our award-winning
  technical support team at (212) 555-2222 and provide them with
  the following information:
<br>
<%=exception.toString()>

 </body>
</html>
```

JAVA BEANS

JavaBeans specification defines *a bean* as a Java class that implements the `Serializable` interface and that has a public no-argument constructor, private fields, and public setter and getter methods. The similar concept of Data Transfer Objects (DTOs) was introduced in Chapter 21 (see Listing 21-2). Java beans are used mainly for data storing and exchange. In JSP they help avoiding mixing Java code and HTML (see also the section "Tag Libraries" later in this lesson; they also help to avoid mixing Java and HTML).

Think of the MVC pattern implemented in JSP-based web applications. The JSP belongs to the view tier; the servlet can play a role of a controller; and the Java bean can represent a model. Instead of programming business logic inside JSP, separate presentation from business logic processing and data storage. First, this enables you to split the work more easily between Alex and Matilda, and second, you're able to have more than one presentation solution (for example, a different UI for mobile devices) while reusing the same Java code.

Using Java beans is the first step in separating processing logic and presentation. Listing 27-2 shows an example of a bean, called `Student`.

LISTING 27-2 Student bean

```
import java.io.Serializable;

class Student implements Serializable{
          private String lastName;
          private String firstName;
          private boolean undergraduate;

          Student(){
              // constructor's code goes here
          }

          public String getLastName(){
                return lastName;
          }
          public String getFirstName(){
                return firstName;
          }
          public void setLastName(String value){
                   lastName = value;
          }
          public void setFirstName (String value){
                   firstName = value;
          }
          public void setUndergraduate(boolean value){
                   undergraduate = value;
          }
          public boolean isUndergraduate (){
                   return undergraduate;
          }
}
```

Don't confuse JavaBeans with Enterprise Java Beans (EJB), which is a different concept that's covered in Chapter 31.

Using JavaBeans in JSP

To use a bean with JSP, first you need to specify its name and location, and after that you can set or get its properties. Following are some examples of bean usage:

```
<jsp:useBean id="Student" class="com.harvard.Student" />
<jsp:getProperty name="Student" property="LastName" />
<jsp:setProperty name="Student" property="LastName" value="Smith"/>
```

The next code snippet populates the `Student` bean's properties `LastName` and `FirstName`. This code snippet can be located in the HTML document with the tag `<form>`, which has two HTML text input fields called `LName` and `FName`:

```
<jsp:setProperty name="Student" property="LastName"
                 value="<%= request.getParameter("LName") %>" />

<jsp:setProperty name="Student" property="FirstName"
                 value="<%=request.getParameter("FName") %>" />
```

If all bean property names are the same as the names of the HTML form fields, mapping the HTML form's and the bean's fields becomes even simpler with the asterisk notation:

```
<jsp:setProperty name="Student" property="*" />
```

How Long Does a Bean Live?

If a JSP variable is declared inside a scriptlet, it has a local scope. To give it an instance scope, declare the variable using the declaration `tag`. You can define a bean's scope using the `scope` attribute of the tag `jsp:useBean`. The following list defines the various scopes.

- `page`: The bean is available only within the current page and will be destroyed as soon as the user exits the page. This is a default scope. For example:

```
<jsp:useBean id="Student" class="com.harvard.Student"
                                     scope="page" />
```

- `request`: The bean is alive for as long as the `request` object is alive. Even if the control is redirected to a different JSP by means of the tag `jsp:forward`, the bean remains available on the new page because it's using the same `request` object, like this:

```
<jsp:useBean id="Student" class="com.harvard.Student"
                                     scope="request" />
```

- `session`: The bean is available for all pages until the user's session ends (see the section "Session Tracking" in Chapter 26).

```
<jsp:useBean id="Student" class="com.harvard.Student"
                                    scope="session" />
```

➤ `application`: The bean is available for all users and all pages—this is a global bean.

```
<jsp:useBean id="Student" class="com.harvard.Student"
                                scope="application" />
```

LOADING JSP FROM SERVLETS

In line with the separation of presentation and processing, JSP should have a bare minimum of any processing. When the servlet receives the data to be sent to the user, instead of sending hard-coded HTML tags to the client it should load and send the JSP page to the client. The JSP should be laid out by a web designer.

SHOULD SERVERS BE PREPARING WEB PAGES?

While sending a pre-created JSP to the clients is better than hard-coding HTML inside servlets, the trend is to have the server sending only the data to the client without any layout. In modern web applications, the UI is programmed using HTML, JavaScript, and Cascading Style Sheets (CSS), and you should consider sparing servers from laying out web pages. In Lesson 33 you find out how to create RESTFul Web Services, where server-side POJOs send only the data to the web browser. Learning how to develop web pages in HTML and JavaScript is out of the scope of this book, but this process is described in detail in another book I co-authored: *Enterprise Web Development* (*`http://shop.oreilly.com/product/0636920028314.do`*) (O'Reilly, 2014).

Let's say you have a servlet that needs to load a JSP based on the user's selection in the HTML window. If you don't need to get new copies of the `request` and `response` objects you'll need to create an instance of the `RequestDispatcher` class and call its method `forward()`, providing `HttpServletRequest` and `HttpServletResponse` as arguments, as shown in Listing 27-3. The servlet `MyServlet` returns to the web browser, either the JSP showing the data of the Toyota dealership or the JSP showing the data about Nissan vehicles.

LISTING 27-3 Servlet loading JSP

```
public class MyServlet extends HttpServlet{
    public void doGet(HttpServletRequest req,
                      HttpServletResponse res)
                                throws ServletException {

      ServletContext context = getServletContext();
      RequestDispatcher requestDisp = null;

      String make = req.getParameter("carMake");
```

```
            if (make.equals("Toyota") {
              requestDisp = context.getRequestDispatcher("/Toyota.jsp");
              requestDisp.forward(req,res);
            }
            else if (make.equals("Nissan") {
              requestDisp = context.getRequestDispatcher("/Nissan.jsp");
              requestDisp.forward(req,res);
            }
        }
    }
```

In some cases the current servlet performs all interactions with the user and just needs to load the code of another servlet or JSP. For this purpose, use the method `include()` instead of `forward()`:

```
requestDisp.include(req,res);
```

Because this redirection happens on the server side, the initial URL is still displayed in the web browser's address bar. To provide the new URL (to allow the user to bookmark the resulting page, for example), use `response.sendRedirect("/some_new_URL")`.

TAG LIBRARIES

Yet another way of minimizing the amount of code in JSP is to use tag libraries containing custom and reusable tags—either your own original library or a library created by someone else. Each custom tag looks similar to a regular one, but under the hood it can be supported by a Java class (or classes) written by a programmer to provide the required functionality.

If you want to create your own custom tags to be used with JSP you have to do the following:

- Create a tag library descriptor—an XML file with the extension `.tld`. It has to be deployed in the directory `WEB-INF/tags`.
- Create Java classes that provide business logic supporting the tags. Such classes are usually deployed as jars in the `WEB-INF/lib` directory.
- Register the tag library with the web application.

Listing 27-4 shows a sample tag library descriptor file. The tag `DowJones` should display a Dow Jones index value. The empty value in `<bodycontent>` means that this is a simple JSP tag with no content and could be used like this: `<sts:DowJones/>`.

LISTING 27-4 Sample .tld file

```
<?xml version="1.0" encoding="UTF-8" ?>
<taglib xmlns="http://java.sun.com/xml/ns/j2ee"
  xmlns: xsi="http://www.w3.org/2001/XMLSchema-instance"
  xsi: schemaLocation="http://java.sun.com/xml/ns/j2ee
  http://java.sun.com/xml/ns/j2ee/web-jsptaglibrary_2_0.xsd"
```

```
    version="2.0" >
    <tlib-version>1.0</ tlib-version>
    <shortname>sts</shortname>
    <uri>http://www.mystockserver.com:8080/taglib</uri>
    <info>Wall Street tag library</info>

    <tag>
      <name>DowJones</name>
      <tagclass>DowJonesHandler</tagclass>
      <bodycontent>empty</bodycontent>
      <info>Displays the Dow Jones index</info>
    </tag>
  </taglib>
```

The class supporting a JSP tag (for example, DowJonesHandler) has to implement the interface javax.servlet.jsp.tagext.SimpleTag or extend SimpleTagSupport. The JSP container will call DowJonesHandler's methods to set the JSP context (setPageContext()) to start the execution of the tag's code — doStartTag(), and so on. This class gives you a default implementation of the SimpleTag interface and initialized references to the pageContext and parent. Place required logic for the tag in the doTag() method, which is called by the container at request time:

```
import javax.servlet.jsp.*;
import javax.servlet.jsp.tagext.*;
import java.io.*;

public class DowJonesHandler extends SimpleTagSupport{

  public int doTag() throws JspException, IOException{

      String dowQuote;
     //  Obtain the DowJones quote by accessing
     //  http://finance.yahoo.com/q?d=t&s=^DJI or similar
        dowQuote=...;

     //  and write it to the client
     JspWriter out = getJspContext().getOut();
     out.print("The last price is " + dowQuote);
  }
}
```

To make a tag library recognizable by your JSP container, you should register it by inserting the following fragment into the file web.xml:

```
<taglib>
     <taglib-uri>
           http://www.mystockserver.com/taglib
     </taglib-uri>
      <taglib-location>
            /WEB-INF/taglib.tld
     </taglib-location>
</taglib>
```

When you've done all this, create a simple file called `test.jsp` and start using your tag library. The sample JSP in Listing 27-5 uses the tag `<DowJones>`.

LISTING 27-5 Using a custom tag in a JSP

```
<html>
<head>
   <%@ taglib uri=http://www.mystockserver.com/taglib
                                                  prefix="sts" %>
</head>
<body>
   Today's Dow Jones index: <sts:DowJones/>
</body>
</html>
```

If a tag requires some parameters, they should be specified in the `.tld` file with the tag `<attribute>`; for example:

```
<tag>
   ...
   <attribute>
      <name>tradeDate</name>
      <required>false</required>
   </attribute>
</tag>
```

The setter method has to be provided in the tag handler class for each parameter. Setters have to be named according to the same naming convention as Java beans:

```
public void setTradeDate(String tradeDate){
...
}
```

Custom tag libraries are created by application developers to fit the needs of a specific project(s). Third parties can also provide non-standard-based tag libraries. Apache hosts standard tag libraries (`http://tomcat.apache.org/taglibs/standard/`) based on the JSTL described next.

JSTL

JSP Standard Tag Library (JSTL) is a standardized specification for library components that includes actions that are reusable for many JSP-based applications. Standard JSTL guarantees that any Java EE–compliant JSP container will include and support these components. There are five JSTL libraries. They contain an iterator, `if` statements, tags for XML processing, tags for executing SQL, tags for internationalization, and commonly used functions.

Whereas the JSP in Listing 27-3 had to specify the location of the tag library on your server, standardized libraries have predefined URLs. For example, to use the `forEach` iterator you'd need to specify the following URI:

http://java.sun.com/jsp/jstl/core. XML processing tags are located at the following URI: http://java.sun.com/jsp/jstl/xml. Accordingly, the code fragment that uses the iterator can look like this:

```
<%@ taglib uri="http://java.sun.com/jsp/jstl/core" prefix="c" %>

<c:forEach var="item" items="${sessionScope.cart.items}">
    ...
</c:forEach>
```

For learning programming with JSTL and Expression Language please refer to the Oracle tutorial at the following URL: http://download.oracle.com/javaee/5/tutorial/doc/bnake.html.

TRY IT

Rewrite the sample stock server application that you created in the "Try It" of Chapter 26, but this time do it using JSP and Java beans. Write a simple HTML client with one text input field and a Submit button. The user should be able to enter the stock symbol she wants to get a price quote for. When the user clicks on the button generate a random quote and return a web page with the quote. Create a JSP that the server uses to provide the resulting page to the client. Reuse the code of `StockServerImpl` from Listing 24-2 from Lesson 24 for generating the price quotes.

Lesson Requirements

You should have Java installed.

> **NOTE** *You can download the code and resources for this "Try It" from the book's web page at* www.wrox.com/go/javaprog24hr2e. *You can find them in the Lesson27.zip file in the download.*

Step-by-Step

1. In the document root folderof Eclipse project Lesson27 create an HTML file `GetPriceQuote.html` that has a `<form>` tag with two `<input>` fields—a text and a Submit button—so the user can enter the stock symbol and send a request for the price quote.
   The `action` attribute of the form should point at the URL of the `StockQuote.jsp` . The `<body>` section of `GetPriceQuote.html` may look like this:

```
<body>
    <form action=http://localhost:8080/Lesson27/StockQuote.jsp
          method=Get>

        <input type="text" name="symbol"
               placeholder="Enter stock symbol">
        <input type="submit" value="Get Price Quote">
   </form>
</body>
```

2. In document root create a new JSP file named `StockQuote.jsp` that should display a requested price quote.

3. Create a Java package `lesson27.tryit`.

4. Create a class called `lesson27.tryit.StockPriceGenerator` to implement randomly generated stock quotes for the specified stock with code similar to what is shown in Listing 24-2 from Lesson 24, but it has to be a POJO.

5. Create a Java bean `lesson27.tryit.Stock` that has a private field `symbol` and public getter and setter method to get and set the symbol's value. The class `Stock` should implement `Serializable`.

6. Use JSP tags to include the `StockPriceGenerator` Java class in `StockQuote.jsp`, and display the price quote generated by its method `getQuote()` as well as the list of all available stock symbols by calling `getNasdaqSymbols()`.

7. The JSP should use `StockPriceGenerator`, `Stock`, `<jsp:useBean>`, and `<jsp:setProperty>`. For example:

```
<%@page import="lesson27.tryit.StockPriceGenerator"%>
...
<body>
  <jsp:useBean id="stock" class="lesson27.tryit.Stock" />
  <jsp:setProperty property="*" name="stock" />
  <%!StockPriceGenerator stockServer=new StockPriceGenerator();%>

   Symbol: <%=stock.getSymbol()%>
   Price: <%=stockServer.getPrice(stock.getSymbol())%>
</body>
```

8. Restart GlassFish server if it's already running. Run and test `GetPriceQuote.html` from Eclipse and your web browser. Figure 27-3 shows how it looks in my Eclipse internal web browser.

FIGURE 27-4: Running GetPriceQuote.html

> **TIP** *Please select the videos for Lesson 27 online at* `www.wrox.com/go/javaprog24hr2e`. *You will also be able to download the code and resources for this lesson from the website.*

28

Developing Web Applications with WebSockets

HTTP-based technologies like Java Servlets, JSP, or JSF use the request-response model. A web browser establishes a connection with the web server and sends a request, and then the server responds using the same connection; this is called a *half-duplex* communication. Think of a narrow bridge where cars can go only in one direction at a time.

As opposed to HTTP, WebSocket protocol (`https://en.wikipedia.org/wiki/WebSocket`) is a two-way street (a *full-duplex* communication). The data travels in both directions over the same connection. The client doesn't have to initiate the request; the server can push the data to the client when the new data is available.

Another important advantage that WebSocket protocol has over HTTP protocol is that the former adds almost no overhead to the data payload. The following list includes some of the web applications that can benefit from using the server-side data push with WebSocket protocol:

- Live trading/auctions/sports notifications
- Controlling medical equipment over the web
- Chat applications
- Multiplayer online games

Although you can create a Java client that uses raw socket connections and the Java can push the data to the client as needed, the server may be located behind the firewall or a proxy server and the company policy wouldn't allow the opening of arbitrary ports for connections. Similarly to HTTP/HTTPS, the WebSocket protocol uses standard port 80 for requests and port 443 for secure connections. These ports are usually open. Besides, all HTML5-compliant web browsers support WebSocket protocol out of the box.

WebSocket protocol was standardized (`https://tools.ietf.org/html/rfc6455`)by the open standards organization Internet Engineering Task Force (IETF), and is supported by HTML5 and Java EE 7 (JSR 356).

Besides the Java EE applications servers, websockets are supported by such popular servlet containers as Apache Tomcat 8 and Jetty 9.

This lesson shows you how to use websockets for the data exchange between web browsers and Java EE servers. But first, let's go over the limitations of HTTP protocol.

HTTP DRAWBACKS

When you see constantly refreshing data on a web page (for example a new mail notification or a stock price change), the browser actually makes multiple requests in certain time intervals asking the server, "Do you have something for me?" If the new data is available, the browser refreshes a specified location on a web page. Just visit an actively traded stock (`https://www.google.com/finance?q=AAPL`) on the Google Finance page during the stock exchange business hours, and it'll give you an impression that the server *pushes* the latest prices, but this is not the case. The Google Finance web application makes multiple AJAX requests asking for data, and the server responds.

To see it, open the Developer Tools panel in Chrome web browser (using View → Developer → Developer Tools). Then select the Network tab and click the XHR tab, where you can see the AJAX (`https://developer.mozilla.org/en-US/docs/AJAX`) requests issued by the browser. In Figure 28-1 you can see a snapshot of my screen while I was monitoring the price of Apple stock.

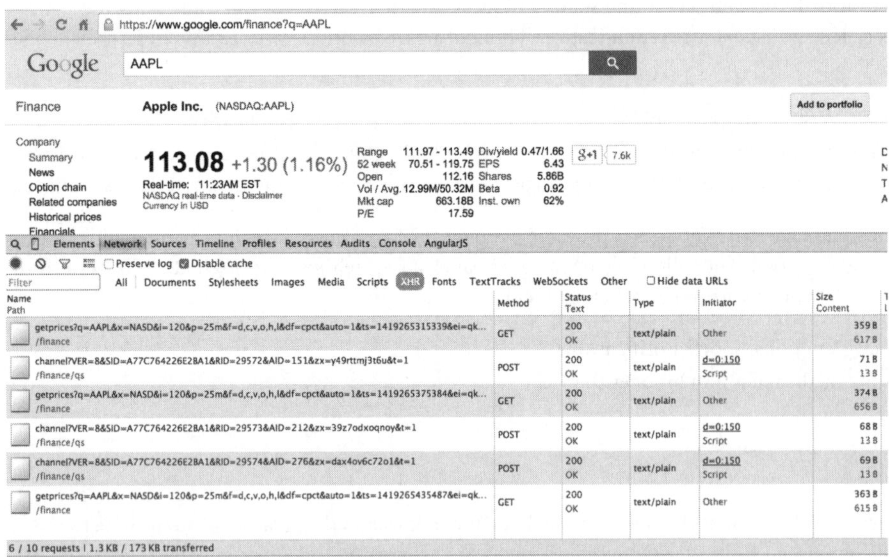

FIGURE 28-1: Monitoring AJAX requests in the Chrome browser

Note the size of these HTTP GET and POST requests on the right. Web browsers add hundreds of bytes to the actual data in the form of HTTP requests, and the server adds HTTP headers to the response, too. Besides, some of the polling requests might not even be needed because the stock price has not changed!

HTTP Hacks for Server-Side Data Push

Because HTTP doesn't support a real server-side data push, software developers came up with several hacks to emulate the push. Before the WebSocket protocol was created, the following hacks were used to update the data on the web page without requiring a user to click or touch the graphical user interface (GUI) controls such as buttons, links, and so on:

- Polling
- Long polling
- Streaming
- Server-Side Events

With polling, the web browser in the specified time intervals establishes the connection with the server and polls the server asking for new data. Many such requests may return no new data, so each client sends and receives hundreds of bytes that contain only HTTP request and response objects without any useful data payload. With polling, the web browser connects-disconnects-reconnects with the server for each request.

With long polling, the web browser establishes one HTTP connection with the server and keeps it alive until the new data arrives from the server and then reconnects.

Typically a connection is established using the browser's `XmlHttpRequest` object (for more information you need to get familiar with AJAX techniques (`http://en.wikipedia.org/wiki/Ajax_%28programming%29`), which is not covered in this book).

With streaming, the web browser establishes one HTTP connection with the server. As soon as the server gets the data ready, it starts streaming content (adding more and more data to the HTTP response object) without closing the connection. The server pushes the data to the client, pretending that the HTTP response never ends.

With Server-Side Events (`http://dev.w3.org/html5/eventsource/`) (SSE), web browsers can subscribe to events sent by a server. All modern browsers support the `EventSource` object, which can handle the Document Object Model (DOM) events. SSE allows the switch from a request-response model to a one-directional data push from server to browser.

All of the methods described here emulate a server-side data push while using request-response-based HTTP. With the WebSocket protocol you become HTTP-free, and web browsers use a bidirectional TCP-based communication with the server.

CLIENT-SERVER COMMUNICATION WITH WEBSOCKETS

When a client communicates with the server via WebSocket protocol, we say that they use *websockets*. This section discusses the entire client-server data flow starting from the client's requesting upgrade from HTTP to WebSocket protocol and ending with the client receiving the data from the server.

Besides being bidirectional, websockets have literally no overhead as only a couple of extra bytes are being added for framing the payload (the exact number of bytes varies depending on the size of the payload). Compare that with the hundreds of bytes in HTTP-based communications. The smaller overhead reduces the latency between the client and the server.

Web Browser as a WebSocket Client

A WebSocket client is typically programmed in JavaScript running inside a web browser. All web browsers released in 2012 or later support the `WebSocket` object, and the website http://caniuse.com/websockets (`http://caniuse.com/websockets`) can tell you if a specific older version of a web browser supports it, too. In JavaScript, you start with creating an instance of this object establishing a connection to the server, and then the client's part of communications comes down to processing events dispatched by the browser when the connection is opened, the message arrives from the server, and so on. Accordingly, your client-side code can perform the following actions:

1. Initiate the connection to the server's endpoint—create an instance of the `WebSocket` object providing the server's URL
2. Write an `onOpen()` callback function
3. Write an `onMessage()` callback function
4. Write an `onClose()` callback function
5. Write an `onError()` callback function

Because this book doesn't cover JavaScript programming, here I just show you an easy-to-read code fragment that performs all of the preceding steps in JavaScript running in a web browser. If you're interested in reading more about HTML5 programming, you could read *Enterprise Web Development* (`http://www.amazon.com/Enterprise-Web-Development-Building-Applications/dp/1449356818`) (O'Reilly Media, 2014), which I coauthored. The following sample JavaScript code connects to the WebSocket echo server and defines all possible callback functions:

```
if (window.WebSocket) {
    ws = new WebSocket("ws://www.websocket.org/echo");

    ws.onopen = function() {
        console.log("onopen");
    };

    ws.onmessage = function(e) {
       console.log("echo from server : " + e.data);
    };

    ws.onclose = function() {
       console.log("onclose");
    };
    ws.onerror = function() {
       console.log("onerror");
    };

} else {
   console.log("WebSocket object is not supported");
}
```

When the new instance of the `WebSocket` is created, it makes a handshake request to the server specified as a URL. The URLs start with `ws` and `wss` as opposed to `http` and `https`. The handshake's HTTP header includes the following attributes:

```
Upgrade: websocket
Connection: Upgrade
```

The request header also contains a unique value in the `Sec-Websocket-Key` attribute. If the server supports the WebSocket protocol, it returns HTTP status code 101 (switching protocols). The server applies a special hash code to `Sec-Websocket-Key`, generates another key, and places it in the `Sec-Websocket-Accept` attribute of the HTTP response header. This proves that the server supports the WebSocket protocol. After that, the client opens a WebSocket connection with the server. Now both the client and the server know each other and can start sending messages to each other without any further ceremony. If the server doesn't support websockets, it returns the status code 400—*bad request*.

When the server's message is received, the callback method annotated with `@OnMessage` is invoked on the client.

If the client sends a message, the callback method annotated with `@OnMessage` is invoked on the server. If the server returns an error, the `@OnError` callback is invoked on the client. The `@OnClose` annotated method is invoked when the connection is closed.

Similar to raw socket connections, websockets do not define the data format of the message exchange. It's the responsibility of the application to decide which *subprotocol* to use, and when the client instantiates a `WebSocket` object, it can pass to the constructor an optional parameter for the subprotocol, in which case the handshake will include the additional attribute `Sec-WebSocket-Protocol`.

To send a message from JavaScript, you can use one of the overloaded methods `send()`, which can take string or binary data (`Blob` or `ArrayBuffer`). When the client receives a message, you can do the type check in JavaScript as follows:

```
webSocket.onmessage = function(messageEvent) {
   if (typeof messageEvent.data === "string"){
      console.log("Received text data: " + messageEvent.data);
   } elseif (messageEvent.data instanceof Blob){
      console.log("Received blob data")
   } elseif (messageEvent.data instanceof ArrayBuffer){
      console.log("Received ArrayBuffer data")
  }
};
```

Communication with the Server Using WebSockets

There are two ways of implementing a WebSocket endpoint in Java on the server. To create a *programmatic endpoint* you need to extend your class from `javax.websocket.Endpoint` and override the methods `onOpen()`, `onMessage()`, `onError()`, and `onClose()`.

To create an *annotated endpoint* you need to annotate a POJO with `@ServerEndPoint`, and each of the callback methods with `@OnOpen`, `@OnMessage`, `@OnError`, and `@OnClose`. This lesson uses only the annotated end-points, which are easier to write and read.

Server-side WebSocket endpoints are deployed in `.war` files of your web modules. No other configuration is needed. In Lesson 36, you'll see how to automate deployment with Gradle.

With websockets, the client and server are peers and can initiate the message exchange independently from each other. Hence they need to know about each other. When a server-side callback method is invoked, it gets a `Session` object, which you can use to get a reference to the peer—the client—and start sending messages to it without the need of receiving any special requests. The next section demonstrates how to do such a server data push.

Hello WebSocket Example

Let's create a Hello World-style WebSocket application. I'm not going to create an example, where the client makes a request and the server responds to it. I want the server to send the message to the client first. On the Java side I'm using just one callback method, `greetTheClient()` annotated with `@OnOpen`, that will be invoked on the server as soon as the client connects. The endpoint class will be annotated with `@ServerEndPoint`.

In Eclipse, create a Dynamic Web Project called `Lesson28` with the target runtime GlassFish. Then create a Java class `HelloWebSocket` that looks like this:

```
import java.io.IOException;
import javax.websocket.OnOpen;
import javax.websocket.server.ServerEndpoint;
import javax.websocket.Session;

@ServerEndpoint("/hello")
public class HelloWebSocket {

  @OnOpen
  public void greetTheClient(Session session){
     try {
        session.getBasicRemote().sendText("Hello stranger");

     } catch (IOException ioe) {
        System.out.println(ioe.getMessage());
     }
  }
}
```

When the client connects to this WebSocket endpoint, the callback method `greetTheClient()` is invoked and the `Session` object that represents a conversation between peers is passed as an argument. The method `getBasicRemote()` returns the reference to the client's endpoint, and `sendText()` sends a text message to this client. There is no special data request from the client; the server sends the message "Hello stranger" as soon as the connection is opened.

Now let's create a simple HTML client that receives and displays the server's message. In Eclipse, right-click the document root folder `WebContent`, and create there an HTML file `index.html` by using the menu File → New → Other → HTML File. When you see a Select HTML Template pop-up window, just select the template New HTML File (5). Eclipse creates a new file with the following HTML content:

```
<!DOCTYPE html>
<html>
<head>
  <meta charset="UTF-8">
  <title>Insert title here</title>
</head>
<body>

</body>
</html>
```

Now add one empty HTML tag <span> where the server's message will be displayed. You also need a simple JavaScript code that opens the connection and declares the function to handle the onmessage callback. This is how your client should look (the manually added content is shown in bold):

```
<!DOCTYPE html>
<html>
<head>
<meta charset="UTF-8">
<title>Insert title here</title>
</head>
<body>
  <span id="messageGoesHere"></span>

  <script type="text/javascript">
    var ws = new WebSocket("ws://localhost:8080/Lesson28/hello");

    ws.onmessage = function(event) {
      var mySpan = document.getElementById("messageGoesHere");
      mySpan.innerHTML=event.data;
    };

</script>
</body>
</html>
```

When the web browser loads this file, it runs the script, instantiates the WebSocket object, and registers the onmessage() callback function. There you get a reference to the <span> tag by calling getElementById() and set its content to the payload event.data, which contains "Hello stranger."

Deploy the project Lesson28 under GlassFish (right-click the server and select the "Add and Remove" menu), right-click the file index.html, and run it on the server. You see a web page with the text Hello stranger.

PASSING PARAMETERS WITH @PATHPARAM

If you want to make your Hello WebSocket application more personal, you could ask the user for her name, save it in a JavaScript variable, and attach the name to the URI so the web client would connect to the following URI:

```
ws://localhost:8080/Lesson28/hello/Mary
```

Accordingly, on the server side you need to use a different URI value in `@ServerEndpoint` and the `@PathParam` annotation:

```
@ServerEndpoint("/hello/{userName}")
public class HelloWebSocket {

  @OnOpen
  public void greetTheClient(Session session,
                       @PathParam String userName){
   ...
  }
```

The value "Mary" is injected in the method argument `userName`, and you can process it as any other method argument.

That's all there is to it. This was an example of a server data push to the client. Now imagine that the server would be retrieving stock quotes or auction bids from a third-party server. The same technique can be used for refreshing the data in the browser's window without any polling requests from the client.

Monitoring WebSocket Network Traffic

Google Chrome browser allows monitoring of the WebSockets traffic. I'm using the `HelloWebSocket` example from the previous section to show you what went over the wire. First, open the URL `http://localhost:8080/Lesson28/index.html` in Chrome, and then open Developer Tools and refresh the web page. The Network tab includes the WebSockets section. The data is sent in chunks called *frames*, and you can see "Hello stranger" in the Data column under the tab Frames, as shown in Figure 28-2.

In Figure 28-2, note that the length of the frame is only 14 bytes, where the length of the data is 13 bytes. No HTTP headers are present during the message exchange. The headers were only present during the initial handshake and the protocol upgrade. You can see them under the Headers tab, as shown in Figure 28-3.

You can see that the request header asked for a connection upgrade, and the GlassFish server has accepted it in the response header.

Chrome Developer Tools offer an easy way to monitor traffic between WebSocket peers. But if you'd like to peek inside the frames of WebSocket messages, use the network packet analyzer called WireShark (`http://www.wireshark.org`).

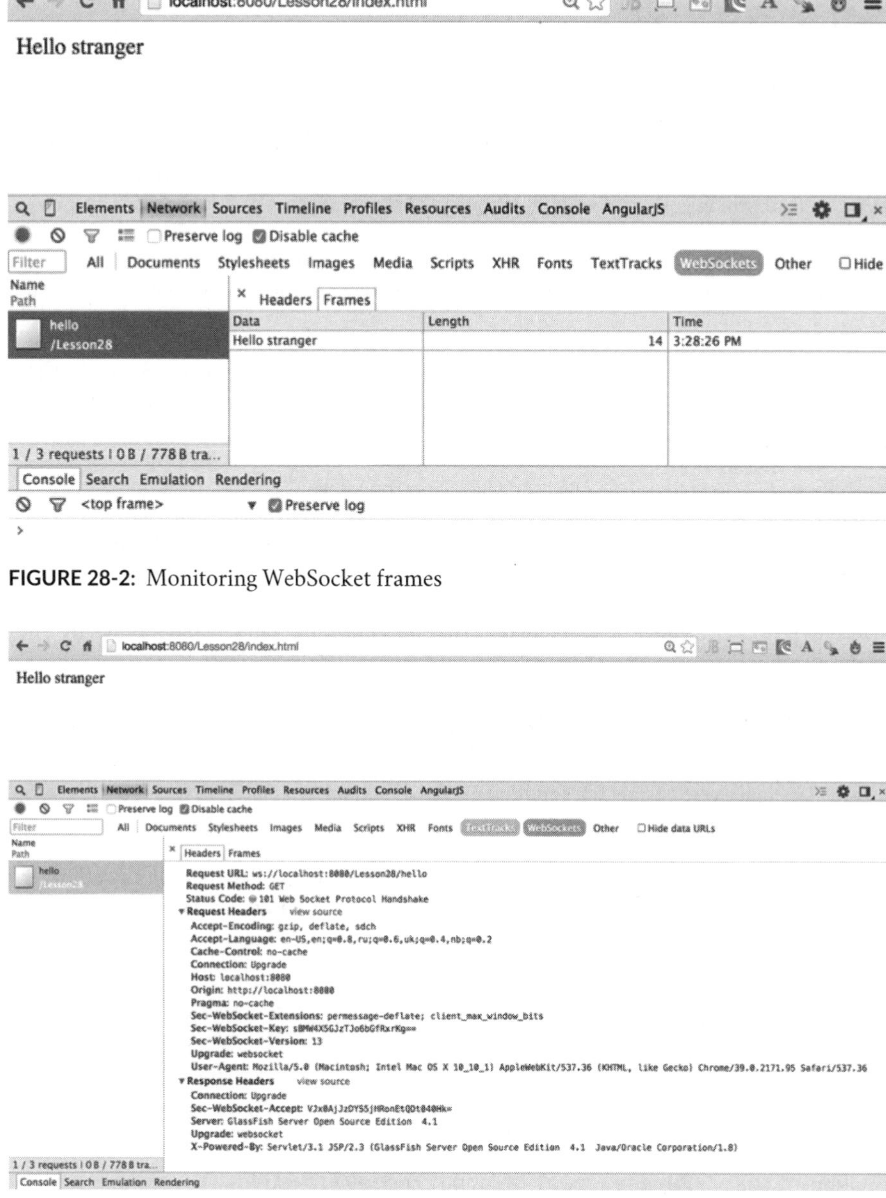

FIGURE 28-2: Monitoring WebSocket frames

FIGURE 28-3: The handshake HTTP headers

Sending Messages

If you want to send the message from a JavaScript client, just use the method `WebSocket.send()`, which can take text or binary objects as arguments. On the Java side you use different methods of sending data depending on the object data type. For example, use the method sendText() from the object javax.websocket.RemoteEndpoint.Basic as you did in the HelloWebSocket example:

```
session.getBasicRemote().sendText("Hello stranger");
```

The method getBasicRemote() returned an instance of the RemoteEndpoint.Basicobject, which performs a blocking call to the peer. For sending asynchronous non-blocking messages, use the object RemoteBasic.Async instead, which you can obtain by calling getAsyncRemote() on the Session object.

If you're not planning to send text, use such methods as sendObject(), sendBinary(), or sendStream(). The sender and receiver should ensure that the data types of the messages being sent are the same.

The server can also send a special control message known as *ping* to check whether the connection is alive. The ping may contain a small amount (up to 125 bytes) of application data, but usually it's just some control word to identify the ping:

```
session.getBasicRemote().sendPing(ByteBuffer applicationData);
```

If the connection is alive, the web browser returns a *pong* of type PongMessage, which can be handled by the server endpoint in the @OnMessage annotated method.

The client can't initiate a ping, though. You need to manually program some ping counter, and if pings are not coming from the server for more than a specified time interval, the client should reconnect.

Receiving Messages Using @OnMessage

The method in your Java class that's responsible for handling messages should be annotated with @OnMessage annotation. The method must have at least one argument defining the type of the expected message.

If such a method returns a value, it's sent to the peer as a message and should be handled there as any other WebSocket message. For example, the following message handler expects a String message and returns a String that is sent as a message to the peer:

```
@OnMessage
public String getStockPrice(String symbol){
    String stockPrice;
    // The code to get the stock price goes here
    return stockPrice;
}
```

The online documentation (https://javaee-spec.java.net/nonav/javadocs/javax/websocket/OnMessage.html) for the @OnMessage annotation offers a choice of parameters:

- Exactly one parameter (text, binary, or a PongMessage)
- Zero to n String or Java primitive parameters annotated with the PathParam (https://javaee-spec.java.net/nonav/javadocs/javax/websocket/server/PathParam.html) annotation for server endpoints
- An optional Session parameter

The `String` type parameters are used for sending textual data, `ByteBuffer` is for any binary data-like images, videos, or any BLOB. The server-side ping and the client side pong (the `PongMessage`) are used in WebSockets for heartbeats—to keep the client-server connection alive.

Your endpoint class can declare up to three message handlers annotated with `@OnMessage`: one for each message type (text, binary, and pong).

An optional parameter `Session` (you used it in the `HelloWebSocket` example with `@OnOpen`) is needed if the server has to perform actions like sending a message to a specific client, getting parameters associated with the client's request (for example, user preferences), or close the current conversation.

ENDPOINT INSTANCES

By default, a WebSocket container creates a separate endpoint instance for each client's connection, and the `Session` object can be used for storing the client's state on the server. If you prefer to have one endpoint instance shared by multiple clients, you need to use the `@OnOpen` annotation with an additional optional parameter `ServerEndpointConfig.Configurator` (see the javadoc (`http://docs.oracle.com/javaee/7/api/javax/websocket/server/ServerEndpointConfig.Configurator.html`) for details) and override the method `getEndpointInstance()` on the configurator.

A message handler method can return `void`, primitives and their wrapper classes, a byte array `byte[]`, `ByteBuffer`, or your custom objects for which the encoder exists (covered in the next section).

JAVA-BASED WEBSOCKET CLIENTS

JSR 356 describes how to write WebSocket clients in Java using an annotation `@ClientEndpoint`. Programming WebSocket Java clients is very similar to what you did on the server; you still need to annotate methods with `@OnOpen`, `@OnMessage`, and so on.

A web browser offers an instance of the `WebSocket` object so it can connect to the server endpoint without any special preparations. But if you write a WebSocket client in Java, you need to obtain the reference to the `WebSocketContainer` object first, and then you can connect to the server with the method `connectToServer()` providing the URI of the server's endpoint. To compile a Java client, you have to include in the CLASSPATH some implementation (jars) of JSR-356 for the client —for example, Project Tyrus (`https://tyrus.java.net/dependencies.html`). Refer to Oracle's WebSocket tutorial (`https://docs.oracle.com/javaee/7/tutorial/websocket.htm#GKJIQ5`) for details of developing WebSocket clients in Java.

ENCODERS AND DECODERS

WebSocket protocol doesn't define an application-specific protocol for data exchange, but it has a place to specify one of the supported subprotocol names (`https://www.iana.org/assignments/websocket/websocket.xml#subprotocol-name`) that can be used in your application. For example, one of the popular messaging protocols is called STOMP (`http://stomp.github.io/`), and you can find some relevant examples by searching for "Stomp Over WebSocket" online.

Besides, the Java implementation of the WebSocket protocol allows you to transform the message payload from one format to another during the client-server data exchange. Custom classes that perform this transformation are called *decoders* and *encoders*.

For example, a web browser sends a JSON-formatted string (see Lesson 33 if you're new to JSON) to your Java WebSocket endpoint. You can create a class `JsonToPojoDecoder` that parses the incoming string and turns it into a POJO of specified type. Similarly, you can create a class `PojoToJsonEncoder` that serializes each POJO to a JSON string on the way from the Java EE server to the user's web browser. The diagram in Figure 28-4 depicts the decoder and encoder classes in a message exchange.

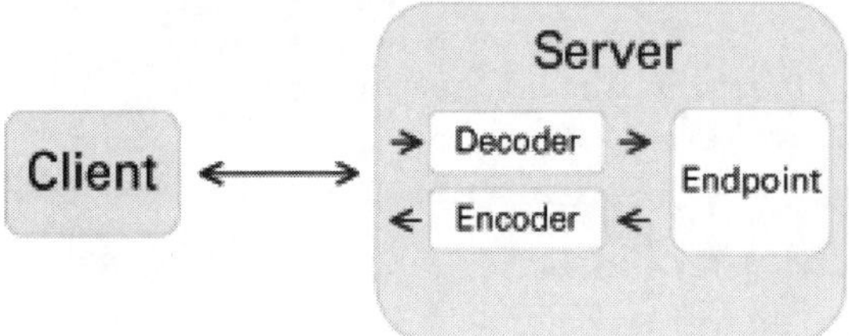

FIGURE 28-4: Encoders and decoders in the message exchange

Now I'll show a sample application to get a stock price quote that uses a decoder and encoder.

Earlier, in the `HelloWebSocket` example, you used only the `value` parameter `"/hello"` in the annotation `@ServerEndpoint`. But this annotation has four more optional parameters: `decoders`, `encoders`, `subprotocols`, and `configurator`. You use the decoders and encoders parameters in the class `StockServerEndpoint` shown next (import statements are omitted for brevity):

```
@ServerEndpoint(value = "/stockprice",
                encoders = {StockEncoder.class},
                decoders = {StockDecoder.class})
public class StockWebsocketEndpoint {

    @OnMessage
    public Stock getPriceQuote(Stock stock){

        stock.price =Math.random()*100;
        return stock;
    }
}
```

This endpoint invokes the method getPriceQuote() when the message arrives from the peer. This method generates a random stock price. Note that both the argument and the return value of the method getPriceQuote() are of Java type Stock shown next:

```
public class Stock {
    public String symbol;
    public double price;
}
```

If a WebSocket client is also written in Java there is no problem here. But a typical client is written in JavaScript, which runs in a browser and sends the data to the server as text. Accordingly, the client running in the web browser may expect the data as a formatted text and not a Java object.

To do these data conversions, write a decoder that converts the text into the Stock object and an encoder that converts a Stock object into text. The decoder class has to implement either Decoder.Text or Decoder.Binary interface. Our class StockDecoder implements Decoder.Text:

```
public class StockDecoder implements Decoder.Text<Stock>{

    @Override
    public void init(EndpointConfig config) {}

    public Stock decode(String symbol) throws DecodeException {
        System.out.println("In Decoder: converting " + symbol +
                           " into Stock object");
        Stock stock = new Stock();
        stock.symbol=symbol;
        return stock;
    }

    public boolean willDecode(String symbol) {
        System.out.println("Allowing decoding");
        return (symbol != null);
    }

    public void destroy() {}
}
```

You can find details of the Decoder.Text in the online documentation (http://docs.oracle.com/javaee/7/api/javax/websocket/Decoder.Text.html). In short, the method decode() intercepts the incoming message from the client, and your code transforms the message into a required Java object. The returned value from decode() is passed to the getPriceQuote() method of the StockWebsocketEndpoint class. The method decode() just creates an instance of the Stock object and assigns the received name of the stock to its field symbol.

The method willDecode() checks whether the given String can be encoded into the requested object—the Stock. You just checked it for null, but if some prerequisites would have to be met to allow the transformation, you could implement that logic here. In the example you don't need to perform any actions on initialization or destruction of the decoder instance; hence why the mandatory methods init() and destroy() have no code.

The encoder class is engaged when the method `getPriceQuote()` is returning the instance of the `Stock` object with populated `symbol` and `price`. You need to serialize the Java object into text to be sent to the browser. This is how your class `StockEncoder` will look:

```
public class StockEncoder implements Encoder.Text<Stock>{

    public void init(EndpointConfig config) {}

    public String encode(Stock stock) throws EncodeException {
        System.out.println(
              "In Encoder: Serializing Stock object into String");

        return stock.symbol + ": " + stock.price;
    }

    public void destroy() {}
}
```

The method encode takes a `Stock` object as an argument and turns it into a `String` by concatenating `symbol` and `price`. I purposely use such simple conversion because my goal is to explain how the encoder works and not the conversion options. But you can implement any transformation you like here. Most likely, you'll be doing Java to JSON conversion if the client runs in a web browser.

You're done coding the server side. The code is for the HTML page `decodersdemo.html` that will be sending the price quote requests:

```
<!DOCTYPE html>
<html>
<head>
<meta charset="UTF-8">
<title>Insert title here</title>
</head>
<body>
  <form>
    <input id="stockSymbol" type="text">
    <input onClick= "getPriceQuote()" type="button"
                                        value="Get Price">
  </form>

  <span id="priceQuote"></span>

  <script type="text/javascript">
    var ws = new WebSocket(
                      "ws://localhost:8080/Lesson28/stockprice");

    ws.onmessage = function(event) {
       var mySpan = document.getElementById("priceQuote");
       mySpan.innerHTML=event.data;
    };

    function getPriceQuote(){
        var symbol = document.getElementById("stockSymbol");
        ws.send(symbol.value);
```

```
    }

</script>
</body>
</html>
```

This web page has an input field and a Get Price button. When the browser loads this page, it executes the JavaScript code that connects to the server endpoint `ws://localhost:8080/Lesson28/stockprice`. The user enters the stock symbol and clicks the button, which invokes the JavaScript function `getPriceQuote()` that sends the entered symbol to the WebSocket server for processing.

On the server, the decoder converts the symbol into a `Stock` object, and the Java method `getPriceQuote()` populates its price field. The encoder turns the `Stock` object into text and sends it back to the web browser.

Figure 28-5 shows how my web page looked when I directed my web browser to `http://localhost:8080/Lesson28/decodersdemo.html`, entered IBM in the input field, and clicked the Get Price button.

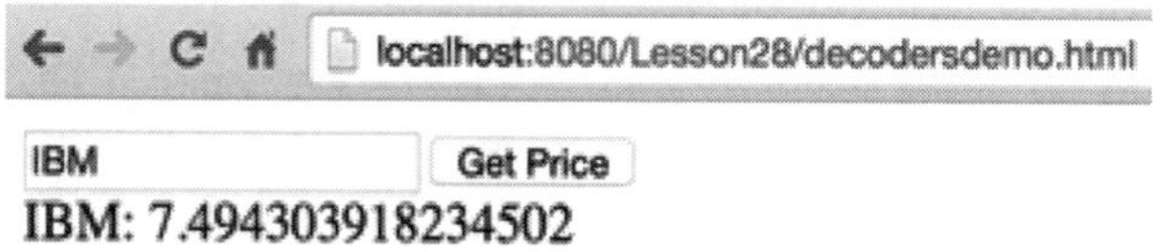

FIGURE 28-5: Testing decodersdemo.html

> **DEBUGGING JAVASCRIPT**
>
> Google Chrome (as well as all other web browsers) offers an easy way to debug JavaScript. For example, I made a typo in the JavaScript function `getPriceQuote()`, but there is no compiler that could have pointed out my error. The symbol was arriving to my Java endpoint as `undefined`. Using Chrome Developer Tools I put a breakpoint inside the function `getPriceQuote()` and quickly found the typo. You can read about debugging JavaScript in Chrome in the product documentation (`https://developer.chrome.com/devtools/docs/javascript-debugging`).

PUBLISHING TO ALL CLIENTS

Pretty often you need to write a program that publishes the same message to all connected clients. For example, multiple clients of the online auctions have to be notified when a new bid is placed on the product. Another example is when a new stock price quote needs to be pushed from the server to all connected clients. With WebSockets it's a pretty easy task.

I'll show you a basic example when a WebSocket endpoint pushes the server's time to all connected clients. If you can publish the server's time to all connected clients, you can publish any application-specific data.

The following endpoint `WebSocketClock` schedules the task that gets and formats the server's time every second and publishes the time to all connected clients. I schedule this timer once when the first client connects to the endpoint. The method `sendTimeToAll()` finds all connected clients by invoking `getOpenSessions()` on the `Session` object. Then on each session it calls `getBasicRemote().sendText()`.

```
@ServerEndpoint("/clock")
public class WebSocketClock {

  static ScheduledExecutorService timer =
       Executors.newSingleThreadScheduledExecutor();

  private static Set<Session> allSessions;

  DateTimeFormatter timeFormatter =
          DateTimeFormatter.ofPattern("HH:mm:ss");
  @OnOpen
  public void showTime(Session session){
      allSessions = session.getOpenSessions();

      // start the scheduler on the very first connection
      // to call sendTimeToAll every second
      if (allSessions.size()==1){
        timer.scheduleAtFixedRate(
             () -> sendTimeToAll(session),1,1,TimeUnit.SECONDS);
      }
     }

   private void sendTimeToAll(Session session){
     allSessions = session.getOpenSessions();
     for (Session sess: allSessions){
        try{
          sess.getBasicRemote().sendText("Local time: " +
                    LocalTime.now().format(timeFormatter));
          } catch (IOException ioe) {
              System.out.println(ioe.getMessage());
          }
     }
  }
}
```

The web client looks similar to the Hello WebSocket example:

```
<!DOCTYPE html>
<html>
<head>
<meta charset="UTF-8">
</head>
<body>
  <span id="messageGoesHere"></span>

  <script type="text/javascript">
    var ws = new WebSocket("ws://localhost:8080/Lesson28/clock");
```

```
    ws.onmessage = function(event) {
      var mySpan = document.getElementById("messageGoesHere");
      mySpan.innerHTML=event.data;
    };

    ws.onerror = function(event){
        console.log("Error ", event)
    }
</script>
</body>
</html>
```

Figure 28-6 shows a screenshot where the Eclipse internal browser, Chrome, and Firefox show the current time published by the WebSocket endpoint.

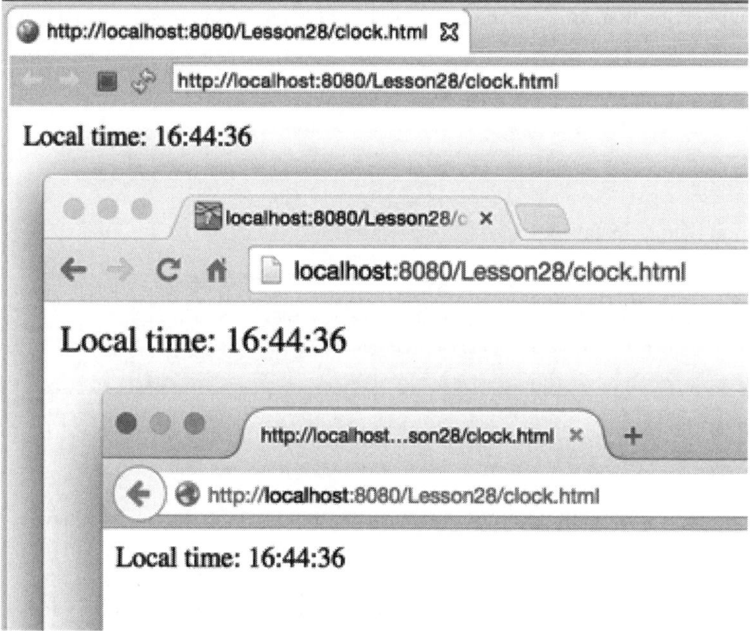

FIGURE 28-6: Three web clients get current time published by a WebSocket endpoint

You'll find this example useful while working on the "Try It" assignment, where you'll need to push the stock price quote to multiple clients.

OPTIMIZING PERFORMANCE IN MESSAGE PUBLISHING

Iterating through all open sessions works fine if the number of connected clients is small. But if you have hundreds of clients, consider grouping the `Session` objects into separate collections in an `@OnOpen` message handler and sending messages to each group in parallel from multiple threads. Important: By default, a Java EE server creates a new instance of the server endpoint class for each client's connection, so if you'll be creating your own session collections they must be `static`:

```
private static Set<Session> sessionsChunk1 =
           Collections.synchronizedSet(new HashSet<>());
private static Set<Session> sessionsChunk2 =
           Collections.synchronizedSet(new HashSet<>());
...
```

TRY IT

Rewrite the sample Stock Server application that you created in the "Try It" of Lesson 27, but this time do it using WebSockets. Create an HTML-based WebSocket client.

Lesson Requirements

You should have Java, GlassFish, and Eclipse installed.

> **NOTE** *You can download the code and resources for this "Try It" from the book's web page at* `www.wrox.com/go/javaprog24hr2e`. *You can find them in the Lesson28 folder in the download.0*

Step-by-Step

1. Reuse the dynamic web project `Lesson28` that you created earlier in this lesson. If you don't have it, download and import it from the book's website.
2. Create an HTML client `GetPriceQuote.html` similar to the one from the section Decoders and Encoders. It should have one text input field to enter the stock symbol and the Get Price button. The user has to enter the stock symbol she wants to get a price quote for and press the button. The server should generate random quotes for the selected stock.
3. Create a server endpoint similar to the class `StockWebSocketEndpoint`from the section Decoders and Encoders, but this time reuse the classes `Stock` and `StockPriceGenerator` from the Try It section from Lesson 27.
4. Implement a timer that generates a new random price quote every five seconds. For the reference use the `ScheduledExecutorService` from the class `WebSocketClock` from the section "Pushing to All Clients."
5. Deploy the project `Lesson28` in GlassFish and start the server.

6. Run the web page `GetStockPrice.html` inside Eclipse or in your web browser and test the application. Enter one of the stock symbols; the web page should should refresh the stock price every five seconds. The user should be able to enter a new stock symbol at any time and the price for the newly selected stock should be displayed and refreshed.

> **TIP** *Please select the videos for Lesson 28 online at* `www.wrox.com/go/javaprog24hr2e`. *You will also be able to download the code and resources for this lesson from the website.*

29

Introducing JNDI

Instead of having distributed Java programs that instantiate lots of reusable objects over and over again, it's better if these objects are pre-created and published at a known server, where they can be easily and quickly found. Lesson 24 introduces a registry concept, in which a Java object can be published under some name so the client can look it up.

Java Naming and Directory Interface (JNDI) is also about registering and finding objects in distributed applications. JNDI is an application programming interface (API) that can be used for binding and accessing objects located in Java EE or specialized naming servers that play roles similar to that of a company telephone directory assistance service. But instead of looking for people's information, you look for objects. Various software vendors offer specialized directory assistance software, and JNDI provides a standard API to read from and write to such directories.

Every Java EE application server comes with an administrator's console that allows you to manage objects in a JNDI tree. This lesson introduces you to the JNDI concepts, and you see how to use JNDI for publishing (and looking up) *administered objects* (that is, configured by the server administrator). Some examples of administered objects are database connection pools and message queues (explained in Lesson 30).

NAMING AND DIRECTORY SERVICES

A *naming service* enables you to add, change, or delete names of objects that exist in some naming hierarchy so other Java classes can look them up to find their location. One more analogy: In a library, you find the name of the physical location of the book in a directory and then go to the shelf to pick up the book. A naming service provides a unique name for every entry that is registered with (*bound to*) this service. Every naming service has one or more *contexts*—think of directories and subdirectories in a file system, where any directory tree with children is a context. The naming tree originates from a root node, which is also known as an *initial context* (like a root directory on the disk).

A *directory service* enables you to search the naming tree by object attributes rather than object names. One example is that of the domain name system, which is a distributed naming system that takes the domain name of a networked computer or service and returns the IP address and port number of the resource.

To allow clients to do lookups, there has to be a process that initially binds the objects to a naming tree. This can be handled via a sever administration console or an independent program that (for example) binds employee names to a directory server of some organization. Java EE servers bind such objects as EJB, Servlets, JMS, and database connection pools to their naming servers during startup.

All classes and interfaces that support JNDI are located in the package `javax.naming` that comes with Java EE SDK.

USING THE CLASS INITIALCONTEXT

The class `InitialContext` represents the root of a JNDI tree in a naming server. There are two ways of getting a reference to a particular resource that was bound to this tree:

- If your Java code runs inside Java EE server, it can can *inject* the JNDI resource into your program by using `@Resource` annotation. Your program can also run a `lookup()` on the `InitialContext` object.
- If an external Java program needs a JNDI resource (for example, a standalone messaging program needs to get references to the message queues bound to the JNDI tree of an application server), it has to get a reference to the `InitialContext` and then invoke the method `lookup()`.

Getting a Reference to InitialContext

Explicit instantiation of `InitialContext` is needed only if you are planning to use `lookup()` as opposed to resource injection, which is explained in the next section. If a Java program runs inside the application server, instantiating the `InitialContext` object comes down to one line of code:

```
Context initContext = new InitialContext();
```

If a Java program runs outside of the application server, you need to specify the location of the server, the names of the vendor-specific classes implementing `InitialContext`, and the access credentials. For example, for the WildFly application server, the following code may be used (given that you know the security credentials):

```
final Properties env = new Properties();
env.put(Context.INITIAL_CONTEXT_FACTORY,
        "org.jboss.naming.remote.client.InitialContextFactory");
env.put(Context.PROVIDER_URL, "http-remoting://127.0.0.1:8080");
env.put(Context.SECURITY_PRINCIPAL, "Alex123");
env.put(Context.SECURITY_CREDENTIALS, "MySecretPwd";

Context initContext = new InitialContext(env);
```

If an external program needs to access the `InitialContext` object in the GlassFish server, the code may look like this:

```
final Properties env = new Properties();
env.setProperty("java.naming.factory.initial",
           "com.sun.enterprise.naming.SerialInitContextFactory");
env.setProperty("java.naming.factory.url.pkgs",
           "com.sun.enterprise.naming");
env.setProperty("java.naming.factory.state",
    "com.sun.corba.ee.impl.presentation.rmi.JNDIStateFactoryImpl");
env.setProperty("org.omg.CORBA.ORBInitialHost", "localhost");
env.setProperty("org.omg.CORBA.ORBInitialPort", "8080");

InitialContext initContext = new InitialContext(env);
```

You need to read the documentation that comes with your application server to get the proper code for accessing JNDI from an external program.

After receiving a reference to `InitialContext`, you can invoke a `lookup()` method specifying the name of the required resource. Lesson 30 explains Java messaging in detail, but for now I'll just show you an example of getting a reference to a message queue named `test`:

```
Destination destination = (Destination)
                     initContext.lookup("jms/queue/test");
```

The next code samples show how to get a reference to an EJB and a default JDBC data source:

```
MySessionBean msb = (MySessionBean) initContext.lookup(
                                "java:comp/env/ejb/mySessionBean");

DataSource ds = (DataSource) initContext.lookup(
                          "java:comp/env/jdbc/DefaultDataSource");
```

The next section shows you an example of preferable way of getting JNDI resources by injection.

Injecting JNDI Resources

Most likely, your Java programs that need JNDI resources will run inside some Java EE application server, which greatly simplifies getting a hold of such resources. In this case you don't even need to instantiate `InitialContext` or invoke `lookup()`.

Resource injection with the annotation `@Resource` is a cleaner and simpler way of providing these resources to your Java EE components. In Lesson 30 you use resource for getting references to JMS objects, which look as follows:

```
import javax.annotation.Resource;
...
@Resource(name="MyTestConnectionFactory")
private ConnectionFactory factory;

@Resource(name="MyJMSTestQueue")
private Queue ioQueue;
```

For example, you could place this code in a Java servlet, which sends messages to a `Queue` bound to the JNDI tree under the name `MyJMSTestQueue` with the help of the `ConnectionFactory` that has the JNDI name `MyTestConnectionFactory`. These resources are injected into variables `ioQueue` and `factory` by the servlet container—no need to do a lookup.

Depending on its location, the time of injection varies. If you put the `@Resource` annotation at the class level, the resource is injected during run time when the application looks it up. If you put this annotation above the field or setter method declaration, the resource is injected in the component when the application is initialized.

If you need to override resources specified in annotations, you can do it in XML configuration files. You see more examples of using resource injection with EJB in Chapter 31. Later in this lesson you use resource injection of JDBC `DataSource`. Meanwhile, take a look at the GlassFish Administration Console.

ADMINISTERING JNDI OBJECTS IN GLASSFISH

Each Java EE application server offers a tool that allows administration of its service modules; we are interested in binding objects to their directory names. When you start GlassFish there is a message on the console: "Waiting for DAS to start..." DAS stands for Domain Administration Server, which authenticates the user with administrative privileges and responds to requests from a graphical web browser-based Admin Console. To use the console enter the following URL in your browser: `http://localhost:4848/`. You see the console, as in Figure 29-1.

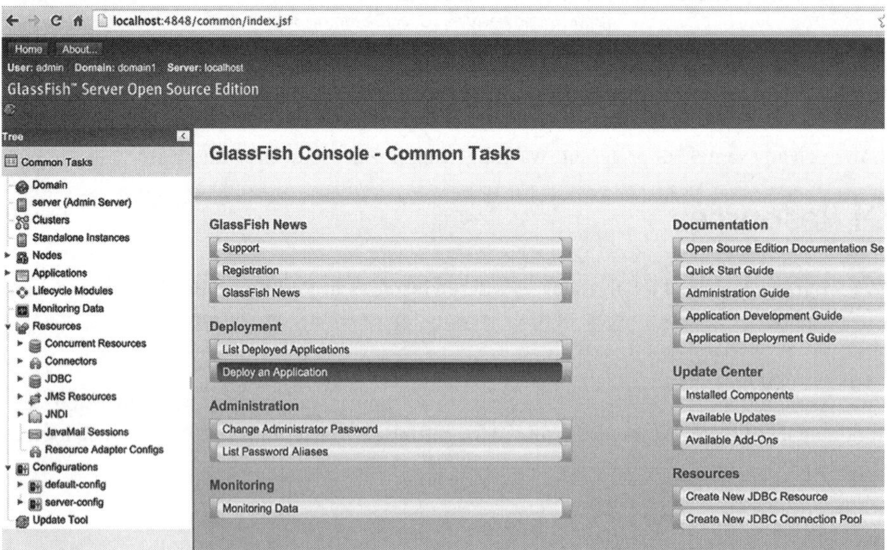

FIGURE 29-1: GlassFish Administration Console

Administration Console enables you to configure your instance(s) of GlassFish server and administer various resources that should be available to Java EE applications. In Lesson 30 you see how to configure JMS resources.

DATASOURCE AND JNDI

In Lesson 21, in the section "Connection Pools and Datasource," you learn that creating a new connection object for each request is a slow operation, and it's better to work with database connection pools that reuse pre-created JDBC connections.

Typically the administrator of the Java EE server pre-creates the pools of database connections and configures the minimum and maximum number of connections and some other parameters on connection pools. To configure a new DBMS connection pool in GlassFish, use the Administration Console's entry JDBC Connection Pools (see Figure 29-2) and press the button New.

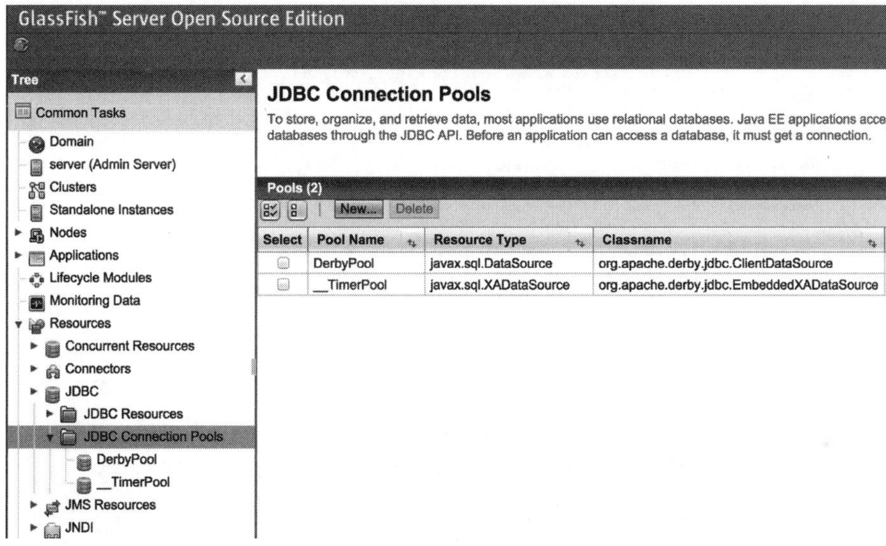

FIGURE 29-2: JDBC connection pools in GlassFish

Then you'd need to add parameters for the new pool. GlassFish includes DerbyDB database server and has a preconfigured pool for it. Figure 29-3 shows a snapshot of the GlassFish administration console, where the existing resource named `DerbyPool` represents a pool of JDBC connections. The object `javax.sql.DataSource` is a *factory* of database connections. The administrator configures this factory as a JNDI resource, specifying what JDBC driver to use, how many connections to create initially, and the maximum number of connections allowed.

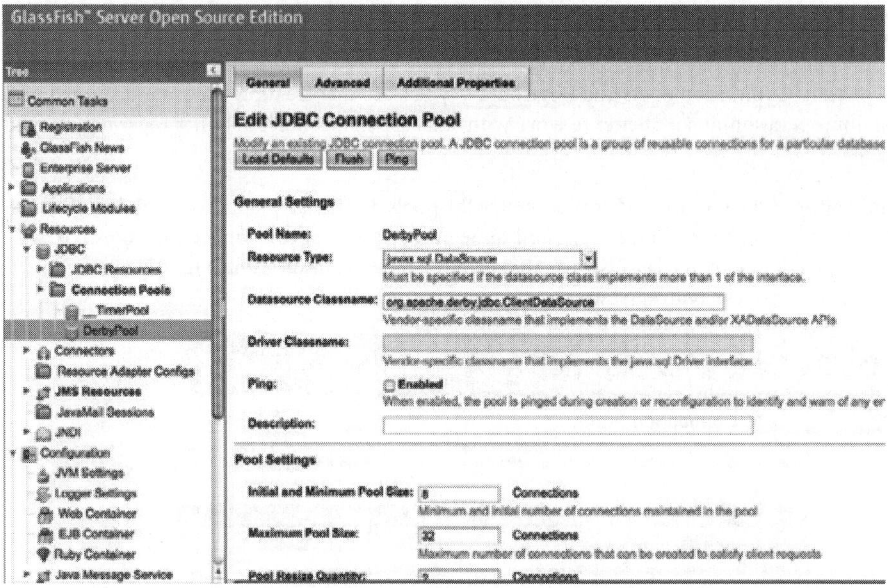

FIGURE 29-3: DerbyPool is configured to have from 8 to 32 connections

CONFIGURING GLASSFISH RESOURCES

GlassFish (and other Java EE servers) has an alternative way of creating and configuring resources by using an XML configuration file. GlassFish resources can be specified in the file `glassfish-resources.xml` that the server loads on startup.

The Java program that needs a JDBC connection gets access to the connection pool by its JNDI name (`DerbyPool` in this case) and makes a `getConnection()` call on this resource. If unused connections are available, the Java class immediately gets an instance of the `Connection` object that internally implements `PooledConnection`. If many users are making concurrent requests, all connections may be taken, and there is a slight delay until one of the busy connections is returned to the pool. Connection is auto-closable, and it gets returned to the pool on closing. Connections returned to the pool are not destroyed; they are preserved by the application server for future requests.

You can do either a JNDI lookup of the `DataSource` object or inject it to your Java code. In Lesson 21 you've been using a standalone Java program, which invoked `DriverManager.getConnection()` to get the `Connection` object. But now you can use `getConnection()` on the `DataSource` object taken from the pool. If the name of the configured `DataSource` object is `DerbyPool`, the sample code to obtain a pooled database connection may look as follows:

```
InitialContext ic = new InitialContext();
DataSource ds = (DataSource) ic.lookup("DerbyPool");
```

```
Connection myConnection = ds.getConnection();
//The rest of the JDBC processing goes here as in Lesson 21
```

Injecting a `DataSource` using the `@Resource` syntax would look like this:

```
@Resource(name="java:global/DerbyPool")
DataSource ds;
```

You have a chance to work with the `DataSource` while working on the assignment from the "Try It" section of this lesson.

LIGHTWEIGHT DIRECTORY ACCESS PROTOCOL

Lightweight Directory Access Protocol (LDAP) servers are specialized software products that store directory entries in hierarchical trees and are highly optimized for reading. This makes them a good choice for such directory services as employee lists or phone directories in an organization. Directories are mainly read, not changed, and this is where LDAP servers shine.

From the enterprise Java perspective you should keep LDAP solutions in mind when a really fast lookup of some Java objects is needed, such as with JMS connection factories, queues, or topics. Java developers use the JNDI API to bind, look up, and update the entries in LDAP. JNDI is to LDAP servers as JDBC is to DBMSes.

These are some popular LDAP servers:

- Oracle Directory Server (Oracle)
- Microsoft Active Directory (Microsoft)
- OpenLDAP (open-source, community developed)
- ApacheDS (open-source, Apache)
- OpenDJ (open-source, community developed)

The LDAP directory tree has a root entry, which consists of one or more *distinguished names* (unique identifiers). Typically the top of the hierarchy is an object with the prefix *o* for *organization*. One level below has the prefix *ou* for *organizational unit*, *cn* stands for *common name*, and so on. Unlike with other naming services, the search string starts from the very lowest hierarchical entry and the root entry has to be specified last. Here's an example of a distinguished name that can be used in a search:

```
cn=jsmith, ou=accounting, o=oracle.com
```

This means "Find the entry that goes by the name jsmith located under accounting node, which in turn is located under oracle.com." The preceding search string corresponds to the following hierarchy in an LDAP tree:

```
o = oracle.com
  ou = accounting
     cn = jsmith
```

The next Java code snippet specifies the JNDI properties, connects to the LDAP server running on port 389, and looks for the object called `CustomerHome`there:

```
Hashtable<String, String> env = new Hashtable<>();
env.put(Context.INITIAL_CONTEXT_FACTORY,
                        "com.sun.jndi.ldap.LdapCtxFactory");
env.put(Context.PROVIDER_URL, "ldap://localhost:389");
env.put(Context.SECURITY_AUTHENTICATION,"simple");
env.put(Context.SECURITY_PRINCIPAL, "cn=Directory Manager");
env.put(Context.SECURITY_CREDENTIALS,"myPassword");

DirContext ctx = new InitialDirContext(env);

CustomerHome custHome =(CustomerHome) ctx.lookup("cn=CusomerHome,
ou=RealBigProject, o=trump.com");
```

To study distributed applications you can run all the examples from this book (clients and servers) on a single computer, but real-world distributed applications can be constructed in various ways; for example:

- Computer #1 runs the LDAP server.
- Computer #2 runs an application server that has registered (published) some objects with the LDAP server on Computer #1.
- Computer #3 has a client program that finds object references on Computer #1 and invokes their methods on Computer #2.
- Computer #4 runs a DBMS server that is being used by the application server running on Computer #2.
- Computer #5 publishes financial market data, and Computer #2 subscribes to this service.

...and so on, and so on.

SEPTEMBER 11

When the terrorists attacked and destroyed the World Trade Center, I was working for a firm that lost the data center as a result of this attack. I was working on a financial trading application that utilized messaging. The JMS objects that were using New York's data center were bound to an LDAP server located in North Carolina. When the reserved data center started functioning in New Jersey, we just ran the program to rebind the JMS objects to the LDAP server so they would point at the messaging server in a new location. Because of such a flexible architecture, the firm's trading application was not operational for only three days.

This lesson has shown you how to use JNDI and given some examples of why you may want to use it. Comparing the code in Listing 30-1 with the one in messageservlet is just one example that shows that naming and binding specific physical objects under a generic JNDI name enables you to remove these physical locations from your program code. Lesson 30 and Chapter 31 give more examples of using JNDI.

TRY IT

In this assignment you need to create a servlet deployed under GlassFish server, which should obtain a connection to DerbyDB by using the resource injection of a `DataSource` object.

Lesson Requirements

You should have Java and GlassFish 4 installed. GlassFish has to be configured in Eclipse IDE as described in Lesson 26 in Configuring GlassFish in Eclipse IDE.

> **NOTE** *You can download the code and resources for this "Try It" from the book's web page at* `www.wrox.com/go/javaprog24hr2e`. *You can find them in the file* `Lesson29.zip`.

Step-by-Step

1. Open the command (or Terminal) window, switch to the folder `glassfish/javadb/bin` and start the instance of the DerbyDB that comes with GlassFish. You need to run `startNetworkServer.exe` (or `startNetworkServer` if you use Mac OS).
2. Start GlassFish from the Eclipse IDE.
3. In Eclipse, create a new Dynamic Web Project Lesson29 specifying GlassFish as the target run time.
4. Create a new servlet called `MyDerbyClientServlet`. This servlet should get the `DataSource` injected and use it for a connection to DerbyDB. Modify the generated code so the servlet looks as follows:

```
@WebServlet("/MyDerbyClientServlet")
public class MyDerbyClientServlet extends HttpServlet {

  @Resource(name="java:global/DerbyPool")
  DataSource ds;

  protected void doGet(HttpServletRequest request,
                       HttpServletResponse response)
                        throws ServletException, IOException {

     try {
         Connection myPooledConnection = ds.getConnection();
         System.out.println("Got pooled connection to DerbyDB");

     } catch (SQLException e) {
          e.printStackTrace();
     }
  }
}
```

5. Deploy the servlet: Right-click GlassFish in the Server view and select Add and Remove. Check the Eclipse console and locate the message that the Lesson29 application is loaded.
6. Right-click the servlet name and select Run on Server. You should see the message "Got pooled connection to DerbyDB" in the Console view.
7. Open GlassFish Administration Console and go to the Additional Properties tab of DerbyPool. Modify the database name to be Lesson29.

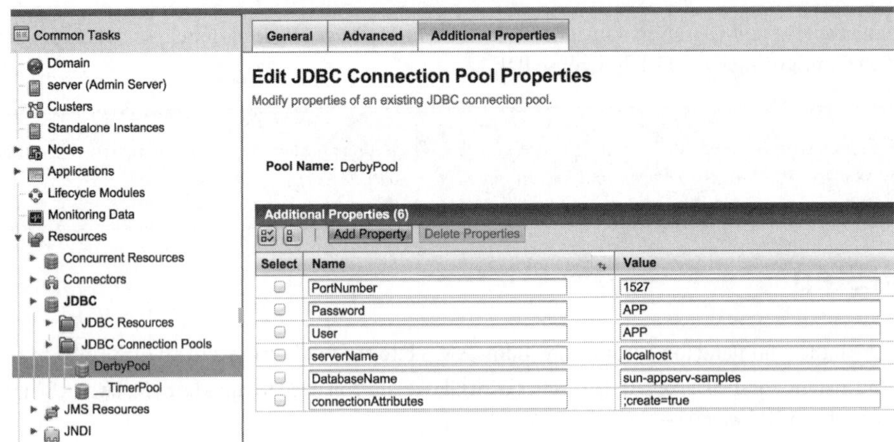

FIGURE 29-4: Additional Properties of the connection pool

8. Revisit Lesson 21 and create the `Employee` table as described in "Installing Derby DB" and "Creating a Database."
9. Add the code to `MyDerbyClientServlet` that retrieves the data from `Employee` table (use employeelist_program as a reference).
10. Run the servlet `MyDerbyClientServlet`. It should retrieve the data from `Employee` and print them in Eclipse Console view.

> **TIP** *Please select the videos for Lesson 29 online at* `www.wrox.com/go/javaprog24hr2e`. *You will also be able to download the code and resources for this lesson from the website.*

30

Introducing JMS and MOM

People send messages to each other via e-mail, instant messages, Twitter, Facebook, and so on. People can also communicate using more traditional methods by sending regular mail. You just need to drop a letter in a mailbox, and the rest is taken care of by postal service providers and logistics companies such as USPS, FedEx, UPS, and DHL.

Applications can send messages to each other using specialized servers known as message-oriented middleware (MOM), which plays a role similar to that of the delivery services. A program "drops the message" into a *message queue* (think *mailbox*) using the Java Messaging Service (JMS) application programming interface (API), and the message is delivered to another application that reads messages off of this queue. In short, JMS is an API for working with MOM servers.

Although JMS is a part of the Java EE specification, you can use it with Java SE applications without needing to have any Java application server—just make a `.jar` file containing JMS classes available to your program. This lesson shows you how to write both standalone Java clients and those that live inside a Java EE server. These clients send and receive applications with the JMS API via a MOM provider. In Lesson 31 you learn about the value that message-driven beans bring to the table.

MESSAGING CONCEPTS AND TERMINOLOGY

You have already learned several methods of data exchange in distributed Java applications: direct socket communication, RMI, and HTTP-based interactions. But all of them were based on remote procedure calls (RPC) or the request/response model. MOM enables you to build distributed systems that communicate *asynchronously*.

JMS itself isn't the transport for messages. JMS is to MOM what JDBC is to a relational DBMS. Java applications can use the same JMS classes with any MOM provider. Here's a list of some popular MOM software:

- WebSphere MQ (IBM)
- EMS (Tibco Software)
- SonicMQ (Progress Software)

- ActiveMQ (open source, Apache)
- Open MQ (open source, Oracle)

If you place an order to buy some stocks by invoking the method `placeOrder()` on a remote machine, that's an example of a *synchronous* or blocking call (also known as remote procedure call). The calling program can't continue until the code in the `placeOrder()` method is finished or has thrown an error.

With *asynchronous* communications it's different. You can place an order but don't have to wait for its execution. Similarly, when you drop a letter in a mailbox you don't have to wait for a mail truck to arrive to the recipient. The same applies to e-mail—press the Send button and continue working on other things without waiting until your message has been delivered. Recipients of your e-mails also don't have to be online when you send a message; they can read it later.

The process of placing a trade order comes down to putting a Java object that describes your order into a certain *message queue* of your MOM provider. After placing an order, the program may continue its execution without waiting until the processing of the order is finished. Multiple users can place orders into the same queue. Another program (not necessarily in Java) should be *de-queueing* and processing messages. Figure 30-1 shows how a trading application can place orders (and receive executions) with another application running on a stock exchange.

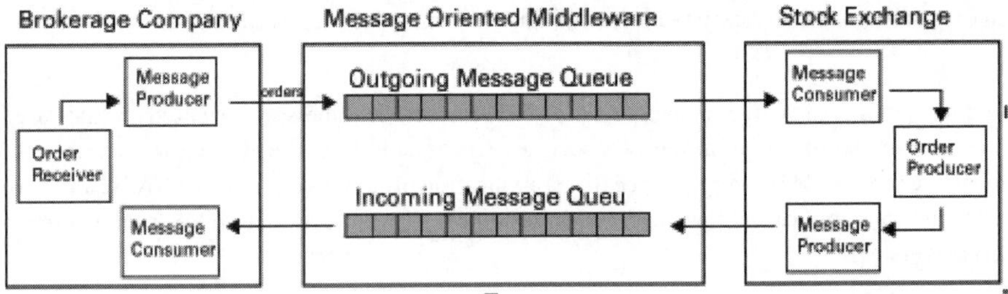

FIGURE 30-1: Brokerage company communicates with a stock exchange via MOM

Even from this very high-level representation of a trading application you can see that messaging allows you to build loosely coupled distributed systems. Say, the stock exchange server is down, the brokerage company servers can still take customers' orders and send them to MOM. As soon as the stock exchange servers become operational, they start retrieving orders from the MOM queues. If the brokerage company would make synchronous RPC-type calls to the stock exchange, the entire trading application would stop functioning it the stock exchange servers were down.

The trading orders are placed in one queue, and when they are executed at the stock exchange the confirmations go into another queue and, if the application at the brokerage firm is active at that time, it will de-queue the messages immediately upon their arrival. If your application is not running, but you've opted for guaranteed delivery, the messages will be preserved in the queue by the MOM provider.

To increase the throughput of your messaging-based application, add multiple parallel consumers reading messages off of the same queue. You can create a consumer Java program that starts multiple threads, each of them de-queuing messages from the same queue. But a better way is to configure multiple consumers using message-driven beans (MDB), which I explain in Chapter 31.

With guaranteed message delivery, MOM—just like the post office—keeps the message in a queue until the receiver gets it. In this mode messages are *persistent*—the MOM provider stores them in its internal storage, which can be a DBMS or a filesystem. In a non-guaranteed mode, MOM delivers a message only to the receiving applications that are up and running at the moment that the message arrives.

TWO MODES OF MESSAGE DELIVERY

A program can *send* or *publish* a message. When it sends a message to a particular queue and another program receives the message from this queue it's called *point-to-point (P2P)* messaging. In this mode a message is removed from a queue as soon as it's successfully received. Figure 30-2 shows that each message goes to only one consumer.

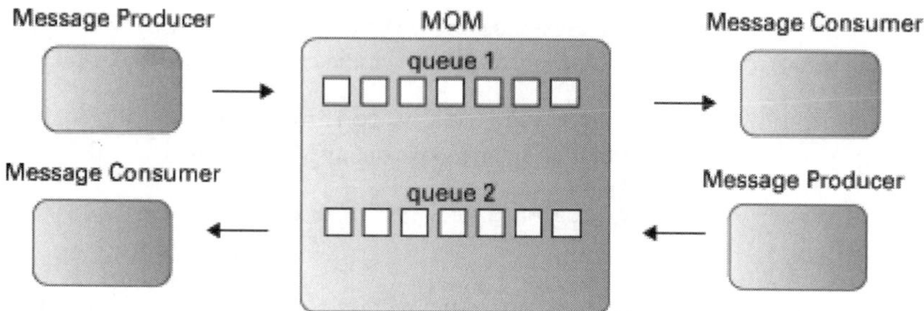

FIGURE 30-2: P2P messaging

If a program publishes a message to be consumed by multiple recipients, that's *publish/subscribe (pub/sub)* mode. A message is published to a particular *topic* and many subscribers can subscribe to receive it. Figure 30-3 illustrates pub-sub, where on message can be consumed by multiple subscribers.

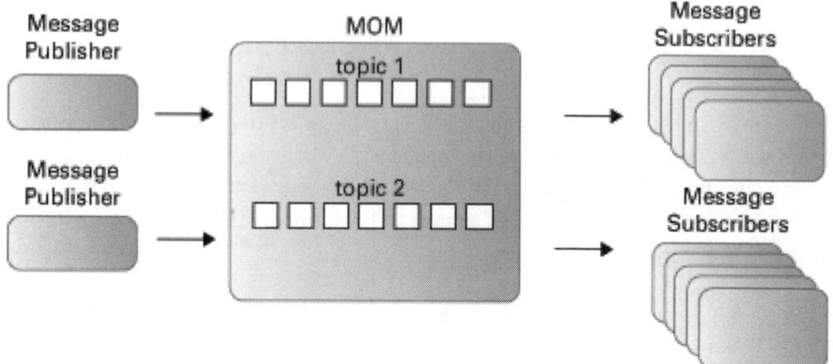

FIGURE 30-3: Pub/sub messaging

A topic represents some important news for applications and/or users; for example, `PriceDropAlert`, `BreakingNews`, and so on. In pub/sub mode, a message is usually removed from a queue as soon as all subscribers receive it (read about durable subscribers in the section How to Subscribe for a Topic).

Another good example of a pub/sub application is a chat room. A message published by one person is received by the other people present in the chat room. Developing a chat room with JMS and MOM is a pretty trivial task.

INTRODUCING OPENMQ MOM

To learn JMS, you need to install a messaging server and configure some message queues there. You can use an open source MOM provider called Open MQ. As a bonus, it comes with GlassFish. You already have it installed in the `mq` directory in your GlassFish install. If you want to use Open MQ with any other application server you could download Open MQ as a separate product from `https://mq.java.net/downloads/index.html`.

First, I'm not going to use Java EE server. The goal is to test standalone Java clients communicating with Open MQ directly, without the middlemen. You need to start the Open MQ server and create a named queue there.

Edit the configuration file `glassfish4/glassfish/mq/etc/imqenv.conf` to specify the location of Java 8 on your computer. For example, this is how this configuration line looks on my Mac computer:

```
IMQ_DEFAULT_JAVAHOME=/Library/Java/JavaVirtualMachines/jdk1.8.0_25.j
dk/Contents/Home
```

Open a command (or Terminal) window to the `glassfish4/mq/bin` directory, and start the Open MQ broker. In Windows you need to run the program `imqbrokerd.exe`. If you use Mac OS, enter the following command:

```
./imqbrokerd
```

You see a message informing you that the broker is ready on port 7676. Now open another command window, change to the `glassfish4/mq/bin` directory, and start the admin graphical user interface (GUI) tool imqadmin to create the required messaging destinations:

```
./imqadmin
```

The administration console opens. In Open MQ there are applications called brokers that manage all message exchanges between clients. So you configure a message broker that manages messages related to stock trading. Right-click the `Brokers` node and add a new broker named `StockBroker`, enter the password *admin*, and click OK. Then right-click `StockBroker` and select Connect to Broker from the menu. Figure 30-4 shows a snapshot of my screen after these steps.

Now create a physical destination—a queue for placing trading orders. Right-click the Destinations under the `StockBroker` node and select Add Broker Destination. In the pop-up window, enter the name of the destination: `TradingOrdersQueue`, as in Figure 30-5.

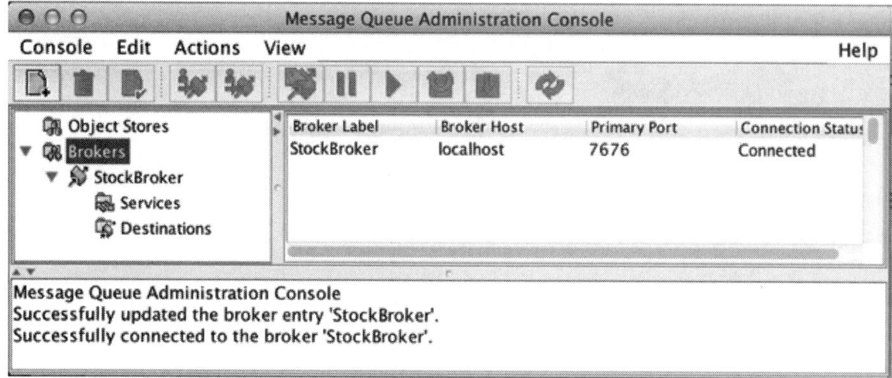

FIGURE 30-4: Open MQ console with newly created StockBroker

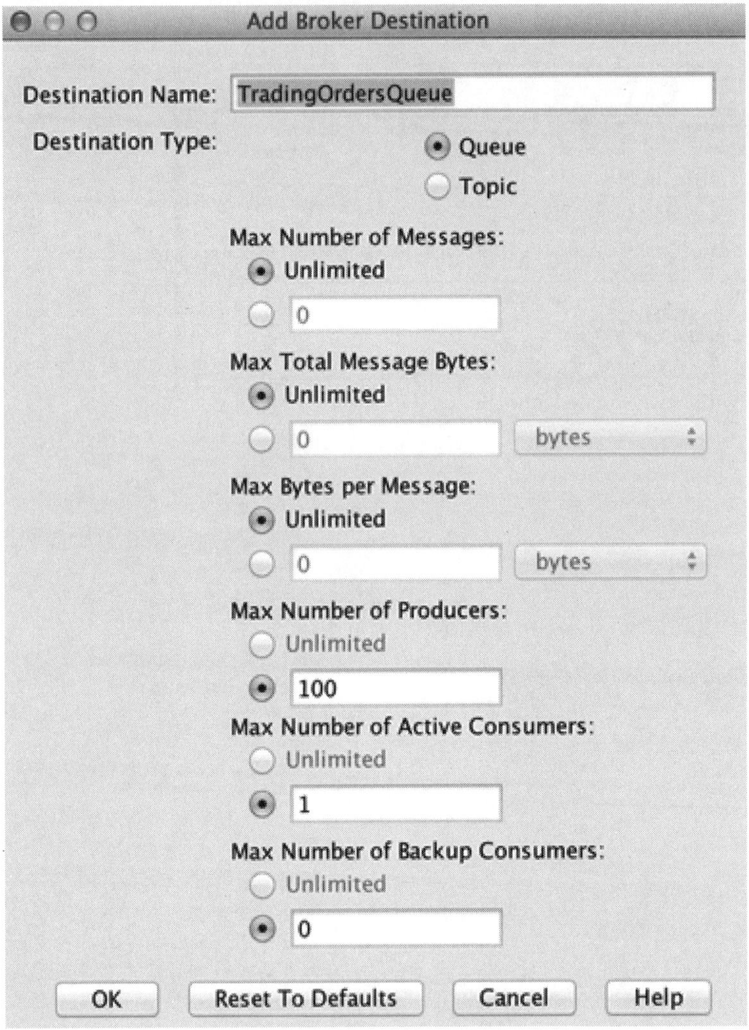

FIGURE 30-5: Configuring a destination in Open MQ

If you want to create a topic rather than a queue you just need to select the Topic radio button. As you can see, there are some other parameters you can set on a destination.

It's out of the scope of this book to include a detailed overview of Open MQ MOM; try reading the Open MQ Administration Guide (`https://glassfish.java.net/docs/4.0/mq-admin-guide.pdf`) for more information. As long as you have a MOM server running and the messaging destination is configured, you can start writing programs that send and receive messages to/from this destination.

JMS API OVERVIEW

JMS API that includes Java classes that enable you to send and receive messages. In this lesson you discuss JMS 2.0 introduced in Java EE 7. If you have to work with application servers that support only older Java EE specifications look for tutorials describing JMS 1.1 API. All of the supporting classes and interfaces are defined in the package `javax.jms`, and you can read about them at `http://docs.oracle.com/javaee/7/api/javax/jms/package-summary.htm (http://docs.oracle.com/javaee/7/api/javax/jms/package-summary.html)`.

In the old JMS specification you'd need to use multiple classes and interfaces such as `Queue`, `QueueConnection`, `QueueConnectionFactory`, `QueueSession`, `Connection`, `QueueSender`, `QueueReceiver`, `Topic`, `TopicPublisher`, and more. With JMS 2.0 this list is shorter. You can send and receive messages using just the few classes and interfaces listed here:

- `JMSContext` combines the JMS `Connection` and `Session` objects. To communication with MOM you need to connect to it and all your messaging exchanges are done within a session.
- `ConnectionFactory` is an object that creates `Connection` object(s) encapsulated in the `JMSContext`.
- `Destination` is a queue or a topic. Both `Queue` and `Topic` interfaces are inherited from `Destination`.
- `JMSProducer` is an interface that has methods to send messages to a destination.
- `JMSConsumer` is an interface that has methods to retrieve messages from a destination.
- `Message` is a root interface for all messages. It consists of a header and a body.

Types of Messages

Every message contains a header and optional body and has facilities for providing additional properties. The header contains the message identification (unique message ID, destination, type, and so on). The optional properties can be set by a program to tag a message with application-specific data; for example, `UrgentOrder`.

The optional body contains a message that has to be delivered. Following are the types of JMS messages that you can place in a message body. All these interfaces are inherited from `javax.jms.Message`.

- `TextMessage` is an object that can contain any Java `String`.
- `ObjectMessage` can hold any `Serializable` Java object.
- `BytesMessage` holds an array of bytes.
- `StreamMessage` has a stream of Java primitives.
- `MapMessage` contains any key/value pairs; for example, `id=123`.

Typically the message producer creates an object of one of the preceding types, initializes it with the application data, and then sends it to a MOM queue or topic. The only exception is `String` messages, which can be sent as-is without wrapping them inside the `TextMessage`. The consumer application extracts the message content by invoking a method `Message.getBody()`, which returns the message body (`http://docs.oracle.com/`

javaee/7/api/javax/jms/Message.html#getBody(java.lang.Class)) of a specified type; for example:

```
msg.getBody(String.class); // msg is a reference to received message
```

If you'd need to send an object of, say Order type (must be Serializable), the message producer needs to wrap it up into the ObjectMessage—for example:

```
Order order = new Order();
ObjectMessage objMsg = context.createObjectMessage(order);
```

then the invocation of getBody() on the message consumer would look like this:

```
Order receivedOrder = msg.getBody(Order.class);
```

How to Send a Message Directly to MOM

This section and the following section show you how a Java SE client can communicate with MOM directly without using any Java EE server as a middleman. This mode isn't often used, but it'll help you to understand the benefits that Java EE and JNDI bring to the table when it comes to messaging. After you see these simple examples, you can rewrite them for a Java EE server using JNDI.

To send and receive messages, queues or topics should be preconfigured in MOM and their names must be known before a program can start sending messages. I used the world *should,* because even if you wouldn't preconfigure the queue, some MOM providers (Open MQ included) may create a temporary queue in memory, which will be destroyed on server restart.

In the real world, a MOM server administrator manages queues and other messaging artifacts, but for the training purposes you already did it in the previous section with the queue TradingOrdersQueue .

To send messages directly to a MOM provider, a program has to perform the following steps:

1. In a Java class create a ConnectionFactory object using the implementation classes provided by the MOM vendor.
2. Create a JMSContext object.
3. Using the JMSContext create a Destination (for example, invoke createQueue()).
4. Create a JMSProducer object.
5. Create one of the Message objects and put some data in it.
6. Call the send() method on the JMSProducer providing Destination and Message as arguments.

Listing 30-1 shows the class DirectMessageSender that implements all of the preceding steps except creating a Message instance - for strings it's not required. This code sends a message to a queue TradingOrdersQueue.

LISTING 30-1 Sending a message directly to MOM

```
public class DirectMessageSender{
 public static void main(String[] args){

   // Vendor-specific factory implementation
   ConnectionFactory factory=
                   new com.sun.messaging.ConnectionFactory();

   try(JMSContext context=factory.createContext("admin","admin")){

      factory.setProperty(ConnectionConfiguration.imqAddressList,
                   "mq://127.0.0.1:7676,mq://127.0.0.1:7676");

      Destination ordersQueue =
                        context.createQueue("TradingOrdersQueue");
      JMSProducer producer = context.createProducer();

      // Send msg to buy 200 shares of IBM at market price
      producer.send(ordersQueue,"IBM 200 Mkt");

      System.out.println("Placed an order to purchase 200
                            shares of IBM to TradingOrdersQueue");
     } catch (JMSException e){
              System.out.println("Error: " + e.getMessage());
     }
  }
}
```

The class `DirectMessageSender` uses an Open MQ–specific implementation of JMS's `ConnectionFactory`, which is located in the vendor's package `com.sun.messaging`. If you decide to change MOM providers or the server address, you would need to modify, recompile, and redeploy this code. This is not great, but you'll fix this issue in the Java EE version of this client.

How to Receive a Message Directly from MOM

The program that receives messages is called a *message consumer* (a listener). It can be a standalone Java program or a message-driven bean. You can receive messages either synchronously, using the `receive()` method, or asynchronously by implementing the `MessageListener` interface and programming a callback `onMessage()`. The `receive()` method is rarely used because it engages a polling mechanism that constantly asks for a message.

Using an asynchronous callback method `onMessage()` on a message consumer is a preferred way to receive messages. The callback method `onMessage()` is invoked immediately when a message is put in the queue. The consumer class has to perform the following steps to receive messages asynchronously:

1. Create a class that implements the `MessageListener` interface and instantiate it.

2. Create a `ConnectionFactory` object using the implementation classes provided by the MOM vendor.
3. Create a `JMSContext` object.
4. Using the `JMSContext` to create a `Destination` (for example, invoke `createQueue()`).
5. Create a `JMSConsumer` object and invoke on it `setMessageListener()`, specifying the object that implements `MessageListener`.
6. Implement `onMessage()` to handle the message when it arrives.

The sample class `MyReceiver` in Listing 30-2 shows how to consume messages from the `TradingOrdersQueue` asynchronously. Its constructor creates JMS objects and registers itself as a message listener. The callback `onMessage()` has code for processing the received messages.

LISTING 30-2 Receiving a message

```
public class DirectMessageReceiver implements MessageListener{

  ConnectionFactory factory =
                    new com.sun.messaging.ConnectionFactory();
  JMSConsumer consumer;

  DirectMessageReceiver(){
   try(JMSContext context=factory.createContext("admin","admin")){
       factory.setProperty(ConnectionConfiguration.imqAddressList,
                    "mq://127.0.0.1:7676,mq://127.0.0.1:7676");

       Destination ordersQueue = context.createQueue(
                                      "TradingOrdersQueue");

       consumer = context.createConsumer(ordersQueue);

       consumer.setMessageListener(this);

       System.out.println(
                    "Listening to the TradingOrdersQueue...");

              // Keep the program running - wait for messages
              Thread.sleep(100000);

   } catch (InterruptedException e){
       System.out.println("Error: " + e.getMessage());
   } catch (JMSException e){
       System.out.println("Error: " + e.getMessage());
   }
 }

  public void onMessage(Message msg){

      try{
```

```
            System.out.println("Got the text message from " +
              "the TradingOrdersQueue: " + msg.getBody(String.class));

            System.out.println("\n === Here's what toString()
                                on the message prints \n" + msg);

        } catch (JMSException e){
            System.err.println("JMSException: " + e.toString());
        }
    }

    public static void main(String[] args){
        new DirectMessageReceiver();  // instantiate listener
    }
  }
```

The class `DirectMessageReciever` calls the method `sleep(100000)` to prevent the program from termination for 100 seconds. I did it for testing purposes so you can send messages to the queue and see that they are being received. If you place a message in a queue by running `DirectMessageSender` the `DirectMessageReciever` gets it, producing output on the console that might look like this:

```
Got the text message from the TradingOrdersQueue: IBM 200 Mkt

 === Here's what toString() on the message prints

Text:     IBM 200 Mkt
Class:              com.sun.messaging.jmq.jmsclient.TextMessageImpl
getJMSMessageID():     ID:7-192.168.1.113(d8:86:af:a3:e1:8d)-62948-
                         1412631694897
getJMSTimestamp():     1412631694897
getJMSCorrelationID():     null
JMSReplyTo:          null
JMSDestination:          TradingOrdersQueue
getJMSDeliveryMode():     PERSISTENT
getJMSRedelivered():     false
getJMSType():          null
getJMSExpiration():     0
getJMSDeliveryTime():     0
getJMSPriority():     4
Properties:          {JMSXDeliveryCount=1}
```

The first line is the result of extracting the text of the message by calling `getBody()`.

```
msg.getBody(String.class)
```

The argument `String.class` means "cast the message body to type `String`."

The rest of the console output is produced by the `toString()` method on the `Message` object. I used it in `DirectMessageReceiver`just to show you that besides message body there are a number of properties (`https://javaee-spec.java.net/nonav/javadocs/javax/jms/Message.html`) that can be retrieved by the corresponding getter.

How to Publish a Message

Programs publish messages to topics, which should be created in advance by the MOM system administrator. In the case of Open MQ, you need to select the Topic radio button in the window shown in Figure 30-5. Multiple subscribers can get messages published to the same topic (this is also known as *one-to-many mode*).

Message publishing is very similar to message sending, but the program should create a `Topic` instead of a `Queue`; the rest is the same. Listing 30-3 shows how to change the `DirectMessageSender` to publish a text message with a price quote to a topic called `PriceQuoteTopic`:

LISTING 30-3 Publishing a message to a topic

```
Destination priceQuoteTopic  = context.createTopic(
                                         "PriceQuoteTopic");

// Publish a price quote msg to subscribers of PriceQuoteTopic
producer.send(priceQuoteTopic,"IBM 187.22");
```

Multiple subscribers can receive the same message.

How to Subscribe for a Topic

Subscribers can be *durable* or *non-durable*. Durable subscribers are guaranteed to receive their messages; they do not have to be active at the time a message arrives. Non-durable subscribers receive only those messages that come when they are active. With non-durable subscriptions, MOM removes the message from its internal storage as soon as all active subscribers have acknowledged message delivery. With durable subscriptions MOM retains the message until it's delivered to all subscribers.

Some applications don't need durable subscriptions. For example, if a subscriber missed a stock price published a second ago it's okay. But this is not the case if a brokerage company has to report a suspicious transaction to several financial fraud prevention organizations—make such subscriptions durable.

If you were to change the `DirectMessageRetriever` into a non-durable topic subscriber, the following slight change would do the trick:

LISTING 30-4 Creating a non-durable subscriber

```
Destination priceQuoteTopic =
                          context.createTopic("PriceQuoteTopic");

consumer = context.createConsumer(priceQuoteTopic);
```

Durable subscribers are created by invoking `createDurableConsumer()`, and each durable subscriber must have a unique client ID. Each durable subscription is identified by a combination of the topic name, subscriber's name, and the client ID. This is how you can create a durable subscriber named `FraudPreventionUnit`:

LISTING 30-5 Creating a durable subscriber

```
Destination priceQuoteTopic =
                        context.createTopic("PriceQuoteTopic");
context.setClientID("client123");

consumer = context.createDurableConsumer((Topic)priceQuoteTopic,
                                     "FraudPreventionUnit");
```

For scalability reasons, the same subscription can be shared by multiple standalone consumers working in parallel (for example, running on different JVMs). In this case, a *shared consumer* has to be created (it can be durable or non-durable). For example, you can create a shared durable subscriber, as shown in Listing 30-6:

LISTING 30-6 Creating a shared durable subscriber

```
Destination priceQuoteTopic =
                        context.createTopic("PriceQuoteTopic");
context.setClientID("client123");

consumer = context.createSharedDurableConsumer(
                (Topic)priceQuoteTopic,"FraudPreventionUnit");
```

PARALLEL SUBSCRIPTIONS WITH MDBS

In standalone Java applications you can't create multiple threads to create several durable topic subscriptions; using a shared subscription is your only option. But if subscribers are created as message-driven beans in a Java EE server, more than one bean can consume messages from the same subscription.

At any time an application can unsubscribe from a topic by calling the method `unsubscribe()` on the `JMSContext` object, for example:

```
context.unsubscribe("FraudPreventionUnit");
```

Message Acknowledgments and Transactions Support

When the message is successfully delivered, the MOM physically removes it from the queue. But what does "successfully delivered" means? Is it when the message was passed to the method `onMessage()`? But if the code in `onMessage()` fails due to some error, you want the message to remain in the queue!

JMS API has a concept of a messaging session in which you can specify either *acknowledgments modes* or request transaction support to give the applications control over message removals from queues or topics.

There are three acknowledgments modes:

- AUTO_ACKNOWLEDGE mode sends the acknowledgment back as soon as the method onMessage() is successfully finished. This is a default acknowledgment mode.
- CLIENT_ACKNOWLEDGE mode requires explicit acknowledgment by calling the method acknowledge() from the message receiver's code.
- DUP_OK_ACKNOWLEDGE mode is used in case the server fails; the same message may be delivered more than once. In some use cases it's acceptable—for example, receiving a price quote twice doesn't hurt.

The message acknowledgment mode is defined when the JMSContext is created. So far, our code samples DirectMessageSender and DirectMessageReceiver have created the JMSContext object by specifying two arguments: user ID and password. But you could also use an overloaded createContext() method to specify a messaging session mode; for example:

```
JMSContext context = factory.createContext("admin","admin",
                            JMSContext.CLIENT_ACKNOWLEDGE));
```

As an alternative to using acknowledgments, you can request transaction support for message consumers. Imagine if a received message contains the data that must be saved in a database and forwarded to a Web Service as one unit of work, so unless both operations are successful the entire transaction must be rolled back. You may need transaction support on the JMS producer side, too. For example, if you need to send two messages as one logical unit of work—either both messages were successfully sent or rolled back the transaction. The following code snippet shows how to create JMSContext and a JMSProducer object that sends two messages in different queues as one transaction.

```
try(JMSContext context = factory.createContext("admin","admin",
                                    JMSContext.TRANSACTED)){

   JMSProducer producer = context.createProducer();

   Destination queue1 = context.createQueue("Queue1");
   Destination queue2 = context.createQueue("Queue2");

   producer.send(queue1,"Msg1");
   producer.send(queue2,"Msg2");

   context.commit(); // commit the JMS transaction

} catch (JMSException e){
    context.rollback(); // rollback the JMS transaction
    System.out.println("Error: " + e.getMessage());
}
```

If both sends went through fine, the Session object (encapsulated inside JMSContext) issues a commit. If the exception is thrown, no messages are placed in any of the queues.

Message Selectors

If you have to share a queue with some other applications or developers from your team, use *message selectors* (also known as *filters*) to avoid "stealing" somebody else's messages. For example, in the message consumer application you can opt for receiving messages that have a property `symbol` with the value `IBM`:

```
String selector = "symbol=IBM";
Context.createConsumer(ordersQueue, selector);
```

In this case the queue listener dequeues only those messages that have a `String` property `symbol` with the value `IBM`. Accordingly, the message producers have to set this property on the message object:

```
TextMessage outMsg = context.createTextMessage();
outMsg.setText("IBM 200 Mkt");
outMsg.setStringProperty("symbol", "IBM");

Destination ordersQueue=context.createQueue("TradingOrdersQueue");

JMSProducer producer = context.createProducer();
producer.send(ordersQueue, outMsg);
```

Remember that message selectors slow down the process of retrieval. Messages stay in a queue until the listener with the matching selector picks them up. Selectors really help if your team has a limited number of queues and everyone needs to receive messages without interfering with the others. But if someone starts the queue listener without selectors, it just drains the queue.

SENDING MESSAGES FROM JAVA EE CONTAINERS

Now that you know how the messaging works, you can see how to send messages to MOM destinations from the Java objects that live inside a Java EE container. This time you bind MOM objects like `ConnectionFactory`, `Queue`, and `Topic` to the JNDI tree, and Java messaging clients get them from there. Figure 30-6 shows a high-level picture of JMS clients communicating with MOM with or without Java EE.

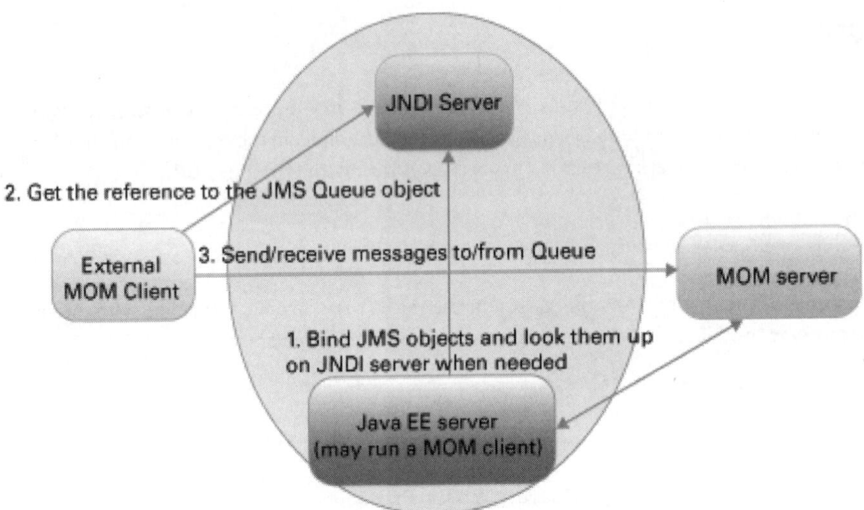

FIGURE 30-6: Bringing together JMS, Java EE , and MOM

An external client can talk to a MOM server directly or from inside the Java EE server represented by the oval. When the Java EE server starts, it binds MOM objects to the JNDI tree as JMS objects. So if a Java servlet or other object deployed in Java EE server needs to send messages to MOM, it gets the references to administered objects by using `lookup()` or resource injection.

I'll give you an example of a Java Servlet that reuses most of the code shown in the `DirectMessageSender` class. Assuming that you are familiar with the JNDI concepts from Lesson 29, the code of the `MessageSenderServlet` should be easy to understand.

```
@WebServlet("/MessageSenderServlet")
public class MessageSenderServlet extends HttpServlet {

   @Resource(lookup ="java:comp/DefaultJMSConnectionFactory")
   ConnectionFactory factory;

   @Resource(lookup = "OutgoingTradeOrders")  // JNDI queue name
   Destination ordersQueue;

   protected void doGet(HttpServletRequest request,
                        HttpServletResponse response)
                              throws ServletException, IOException{

     try(JMSContext context=factory.createContext("admin","admin")){

          JMSProducer producer = context.createProducer();

          // Send msg to buy 200 shares of IBM at market price
          producer.send(ordersQueue,"IBM 200 Mkt");
```

```
            System.out.println("Placed an order to purchase 200" +
                              "shares of IBM to OutgoingTradeOrders");
        }
      }
    }
```

For the `MessageSenderServlet` to work, you need to configure JMS objects using the administration console of the Java EE server. In this example, I use the JNDI queue name `OutgoingTradeOrders` that will be mapped to the physical queue name `TradingOrdersQueue`. In the next section I show you how to do it in GlassFish.

Administering JMS Objects in GlassFish

Configuring JMS objects comes down to mapping JNDI names to physical MOM objects. Assuming that Open MQ and GlassFish servers are up and running, open GlassFish Administration Console by visiting http://localhost:4848. There is a JMS Resources node in the navigation tree on the left. Click the server node, and you see a tab for adding the JMS physical destination, as shown Figure 30-7.

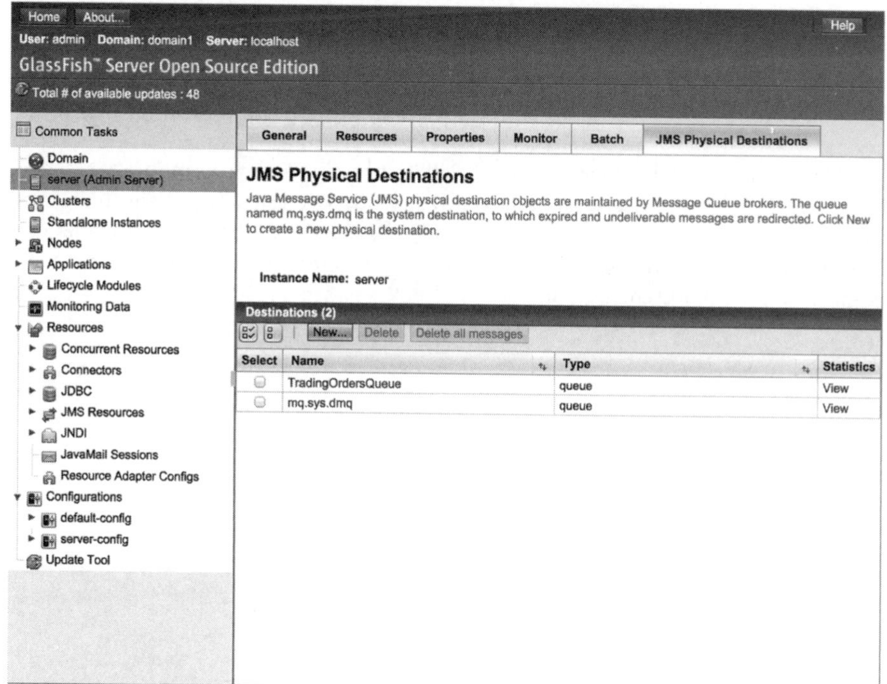

FIGURE 30-7: JMS Physical Destinations in GlassFish

The only reason the destination `TradingOrdersQueue` is known is because Open MQ is integrated with GlassFish. To configure another MOM server you'd need to create a new JMS host by using the Configurations node in the navigation panel.

Now you need to create a GlassFish JMS entry mapped to the physical MOM queue. Add the new destination resource to JMS Resources (see Figure 30-8). I gave it a JNDI name `OutgoingTradeOrders`.

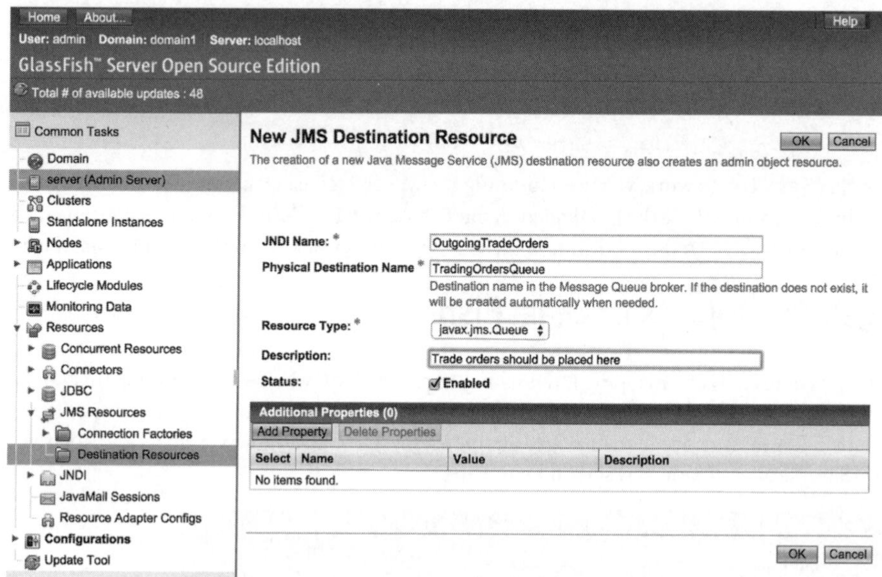

FIGURE 30-8: Mapping JNDI name to a physical queue

Creation and closing of JMS connections (it's done internally by `JMSContext`) are slow operations; you should consider using JMS connection pools. Java EE servers enable you to automatically create such pools by configuring a connection factory. Figure 30-9 shows how to configure a connection factory to use pooled connections. I set it to create 20 JMS connections on the GlassFish server startup and, as the number of users increases, the pool size will grow to the maximum size of 100 connections.

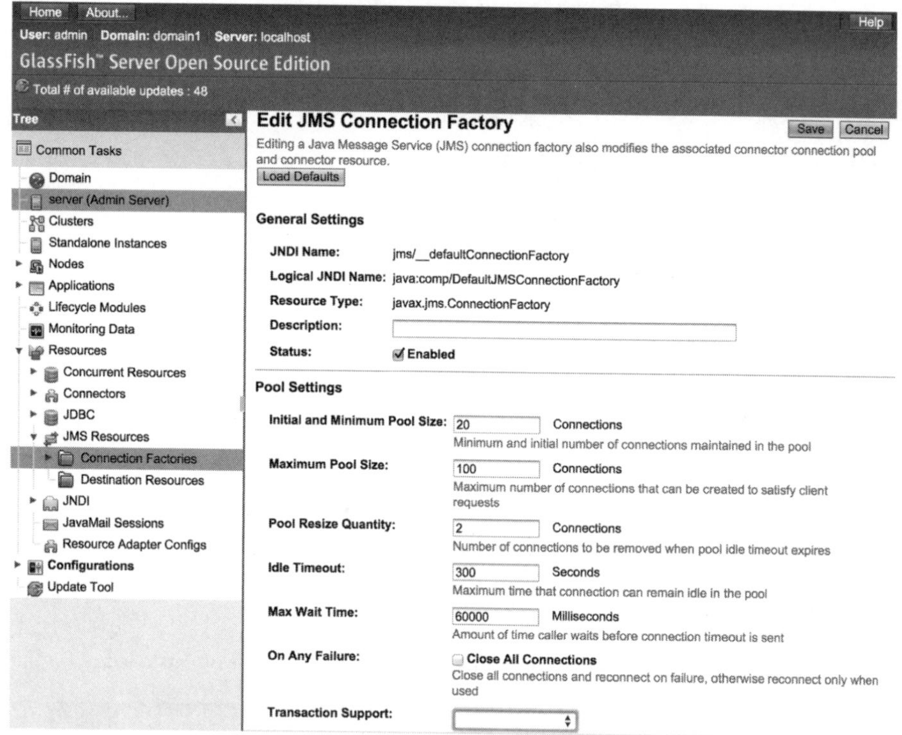

FIGURE 30-9: Configuring JMS connection factory

Now you can create, deploy, and run the servlet `MessageSenderServlet` in GlassFish. Do it in Eclipse as explained in Lesson 26. Create an Eclipse Dynamic Web Project specifying GlassFish as a target run time. Then create a servlet `MessageSenderServlet` with the code shown earlier in this section. Finally, deploy this Eclipse project using the right-click menu Add and Remove on the GlassFish server and run it.

Lesson 31 shows you how to retrieve messages from a queue or topic using message-driven beans. The "Try It" section has instructions on how to use a standalone message consumer.

TRY IT

The goal is to use a standalone message consumer `DirectMessageReceiver` to retrieve messages sent by the Java servlet. Test the messaging scenario depicted in Figure 30-10.

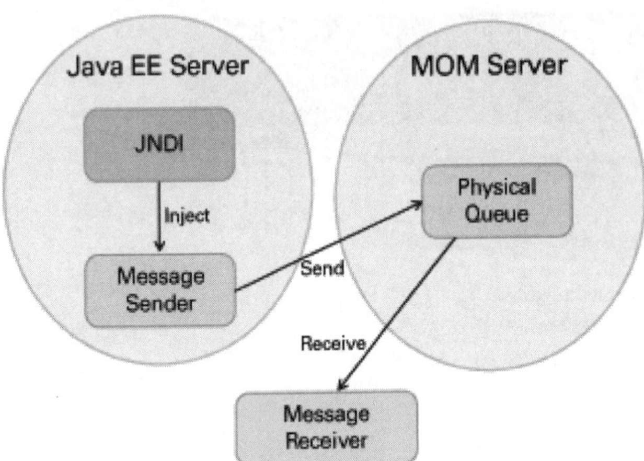

FIGURE 30-10: Java EE message sender and a standalone receiver

Lesson Requirements

You should have Eclipse for Java EE Developers and GlassFish 4.1 (it comes with Open MQ) installed.

> **NOTE** *You can download the code and resources for this "Try It" section from the book's web page at* `www.wrox.com/go/javaprog24hr2e`. *You can find them in the* `Lesson30.zip`.

Hints

Open MQ started independently with `imqbrokerd` runs on a different port than embedded Open MQ started by GlassFish.

Step-by-Step

1. Stop both the Open MQ server started independently and GlassFish.
2. Open the file `glassfish/domains/domain1/config/domain.xml` and change the value of the system variable `JMS_PROVIDER_PORT` to be 7676. By default, GlassFish starts embedded Open MQ server on the port 27676, but our `DirectMessageReceiver` uses hardcoded 7676 as a port value.
3. Restart GlassFish. Now it starts embedded JMS provider on port 7676.
4. Make sure that the `OutgoingTradeOrders` is configured in the GlassFish, as shown on Figure 30-8.

5. Run the `MessageSenderServlet` as explained earlier. It'll send the message to the queue that is known as `OutgoingTradeOrders` in the GlassFish JNDI tree.

6. Run `DirectMessageReceiver`. It prints on the console the message "Listening to the TestQueue" and then retrieves and prints the message from the physical queue named `TradingOrdersQueue`.
7. Modify the code of `DirectMessageReceiver` so it has no hardcoded values of the Open MQ server.
8. Self-study the use of the `QueueBrowser` class and write a program that prints the content of a queue without de-queuing messages.

> **TIP** *Please select the videos for Lesson 30 online at* `www.wrox.com/go/javaprog24hr2e`. *You will also be able to download the code and resources for this lesson from the website.*

31

Introduction to Enterprise JavaBeans

This lesson introduces you to one of the Java EE technologies, Enterprise JavaBeans (JSR 345 (`http://download.oracle.com/otndocs/jcp/ejb-3_2-fr-spec/index.html`)), which can be used for implementing the business tier in a distributed application (refer to Figure 25-1 in Lesson 25). Chapter 26 and Chapter 27 were about various ways of programming the presentation tier on the web; in Chapter 30 and Chapter 29 you learned how to organize communication between the different tiers of the application using messaging. The application business logic was programmed in POJOs.

In this lesson you see how to program the business tier in EJBs, which are also POJOs, but managed by an EJB container. Java EE 7 includes EJB 3.2 and the Java Persistence API (JPA) 2.1 that offer you a standardized way to implement solutions for business logic and data persistence. Using EJBs as JMS listeners makes your enterprise application more scalable without the need to write additional code.

This lesson introduces you to various types of EJBs, and the next lesson is about persisting data with JPA.

WHO NEEDS EJB CONTAINERS?

What's wrong with POJOs? Why not just implement business logic there? You certainly can, but most likely you'd need to spend additional time manually programming a multithreaded environment for them. The chances are that your application needs transactional support. If the business logic is located in POJO 1 and POJO 2, and the second one fails, you want to roll back whatever has been completed by the first one.

It's great that you know how to program message receivers using JMS, but how can you make this solution scalable? What if you need a couple of dozen message listeners that concurrently dequeue the messages? Don't forget about the tasks of integrating your POJOs with other tiers to perform authentication and JDBC operations.

EJB containers take care of all these infrastructure-related concerns without requiring manual programming on your side. Application servers allow you to configure pools of *message-driven beans* (MDBs) if you need multiple message listeners. You can turn on transactional support if need be. You don't need to worry about multithreading problems if your beans operate in an EJB container. Turning a POJO into an EJB is as simple as adding Java annotations in the EJB classes. Intercommunication among beans is done via dependency injection or singleton beans.

If you need to scale a distributed application, EJB containers offer clustering and failover support. Security authorization is also the container's responsibility. Without the need to manually code all these infrastructural functionalities, the code of your EJBs becomes really light.

The other interesting service offered by EJB containers is *asynchronous method invocation*, which enables asynchronous processing.

EJB supports embeddable containers (`https://docs.oracle.com/javaee/7/tutorial/ejb-embedded.htm#GKCQZ`). You can run EJB applications in a Java SE environment outside of any application servers. This is a good idea for tasks such as testing because there's no need to depend on the readiness of a Java EE server; you can just test your EJBs locally. Creating an embeddable container comes down to executing one line of code:

```
EJBContainer myContainer = EJBContainer.createEJBContainer();
```

If the originally selected application server doesn't deliver the performance or reliability you expected, deploy your EJBs in a different Java EE 7-compliant server without changing a line of code.

TYPES OF EJBS

There are two major types of EJB: *session beans* and *message-driven beans*. MDBs specialize in retrieving messages from JMS queues or topics—this is all they can do. Your application business logic resides in the session beans. There are three types of session beans:

- A *stateless* session bean is one that contains business logic but doesn't support state. In other words, it doesn't "remember" any data specific to the client. If the same client invokes two methods in a row on the stateless bean `FindBooks`, the container may decide to use two separate instances of the `FindBooks` bean, as it doesn't store any intermediate data specific to the client.
- A *stateful* session bean is one that contains business logic and state. The EJB container allocates a specific instance of the session bean to the client and can store results between subsequent method invocations.
- A *singleton* session bean is instantiated once per application. Think of a singleton bean as a global repository in which one bean can put some data to be used by another bean. Singleton session beans not only provide easy access to common data but also ensure that there are no race conditions in cases of concurrent access.

Older EJB specifications defined *entity beans* for data persistence. Formally they still exist in the current EJB specification, but they are pruned (made optional for implementation by the vendors of Java EE 7-compliant application servers).

An EJB container creates and maintains pools of session beans. The instances of the stateless beans are allocated to clients for much less time than stateful ones. Therefore, if you are working on a multiuser application with hundreds or thousands of concurrent requests to the EJB container, stateless beans offer a much more scalable solution because a smaller pool can serve more users' requests.

But even with stateful session beans, the EJB container is playing smart, and those instances sitting in memory without active interaction with the client are being *passivated*—removed from memory and stored on the disk. When the client issues another request to a stateful bean that has been passivated, the container *activates* it again.

STATELESS SESSION BEANS

I'll introduce you to stateless session beans by creating a simple example featuring an EJB that contains the business logic to return the message "Hello World."

The Bean

Having a class that just returns "Hello World" and lives in a the container can be easily implemented as a stateless session bean: It has only one method, and there is no state to remember. Listing 31-1 shows you how to program such a bean.

LISTING 31-1 HelloWorld session bean, take 1

```
@Stateless
public class HelloWorldBean {

    public String sayHello(){
        return "Hello World!";
    }
}
```

Basically, you create a POJO and annotate it with one or more Java annotations. There are no special interfaces to be implemented to turn a POJO into an EJB. Accordingly there are `@Stateful`, `@MessageDriven`, and `@Singleton` annotations to mark other types of session beans.

The preceding version of `HelloWorldBean` doesn't specify how the clients can access this so-called *no interface view* bean, which means that when a client gets a reference to the bean it can only be of the bean's data type (`HelloWorldBean` in our case). You cannot declare a reference variable of an interface type because the bean doesn't implement any. Classes that are deployed in the same archive file can access the method `sayHello()` using resource injection with the `@EJB` annotation:

```
@EJB HelloWorldBean myBean;
myBean.sayHello();
```

The Client's View

The bean shown in Listing 31-1 runs on the server, but the client that invokes the `sayHello()` method can run either in the same Java Virtual Machine (JVM) (for example, a servlet or another bean) or in another one (for example, a standalone Java SE application or Java EE class deployed in another container). Beans may or may not implement interfaces. If `HelloWorldBean` will be used only by clients running in the same JVM, you can mark it with an optional `@LocalBean` annotation to show that it's a no-interface bean. If `HelloWorldBean` in addition to a no-interface view can also be exposed to other clients, the `@LocalBean` has to explicitly annotate the bean.

If you'd like to expose only certain business methods to local clients, you can create a business interface, declare these methods there, have your bean implement them, and mark the bean with a `@Local` annotation. The `@Local` annotation can be used with either a business interface or with the session bean itself.

If you'd like to expose some methods to remote clients, create an interface, declare the business methods there, implement them in the bean, and mark it as `@Remote`.

Local No-Interface Beans

I am planning to use `HelloWorldBean` from the servlet running in the same JVM, so the final version of the code looks like Listing 31-2.

LISTING 31-2 HelloWorld session bean, take 2

```
import javax.ejb.LocalBean;
import javax.ejb.Stateless;

@LocalBean
@Stateless
public class HelloWorldBean {

    public String sayHello(){
        // You can instantiate and use other POJOs
        // here if need be

        return "Hello World!";
    }
}
```

Any EJB can use regular Java classes to implement business logic: For example, the `sayHello()` method can create instances of other Java classes with the `new` operator and invoke their business methods if need be. Or even better, you can instantiate POJOs using Context Dependency Injection (CDI), which is explained in Lesson 33.

Now it's time to do it hands-on. Create a new Dynamic Web Project in Eclipse named `Lesson31`. Then create a new servlet class, `HelloWorldServlet`, in the package `lesson31.client` (select File → New → Servlet).

You use only the doGet() method in this servlet. This servlet becomes your client, communicating with the EJB.

Next create a Java class called HelloWorldBean in the package lesson31.ejb by selecting File → New → Other → EJB → Session Bean (EJB 3.x). Do not select any local or remote business interfaces. By default, Eclipse generates a no-interface view bean and annotates it as @Stateless @LocalBean. Eclipse creates a class with a default constructor. Add to this class the method sayHello() shown earlier in Listing 31-2, and the EJB is ready for use.

The next step is to inject the HelloWorldBean into the servlet code with the @EJB annotation:

```
@EJB HelloWorldBean myBean;
```

Eclipse marks this line with a red error bullet. Right-click it and select Quick Fix to automatically insert two import statements: one for the @EJB annotation and the other for HelloWorldBean.

Using JNDI remains an alternative to injecting the bean into the client. Java EE supports portable JNDI names that don't depend on the application server's implementation. Instead of the @EJB annotation you could (but we won't) use the following code:

```
Context ctx = new InitialContext();
HelloWorldBean myBean = (HelloWorldBean)
                  ctx.lookup("java:global/Lesson31/HelloWorldBean");
```

Now add the following two lines in the doGet() method of the servlet to make it invoke the method sayHello() on the EJB:

```
PrintWriter out = response.getWriter();
out.println(myBean.sayHello());
```

That's all there is to it. The complete code of the servlet is shown in Listing 31-3.

LISTING 31-3 Servlet client for HelloWorldBean

```
package lesson31.client;
import java.io.IOException;
import java.io.PrintWriter;
import javax.ejb.EJB;
import javax.servlet.ServletException;
import javax.servlet.annotation.WebServlet;
import javax.servlet.http.HttpServlet;
import javax.servlet.http.HttpServletRequest;
import javax.servlet.http.HttpServletResponse;
import lesson31.ejb.HelloWorldBean;

@WebServlet(urlPatterns = { "/HelloWorldServlet" })
public class HelloWorldServlet extends HttpServlet {

  @EJB HelloWorldBean myBean;
```

```
    protected void doGet(HttpServletRequest request,
                         HttpServletResponse response)
                          throws ServletException, IOException {

        PrintWriter out = response.getWriter();
        out.println(myBean.sayHello()); }
}
```

Deploy the project `Lesson31` in GlassFish server (right-click the server name and use Add and Remove menu) and start the server. Right-click the servlet HelloWorldServlet and select Run As → Run on Server. The servlet calls the method on the EJB, and you see what's shown in Figure 31-1 in the Eclipse internal web browser.

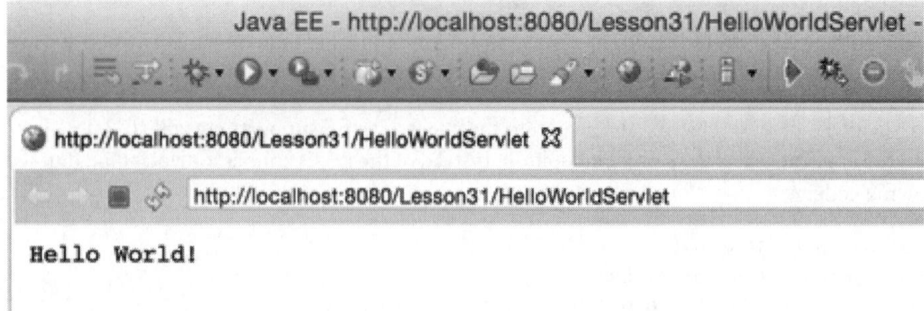

FIGURE 31-1: Running the servlet, an EJB client

You can copy the servlet's URL in your web browser and the resulting web page will be the same.

Printing Hello World from an EJB may not look too impressive, but my goal was to illustrate how to move the application logic from servlet to the EJB.

AUTOMATIC REDEPLOYMENTS ON THE SERVER

While working on your project you might want to make sure that the server performs automatic redeployment of your application when the Java code changes. Just double-click the GlassFish server in the Servers view, which will open the Overview window describing the server. Expand the Publishing panel there and select the option Automatically Publish When Resources Change.

Local Beans

Now to expose a business method to local clients, you can declare the interface marked with the `@Local` annotation. In Eclipse create a new session bean named `HelloWorldLocal`, select the Local checkbox, and enter `Authorizable` as the name of the business interface, as shown in Figure 31-2.

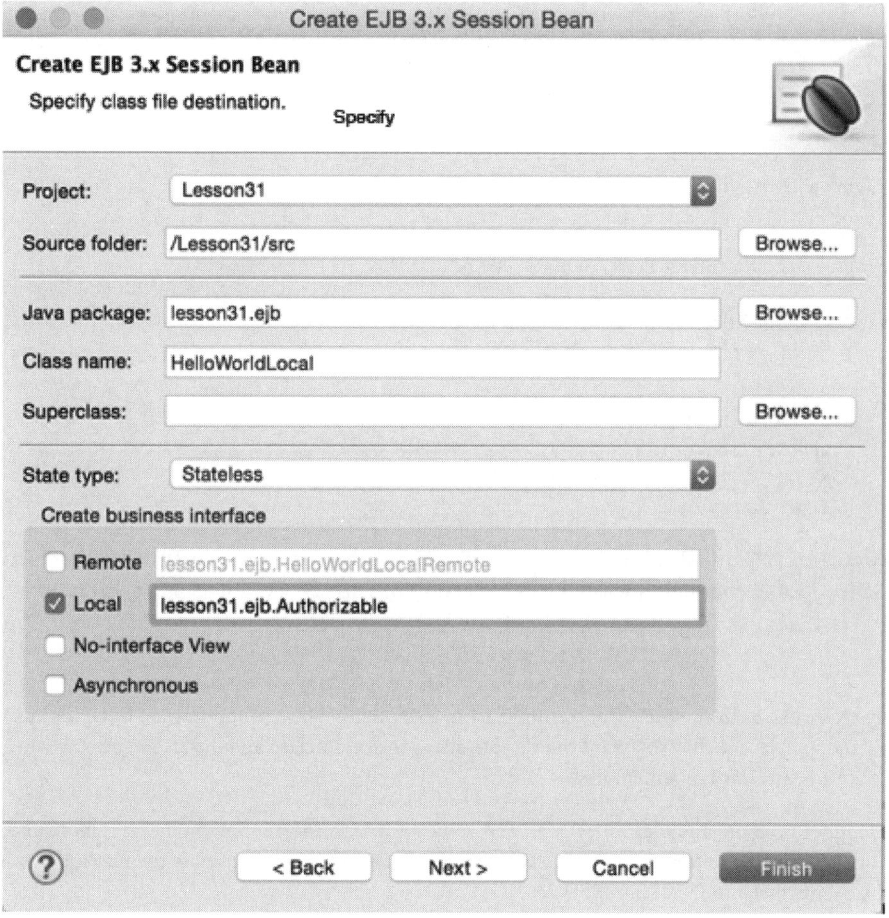

FIGURE 31-2: Creating an EJB with a business interface

Eclipse generates the interface `Authorizable` and the EJB class that should implement it.

After I've added the declaration of the method `authorize()`, this interface looks as follows:

```
package lesson31.ejb;

import javax.ejb.Local;

@Local
public interface Authorizable {
   public String authorize();
}
```

Now you can implement the method `authorize()` and add `sayHello()` as before.

LISTING 31-4 Local interface and bean

```
package lesson31.ejb;

import javax.ejb.Stateless;

@Stateless
public class HelloWorldLocal implements Authorizable {

     public String authorize(){
            return "The user is authorized!";
     }

     public String sayHello(){
         return "Hello World!";
     }
}
```

The difference between `HelloWorldBean` and `HelloWorldLocal` is that the former doesn't implement any interfaces, but the latter does. Accordingly, the latter exposes a `Authorizable` view to the local clients.

Remote Beans

For clients that may access the bean remotely (for example, from a standalone Java program via a JNDI lookup), you can expose only the interface(s) that you want the remote client to see. Declare an interface marked with `@Remote` and have your bean class implement it.

An EJB can implement both remote and local interfaces, and you can expose different methods for remote and local clients, too. For example, the following bean `HelloWorldLocalRemote` exposes only the method `sayHello()` to the clients that run in a different JVM.

LISTING 31-5 An EJB that implements local and remote interfaces

```
@Local public interface Authorizable {
    public String authorize(); }

@Remote
public interface Greeting {
   public String sayHello();
}

@Stateless
public class HelloWorldLocalRemote
                       implements Authorizable, Greeting {

     public String authorize(){
            return "The user is authorized!";
     }
```

```
        public String sayHello(){
            return "Hello World!";
        }
    }
```

The clients find remote beans by performing JNDI lookups. Because the remote client runs in different JVMs, all arguments of the remote methods must be serializable.

Asynchronous Methods and Concurrency

There is one more feature in stateless beans that I'd like you to be aware of: *asynchronous methods*. Imagine that `sayHello()` is a long-running method performing some lengthy calculations, and you'd like to call it and continue with other operations without waiting for it to complete. In a Core Java application you would start a thread that would eventually return the `Future` object, as explained in Lesson 17.

Prior to Java EE 7, it was not safe to create and start threads from the Java EE container, which was taking care of all multithreading issues for you. So asynchronous methods were introduced to start a parallel process and free the EJB for handling other clients' requests.

Just mark the bean's method with the `@Asynchronous` annotation and have it return an object of type `javax.ejb.AsyncResult`, which is an implementation of the `Future` interface:

```
@Asynchronous
public Future<String> modelStockPrices(){

    // Some lengthy calculations go here
    //...

   return new AsyncResult<String>("The best stock to buy is...");
}
```

The client would make a call to `modelStockPrices()` then execute some other code without waiting for `modelStockPrices()` to complete. At some point it would request `Future` by making a blocking call, `get()`, as in the following code snippet:

```
//Asynchronous call
Future<String> myFutureStockToBuy = myBean.modelStockPrices();

// Some other code that is executed immediately without
// waiting for modelStockPrices() to complete goes here

// Sometime later the client's code makes a blocking call and starts
// waiting for the result of modelStockPrices()
String stockRecommendations = myFutureStockToBuy.get();
```

You can also use asynchronous methods if a client needs to start more than one method on the EJB to run in parallel threads. The methods don't even need to return values; say one is generating large PDF files and the other prepares shipments based on today's orders. In this case you don't even need to process returned values; just declare the methods as asynchronous and invoke them from the client (fire and forget). They start immediately and run in parallel. Such asynchronous methods need to return `void` instead of `<Future>`.

The Java EE 7 specification includes JSR 236 (`https://jcp.org/en/jsr/detail?id=236`) (Concurrency Utilities) that allows you to create threads from the application code. These threads are controlled by the Java EE container, so your application remains thread safe. In Java EE code, you can use `javax.enterprise.concurrent.ManagedExecutorService`, which is a peer of the Java SE `ExecutorService`. You can obtain the reference to the `ManagedExecutorService` using standard resource injection:

```
@Resource(lookup="java:comp/DefaultManagedExecutorService")
ManagedExecutorService myExecutor;
```

The JNDI lookup is supported as well. After obtaining the reference to the instance of `ManagedExecutorService`, you can execute a task—the class that implements either `Runnable` or `Callable` interface; for example:

```
myExecutor.execute(new Runnable(...));

Future future = meExecutor.submit(new Callable(...));
```

The rest of the thread processing is done similarly to the Executor Framework routines with the help of Concurrency Utilities for Java EE (`https://docs.oracle.com/javaee/7/tutorial/concurrency-utilities.htm#GKJIQ8`).

STATEFUL SESSION BEANS

Although stateless session beans are given to the client just for the time one method execution takes, stateful beans are allocated to the client for longer. They have state; they remember the results of the execution of previous method(s). For example, you can use a stateful bean to implement shopping cart functionality, enabling the user to add more than one item to the cart while browsing the company's catalog. When the client ends the session the stateful bean can be allocated to another client.

Suppose you have a stateful EJB called `MyShoppingCart`. The client's application looks up this bean using JNDI (or gets it injected) and makes the first call to the method `addItem()`. Then the user continues browsing and adds another item to the shopping cart. Then the user decides to complete the purchase and calls the method `placeOrder()`. All these method invocations are done on the same instance of the stateful bean `MyShoppingCart`:

```
MyShoppingCart myCart = (MyShoppingCart)
               ctx.lookup("java:global/OnlineStore/MyShoppingCart");

// The client is browsing the catalog and finds the first item
// to buy
// ...
myCart.addItem(myFirstItem);
// The client continue browsing the catalog and finds the second
// item to buy
```

```
...
myCart.addItem(mySecondItem);

// The client is ready to complete the purchase
// ...

myCart.placeOrder();
```

To complete the shopping process and release the stateful bean for other users, the program needs to call one of the bean's MyShoppingCart methods marked with the @Remove annotation. In the preceding example the method placeOrder() should be marked with this annotation. You should also provide another @Remove method on the bean to allow the client to cancel the order and release the bean.

There is one more way to release a stateful bean—by using the @StatefulTimeout annotation, which enables you to specify how long a bean can stay allocated to the client without any activity. When this time expires the session times out and the bean is released.

SINGLETON BEANS

Pretty often an application needs a place to keep data that are shared by all the beans. This is when a singleton bean comes in handy. Another use case for a singleton is to control access to some external resources. For example, if a limited number of connections are available to some external Web Service, you can create a singleton that implements throttling for EJBs that need these connections. A singleton bean can be used as global storage (or a cache) for the application; the state of this bean is shared among clients.

Only one singleton bean with any given name can exist per JVM per application. If you need several singletons in an application, give them different names. An EJB container doesn't create pools of singleton beans. To create a singleton EJB just mark a POJO with the @Singleton annotation:

```
@Singleton
public class MyGlobalStorage {
...
}
```

When is the singleton bean created? It's up to the EJB container to decide, unless you specifically want to request that this bean be created on application startup. This is called *eager initialization,* and there is a special annotation, @Startup, for it:

```
@Startup
@Singleton
public class MyGlobalStorage {

    // a storage for objects to be shared
    private Map<String, Object> = new HashMap<>();

    addToStorage(String key, Object objToStore){...}

    removeFromStorage(String key){...}
}
```

Let's say that you'd like to create a program that at certain times sends some messages into a queue. Write a singleton bean, request that the EJB container instantiates it on application start-up, and start pushing the messages immediately after the singleton has been constructed. There is another handy annotation, `@PostConstruct`, that causes the container to invoke a method immediately after the bean's constructor is finished:

```
@Startup
@Singleton
public class MyStockQuoteServer {
...
@PostConstruct
void sendPriceQuotes(){
   // The code connecting to the stock prices feed and
   // sending messages to a queue goes here
 }
}
```

To get access to the business methods of a singleton, the client Java classes need to call the public static method `getInstance()` on the specific singleton, as shown in the following code snippet. If you'll be implementing the singleton design pattern manually in Java SE you need to declare a private constructor and a public static `getInstance()` in the class:

```
MyGlobalStorage.getInstance()
               .addToStorage("emplOfTheMonth", bestEmployee);
```

But in Java EE, the EJB container takes care of this. The EJB container allows concurrent access to singleton beans, and by default it applies the *container-managed concurrency* policy, sparing the developer worry about race conditions and such. You just need to use the `@Lock` annotation, specifying whether you want a resource to be locked during the read or write operation. If you prefer to write thread-synchronization code by yourself, switch to *bean-managed concurrency*. You set the type of concurrency using the `@ConcurrencyManagement` annotation, as shown here:

```
@Singleton
@ConcurrencyManagement(ConcurrencyManagementType.BEAN)
public class MyGlobalStorage {
...
}
```

DEPLOYING EJB

Before deployment to any application server, EJBs are usually packaged into one archive file, which could be a jar; an *Enterprise Archive* (ear), which is a Java archive with an `.ear` file name extension; or a `.war` in case of web applications. Even a simple web application should be compressed and deployed as one file. If your client's code is located in a web application it's convenient to keep the EJB inside a `.war` file, too.

The right way to package the application in an archive file is to use a build automation system like Ant, Maven, or Gradle (see Lesson 36). But for training purposes you can create a `.war` file in Eclipse, too. Right-click the Deployment Descriptor section in the Eclipse project Lesson31 and select Export → WAR file. In a second you get the file `Lesson31.war` that contains both the servlet and the EJB.

This file can be deployed in any Java EE-compliant application server. This `.war` file is small: less than 4 KB! Java EE makes EJB components really lightweight. If you have multiple EJB classes, put them in one or more jars in the `WEB-INF/lib` directory.

If your client is not a small web application, or you want to keep EJBs deployed separately, you can package them inside a separate `.jar` or `.ear` file. The root directory that you'll be using to create `.ear` files has to have all compiled Java classes and, if applicable, the optional `ejb-jar.xml` file. As a matter of fact, you can create an `.ear` file that contains not only your EJBs, but also the `.war` file.

The optional configuration file `ejb-jar.xml` allows you to specify metadata for the EJB, and if you need to change the metadata on a production system without recompiling the code, make the changes in `ejb-jar.xml`. They override the values specified via annotations. For standalone applications, this file is stored in the application server's directory `META-INF`. If the EJBs are packaged with the web application inside the `.war` file, the `ejb-jar.xml` has to be located in the directory `WEB-INF`.

JAVA ARCHIVES - JARS

A typical Java application, library or framework consists of multiple classes, interfaces and configuration files. To simplify deployment and distribution, all these files are packaged into a small number of Java archives (JARs). Most of the third party libraries are distributed as JARs. Both JRE and Java SDK include dozens of JARs. In Eclipse you can see them by opening project properties.

Java comes with a *jar* utility that is used to archive multiple Java classes and other files into a file having the name extension `.jar`. Internal formats of `.jar` and `.zip` files are the same.

To create a jar that will contain all files with extension .class, open the Command or Terminal window, get into the folder where your classes are, and type the following command:

```
jar cvf myClasses.jar *.class
```

After the word jar you should specify the options for this command. In the last example `c` is for creating a new archive, `v` is for displaying what goes in there, and `f` means that the file name of the new archive is provided.

To *unjar* (extract) the files from the archive `myClasses.jar`, type the following command:

```
jar xvf myClasses.jar
```

All files will be extracted into the current directory. In this example the option `x` is for extracting files from the archive.

If you just want to see the content of the jar without extracting the files, use the next command where `t` is for the table of contents:

```
jar tvf myClasses.jar
```

If a JAR includes a manifest file (`http://docs.oracle.com/javase/tutorial/deployment/jar/appman.html`) that includes the `Main-Class` entry, you can run such a Java application from a command line without the need to unzip the JAR:

```
java -jar myApplication.jar
```

If your project needs to include a third-party library you should add its JAR(s) to the `CLASSPATH` environment variable. For example, in Lesson 21 we had to add the file `derbyclient.jar` that contained database drivers for Derby DB to the `CLASSPATH`. In Eclipse IDE you do this by adding external JARs to the Build Class Path of the project. For more information read Oracle's tutorial "Packaging programs in JAR Files (`http://docs.oracle.com/javase/tutorial/deployment/jar`)."

MESSAGE-DRIVEN BEANS

MDBs (message-driven beans) perform only one function: They retrieve messages from queues and topics via the JMS API. The clients never need to look them up or invoke their methods. The client just needs to drop a message in a queue or publish it to a topic, and the MDBs that were listening to the messages at these destinations get invoked automatically.

MDBs must implement the `MessageListener` interface. All configuration parameters can be specified in the parameters of the `@MessageDriven` annotation, as shown in the following example.

LISTING 31-6 MDB MyMessageBean

```
@MessageDriven(mappedName="jms/testQueue", activationConfig = {
      @ActivationConfigProperty(propertyName = "acknowledgeMode",
                                propertyValue = "Auto-acknowledge"),
      @ActivationConfigProperty(propertyName = "destinationType",
                                propertyValue = "javax.jms.Queue")
   })
public class MyMessageBean implements MessageListener {

MessageDrivenContext ctx;

   // A no-argument constructor is required
   public MyListener() {}

   public void onMessage(Message message){
      // The business logic is implemented here.
   }
}
```

When a message appears in the queue named `testQueue`, the EJB container picks one of the MDBs from the pool and invokes its callback method `onMessage()`, passing the message from the queue as an argument. Unlike with the standalone message receivers described in Chapter 30, with MDBs the container gives you excellent freebies: distributed transaction processing, automatic pooling, co-location of receivers and other beans, and simple assignment of queues or topics to the receivers in deployment descriptors. In addition, you can easily configure the number of receivers by specifying the pool size in the deployment descriptor.

You can use any client to send a message in a queue. It can be a standalone client (as shown in how_to_send_a_message), a servlet, an EJB, and so on.

EJB AND TRANSACTIONS

Java EE specification includes Java Transaction API (JTA), which is a standard interface for demarcating transactions in EJB and web containers. Lesson 21 explains how to do transactional updates while working with relational databases. But a logical unit of work may include actions other than updating the database. For example, your application may need to update a database and send a message using JMS in one transaction. If any of these operation fails, the entire transaction should be rolled back.

More than one EJB can perform actions that should be considered a single transaction. The term *transaction scope* defines all participants of the transaction, which may be declared on the same or different EJBs. For example, one session bean can have a method `saveOrder()`, which implements the logic for saving order and calls a method `notifySupplier()` on another bean. If any of these methods fails, the entire transaction should be rolled back.

Say, a transaction started in the method `saveOrder()`, which called `notifySupplier()`. Should the code of the latter work as a part of the existing transaction or create a new one? Should a method simply ignore an existing transaction and its failure should not affect the transaction? There are other questions to answer, too.

JTA transactions in EJB containers can be of two types: *container-managed* and *bean-managed*. Container-managed transactions are managed by the EJB container, and you just specify transactional behavior in a declarative way by using the annotations `@TransactionAttribute` that instruct the EJB container when to consider a transaction successful. With a bean-managed transaction you'd need to invoke the methods `begin()`, `commit()`, and `rollback()` of the `UserTransaction` interface.

But using container-managed declarative transaction is a lot easier. The enum `TransactionAttributeType` declares a handful of transaction attributes:

- `MANDATORY`: This method must always be a part of the transaction of the invoking method. If the invoking method has no transaction, the exception `EJBTransactionRequired` is thrown.
- `REQUIRED` : This method must be invoked within a transaction scope. If the invoking method was not transactional, the container will create a new transaction.
- `REQUIRES_NEW`: Always start a new transaction for this method even if the invoking method has its own transaction
- `SUPPORT`: Execute the code of this method as a part of the transaction of the invoking method.
- `NOT_SUPPORTED`: Suspend the transaction of the invoking method until this method is complete. If the invoking method is not executed within a transaction, this method also won't be transactional.
- `NEVER`: This method must never be a part of the transaction. If the invoking method has a transaction, the `EJBException` is thrown.

If the class is annotated with a transaction attribute, it applies to all methods from the class. You can override the class attribute on the method level. The next example shows a stateless bean that declares that container must create a new transaction for each method except `method3()`, which should never be executed inside a transaction:

```
@Stateless
@TransactionAttribute(TransactionAttributeType.REQUIRES_NEW)
class MySessionBean {

  public void method1(){...}

  public void method2(){...}

  @TransactionAttribute(TransactionAttributeType.NEVER)
  public void method3(){...}

}
```

Message-driven bean can use only `NOT_SUPPORTED` or `REQUIRED` transaction attributes.

TIMER SERVICE

Many enterprise applications require the use of schedulers to perform certain repetitive tasks at certain times. Cron is a widely used scheduler for UNIX-based applications. Windows also has a task scheduler (Control Panel → Scheduled Tasks). The open-source Quartz Scheduler is also popular among Java developers.

EJB supports the `@Schedule` annotation, which takes a calendar-based expression so you can schedule the execution of required functionality in your beans. For example, you can create expressions that invoke some business method every second, minute, hour, Monday, weekday, midnight, and so on.

The next code snippet shows how you can create a timer that invokes the method `getPriceQuotes()` every second during weekdays from 9:30 a.m. to 4:00 p.m.:

```
@Stateless
public class MyStockQuoteFeed {

    @Schedule(second="*", minute="*", hour="9:30-16:00",
              dayOfWeek="Mon-Fri")
    public List getPriceQuotes(){
        // The code to connect to price quote feed goes here
        ...
    }
}
```

You can also create timers programmatically using the `TimeService` class and its methods `createTimer()`, `createSingleActionTimer()`, `createIntervalTimer()`, and `createCalendarTimer()`.

In addition to using `@Schedule` and programmatic timers, you can configure timers in the deployment descriptor `ejb-jar.xml`.

SUMMARY

Enterprise Java Beans technology is a powerful solution for creating a scalable, easy-to-develop and -deploy, and lightweight solution for enterprise applications. Even a small-scale applications can benefit from EJB. If your application doesn't need all the features mandated by the EJB specification, consider using EJB Lite, which is a subset of the full specification.

It's not possible to cover all the features offered by EJB containers in one short lesson. I've introduced you to the main EJB concepts, but if you'd like more in-depth coverage, read the EJB section (`https://docs.oracle.com/javaee/7/tutorial/partentbeans.htm#BNBLR`) in Oracle's Java EE 7 tutorial.

TRY IT

> **NOTE** *You can download the code and resources for this "Try It" from the book's web page at* `www.wrox.com/go/javaprog24hr2e`. *You can find them in* `Lesson31.zip`.

The assignment for this lesson is to implement the `StockServer` class as an EJB and to use the timer to automatically generate and print stock price quotes every second. The new quotes should be sent to `testQueue` via the JMS API and consumed by a message-driven bean. Reuse the code of the sample stock server application of the `StockServerImpl` from Listing 24-2 to generate the price quotes.

Lesson Requirements

You should have Java and GlassFish installed.

Hint

If you want to push the stock prices to the end users, consider creating a JMS topic (for example, `PriceQuotes`) to which the method `getQuote()` publishes the latest prices. The Java client should subscribe to this topic to get the fresh quotes every second.

Step-by-Step

1. In Eclipse project Lesson31, create a new stateless session bean, `StockServerBean`, that includes the method `getQuote()`. The initial version of the bean may look as follows:

```
@Stateless
public class StockServerBean {
  private String price=null;
  private List<String> nasdaqSymbols = new ArrayList<>();

  public StockServerBean(){
```

```
        // Define some hard-coded NASDAQ symbols
        nasdaqSymbols.add("AAPL");
        nasdaqSymbols.add("MSFT");
        nasdaqSymbols.add("YHOO");
        nasdaqSymbols.add("AMZN");
    }

    public void getQuote(String symbol){

      if(nasdaqSymbols.indexOf(symbol.toUpperCase()) != -1) {

          // Generate a random price for valid symbols
          price = (new Double(Math.random()*100)).toString();
      }
      System.out.println("The price of "+ symbol + " is " + price);
     }
    }
```

2. Use the `@Schedule` annotation to have the `getQuote()` method invoked every second.
3. Replace the `println()` statement in the method `getQuote()` with the code sending a text message with the generated price quote to the queue `MyJMSTestQueue` configured in Chapter 29.
4. Create an MDB called `MyPriceConsumer` to retrieve and print messages from the queue `MyJMSTestQueue`.
5. Deploy this application in GlassFish and test it.

> **TIP** *Please select the videos for Lesson 31 online at* `www.wrox.com/go/javaprog24hr2e`. *You will also be able to download the code and resources for this lesson from the website.*

32

Overview of the Java Persistence API

In the previous lesson you learned about various types of Enterprise Java Beans in which you could program the business logic of your application. Now it's time to talk about persisting data. If an online store allows users to place orders with session beans, there should be a mechanism for saving the data, too. Typically, the data is persisted in the relational or NoSQL DBMS.

The Java Persistence API (JPA) defines a standard way of mapping the Java classes to their relational database peers. This process is also known as *object-relational mapping (ORM)*. JPA allows you to work with DBMSes using Java objects rather than with SQL. All SQL queries are generated under the hood by the library that implements JPA. The most popular implementation of JPA is Hibernate (`http://hibernate.org/`), and there is a reference implementation called EclipseLink (`http://eclipse.org/eclipselink`). You use EclipseLink in the "Try It" section of this lesson.

This lesson is a brief introduction to the standard JPA 2.1 that's implemented by Java EE 7-compliant servers. You'll also get familiar with the data validation process offered by the Bean Validation framework.

THE BIG PICTURE

In the past, J2EE (currently Java EE) specifications recommended using Entity EJB to provide all interactions with databases. Entity beans have been pruned from the current Java EE specification, and you should use JPA instead to deal with your application's data querying and persistence. As a matter of fact, you can use JPA from Java SE applications, too.

JPA enables you to specify and run queries and update data without needing to write SQL statements as you did in Chapter 21 while studying JDBC. Starting from JPA 2.1 you can invoke stored procedures located in relational DBMSes.

JPA enables you to map Java classes to database tables using metadata, and perform create, retrieve, update, and delete (CRUD) operations using Java Persistence Query Language (JPQL), the Persistence Criteria API, and native database queries in SQL language. The idea is to create an application-specific domain model as a set of interrelated Java classes and map it to the corresponding data storage (the DBMS).

If a Java class marked with the `@Entity` annotation has no argument constructor you can call it an *entity:*

```
@Entity
public class Employee{
  ...
}
```

If a persistent storage is a relational DBMS, each entity instance corresponds to a row in a database table. If you start with an empty database, JPA tools enable you to create database tables based on Java entities. You can also map Java entities to the existing database tables. Just like database tables, Java entities can have one-to-one relationships (such as an `Employee` entity with one corresponding `OfficeAddress` entity); one-to-many relationships (such as one `Customer` with many `Orders`); many-to-one relationships (the opposite of one-to-many relationships); and many-to-many relationships (for example, a `UniversityClass` has many enrolled `Students`, but each `Student` can enroll into multiple classes).

JPA AND NOSQL

In NoSQL DBMS, a Java class entity corresponds to an object in the database. Format of the object varies depending on the DBMS. Popular formats are JSON and BSON (binary JSON). For details, refer to the documentation of your JTA providers. For example, refer to the online documentation of Hibernate Object/Grid Mapper (`http://docs.jboss.org/hibernate/ogm/3.0/reference/en-US/pdf/hibernate_ogm_reference.pdf`) and EclipseLink (`https://wiki.eclipse.org/EclipseLink/Examples/JPA/NoSQL`).

Every entity class must define a field containing a unique value, which is the equivalent of a primary key in a database table. You can either work directly with the fields of an entity class or use setters and getters as defined in the JavaBeans specification (`http://www.oracle.com/technetwork/java/javase/overview/spec-136004.html`). In the latter case, persistent fields must not be `public` and should be accessed by `public` methods, and the entity class must have a no-argument constructor.

The `EntityManager` class deals with objects. Before persisting data you can validate the values using the Bean Validation API illustrated later in this lesson.

While JPQL provides string-based SQL-like syntax for working with entities, the Criteria API enables you to dynamically construct queries from strongly typed objects.

MAPPING OBJECTS TO DATABASE TABLES

You can map Java classes to database tables via annotations, XML configuration files, or both. For example, common fields can be mapped with annotations, and DBMS-specific mapping can be done in XML files. It does not have to be one-to-one mapping; one Java entity can be mapped to a set of columns from more than one database table.

Besides having fields mapped to table columns, Java entities can have embeddable classes, like `Address` in the `Employee` entity.

Typically a database table has a *primary key*—one or more columns that uniquely identify each row. Accordingly, Java entities must have one or more fields making each instance unique. For a one-field key, an entity ID is marked with the `@Id` annotation. A composite key is declared in separate classes, and the entity class is denoted with `@IdClass` (or `@EmbeddedId` if the key defined in embeddable class). You can request your JPA provider to auto-generate the ID by adding the annotation `@GeneratedValue` to the entity class. Listing 32-1 shows an example of an `Employee` entity.

LISTING 32-1 Employee entity

```
@Entity
public class Employee{

  @Id
  @GeneratedValue(strategy=GenerationType.IDENTITY)

  @NotNull
  @Size(max=10)
  private String firstName;

  @NotNull
  @Size(min=2, max=20)
  private String lastName;

  @Column(name="boss_name")
  private String managerName;

  @OneToMany (mappedBy = "employee")
  private List<Address> addresses = new ArrayList<Address>();

  // constructor
  public Employee(){ ...}

  // getters and setters go here
}
```

If you don't specify an annotation containing the database table name in the entity class, JPA assumes that there is a corresponding database table with the same name as the entity class, which in our example is `Employee`. The specified strategy `GenerationType.IDENTITY` means that DBMS has an auto-generated primary key with auto-increment. Many database management systems support either identity columns or sequence objects with similar functionality.

The fields that must have values are marked as `@NotNull`. If an instance of the preceding `Employee` entity won't have values in the `firstName` or `lastName` fields, Bean Validation can catch this and generate an error. The entity fields that don't have to be persisted should be marked with the `@Transient` annotation.

If a table column name is not the same as the name of the entity field, you can specify the column name using `@Column`. According to the code sample Listing 32-1, the database column name `boss_name` corresponds to the field `managerName` of the entity `Employee`.

Not every Java class that corresponds to some data in the database has to be an entity. You can have embeddable classes that define a group of arbitrary properties that belong to an entity. Let's say a company gives to each employee a smartphone identified by a phone number and model number. You can create a Java class to represent such a device and mark it with `@Embeddable`:

```
@Embeddable
public class SmartPhone implements Serializable{

   @Size(max=10)
   public String phoneNumber;

   public String model;
}
```

Now the `Employee` entity can embed the property of the `SmartPhone` type along with other fields:

```
@Entity
public class Employee{

  @Id
  @GeneratedValue(strategy=GenerationType.IDENTITY)

  @NotNull
  public String firstName;

  // some other fields go here
  // ...

  @Embedded
  public SmartPhone companyPhone;

}
```

The code in Listing 32-1 illustrates the mapping of one-to-many relations between the entities `Employee` and `Address` (not shown). One employee can have multiple addresses, so `Employee` references a collection of the `Address` entities.

You can also use `@Embeddable` class to declare a composite primary key for an entity class.

QUERYING ENTITIES

JPA offers two ways of querying entities: Java Persistence Query Language (JPQL) and the Criteria API.

JPQL

JPQL is a SQL-like query language. But SQL operates with the DBMS objects like schemas, tables, and stored procedures, and JPQL manipulates with Java objects and their attributes from the domain model. The application doesn't need to know details of the underlying data storage objects to perform JPQL queries.

If you know the queries in advance you can precompile them; otherwise you can build them dynamically during the run time. Similarly, in JDBC you can use either `PreparedStatement` or `Statement`.

JPQL includes (case-insensitive) keywords that are pretty easy to remember: `SELECT`, `FROM`, `WHERE`, `ORDER BY`, `GROUP BY`, and so on. Here's how you would write a JPQL query to find all managers who have subordinates with the last name Smith:

```
SELECT e.managerName,
FROM Employee AS e
WHERE e.lastName='Smith'
```

Don't be misled by the `SELECT`, `FROM`, and `WHERE` clauses; it's not SQL, and this queries the Java Entity class, which in turn will generate SQL under the hood. The `e` serves as an alias name here to refer to the `Employee` entity name. The result of this query can be a collection of Java objects that contains zero or more instances.

The next query finds all employees who were given iPhones by the firm. Note the dot notation to find the phone model from the embedded class:

```
SELECT e.firstName, e.lastName
FROM Employee AS e
WHERE e.companyPhone.model='iPhone'
```

To populate all fields of certain entities (the equivalent of `Select *` in SQL) just specify the alias name of the entity right after the `SELECT` clause:

```
SELECT e FROM Employee AS e
```

The `Employee` and `Address` entities have a one-to-many relationship. If you'd like to find all employees who live in New York, this is the join written in JPQL:

```
SELECT DISTINCT e
FROM Employee AS e JOIN e.addresses as a
WHERE a.city='New York'
```

Criteria API

Although JPQL is a string-based query language, the Criteria API allows the creation of strongly typed object-based queries. On one hand it's more verbose than JPQL, but on the other there is no need to do data-type conversion when processing query results. Because Criteria API is strongly typed, Java compiler catches all the type-related errors during the compilation time, whereas string-based JPQL needs to be parsed during the run time.

These are some core interfaces in the Criteria API:

- `CriteriaBuilder`: A utility class that can create criteria queries.
- `CriteriaQuery`: This is an object that contains all parts of the query, such as `SELECT`, `FROM`, and `WHERE`. It's like a memory graph, in which each node represents some clause of the query.
- `Root`: Represents the root of the query.
- `TypedQuery`: A query prepared for execution.
- `Join`: An object that represents a `JOIN` clause.

The next code fragment shows an equivalent of the JPQL query `SELECT e FROM Employee AS e` written using the Criteria API:

```
EntityManager em;
...
CriteriaBuilder cb = em.getCriteriaBuilder();

CriteriaQuery<Employee> crQuery = cb.createQuery(Employee.class);
Root<Employee> employee = crQuery.from(Employee.class);
crQuery.select(employee);

TypedQuery<Employee> tQuery= em.createQuery(crQuery);
List<Employee> employees = tQuery.getResultList( );
```

Start with asking `EntityManager` to create `CriteriaBuilder`, which in turn creates the instance of `CriteriaQuery`. Note that via generics, the `CriteriaQuery` is typed based on the expected results. After that you add instances of required objects (`SELECT`, `FROM`, `WHERE`, and so on) to `CriteriaQuery`.

Finally, the `EntityManager` prepares the executable `TypedQuery` that produces strongly typed results by executing `getResultList()`. If you expect just one record back, use the `getSingleResult()` method. You can chain several clauses in the query:

```
crQuery.select(employee).where(...).orderBy(...);
```

Because we are building the object graph, the order of the query classes in the preceding line is not important. The `Root` object can serve as a starting point for joining entities:

```
Root<Employee> employee = crQuery.from(Employee.class);
Join<Employee, Address> empJoin = employee.join(...);
```

The next example shows how to add the `LIKE` clause to get all employees with the last name Thompson:

```
Root<Employee> employee = crQuery.from(Employee.class);
crQuery.select(employee).where(
          cb.like(employee.<String>)get("lastName"),
          cb.parameter(String.class, "lname"));

TypedQuery<Employee> tQuery= em.createQuery(crQuery);
tQuery.setParameter("lname", "%Thompson%");
List<Employee> employees = tQuery.getResultList( );
```

ENTITY MANAGER

Entities are managed by the entity manager `javax.persistense.EntityManager`, which is the centerpiece of persistence mechanism; it executes all your JPA requests to read from or write into a database. Often each instance of `EntityManager` is associated with a set of entities. Such a set is called a *persistence context.*

A JTA transaction usually involves invocation of more than one application component and is annotated with `@PersistenceContext`. In Java EE containers the `EntityManager` can be injected as a resource—for example:

```
@PersistenceContext
EntityManager em;
```

With a container-managed entity manager, its persistence context is automatically propagated by the container to application components. If you want your application to manage multiple instances of `EntityManager` , you need to instantiate it programmatically using `EntityManagerFactory`:

```
private EntityManagerFactory factory;

private static final String PERSISTENCE_CONTEXT_NAME = "employees";
...
factory = Persistence.createEntityManagerFactory(
                                          PERSISTENCE_CONTEXT_NAME);
EntityManager em = factory.createEntityManager();
```

The entity manager can create, update, remove, and find entities by IDs or using a query. The code to find an `Employee` entity with the ID `1234` can look like this:

```
Employee employee = em.find(Employee.class, 1234);
```

To create a new row in the `Employee` database table, create an instance of the entity `Employee` and invoke the method `persist()` on the `EntityManager`. To delete a row, call `remove()`. Your application can explicitly begin and commit transactions when the persistence is successfully completed:

```
@PersistenceContext
EntityManagerFactory factory;
EntityManager em;

@Resource
UserTransaction userTransaction;
...
em=factory.createEntityManager();

Employee newEmployee = new Employee();
newEmployee.firstName="Mary";
newEmployee.lastName="Thompson";
...
try{
  userTransaction.begin();
  em.persist(newEmployee);
  em.remove(oldEmployee);
```

```
userTransaction.commit();

}
catch (SystemException e){ //other exceptions can be thrown here
  e.printStackTrace();
  try{
   userTransaction.rollback();
   } catch(SystemException e1){e1.printStackTrace()}
}
```

To select the manager name of the employee with the `firstName` Mary and the `lastName` Thompson, ask the `EntityManager` to run the following JPQL query:

```
EntityManager em;
List employees;
...employees = em.createQuery(
"SELECT e.managerName FROM Employee AS e WHERE e.firstName='Mary' "
      + " AND e.lastName='Thompson'").getResultList();
```

This static query works only for employees whose full names are Mary Thompson. Note that the method `getResultList()` is invoked on the created query object. If you expect just one entity as a result, call the method `getSingleResult()` instead. To specify the first and last names dynamically, you should use parameters; for example:

```
EntityManager em;
List<Employee> employees;

// parameters
String firstName = "Mary";
String lastName = "Thompson";
...

employees = em.createQuery(
"SELECT e.managerName FROM Employee AS e WHERE " +
  "e.firstName= :fname AND lastName= :lname")
   .setParameter("lname", lastName)
   .setParameter("fname", firstName)
   .getResultList();
```

One instance of `EntityManager` manages a *persistence unit*—a set of classes specified in the configuration file `persistence.xml`, which is located in the `META-INF` directory of the deployed EJB jar. If you package the application in the `.war` file, this file has to be located either in the directory `WEB-INF/classes/META-INF` or in a jar under `WEB-INF/lib`.

The file `persistence.xml` specifies the name of the `.jar` file that contains managed persistence classes and their names. It also contains the name of the JDBC data source (not the specific JDBC driver) used for communication with DBMS; for example:

```
<persistence>
    <persistence-unit name="EmployeeManagement">
        <description>This unit manages Acme Employees </description>
```

```
        <jta-data-source>jdbc/HRDatabase</jta-data-source>
        <jar-file>MyEmployeeApp.jar</jar-file>
        <class>lesson32.Employee</class>
        <class>lesson32.Address</class>
    </persistence-unit>
</persistence>
```

The `<persistence-unit>` element must specify a name that is unique to the persistence unit scope. All classes included in a persistence unit have to work with a single data store defined in the element `<jta-data-source>`, which must be preconfigured as a JNDI resource in your Java EE application server.

BEAN VALIDATION

When the user enters the data, she can make a mistake. The input validation can and should be done on the client's side to prevent unnecessary server requests if the entered data is wrong or incomplete.

Then the data travels to the server, which also has to perform the validation before handling or persisting the data. Think of a web application where the user enters the data in the form, the client-side validation passed, and an HTTP request is made to the server. You should revalidate the data on the server side to protect against the malicious user who might have hijacked and modified the data en route.

Then you need to perform the data validation prior to persisting the data. The Bean Validation framework is supported by all Java EE-compliant servers. It's a Java API for ensuring that the values in entities are correct. You can declare the constraints on your entities, and the validation is automatically initiated when you are about to create, update, or remove an entity. Standard bean validation is done by placing built-in annotations (`https://docs.oracle.com/javaee/7/tutorial/bean-validation001.htm#GKAGK`) on a class, field, or a method of a managed bean. Custom bean validation is done by declaring a custom annotation and implementing the `isValid()` method of the `ConstraintValidator` interface.

The code sample Listing 32-1 declared the field validation using `@NotNull` and `@Size` built-in constraints defined in the package `javax.validation.constraints`, but you can create and implement custom validation rules as well. You can validate non-static methods of the entity class.

The entity life-cycle callback methods marked with the annotations `@PrePersist` and `@PreRemove` are invoked on the entity before the `EntityManager` persists or removes this entity. Accordingly, another pair of annotations, `@PostPersist` and `@PostRemove`, are invoked after these operations.

For example, you can put the validation code in the method `transferEmployee()` to ensure that the transfer has been approved by the employee's manager. Throwing an exception invalidates the operation:

```
@PrePersist
public void validateTransfer(){
   if (!transferApproved()){
     throw new TransferException("Manager didn't approve transfer");
  }
}
```

To prevent `NullPointerExceptions`, you can add a `@NotNull` constraint to the return value of a method:

```
@NotNull
public Employee getEmployee() {
  ...
}
```

If you need to validate a group of fields, you can create a cross-parameter validation on the constructor or a method level. For example, you can create a custom constraint `@EmploymentDates` that ensures that the employee's hire date is older than the resignation date, and none of these dates are Saturday, Sunday, or a company holiday. Such a custom validation can be applied to the class `Employee`:

```
@ValidateEmploymentDates (start="hireDate", end="resignationDate")
public class Employee{
  Date hireDate;
  Date resignationDate;
  ...
}
```

To create a custom validation, you need to declare a custom annotation and implement it. For example, you could declare the custom annotation as follows:

```
@Target( { TYPE, ANNOTATION_TYPE })
@Retention(RUNTIME)
@Constraint(validatedBy = {EmploymentDatesValidator.class} )
@Documented public
@interface ValidateEmploymentDates {
    String message() default "{end} should be later than {start}
                    and can't fall on weekends and holidays";
    String start();
    String end();
    Class[] groups() default {};
    Class[] payload() default {};
}
```

This annotation allows two parameters: `start` and `end`. According to the Bean Validation specification, it must include three mandatory attributes: `message`, `groups`, and `payload`. The `message` attribute is needed to specify an error message if the constraint is violated. An attribute `groups` can be used to group constraints, and must default to an empty array. The `payload` attribute can be used to assign custom payloads required for validation. It also must default to an empty array.

The class that implements this validation has to implement the interface `javax.validation.ConstraintValidator`, that declares two methods: `initialize()` and `isValid()`. The first method initializes the values to be validated, and the second implements the validation logic:

```
public class EmploymentDatesValidator implements
            ConstraintValidator(ValidateEmploymentDates, Employee){

  private String start;
  private String end;
  public void initialize(ValidateEmploymentDates validateEmpDates){
    start = validateEmpDates.start();
    end = validateEmpDates.end();
```

```
    }

    public boolean isValid(Employee employee,
            ConstraintValidatorContext constraintValidatorContext) {

        // Implement the validation logic here.
        // Return true if valid, and false if invalid
    }
}
```

The content of this section should give you an idea how to validate entities. For more details about the Bean Validation API, refer to the Oracle tutorial (`https://docs.oracle.com/javaee/7/tutorial/part-beanvalidation.htm#sthref1322`).

This lesson gives you a very high-level overview of the Java Persistence API. You can find more detailed explanation of JPA in the online Oracle tutorial (`https://docs.oracle.com/javaee/7/tutorial/part-persist.htm#BNBPY`).

TRY IT

The GlassFish 4 server includes the binaries of the JPA 2.1 provider EclipseLink (`http://eclipse.org/eclipselink`), which is an open source mapping and persistence framework. You'll be using EclipseLink to auto-generate the Java entity class `Employee` based on the existing database table `EMPLOYEE`. This serves as an example of object-relational mapping, when Java entities are generated based on the existing database. In this walkthrough you reuse the database named `Lesson21` with a table `Employee` that was created in Lesson 21.

Lesson Requirements

You should have installed Java, Eclipse, GlassFish, and Derby DB , which comes with GlassFish.

You can download the code and resources for this "Try It" from the book's web page at www.wrox.com/go/javaprog24hr2e. *You can find them in* `Lesson32.zip`.

Step-by-Step

1. This time you create a new type of Eclipse project. Create a new JPA project by selecting File → New → JPA → JPA project. Name it `Lesson32`. Select GlassFish 4 as a target run time and JPA Configuration 2.1, as shown in Figure 32-1.

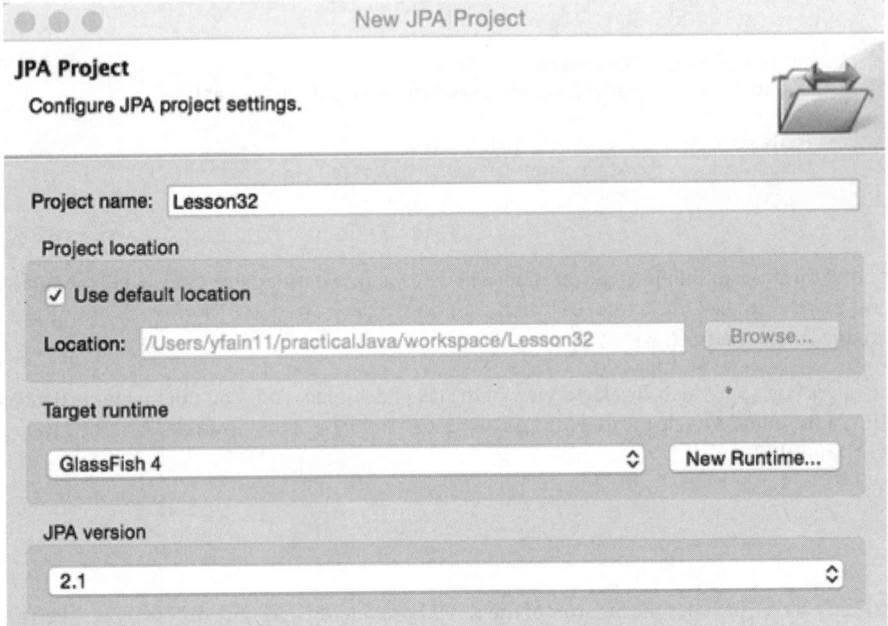

FIGURE 32-1: A fragment of the JPA project configuration window

2. A pop-up suggesting the name of the default output folder displays. Don't change anything there; click Next.
3. The JPA Facet window enables you to select the JPA implementation—the library that implements JPA specification. The User Library box is initially empty.Press the little Preferences icon next to it and then click New in the Preferences window to configure a new library. Call it `EclipseLink`.
4. To include full EclipseLink implementation, add the following external jars from the folder `glassfish4/glassfish/modules` to your EclipseLink user library:

```
org.eclipse.persistence.antlr.jar
org.eclipse.persistence.asm.jar
org.eclipse.persistence.core.jar
org.eclipse.persistence.dbws.jar
org.eclipse.persistence.jpa.jar
org.eclipse.persistence.jpa.jpql.jar
org.eclipse.persistence.jpa.modelgen.processor.jar
org.eclipse.persistence.moxy.jar
org.eclipse.persistence.oracle.jar
javax.persistence.jar
```

5. Click the Finish button and the generation of the Eclipse JPA project will be finished. The structure of your project should look similar to Figure 32-2.

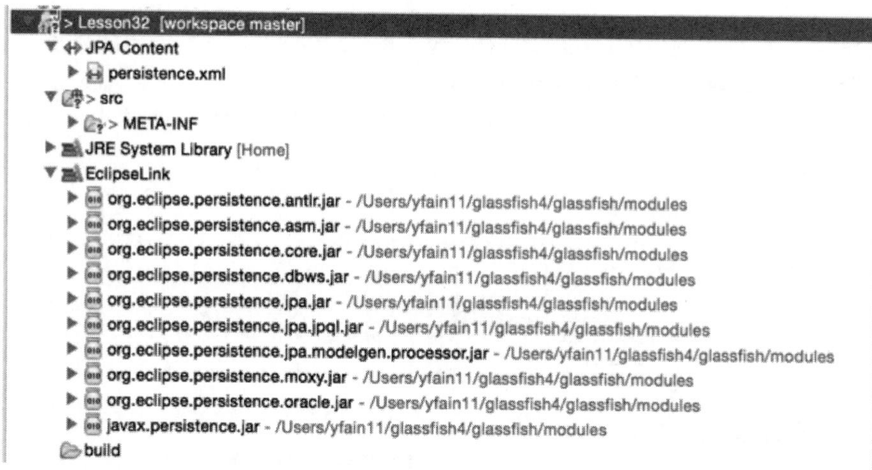

FIGURE 32-2: Newly generated Eclipse JPA project with EclipseLink support

6. Start your Derby database server using the `startNetworkServer` command, as explained in creating_a_database_with_derby in Lesson 21.
7. Using the ij utility in a separate command window, check to see that the database `Lesson21` exists and the table `Employee` (created in Lesson 21) is still there. If not, re-create it and populate it with data.
8. Add the file `derby/lib/derbyclient.jar` to the build path of your Eclipse project (right-click the project Lesson32, select Properties → Java Build Path → Libraries → Add External Jars). This is where the Derby DB implements the JDBC driver.
9. In the project's Data Source Explorer view, right-click Database Connections (see Figure 32-3) and create a new Connection Profile.

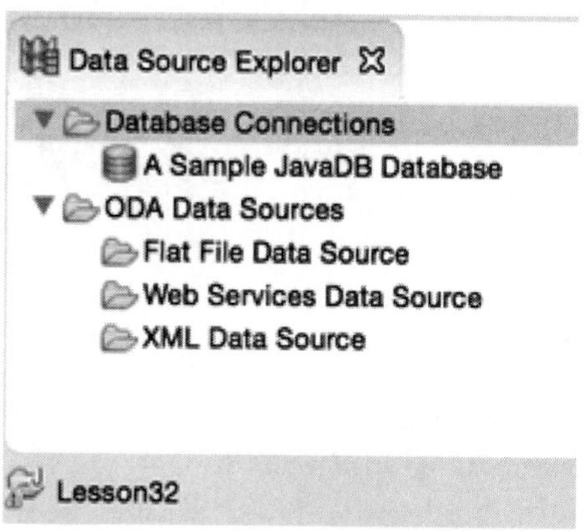

FIGURE 32-3: The Data Source Explorer View

10. In the pop-up window, configure your new connection into the database Lesson21 that you created in Chapter 21Chapter 21. The default user id is `user` and the password is `sys`. (See Figure 32-4.)

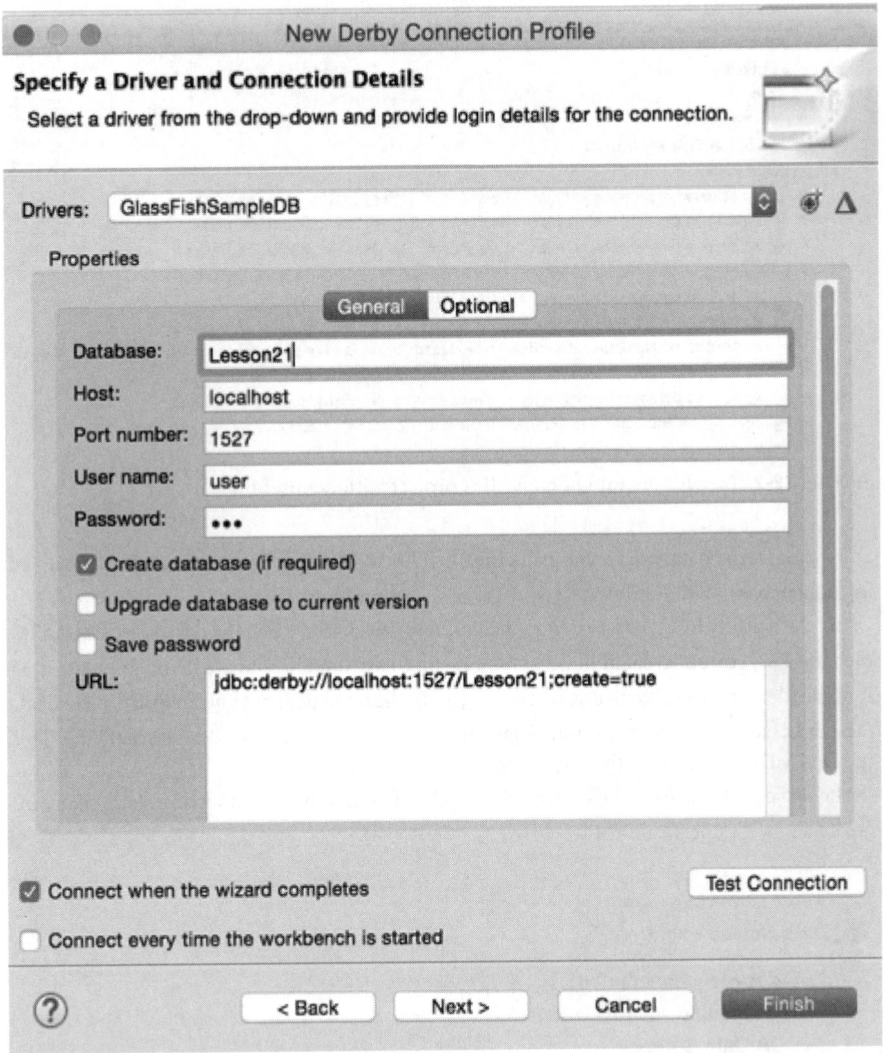

FIGURE 32-4: Configuring new connection profile

11. Click Test Connection to ensure the connection is successful.

12. Using the view Data Source Explorer, connect to the database using the newly configured profile and see that the table Employee exists in the APP schema, as shown in Figure 32-5.

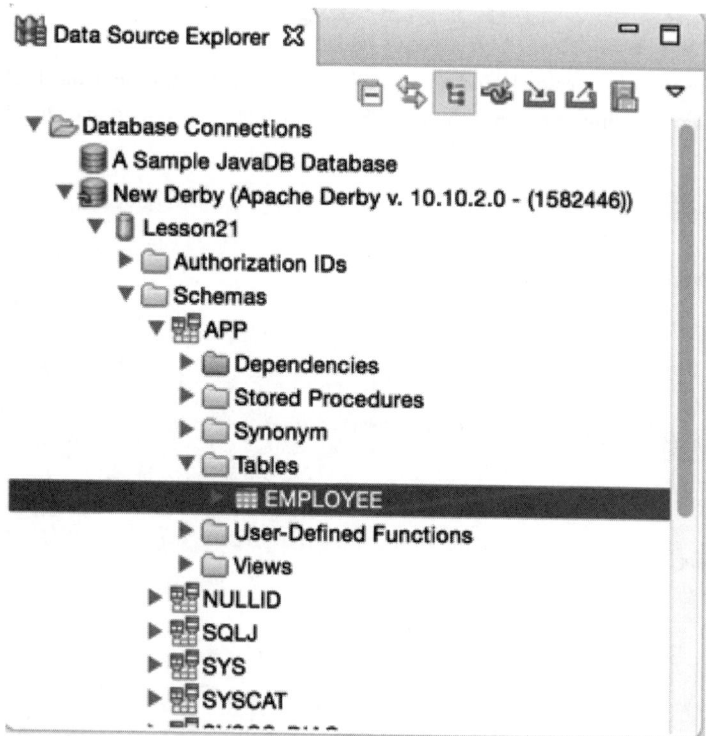

FIGURE 32-5: Verifying that the table Employee exists

13. You can see the data in Eclipse, as shown in Figure 32-6; right-click the table `Employee` and select Data → Sample Contents.

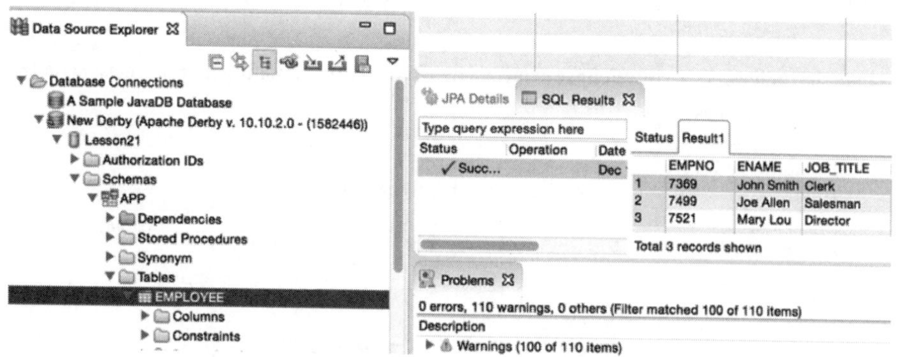

FIGURE 32-6: Sampling the data from a table

14. JPA requires database tables to have primary keys, but our table Employee didn't define one. You need to fix this by making the column `empno` a primary key. You can do it from the command line via the *ij* utility (see working_with_databases_using_jdbc) by issuing the following command:

```
alter table APP.Employee add primary key (empno);
```

15. Right-click the name of project Lesson32 and select JPA Tools → Generate Entities from Tables. In the pop-up window, select the connection, the schema APP, and the table `Employee` and click Finish as shown in Figure 32-7.

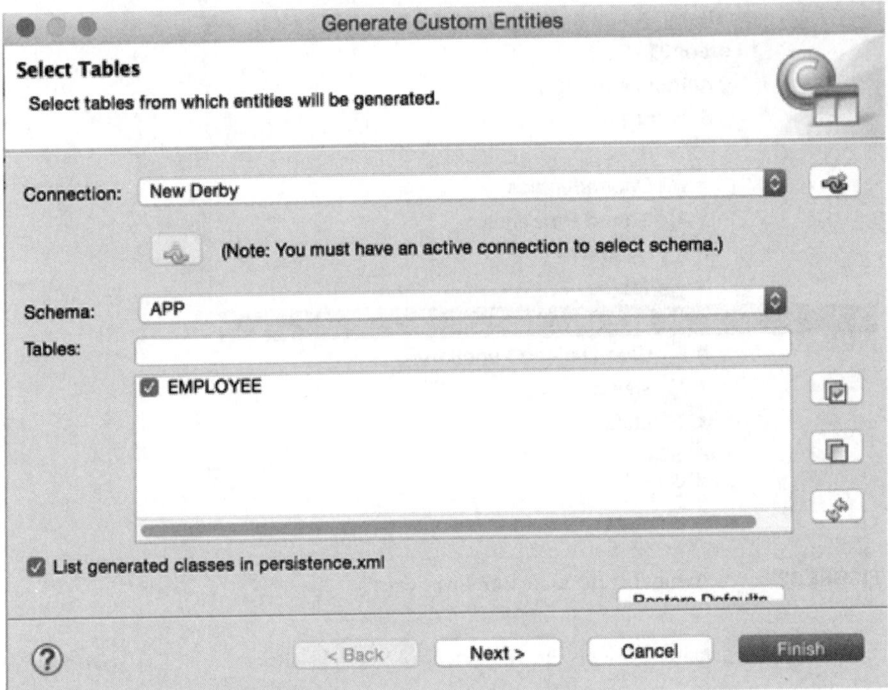

FIGURE 32-7: Generating an entity from the existing table

16. Open the folder `src` in your Eclipse project, where you'll find a freshly generated class called `Employee` that looks as follows:

```
package model;
import java.io.Serializable;import javax.persistence.*;

/** * The persistent class for the EMPLOYEE database table. * */

@Entity
@NamedQuery(name="Employee.findAll",
            query="SELECT e FROM Employee e")
public class Employee implements Serializable {
  private static final long serialVersionUID = 1L;

  @Id private int empno;
  private String ename;
  @Column(name="JOB_TITLE") private String jobTitle;
```

```
    public Employee() { }

    public int getEmpno() { return this.empno; }

    public void setEmpno(int empno) { this.empno = empno; }

    public String getEname() { return this.ename; }

    public void setEname(String ename) { this.ename = ename; }

    public String getJobTitle() { return this.jobTitle; }

    public void setJobTitle(String jobTitle) {
     this.jobTitle = jobTitle; }
}
```

Finally, open the folder META-INF, where you'll find the file persistence.xml:

```
<?xml version="1.0" encoding="UTF-8"?>
<persistence version="2.1"
  xmlns="http://xmlns.jcp.org/xml/ns/persistence"
  xmlns:xsi="http://www.w3.org/2001/XMLSchema-instance"
  xsi:schemaLocation="http://xmlns.jcp.org/xml/ns/persistence
  http://xmlns.jcp.org/xml/ns/persistence/persistence_2_1.xsd">

    <persistence-unit name="Lesson32">
        <class>model.Employee</class>
    </persistence-unit>

</persistence>
```

Eclipse has generated the Java entity class Employee from an existing database table. This completes your assignment.

The reverse workflow is also supported. Eclipse can generate a database table based on the entity class definition. To do this, you'd need to use the option JPA Tools → Generate Tables from Entities.

> **TIP** *Please select the videos for Lesson 32 online at* www.wrox.com/go/javaprog24hr2e. *You will also be able to download the code and resources for this lesson from the website.*

33

Working with RESTful Web Services

In the 1990s the web became widely used, and newly created web applications were consumed by millions of people around the world. At the same time lots of legacy applications were available for use only within corporate walls. They were written in a variety of programming languages and deployed on many types of hardware. There was a need to expose corporate data to wider audiences, which resulted in the creation of the standard interface for consuming data over the web.

The difference between traditional JSP/Servlet/JSF web applications and Web Services is that the latter offer just the data and have no interest in what the client's user interface (UI) looks like. For example, an insurance company could offer information about its products, or a mutual fund could expose its data as a Web Service returning XML documents. Clients didn't need to know that this insurance company was running its applications using a server from Oracle or that the mutual fund was running on mainframe computers from IBM.

Java EE includes specification for two different implementations of Web Services—JAX-WS and JAX-RS, which I discuss next. Take another look at the sample architectural diagram in Lesson 25 and notice that I put these APIs in two places—one in the Presentation tier and another in the Data tier. Just think of Web Services as a mechanism to expose useful data that can be retrieved using HTTP requests.

Thousands of publicly available Web Services offer various APIs to get the data of some kind. You can find plenty of useful Web Services at the ProgrammableWeb (`http://www.programmableweb.com/apis/directory`) directory. Enterprises use private Web Services for their internal needs, too.

THE SOAP WEB SERVICES

The first standard for publishing and consuming Web Services was the XML-based Simple Object Access Protocol (SOAP). Web clients would form HTTP requests and receive responses using the SOAP syntax.

The clients needed to know the directory of services available from this particular organization, the names of the offered operations (functions), and the address of the *endpoint* to connect to in order to consume this service.

The directory of services could be published with the XML-based Web Services Description Language (WSDL (`http://en.wikipedia.org/wiki/Web_Services_Description_Language`)), which is pretty verbose. In the Java EE world, SOAP messages could be processed by means of JAX-WS API without the need for a directory of services.

Even though SOAP Web Services are verbose, they are still being used as a means of integration with the software produced by third parties. Some SOAP services are publicly available. For example, the web page www.webservicex.net offers descriptions and WSDL locations of such information and services as weather forecasts, U.S. address verification, currency converters, and stock quotes. You can integrate these into your application, but providing a user interface for them remains your responsibility.

THE RESTFUL WEB SERVICES

REST stands for *representational state of transfer*. A Web Service built on REST principles is called a RESTful Web Service. As opposed to SOAP, REST is not a protocol, but a lighter-than-SOAP architectural style of building Web Services. Dr. Roy Fielding (`http://en.wikipedia.org/wiki/Roy_Fielding`) identified the REST principles in his PhD dissertation:

- Every resource on the web has a unique ID.
- Use uniform interface: HTTP `Get`, `Post`, `Put`, `Delete`, and so on.
- A resource can have multiple representations (text, JSON, XML, PDF, and so on).
- Requests are stateless; no client-specific information is stored between requests.
- You can link one resource to another.
- Resources should be cacheable.
- A REST application can be layered.

To put it simply, a *resource* is anything that you can access with a hyperlink. Each resource has a uniform resource identifier (URI). For example, `www.dice.com/yakovsresume` identifies a unique resource with Yakov's résumé on the server `dice.com`. The résumé might be stored on the server as a file in a plain text format, or it may be located in the database and has to be retrieved by a JDBC query, but in any case it can be represented (served) in different formats like PDF, XML, or JSON.

REST resources have to support standard stateless HTTP requests. If with SOAP creators have to come up with arbitrary names of the supported operations (for example, `getCityByZipCode`), with REST you use the standard HTTP methods like `Get`, `Post`, `Put`, and `Delete`.

I've seen many web applications that used only the HTTP methods `GET` for reading the server-side content and `POST` for updating the content or hiding HTTP parameters inside the HTTP header, but REST is stricter about this. In the RESTful world you should use `GET` for retrieving the data, `POST` for creating new resources, `PUT` for updates, and `DELETE` for resource removal.

Each of the standard HTTP methods has certain characteristics:

- GET: Safe, idempotent, cacheable
- PUT: Idempotent
- DELETE : Idempotent
- POST : None of the above

Safe means that this method doesn't modify the resource. *Cacheable* means that the client application can cache the result. *Idempotent* means that no matter how many times you call this method, the result will be the same. For example, if you update a person's name from Smith to Johnson, no matter how many times you try to update this person's resource with the name Johnson, the last name will still be Smith.

On the same note, no matter how many times you try to delete the resource with the unique ID, it results in removal of this resource only without harming any other data.

While the client communicates with the server both can send application data to each other in various formats. Let's discuss the most popular format used in web applications: JSON.

WORKING WITH JSON-FORMATTED DATA

JSON format is based on the syntax of the JavaScript object literals. All web browsers know how to parse JSON without the need to use any add-ons or plug-ins. Because the majority of today's web applications use JavaScript on the client side, no wonder that JSON became a de facto standard way of data formatting on the web, replacing XML, which was popular in the 1990s.

Here's an example of how an instance of the `Stock` entity can be represented in XML:

```
<stock>
  <country>USA</country>
  <currency>USD</currency>
  <price>43.12</price>
  <symbol>IBM</symbol>
</stock>
```

In JSON, the same resource would be represented like this:

```
"stock": {
  "country": "USA",
  "currency": "USD",
  "price": 43.12,
  "symbol": "IBM"
}
```

COMPARING XML AND JSON

The public community domain `www.geonames.org` enables you to search for geographical and statistical information about countries, cities, and so on. For the most part, this website uses RESTful

Web Services. To compare how the same data is represented in XML and in JSON, visit this web page: `www.geonames.org/export/ws-overview.html`.

Development of so-called Single-Page Applications (SPA) is a trend in today's HTML5 world. SPA refers to the applications that don't refresh the entire web page but rather update the portions of it retrieving the fresh data by making AJAX (`http://en.wikipedia.org/wiki/Ajax_(programming)`) requests. Google's GMail client is a good example of SPA; when a new e-mail arrives, just one new line is added to a single web page that shows the content in the inbox. The server sends only the preformatted data, which the web client positions on the screen using HTML, JavaScript, and CSS. No HTML markup is generated by the server as it's done by Java Servlets, JSP, or JSF.

REST OR WEBSOCKETS

Because RESTful Web Services send only the data (without HTML markup) in client-server communications, they are more efficient in terms of the network throughput compared to servlets, JSP, or JSF. But RESTful Web Services are based on HTTP protocol, which adds an overhead by attaching HTTP headers to the data sent by both the client and the server. If you need to substantially increase the data throughput, by removing these heavy headers consider using websockets, explained in Lesson 28. For real-time applications that need to push the server-side data to a web client, switching from REST to websockets substantially increases the number of messages sent per second. With websockets, the application responsiveness is also increased because there is no need to re-establish the HTTP connection for each request, and there is almost no overhead in the data payload.

SPA needs to use some data format between the client and the server. Because of JSON popularity, Java EE specification standardized its processing in JSR 353. Usually Java application servers implement the JSON processing specification in a separate jar, so you can use it with standalone Java SE applications, too. For example, GlassFish comes with a file, `glassfish4/glassfish/modules/javax.json.jar`, which you can add to any standalone application.

The package `javax.json` includes classes supporting two ways of producing JSON from Java:

- **Object Model API:** With this API your Java code should first create an object tree representing JSON data in memory, and then send it to an I/O stream.
- **Streaming API:** This is an event-driven API that dispatches events when the beginning or end of the JSON object is found, or when it finds a key or a value in the data load. The streaming API generates the output into a given stream (for example, a file or a network connection).

Although you can create a Java client application that parses or generates JSON, typically JSON is produced or consumed by JavaScript in web browsers (`https://developer.mozilla.org/en-US/docs/Web/JavaScript/Reference/Global_Objects/JSON`). This lesson includes the examples of parsing JSON in server-side Java, assuming that the server receives or builds a JSON-formatted string. For complete coverage of JSON on both the client and the server, see JSON Processing Tutorial (`http://docs.oracle.com/javaee/7/tutorial/jsonp.htm#GLRBB/jsonp.htm#GLRBB`) by Oracle.

Reading JSON with the Streaming API

The following code snippet shows how reading JSON-formatted data with the streaming API can be structured. The parser dispatches the appropriate event as it parses the JSON string, and you should write the code to process events you're interested in:

```
JsonParser parser = Json.createParser(new StringReader(jsonData));
while (parser.hasNext()) {
    JsonParser.Event event = parser.next();
    switch(event) {
        case START_ARRAY:
        case END_ARRAY:
        case START_OBJECT:
        case END_OBJECT:
        case VALUE_FALSE:
        case VALUE_NULL:
        case VALUE_TRUE:
            System.out.println(event.toString());
            break;
        case KEY_NAME:
            System.out.print(event.toString() + " " +
                    parser.getString() + " - ");
            break;
        case VALUE_STRING:
        case VALUE_NUMBER:
            System.out.println(event.toString() + " " +
                    parser.getInt());
            break;
    }
}
```

In this example, the code handles only the parser events (`http://docs.oracle.com/javaee/7/api/javax/json/stream/JsonParser.Event.html`): `VALUE_TRUE` a (a JSON element has a value of `true`), `KEY_NAME` (a name in a key/value pair is found), and `VALUE_NUMBER` (a numeric value is found.)

Writing JSON with the Streaming API

The following class—`JavaToJSONStreaming`—creates an instance of a `Product` class , turns it into a JSON-formatted string, and saves it in a file named `product_from_stream.json`:

```
public class JavaToJSONStreaming {

 public static void main(String[] args) {

   Product prd1 = new Product(777, "Gucci Handbag", 1000.00);

   try (OutputStream fos =
             new FileOutputStream("product_from_stream.json");
        JsonGenerator jsonGenerator = Json.createGenerator(fos);) {

      jsonGenerator.writeStartObject();
```

```
        jsonGenerator.write("id", prd1.id);
        jsonGenerator.write("description", prd1.description);
        jsonGenerator.write("price", prd1.price);

       // To create nested JSON objects enclose each of them
       // into a pair of writeStartObject() and writeEnd()

        jsonGenerator.writeEnd();
    } catch (IOException ioe) {
        ioe.printStackTrace();
    }
  }
}
```

The Json object creates a generator JsonGenerator that writes JSON data to an output source in a streaming way. In this example, the output source is a file represented by the variable fos.

I omitted the declaration of the Product class for brevity, but both classes Product and JavaToJSONStreaming come with the book's code samples. If you run this program, it creates a file with the following content:

```
{"id":777,"description":"Gucci Handbag","price":1000.0}
```

Keep in mind that to make this program work as a standalone application you need to include the jar that implements the JSON Processing API (also known as JSON-P API) in the CLASSPATH of your application. If this program will run on the server side, each Java EE server already includes such a jar, and no modification of the CLASSPATH is needed.

Writing JSON with the Object Model API

As opposed to streaming, the Object Model API requires you to build the entire JSON object in memory, and only after to write the whole thing to the destination of your choice. To illustrate this, I re-write the class JavaToJSONStreaming from the previous section:

```
public class JavaToJSONObject {

   public static void main(String[] args) {

     Product prd1 = new Product(777, "Chanel Handbag", 1000.00);

     try (OutputStream fos =
                new FileOutputStream("product_from_object.json");
         JsonWriter jsonWriter = Json.createWriter(fos);) {

         JsonObjectBuilder prdBuilder = Json.createObjectBuilder();

         prdBuilder.add("id", prd1.id)
                   .add("description", prd1.description)
                   .add("price", prd1.price);

         JsonObject prdJsonObject = prdBuilder.build();
```

```
            System.out.println("prdJsonObject: " + prdJsonObject);

            jsonWriter.writeObject(prdJsonObject);

            // Read and parse the newly created file back
            JsonReader jsonReader =
            Json.createReader(new FileReader("product_from_object.json"));
            JsonObject jsonObject = jsonReader.readObject();
            System.out.println(jsonObject);


        } catch (IOException e) {
            e.printStackTrace();
        }
      }
  }
```

`JsonObjectBuilder` initializes the model and allows you to add key/value pairs to represent the JSON object. The class `Json` has methods to create the builder object, which includes a method `build()` to create a JSON-formatted string. The `JsonWriter` writes the JSON object to a file, and `JsonReader` reads and parses the newly created file. If you don't need to write a `JsonObject` to a file you can convert it to a `String` by calling `prdJsonObject.toString()`. Then, for example, you can send this `String` to a web client.

THE RESTFUL STOCK SERVER

The Java EE specification includes the JAX-RS API for creating the server- and client-side programs for RESTful Web Services. All Java EE-compliant application servers implement JAX-RS. I'll continue using the GlassFish server, which comes with the JAX-RS implementation known as Jersey, and you won't need to download any additional libraries to run the sample code from this lesson. Let's see how to implement RESTful Web Services by redesigning a familiar stock server example. The representation of the resources (in this case, stocks) can vary and is determined by media type.

Development of a RESTful application with JAX-RS is pretty straightforward:

1. Create a small Java class that extends `javax.ws.rs.core.Application`, which registers your application with a Java EE server.
2. Create and properly annotate a *REST endpoint*, which is a POJO.
3. Define a Java bean that will be converted into XML, JSON, or some other format for communicating with the client's application.
4. Create any number of helper classes that implement application logic.

The following sections show you how this can be done.

Creating the Application

The same Java EE server may host multiple RESTful Web Services. To help the server with routing the client's requests to the proper application, each application should be mapped to a specific URL pattern. In older versions of Java EE it could be done only by adding a configuration to the file called `web.xml`. This is not required any longer. Just create a class that extends `javax.ws.rs.core.Application`, and mark it with an `@ApplicationPath` annotation containing a URL fragment identifying your application. This is how your application class `StockQuoteApplication` will look:

```
package lesson33;

import javax.ws.rs.ApplicationPath;
import javax.ws.rs.core.Application;

@ApplicationPath("resources")
public class StockQuoteApplication extends Application {
}
```

This is all that the Java EE server needs to redirect to your application all requests containing the pattern `resources` in the URL. This is how the routing begins, but any application can have multiple endpoints. To identify the right one you need to use the `@Path` annotation, which you see in the section "Creating the Endpoint StockService."

Creating the Java Bean Stock

The client and the RESTful server needs to agree on the data format for communications—for example, JSON, XML, and so on. Although JAX-RS is a specification for implementing Java-based RESTful Web Services, JAXB is a specification for converting data to/from XML format. For example, annotating a Java bean with `@XmlRootElement` can bring into action the JAXB framework for processing XML, which turns a Java bean into an XML or JSON document before sending it to the web client that has no knowledge of the Java object format. Listing 33-1 shows a Java bean called `Stock` annotated with `@XmlRootElement`.

LISTING 33-1 A Java bean Stock

```
import javax.xml.bind.annotation.XmlRootElement;

@XmlRootElement
public class Stock {
    private String symbol;
    private Double price;
    private String currency;
    private String country;

    public Stock() {
    }

    public Stock(String symbol,Double price, String currency,
```

```
                                                        String country) {
        this.symbol = symbol;
        this.price = price;
        this.currency = currency;
        this.country = country;
    }

    public String getSymbol() {
        return symbol;
    }

    public void setSymbol(String symbol) {
        this.symbol = symbol;
    }

    public Double getPrice() {
        return price;
    }

    public void setPrice(Double price) {
        this.price = price;
    }

    public String getCurrency() {
        return currency;
    }

    public void setCurrency(String currency) {
        this.currency = currency;
    }

    public String getCountry() {
        return country;
    }

    public void setCountry(String country) {
        this.country = country;
    }
}
```

The server-side Java code can retrieve the data about a particular stock and create an instance of the `Stock` class, which has to be converted into the requested data format and sent to the web client. In the JSON section of this lesson I give examples of how a Java class can be converted into a JSON string.

Creating the Endpoint StockService

The endpoint class is an entry door to a particular Web Service. Its role is to find and invoke the Java method with a signature that matches the client's request. For example, if the endpoint received an HTTP GET request with one parameter, the endpoint class should have a method that takes one argument and is marked with an `@GET` annotation.

You need to mark an endpoint class with an @Path annotation, so the server redirects only specific client requests to this class. You also need to annotate the methods of this class to specify which method should be handling GET requests, which - PUT, et al.

Here is a list of the most popular annotations that are used with REST endpoints:

- @Path: A root resource class (POJO). This annotation specifies the URL pattern that this class handles. The endpoint class has at least one method annotated with @Path.
- @GET: The class method that should handle HTTP GET requests. You can have multiple methods annotated with @GET, and each can produce the result in a different MIME type (http://www.iana.org/assignments/media-types/media-types.xhtml).
- @POST: The class method that handles HTTP Post requests.
- @PUT: The class method that handles HTTP Put requests.
- @DELETE: The class method that handles HTTP Delete requests.
- @Produces: Specifies the MIME type(s) for response; for example,"application/json".
- @Consumes: Specifies the MIME type(s) that a resource can consume when sent by the client.
- @PathParam: Injects the URI fragment into a method parameter (for example, IBM).
- @QueryParam: Injects the parameter from the URL into a method parameter (or example, stock=IBM). It is used with HTTP GET requests.
- @FormParam: Injects the value from an input field of an HTML form into the provided Java variable or a method argument.

The following class StockService is an example of a RESTful endpoint that may return the stock that's identified by the URI like http://localhost:8080/Lesson33/resources/stock/IBM. The class StockService is sprinkled with annotations. First comes the annotation @Path, which can be used with either a class or a method. JAX-RS maps clients' requests to class methods. If more than one annotation @Path are used in a class, their values are going to be compared with the URL fragments for finding the matching method.

LISTING 33-2 REST endpoint StockService

```
@Path("/stock")
public class StockService {

    @Produces({"application/xml","application/json"})
    @Path("{symbol}")
    @GET
    public Stock getStock(@PathParam("symbol") String symbol) {

        Stock stock = StockServiceHelper.getStock(symbol);

        if (stock == null) {
            return new Stock("NOT FOUND", 0.0, "--", "--");
        }

        return stock;
    }
```

```
        @POST
        @Consumes("application/x-www-form-urlencoded")
        public Response addStock(
                        @FormParam("symbol") String symbol,
                        @FormParam("currency") String currency,
                        @FormParam("price") String price,
                        @FormParam("country") String country) {

            if (StockServiceHelper.getStock(symbol) != null)
                return Response.status(Response.Status.BAD_REQUEST)
                        .entity("Stock " + symbol + " already exists")
                        .type("text/plain").build();

            double priceToUse;
            try {
                priceToUse = new Double(price);
            }
            catch (NumberFormatException e) {
                priceToUse = 0.0;
            }

            StockServiceHelper.addStock(new Stock(symbol, priceToUse,
                                                    currency, country));

            return Response.ok().build();
        }
    }
```

One of the methods in `StockService` is marked with an `@GET` annotation and the other one with `@POST`. One of these methods is automatically invoked to process the corresponding HTTP requests.

Let's see how our Java EE server routes the HTTP GET request to get the resource—the data about the IBM's stock—represented by the following URI: `http://localhost:8080/Lesson33/resources/stock/IBM`. First, the Java EE server parses the URI and tries to find the Java class that matches the value from the `@ApplicationPath`, which is `resources` in our case (see the section Creating the Application). Then the RESTFul server looks for the class annotated with `@Path("/stock")` and routes this request to the class `StockService`.

Because the URI doesn't end with `/stock`, the matching process continues. Our URI has a stock symbol after the word `stock`, (`/IBM`), and the method-level annotation `@Path("{symbol}")` helps the server to find (and invoke) the matching method: `getStock()`.

The annotation `@PathParam("symbol")` indicates that the server should inject the value of the stock symbol included in the URI into the `symb` argument of the method `getStock()`. Figure 33-1 shows the annotations that were involved in the parsing process of our URI.

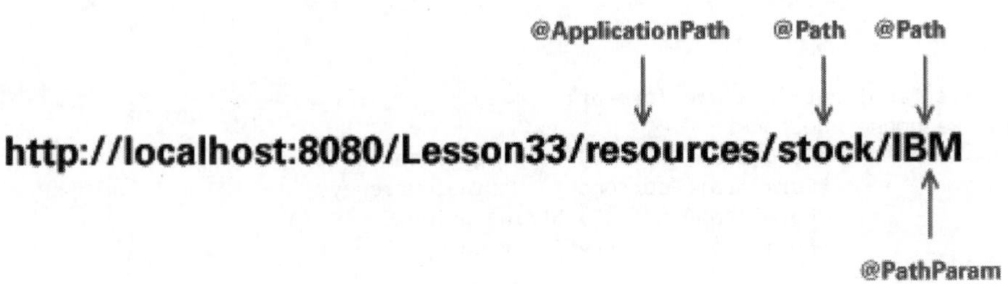

FIGURE 33-1: Parsing the URI with annotations

The MIME type specified in the annotation `@Produces` means that the method `getStock()` can produce the data either in XML or in JSON format. Software developers responsible for creating the client part need to make sure that the header of the client's HTTP request includes the required MIME format in its `Accept` header. If no methods that produce the content in the requested MIME type are found, the client gets the HTTP error 406, which you see in action in the "Try It" section. One HTTP client may request the stock data in JSON and another requests it in the XML format, but both of them are served by the same method `getStock()`.

The `addStock()` method is marked with the `@Consumes` annotation to consume the HTML form's data sent by the client. The method `addStock()` is called when the HTTP `POST` request is received. If the REST endpoint is unable to consume the requested MIME type, the client gets HTTP error 415.

The `@FormParam` annotation injects the values entered in the HTML form into the method `addStock()`. If the web client wouldn't be using an HTML form but was sending an HTTP `GET` request with parameters, you'd have to use the annotation `@QueryParam` instead of `@FormParam`.

The stock MSFT is considered another resource and can be represented by the URI `http://localhost:8080/Lesson33/resources/stock/MSFT`. So your `StockService` endpoint can provide the data about different stocks as long as you know their URIs.

The class `StockService` uses the helper class `StockServiceHelper`, shown in stockservicehelper_class. For simplicity, this class has two hard-coded stocks, but in the real world it would be connected to one of the financial data feeds. This class uses static initializer, which calls the method `generateStocks()` on the first reference to `StockService`.

LISTING 33-3 StockServiceHelper class

```
public class StockServiceHelper {
    public static void addStock(Stock stock) {
        stocks.put(stock.getSymbol(), stock);
    }

    public static void removeStock(String symbol) {
        stocks.remove(symbol);
    }

    public static Stock getStock(String symbol) {
        return stocks.get(symbol);
```

```
        }

        private static Map<String, Stock> stocks = new HashMap<>();

        static {
            generateStocks();
        }

        private static void generateStocks() {
            addStock(new Stock("IBM", 43.12, "USD", "USA"));
            addStock(new Stock("AAPL", 120.0, "USD", "USA"));
         }
}
```

Creating RESTFful Clients

A client application that communicates with the server-side endpoint can be written in any programming language that supports HTTP requests. Typically, the REST clients are HTML applications that use JavaScript functions that issue such requests. Because this book is about Java programming, I do not cover how to do this in the JavaScript, but in the "Try It" section, I show you how to use a tool called Postman that can be used to test RESTful services from the Chrome web browser.

Because RESTful applications can be layered, the following sample scenario is possible: An HTML client requests a resource implemented in Java, which in turn becomes a client for another resource implemented on another, say, .NET server. This is perfectly legal because both technologies support JSON as a data exchange format.

If you need to write RESTful clients in Java, use the JSON API discussed earlier in the section "Working with JSON-Formatted Data."

CONTEXTS AND DEPENDENCY INJECTION

When your Java code runs in a Java EE container, it may need to use instances of some objects. Lesson 29 familiarized you with injecting JNDI resources, but you can inject instances of your application objects as well. The Java EE specification includes JSR 346, which defines Contexts and Dependency Injection (CDI).

For example, the `StockService` class might have needed a modeling engine that would apply some technical analysis algorithms to give recommendations on buying or selling a stock. As an example, you can write a class `TechAnalysisEngine` that implements the `Recommendations` interface, and with CDI you don't need to create an instance of this class yourself; you could ask the container to inject the instance of this class into your code using the CDI annotation `@Inject`, which could be placed before the field, constructor, or a method. The following example injects the method argument:

```
@Path("/stock")
public class StockService {

  Recommendations theEngine;
```

```
      @Inject
      public void setRecommendationsEngine(Recommendations theEngine){
          this.theEngine = theEngine;
      }

    @Produces({"application/xml","application/json"})
    @Path("{symbol}")
    @GET public Stock getStock(@PathParam("symbol") String symbol) {
        Stock stock = StockServiceHelper.getStock(symbol);

        String tradeRecommendations =
                                theEngine.getRecommendations(stock);
    }

    ...
}
```

CDI bean is a POJO that can be managed by Java EE container. If you are planning to use CDI, you need to add an empty file `bean.xml`, which signals the Java EE container to discover CDI beans in the application. To continue the example with the technical analysis engine, you could define it as follows:

```
public interface Recommendations {
   public String getRecommendations (Stock stock);
}
```

Accordingly the CDI bean could be declared like this:

```
public class TechAnalysisEngine implements Recommendations{

    public TechAnalysisEngine(){
    }

    public String getRecommendations(Stock stock){
     String recommendations;
     // Implement the technical analysis logic here
     return recommendations;
    }
}
```

A USE CASE FOR A SINGLETON

You don't want Java EE container to create multiple instances of the class `TechAnalysisEngine`. The same instance can serve multiple client requests. Just annotate the class `TechAnalysisEngine` as `@Singleton`, and CDI injects it only once. To ensure that you use CDI, import the `javax.inject.Singleton` implementation of the annotation `@Singleton`, which is not the same as creating a singleton EJB implemented in `javax.ejb.Singleton`.

But what if more than one class implements the `Recommendation` interface? How will the container know which implementation to inject? To avoid ambiguity you should use custom qualifier annotations. For example, you can declare an annotation `@Fundamental` like this:

```
@Qualifier
@Retention(RUNTIME)
@Target({TYPE, METHOD, FIELD, PARAMETER})
public @interface Fundamental {}
```

Now you can annotate with `@Fundamental` another class that also implements the `Recommendations` interface:

```
@Fundamental
public class FundamentalAnalysisEngine implements Recommendations{

  public FundamentalAnalysisEngine(){
  }

  public String getRecommendations(Stock stock){
    String recommendations;
    // Implement the fundamental analysis logic here
    return recommendations;
  }
}
```

The line that injects the instance of the `FundamentalAnalysisEngine` class into `StockService` looks like this:

```
@Inject @Fundamental
public void setRecommendationsEngine(Recommendations theEngine) {
    ...
}
```

The ambiguity is resolved!

Because you are not creating the instances of the objects manually, you need to have a way to specify how long the injected instance will live. This is done using CDI scope annotations: `@RequestScoped`, `@SessionScoped`, `@ApplicationScoped`, `@Dependent`, and `@ConversationScoped`. You can find more details about these annotations in the CDI chapter (`https://docs.oracle.com/javaee/7/tutorial/partcdi.htm#GJBNR`) of the Java EE Tutorial.

JAVA EE SAMPLES

This lesson concludes the coverage of selected Java EE 7 technologies. Refer to the GitHub repository `https://github.com/javaee-samples/javaee7-samples` that contains lots of Java EE 7 code samples that illustrate the usage of all Java EE 7 JSRs.

TRY IT

Your assignment is to make the code related to the stock quote examples work. You need to create an Eclipse project and copy the code samples from the book's web page at *working_with_restful_web_services* there. Then you need to deploy this project in GlassFish and run it.

Lesson Requirements

You should have Java and GlassFish v4 server installed.

> **NOTE** *You can download the code and resources for this "Try It" from the book's web page at* `www.wrox.com/go/javaprog24hr2e`. *You can find them in the working_with_restful_web_services folder in the download.*

Hints

Eclipse IDE for Java EE Developers has a template for the creation of REST resources. After the Eclipse project is created, right-click the project name, select New, and then select RESTful Web Service from Pattern (Java EE 7). Eclipse creates for you an annotated class similar to the one from rest_resource_stockresource, which you can edit to meet your application's requirements.

Step-by-Step

1. Create a dynamic web project called `Lesson33` in the Java EE perspective of Eclipse.
2. Download the source files for Lesson 33 from the *working_with_restful_web_services* folder.
3. Create packages called `lesson33` and `lesson33.service`.
4. Copy the class `StockQuoteApplication` to the folder `lesson33`.
5. Copy the classes `Stock`, `StockService`, and `StockServiceHelper` from the downloaded code samples into the folder `lesson33/service`.
6. Deploy the project `Lesson33` under GlassFish. Right-click the server name, select Add and Remove, and in the pop-up window move the entry Lesson33 from the left box to the right one by clicking Add. Then click Finish. The RESTFul service is deployed on the server.
7. For the client, use Google Chrome Web browser with the Postman REST Client add-on. Open Chrome browser and launch the Postman from `http://bit.ly/18JpMha`.
8. In the URL field on top enter the following URL: `http://localhost:8080/Lesson33/resources/IBM`.
9. Click the Send button, and your RESTful service responds with the JSON-formatted data. Your Postman window should look similar to Figure 33-2.

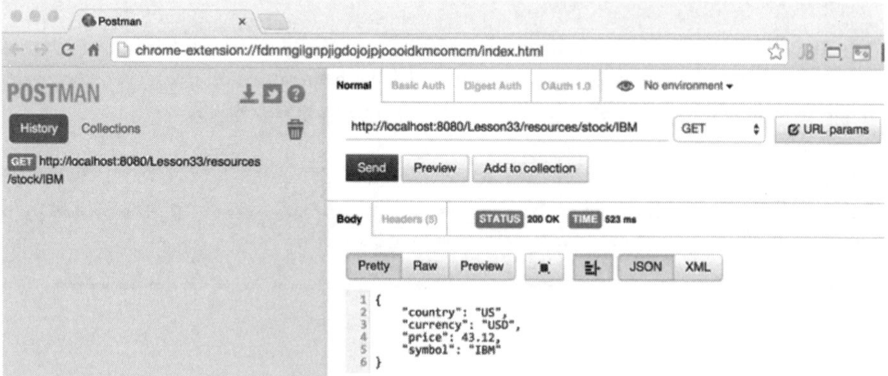

FIGURE 33-2: Getting the stock/IBM resource using Postman REST Client

The GlassFish Server found the REST endpoint `StockService` and invoked the method `getResource("IBM")` on it.

10. Remove IBM from the URL, so it looks like this: `http://localhost:8080/Lesson33/resources`. Press Send, and you get the error 405 because the endpoint `StockService` from rest_resource_stockresource has no @GET annotated methods that don't require arguments.
11. To test the Add New Stock functionality, select POST in the method drop-down menu, select the `x-www-form-urlencoded` tab, click the URL Params button, and fill out the parameters required by the method `addStock()` of `StockService` from rest_resource_stockresource. After you click the Send button, your Postman window should look like Figure 33-3.

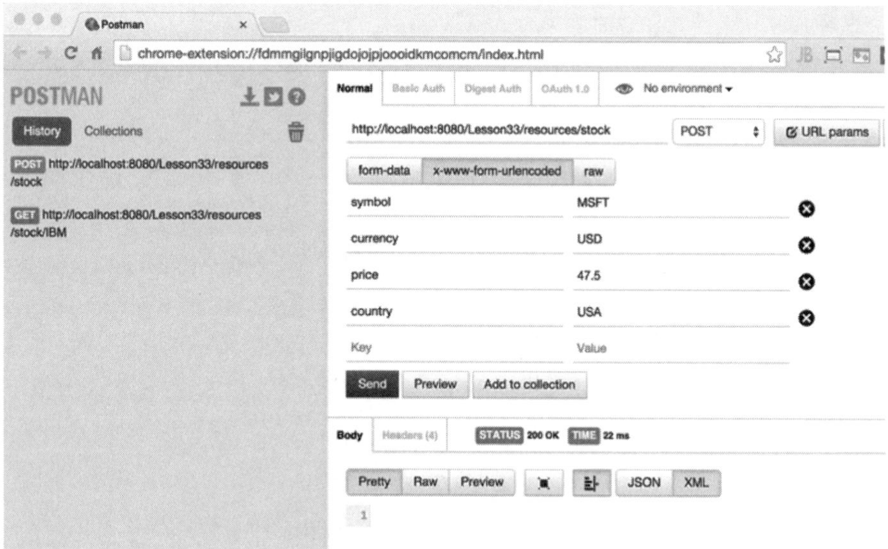

FIGURE 33-3: Added new stock using the POST request

The RESTful endpoint properly matched the `@POST` annotated method `addStock()` with four arguments. To ensure that the information about MSFT has been added on the server side, issue a GET request: `http://localhost:8080/Lesson33/resources/MSFT`.

> **TIP** *Please select the videos for Lesson 33 online at* `www.wrox.com/go/javaprog24hr2e`. *You will also be able to download the code and resources for this lesson from the website.*

34

Java Logging API

Every Java program performs various functions during its life cycle—for example, it opens files, connects to databases or remote services, or it performs some calculations. Often software developers need to print application-specific messages from various parts of the program. Sometimes developers need to confirm that a program visited a certain method or print the results of intermediate calculations.

Proper reporting of runtime errors is even more important. You may want to print not only the error messages, but also the messages that inform about the control flow of the program (for example, an order has been placed or cancelled). If your Java application server won't start, the first place to check is its log files, which may have a description of an issue, or at least you can see at which stage the launch process stopped working.

Until now, in most of the code samples in this book (except graphical user interface applications) I've used the tried and true method `System.out.println()`, but this approach has several issues:

1. It's not easy to "turn off" multiple informational `println()` calls when the application goes into quality assurance (QA) or production. You need to find and comment out these statements that are sprinkled through your application code. And if a bug is reported in the production application, you need to uncomment several `println()` statements and potentially add more of them.

2. There is no trace of what's happened in the application after it's complete.

3. If one of many users of a server-side Java application calls the support team about an issue, the support personnel needs to be able to quickly identify and analyze the messages related to this particular user's interaction—when the issue happened and in which software module it occurred.

Replacing `println()` statements with a Java Logging application programming interface (API) or a third-party logging framework addresses these issues, and you should use in all applications both on the server and the client sides. Logging is used both in development and production. The logging messages can be directed to the end users as well.

There are many Java logging frameworks (`http://en.wikipedia.org/wiki/Java_logging_framework`). But the majority of this lesson is dedicated to the Java Logging API, which is a part of Java SE.

JAVA LOGGING API

The Java Logging API is implemented in the package `java.util.logging`. The two main classes of the logging API are `Logger` and `Handle`. An application obtains an instance of the `Logger` object, which creates an instance of the `LogRecord` and gives it to a `Handler` object for publishing. The Java Logging API includes several types of handlers, and the default one is `ConsoleHandler` that publishes messages on the system console.

For a simple application, you can create one *global logger* that takes care of all message logging. In more complex applications, you can create a hierarchy of loggers where each package or class has its own logger.

The Java Logging API enables you to group messages by different levels. For example, you can assign the `INFO` level to the messages that do not report errors, and you can assign serious error messages the `SEVERE` level. These are the logging levels defined in the class `Level`:

1. `SEVERE`
2. `WARNING`
3. `INFO`
4. `CONFIG`
5. `FINE`
6. `FINER`
7. `FINEST`

The order of these levels is important as these levels represent ordered integers. `SEVERE` is the highest number and `FINEST` is the lowest. The default logging level is `INFO`, which means that all log messages marked as `INFO`, and the higher levels (`WARNING` and `SEVERE`) will be logged. If you change the default logging level to `WARNING`, then only the messages of the levels `WARNING` and `SEVERE` are logged.

The levels `FINE`, `FINER`, and `FINEST` are used to create log records with more descriptive messages. To turn on all logging levels, set the level to `Level.ALL`, and to turn the logging off set the level to `Level.OFF`. For more details of the logging level refer to Oracle javadoc (`http://docs.oracle.com/javase/8/docs/api/java/util/logging/Level.html`) for the class `Level`. Regardless of what level you decide to use, make sure that the log messages are informative.

You can set the log level on both the `Logger` and the `Handler` objects. You do this programmatically or in a configuration file. The latter allows you to change the default level during the run time for a deployed application. One logger object can have several handlers that publish messages to different destinations, and each of the handlers can have a different log level.

Writing lots of logging messages can affect the performance of your application. When you change the default log level you minimize the performance burden in applications that are deployed in production. I explain how you set and change log levels a bit later, but for now let's create a very basic logging application.

Hello World with the Java Logging API

Everyone starts learning Java by writing a simple program that prints `Hello World` on the system console using the following statement:

```
System.out.println("Hello World");
```

It's time to replace this statement with the Java Logging API.

Hello World with a Global Logger

Start with creating an Eclipse Java project called Lesson34. In it, create a new class `HelloLoggingWorld` in a package `com.lesson34`. In the `main()` method of this class you're going to use the `Logger` object to greet the world as follows:

```
package com.lesson34;

import java.util.logging.Logger;

public class HelloWorldGlobalLogger {

    private static Logger logger =
            Logger.getGlobal();

    public static void main(String[] args) {

        logger.fine("Hello fine world!");
        logger.info("Hello info world!");
        logger.severe("Hello severe world!");
    }
}
```

Although an application can have a hierarchy of loggers, this simple program uses a single global logger obtained by calling the method `getGlobal()`. The program starts with initializing the `logger` variable with the `Logger` object. Then the program invokes three methods on this logger: `fine()`, `info()`, and `severe()`. The names of the methods correspond to the logging levels. But if you run this program, only two messages are printed on the system console:

```
Jan 28, 2015 11:27:17 AM com.lesson34.HelloWorldGlobalLogger main
INFO: Hello info world!
Jan 28, 2015 11:27:17 AM com.lesson34.HelloWorldGlobalLogger main
SEVERE: Hello severe world
```

Because the default logging level is `INFO`, the message of the `FINE` level was not printed. By default the log records published on the console include the date and time, the name of the class, the level, and the message.

Hello World with a Class-Level Logger

The application can have more than one logger, all of which are children of the global logger. For example, you can create a class-level logger identified by a hierarchical name that looks similar to a fully qualified class name. You can create a Java class that creates the logger specifically for this class:

```
private static Logger logger =
            Logger.getLogger("com.lesson34.HelloWorldClassLogger");
```

To avoid hardcoding the class name (it can be moved to a different package) you can ask Java to obtain a fully qualified class name, as shown here:

```
private static Logger helloLogger =
         Logger.getLogger(HelloWorldClassLogger.class.getName());
```

The following program purposely divides by zero just to show the use of the class-level logger:

```
package com.lesson34;

import java.util.logging.Logger;

public class HelloWorldClassLogger {

    private static Logger helloLogger =
            Logger.getLogger(HelloWorldClassLogger.class.getName());

    public static void main(String[] args) {

        helloLogger.info("Trying to divide by zero");
        try{
            int result = 25/0;
        } catch(ArithmeticException e){
            helloLogger.severe("Division by zero");
        }
    }
}
```

The output of this program is shown here:

```
Jan 28, 2015 2:54:26 PM com.lesson34.HelloWorldClassLogger main
INFO: Trying to divide by zero
Jan 28, 2015 2:54:26 PM com.lesson34.HelloWorldClassLogger main
SEVERE: Division by zero
```

Software developers often create a separate logger not only for each class but also for each package. But the procedure remains the same; just specify the name of the package as the logger name:

```
private static Logger logger = Logger.getLogger(
               HelloWorldClassLogger.class.getPackage().getName());
```

Using Handlers and Setting Log Levels

The Logger object doesn't log messages on its own. It creates a LogRecord and passes it to a Handler object for publication to a specified destination. So far the log messages from the code examples have been sent to the system console because the Java Logging API uses a ConsoleHandler object by default. It was a ConsoleHandler that printed the log messages.

To set the logging level, you need to call a method setLevel(); for example, to set the FINE logger level you need to call a method setLevel(Level.FINE). You can set the severity level of the log messages on both the logger and the handler, and they don't have to be the same. For example, you may want to record only SEVERE messages in the log file, while sending to the console messages of the level INFO and higher.

You can also log one message under different logging level without changing the current level by using the method log():

```
log(Level.FINE, "Hello fine world");
```

You can assign one or more handlers to the Logger objects so the log messages are published in one or more destinations. The Java Logging API supports the following handlers:

- ConsoleHandler: A handler for writing log records to the System.err object (by default it points at the same device as System.out).
- FileHandler: A handler that writes log records either to a single file or to a set of rotating log files.
- StreamHandler: A handler for writing log records to an OutputStream.
- SocketHandler: A handler that writes log records to local or remote Transmission Control Protocol (TCP) ports.
- MemoryHandler: A handler that buffers log records in memory.

To assign a handler(s) to a logger object you need to create an instance of one of the previously listed handlers and add it to the Logger object by invoking the method addHandler():

```
FileHandler helloFileHandler
helloFindHandler = new FileHandler("helloWorld.log");
helloLogger.addHandler(helloFileHandler);
```

Now write yet another small program that publishes log messages on the console and in a log file. The logger that you've used in the previous examples internally created an instance of the ConsoleHandler class that published messages on the system console. Now you're adding another handler, FileHandler, to write log messages into a file, so you have the logs in the system console as well as in a file. To make this example more interesting, publish only WARNING and SEVERE messages in a file and have the console get the messages of the level FINE and above.

Create the directory named logs in the root of your Eclipse project, and see whether the following program HelloWorldHandlers properly publishes messages in the log file and system console:

```
package com.lesson34;

import java.io.IOException;
```

```
import java.util.logging.ConsoleHandler;
import java.util.logging.FileHandler;
import java.util.logging.Level;
import java.util.logging.Logger;

public class HelloWorldHandlers {

    private static Logger helloLogger =
            Logger.getLogger(HelloWorldClassLogger.class.getName());

    public static void main(String[] args) {

        FileHandler helloFileHandler;
        try {
          helloFileHandler = new FileHandler("logs/helloWorld.log");
          helloLogger.addHandler(helloFileHandler);
          helloFileHandler.setLevel(Level.WARNING);

        } catch (SecurityException se) {
           System.out.println(se.getMessage());
        } catch (IOException ioe) {
           System.out.println(ioe.getMessage());
        }

        helloLogger.fine("Hello from fine world");
        helloLogger.info("Trying to divide by zero");
        try{
            int result = 25/0;
        } catch(Exception e){
            helloLogger.severe("Division by zero");
        }
    }
}
```

The program `HelloWorldHandlers` adds a `FileHandler` to the logger to publish messages to the file `logs/helloWorld.log`. You can create and assign a `Formatter` object to the handler to format the output in a way that fits your needs. `XMLFormatter` is the default formatter for `FileHandler`. Having log files in the XML format allows writing programs that can read and parse log files, which can be pretty useful for large log files.

Creating an instance of the `FileHandler` may throw `SecurityException` if access to log files was protected by Java Security Manager (`http://docs.oracle.com/javase/tutorial/essential/environment/security.html`), which is not the case in our example.

Run `HelloWorldHandlers` and it creates a file `helloWorld.log` in the `logs` directory of your Eclipse project (you may need to refresh the project view to see it). Here's the content of this log file:

```
<?xml version="1.0" encoding="UTF-8" standalone="no"?>
<!DOCTYPE log SYSTEM "logger.dtd">
<log>
<record>
  <date>2015-01-28T17:20:38</date>
  <millis>1422483638650</millis>
  <sequence>1</sequence>
```

```
    <logger>com.lesson34.HelloWorldClassLogger</logger>
    <level>SEVERE</level>
    <class>com.lesson34.HelloWorldHandlers</class>
    <method>main</method>
    <thread>1</thread>
    <message>Division by zero</message>
  </record>
  </log>
```

The preceding file contains only the SEVERE message, which is correct. At the same time, the ConsoleHandler also printed INFO messages on the system console:

```
Jan 28, 2015 5:20:38 PM com.lesson34.HelloWorldHandlers main
INFO: Trying to divide by zero
Jan 28, 2015 5:20:38 PM com.lesson34.HelloWorldHandlers main
SEVERE: Division by zero
```

AVOIDING DUPLICATE LOG MESSAGES

The program HelloWorldHandlers uses a default console handler of the global logger to publish messages on the console. If you add an instance of the ConsoleHandler object to helloLogger, you have two console handlers: one on the class level and one global. This results in displaying duplicate messages on the console because the global logger is a parent of helloLogger, and all handlers in this hierarchy are invoked. If you want to turn the parent loggers off, use the method setUseParentHandlers():

```
helloLogger.setUseParentHandlers(false);
```

But why was the FINE level message "Hello from fine world" not displayed on the console? Invoking helloLogger.setLevel(Level.FINE) from HelloWorldHandlers won't help. The reason is that the Java Runtime Environment (JRE) comes with the configuration file logging.properties, which may supersede the log levels set in the program.

The File logging.properties

If you open the directory jre/lib in your Java distribution, you find the file logging.properties, which sets various logging properties including these:

```
.level= INFO
java.util.logging.ConsoleHandler.level = INFO
```

The first one restricts the default global level across all loggers, and the second limits the messages that are printed on the console. Both levels default to INFO. If you change these values to FINE or ALL, the program HelloWorldHandlers starts publishing FINE messages on the console.

Each application can have its own logging properties file that you can pass as the Java Virtual Machine (JVM) parameter from the command line, for example:

```
java -Djava.util.logging.config.file="myLogging.properties" MyApp
```

You can also load the application-specific logging properties file programmatically as follows:

```
LogManager.getLogManager().readConfiguration(
                        newFileInputStream("mylogging.properties"));
```

If your program creates named loggers, you can override the log levels in your `log.properties` file; for example:

```
com.lesson34.HelloWorldClassLogger.level=ALL
```

More About Logging with FileHandler

Writing log messages into files is the most common practice. The `FileHandler` class has several overloaded constructors. To work with log files in the append mode (log records are being added to the existing file), use a two-argument constructor:

```
helloFileHandler = new FileHandler("logs/helloWorld.log", true);
```

To avoid littering your disk space by tons of log files, you can create rotating log files. You can specify the maximum file size and maximum number of log files. A new file is created as soon as the current log file reaches a specified size. When the new log file is maxed out, another one is created. If the number of the allowed log files is reached the oldest log file is replaced with a new one, and log records are directed there.

For example, the following code snippet creates a `FileHandler` object that initially creates a log file named `helloWorld.log.0`, and as soon as its size grows to 1000 bytes, the handler renames the log file into `helloWorld.log.1` and creates a new one named `helloWorld.log.0` and so on. This `FileHandler` creates not more than three files in total, and logging is done in the append mode:

```
helloFileHandler =
          new FileHandler("logs/helloWorld.log", 1000, 3, true);
```

You see this code in action while working on the assignment from the "Try It" section of this lesson.

Formatters and Filters

Formatters allow you to change the format of logging messages and filters (in addition to log levels), so the handlers can decide if they are interested in a particular `LogRecord`. You can assign formatters to the log handlers. Filters can be assigned to both loggers and handlers.

Formatters

You can format log messages using classes `SimpleFormatter` or `XMLFormatter` included in with Java Development Kit (JDK), or create your own custom formatter. By default, console handlers use `SimpleFormatter`, and file handlers use `XMLFormatter`.

SimpleFormatter outputs the time-stamp, class name, method name, level, log message, and possible exception. XMLFormatter outputs messages in a form of an XML structure as XML-formatted messages as you've seen in the section on log handlers.

To create a custom formatter, declare a class the extends an abstract class Formatter and override its method format(). You can implement any formatting you like. Just prepare a String with the required content and let the method format() return it. The following example shows a simple custom formatter that doesn't print a timestamp and uses the symbols ==> as a separator between the fields of the LogRecord:

```
package com.lesson34;

import java.util.Date;
import java.util.logging.Formatter;
import java.util.logging.LogRecord;

public class MyFormatter extends Formatter {

    @Override
    public String format(LogRecord logRecord) {
        return logRecord.getSourceClassName()+"==>"
                + logRecord.getSourceMethodName()+"==>"
                + logRecord.getMessage()+"\n";
    }
}
```

Open your logging.properties file and assign this class to be a formatter for the console handler:

```
java.util.logging.ConsoleHandler.formatter=com.lesson34.MyFormatter
```

Now if you run the HelloWorldHandlers (or any other sample from this lesson), the output of the logger should look like this:

```
com.lesson34.HelloWorldHandlers==>main==>Hello from the fine world
com.lesson34.HelloWorldHandlers==>main==>Trying to divide by zero
com.lesson34.HelloWorldHandlers==>main==>Division by zero
```

Invoking the method setFormatter() on the handler object is an alternative to specifying a formatter to a handler from the command line.

Filters

With filters, you can program application logic to decide if a particular LogRecord should be logged. If you don't want to publish a particular LogRecord, simply return false and it won't be published. Otherwise, return true. Filter is an interface with a single method isLoggable(). Remember functional interfaces from Lesson 13? You can implement a filter with a lambda expression.

The following example generates random prices for stocks, but it logs only those prices that are greater than $60:

```
package com.lesson34;
import java.util.logging.Filter;
import java.util.logging.Level;
import java.util.logging.Logger;

public class StockQuotePublisher {

    private static Logger stockLogger =
            Logger.getLogger(StockQuotePublisher.class.getName());

   // A lambda expression
   static Filter expensiveStocks = (logRecord) -> {
        Object[] parameters = logRecord.getParameters();
        double price = ((Double)parameters[0]).doubleValue();
        return ( price > 60) ? true: false;
    };

    public static void main(String args[]){

        stockLogger.setFilter(expensiveStocks);

        getPrice("IBM");
        getPrice("MSFT");
        getPrice("AAPL");
        getPrice("CAT");
        getPrice("VZ");
    }

    private static double getPrice(String stockSymbol){

        double price = Math.random()*100;

        stockLogger.log(Level.INFO, stockSymbol + ":"
                                                + price, price);
        return price;
    }
}
```

The method `getPrice()` generates prices in the range between 0 and 100. This method logs messages using a different logging API—the method `log()`—which has several overloaded versions. In this case, I use the version with three arguments: level, message, and an object. The last argument can be any object; it's considered a parameter of the `LogRecord`. Even though it seems that you log the price value of the primitive `double`, Java knows that an object is required and uses the autoboxing feature to create an instance of the `Double` wrapper.

The program calls `getPrice()` from the `main()` method for five different stocks. If you didn't apply a filter, all generated prices would be published on the console. But the class `StockQuotePublisher` declares a lambda expression `expensiveStocks` that implements the functional interface `Filter` , which returns `true` only if the stock price is greater than 60. This filter is assigned to the logger:

```
stockLogger.setFilter(expensiveStocks);
```

You can assign a filter to a `Handler` the same way you assign it to a `Logger` object. Log filters go one step further than log levels: they offer data-driven logging. Running `StockQuotePublisher` produces different results on each run because of the random price generation. But none of the published log records show a price lower than 60. Here's a sample console output:

```
Jan 29, 2015 8:29:29 PM com.lesson34.StockQuotePublisher getPrice
INFO: AAPL:92.09444632063976
Jan 29, 2015 8:29:29 PM com.lesson34.StockQuotePublisher getPrice
INFO: VZ:85.58149465560332
```

LOGGING FRAMEWORKS

Although the Java Logging API is a good solution for small and mid-size applications, it may present a performance bottleneck in high-load multiuser applications where adding a couple of hundred milliseconds for publishing each message is not acceptable. There are numerous open-source logging frameworks on the market, which you can easily learn if you're familiar with the Java Logging API.

Apache Log4J 2 (`http://logging.apache.org/log4j/2.x/`) is the most popular framework used in commercial Java applications. It's a newer version of Log4J. Log4J also has a logger object. Appenders perform the same role as handlers. Layouts are similar to formatters. A log record is represented by a log event in Log4J. Whereas the Java Logging API allows file rotation by size only, Log4J supports file rotation by date/time.

But Log4J 2 also supports asynchronous loggers and appenders, which can make it an order of magnitude faster than the Java Logging API. Log4J 2 is the right choice for high-performance logging. To see how many messages Log4J 2 can publish per second, see the statistics on low-latency logging (`http://logging.apache.org/log4j/2.x/manual/async.html#Performance`).

The second popular logging framework is called Logback (`http://logback.qos.ch/reasonsToSwitch.html`). It's similar to Log4J as it was founded by the same developer. Logback is faster than Log4J, but Log4J 2 asynchronous logging is faster than Logback's. Start your next project with one of these frameworks, and if your application requires some special logging features, see if there is a framework that offer them out of the box.

To minimize the dependency of any particular logging framework, it is recommended to use an abstraction layer that will allow you to easily switch logging frameworks, if need be. Simple Logging Facade for Java (SLFJ) is the most popular implementation of such a layer. SLFJ (`http://www.slf4j.org/`) allows you to decouple the logging API from a particular implementation. For example, no matter what logging framework you use, creating a `Logger` object and publishing an `INFO`-level message looks the same in SLFJ:

```
Logger logger = LoggerFactory.getLogger(HelloWorld.class);
logger.info("Hello World");
```

With SLFJ you're not afraid that you picked the wrong logging framework; you can easily change it without modifying even one line of code. SLFJ logging levels include `ERROR`, `WARN`, `INFO`, `DEBUG`, and `TRACE`, which correspond to the `SEVERE`, `WARNING`, `INFO`, `FINE`, `FINER` levels of the Java Logging API or similar levels in other frameworks. Watch this video (`https://www.youtube.com/watch?v=tMLEbGJ2z7I&hd=1;`) to see how easy it is to switch from one logging framework to another.

To add SLFJ you need to add two JARs to your project: one with the SLFJ API, and another that binds a particular logging framework to SLFJ. In Lesson 36, you'll learn how to automate getting required JARs from public repositories of binaries. If you decide to try using SLFJ with the Java Logging API, you can find the required two JARs in Maven Central (`http://search.maven.org/#search%7Cga%7C1%7Cslf4j-api`) by searching for the following artifacts: `slf4j-api` and `slf4j-jdk14`.

But no matter what logging framework you choose, the sooner you stop using `System.out.println()` the better.

TRY IT

In this excercise, you create, configure, and use an application-specific `logging.properties` file. You also use a rotating file handler to control the size and number of your log files.

Lesson Requirements

You should have Java installed.

> **NOTE** *You can download the code and resources for this "Try It" from the book's web page at* `www.wrox.com/go/javaprog24hr2e`. *You can find them in the Lesson34 folder in the download.*

Step-by-Step

1. Copy the file `logging.properties` from your `jre/lib` directory into the root directory of the project Lesson34. Rename this file to `myLogging.properties`. I'm assuming that you previously created the `logs` directory.
2. Set the levels of the logger and the console handler to `FINE` in `myLogging.properties`:

```
.level= FINE
java.util.logging.ConsoleHandler.level = FINE
```

3. In Eclipse create a package `tryit` and copy the file `HelloWorldHandlers.java` there. Rename this file and refactor the code so it uses the class name `RotatingFilesLogger`.

4. Open the Run Configurations window for the class `RotatingFilesLogger`, select the Arguments tab, and add the following JRE property in the VM Arguments text field:

```
-Djava.util.logging.config.file="myLogging.properties"
```

5. Modify the line in `RotatingFilesHandler` to direct the log records to the file `logs/rotating.log`.

6. Run the `RotatingFilesLogger` program. It should publish `FINE`, `INFO`, and `SEVERE` messages into Eclipse console view regardless of the settings in the JRE's global `logging.properties` file. This version of the program also creates a log file `rotating.log` in the `logs` directory. We implement file rotation in the next step.

7. Modify the line that creates `FileHandler` to use the constructor for rotating files in the append mode:

```
helloFileHandler =
          new FileHandler("logs/rotating.log", 1000, 3, true);
```

8. Run the program several times and monitor the content of the `logs` directory. After several runs you should see the files named like `rotating.log.0`, `rotating.log.1`, and `rotating.log.2` there. The numeric suffix will never go higher than 2 as the logger creates and rotates only three log files. The name of the newest log file always has the suffix 0.

> **TIP** *Please select the videos for Lesson 34 online at* `www.wrox.com/go/javaprog24hr2e`. *You will also be able to download the code and resources for this lesson from the website.*

35

Introduction to Unit Testing with JUnit Framework

Software developers are not perfect, and bugs happen. Even if your program has no bugs, you may have used someone else's code, which does have bugs. Moreover, code modification in one class or interface can break previously working code in another; this is called *regression*. Thorough testing is an important phase of any software development project.

Every developer knows how to test his or her code manually, and they do it. Periodically. But manual testing is a pretty boring routine. Would you want to start each day with manual testing to see if creating, updating, and deleting a sample purchase order still works? Neither do I. Testing should be automated.

The sooner your project team implements automated testing routines, the shorter the development cycle will be. The concept of *test-driven development* (TDD (`http://en.wikipedia.org/wiki/Test-driven_development`)) suggests that testing should be embedded in the software development process from the very start of any new project.

There are different types of testing routines that have different goals. Here's a description of the main types of testing (see more at the Wikipedia article Software Testing (`http://en.wikipedia.org/wiki/Software_testing`)):

- **Unit testing** is performed by a software developer and is targeted at small pieces of code. For example, if you invoke a method `calcTax()` with particular arguments, it should return the expected result. Java classes performing application-specific unit tests are written by software developers. Sometimes unit testing is called *white-box* testing because a developer is familiar with the code being tested.
- **Integration testing** is a process when several unit tests are combined to ensure that different pieces of code work properly with each other. In other words, the goal here is to test interfaces between different software components. If John wrote the method `calcTax()`, which uses the method `getTaxBrackets()` that Mary wrote, there is a chance that Mary decided to change this method's signature without notifying John about the change.

- If John and Mary work with the same source code, the Java compiler may catch this error. But what if Mary packages compiled code in a JAR that John adds to the runtime `CLASSPATH` variable? The application would break. Integration tests ensure that all pieces of software work well together. Integration tests are written by software developers.
- **QA testing** is not performed by software developers; instead specially trained IT people use the application written by software developers and identify issues in the functionality—for example, a Place Order button in the graphical user interface (GUI) allows the user to place an order even though the user hasn't entered the shipping address.
- In some scenarios, QA engineers test the software manually, but in many cases they use test-automation software (`http://en.wikipedia.org/wiki/Test_automation`) (such as Selenium (`http://docs.seleniumhq.org/`) or QuickTest Pro (`http://www8.hp.com/us/en/software-solutions/unified-functional-automated-testing/index.html`)). They write scripts for different use cases using scripting languages. All errors are reported in an issue-tracking system (such as Redmine (`http://www.redmine.org/`) or JIRA (`https://www.atlassian.com/software/jira`)) and are assigned to software developers for providing code fixes.
- **User-acceptance testing** is performed by end users. It is often referred as *black-box* testing because the users don't know how the software was constructed. Although QA engineers can catch a large number of usability issues, they're not experts in the business domain for which the software was written. For example, an application for insurance agents should check that the agent is licensed for business in certain states and her license is not expired. These kind of errors can be caught by the business users.
- **Stress or load testing** must ensure that the application remains operational if a large number of users decide to use the application simultaneously. Load-testing tools (such as Apache JMeter (`http://en.wikipedia.org/wiki/Apache_JMeter`) or NeoLoad (`http://www.neotys.com/product/overview-neoload.html`)) make it possible to set up several computers that emulate a large number of users working with your application. How good is an application that works fine for 10 users but becomes unresponsive if the number of users increases to 100?

Ideally, there should be a written document called Service Level Agreement (SLA) that defines the number of concurrent users and acceptable response time for the software being developed. A savvy project manager signs an SLA with the users before the software development begins. If a user starts complaining about a 10-second wait, you should check the SLA and either improve the response or reject the user's request.

This lesson covers just the unit testing procedures as they apply to the software developed in Java. JUnit is the most popular tool for testing Java framework.

INTRODUCTION TO JUNIT

JUnit is a an open source unit testing framework available for download at `http://junit.org`. Before you start writing test classes, you should get familiar with the JUnit terminology:

- Assertions compare expected and received results.
- Test setup is a process of preparing the test data before running the test.
- Test teardown means getting rid of the test data after it runs.
- Test suite is a group of test classes that run together.

- Exceptions testing checks that an exception is thrown where it should be or is not thrown where it shouldn't.
- Test runner is a utility that can run tests.
- Rules allow to add functionality that applies to all tests within a test class, but in a more generic way.
- Theories allow to combine assertions to state the test assumptions more clearly.
- Assumptions selectively ignore certain tests based on some criteria.
- Parameters allow you to prepare a set of data and pass it to a test as parameter.

A class that unit-tests the application's code is a Plain Old Java Object (POJO) that includes methods marked with the `@Test` annotation. Each method represents a test case.

To run a unit test you need the following:

- A test Java class
- System Under Test (SUT), which is a class method
- A test runner

Installing JUnit

JUnit is so popular that all major integraged development environments (IDEs) include the JUnit library, so you don't even need to download it unless you want to use a newer JUnit version. In Eclipse, you simply add the JUnit library to the Project Build Path. You can run JUnit tests right from Eclipse or from a command line using test runners.

If you're not using an IDE or prefer running tests from a command line, you need to download JUnit; no installation is required. JUnit is packaged in two JAR files `junit.jar` and `hamcrest-core.jar`, and you need to add them to the `CLASSPATH` of your application. You can download these JARs from the Maven Central repository (`http://search.maven.org/`). Search for these files by names and click the jar link to download. Lesson 36 shows you how to automate downloading required JARs from Maven Central using build tools.

Changing the Default Directory Structure in Eclipse

Popular build tools like Maven and Gradle recommend the following standard directory structure for Java sources:

```
src
  main
    java
  test
    java
```

The source code of the application classes should originate from `src/main/java`, and the test classes originate from `src/test/java`. But Eclipse originates all Java sources from the directory `src`, and it doesn't force you to write test classes. If you create a new Eclipse project, change the directory structure up front to be prepared for automating the build process in the future.

Create a new Eclipse Java project called Lesson35 and change its default directory structure. Open the project properties and select the Java Build Path option. Open the Source tab and remove the src folder from the Source Folders on the Build Path field. After that add the folders src/main/java and src/test/java. This is it. Your project directory structure should look like Figure 35-1.

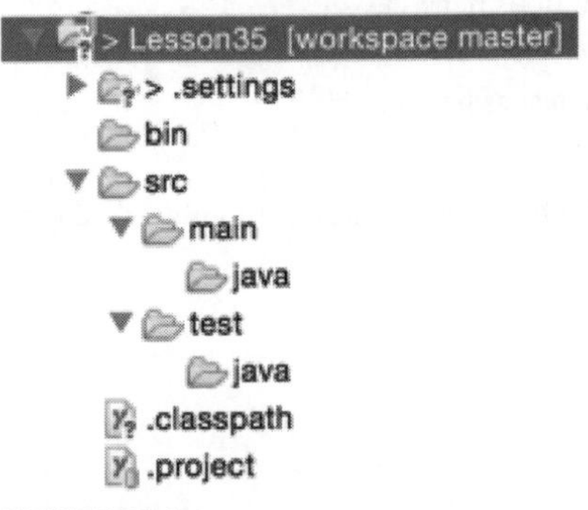

FIGURE 35-1:
New Eclipse project with modified directory structure

Now your test classes are separated from your application source code.

Your First JUnit Test Case

Following standard naming conventions you name the test class the same as the class under test but with the additional suffix Test. For example, if you are planning to unit test the class Tax, the name of the test class should be TaxTest. Start with creating a new package tax in the directory src/main/java. Then create a new interface Taxable and the class Tax there. The interface Taxable has the following content:

```
package tax;

interface Taxable {

  double calcTax(double grossIncome, int dependents)
                                   throws IllegalArgumentException;

  double applyStudentDeduction(double taxAmount, int numOfStudents);
}
```

The class Tax implements Taxable as follows:

```
package tax;
class Tax implements Taxable {

    final static double STUDENT_DEDUCTION = 300.00;

    public double calcTax(double grossIncome, int dependents)
                                  throws IllegalArgumentException{

       if (grossIncome <0 ){
```

```
            throw new IllegalArgumentException(
                               "Gross income can't be negative");
         }

         return (grossIncome*0.33 - dependents*100);
      }

      public double applyStudentDeduction(double taxAmount,
                                          int numOfStudents){

         return taxAmount - STUDENT_DEDUCTION*numOfStudents;
      }
   }
```

WHY USING AN INTERFACE?

You may ask, "Why do I even need to create a separate interface for such a simple class?" Designing to interfaces is a good idea in general, as it clearly declares the application programming interface (API) and allows changing implementation without the need to change classes that use this API. From the testing perspective, interfaces clearly expose the methods that should be unit tested.

Now create a package `tax` inside `src/test/java`. Select this package and ask Eclipse to generate a test class by selecting the menu File → New → JUnit Test Case.

Eclipse displays a window where you enter the class name as `TaxTest` and the name of the class under test as `tax.Tax`. (See Figure 35-2.)

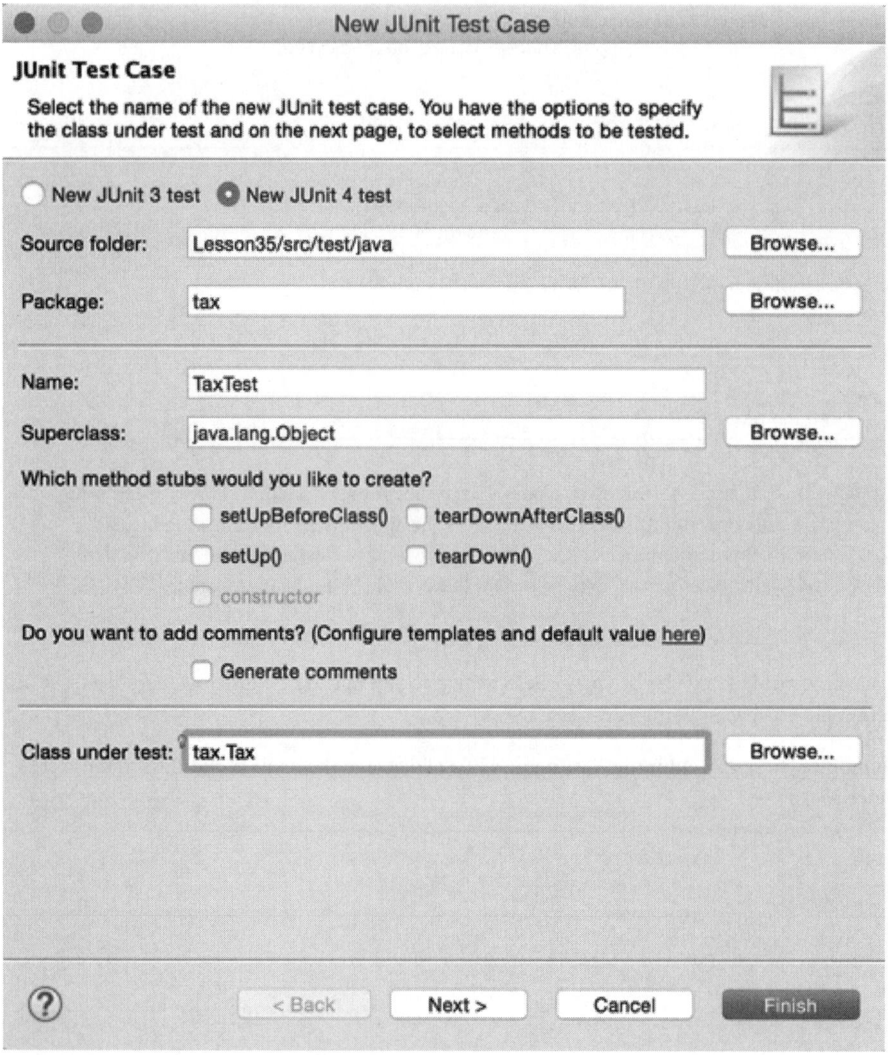

FIGURE 35-2: Creating a new JUnit Test Case in Eclipse

Click the Next button, and you can select the methods from the class `Tax` that you want to test, such as `calcTax()`. Then Eclipse displays a pop-up message asking if JUnit 4 should be added to the build path of the project. Agree to this and you see a newly generated class that looks like the following:

```
package tax;

import static org.junit.Assert.*;
import org.junit.Test;

public class TaxTest {
```

```
        @Test
        public void testCalcTax() {
            fail("Not yet implemented");
        }
    }
```

Now run this test. Right-click the TaxTest class name and select Run As → Unit Test.

Eclipse starts its default JUnit test runner, which displays a red bar and a test failure message producing the AssertionError with a message "Not yet implemented," as shown in Figure 35-3.

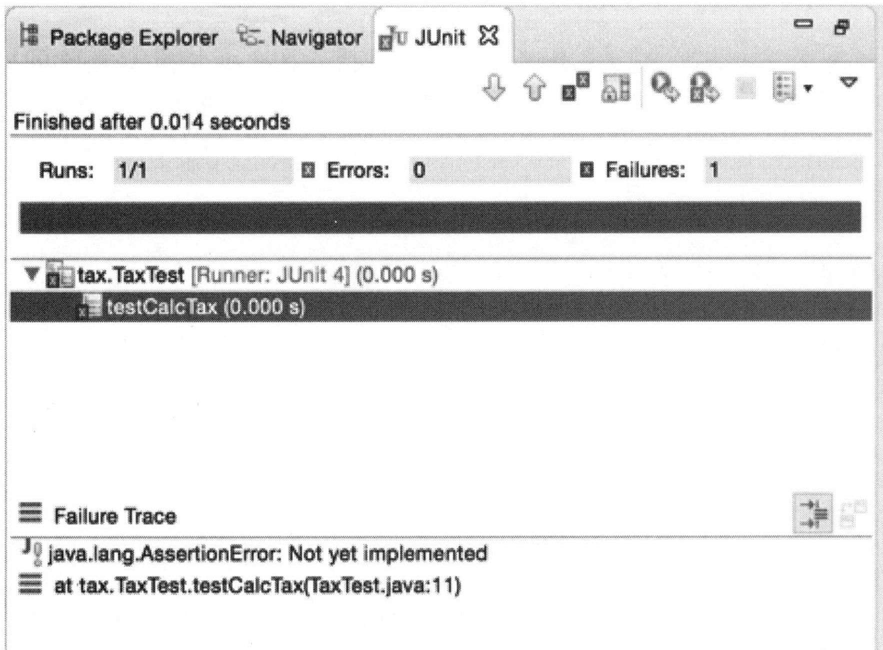

FIGURE 35-3: The first test failed: Not yet implemented

The test runner found one method annotated with @Test and ran it. The invocation of JUnit's method fail() reported an error with the message "Not yet implemented." If you comment out the fail() method and rerun the test, it passes and you see a green bar. Before learning how to write the real tests, the next section familiarizes you with JUnit annotations.

JUnit Annotations

JUnit comes with a handful of annotations that you need to use in your test classes. The test runner reads these runtime annotations and performs the testing according to your code. Here's the list of selected JUnit annotations:

- @Test annotation declares that a public void method is a unit test.
- @Before is used with a method to write some code to be executed before each test.
- @After is used with a amethod to be executed after each test.

- `@BeforeClass` is used with a method to be executed before the very first test starts.
- `@AfterClass` is used with a method to be executed after the very last test is complete.
- `@Ignore` disables a test (the test runner skips such a method).

You can use the `@Test` annotation with optional parameters `expected` and `timeout`. For example, the annotation `@Test(expected=Exception.class)` fails the test if the specified exception is not thrown. The annotation `@Test(timeout=1000)` fails the test if it runs longer than 1000 milliseconds.

Applying Annotations for Testing Tax

It's time to see the `@Test` annotation in action. You're going to write a test to ensure that if you assign zero values to the arguments `grossIncome` and `dependents`, the method `calcTax()` returns a zero tax. For that you use the `static` method `assertEquals()` from the class `org.junit.Assert`. Names of the test methods should be descriptive; call it `testZeroTax()`. The new version of your class `TaxTest` is shown next:

```
package tax;

import static org.junit.Assert.*;
import org.junit.Test;

public class TaxTest {

    @Test
    public void testZeroTax() {
        Tax tax = new Tax();
        assertEquals("Tax on zero income is not zero",
                                  0, tax.calcTax(0, 0), 0 );
    }
}
```

The class `Assert` has several overloaded versions of the method `assertEquals()`, which checks whether the expected value is equal to the actual. I used the method with the following four arguments:

- The message to display if the test fails
- The expected value
- The method to invoke on the test subject
- The maximum difference (delta) between `expected` and `actual`, for which both numbers are still considered equal

Executing this test with the test runner returns success. Change the expected value or delta while invoking `assertEquals()` in the preceding example, and the test fails. JUnit has many flavors of the `assert()` method, for example, `assertTrue()` that check that the boolean value is true and `assert NotNull()` checks that the value is not null. The names of these methods are self-explanatory and are pretty easy to understand.

STATIC IMPORTS

In the class TestTax, I use the `import static` keywords to import the class `Assert`. This allows me to use the `static` method `assertEquals()` without specifying the name of the class where it was declared. With a regular `import` statement I should have written `Assert.assertEquals()`. In general static imports should be used rarely, as the code is more difficult to understand.

In a small program such as `TaxTest`, you remember that the method `assertEquals()` was declared in JUnit, but in larger classes with lots of import statements static imports would make it less obvious where a method without the class qualification was declared.

Add one more test to see if the tax deduction is properly applied for a household with one student. The class Tax has a method `applyStudentDeduction()` that should deduct $300 per student. The method `testOneStudentTaxDeductionIs300()` in the following class `TaxTest` asserts this:

```
package tax;
import static org.junit.Assert.*;
import org.junit.Test;

public class TaxTest {

    @Test
    public void testZeroTax() {
        Tax tax = new Tax();

        assertEquals("Tax on zero income is not zero", 0,
                            tax.calcTax(0, 0),0 );
    }

    @Test
    public void testOneStudentTaxDeductionIs300(){
         Tax tax = new Tax();

         assertEquals("The $300 student discount was not applied",
                    2000, tax.applyStudentDeduction(2300, 1), 0);
    }
}
```

The test runner runs both `testZeroTax()` and `testOneStudentTaxDeductionIs300()`, and both of them are successful. By default, JUnit runs tests in arbitrary order unless you use a special annotation `@FixMethodOrder` that expects you to name the test methods in alphabetical order (`http://junit.czweb.org/apidocs/org/junit/FixMethodOrder.html`).

If you replace one of the `@Test` annotations with `@Ignore`, the test runner won't run this test.

Let's improve the code of the class `TestTax` a little bit. I don't like that we create a new instance of `Tax` in each test method. You can create a *set up* method that instantiates `Tax` so it's available for each test method. To perform some actions before the first test method run, you should use a set up method (for example, connect to a database and insert test data) annotated with `@BeforeClass`. If you need to run some cleanup procedure (for example, remove the test data from a database and disconnect) add a *tear down* method annotated with `@AfterClass`. The following version of the class `TestTax` illustrates the use of the annotations `@BeforeClass` and `@AfterClass` (the latter just prints the "In tearDown" message on the console):

```
package tax;

import static org.junit.Assert.*;

import org.junit.*;

public class TaxTest {

    static Tax tax;

    @BeforeClass
    public static void setUp(){
        tax = new Tax();
        System.out.println("In setUp");
    }

    @Test
    public void testZeroTax() {
        assertEquals("Tax on zero income is not zero", 0,
                            tax.calcTax(0, 0),0 );
    }

    @Test
    public void testOneStudentTaxDeductionIs300(){

         assertEquals("The $300 student discount was not applied",
                    2000, tax.applyStudentDeduction(2300, 1), 0);
    }

    @AfterClass
    public static void tearDown(){
        System.out.println("In tearDown");
    }
}
```

If you want to create a test class that invokes `setUp()` and `tearDown()` before invoking each test method, replace `@BeforeClass` and `@AfterClass` with `@Before` and `@After`, respectively. Although `@BeforeClass` and `@AfterClass` annotations can be used only with static methods, `@Before` and `@After` don't have this restriction.

Test Suites

A test suite is a container for test classes that the test runner should execute together. In large applications test cases are grouped into suites by some criteria—for example, long running tests, or tests that should check a particular software module of the application.

For a demonstration of how to create a test suite, create a second JUnit test case in the same folder as `TaxTest`. Name this class `TaxExceptionTest`; it has one test method to check whether the exception is thrown if the method `Tax.calcTax()` gets a negative number as `grossIncome`:

```
package tax;

import static org.junit.Assert.*;

import org.junit.Test;

public class TaxExceptionTest {

    @Test(expected=IllegalArgumentException.class)
    public void testForNegativeGrossIncome() {
      Tax tax = new Tax();

      tax.calcTax(-100, 2);
      fail("grossIncome in calcTax() can't be negative.");
    }
}
```

The test `TaxEceptionTest` is considered successful when the `calcTax()` throws an `IllegalArgumentException` if it gets the negative number in `grossIncome`. If you want to see it fail, comment out the `throw` statement in the method `calcTax()`. In this example, I was using `IllegalArgumentException`, which is included in Java SE. But you can use the same mechanism with custom exceptions as well.

Now create a test suite that consists of two test cases: `TaxTest` and `TaxExceptionTest`. In Eclipse select File → New → Other → Java → JUnit → JUnit Test Suite; you see the window shown in Figure 35-4.

Click the Finish button and Eclipse generates the class `AllTests` with the following content:

```
package tax;

import org.junit.runner.RunWith;
import org.junit.runners.Suite;
import org.junit.runners.Suite.SuiteClasses;

@RunWith(Suite.class)
@SuiteClasses({ TaxExceptionTest.class, TaxTest.class })
public class AllTests {

}
```

The annotation `@RunWith` instructs the test runner `Suite` to be used instead of a default test runner. The annotation `@SuiteClasses` includes both of the test classes: `TaxExceptionTest` and `TaxTest`. Run the test suite `AllTests` as JUnit Test Case and you see that all of the tests have succeeded, as shown in Figure 35-5.

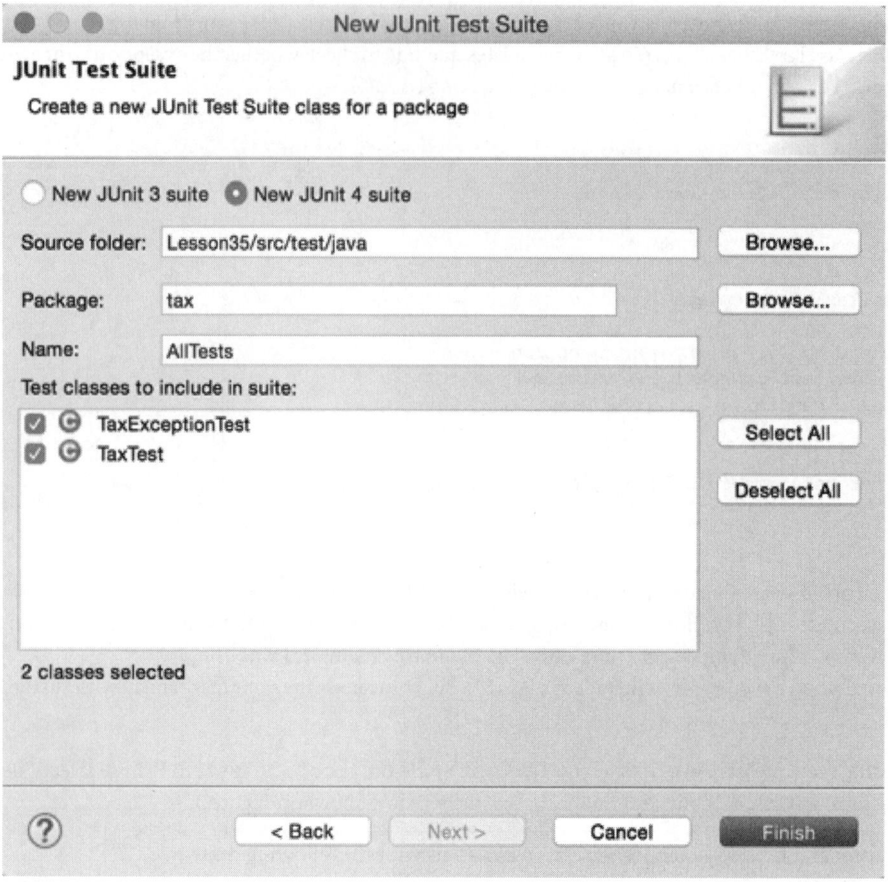

FIGURE 35-4: Creating a test suite in Eclipse

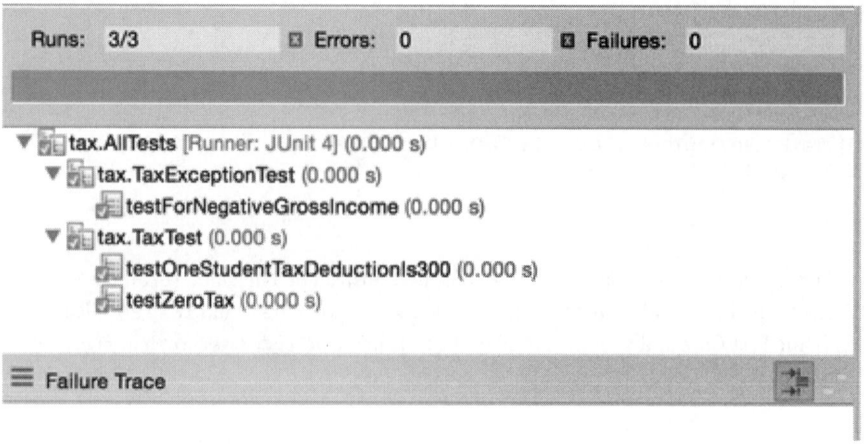

FIGURE 35-5: Running a test suite in Eclipse

JUnit Test Runners

JUnit comes with several test runners (`https://github.com/junit-team/junit/wiki/Test-runners`) classes located in the package `org.junit.runner`. The class `JUnit4` is a default runner that was used for most of the examples in this lesson. To specify a non-default runner you need to use the annotation `@RunWith`. As you saw in the previous section, the test suite `AllClasses` used the runner implemented in the `Suite` class:

```
@RunWith(Suite.class)
```

There are other specialized runners implemented in the classes `Parameterized`, `Categories`, and `Enclose`. There are also several third-party runners.

Using test runners inside Eclipse is convenient for development, but in real-world projects you should incorporate unit tests into build scripts. Hence you need to know how to launch JUnit test runners without an IDE. You can launch the runners outside of any IDE using one of these methods:

- Create a Java class that invokes the method `run()` on the `JUnitCore` object.
- Run the `JUnitCore` from a command line providing the names of the test classes as command-line arguments.

With the first method, you need to create a Java class, instantiate `JUnitCore`, and invoke its method `run()` providing test classes or a test suite as arguments. For example:

```
JUnitCore junitCore= new JUnitCore();
Result result = junitCore.run(AllTests.class);
```

Then you can get a collection of the `Failure` objects each of which represents one failed test, if any:

```
List<Failure> failedTests = result.getFailures();
```

To have better control and improved logging during the test run, you can create a listener—a subclass of `RunListener`—and assign it to the instance of the `JUnitCore` object using the method `addListener()`:

```
JUnitCore junitCore= new JUnitCore();
jUnitCore.addListener(new MyRunListener());
jUnitCore.run(AllTests.class);
```

In the listener class, you can override methods `testStarted()`, `testFinished()`, `testFailure()`, and several others. Then add logging statements inside these methods.

If you decide to run `JUnitCore` directly from the command line, you need to make sure that the JUnit JAR and the directories of your test classes and the classes under test are included to the `CLASSPATH` variable in your runtime environment. Then you can run a command similar to this one:

```
java org.junit.runner.JUnitCore tax.TaxTest
```

Lesson 36 explains how to automate builds with Gradle. If you've written unit tests for your application, you can easily incorporate them into the build process, so they run without manual interaction via an IDE. In the "Try It" section you practice using JUnit test runners from the command line.

In this lesson you've learned how to write simple unit tests using JUnit framework. For writing more advanced tests you should study JUnit online documentation (`https://github.com/junit-team/junit/wiki`). The other popular frameworks that can be used for unit testing are TestNG (`http://testng.org/doc/index.html`) and Spock (`https://code.google.com/p/spock/`). I can also recommend you to watch a presentation "Tooling for Test-Driven Development in Java (`http://www.java-tv.com/2015/02/09/tooling-for-java-test-driven-development/`)" by Pawel Lipinski.

TRY IT

In this assignment you need to run the test classes described in this lesson from the command line. First, you create a Java class with the code that invokes a test runner. Then you try an alternative way of launching the test runner; you start the `JUnitCore` runner directly from a command line.

Lesson Requirements

You should have Java installed and the JUnit JARS available.

> **NOTE** *You can download the code and resources for this "Try It" from the book's web page at* `www.wrox.com/go/javaprog24hr2e`. *You can find them in the Lesson35 folder in the download.*

Step-by-Step

1. Continue using the directory structure created for Eclipse project Lesson35. In the directory `src/test/java/tax` create a class `TaxCommanLineRunner` with the following code:

```
package tax;
import java.util.List;
import org.junit.internal.TextListener;
import org.junit.runner.JUnitCore;
import org.junit.runner.Result;
import org.junit.runner.notification.Failure;

public class TaxCommandLineRunner {

    public static void main(String[] args) {

        JUnitCore junitCore = new JUnitCore();

        Result result = junitCore.run(AllTests.class);

        if (result.wasSuccessful()){
```

```
                System.out.println(
                            "All Tax Test cases ran successfully");
            } else{

                System.out.println("These Tax Test cases failed:");

                List<Failure> failedTests = result.getFailures();
                failedTests.forEach(failure ->
                        System.out.println(failure.getMessage()));
            }
        }
    }
```

This program runs the `AllTests` suite and either prints the message that all tests were successful or prints specific error descriptions from the failed tests.

2. Open the Command or Terminal window and change to the `bin` directory of the project Lesson35 where all the compiled classes are located.

3. Run `TestCommandLineRunner` adding the JARs `junit.jar` and `hamcrest-core.jar` to the CLASSPATH (the option `-cp`). In my case these JARs were located in the directory `/Users/yfain11/junit`, and Figure 35-6 shows how I launched my test runner in the Terminal window.

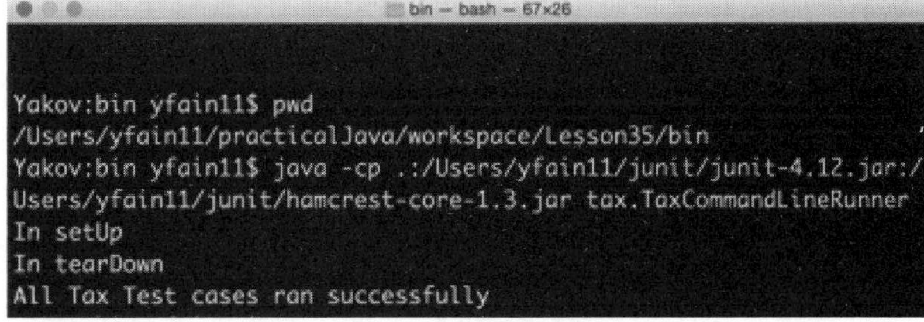

FIGURE 35-6: Running TaxCommandLineRunner in Mac OS

4. Replace the `System.out.println()` calls with logging as explained in Lesson 34.

5. Use an alternative way of invoking the `JUnitCore`. Run it directly from a Command or Terminal window specifying the test suite `AllTests` as a command-line argument. I did it, as shown in Figure 35-7.

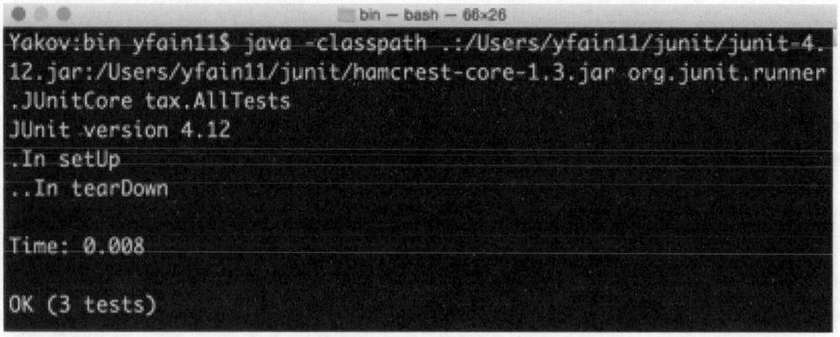

```
bin — bash — 66×26
Yakov:bin yfain11$ java -classpath .:/Users/yfain11/junit/junit-4.
12.jar:/Users/yfain11/junit/hamcrest-core-1.3.jar org.junit.runner
.JUnitCore tax.AllTests
JUnit version 4.12
.In setUp
..In tearDown

Time: 0.008

OK (3 tests)
```

FIGURE 35-7: Invoking org.junit.runner.JUnitCore directly

The output of the `AllTests` program looks a little different now, but the results are the same: All tests completed successfully.

> **TIP** *Please select the videos for Lesson 35 online at* `www.wrox.com/go/javaprog24hr2e`. *You will also be able to download the code and resources for this lesson from the website.*

36

Build Automation with Gradle

While studying Java and trying to work on hands-on assignments, you've been compiling, deploying, and running Java programs in the integrated development environment (IDE). These actions were required to *build projects*. For a real-world project, the build process usually includes more steps before the application goes into production. For example:

- Running unit and integration tests
- Creating scripts for continuous integration
- Working with version control systems and code repositories
- Managing dependencies (ensuring that the right versions of the third-party libraries are linked to the code)
- Generating program documentation
- Deploying the application on development, quality assurance (QA), and production servers
- Sending notification e-mails about successful or failed builds

In the enterprise setup, creating, customizing and maintaining build scripts is a project in its own, which should be started in early stages of application development.

The build process should not depend on any particular IDE or on the presence of any guru-developer who knows how to compile all the code, link it with required libraries, and deploy it to the right computer. Compiling, building, and deploying the code should be run by scripts. A typical enterprise Java project consists of more than one software module and hundreds of classes, and it is developed by a team (or teams) of programmers, who may use different IDEs.

Continuous Integration (`http://en.wikipedia.org/wiki/Continuous_integration`) (CI) is a practice that requires developers to check the code into a code repository several times a day, and every check-in may initiate a new automated build of the entire project. Besides, there could be scheduled builds that run nightly or weekly regardless of whether the new code was checked in. Teams that practice test-driven development (`http://en.wikipedia.org/wiki/Test-driven_development`) (TDD) include running of multiple tests into the build script to get the reports and act on any issues early. Continuous Delivery (`http://`

en.wikipedia.org/wiki/Continuous_delivery) practice goes even further than CI; delivery of software to the test or production servers is scripted and automated, too. When a programmer sees a "Who broke the build?" message in the team's chat window, his first thought is, "It better not be me."

Implementing build scripts improves the discipline in the team . You better think (or test) twice before submitting a piece of the new functionality to the code repository without testing it as it might break the build.

This lesson starts with very brief introduction to the older build tools Ant and Maven, and then you get familiar with the modern build automation tool called Gradle (https://www.gradle.org/).

HELLO WORLD IN ANT

About fifteen years years ago, Apache Ant (http://ant.apache.org/) was the most popular build tool in the Java world. The build in Ant is described in a file that contains several *targets* that the build should achieve a sequence—for example, compile, jar, and run. A target consists of *tasks*, such as mkdir and javac.

Say you wrote a class HelloWorld, saved it in the file HelloWorld.java, and want to configure an Ant build process. Create a file build.xml with the following content:

```
<project default="main">
  <target name="clean">
     <delete dir="build"/>
  </target>

   <target name="compile" depends="clean">
     <mkdir dir="build/classes"/>
     <javac srcdir="src" destdir="build/classes"/>
  </target>

  <target name="jar"  depends="compile">
      <mkdir dir="build/jar"/>
      <jar destfile="build/jar/HelloWorld.jar"
                                         basedir="build/classes">
        <manifest>
          <attribute name="Main-Class" value="HelloWorld"/>
        </manifest>
     </jar>
  </target>

  <target name="run" depends="jar">
    <java jar="build/jar/HelloWorld.jar" fork="true" />
  </target>

  <target name="main" depends="clean, compile, jar, run">
  </target>

</project>
```

This file describes five targets: `clean`, `compile`, `jar`, `run`, and `main`. The `clean` task deletes the directory `build`. The `compile` target consists of two tasks: create a directory build and compile all classes located in the directory `src` into the directory `build/classes`.

The `jar` target creates a directory `build/jar` and then creates a jar file from compiled classes assigning the class `HelloWorld` as a runnable program. The `run` target launches the application. The `main` target runs by default if you go to the directory where the `build.xml` is located and enter the `ant` command without parameters.

You may also add custom `<property>` tags (for example, naming the source or destination directories) and the `<path>` element listing JAR files that otherwise should have been added to the `CLASSPATH` environment variable.

Most of the targets depend on the success of another (see the `depends` attributes). The target's executional unit fails if any of the targets listed in the `depends` attribute fail. Writing such detailed instructions on what has to be done is known as the *imperative way* of describing builds.

You can run one or more targets by specifying their names in the command line. For example, this is how to run several targets with one command:

```
ant clean compile jar run
```

All Java IDEs support Ant, and you can run the target without even going to the command window. For example, Eclipse has an Ant view, and you can run each of the tasks from the right-click menu, as shown in Figure 36-1.

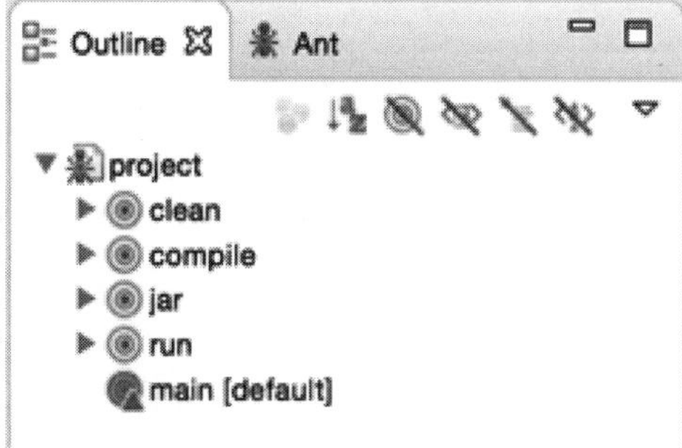

FIGURE 36-1:
Ant view in Eclipse IDE

HELLO WORLD IN MAVEN

In 2004 Apache Maven (`http://maven.apache.org/`) was released, and it soon became the de facto standard for building Java projects. Maven is not just a build tool; it's a project management tool. Based on the project object model (POM) defined in one or more `pom.xml` files, Maven can manage the project's build process and pull all dependencies either from a local server or a central repository (`http://search.maven.org/`). Maven's functionality can be extended using numerous existing plug-ins or with those you write on your own.

The smallest unit of work in Maven is called *a goal*. You can start development with the generation of the standard project structure by opening a Command or a Terminal window and entering the `mvn` command with the goal `archetype:generate`:

```
mvn archetype:generate -DgroupId=hello.app -DartifactId=Lesson36
-DarchetypeArtifactId=maven-archetype-quickstart
-DinteractiveMode=false
```

In several seconds the directories and files shown in Figure 36-2 are generated in the directory `Lesson36`.

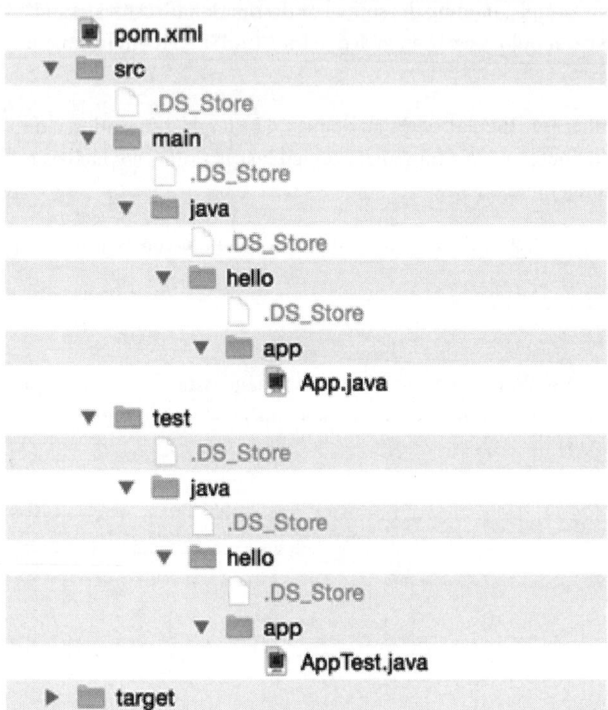

FIGURE 36-2: Maven-generated project

Per Maven's conventions, the source code is located in the directory `src/main/java`, and the compiled code goes into the directory `target` (it doesn't exist yet). The file `App.java` contains the Java class with the code to print Hello World on the console. The file `AppTest.java` creates the code for unit testing using the JUnit framework covered in Lesson 35. The content of the generated file `pom.xml` is shown here:

```
<project xmlns="http://maven.apache.org/POM/4.0.0"
            xmlns:xsi="http://www.w3.org/2001/XMLSchema-instance"
            xsi:schemaLocation="http://maven.apache.org/POM/4.0.0
            http://maven.apache.org/maven-v4_0_0.xsd">
  <modelVersion>4.0.0</modelVersion>
  <groupId>hello.app</groupId>
  <artifactId>Lesson36</artifactId>
  <packaging>jar</packaging>
```

```
    <version>1.0-SNAPSHOT</version>
    <name>Lesson36</name>
    <url>http://maven.apache.org</url>
    <dependencies>
      <dependency>
        <groupId>junit</groupId>
        <artifactId>junit</artifactId>
        <version>3.8.1</version>
        <scope>test</scope>
      </dependency>
    </dependencies>
  </project>
```

With Maven you can, but don't have to, specify step-by-step instructions for the build process. You describe the project in a *declarative way* by specifying packaging and dependencies. You described *what* has to be done, but not *how* to do it as it's done with Ant. For example, when you declare that a `<packaging>` element of the project is JAR, WAR, or EAR, you don't have to specify detailed executional units because Maven automatically creates a number of goals that have to be executed to create a requested packaging.

Maven promotes the *convention over configuration* paradigm, where each project has a standardized layout. For example, Maven knows that the source code of the project is located in the directory `src/main/java`. Standard conventions work well unless you need to create build scripts for several modules that use different conventions. Customizing builds requires writing Maven plug-ins so the final build consists of a mix of XML and scripts written in the Java or Groovy languages.

The results of a Maven build are called artifacts. In the example, the artifact named Lesson36 depends on the artifact junit of version 3.8.1 (the current version of junit is 4.12).

Maven's build life cycle (`http://maven.apache.org/guides/introduction/introduction-to-the-lifecycle.html`) consists of phases (such as `install` and `clean`), which can run goals (for example, `clean:clean` or `dependency:copy-dependencies`). To build the project, you need to go to the directory that contains `pom.xml` and execute the phase `package`, which compiles and deploys it according to the `<packaging>` tag:

```
mvn package
```

The phase package compiles and creates the JAR file, attaching the prefix specified in `<version>` to the filename. You can find this file in the directory `target` as shown in Figure 36-3.

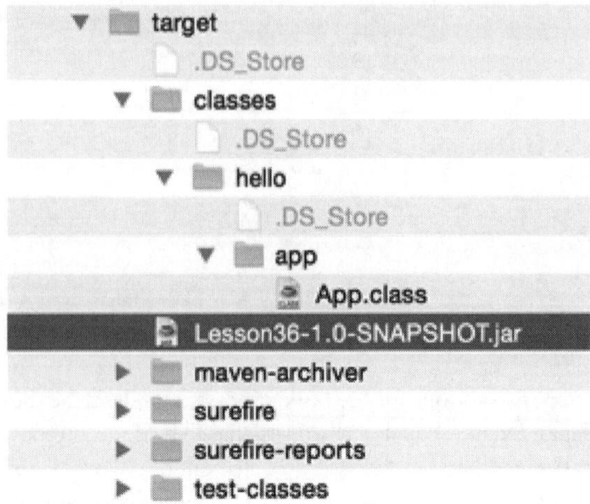

FIGURE 36-3: The target directory after running the phase package

If you didn't want to package the compiled classes into a JAR, you could just run the `mvn` compile command and Maven would compile the classes into the `target/classes` directory. To see the Hello World message on the console run the following command:

```
java -cp target/Lesson36-1.0-SNAPSHOT.jar hello.app.App
```

To run tests that were generated in the test directory run the `verify` goal:

```
mvn verify
```

Both Ant and Maven describe the control flow of the build in XML format. Because XML is not a programming language, the ability to customize and adapt builds for changing environments may not be easy. In our Hello World projects, XML files were rather small, but in real-world projects they could consist of hundreds of lines.

GRADLE BASICS

Gradle is written in Java, and it doesn't use XML to describe builds. Gradle uses a Domain Specific Language (DSL) based on Groovy, which is a dynamic language that runs in Java Virtual Machine (JVM). The build script is written in a text file, which has a `.gradle` extension. But this file is not just data formatted in XML or another way. It's a program.

The main Gradle concepts are *projects* and *tasks*. By default, the name of the directory where the build script is located is a name of the project. Each build consist of tasks. A task is an equivalent of the Ant's target. A task consists of *actions*. Gradle may decide to run certain tasks in parallel or not run at all. For example, if the source code has not been changed, Gradle won't run the compile task.

Installing Gradle is a pretty simple process described in these installation instructions (`http://www.gradle.org/installation`). Just download and unzip the file with the latest Gradle release and add the Gradle's `bin` directory to the `PATH` environment variable on your computer.

Gradle has a user guide in both HTML and PDF formats, which you can find in the docs/userguide directory of your Gradle install. There is also a javadoc for the Gradle API in the directory docs/javadoc. There you can find a description of interfaces Project, Task, Action, and many others.

Similarly to Maven, Gradle uses a certain convention about the default project directory layout (it can be customized). Because we'll be creating a Java build, the default location of the Java source files is the directory src/main/java. The directory src/main/resources is a default location for all project resources that are usually packaged inside a JAR file with compiled Java classes. By default, the build output goes into the directory called build.

The next section starts familiarizing you with Gradle by showing you how to compile and run a HelloWorld class that should print Hello World on the system console.

Hello World in Gradle

In this example you're going to place the HelloWorld class in the package hello. Start with creating a directory src/main/java/hello and save the file HelloWorld.java there.

Building Hello World

Although core Gradle doesn't provide much functionality, you can use it as a build tool for different programming languages. All language-specific features are provided as plug-ins, and you add only those that are needed for your project. Some plug-ins are available out of the box, and you can extend Gradle by writing your own plug-ins.

Here's a simple script, build.gradle, that can perform several tasks. In particular, it can compile Java classes located in the directory src/main/java:

```
apply plugin: 'java'
```

The file build.gradle should be located in the same directory as src. To run the build, open the Command or Terminal window in this directory and run the build task:

```
gradle build
```

Although you've never declared the build task in build.gradle, it's already a part of the Java plug-in. You'd need to read the documentation to learn what a specific plug-in can do for you. For example, the documentation (http://www.gradle.org/docs/current/userguide/java_plugin.html) for the java plug-in describes 22 tasks (for example, clean, compileJava, jar, and build). The test task runs the tests created with JUnit covered in Lesson 35. After running the build task, my Terminal window looked like Figure 36-4.

```
Total time: 3.15 secs
Yakov:HelloWorld yfain11$ gradle build
:compileJava
:processResources UP-TO-DATE
:classes
:jar
:assemble
:compileTestJava UP-TO-DATE
:processTestResources UP-TO-DATE
:testClasses UP-TO-DATE
:test UP-TO-DATE
:check UP-TO-DATE
:build

BUILD SUCCESSFUL

Total time: 3.675 secs
```

FIGURE 36-4: Running the Gradle build command the first time

Note that the `build` task initiated a series of other tasks: `compileJava`, `processResources`, `classes`, `jar`, and so on . Actually, some of the tasks were marked as UP-TO-DATE—they were not run because you don't have any resources under `src/main/resources` or test classes under `src/test/java`. You also haven't included another plug-in that can check the quality of your code. Now run the Gradle build task again. The output looks a little different, as shown in Figure 36-5.

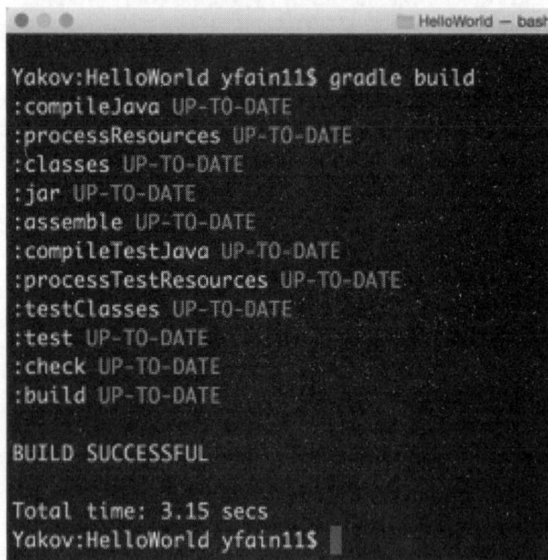

FIGURE 36-5: Running Gradle build again

This time Gradle had nothing to do because everything, including compiled classes and the JAR, was up to date. This feature is called *incremental build*—Gradle doesn't run the tasks, which would produce the same results.

The `compileJava` task supports incremental Java compilation, which saves time by compiling only those classes that have been modified.

I started the build having only class `HelloWorld` in the folder `src/main/java/hello`. Gradle's `build` task has created the `build` directory with the content shown in Figure 36-6.

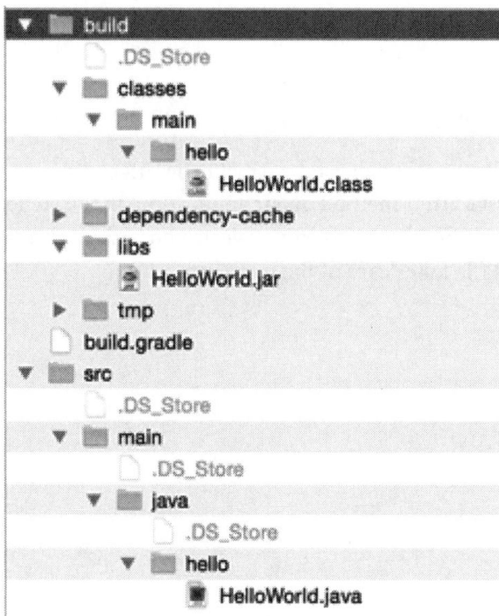

FIGURE 36-6: The Hello World project after running the Gradle build task

The `classes` directory contains the compiled classes, and the `lib` directory contains the JAR file with `HelloWorld.class` inside (it was created by the task `jar`).

SPECIFYING THE BUILD FILENAME

By default, Gradle assumes that the name of the build script is `build.gradle`. But if you'd like to keep more than one build file in the same directory, you can always use the –b command-line option and enter the build filename; for example:

```
gradle -b mySecondBuildFile.gradle build
```

Running Hello World

You can run the compiled `HelloWorld` class as any other Java program by entering the following command:

```
java -cp build/classes/main hello.HelloWorld
```

On the other hand, you can add to `build.gradle` the `application` plug-in that has tasks to run programs. Because your project may have multiple classes, you also need to specify the name of the class with the `main()` method that you want to run:

```
apply plugin: 'java'
apply plugin: 'application'

mainClassName="hello.HelloWorld"
```

Now enter `gradle run` on the command line, and you see the Hello World message printed on the console.

Next, configure the manifest property of the jar object (yes, Gradle tasks are objects). To make the JAR executable, it has to include the manifest file that specifies the class with the `main()` method in our application. In the Hello World example, you have a single class, which has the `main()` method. But in larger projects you have multiple files, and only one of them is the main one. The following build file takes care of the manifest:

```
apply plugin: 'java'
apply plugin: 'application'

mainClassName="hello.HelloWorld"

jar {
  manifest {
    attributes 'Main-Class': 'hello.HelloWorld'
  }
}
```

After running the build task, you can go to the `build/libs` directory and run the `HelloWorld` application as follows:

```
java -jar HelloWorld.jar
```

If you want to see the content of the manifest file that Gradle created and placed inside the JAR, visit the `build/tmp/jar` directory where you'll find a `MANIFEST.MF` file with the following content:

```
Manifest-Version: 1.0
Main-Class: hello.HelloWorld
```

Your `build.gradle` file looks a lot shorter than the `build.xml` shown in the section Hello World with Ant, but with Ant it's easier to understand what the build process can do. On the other hand, on large projects you need to write lots of Ant targets whereas Gradle plug-ins include multiple tasks out of the box.

CHANGING GRADLE CONVENTIONS

Software developers may be accustomed to certain project layouts, which may not necessarily match Gradle default conventions. This section shows you how to change Gradle's conventions on where the sources and resources are located, and where the output files should go.

Say that I want to keep the Java source code in the `src` directory, and not `src/main/java`, which is Gradle's default. I want to keep additional resource files in the `resources` directory instead of `src/main/resources`. I also want to change my output directory from `build` to `bin`.

The SourceSet API (`http://www.gradle.org/docs/current/dsl/org.gradle.api.tasks.SourceSet.html`) enables you to change Gradle conventions of the Java projects. A source set is a concept of a Java plug-in that represents a group of files (classes and resources) that are compiled and executed together. The Java plug-in defines two standard source sets: `main` and `test`. Because you haven't written any test classes; you can just redefine the directory for the source set `main`.

For illustration purposes, this example also shows you how to have Gradle create the `libs` directory as a sibling to `src` and `bin` using the property `libsDirName`. Use the same `HelloWorld` example to try this out. I'm using the `build.gradle` from the previous section and adding a `sourceSets` code block to it:

```
apply plugin: 'java'
apply plugin: 'application'

mainClassName="hello.HelloWorld"

jar {
  manifest {
    attributes 'Main-Class': 'hello.HelloWorld'
  }
}
sourceSets{
   main{
     java{
        srcDirs=['src']
        output.classesDir='bin'
     }
     resources {
        srcDir 'resources'
     }
   }
}

libsDirName='../libs'
```

Now move `hello/HelloWorld.java` from `src/main/java` to `src` and run the preceding build to see the `bin` and `libs` directory at the same level as `src`, as shown in Figure 36-7.

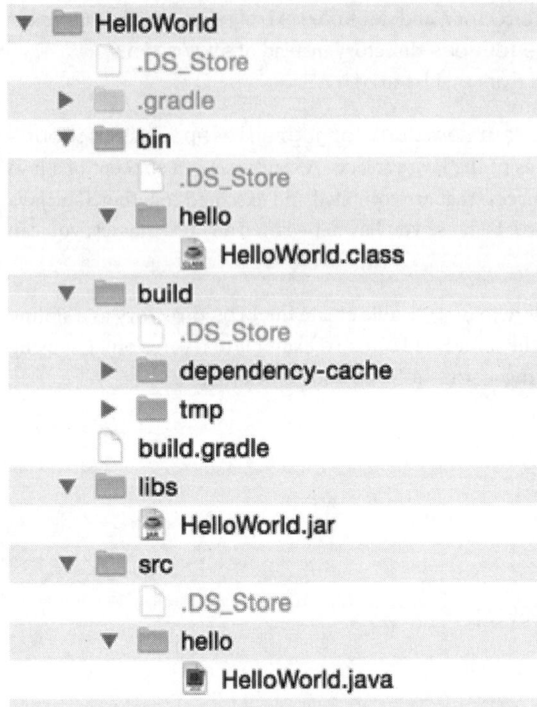

FIGURE 36-7: Running the build after changing Gradle's defaults

I'm not encouraging you to change the default project layout, but in some cases you need to introduce Gradle in the existing projects with a different directory structure, so having this type of flexibility helps.

MANAGING DEPENDENCIES WITH GRADLE

Real-world Java projects often depend on external libraries. For example, the JDBC example from Lesson 21 wouldn't work without the Derby DB drivers packaged in the file `derbyclient.jar`. Hence, to create a build script for the application that works with Derby DB, you need to add this JAR to the `build.gradle` script.

But knowing *what* JAR files to add is not enough. You also need to specify *where* these files are located. Accordingly, the `dependencies` code block answers the *what* question, and `repositories` points at the location *where* these files are stored.

Dependency Management is well described in the Gradle tutorial (`http://www.gradle.org/docs/current/userguide/artifact_dependencies_tutorial.html`), but this section shows you how to work with repositories and dependencies while working on a concrete example, namely the `EmployeeList` program from Lesson 21. This program retrieves a list of employees from the Derby DB database. Start with creating a directory `derbySample`; the `build.gradle` goes there. Then create subdirectories `src/main/java` and copy to there the file `EmployeeList.java` from Lesson 21:

```
// Class EmployeeList displays Employees from the table EMP
// using JDBC drivers of type 4

import java.sql.*;

class EmployeeList {

  public static void main(String argv[]) {

   String sqlQuery = "SELECT * from Employee";

   // Open autocloseable Connection, Statement
   // and get the result set
   try (Connection conn = DriverManager.getConnection(
                           "jdbc:derby://localhost:1527/Lesson21");
        Statement stmt = conn.createStatement();
        ResultSet rs = stmt.executeQuery(sqlQuery); ) {

      // Process the result set - print Employees
      while (rs.next()){
         int empNo = rs.getInt("EMPNO");
            String eName = rs.getString("ENAME");
         String job = rs.getString("JOB_TITLE");
         System.out.println(""+ empNo + ", " + eName + ", " + job );
      }
   } catch( SQLException se ) {
      System.out.println ("SQLError: " + se.getMessage ()
           + " code: " + se.getErrorCode ());

   } catch( Exception e ) {
      System.out.println(e.getMessage());
   }
  }
}
```

In the directory derbySample, create the gradle.build file that looks like this:

```
apply plugin: 'java'
apply plugin: 'application'

mainClassName="EmployeeList"
```

Running the task gradle build produces no errors and creates the file EmployeeList.class in the directory build/classes/main and derbySample.jar in the directory build/libs. But when I executed the command gradle run it gave me the runtime exception "No suitable driver," as shown in Figure 36-8.

```
Yakov:derbySample yfain11$ gradle run
:compileJava UP-TO-DATE
:processResources UP-TO-DATE
:classes UP-TO-DATE
:run
SQLError: No suitable driver found for jdbc:derby://localhost:1527/Lesson21
```

FIGURE 36-8: Running Gradle results in an exception

You know why: Java could not find JDBC drivers to work with Derby DB. In other words, the application `EmployeeList` depends on the file `derbyclient.jar`., which was not included in the `CLASSPATH`. I broke the build! Let's fix it by adding repositories and dependencies.

Repositories

Repositories of the code that a project depends on can be local or remote. You may have a dedicated server within the organization where all third-party and homemade JARs are located. In another scenario, the JAR (or JARs) you project may be created as a part of another project build and published in a predefined location.

There are many software source code hosting facilities on the Internet. Some of them are public, and some are private. Some of them host source code (`http://en.wikipedia.org/wiki/Comparison_of_source_code_software_hosting_facilities`), and some host-compiled code (or binaries). In the Java world, the most popular repositories of the compiled code are Maven Central, Apache Ivy, and Bintray by JFrog. This section uses Maven Central to look for the `derbyclient.jar`. A quick search in Maven Central produces the result shown in Figure 36-9.

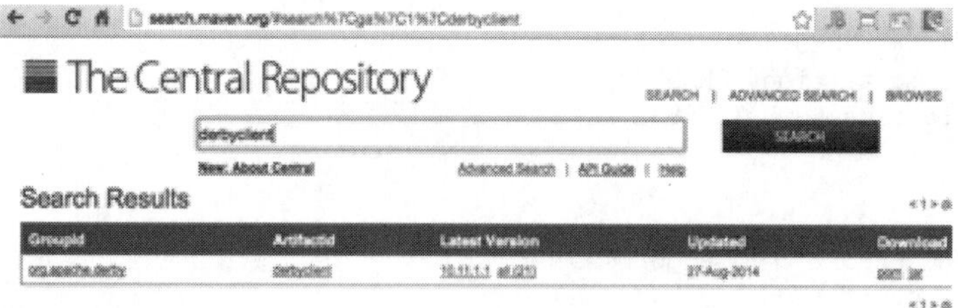

FIGURE 36-9: Derby Client at Maven Central

Every artifact in Maven Central has such attributes as `group id`, `artifact id`, and `version`. If you click on the Latest Version link, you find a detailed information about this artifact, and you can even copy the string with dependencies for automatic download of this artifact. You use `group id`, `artifact id`, and `version` in the dependencies section of the build in the next section. For now, just add Maven Central in the repositories block of the build script:

```
apply plugin: 'java'
apply plugin: 'application'

mainClassName="EmployeeList"

repositories{
   mavenCentral()
}
```

I'll use Maven Central repository, but if you want to store the artifacts in one of your company servers, you could specify it as follows:

```
repositories{
    mavenLocal()
}
```

By default, Gradle uses the directory *USER_HOME/.m2/repository* on the local computer. This location can be changed in the file `settings.gradle` (see Gradle documentation (`http://www.gradle.org/docs/current/dsl/org.gradle.api.initialization.Settings.html`) for details).

You're done with the first part. Your build script knows where to look for project dependencies, which are covered in the next section.

Dependencies and Configurations

Your build process may depend on certain JARs during different phases of its control flow. In some cases, your code won't even compile if a certain JAR is not available in the `CLASSPATH`. For example, when you've been creating Dynamic Web Projects in Eclipse, all references to the Java EE classes, interfaces, or annotations (for example, `HttpServlet` or `@Stateless`) were known to the project during the compilation. The reason being that when Eclipse creates a Dynamic Web Project for a specific target server, it adds all JARS (dependencies) to the project. Open the Build Path of any of your GlassFish Eclipse projects, and you'll find there an entry called GlassFish System Libraries that includes dozens of JARs.

In some cases (as with the `EmployeeList` program), the code compiles but generates errors during the run time. The same applies to compiling and running test programs.

In Gradle, when you declare a dependency, you need to specify the *configuration* where this dependency should be used. Run the task `gradle dependencies` in the Command window to see a list of available configurations for Java projects, as shown in Figure 36-10.

As you can see, dependencies can be configured (`http://www.gradle.org/docs/current/userguide/java_plugin.html#tab:configurations`) for compilation, run time, archiving, and testing tasks. Add the dependencies section to your `gradle.build` from the `derbySample` directory:

```
apply plugin: 'java'
apply plugin: 'application'

mainClassName="EmployeeList"

repositories{
   mavenCentral()
}

dependencies {
  runtime group: 'org.apache.derby', name: 'derbyclient',
                 version: '10.11.1.1'
}
```

If you execute the `gradle run` task now, the "No suitable driver" exception isn't thrown. The task `run` downloads the dependency from Maven Central and the JDBC driver is found. You get the server connection error because the Derby DB server is not running, but it's a different problem to address (see Figure 36-11).

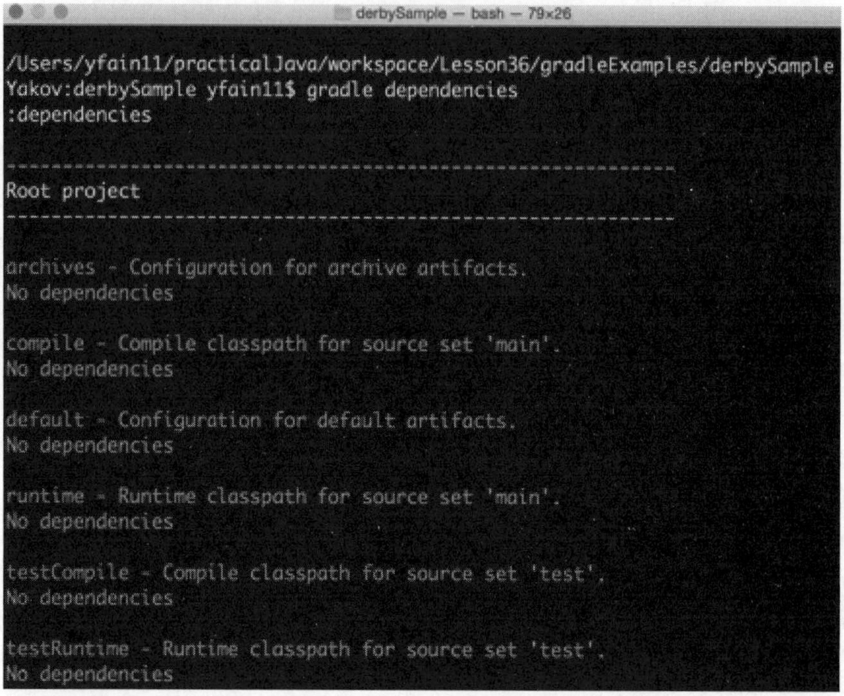

```
derbySample — bash — 79×26
/Users/yfain11/practicalJava/workspace/Lesson36/gradleExamples/derbySample
Yakov:derbySample yfain11$ gradle dependencies
:dependencies

------------------------------------------------------------
Root project
------------------------------------------------------------

archives - Configuration for archive artifacts.
No dependencies

compile - Compile classpath for source set 'main'.
No dependencies

default - Configuration for default artifacts.
No dependencies

runtime - Runtime classpath for source set 'main'.
No dependencies

testCompile - Compile classpath for source set 'test'.
No dependencies

testRuntime - Runtime classpath for source set 'test'.
No dependencies
```

FIGURE 36-10: Running Gradle dependencies shows available configurations

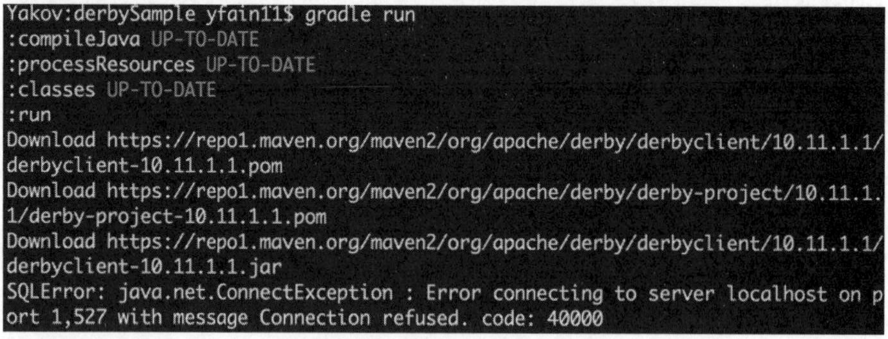

```
Yakov:derbySample yfain11$ gradle run
:compileJava UP-TO-DATE
:processResources UP-TO-DATE
:classes UP-TO-DATE
:run
Download https://repo1.maven.org/maven2/org/apache/derby/derbyclient/10.11.1.1/
derbyclient-10.11.1.1.pom
Download https://repo1.maven.org/maven2/org/apache/derby/derby-project/10.11.1.
1/derby-project-10.11.1.1.pom
Download https://repo1.maven.org/maven2/org/apache/derby/derbyclient/10.11.1.1/
derbyclient-10.11.1.1.jar
SQLError: java.net.ConnectException : Error connecting to server localhost on p
ort 1,527 with message Connection refused. code: 40000
```

FIGURE 36-11: Gradle's run task downloads dependency derbyclient-10.11.1.1.jar

The shorter way of declaring the same dependency would look like this:

```
dependencies {
  runtime 'org.apache.derby:derbyclient:10.11.1.1'
}
```

If you wouldn't need to specifically request the version 10.11.1.1, you could request any version of the `derbyclient.jar` that's greater than 10:

```
dependencies {
   runtime 'org.apache.derby:derbyclient:10+'
}
```

Gradle caches the downloaded artifacts and stores them in your home directory under the `.gradle` directory. On my computer, I found the downloaded file `derbyclient-10.11.1.1.jar` in the following directory:

```
/Users/yfain11/.gradle/caches/modules-2/files-2.1/org.apache.derby
```

If you want to be able to print the exact location of the cached runtime artifacts on your computer, you can add the task `showMeCache` (the name can be different) to your `gradle.build` file:

```
task showMeCache << {
  configurations.runtime.each { println it }
}
```

Running `gradle showMeCache` prints the location of the derbyclient JAR. Similarly, the task printing the cache content of the compile configurations could look like this:

```
task showMeCache << {
  configurations.compile.each { println it }
}
```

Packaging Dependencies Inside a JAR

Knowing that dependencies are cached in the `.gradle` directory helps if you want to know where they are located during development, but if you're deploying the `debrySample.jar` on another computer the derbyclient JAR won't be there. At this point the `derbySample.jar` includes only one file: `EmployeeList.class`. It doesn't even have a manifest file making this JAR executable. You can customize and add the jar task to your build script so it packages the `derbyclient-10.11.1.1.jar` inside `derbySample.jar`.

So far you have Derby client as a `runtime` dependency. But the `derbySample.jar` is created before you run the application. So specify your dependency earlier in the compile configuration. This way the `build` task downloads it during the project compilation. You also need to customize the jar section to copy the dependencies inside the output jar. This is how I did it:

```
apply plugin: 'java'
apply plugin: 'application'

mainClassName="EmployeeList"

repositories{
   mavenCentral()
}

dependencies {
   compile 'org.apache.derby:derbyclient:10+'
}

jar {
```

```
        from configurations.compile.collect {entry -> zipTree entry}

        manifest {attributes 'Main-Class': 'EmployeeList'
      }
    }
```

It takes just one line to loop through the file hierarchies of all `compile` configurations. In this case, the file hierarchy represents the content of `derbyclient-10.11.1.1.jar`, and the following action extracts all its content:

```
    from configurations.compile.collect {zipTree it}
```

The method `collect` gets a reference to all compile configurations, and the `zipTree` method extracts the entire file hierarchy from the file in a zip format. Then the `jar` task includes these file hierarchies inside the output JAR. After running `gradle build` I unzipped the `derbySample.jar`. It included all derby classes that were initially located inside the file `derbyclient-10.11.1.1.jar`, as shown in Figure 36-12.

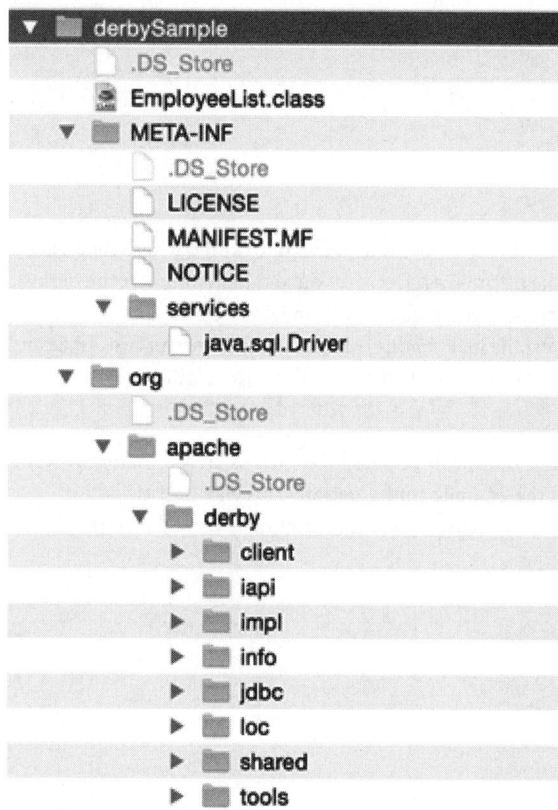

FIGURE 36-12: The content of the derbySample.jar

Now the `derbySample.jar` is a self-contained application, and if you open a Command window and change the directory to `build/libs`, you can run the application by running the standard Java command:

```
java -jar derbySample.jar
```

The file `derbySample.jar` can be copied on any server now. You can read about available file operations in Chapter 16 (`http://www.gradle.org/docs/current/userguide/working_with_files.html`) of the Gradle User Guide.

If you really want to see the employee list retrieved from the database created in Lesson 21, start Derby DB server in a separate command window and rerun the preceding command. Figure 36-13 shows my result.

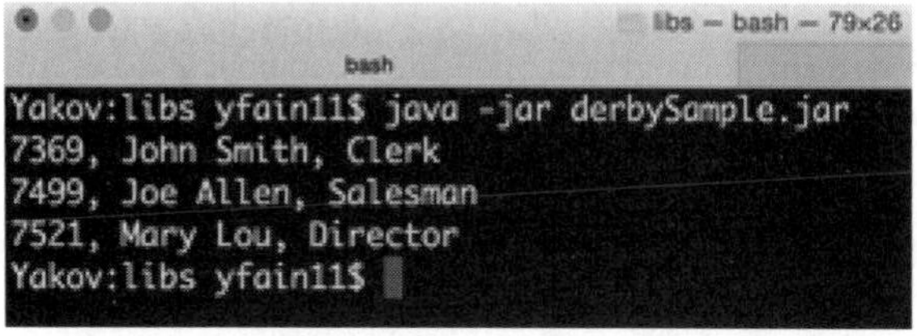

```
Yakov:libs yfain11$ java -jar derbySample.jar
7369, John Smith, Clerk
7499, Joe Allen, Salesman
7521, Mary Lou, Director
Yakov:libs yfain11$
```

FIGURE 36-13: Getting employees from Derby DB database

GRADLE WRAPPER

When a team of programmers works on a project, you may run into a situation when developers have different versions of Gradle run time. If a new developer joins the team, she may not even have Gradle installed yet. The Gradle Wrapper (`http://www.gradle.org/docs/current/userguide/gradle_wrapper.html`) allows to run build scripts without worrying about incompatible versions of the runtime. The Wrapper ensures that the build script runs with a specific version of Gradle. It automatically downloads and installs the proper version of Gradle if need be.

You need to create the wrapper task. For example:

```
task wrapper (type: Wrapper) {
    gradleVersion = '2.2.1'
}
```

Then run it:

```
gradle wrapper
```

This creates two scripts for executing Gradle commands—`gradlew` and `gradlew.bat`—and a directory `gradle/wrapper` with two files in it: `gradle-wrapper.jar` and `gradle-wrapper.properties`. The JAR file contains the library to download and unpack Gradle's distribution. The properties file contains the wrapper's metadata. If you already have the right version of Gradle running, the `wrapper` task won't do anything.

After all these files have been added to your project, you should use `gradlew` instead of `gradle` to execute all your build tasks. When a person without Gradle (or with the wrong version) runs any task for the first time using the `gradlew` script, the Gradle distribution is downloaded and unpacked in `.gradle/wrapper/dist` in her home directory.

Building a WAR file

If you need to compile a web application and package it in a WAR file, you need to add the `war` plug-in (it extends the `java` plug-in) to your build file:

```
apply plugin: 'war'
```

But your code becomes dependent on the availability of certain JARs that come with your Java EE server. In Eclipse IDE, when you create a Dynamic Web Project and select GlassFish (or any other Java server) as a target run time, and all required JARS become automatically available for your project during the compilation and run time. But Gradle doesn't use IDE settings, and it needs to know where these files are located. Say that your web application has the following Java servlet:

```
import javax.servlet.*;
import javax.servlet.annotation.*;

@WebServlet("/books")
public class FindBooksServlet extends HttpServlet {
   // the servlet's code goes here
}
```

Unless you add a repository and dependencies section to your build script, this servlet won't compile because it won't find the declaration of the annotation `@WebServlet` and the class `HttpServlet`. If you run the command `gradle dependencies`, you see that in addition to all configurations available for the `java` plug-in, the `war` plug-in adds two more: `providedCompile` and `providedRuntime`.

The `providedCompile` configuration is for specifying an additional `CLASSPATH` for libraries that shouldn't be part of the WAR file. The word *provided* means that these libraries are provided in the environment where the task runs. `providedRuntime` has a similar use, but it adds a `CLASSPATH` for the run time. Add `providedCompile` and a `repository` to the build file:

```
apply plugin: 'war'
repositories {
    mavenCentral()
}

dependencies {
    providedCompile 'javax.servlet:javax.servlet-api:3.1+'
}
```

If you run the `gradle war` command now, the JAR with servlet 3.1 API is downloaded, the code compiles, and the WAR (not JAR) file is created in the directory `build/libs` of your project. The size of this file is rather small as it contains only the application code.

If you'd like to add not only the servlets but the entire Java EE API, the dependencies section could look like this:

```
dependencies {
    providedCompile 'javax:javaee-api:7+'
}
```

> **BINTRAY REPOSITORY**
>
> In all code samples, I've been using Maven Central as a repository. However, instead of `mavenCentral()` you could use `jcenter()` if you're getting the JARs from Bintray (`https://bintray.com/`).

USING GRADLE IN ECLIPSE IDE

Gradle supports all major Java IDEs. Each IDE has its own proprietary project structure, which depends on the project type. For example, when you create a Dynamic Web Project in Eclipse, it creates certain directories (for example, `WebContent` and `WEB-INF`), which would not be created for a regular Java project. To add a JAR to the Java `CLASSPATH`, you open project properties and add the required file using the Project Build Path window.

Eclipse stores the project structure in the files `.project`, `.classpath`, and in an optional directory `.settings`. If a zip file or a directory contains an Eclipse project file, you can create an Eclipse project by selecting File → Import → General → Existing Project into Workspace.

The creators of Gradle added support of Eclipse projects in the form of Gradle plug-ins for Eclipse, which are covered in the next section.

Gradle Eclipse Plug-ins

Gradle comes with two Eclipse plug-ins (`http://www.gradle.org/docs/current/userguide/eclipse_plugin.html`): `eclipse` and `eclipse-wtp`:

- The `eclipse` plug-in is used for creating regular Eclipse Java projects.
- The `eclipse-wtp` plug-in is used for creating Dynamic Web Projects. Internally it uses the settings from Web Toolkit Platform (`https://www.eclipse.org/webtools/`)—hence the wtp suffix. If you decide to use `eclipse-wtp`, it supports all the tasks available in the `eclipse` plug-in, too.

To see the `eclipse` plug-in in action, create a copy of the `HelloWorld` directory from hellogradle and call it `HelloWorldEcipse`. It has the `HelloWorld` class in the directory `src/main/java/hello`. The `build.gradle` file should have the following content:

```
apply plugin: 'java'
apply plugin: 'eclipse'
```

Run the `gradle eclipse` command, and it generates two new files—`.classpath` and `.project`—and the directory `.settings`. Open Eclipse and select File → Import → General → Existing Projects into Workspace, and point at the `HelloWorldEclipse` as the root directory. Eclipse imports the project, and you can run it as you did all other projects. Figure 36-14 shows how the imported project looks on my computer.

FIGURE 36-14: Gradle-generated project in Eclipse

A simple `build.gradle` file for generating an Eclipse Dynamic Web Project can look like this:

```
apply plugin: 'war'
apply plugin: 'eclipse-wtp'
```

The `war` plug-in (`http://www.gradle.org/docs/current/userguide/war_plugin.html`) extends the `java` plug-in and adds support for assembling WAR files for web application deployments.

To generate an Eclipse Dynamic Web Project you still need to run the `gradle eclipse` command, but the content of generated files `.project` and `.classpath` will be different. In the "Try It" section of this lesson you generate, import, and deploy an Eclipse project using the `eclipse-wtp` plug-in.

If you need to regenerate Eclipse project files from scratch, run the `gradle cleanEclipse` command to delete the existing project files.

Eclipse IDE and Gradle

Gradle supports IDEs, and IDEs support Gradle. Gradle Integration for Eclipse (`http://marketplace.eclipse.org/content/gradle-integration-eclipse-44`) is an Eclipse IDE plug-in created by Pivotal. It allows creating and importing Gradle projects, and you can run builds right from the Eclipse IDE.

After installing the plug-in, I imported the `HelloWorldEclipse` project from the previous section by using File → Import → Gradle → Gradle Project. The right-click menu on the `build.gradle` now has an option Run As → Gradle Build. You can either manually enter the task to run or open the tasks view by selecting Window → Show View → Gradle → Gradle Tasks. Figure 36-15 shows a Gradle Task View in Eclipse for my imported project `HelloWorldEclipse`.

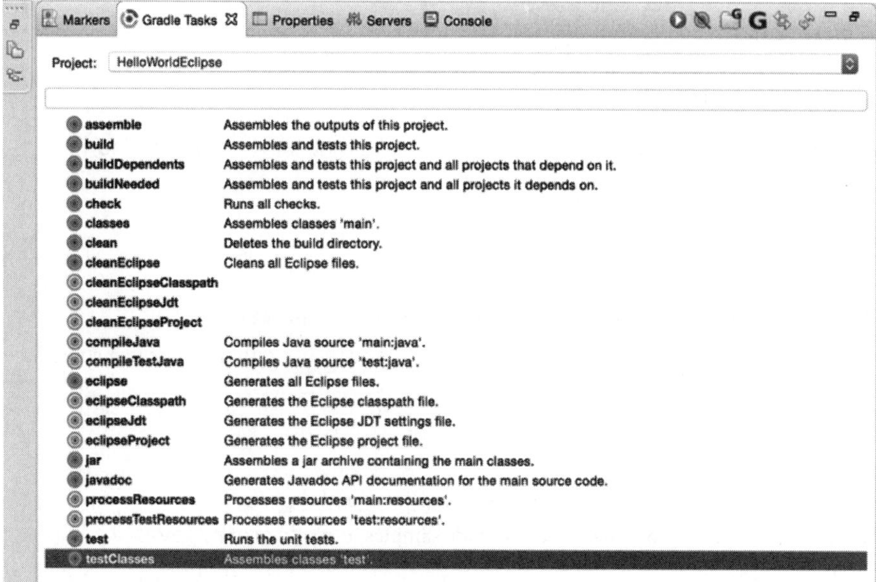

FIGURE 36-15: Gradle Tasks View in Eclipse IDE

You can select and execute a task by pressing the green play button on the status bar on the top.

Eclipse Marketplace has yet another product that includes Gradle Integration. It's called Gradle ID Pack (`http://marketplace.eclipse.org/content/gradle-ide-pack`), and it offers additional utilities for code block highlighting, an archive editor, and more.

> **IF GRADLE INTEGRATION FOR ECLIPSE WON'T INSTALL**
>
> If you run into issues during the Gradle Integration plug-in installation, turn off all Spring-related options on the confirmation window displayed during install.

This concludes my introduction to Gradle. I haven't covered the subject of creating custom tasks in Gradle. For this and other Gradle features, please refer to the book *Building and Testing with Gradle*, which is available as a free online version (`http://gradleware.com/registered-access?content=books%2Fbuilding-and-testing%2F`).

TRY IT

In this assignment you need to create and use a Gradle build script to generate an Eclipse Dynamic Web Project. Then you import it into the Eclipse IDE, deploy it under GlassFish, and confirm that the web application works. In this assignment you use the `FindBooksServlet` class from Lesson 26.

Lesson Requirements

You should have Java, GlassFish, and Gradle installed.

You can download the code and resources for this "Try It" from the book's web page at `www.wrox.com/go/javaprog24hr2e`*. You can find them in the Lesson36 folder in the download.*

Step-by-Step

1. Create a directory `FindBookGradle` with two subdirectories: `src` and `WEB-INF`.
2. Inside the directory `FindBookGradle` create the `build.gradle` file with the following content:

```
apply plugin: 'war'
apply plugin: 'eclipse-wtp'
```

3. Under the `src` directory, create subdirectories `main` and `java` and copy the file `FindBooksServlet.java` from the Lesson 26 code samples into `src/main/java`.
4. In the Command or Terminal window, change the directory to `FindBookGradle` and run the command `gradle eclipse`. After this task completes, you find there files `.classpath`, `.project`, and the directory `.settings`.
5. Open Eclipse in the Java EE perspective. You should have GlassFish server configured there. Select File → Import → General → Existing Projects into Workspace. Select `FindBookGradle` as a root directory and press the Finish button. The project is imported to Eclipse.
6. In the project properties menu, select Targeted Runtimes, and then select GlassFish 4 as your server. Click OK.
7. Right-click the GlassFish server in the Servers view and deploy the project `FindBookGradle` using the Add and Remove menu. Because you are deploying the copy of the `FindBookServlet` from Lesson 26, make sure that the project `Lesson26` is not deployed in GlassFish.
8. Enter the URL `http://localhost:8080/FindBookGradle/books` in your web browser, and you should see the message `Hellow from FindBooks`.

TIP *Please select the videos for Lesson 36 online at* `www.wrox.com/go/javaprog24hr2e`*. You will also be able to download the code and resources for this lesson from the website.*

37

Java Technical Interviews

Technical job interviewing is a game with well-defined rules. I've worn the hats of both interviewer and interviewee many times over my Java career. In this lesson I share with you my views on hiring Java developers and on preparing for technical interviews.

Regardless of whether the IT job market is hot or not at any given time, there are some rules and techniques that can increase your interview success rate. The process of getting a job consists of three separate activities:

1. Getting the interview
2. Interviewing successfully
3. Considering the offer

I can't stress enough how important it is to work on each of these tasks *separately*, one step at a time! Let's discuss them one by one.

GETTING THE INTERVIEW

Your résumé is the most important thing in the first step. Unless you are a well-known Java guru (if you were, you wouldn't read this book) your résumé is your main weapon for getting an interview. Adjust the résumé for each position you are applying for. No, I'm not asking you to lie, but you have to highlight your skills that match each particular job opening you're applying to. Make sure it's short and to the point (not more than two pages long).

If you are applying for a Java developer's position, nobody needs to know the details of that Visual Basic project from 10 years ago. Always update your résumé based on the feedback you receive from recruiters or more experienced programmers.

There is a summary section on each résumé, and many people waste this space with some junk like, "I'm looking for a challenging position that will let me improve my talents." What a waste! Use this summary line to show your relevant skills.

Say you've been specializing in Java messaging during the last two years, but this job posting requires web developers. Add a phrase that the messaging architecture was able to support both Java and web clients. Recruiters are not too technical—they do a quick résumé scan to find the presence of the required keywords. Also, chances are that you've developed web applications before; highlight your web experience in the summary section of your résumé. The same day you may be responding to another ad seeking people who know Java messaging.

Modify your summary section accordingly and send a version of your résumé that emphasizes your experience with messaging; your understanding of the web principle is not that important here.

Job requirements are more involved these days, and recruiting companies don't even want to submit your résumé to the client if you have "only" 8 out of 10 required skills. Read the requirements and highlight all the relevant skills you have. Do not be lazy; work with your résumé.

Networking is another great way to get an interview. This time I'm not talking about Java networking; I'm talking about meeting other IT people who may be hiring or know people who are hiring. Attend your local Java Users Group meetings, join online meetups (`http://www.meetup.com/`), follow Java developers on Twitter, and go to professional conferences and seminars.

DOING WELL AT THE INTERVIEW

OK. The interview is scheduled, and now your main goal is to ace it. Remember, your interviewer has a difficult task: He needs to assess your technical skills within 30 to 60 minutes, so help him! In advance of the interview, try to get as many technical details about the job as possible from your recruiter. If the position you are applying for requires knowledge of Java sockets, research working with non-blocking sockets. If the company is building Java EE applications, find out which application server they use and read up on it.

Do your homework and *prepare a short talk* about some interesting and challenging technical problems you might have experienced in one of your college or real-world projects. If you didn't have any super-complex projects, just pick up a topic from one of the multiple online programmers' forums and research it. Another great source of Java tips and tricks is a hugely popular online resource called Stackoverlow. This is a place where software developers ask and answer questions about different programming languages and technologies. Check out the Java section (`http://stackoverflow.com/questions/tagged/java`) at Stackoverflow.

For example, if you have prepared a talk on concurrent collections, you're not allowed to leave the interview without talking about this. But what if the interviewer won't ask you about Java concurrency? It doesn't really matter. Find a way to switch the conversation to the prepared topic and do your best. The interviewer will be happy because he doesn't need to think about what to ask next, and you're happy because you've had a chance to talk about a well-prepared subject.

Will this technique work all the time? No. But it'll work most of the time. Obviously you need to research the selected subject well, or you'll get burned. You must talk about technical challenges you've resolved. You need to remember that your interviewers face a challenging task of figuring out your technical abilities in just 30 minutes. So, you need to help them out. Be in charge.

If you're a junior developer, spend some time answering the multiple-choice computer tests that are usually required for certification exams. You don't need to get certified, but all these books and online mock tests will help you pass similar tests offered by some job agencies. Find some sample interview questions online.

A technical interview is a game with known rules, but in many cases the interviewers are not prepared to run the interviews. Sometimes they just go by a prepared list of questions. Some interviewees take advantage of this and just spend some time studying introductory courses, and then memorize questions and answers for technical interviews. Believe it or not, in many cases this works.

What does a good enterprise Java developer have to know in addition to understanding the difference between abstract classes and interfaces? Usually employers are looking for people with knowledge of the following: Java Servlets, JSP, Spring framework, JMS, any commercial message-oriented middleware, JDBC, JNDI, HTML, XML, Hibernate, build tools, SQL, one of the major application servers, and a couple of relational database management systems.

Understanding why a particular Java EE component is being used in your current project is equally important. If the interviewer asks you, "Why did you use EJB in this project?" please do not answer, "That decision was made before I joined the project." Even if it was, have your own opinion and explain why you think it was a good or bad choice for this particular project.

Here's another tip: Don't critique the application architecture of your potential employer. You'll have plenty of chances to provide technical advice if you're hired, so just focus on getting an offer. Remember, one step at a time!

Be energetic during the interview and show your interest in the job. Even if you are a technical guru, don't behave as if you're doing the interviewer a favor just by showing up. Personality matters. People don't like prima donnas.

Be prepared to write code on a whiteboard and practice that skill. The interviewer may not ask you to do this, but it may be a good idea to start illustrating your thoughts on the board if there is one in the room. If there is no board, use your own notepad. Often interviewers are trying to judge how well you think and approach a problem more than how effectively you've memorized an algorithm, class name, or method arguments.

No need to rush. If you start writing a code fragment on a board, don't be afraid of making mistakes. Think aloud. It may be even beneficial for the interviewer to see how you can identify the wrong approach and then pick the right one. Practice explaining little code fragments to your friends or relatives; they don't need to know Java to participate in these role-playing games.

Questions of data structures and collections are pretty popular during the interviews. For example, you need to be able to explain when using `LinkedList` is better than using `ArrayList`. Some people fail the interview on simple task like "write a program to reverse letters in a word." Get a book on data structures and algorithms and skim through it before going to the interview.

After the interview, as soon as you leave the building, take notes about what just happened. Don't postpone it until you get home; you may forget important details. Make a note to work on the questions you might have not answered correctly. These questions require your attention and research. Improve your technical skills after each interview.

CONSIDERING THE OFFER

You've got an offer! Now think hard about whether you want to accept it. Have I mentioned that you should look for a new job not when your employer decides to let you go or your contract ends, but when you have a stable job, the sky is blue, and the grass is green? This gives you a tremendous advantage: You can consider the offer without being under pressure from unpaid bills.

Don't accept an offer just because the new job pays an extra $5,000 a year, which comes to less than $300 a month after taxes. Do accept the offer that gives you a chance to work with interesting technologies or business applications even if it won't pay you an extra dime.

Other nonmonetary factors of an offer are health benefits, flexible work hours, ease of commute, or simply a kinship that you feel with the people working for the potential employer. Believe it or not, some people won't accept offers from employers who require you to wear suit and tie. Just make a decision about what's more important for you—having an interesting job or being able to show off your latest tattoos.

No matter what your preferences are, take charge of your career and actively build it the way you want.

INTERVIEWING ENTERPRISE DEVELOPERS

When the job market is healthy, major online job search engines show thousands of openings, and people are competing for these jobs. These days a seasoned developer has to know about 10 different tools or technologies to find a good job and feel relatively secure for a couple of years. Over the last several years I've interviewed lots of Java developers, and this is what I've noticed:

- People do not call themselves Java developers or programmer-analysts anymore; most of them prefer the title *Java architect*. Unfortunately, only some of them really understand how Java EE components operate and can suggest design solutions. Of course, knowledge of Java EE is not all that a Java architect should know.
- Job applicants are more senior, and I barely see any college graduates or junior programmers. Many of the junior positions are being outsourced and the number of graduates with computer science degrees has declined over the past several years.
- Having software certification does not make a résumé stand out. Actually, if a résumé starts with a list of certifications, most likely it's a beginner's. I'm not against certifications, as they help you learn a language or a tool, and show that you are willing to and can study. But a certificate doesn't make someone a skilled professional.
- With the introduction of middle-tier object-relational mapping frameworks such as Hibernate, many people don't even bother learning how database management systems work or how to write a SQL query that performs well — they just map Java classes to database tables.
- On multiple occasions I've interviewed (`http://yakovfain.com/2012/10/11/the-degradation-of-java-developers/`) enterprise Java developers who were trained to use certain frameworks, but without understanding how things work under the hood. A simple question to explain in details what happens between the moments when the user click the button Get Data on a web page and when the data arrive often results in a description of how a certain web framework does it. But what if there is no frameworks, but just a web page and a servlet. Not many programmers can describe such a data flow.
- In a slow economy, be prepared to pass at least four interviews to get hired. Back in 1999 two good interviews would be enough; in 2001 it was very difficult to even get an interview, let alone a job!
- Today large portions of development is done in India. Even though the total cost of development is not low despite the lower hourly rates of offshore developers, Western hiring managers unfortunately have an impression that local candidates must be flexible in their rates, too. Being a native English speaker

> is not enough for you to charge top dollar. Always be technically current, otherwise the more motivated guys from overseas will leave you in the dust.

Good knowledge of the business terminology of your potential employer is also important. I'm not sure about the Silicon Valley or Europe, but here in New York just being a techie may not be good enough to get you a senior job. Of course, interviewing with Google or Microsoft is an exception.

For example, if you're applying for a Java position in a financial brokerage company and don't know what a short sale is, this may be a deal breaker. If you are a senior developer you should be able to hit the ground running: Try to find out from your recruiter as many details as possible about the business. Do your homework, and you'll get the job! Recruiters are desperately looking for good programmers, and you can be one of them.

TO GET OR NOT TO GET CERTIFIED?

Any certification program is a business for the vendor that wants to sell training to award certificates. Oracle is no exception; you can find various certification programs to rate your Java skills. The following website offers various certification programs in Java SE and EE technologies: `http://education.oracle.com/pls/web_prod-plq-dad/db_pages.getpage?page_id=651#5`.

Although most certification programs require you to pass a multiple-choice computer test, some of them (such as those for Java EE architects) give you a challenging task to design and program.

Overall I think it's a good idea to prepare yourself and go through the certification process because it will definitely improve your understanding of the Java language or a specific enterprise technology or framework. In some areas it may also improve the perception of your résumé. It'll also help you slip through computer screening tests that are used by job placement agencies. Just check job postings from your potential employers to see if they insist on having certificates.

I also want to caution you against overestimating the importance of getting Java certification. When I see a résumé that starts with a list of certificates, it tells me that this candidate is good... at passing multiple-choice tests. Having practical hands-on experience working on open-source or enterprise projects is a lot more valuable than any certificate you might have earned. It's fine if you have certificates, but keep them somewhere at the end of your résumé rather than trying to present them as a major achievement.

TECHNICAL QUESTIONS AND ANSWERS

Suggesting a list of technical questions for an interview is a risky business. Seasoned Java developers have different views on what's fair and what's not fair to ask. But junior developers who just completed a Java tutorial can definitely benefit from some guidance in preparing for Java job interviews.

The following are suggested technical interview questions and expected brief answers on various Java-related topics. The questions included in this section are those that I had to answer while working on various projects. In no way is this a complete list of possible questions, but it definitely gives you an idea of what to expect at an interview. Most of the answers to these questions can be found in this book, but some require additional research.

Q: What's the difference between an interface and an abstract class?

A: Prior to Java 8 I'd answered that an abstract class may contain code in method bodies, which is not allowed in an interface. But with introduction of the defender and static methods in interfaces the answer should be different. Abstract classes can implement state in member variables, but interfaces can't. You can extend from one abstract class, but implement multiple interfaces.With abstract classes you have to inherit your class from the abstract one because Java does not allow multiple inheritance.

Q: How do you deploy a web application in the application server that you currently use?

A: In most Java EE application servers you create a web archive (war file) and copy it to the assigned directory per the application server documentation. (You should be able to explain the directory structure in a war file.)

Q: Why were the defender methods introduced in Java 8?

A: Oracle's software engineers wanted to include new methods in the existing interfaces. If they would just add new method declarations, lots of existing code would break because classes that implement those interfaces didn't implement newly introduced methods. The keyword `default` allowed them to add new methods in the interfaces without forcing existing classes implement them.

Q: What's the usage of the keyword `static`?

A: It's used in declarations of methods and variables to make them available without creating an instance of the class. For example, the `main()` method is a `static` one. If a variable is `static`, its value is shared by all instances of the class.

Q: How can you force garbage collection?

A: You can't force garbage collection, but you can request it, because JVM does not guarantee that it'll be started immediately. Invoking `System.gc()` requests Java garbage collection.

Q: Why would you use lambda expression in your code?

A: Lambda expression makes the code more concise and in some cases allows developers to flatten the class hierarchies and eliminate certain classes. For more details read about eliminating polymorphism in Lesson 13.

Q: How do you decide if explicit casting is needed?

A: If you assign a superclass object to a variable of a subclass's data type, you need to use explicit casting. For example:

```
Object a;
Customer b;
b = (Customer) a;
```

Java generics can eliminate the need for explicit casting. For subclass-to-superclass assignments, the casting is performed automatically. You can also cast to interfaces that a class implements.

Q: Can you perform casting between objects of different types?

A: No, you can't. The objects can have a superclass-subclass relationship, or you can cast to interfaces implemented by a class.

Q: Can a Java class be inherited from two classes?

A: No, Java does not allow multiple inheritance, but a class can implement multiple interfaces, which, to some extent, can be used as a workaround.

Q: What's the difference between constructors and regular methods?

A: Constructors must have the same name as the class and cannot return a value. They are invoked only once, while regular methods can be invoked many times.

Q: What's a cookie? Which Java components create them?

A: A cookie is an object that represents a name/value pair. Servlets, JSP, and third-party Java frameworks can create and send cookies to a web browser that saves them on the user's disk in a special directory. Cookies help the server-side code to identify a user and implement session tracking.

Q: Does each abstract class have at least one abstract method?

A: Not necessarily. If a class is declared with the `abstract` keyword, it can be instantiated even if it has no abstract methods. For example, you can declare an abstact class `Animal`, which should never be instantiated, while one can create instances its concrete subclasses `Cat` and `Dog`.

Q: Explain the use of Java packages.

A: Packages offer a way to organize multifile projects. They also help in resolving naming conflicts when different packages have classes with the same names. Package access level also enables you to protect data from being used by unauthorized classes, permitting only the classes from the same package to see each other's member variables.

Q: Explain the usage of the keyword `transient`.

A: The `transient` keyword indicates that the value of this member variable does not have to be serialized with the object. When the class gets deserialized, `transient` variables are initialized with the default values of the variable data types (such as `0` for integers).

Q: What do you know about thread synchronization? Explain the difference between

```
public void synchronized myMethod() { ... }
```

and

```
public void myMethod() {
    ...
    synchronized (some_object) {... }
}
```

A: The keyword `synchronized` is used to prevent race conditions when more than one thread tries to update some values. Synchronized blocks are preferable to synchronized methods because they place locks for shorter periods. The package `java.util.concurrent` includes a class `ReentrantLock`, which can be a better solution than using the `synchronized` keyword.

Q: What's the difference between the methods `sleep()` and `wait()`?

A: The code `sleep(1000)` puts the thread aside for exactly one second. The code `wait(1000)` makes the thread wait for up to one second. A thread can stop waiting earlier if it receives the `notify()` or `notifyAll()` call. The method `wait()` is defined in the class `Object`, but `sleep()` is defined in the class `Thread`.

Q: What's the difference between creating threads subclassing the class `Thread` and implementing the `Runnable` interface?

A: Thread creation with the class `Thread` requires that your class be inherited from it. Then you need to create an instance of your class and call its `start()` method. If a class implements the `Runnable` interface the procedure is different; you have to create the instance of your class, and the instance of the `Thread` object, passing the `Runnable` class to the latter. Using `Runnable` enables you to create threads from classes that have to be inherited from classes other than `Thread` classes. You can implement `Runnable` with lambda expressions.

Q: How can you create a thread that can return a value from its method `run()`?

A: You need to implement the `Callable` interface.

Q: What would you use to compare two `String` variables: the `equals()` method or the == operator?

A: I'd use `equals()` to compare the values of the `Strings`, and the == operator to check whether two variables point at the same `String` object in memory.

Q: What do you know about the MVC design pattern?

A: MVC stands for the model-view-controller design pattern, which is used to separate presentation modules from business logic and data ones. The model part represents the data and the business logic of the application, the view is a visual representation (for example, a UI), and the controller accepts the data from the view and passes it to the model and vice versa.

Q: How can you reduce the time spent by JVM on creating frequently used instances of some objects?

A: I'd create my own or configure existing object pools (for example, `DataSource` can be configured to use object pools of database connections).

Q: Will the following statement create the file `xyz.txt` on disk?

```
File a = new File("xyz.txt");
```

A: No, it just creates an object pointing to this file.

Q: How can a subclass invoke a method defined in a superclass?

A: Java has the keyword `super`. If a method has been overridden, but you'd like to invoke its version defined in the superclass, use the following syntax: `super.myMethod();`. To call a constructor of the superclass, use `super();` with required parameters in the first line of the subclass's constructor.

Q: Can a functional interface declare more than one method?

A: Yes as long as only one of them is abstract. For example, besides abstract methods you can have several defender and static methods in the interface.

Q: What access level do you need to specify for members of the class `Customer` to ensure that only classes from the same directory can access these members?

A: You do not need to specify any access level. In this case, Java uses the default package access level, which guarantees visibility for the `Customer` members only to the classes located in the same directory (package).

Q: What's the use of JNDI?

A: JNDI is a Java API for naming and directory servers. It is used for finding Java objects by name in a distributed application. For example, you can use JNDI to get a reference to the `DataSource` or `JMS` objects.

Q: Can you modify the data in the underlying collection using the Stream API?

A: No you can't. The underlying data set is immutable.

Q: If you need to catch more than one exception (such as `FileNotFoundException` and `IOException`), does the order of the `catch` statements matter?

A: Yes, it does. `FileNotFoundException` is inherited from `IOException`. The exception subclasses have to be caught first.

Q: Explain in detail the data workflow between a web page and a Servlet called `FindBooks` after the user clicks Submit. (In this question interviewers can replace the web page and Servlet with any other client-server components. The main point is to find out if the job applicant understands the entire end-to-end data flow.)

A: The web browser connects to the server located at the specified URL, and if `FindBooks` has not been started yet, the Servlet container starts it, invoking the servlet's `init()` method followed by the `service()` method, which in turn calls `doGet()` or `doPost()`, depending on the method of HTTP request. The objects `HTTPServletRequest` and `HTTPServletResponse` are used for the interaction between the client and `FindBooks`. The Servlet's output can be sent back to the user by means of one of the methods of `HTTPServletResponse`, for example `println()`.

Q: Explain the process of getting the data from a database table in a Java SE program using JDBC. Which classes and methods have to be used?

A: First you load the appropriate JDBC driver using `Class.forName()`. After that you get the `Connection` object using either the `DataSource` object or `DriverManager.getConnection()`. Then you create a `Statement` object and invoke one of its methods, like `executeQuery()` or `executeUpdate()`. Process the `ResultSet`, if any, and close the `Connection`, `Statement`, and `ResultSet` objects. In some cases instead of `Statement` you use `PreparedStatement` or `CallableStatement`.

Q: What are the differences among the Java keywords `final`, `finalize`, and `finally`?

A: Depending on its position, the keyword `final` means either that the variable can be initialized only once, or that you cannot override a method, or that you cannot subclass a class. Parameters in the `catch` block are implicitly `final`.

The method `finalize()`, if defined in your class, is invoked by the garbage collector when it's ready to release a memory used by the instance of your class.

The keyword `finally` is used in a `try/catch` block to place code, that must be executed whether the code in the `try` block succeeds or fails.

Q: Can you declare fields in an interface?

A: You can only declare `final` and `static` variables in an interface.

Q: Can an inner class, declared inside a method, access local variables of this method?

A: It's possible only if the method's variables are `final`.

Q: What could be used to keep track of sessions in web applications?

A: You can use cookies, URL rewriting, and the `HTTPSession` object.

Q: Will session management with cookies always work?

A: No, if a user disables cookies in the web browser, it won't work. In such cases application servers usually automatically switch to URL rewriting.

Q: How can you stop a long-running thread?

A: The class `Thread` has a deprecated method called `stop()`, but this method does not guarantee that the thread will be stopped. Depending on the process that is run by this thread, you could try to close connections or open streams, if any, or use the method `interrupt()`.

Q: When could a Java class be called a bean?

A: You call the class a bean if it has a no-argument constructor, implements the `Serializable` interface, and has public setter/getter methods for its private properties.

Q: What are the advantages of using JSP rather than Servlets?

A: JSP enables you to separate presentation from business logic and the resulting web page can be modified by people who do not know Java.

Q: Give an example that shows the difference between the use of the operators && and &.

A: In the following code snippet, the second expression in the `if` statement is not even evaluated if variable `a` is `null`. If a single ampersand were used here you'd get a `NullPointerException`.

```
String a=null;
if (a != null && a.length()>10) {...}
```

Q: Name some predefined JSP variables.

A: `request`, `response`, `out`, `session`...

Q: How do you deploy a JSP?

A: You can place `.jsp` files in a document root directory of the Servlet container or application server, or create a war file and put a JSP in the document root there.

Q: What's the default port number that web servers use for HTTP-based communications?

A: HTTP requests go through port 80; HTTPS ones go through port 443.

Q: What method of the Servlet class is an equivalent of a constructor in a regular Java class?

A: The Servlet's method `init()` plays a similar role, but because all clients use the same instance of the Servlet, you should initialize only those variables that are allowed to have the same value for each user's request, such as the name of the database server.

Q: Which is faster: array or `ArrayList`?

A: In most cases arrays are faster. An array can be used if you know in advance the number of elements in the array. `ArrayList` is an API on top of an array. You do not need to know its size in advance; new elements can be added as needed. Arrays work faster because JVM allocates memory only once for all elements. But to give you a better answer I'd have to write an appropriate benchmark in context to find out.

Q: What do you know about Java reflection?

A: Reflection is a way of finding information about a Java class internals during run time. For example, you can find out the constructors and the method signatures of a particular class. The class `Class` has such methods as `getConstructor()`, `getFields()`, `getMethods()`, and others.

Q: What would you do if your Java program crashed during the run time with an "out of memory" error?

A: I'd try to increase the size of the JVM's dynamic memory (heap) on program start-up using command-line parameters. For example, you can request the minimum heap size of 512 MB and the maximum heap size of 1024 MB as follows:

```
java -Xms512 -Xmx1024 MyProgram
```

Q: How can you ensure that only one instance of some class can be created in your application?

A: You need to implement the singleton design pattern. Create a class with a private constructor and provide a public getter method that returns the only instance of this class—for example `MyClass.getInstance()`.

Q: What's the major difference between a `Hashtable` and a `HashMap`?

A: The `Hashtable` class is internally synchronized, whereas the `HashMap` is not.

Q: Name some design patterns.

A: Singleton, MVC, data transfer object, facade... While preparing to answer this question, refer to the article on design patterns (`http://en.wikipedia.org/wiki/Software_design_pattern#Classification_and_list`) at Wikipedia.

Q: The word stateless is used to describe a session EJB as well as HTTP protocol. What's the meaning of the word stateless in these two cases?

A: HTTP protocol is page-based, meaning that the web browser does not hold the connection between requests, but in the case of an EJB, *stateless* means that the session bean cannot be used to store the state of a particular client.

Q: Are Java objects passed by value or by reference?

A: Objects are passed by reference, but their reference variables are passed by value.

Q: How can a Java client access a message-driven bean?

A: Java clients don't access MDBs directly; they just place messages into a queue or publish them to topics, and the MDB retrieves them from there.

EPILOGUE

The book is over. Even though it's rather small in size for the number of the covered subjects, I tried to touch on a wide spectrum of topics that most Java practitioners have to know. You may still need to do additional research on certain subjects, depending on your project needs, but at least now you know where to dig.

I really hope that you'll keep this book handy as a quick reference or for a refresher when it's time to start a new Java project or hit the job market. No matter what your motivation is, have fun reading. I certainly had fun writing it. You can send comments and suggestions via e-mail to `yakovfain@gmail.com`. Thank you for reading my book!

INDEX

A

abstract classes, 73
  versus interfaces, 78
abstract keyword, 73
accept( ) method, 205
access levels, 63
acknowledgment modes (MOM), 438
ActionEvent class, 102
ActionListener interface
  components, 101
actionPerformed( ) method, 100, 229
activation of objects, 186
adapter classes, 108
adapters, 109
add( ) method, 129
administered objects, 415
Adobe Flex, 233
@After annotation, 521
@AfterClass annotation, 522
AnchorPane layout, 237
AND operator, 57
annotated endpoints, 399
annotation, 263, 264
  isAnnotationPresent( ) method, 329
annotation processor, 322
annotations, 321
  @After, 521
  @AfterClass, 522
  @Asynchronous, 455
  @Before, 521
  @BeforeClass, 522
  @Consumes, 492
  @DELETE, 492
  @Deprecated, 324
  @Documented, 325
  @Embeddable, 468
  @Entity annotation, 466
  @FormParam, 492
  @FunctionalInterface, 324
  @GET, 491
  @Id, 467
  @Inherited, 324
  @LocalBean, 450
  @MessageDriven, 449
  @OnError, 399
  @OnMessage, 404
  @Override, 323-324
  @Path, 492
  @PathParam, 401, 492
  @POST, 492
  @Produces, 492
  @QueryParam, 492
  @Resource, 417
  @Schedule, 462
  @ServerEndPoint, 400
  @Singleton, 449
  @Stateful, 449
  @SuppressWarning, 323
  @Test, 517, 521
  @TransactionAttribute, 461
  @WebFilter, 374
  @WebServlet, 357
  code generation and, 327
  custom, 325-328
  declaring, 325
  Ignore, 522
  Javadoc, 321
  JUnit framework, 521
  meta-annotations, 325
  parameters, 326
  PUT, 492
  retention policy, 325
    CLASS, 326
    RUNTIME, 326
    SOURCE, 326
  run-time processing, 330-332
  targets, 321
anonymous inner classes, 111, 154
Ant Hello World, 532-533
APIs (application programming interfaces), 38, 415
  Criteria , 469
  Java Logging API, 501
  JDBC, 297
  JMS, 425
  JPA, 465
  JTA (Java Transaction API), 349
  Object Model, 486, 488
  Persistence Criteria, 466
  Stream, 281

Streaming, 487
applets, 83
RMI clients, 341
Application class (JavaFX), 234
application servers versus containers, 348
application variable, 383
applications
containers, 348
distributed , 335
Java Ee, 346
arguments, 37
command-line arguments, 58
lambda expressions, 154
method extractors and, 288
ArrayList collection, 129
ArrayList interface
concurrent access, 131
dynamic arrays, 129-132
interface implementation, 132
List interface, 129
ArrayList objects, populating, 129
arrays, 47-48, 128
byte, serialization, 192
declaring, 128
dynamic, ArrayList, 129-132
loops, 50
populating, 128
size, values and, 47
zero-based, 47
@Asynchronous annnotation, 455
asynchronous communications, 426
asynchronous method invocation, 448
asynchronous servlets, 375
attributes, 21
mutable, 157
autoboxing, 26
AutoClosable interface, 121
AWT (Abstract Windowing Toolkit), 83

B

Bean Validation framework, 473-475
@Before annotation, 521
@BeforeClass annotation, 522
BiFunction interface, 167-169
Big O notation, 139
bind( ) method, 247, 339
bindBidirectional( )method, 247
binding
binding in JavaFX, 246-249
BitSet class, 137-138
BitSet classes
block comments, 27
blocking calls, 426
body of a method, 6
boolean variables, 215
BorderLayout manager, 90
BorderPane layout, 237
bounded type parameters, 147-149
BoxLayout manager, 93
break keyword, 52
browser as WebSocket client, 398-399
buffered streams, 173
BufferedInputStream class, 173
BufferReader class, 174
buffers, 173
builds, 531
Ant "Hello World", 532-533
Gradle "Hello World", 537-540
Maven "Hello World", 533-536
business tier, 347
buttonClickHandler( ) method, 260
buttons
actionPeformed( ) method, 229
operation, 278
byte arrays, serialization
serialization, 192
byte streams, 172

C

calculator with Scene Builder, 251-260
CalculatorEngine class, 100, 101
call( ) method, 225
Callable interface, 210
CallableStatement class, 304
callback methods, 102
callbacks
capturing phase, events, 261
CardLayout manager, 95
casting, 68
downcasting, 69
catch keyword, 118
CDB (Clear Data Builder), 327
CDI (Contexts and Dependency Injection), 495-497
cell editors, 318-319
cell renderers, 318-319
certification, 559
char values, 174
character streams, 174
chat rooms, 428
CI (Continuous Integration), 531
class methods (see methods)
CLASS retention policy, 326
class versioning, 191
classes, 6
abstract, 73-76, 78
access level, 63

ActionEvent, 102
adapter classes, 108
anonymous inner classes, 154
attributes, 21
BitSet, 137-138
BufferedInputStream, 173
BufferReader, 174
CalculatorEngine, 100, 101
CallableStatement, 304
collection classes, 127
Collections, 133
Condition, 225
DataInputstream, 171
DataInputStream, 178
DataOutputStream, 171, 178
declaring, 27, 29
descendant, 162
DirectMessageReceiver, 435
DirectMessageSender, 440
embeddable, 468
EntityManager, 466
Enumeration, 135
Executors, 225-228
fields, 21
File, 179
FileDownload, 199, 200
FileHandler, 508
FileInputStream, 171
FileReader, 171, 174
FileWriter, 174
final keyword, 64
Formatter, 509
generics and, 141-143
Hashmap, 132
Hashtable, 132
ImperativeVsFunctional, 152
InitialContext, 416
inner classes, 110
inner, anonymous, 111
InputStream, 171
instances, heap memory and, 23
Iterator, 135
JavaToJSONStreaming, 487
JTable, 311
LinkedBlockingDeque, 228
LinkedList, 135
methods, 21, 28
    invoking, 335
ObjectInputStream, 188
ObjectOutputStream, 187-188
OutputStream, 171
packages, 61
parameterized, 141
    custom, 146-147
PreparedStatement, 304
Properties, 134
Reader, 171
ReentrantLock, 224
ReflectionSample, 328
RemoteException, 124
ResultSetMetaData, 305
serializable, 186
ServerSocket, 203
SimpleFormatter, 509
Socket, 203
SocketServer, 205
StreamOfDates, 291
StringBuffer, 49
StringBuilder, 49
subclasses, 32
    byte streams, 172
superclasses, 40
Swing, 84
Swingworker, 230
TestCallableThreads, 226
TestGenericBounded, 148
TestTaxLambda, 159
Thread, 210-211, 213, 215
TicTacToeController, 273-276
URL, 199
URLConnection, 198
UserPreferences, 185
variables, declaring, 22
WebSiteReader, 198
wrapper classes, 26
Writer, 171
clients
    fat clients, 347
    RESTful services, 495
    RMI, 339
        applets as, 341
    thin, 347, 357
Closure, 151
closures, 221
    lambda expressions, 167
code
    embedding in HTML, 380-383
    generating, 16-18
        annotations and, 327
collect( ) method, 282
Collection interface, 128
collections, 127
    ArrayList, 129
    forEach( ) method, 160
    interfaces, java.util, 128
    java.util.concurrent package, 228
    LinkedList, 129
    mutable, 289
    selection tips, 138
    sorting, 286

Comparable interface, 286
Comparator interface, 287
Collections class, 133
command-line arguments, 58
lesson, 59-60
comments, 26
block comments, 27
forward slashes, 27
commit( ) method, 308
Comparable interface, 286
Comparator interface, 287, 289
compareTo( ) method, 286
comparing( ) method, 288
compiling
errors, 142
Hello World, 7
composition versus inheritance, 162
concurrency, 209
Condition class, 225
conditional statements, 57
if, 30
switch, 31
config variable, 383
configuration
GlassFish, 359
Gradle and, 545-551
ConsoleHandler object, 505
constructors, 39
@Consumes annotation, 492
container classes, JavaFX layouts, 237
containers
EJB, 447
asynchronous method invocation, 448
embeddable, 448
MDBs, 448
JFrame, 85
versus application servers, 348
contains( ) method, 153
containsKey( ) method, 133
containsValue( ) method, 133
contexts, naming services, 415
continue keyword, 52
Controller class
event handling in JavaFX, 260, 264
convention over configuration paradigm, 535
conventions, 31
cookies, 368
copy( ) method, 181
createDurableConsumer( ) method, 436
createNewFile( ) method, 179
Criteria API, 469
CriteriaBuilder interface, 470
CriteriaQuery interface, 470
CRUD (create, retrieve, update, delete), 466
CSS (Cascading Style Sheets)
JavaFX, 234
selectors, 241
skinning, 241-244
CSS (cascading style sheets)
tic-tac-toe game, 266-273

D

DAS (Domain Administration Server), 418
data
passing between objects, 104-106
passing between view to controller, 263
reading from Internet, 196-198
stream data, 291
data streams, 171, 178
data types, 37
erasure, 143
parameterized, 141
primitive, 24
memory, 24
wrapper classes, 26
raw, 143, 143
type inference, 143
wildcards, 144
databases, 297
@Column, 468
JPQL, 469
lesson, 320
NoSQL, 297
@NotNull, 468
tables
mapping objects to, 466-468
primary keys, 467
transactions
committing, 308
rolling back, 308
datagrams, 203
DataInputStream class, 171, 178
DataOutputStream class, 171, 178
DataSource interface, 308
datasource, JNDI and, 419-421
DBMSes (Database Management Systems), 297
metadata, 321
stored procedures, 298
debugging, 54-56
JavaScript, 409
declarations
generics, 144
JSP, 384
variables, 23
declaring
classes, 27, 29
variables, 22
decode( ) method, 407

decoders, websockets, 406-409
defender methods, 67
@DELETE annotation, 492
DELETE method, 485
dependencies
  Gradle and, 542
    configurations and, 545-551
    repositories, 544
  JAR files, 547
dependency injection, 351
deployment, 58
  EJB, 458
  hot deployment, 365
  JSP (Java Server Pages), 380
  servlets, 358-359
@Deprecated annotation, 324
Deque interface, 228
Derby DB , 298-300
descendant classes, 162
deserialization, 186
  ObjectInputStream class, 188
  properties, 192
design
  MVC (Model-View-Controller), 107
  Observer pattern, 247
destroy( ) method, 367, 375
developer interviews, 558
diamond operator, 142
directives
  JSP
    attribute, 384
    include, 384
    page directives, 384
DirectMessageReceiver class, 435
DirectMessageSender class, 440
directory services, 341, 415
distributed applications, 335
do-while loop, 53
document root, 358
@Documented annotation, 325
doGet( ) method, 358
doInBackground( ) method, 230
DOM (Document Object Model), 397
doPost( ) method, 358
doSomething( ) method, 160, 162
dot notation, 6
doubly linked lists, 135
downcasting, 69
downloading
  Eclipse IDE, 10
  from Internet, 199
driver types, JDBC, 298
DSL (Domain Specific Language), 536
DTOs (Data Transfer Objects), 387
durable subscribers, 436
dynamic arrays, ArrayList, 129-132
dynamic IPs, 195

E

E(fx)clipse plug-in
  JavaFX and, 234-236
eager initialization, 457
ear (Enterprise Archive), 458
Eclipse IDE , 30, 9, 9
  directory structure, 517
  downloading, 10
  GlassFish configuration, 359-362
  Gradle in, 551, 552
    plug-ins, 551
  Hello project, 11
  HelloWorld class, 14
  installation, 10
  RCP (Rich Client Platform), 9
  server adapters, 360
  servlet creation, 362-366
  WAR files, 366
  workbench, 10
Eclipse IDE for Java EE Developers, 10
Eclipse Luna, lambda expressions and, 156
EE (Enterprise Edition), 29
EJB (Enterprise JavaBeans), 346, 447
  containers, 447
    asynchronous method invocation, 448
    embeddable, 448
    MDBs, 448
  deployment, 458
  ear (Enterprise Archive), 458
  entity beans, 448
  HelloWorldBean, 449
  lesson, 463
  local, 452-454
  local no-interface beans, 450
  MDBs, 460
  remote beans, 454
  session beans
    singleton, 448, 457
    stateful, 448, 456
    stateless, 448, 449-456
  timer service, 462
  transactions, 461
@Embeddable annotation, 468
embeddable classes, 468
embedding code in HTML, 380-383
encapsulation, 61, 62
encoders, websockets, 406
entities, 466
@Entity annotation, 466
entity beans (EJB), 448

Entity Manager , 471-473
EntityManager class, 466
Enumeration class, 135
Enumeration interface, 135, 135
enumerations, 135
equals( ) method, 50
error pages (JSP), 386
errors
  compilation and, 142
  I/O, 116
event dispatch thread, 229
event handling
  buttonClickHandler( ) method, 260
  JavaFX, 244-246
    Controller class, 260, 264
event listeners, 99
event-driven programming, 99
events, 99
  bubbles, 261
  capturing phase, 261
  KeyEvent, 262
  source, 261
  sources, 102
EventSource object, 397
exception handling, 115
  final keyword, 64
exception variable, 383
exceptions, 116
  AutoClosable interface, 121
  creating, 123-125
  finally clause, 120
  hierarchy, 117
  lesson, 125
  MalformedURLException, 196
  RemoteException, 124
  subclasses, 117
  throws clause, 119
Executor framework, 225-228
Executors class, 225-228
expressions
  JSP, 384
  lambda expressions, 151, 153
    method references, 155
extended keyword, 147
Externalizable interface, 189

F

fat clients, 347
File class, 179
FileDownload class, 199
  command-line parameters, 200
FileHandler class, 508
FileInputStream class, 171
FileReader class, 171, 174
files
  copying, 181
  downloading from Internet, 199
FileWriter class, 174
Filter interface, 374
filter( ) method, 282
filters
  Java Logging API, 509
  servlets, 373
  streams, 283
final keyword, 23
  classes, 64
  exception handling and, 64
  methods, 64
  variables, 64
final variables, 23
finally clause, 120
finally keyword, 118
firewalls, 195
  HTTP proxy servers and, 198
FlowLayout layout manager, 86-87
FlowLayout manager, 88
FlowPane layout, 237
FocusListener, 108
for loop, 50
for-each loop, 51
forEach( ) method, 51, 160
Formatter class, 509
formatters, Java Logging API, 508
@FormParam annotation, 492
frameworks
  Executor, 225-228
  logging frameworks, 511-512
  ORM, 325
  RIA (Rich Internet Application), 233
full-duplex communication, 395
Function interface, 167-169
functional interfaces, 100, 155
functional programming languages, 151
functional style programming, 151
  versus imperative, 152
@FunctionalInterface, 156
@FunctionalInterface annotation, 324
functions
  hash functions, 133
  higher order, 168
  higher-order, 158
  nested, closures, 221
  passing to methods, 158
  versus methods, 157-160
FXML, 233
  annotation, 264
  GUI and, 233
  tic-tac-toe game, 266-273

G

GC (Garbage Collector), 25
generating code, 16-18
generics, 133, 141
  classes and, 141-143
  declaring, 144
  lesson, 150
  methods, 149
@GET annotation, 491
GET method, 485
Get method (HTTP), 367
get( ) method, 130, 133, 226
getConstructors( ) method, 329
getFields( ) method, 329
getInterfaces( ) method, 329
getProperty( ) method, 134
getSession( ) method, 370
getState( ) method, 219
GlassFish, 30
  configuration, Eclipse IDE, 359-362
  JMS objects, 441-443
  JNDI objects, 418
Gosling, James, 1
Gradle, 536
  conventions, 540-542
  dependencies and, 542
    configurations and, 545-551
    repositories, 544
  Eclipse IDE, 551, 552
    plug-ins, 551
  Hello World, 537-540
  lesson, 553
  projects, 536
  tasks, 536
Gradle Wrapper, 549
GridBagLayout, 94
GridLayout manager, 88
GridPane layout, 237
  sample application, 239-241
Groovy, 536
GUI (graphic user interface), 83
  FXML and, 233
  I/O streams and, 175-177
  skinning with CSS, 241-244

H

half-duplex communication, 395
handlers, Java Logging API, 505-508
hash functions, 133
Hashmap class, 132
Hashtable class, 132
Haskell, 151
hasMoreElements( ) method, 135
HBox layout, 237
  sample application, 238
heap memory, 23
Hello WebSocket, 400-402
Hello World , 5-6
  Ant, 532
  Eclipse IDE, 11
  Gradle, 537-540
  Java Logging API, 503
    class-level logger, 504
    global logger, 503
  Maven, 533
  running, 7
HelloFX project, 235
HelloWorld class, Eclipse IDE, 14
HelloWorldBean, 449
hierarchy exceptions, 117
higher order functions, 168
higher-order functions, 158
hostnames in URLs, 195
hot deployment, 365
HTML (Hypertext Markup Language)
  embedding code, 380-383
HTTP (Hypertext Transfer Protocol), 355
  DELETE method, 485
  drawbacks, 396-397
  Get, 367
  GET method, 485
  Post, 367
  POST method, 485
  PUT method, 485
  server-side data push, 397
  session tracking, 368
    cookies, 368
    HttpSession, 370-373
HTTP proxy servers, 198
HTTPSession interface, 368
HttpSession object, 370-373

I

I/O errors, 116
I/O streams, 171
  buffered streams, 173
  BufferedInputStream class, 173
  byte streams, 172
  character streams, 174
  data streams, 178
  GUI and, 175-177
  NIO, 182-183
  Stream API, 292
@Id annotation, 467
IDE (Integrated Development Environment), 9

if statement, 30, 52, 57-58
if-else statements, 57
@Ignore annotation, 522
imperative programming versus functional , 152
ImperativeVsFunctional class, 152
implicit objects (JSP), 383
include directive, 384
infinite loops, 54
inheritance, 32, 61
  casting, 68-70
  eliminating, 165, 213
  lambda expression comparison, 162-169
  versus composition, 162
@Inherited annotation, 324
init( ) method, 234, 367
InitialContext class, 416
inner classes, 110
  anonymous, 111, 154
InputStream class, 171
installation
  Eclipse IDE, 10
  JDK
    MAC OS, 3
    Windows, 4
instanceof operator, 130
instances, 22
  heap memory, 23
  locks, 217
integration testing, 515
IntelliJ IDEA, 9
interfaces, 65-66
  ActionListener, 101
  AutoClosable, 121
  BiFunction, 167-169
  Callable, 210
  Collection, 128
  collections, java.util, 128
  Comparable, 286
  Comparator, 287, 289
  CriteriaBuilder, 470
  CriteriaQuery, 470
  DataSource, 308
  Deque, 228
  Enumeration, 135, 135
  Externalizable, 189
  Filter, 374
  Function, 167-169
  functional, 100
  functional interfaces, 155
  HTTPSession, 368
  Iterable, 128
  Iterator, 135
  lesson, 79-82
  List, 129
  Map, 129
  marker interfaces, 66
  MessageListener, 433
  methods
    default, 67
    static, 68
  no-interface beans (EJB), 450
  Path, 180
  programming to, 131
  Property, 247
  public, 63
  Queue, 129
  Recommendations, 495
  remote, 336
    implementation, 337
  RMI, 335
  Root, 470
  Rowset, 307
  Runnable, 210, 211-213
  Serializable, 186
  Set, 129
  StockServer, 336
  TableModel, 312-318
  TypedQuery, 470
  versus abstract classes , 78
intermediate operations in streams
  streams, 282
Internet
  file downloads, 199
  reading data from, 196-198
intranet, 195
introspection, 328
  reflection and, 330
invoke( ) method, 330
invoking methods, 335
IoT (Internet of Things), 30, 347
IP (Internet Protocol), 195
IP addresses, dynamic, 195
isAlive( ) method, 219
isAnnotationPresent( ) method, 329
isBound( ) method, 247
ISP (Internet service provider), 195
italic text, 242
ItemListener, 108
Iterable interface, 128
iteration, 135
  forEach( ) method, 160
Iteration interface, 135
Iterator class, 135

J

JARs (Java Archives), 459
Java architect, 558
Java EE, 3, 345

applications
containers, 348
tiers, 346-348
lesson, 352
messages and, 439-441
multithreading, 350
profiles, 350
Project Explorer, 10
pruning, 350
reasons to use, 350
versions, 346
Java Logging API, 501
duplicate messages, 507
filters, 509
formatters, 508
handlers, 502, 505-508
Hello World, 503
class-level logger, 504
global logger, 503
lesson, 512
log levels, 505-508
logging frameworks, 511-512
logging.properties file, 507
message grouping, 502
Java SE (Standard Edition), 3
downloading, 3-5
java.io package, 171
java.nio package, 171
java.util collection interfaces, 128
java.util.Collections class, 133
java.util.concurrent package, 224-229
collections, 228
JavaBeans, 387
bean lifecycle, 388
JSP and, 388
RESTful services, 490
JavaDB (see Derby DB)
Javadoc
annotations, 321
@Deprecated, 324
@Documented, 325
@FunctionalInterface, 324
@Inherited, 324
@Override, 323-324
JavaFX, 83, 233
Application class, 234
binding, 246-249
CSS, 234
E(fx)clipse plug-in, 234-236
event handling, 244-246
Controller class, 260, 264
events
KeyEvent, 262
source, 261
HelloFX project, 235
layout container classes, 237
layouts, 236-239
BorderPane, 236
lesson, 250
mobile devices, 278
properties, 246-249
property classes, 247
root nodes, 234
Scene Builder, 251-260
scene graphs, 233
stages, 233
Swing and, 234
theater terminology, 233
tic-tac-toe game, 265-273
menus, 277
TicTacToeController class, 273-276
web, 278
JavaScript, 151
debugging, 409
JavaToJSONStreaming class, 487
JAX-RS, 483
JAX-WS, 483
JCP (Java Community Process), 346
JDBC
CallableStatement class, 304
connection pools, 308
DataSource interface, 308
drivers, 298
PreparedStatement class, 304
result sets, 302-303
scrollable, 307
ResultSetMetaData class, 305
Rowset interface, 307
sample program, 300-302
JDBC API, 297
JDK (Java Development Kit), 30, 3
MAC OS, 3
Windows, 4
JFrame containers, 85
JMS (Java Messaging Service), 346, 425, 431
asynchronous communications, 426
message types, 431
MOM and, 425
objects in GlassFish, 441-443
OpenMQ MOM, 428-430
JNDI (Java Naming and Directory Interface), 415
administered objects, 415
datasource and, 419-421
InitialContext class, 416
lesson, 423
objects, GlassFish and, 418
resources, 417
join( ) method, 222
joining threads, 222
JPA (Java Persistence API), 465, 469

(see also JPQL)
bean validation, 473-475
Entity Manager, 471-473
lesson, 475
JPQL (Java Persistence Query Language), 466, 469
Criteria API, 469
JRE (Jave Runtime Environment), 3
JSF (JavaServer Faces) , servlets and, 355
JSON (JavaScript Object Notation), 351
Object Model API, 486
writing JSON, 488
RESTful services and, 485-489
Stream API and
reading JSON, 487
Streaming API, 486
writing JSON, 487
XML comparison, 485
JSP (Java Server Pages), 346, 379
actions, 385
declarations, 384
deployment, 380
directives
attribute, 384
include, 384
page directives, 384
error pages, 386
expressions, 384
forward element, 385
JavaBeans in, 388
lesson, 393
objects, implicit, 383
plugin element, 385
servlets and, 355
loading from, 389
tag libraries, 390-392
variables, 383
JSR (Java Specification Request), 346
JSTL (JSP Standard Tag Library), 392
JTA (Java Transaction API), 349, 461
JTable
annotations, 321
cell editors, 318-319
cell renderers, 318-319
UI class, 312
JTable class
MVC and, 311
JUnit framework, 515, 516
(see also unit testing)
annotations, 521
applying, 522-524
Eclipse directory structure, 517
imports, 523
installation, 517
lesson, 528
test case, 518-521
test runners, 527-528
test suites, 524-525
JVM (Java Virtual Machine), 1, 2

K

KeyEvent, 262
KeyListener, 108
keys
Hashmap class, 132
Hashtable class, 132
primary
databases, 467
keywords
abstract, 73
break, 52
catch, 118
continue, 52
extends, 147
final, 23, 64
finally, 118
null, 51
private, 63
public, 6
static, 6, 44
String, 6
super, 40, 149
synchronized, 217, 224
this, 40
throw, 118
throws, 118
transient, 188
try, 118
void, 6
`public, 63

L

lambda expressions, 151, 153
@FunctionalInterface, 156
arguments, 154
closures and, 167
curly braces, 154
inheritance comparison, 162-169
inner class alternative, 112
lesson, 170
Luna and, 156
method references, 155
polymorphism comparison, 162-169
syntax, 154
TableModelListener, 317
LANs (local area networks), 195
late binding, 77

launch( ) method, 234
layout managers (Swing)
    absolute layout, 96
    BorderLayout manager, 90
    BoxLayout, 93
    CardLayout, 95
    combining, 90
    FlowLayout, 86-87, 88
    GridBagLayout, 94
    GridLayout, 88
layouts
    AnchorPane, 237
    BorderPane, 237
    FlowPane, 237
    GridPane, 237, 239-241
    HBox, 237, 238
    JavaFX, 236-239
        container classes, 237
    StackPane, 237
    TilePane, 237
    VBox, 237
LDAP (Lightweight Directory Access Protocol), 421-422
lessons, 30
    command-line arguments, 59
    database, 320
    EJB, 463
    exceptions, 125
    generics, 150
    Gradle, 553
    interfaces, 79
    Java EE, 352
    Java Logging API, 512
    JavaFX, 250
    JNDI, 423
    JPA, 475
    JSP, 393
    JUnit framework, 528
    lambda expressions, 170
    LinkedList modification, 139
    message consumers, 443
    operation buttons, 278
    packages, 70
    RESTful services, 498
    RMI, 341
    run-time annotation, 332
    serialization, 193
    servlets, 376
    socket programming, 207
    streams, 294
    Swing application creation, 232
    websockets, 412
    .zip files, 184
libraries
    Swing, 84
    tag libraries (JSP), 390-392
        JSTL, 392
linked lists, doubly linked lists, 135
LinkedBlockingDeque class, 228
LinkedList class, 135
LinkedList collection, 129
links, symbolic, 180
List interface, 129
    ArrayList interface, 129
listeners, events, 99
lists, double linked, 135
load testing, 516
local scope, 25
@LocalBean annotation, 450
lock( ) method, 224
locks, object instances, 217
Logger object, 505
logging frameworks, 511-512
loops, 50-54
    arrays, 50
    do-while, 53
    for, 50
    for-each, 51
    forEach( ) method, 51
    infinite, 54
    while, 52
Luna, lambda expressions and, 156

M

MAC OS, JDK installation, 3
main method, 59
main( ) method, 6
MalformedURLException, 196
Map interface, 129
maps, streams, 283
marker interfaces, 66
Maven, 533, 536
MDBs (message-driven beans), 426, 448, 460
member variables, access level, 63
memory
    arrays, 128
    heap memory, 23
    primitive data types, 24
message consumer, 433, 443
message queue (MOM), 425
message selectors (MOM), 439
@MessageDriven annotation, 449
MessageListener interface, 433
messages
    onClose( ), 399
    onError( ), 399
    onOpen( ), 399
    websockets
        receiving, 404

sending, 403
MessageSenderServlet, 440
meta-annotations, 325
META-INF directory, 359
metadata, 321
annotations, 321
method extractors, 288
method signatures, 6
methods, 6, 21, 335
(see also RMI (Remote Method Invocation))
accept( ), 205
access level, 63
actionPerformed( ), 100, 229
add( ), 129
arguments, 37
asynchronous method invocation, 448
bind( ), 247, 339
bindBidirectional( ), 247
body, 6
buttonClickHandler( ), 260
call( ), 225
callback methods, 102
calling, 37
classes, 28
collect( ), 282
commit( ), 308
compareTo( ), 286
comparing( ), 288
contains( ), 153
containsKey( ), 133
containsValue( ), 133
copy( ), 181
createDurableConsumer( ), 436
createNewFile( ), 179
data types, 37
decode( ), 407
default, in interfaces, 67
destroy( ), 367, 375
doGet( ), 358
doInBackground( ), 230
doPost( ), 358
doSomething( ), 160, 162
dot notation, 6
equals( ), 50
filter( ), 282
final keyword, 64
forEach( ), 51, 160
generic, 149
get( ), 130, 133, 226
getConstructors( ), 329
getFields( ), 329
getInterfaces( ), 329
getProperty( ), 134
getSession( ), 370
getState( ), 219
hasMoreElements( ), 135
init( ), 234, 367
invoke( ), 330
invoking, 37, 335
isAlive( ), 219
isAnnotationPresent( ), 329
isBound( ), 247
join( ), 222
launch( ), 234
lock( ), 224
main, 59
main( ), 6
newFixedThreadPool( ), 225
nextElement( ), 135
non-implemented, 155
notify( ), 219-222
notifyAll( ), 219-222
onMessage( ), 399, 433
overloading, 38
overriding, 33
parallelStream( ), 285
passing functions to, 158
persist( ), 471
println( ), 6, 501
process( ), 231
processDigit( ), 262
processOperation( ), 262
proxies, 335
publish( ), 231
readExternal( ), 189-191
readObject( ), 188
remove( ), 135
reverse( ), 133
run( ), 210, 211
sendBinary( ), 404
sendObject( ), 404
sendStream( ), 404
service( ), 357, 367
setConstraints( ), 240
setDoOutput( ), 198
setLevel( ), 505
setPriority( ), 217
size( ), 133
sleep( ), 213
sort( ), 133
start( ), 234
static, 68
stop( ), 215
Stream.generate( ), 291
swap( ), 133
tableChanged( ), 318
unbind( ), 247
unbindDirectional( ), 247
useCaches( ), 198
versus functions, 157-160

wait( ), 219-222
willDecode( ), 407
writeExternal( ), 189-191
writeObject( ), 187
mobile devices, JavaFX and, 278
MOM (message-oriented middleware), 348, 425
asynchronous communications, 426
message acknowledgment, 437-438
message consumers, 433
message delivery, 427
message queue, 426
message selectors, 439
messages from Java EE containers, 439-441
OpenMQ, 428-430
persistent messages, 427
topic subscription, 436-438
MouseListener, 108
MouseMotionListener, 108
multithreading, 209
Java EE, 350
mutable attributes, 157
mutable collections, 289
MVC (Model-View-Controller), 177
design patterns, 107

N

names, annotated, 263
naming conventions, packages and, 16
naming services, 341, 415
contexts, 415
nested functions, 221
NetBeans, 9
networking properties, 198
networks
firewalls, 195
HTTP proxy servers, 198-199
intranet, 195
LANs, 195
protocols, 195
WANs, 195
newFixedThreadPool( ) method, 225
nextElement( ) method, 135
NIO, 182-183
NIO.2, 180
non-blocking sockets, 207
non-durable subscribers, 436
non-implemented methods, 155
NoSQL databases, 297
NoSQL DBMS, 466
NOT operator, 58
Notepad, 3
notify( ) method, 219-222
notifyAll( ) method, 219-222
null keyword, 51

O

O(n) , 139
Object Model API, 486
writing JSON, 488
ObjectInputStream class, 188
serialization and, 186
ObjectOutputStream class, 187-188
serialization and, 186
objects
activation, 186
ConsoleHandler, 505
EventSource, 397
implicit, JSP, 383
instances, 22
locks, 217
introspection, 328
JNDI, GlassFish and, 418
Logger, 505
mapping to database tables, 466-468
passing data between, 104-106
passivation, 186
remote registration, 338
RMI, 341
URL, 196
URLConnection, 197, 198
observables, 247, 247
Observer design pattern, 247
onClose( ) method, 399
@OnError annotation, 399
onError( ) method, 399
@OnMessage annotation, 399, 404
onMessage( ) method, 399, 433
onOpen( ) method, 399
OOP (object-oriented programming), 2
classes, 21-23
encapsulation and, 61
inheritance, 32
inheritance and, 61
objects, 21
instances, 22
polymorphism, 61
OpenMQ MOM, 428-430
operators
AND, 57
diamond operator, 142
instanceof, 130
NOT, 58
OR, 58
OR operator, 58
ORM (object-relational mapping), 325, 465
out variable, 383

OutputStream class, 171
overloading methods, 38
@Override annotation, 323-324
overriding methods, 33
OWASP (Open Source Web Application Security Project), 369

P

P2P (point-to-point) messaging, 427
P2P forums, 32
packages, 15, 61
  classes, placing, 61
  java.io, 171
  java.nio, 171
  java.util.concurrent, 224-229
  JavaFX property classes, 247
  lesson, 70
  naming conventions, 16
  reverse domain name, 61
page directives, 384
page variable, 383
pageContext variable, 383
parallel streams, 285
  sorting, 290
parallelStream( ) method, 285
parameterized classes, 141
  custom, 146-147
parameterized data types, 141
parameterized types, 144
parameters, bounded type, 147-149
passing
  data
    between objects, 104-106
    between view and controller, 263
  parameters, websockets, 401
passing values
  by reference, 42
  by value, 42
passivation, 186
@Path annotation, 492
Path interface, 180
@PathParam annotation, 401, 492
persist( ) method, 471
persistence context, 471
Persistence Criteria API, 466
platform independence, 1
plug-ins
  E(fx)clipse, 234-236
  Gradle in Eclipse IDE, 551
POJO (Plain Old Java Object), 348, 355, 447
polling, 397
polymorphism, 61, 76-78
  lambda expression comparison, 162-169
populating arrays, 128
@POST annotation, 492
POST method, 485
Post method (HTTP), 367
Preferences panel, 185
PreparedStatement class, 304
presentation layer, 355
presentation tier, 347
primary keys, databases, 467
primitive data types, 24
  memory, 24
  wrapper classes, 26
println( ) method, 6, 501
private keyword, 63
private variables, 303
process( ) method, 231
processDigit( ) method, 262
processOperation( ) method, 262
@Produces annotation, 492
program life cycle, 2
programmatic endpoints, 399
programming
  functional programming languages, 151
  functional style programming, 151
  imperative versus functional, 152
  socket programming, 203-207
  to interfaces, 131
Project Explorer (Java EE), 10
properties
  Class, 133
  deserialization, 192
  JavaFX, 246-249
  networking properties, 198
Properties class, 133, 134
Property interface, 247
protocols, 195
  WebSocket, 204
proxies, 335
pruning, 350
public interface, 63
public keyword, 6, 63
publish( ) method, 231
publishing with WebSocket protocol, 409-411
push technology, 397
@PUT annotation, 492
PUT method, 485

Q

QA testing, 516
Quartz Scheduler, 462
queries in JPQL, 469
@QueryParam annotation, 492
Queue interface, 129
queues, 228

R

race conditions, 131, 217-219
raw data types, 143, 143
RCP (Rich Client Platform), 9
RDBMSes (Relational Database Management Systems), 297
    (see also databases)
Reader class, 171
readExternal( ) method, 189-191
readObject( ) method, 188
Recommendations interface, 495
ReentrantLock class, 224
reflection, 321, 328
    introspection and, 330
ReflectionSample class, 328
regression, 515
remote interfaces, 336
    implementation, 337
    StockServer, 336
RemoteException class, 124
remove( ) method, 135
repositories, Gradle and, 544
request variable, 383
@Resource annotation, 417
response variable, 383
REST (representational state of transfer), 484
RESTful services, 355, 483, 484
    application creation, 490
    CDI (Contexts and Dependency Injection), 495, 497
    clients, 495
    endpoint class, 491-494
    JavaBeans, 490
    lesson, 498
    websockets comparison, 486
result sets, scrollable, 307
ResultSetMetaData class, 305
reverse domain name, 61
reverse( ) method, 133
reverse-domain name conventions, 16
RIA (Rich Internet Application) framework, 233
RMI (Remote Method Invocation), 335
    application development, 336-341
    clients, 339
        applets as, 341
    distributed applications, 335
    lesson, 341
    object registration, 338
    objects, finding, 341
    remote interfaces, 336
        implementation, 337
    security, 340
    stubs, 335
Root interface, 470
root nodes, JavaFX, 234
Rowset interface, 307
RPC (remote procedure calls), 425
Ruby, 151
run( ) method, 210, 211
run-time binding, 77
Runnable interface, 210, 211-213
runtime annotation processing, 330-332
runtime errors, stack traces, 115
RUNTIME retention policy, 326

S

Scala, 151
scalability, subscriptions and, 437
Scene Builder, 233
    calculator, 251-260
@Schedule annotation, 462
scope, variables, 25, 43
screencasts, 30
security, RMI and, 340
sendBinary( ) method, 404
sendObject( ) method, 404
sendStream( ) method, 404
sequential streams, 285
serial version unique ID, 192
Serializable interface, 186
serialization, 66, 185-186
    byte arrays, 192
    class versioning, 191
    deserialization, 186
    Externalizable interface, 189
    lesson, 193
    ObjectOutputStream class, 187-188
@ServerEndPoint annotation, 400
servers, websocket communication and, 399-402
ServerSocket class, 203
service( ) method, 357, 367
servlets, 346, 355
    asynchronous, 375
    creating, 357
        Eclipse, 362-366
    data flow, 366-367
    deploying, 358-359
    document root, 358
    filters, 373
    HTTP requests, 355
    JSF and, 355
    JSP and, 355, 379
        loading from , 389
    lesson, 376
    online store example, 356
    thin clients, 357
session beans (EJB)
    singleton, 448, 457

stateful , 448, 456
stateless, 448, 449-456
asynchronous methods, 455
session tracking (HTTP), 368
cookies, 368
HttpSession, 370-373
session variable, 383
Set interface, 129
setConstraints( ) method, 240
setDoOutput( ) method, 198
setLevel( ) method, 505
setPriority( ) method, 217
short-circuit stream operations, 293
Silverlight, 233
SimpleFormatter class, 509
@Singleton annotation, 449
singleton session beans (EJB), 448, 457
size( ) method, 133
skinning with CSS, 241-244
SLA (Service Level Agreement), 516
sleep( ) method, 213
versus wait( ), 220
SOAP (Simple Object Access Protocol), 355, 483
Socket class, 203
socket programming, 203-207
lesson, 207
sockets
non-blocking, 207
uses, 204
SocketServer class, 205
sort( ) method, 133
sorting
collections, 286
Comparable interface, 286
Comparator interface, 287
streams, 289
Comparator interface, 289
parallel, 290
source code, 31
SOURCE retention policy, 326
sources, events, 102
SPA (Single-Page Applications), 486
SSE (Server-Side Events), 397
stack trace, 115
StackPane layout, 237
start( ) method, 234
@Stateful annotation, 449
stateful session beans (EJB), 448, 456
stateless protocols, 368
stateless session beans (EJB), 448, 449-456
asynchronous methods, 455
statements
conditional, 30, 57
switch, 31
if, 30, 52, 57
if-else, 57
switch, 31
throw, 122
static final variable, 192
static keyword, 6, 44
static methods, interfaces, 68
stock market price program, 200-203
stock quote server, 204-206
StockServer remote interface, 336
stop( ) method, 215
stored procedures, 298
Stream API, 281
I/O streams, 292
Stream.generate( ) method, 291
Streaming API, 486
reading JSON, 487
writing JSON, 487
StreamOfDates class, 291
streams, 281-285
data generation, 291
filters, 283
finite size, 290
infinite-size, 291
intermediate operations, 282
lazy operations, 282
lesson, 294
maps, 283
parallel , 285
parallelStream( ) method, 285
reduce , 283
sequential , 285
short-circuit operations, 293
sorting, 289
Comparator interface, 289
parallel, 290
terminal operations, 282
streams of data (see data streams)
stress testing, 516
String keyword, 6
StringBuffer class, 49
StringBuilder class, 49
strings, 49-50
stubs (RMI), 335
subclasses, 32
byte streams, 172
exceptions, 117
Sublime Text, 3
super keyword, 40, 149
superclasses, 40
@SuppressWarning annotation, 323
swap( ) method, 133
Swing, 83
AbstractTableModel class, 312
adapters, 109
application creation, 232

classes, 84
DefaultTableModel class, 312
FocusListener, 108
GUI builders, 97
ItemListener, 108
JavaFx and, 234
JTable class, 311
JTable, MVC and, 311
KeyListener, 108
layout managers, 85
absolute layout, 96
BorderLayout, 90
BoxLayout, 93
CardLayout, 95
combining, 90
FlowLayout, 86-87, 88
GridBagLayout, 94
GridLayout, 88
library, 84
listeners, 108, 109
MouseListener, 108
MouseMotionListener, 108
TableModel interface, 312-318
threads, 229-231
widgets, 96
WindowListener, 108
Swingworker class, 230
switch statement, 31
symbolic links, 180
synchronization, 133
synchronized keyword, 217, 224
synchronous calls, 426
syntax of lambda expressions, 154

T

tableChanged( ) method, 318
TableModel interface, 312-318
callbacks, 313-318
TableModelListener, lambda expressions in, 317
tables (databases)
mapping objects to, 466-468
primary keys, 467
tabular data, 311
tag libraries (JSP), 390-392
JSTL, 392
task scheduler, 462
TCP/IP (Transmission Control Protocol/Internet Protocol), 203
TDD (test-driven development), 515
technical interviews, 555-557
developers, 558
offers, 557
questions/answers, 559-567
terminal operations in streams, 282
@Test annotation, 517, 521
TestCallableThreads class, 226
TestGenericBounded class, 148
testing
SLA (Service Level Agreement), 516
types, 515
TestTaxLambda class, 159
text editors, 3
TextEdit, 3
thin clients, 347
servlets, 357
this keyword, 40
Thread class, 210-211
sleep( ) method, 213
stop( ) method, 215
threads
event dispatch thread, 229
joining, 222
priorities, 217
queues, 228
race conditions, 217-219
states, 219
Swing, 229
throw keyword, 118
throw statement, 122
throws clause, 119
throws keyword, 118
tic-tac-toe game, 265-273
menus, 277
strategy, 273-276
TicTacToeController class, 273-276
TilePane layout, 237
topic subscription (MOM), 436-438
@TransactionAttribute annotation, 461
transactions
committing, 308
EJB, 461
rolling back, 308
transient keyword, 188
transient variables, 188, 189
try keyword, 118
try-with-resources, 121
try/catch blocks, 116, 118
try-with-resources, 121
type inference, 143, 162
TypedQuery interface, 470
types, parameterized, 144

U

UDP (User Datagram Protocol), 203
UIs (user interfaces), 9
Swing, 83
UML notation, 163

unbind( ) method, 247
unbindDirectional( ) method, 247
unbound queues, 228
unboxing, 26
unicast communication, 337
unit testing, 515
upcasting, 68
upper bounded wildcard, 148
URL class, 199
URL object, 196
URLConnection class, 198
URLConnection object, 197, 198
URLs (uniform resource locators), 195
  rewriting, 369
useCaches( ) method, 198
user-acceptance testing, 516
UserPreferences class, 185

V

validation, Bean Validation framework, 473-475
values
  passing
    by reference, 42
    by value, 42
variables
  application, 383
  boolean, 215
  class level declaration, 25
  config, 383
  declaring, 22, 23
  dot notation, 6
  exception, 383
  final, 23
  final keyword, 64
  JSP (Java Server Pages), 383
  member variables
    access level, 63
  out, 383
  page, 383
  pageContext, 383
  private, 303
  request, 383
  response, 383
  scope, 25, 43
  session, 383
  static final, 192
  transient, 188, 189
VBox layout, 237
versioning, class versioning, 191
vi, 3
void keyword, 6

W

wait( ) method, 219-222
  versus sleep( ), 220
WANs (wide area networks), 195
WAR files, 366, 550
warning messages, suppressing, 323
Web Services, 484
  (see also RESTful services)
  JAX-RS, 483
  JAX-WS, 483
  SOAP , 483
  WSDL, 484
WEB-INF directory, 359
@WebFilter annotation, 374
@WebServlet annotation, 357
WebSiteReader class, 198
WebSocket clients, browser as, 398-399
WebSocket protocol, 204, 395
  decoders, 406-409
  encoders, 406-409
  Hello WebSocket, 400-402
  Java-based clients, 405
  publishing, 409-411
  Sec-Websocket-Key attribute, 399
  standardization, 395
  traffic monitoring, 402
websockets
  annotated endpoints, 399
  bidirectionality, 397
  client-server communication, 397-405
  data format, 399
  endpoint instances, 405
  lesson, 412
  messages
    receiving, 404
    sending, 403
  parameter passing, 401
  programmatic endpoint, 399
  RESTful services comparison, 486
  server communication, 399-402
  subprotocols, 399
while loop, 52
WhileLoopDemo program output, 53
wildcards, 144
  upper bounded, 148
willDecode( ) method, 407
WindowListener, 108
Windows, JDK installation, 4
workbench (Eclipse), 10
wrapper classes, 26
writeExternal( ) method, 189-191
writeObject( ) method, 187
Writer class, 171

WSDL (Web Services Description Language), 484

XML (eXtensible Markup Language), 233
    JSON comparison, 485

zero-based arrays, 47
.zip files, 184